Manual of Law Librarianship

MANUAL OF LAW LIBRARIANSHIP

The Use and Organization of Legal Literature

Edited by ELIZABETH M. MOYS, BA, FLA
Hon. Editor of *The Law Librarian*

A GRAFTON BOOK

Published for the British and Irish Association of Law Librarians

 ANDRE DEUTSCH

First published 1976 by
André Deutsch Limited
105 Great Russell Street London w c 1

Copyright © 1976 by the British and Irish
Association of Law Librarians
All rights reserved

Printed in Great Britain by
Ebenezer Baylis and Son Limited
The Trinity Press, Worcester, and London

ISBN 0 233 96735 4

Contents

Part III. LAW LIBRARY PRACTICE

Foreword

As one who has spent a fair proportion of the last forty-odd years burrowing in or borrowing from Law Libraries and has benefited from the ever-helpful ministrations of Law Librarians, I am very pleased to accept the invitation to write a short Foreword to this *Manual of Law Librarianship*. Its importance is shown by the fact that it is the first comprehensive manual in English covering both legal bibliography and practical law librarianship.

The project began several years ago as an idea for a small practical handbook to be written by one or two authors. The British and Irish Association of Law Librarians, after it was founded in 1969, agreed to take over the project and to supervise its publication. Meanwhile the proposed volume had expanded into a full-scale manual. The emphasis throughout is on matters special to *law* librarianship, although subjects of more general application are touched on where appropriate. Special attention is given to the *practical* aspects of this subject and of legal bibliography. Readers are given further guidance in the bibliographies at the end of the chapters.

The eighteen chapters are contributed by seventeen librarians and two academic lawyers who are experts in their various fields. The thanks of the Association are due to the contributors, and especially to Miss Elizabeth Moys for her devoted work as Honorary Editor.

I commend this *Manual* to all who are concerned with running or using Law Libraries in the English-speaking world.

Faculty of Law   O. Hood Phillips
University of Birmingham
17 July 1974

Preface

This is intended to be a book to help all people dealing with legal material in libraries, both general and specialized. The pattern adopted is that, after two introductory chapters explaining the general context of law librarianship in the British Isles, about one half of the total volume deals with the literature of law and its use, while the remainder is devoted to other library techniques. As it is somewhat unusual for a library manual to allocate such a high proportion of its space to subject literature, an explanation is offered.

First, it is necessary to consider carefully what is meant by a law library. A workable definition might be 'a collection of materials wholly, or mainly, containing legal information, organized for use'. Concerning the first part of the definition, it will be noted in the following chapters that a very high proportion of legal information, including almost all modern English language texts of the law itself, is published in serial or loose-leaf form. Therefore, any discussion of 'law books' includes serial publications, unless they are expressly excluded. The second part of the definition applies, of course, to any library: a collection that is not organized is a mere jumble, and if it is not for use, it is a museum-piece, not a library. Other characteristics which the term 'library' frequently conjures up, such as lending facilities, subject-classified shelf arrangement, card catalogues and even (I regret to admit) the presence of a qualified librarian, will be seen not to be quintessential.

For many years law libraries have been recognized, albeit reluctantly, as being 'different'. The legal profession is undoubtedly different in detail from the other learned professions, such as medicine. But experience suggests that, from the point of view of those serving them, the older professions have a great deal in common, such as an innate conservatism in their professional outlook and their attitude to members of newer professions. It is not, therefore, the users of law libraries that single them out from other libraries, so much as their contents. The law books themselves *are* different from all other subject literatures, not only in their subject matter, but also in their own innate forms. It is this knowledge that law books are somehow different (and are therefore presumed to be difficult), that can sometimes lead to a willingness on the part of general librarians to set aside their natural centralist tendencies and segregate law books and their users into separate or semi-autonomous libraries.

Hence the emphasis placed on the literature of law in this *Manual*. No one can be an efficient law librarian unless he has acquired a good basic knowledge of the types of material that make up a law library and of how best to obtain access to the information recorded there. A knowledge of the substance of the law itself is undoubtedly useful, but is less so than a good practical knowledge of library techniques, and in any case the librarian is debarred by the nature of his office from giving legal aid or advice. What he must have, in order to provide the service his readers require, is a sound knowledge of basic legal texts (legislation and law reports), reference books, indexes, bibliography, citation methods and the organization of legal literature.

In planning the volume, the Publications Sub-Committee decided to include all types of legal material and all systems of law that might be represented in a law library. Naturally, however, the largest amount of space was allocated to the sources of the law of the British Isles. As Professor Cornish has pointed out, this involves at least six legal jurisdictions: England and Wales, Scotland, Northern Ireland, the Isle of Man, the Channel Islands (where Jersey and Guernsey have some differences) and the Republic of Ireland. There is no implication that all British or Irish law libraries *should* have full coverage of all these jurisdictions – indeed many libraries serve restricted local interests and rarely need to look beyond the law of their local jurisdiction, whichever it may be. However, both individual and corporate persons are becoming increasingly mobile. Any law librarian could suddenly be faced with enquiries about, for example, company laws in tax havens or the validity of a will that had been drawn up almost anywhere in the world.

Over the centuries, successive waves of immigrants from Europe, and other continents, have brought with them additional laws and customs, notably those of religious origin. Academic lawyers may, of course, be interested in yet other systems of law, such as modern international law or classical Roman law. The *Manual* therefore contains short statements and selective bibliographies to give elementary guidance on all foreign and non-jurisdictional legal systems. The placing of the European Communities in the foreign law chapter does not reflect any political views, merely the facts that: firstly, when the volume was initially planned the expansion of the Communities from the original six members was still uncertain (at the time of writing this Preface, the continued membership of the United Kingdom remains uncertain) and, secondly, this position seemed best to fit the pattern of chapters and the inclinations of the contributors. In any future edition, the situation will be reviewed.

The remainder of the *Manual* deals with the organization and operation of law libraries. Contributors were asked to cover the whole range of topics in their respective chapters, so that the volume would provide a complete outline of the subject, and to concentrate their efforts on practical problems giving most attention to those matters where legal literature requires some variation from general librarianship practices. Matters such as charging systems and classification theory have been touched on rather briefly, and readers who require more detailed information have been referred to further literature on these, and many other topics, in the reading lists at the ends of chapters.

Law librarianship, as we have defined it, is such a vast subject that, even in a volume of this size, it is not possible to give a total statement. However, it can truthfully be said that never before have so many aspects of legal literature and librarianship been brought together between the covers of a single volume. It was our intention to provide at least some clue to the solution of any problem likely to occur in a law library and, where space prohibited a full discussion of a topic, references to further sources of information. Even so, most contributors have had to be highly selective in their chapter bibliographies. We are sure that our readers will find in practice that reference to the volumes cited in the *Manual* will soon lead them to still further literature.

A few themes pervade the chapters, showing how important they are to law librarians. One is the fact, already mentioned, that the more important legal texts are in serial form. Another is that no law book, however old, is useless merely by reason of its age. The fact that some thirteenth-century legislation (*eg*, parts of Magna Carta) and legal principles enunciated in some of the medieval law reports are still valid today neatly combines these two themes. Every law librarian needs to develop a sense of historical perspective if he is to begin to understand the books and readers with whom he is working. There are many subject areas in which periodical literature plays an important part, but the degree of use of legal serials dozens, or even hundreds, of years after publication is unique.

At the same time, law libraries have a vital need to keep up to date. While it is no longer true that a client's life depends on the preparation of a case by his legal representatives, it is still true that their reliance on superseded precedents could lose an otherwise good case. Law has always been a well-documented subject, provided with a substantial array of commercially produced indexes, bibliographies and other tools. But this in no way absolves the law librarian from the need to be on top of his subject by scanning in-coming serial literature and maintaining whatever current information indexes and services are appropriate for his readers. These, and other aspects of the special needs of law libraries in the organization and representation of their contents are dealt with at greater length in the *Manual*.

A newcomer to the practice of law librarianship wishing to obtain a clear and concise statement of the professional philosophy he should follow would be well advised to read Wallace Breem's article 'The obligations of a law librarian' (*Law Librarian*, vol. 3, no. 3, 1972, pp. 40–2). The article covers matters such as the librarian's duty to his committee, whether or not he should exercise censorship in book selection and the problem of the conflicting needs of conservation and use of rare material.

Texts of the chapters in the *Manual* were mostly completed during 1974, but some details have been up-dated since then.

Finally I should like to record my gratitude to the contributors for their hard work and cheerful acceptance of editorial comments and suggestions; to Jill McIvor and George Ballantyne, the Consultants for Irish and Scottish matters, who read every chapter and wrote substantial portions of some; and especially to Wallace Breem and Derek Way for their help and encouragement at all stages of the planning and preparation of the *Manual*. The names of people outside the British and Irish Association of Law Librarians who have given help in many and various ways are separately listed.

ELIZABETH M. MOYS

List of Contributors

Miss MURIEL ANDERSON, BA, ALA, Deputy Librarian, Institute of Advanced Legal Studies, University of London.

W. W. S. BREEM, Librarian to the Honourable Society of the Inner Temple, Hon. Secretary/Treasurer, BIALL.

Mrs MARGARET G. CHUBB, BA, MA, Sub-Librarian i/c Readers' Services, Trinity College Library, Dublin.

W. R. CORNISH, LL.B, BCL, Professor of English Law, London School of Economics and Political Science.

D. DAINTREE, MA, FLA, Librarian, Trent Polytechnic, Nottingham, Chairman, BIALL, 1969–75.

Miss SHEILA M. DOYLE, BA, ALA, Assistant Librarian, University of Durham.

R. G. LOGAN, LL.B, ALA, Law Librarian, University of Nottingham.

E. J. MILLER, BA, FSA, FRHist.s, formerly Assistant Keeper, Official Publications Collection, Reference Division, British Library.

Miss ELIZABETH M. MOYS, BA, FLA, Librarian, Goldsmiths' College, University of London, Hon. Editor, *The Law Librarian*.

P. NORMAN, BA, MA, ALA, Assistant Librarian, Institute of Advanced Legal Studies, University of London.

Miss DAPHNE A. PARNHAM, Deputy Librarian, Inner Temple Library.

K. O. PARSONS, MA, Assistant Librarian (Law), British Library of Political and Economic Science.

PROFESSOR OWEN HOOD PHILLIPS, QC, DCL, JP, formerly Pro-Vice-Chancellor and Vice-Principal, University of Birmingham, President, BIALL.

F. P. RICHARDSON, FLA, Librarian, Law Society, London, Chairman, BIALL, 1975– .

I. M. SAINSBURY, BA, ALA, Law Librarian, University of Reading.

W. A. STEINER, LL.M, MA, ALA, Barrister-at-Law, Librarian, Institute of Advanced Legal Studies, University of London.

MISS BARBARA M. TEARLE, LL.B, ALA, Law Librarian, University College, London.

D. J. WAY, MA, FLA, Sub-Librarian, University of Liverpool (Faculty of Law).

Acknowledgments

The editor and contributors are grateful to the following for help received: American Association of Law Libraries; Professor Sir J. N. D. Anderson, Director, Institute of Advanced Legal Studies; Aslib; Miss Margaret A. Banks, Law Librarian, University of Western Ontario; Mr P. C. M. Curtis-Bennett, Barrister-at-Law of the Inner Temple; Mr B. A. Custer, Editor, Dewey Decimal Classification; Mr Forrest S. Drummond, Librarian, Los Angeles County Law Library; Mrs M. G. Gallagher, Law Librarian, University of Washington, Seattle; Professor B. J. Halévy, Law Librarian, York University, Ontario; Mr G. A. Lloyd, Head, Classification Department, Fédération Internationale de Documentation; Mr B. McKenna; Mgr. L. L. McReavy, Ushaw College, Durham; Mr Jack Mills, Polytechnic of North London; Miss L. J. Mitchell, graduate trainee, Goldsmiths' College; Miss D. M. Priestly, formerly Law Librarian, University of Western Ontario; Mrs E. Richardson; Mr Gordon H. Scott, Barrister-at-Law of the Inner Temple; Mr M. I. Staig, Cataloguer, Goldsmiths' College; Mrs B. K. Steiner; the late Mr E. E. Thorogood, Chief Cataloguer, Goldsmiths' College; Mr W. J. Welsh, Director, Processing Department, Library of Congress.

The following have kindly granted permission for reproduction of copyright material in the text:

Architectural Press Ltd (Ch. 17, figs. 1 and 2)
Butterworth and Co. (Publishers) Ltd (Ch. 4, fig. 1; Ch. 5, figs. 1, 2, 4)
Don Gresswell Ltd (Ch. 13, fig. 5)
Controller of HM Stationery Office (Ch. 3, figs. 1–6)
Incorporated Council of Law Reporting for England and Wales (Ch. 4, fig. 2)
Polytechnic of Central London (Ch. 13, figs. 1 and 2)
Roneo Ltd (Ch. 13, figs. 3 and 4)
Sweet and Maxwell Ltd (Ch. 5, fig. 3)

Abbreviations

AA code	Cataloguing rules, author and title entries, 1908
AACR	Anglo-American Cataloguing Rules, 1967
AALL	American Association of Law Libraries
AC	Law Reports, Appeal Cases
ADP	Automatic data processing
AJ	Architects' Journal
ALA code	A[merican] L[ibrary] A[ssociation] cataloguing rules for author and title entries. 2nd edition 1949
Algol	Algorithmic language
All ER	All England Law Reports
Aslib	Association of Special Libraries and Information Bureaux
BC	(1) Before Christ
	(2) Bibliographic Classification (H. E. Bliss)
BIALL	British and Irish Association of Law Librarians
BLLD	British Library Lending Division
BLRD	British Library Reference Division
BM	British Museum
BNB	British National Bibliography
BS(I)	British Standard(s Institution)
BUCOP	British Union Catalogue of Periodicals
C	Command papers (1870–1899)
CA	Cases on Appeal
CBI	Cumulative Book Index
Cd	Command papers (1900–1918)
CL	Current Law
CLYB	Current Law Year Book
Cmd	Command papers (1919–56)
Cmnd	Command papers (1956–)
Cobol	Common business-orientated language
CODEN	System of coding serial publications devised by the American Society for Testing and Materials
CPU	Central processing unit

CREDOC	An information retrieval system, based on keyword indexing, for Belgian lawyers
DDC	Dewey Decimal Classification
ECSC	European Coal and Steel Community
EEC	European Economic Community (Common Market)
ENIAC	Electronic numerical integrator and calculator
ER	English Reports
Euratom	European Atomic Energy Community
ex.rel.	*ex relatione*
F	Fahrenheit
FAO	Food and Agriculture Organization
FID	Fédération International de Documentation
FIRA	Fontes iuris (or juris) Romani anteiustiniani
FLA	Fellow of the Library Association
Fortran	Formula translator
ft.^{2}	square feet
GPSL	Government publications sectional list
HL	House of Lords
HLRO	House of Lords' Record Office
HMC	Historical Manuscripts Commission
HMCR	Historical Manuscripts Commission's Reports
HMSO	Her (His) Majesty's Stationery Office
IAEA	International Atomic Energy Agency
IALL	International Association of Law Libraries
IALS	Institute of Advanced Legal Studies
IBM	International Business Machines (firm)
ICAO	International Civil Aviation Organization
ICCP	International Conference on Cataloguing Principles, Paris, 1961
ICJ	International Court of Justice
ICL	International Computers Limited (firm)
ICLQ	International and Comparative Law Quarterly
ICR	Industrial Court Reports
IFLA	International Federation of Library Associations
IFLP	Index to Foreign Legal Periodicals
ILO	International Labour Organization
ILP	Index to Legal Periodicals
ILTR	Irish Law Times Reports
INSPEC	Information service in physics, electrotechnology, computers and control (Institution of Electrical Engineers, London)

Interdoc	International Association for Legal Documentation
IR	Irish Reports
Ir	Ireland
ISBN	International Standard Book Number
ISDS	International Serials Data System
ISSN	International Standard Serial Number
JSPTL	Journal of the Society of Public Teachers of Law
K	A thousand units (especially in connection with computer hardware)
KB	King's Bench
KWIC	Key word in context indexing system
KWOC	Key word out of context indexing system
LA	Library Association, London
LACLL	Los Angeles County Law Library
LASER	London and South Eastern Region
LC	Library of Congress (USA)
m²	square metres
M&W	Meeson and Welby
MARC	Machine-readable catalogue
MASS	MARC-based Serials System
NALGO	National Association of Local Government Officers
NBT	Notable British Trials
NCL	National Central Library
NIJ & LG	New Irish Jurist and Local Government Review
NILR	Northern Ireland Law Reports
NS (or ns)	New series
OBAR	Ohio State Bar Automated Research System
OSTI	Office for Scientific and Technical Information (a part of the Department of Education and Science, now the British Library Research and Development Department)
PA	Publishers' Association
PRECIS	Preserved context indexing system
PRO	Public Record Office
QBD	Queen's Bench Division
R	Rex; Regina; Regum; Reginam
RCJ	Royal Courts of Justice
RECON	Project for possible retrospective conversion of the US Library of Congress catalogue to machine-readable form

RIAA	Reports of International Arbitral Awards
RS	Rolls Series [of Year Books]
SCONUL	Standing Conference of National and University Libraries
SDI	Selective dissemination of information
SI	Statutory Instrument
SLIC	Selective listing in combination
SLL	Squire Law Library, University of Cambridge
SLT	Scots Law Times
SLTR	Scots Law Times Reports
SPTL	Society of Public Teachers of Law
SR & Os	Statutory Rules and Orders
SS	Selden Society
STATUS	Statute search project
STC	Pollard, A. W. and Redgrave, G. R.: A short-title catalogue of books printed . . . 1475–1640
TIAS	Treaties and other International Acts Series (US)
TRHS	Transactions of the Royal Historical Society
UDC	Universal Decimal Classification
UGC	University Grants Committee
UK	United Kingdom of Great Britain and Northern Ireland
UN	United Nations
UNDEX	United Nations documents computer-assisted indexing programme
UNDI	United Nations Documents Index
Unesco/UNESCO	United Nations Educational, Scientific and Cultural Organization
Unidroit	Institute for the Unification of Private Law, Rome
UNISIST	Proposed world science information system
UST	United States Treaties and other International Agreements
WHO	World Health Organization
WLR	Weekly Law Reports
YB	Year Books [Medieval]

Glossary

Administrative tribunals: quasi-judicial bodies exercising some of the functions of courts of law, but outside the conventions of the legal system.

Abridgment: older form of digest or encyclopedia.

Accessioning: process of cross-checking contents of parcels, order records, invoices, etc., to ensure accuracy, and the subsequent taking into stock of the newly-received material.

Balance area: space within a building that is not assigned to specifically library functions, but is essential for services, circulation, toilets, etc.

Bay (shelving): group of shelves one shelf wide.

Blanket/block order: standing order with a supplier for all materials published in a special category.

Breviate: short account.

Broad classification: classification into a relatively small number of large categories without detailed sub-division.

Bull: edict or mandate issued by a pope or bishop.

By-laws: subordinate legislation promulgated by local authorities and other bodies under statutory authority.

Call mark: total finding symbol for a book, including, for example, location, class and cutter numbers.

Canon: rule, law or decree of the Church, especially one laid down by an ecclesiastical council.

Carrel: small individual study or screened table which may be allocated to a serious worker who requires the uninterrupted use of certain books for long periods.

Casebook: compilation of extracts from leading cases on a particular subject, designed as a teaching aid.

Charging: process of recording loans in a library.

Citation order: order in which the various facets (qv) of a complex subject are dealt with in a classification scheme.

Citator: volume or section of a volume containing tables of cases or legislation that have been judicially noticed in subsequent cases.

Civil law: (1) private rights of action for redress, contrasted with criminal law;
(2) the family of legal systems where the influence of Roman law has been strong.

Class mark: notation symbol representing the total subject of a book or document.

Classificationist: creator of a classification scheme.

Classifier: librarian who applies an existing classification scheme to materials in a library.

Codifying Acts: Acts passed to codify the whole of the existing law, both statutory and common law, on a subject.

Collating: checking all pages, plates, maps, or other contents of a publication to ensure that the text is complete, undamaged and in the correct order.

Collation: (1) make-up of a book from the printer's sections, etc.;
(2) part of a catalogue entry giving full or part details of collation (see above).

Common law: (1) judge-made law, as distinct from legislation and the rules of equity;
(2) family of legal systems deriving from the law of England.

Compiler: a computer program (*qv*) which converts a program written in one of the higher-level computer languages, *eg*, Cobol, into machine code.

Concordat: treaty or agreement with the force of international law, between the Church and a secular government.

Conflict of laws: that part of the law of a country which governs cases involving a foreign element.

Consolidating Acts: Acts passed to consolidate the statute law only on a subject, without necessarily affecting case law.

Constitutiones principum: Roman Imperial enactments, the sole form of legislation in the third century AD.

Convention: agreement between states, of less formality or importance than a treaty.

Cutter number: filing symbol ensuring alphabetical arrangement, consisting of letters and numbers (after C. A. Cutter).

Dáil Eireann: lower house of the Irish Parliament.

Delegated legislation: legislation made by a person or body, other than the sovereign in Parliament, by virtue of powers conferred either by statute or by legislation which is itself made under statutory powers.

Digest: (1) in common law jurisdictions: a compilation of the head-
notes (*qv*) of decided cases, arranged alphabetically or
systematically by subject;
(2) collection of principles or rules of law, compiled privately;
(3) major part of the *Corpus Juris Civilis* of Justinian.

Documentation: recording the contents of a library collection,
usually detailed analysis of the subject content for the purpose of
specialist information retrieval.

Equity: body of legal rules and remedies developed by the Court of
Chancery parallel to but separate from the common law (*qv*).

Facet (classification): one of the constituent categories of a complex
subject, *ie*, the group of divisions produced by the application of
a single characteristic of division (*eg*, place) to the subject.

Filing title: word or words inserted before the title statement in a
catalogue entry, to ensure correct filing order for entries under
the same heading. This may be a uniform title (*qv*) or some other
word(s) selected by the cataloguer.

Flow-chart: diagrammatic representation of the logical steps in the
task to be performed.

Fore-edge: edge of a volume opposite to the spine.

Foxing: brown stains caused by the growth of mould in paper, due
to dampness in the atmosphere.

Head-note: concise statement of the legal principles contained in a
law report.

Hospitality (classification): ability of a classification scheme to
accommodate changes, especially additional subjects, after initial
publication.

Housekeeping routines: routine library operations, such as ordering
and cataloguing, as distinct from textual scanning, usually in
connection with mechanization.

Imprint: (1) publisher's name and address as printed on the title
page;
(2) part of a catalogue entry giving place and date of
publication and publisher's name.

Information retrieval system: that part of a library's organization
designed to give access to the subject information contained in its
stock, *eg*, catalogues, indexes, shelf arrangement, etc.

International law: (1) private: *see* Conflict of laws;
(2) public: law concerning the rights and duties
of sovereign states towards each other, both
in peace and war.

Interpretatio: opinions of Roman jurists (interpreters of the law, not advocates) who did not usually appear in court; not originally binding but, by the Law at Citations, AD 426, the opinions of five jurists acquired binding force.

Leges publicae: statutes passed by the vote of the Roman people in the popular assemblies. The great bulk of the leges was of temporary political interest.

Literary warrant: theory of bibliographic classification that the divisions in a classification scheme should match the volume of literature rather than abstract concepts.

Local and Personal Acts: Acts of Parliament with restricted local or personal application, enacted on petition from the local or personal sponsor.

Municipal law: law of an individual sovereign state, as contrasted with public international law.

Noting up: noting that a reported case has been cited, and with what effect, in a later reported case, by means of a manuscript annotation, printed label, card index, printed supplement, etc. (*see also* Shepardize).

Oireachtas: Parliament of the Republic of Ireland.

Open entry: catalogue entry for a multi-volume work whose publication is not yet complete, with some details of the entry left open to allow for future additions.

Periodical: serial publication (*qv*) usually produced at regular intervals of less than a year and containing at least some articles and/or news items, as distinct from legislation and case reports.

Phase (classification): relationship between two subjects or two facets (*qv*) of one subject.

Practice book: volume devoted to the practice of a court or category of courts; it usually includes: court rules, court forms, practice directions, etc.

Practick: in Scots law: a precedent that is not necessarily binding.

Praetorian edicts: yearly Roman proclamations in which the new praetors made known those legal rules which they would apply to the administration of justice.

Precedent book: volume containing standard legal forms, precedents, or other documents.

Prelims: all parts of a volume preceding the main text; these may include half-title, title, contents list, foreword, introduction, etc.

Primary materials: texts consisting wholly or substantially of the law itself, *eg*, legislation, codes, law reports.

Private Act: Act of Parliament not held to be of general application; it may be local or personal.

Private international law: *see* Conflict of laws.

Program: set of instructions to a computer to perform a specific task.

Promulgation: official publication of a new law, putting it into effect.

Reception: adoption in whole or in part of the law of one jurisdiction by another jurisdiction.

Record: any document that is specially created as being authentic evidence of a matter of legal importance.

Roman-Dutch law: system of law of Holland from the mid-fifteenth century to the early nineteenth century, based on a mixture of Germanic customary law and Roman law as interpreted in medieval law schools.

Seanad Eireann: Upper House of the Irish Parliament.

Secondary legislation: *see* Delegated legislation.

Secondary materials: texts consisting mainly of commentary on the law, rather than the law itself, *eg*, exposition, criticism, history, philosophy.

see also reference: reference linking catalogue entries under one heading with entries under one or more related headings.

see reference: reference from a heading not used in the catalogue to the heading selected for use.

Selective dissemination of information: information service tailored to the specialized interests of individual readers.

Senatus consulta: Advice from the Roman Senate which had no legal weight, although it was usually followed, until the second century AD, when it became the expression of the imperial will.

Serial publication: any publication issued at intervals over a long period, *eg*, any newspaper or journal, most law reports, legislative and treaty series. Many libraries treat annuals and loose-leaf and other encyclopedias as serials.

Shelf list: form of catalogue, arranged strictly in shelf order, with one entry only per item.

Shepardize: in United States practice, to produce a complete citator (*qv*) for a series of legislation or court reports.

Sizing: strengthening water-stained or soft leaves of a book by passing them through a bath of hot glue size, after which they are hung to dry.

Slip laws: individual pamphlets containing one enactment in each.

Sources of law: those repositories of legal rules to which lawyers, especially judges, turn in order to discover what the law is.

Standard stack section: bay (*qv*) of shelving 7' 6" (2290 mm) high and 3' 0" (915 mm) wide.

Subordinate/subsidiary legislation: *see* Delegated legislation.

Tag: form of coded label attached to an element of information input to a computer to distinguish one category of information from another, *eg,* order number, author, title, etc.

Textbook: volume containing opinions, and sometimes texts, on the law. It has no legal authority.

Uniform title: version of the title of a work selected as the filing medium for all editions and versions of the work, whatever the title-page title may be.

Unit entry: standard catalogue entry, to which may be added headings for co-authors, editor, title, series, subject, etc.

Year Books: law reports, highly subjective, of medieval English society.

Part I Introduction

1. Law Libraries and Their Users

D. DAINTREE, MA, FLA
Librarian, Trent Polytechnic, Nottingham

Law libraries in the British Isles have a long history (the library of Lincoln's Inn for example can be traced back to 1475) and today they form a distinct group characterized by their common interest in a specific subject area. However, although they all share this common subject interest in law, at the same time they vary considerably, for example in size, in the type of user to be served, in their administration, finance, etc. It is the purpose of this survey to examine the various categories of law libraries, so that the chapters which follow may be seen in relation to the pattern of libraries, whose staffs this *Manual* is intended to assist.

It seems only fitting that we should begin this survey with the national libraries, for while they are not specialized law libraries, as are many of those shortly to be examined, their collections of legal material are often more extensive than the latter.

NATIONAL LIBRARIES

In terms of users, the national libraries are distinct from most other categories which will be dealt with later in this chapter. Instead of being restricted, for example, to members of a society, students of an academic institution, or staff of a government department, their services are available to the nation with but few formalities save those necessary for their efficient operation or brought about by space restrictions. At a time when all but the largest law libraries are unable to claim self-sufficiency (and even these are beginning to feel the effect of financial stringencies) the value of the national libraries holdings as back-up resources needs no further elaboration.

England

There is no national law library in the United Kingdom as exists, for example, in the United States; but because it is a legal deposit library, the British Library Reference Division in London (more commonly known by its previous name – the British Museum Library) possesses rich resources in English law; its holdings of English legal periodicals, for example, are unmatched in this country. Unfortunately, this legal material is not kept together as a separate law collection but is disseminated throughout the library's holdings. Neither are there specially qualified subject staff (as in its American counterpart) to select, organize and exploit the collections in this subject field. The result is that, despite the breadth and depth of its stock in law, for all but the more determined research worker the library is not of great practical value.

In an attempt to improve its provision for lawyers, a memorandum was submitted to the British Library Board in 1973 by the BIALL.[1] Its main recommendation was that the plans for the reference service should incorporate a separate subject department for law, with a specialist staff and as comprehensive a collection as possible, the most frequently used materials being on open access. It is hoped that facilities for the profession will thus at least be considerably expanded in the proposed new library premises, if not in its present ones.

In addition to its holdings of monographs and journals, the library, in its State Paper Room, possesses a wealth of government documentation (including legislation) from both this country and many countries overseas – much of which is of great value to the lawyer.

All of this material is for reference use only (though photocopying facilities are available) and it is the British Library Lending Division at Boston Spa in Yorkshire which provides borrowing facilities. Because this division is of much more recent origin than the Reference Division (it was originally established in 1959 as the National Lending Library for Science and Technology and later absorbed the National Central Library), its holdings of older legal materials are

---

[1] British and Irish Association of Law Librarians. Provision for law in the British Library. *Law Librarian*, vol. 5, 1974, pp. 25–6.

relatively small; but by means of its union catalogue of stock held in many British libraries it is frequently able to obtain such items through the inter-library loan network. For more recent material, however, its collections are now becoming more comprehensive – not least in the field of law. It has a larger collection of current English language legal periodicals than any other library in the country and now purchases all British monographs costing over £10, all law books from American university presses, and all other worthwhile English language books in our subject field (the exception in these latter cases being 'technical' law books). In addition, it has significant holdings of British government publications, and special collections of research reports, theses and conference proceedings – many of which can be of value to the lawyer.

All of this material is available for loan, either in the original or as photocopies or microforms.

Other parts of the British Isles

In Wales, the privilege of legal deposit is accorded to the National Library of Wales in Aberystwyth, and although Scotland possesses its own national library in the National Library of Scotland, for historical reasons the Advocates' Library (see page 38) holds the legal deposit collection in law. Both the above libraries are basically reference collections and neither Wales nor Scotland possess lending facilities comparable to those of the British Library Lending Division. In the Republic of Ireland, the function of the national library is performed by Trinity College Library in Dublin (see page 50).

SOCIETY LIBRARIES

Extensive though the collections of the relevant national library in law may now be, the first library to which the practitioner turns for assistance is that of his professional body.

England and Wales

In England and Wales the legal profession is divided into two well defined branches – barristers (collectively known as the

2

Bar) and solicitors. The Bar is traditionally the senior of the two branches and barristers are chiefly concerned with the drafting of legal documents, the writing of opinions, advising clients and the preparation and pleading of cases heard in courts of law – they in fact have the monopoly of pleading before the higher courts. There were approximately 3,000 barristers in practice in 1973, the majority of whom were to be found in London. All barristers are members of one of the four Inns of Court (*ie*, Lincoln's Inn, Gray's Inn, the Inner Temple, and the Middle Temple) whose origin can be traced back to the fourteenth century. The Inns are independent entities with the legal status of unincorporated associations and they were originally founded to provide legal instruction for prospective lawyers. Apart from providing focal points for the profession and space within their confines for the establishment of chambers, they are, through their Senate and together with the Bar Council (*ie*, representatives of the practising barristers) responsible for many important matters affecting the profession, such as discipline and education – though the actual teaching and examination is performed by the Council of Legal Education on behalf of all the Inns.

Solicitors, on the other hand, are concerned with a wide variety of general legal matters as distinct from the more specific tasks of the barrister (the comparison is frequently made with the medical profession, whereby the barristers are regarded as the 'specialists' and the solicitors the 'general practitioners'). They deal with, among other matters, conveyancing, probate, the formation of companies, the preparation of miscellaneous documents, the giving of legal advice to clients, matrimonial disputes, taxation questions, preliminary work in cases going for trial, and actual pleading in the lower courts.

The part played by the Inns of Court in relation to barristers is played by the Law Society in relation to solicitors. The society was founded in 1825 (though an earlier body known as the Society of Gentlemen Practicers in the Courts of Law and Equity preceded it in the eighteenth century) and now regulates the solicitors' branch of the profession by conducting qualifying examinations, granting annual certificates of practice, and maintaining a code of professional ethics. In addition, many of the other functions expected of a professional society are provided (*eg*, publications, social facilities and – not least important – a library). Solicitors are much more numerous than barristers (there were approximately 24,000 in practice in 1973) and are found throughout the length and breadth of the country. Because of this geographical scatter provincial law societies exist in most of the large centres of population; these provide services similar to the national society at the local level.

The printed word has always been to the legal practitioner what tools are to the craftsman or apparatus to the scientist, hence libraries or collections of legal texts have long been regarded as essential by the Inns and (although of much later foundation) the Law Society.

It is perhaps of interest at this point to notice the intense concentration of practitioners' libraries in London. This is directly due to the fact that the major courts in England and Wales have been located in that city since the thirteenth century. It is only natural, therefore, that the various professional bodies should also establish themselves there. Since the Inns and (at a later date) the Law Society were also responsible for the education of their members – in the absence of academic courses in law at the universities (see page 43) – their libraries assumed a wider role than that of merely providing day to day information for the practising solicitor or barrister. The net result has been, in a sense, an over-provision of legal resources in the capital while many other parts of the country lag far behind – an inequitable distribution which the SPTL attempted unsuccessfully to remedy for all users of legal literature in their evidence to the Dainton Committee in 1969.[1]

Inns of Court

The exact date of the foundation of the Inn libraries is uncertain, but the records available indicate that such were in existence in 1475 (Lincoln's Inn), 1506 (Inner Temple), 1521 (Gray's Inn) or, in the case of the Middle Temple, some time in the early sixteenth century. Today their collections are of some significance, figures for their holdings being in the region of 35,000 (Gray's Inn), 106,000 (Lincoln's), 85,000 (Inner

[1] Great Britain. National Libraries Committee. Report. HMSO, 1969. (Cmnd. 4028) (ISBN 0 10 140280 5).

Temple) and 103,000 (Middle Temple). Because of their long history, all the libraries possess significant amounts of rare historical material – though owing to the depredation of enemy bombs during the Second World War, much that was irreplaceable was destroyed. In common with many other society libraries whose origins precede the present century, their collections are much more cosmopolitan than their present-day subject interests would indicate; apart from a wide range of legal material there are significant holdings in history, literature, topography, biography and similar enlightening subjects. At the present time, however, such excursions into non-legal subjects are restricted by financial limitations and available funds are used to ensure that there is adequate provision for the current needs of their users – including material on jurisdictions other than our own. Thus attempts are made to cover American and Commonwealth law, but at present there is especial interest in the law of the European Communities and one of the few moves towards formal co-operation between the four Inn libraries was made in 1972 when, following a study by a Committee of the Inns under the chairmanship of Lord Diplock, an Inns of Court European Communities Law Library was established. This is housed in the Middle Temple Library and aims to establish a comprehensive collection of community law material together with that of the law of the major member countries. It is designed for the use of members of the Bar, and of solicitors by arrangement with the Law Society.

The Inn libraries serve two groups of user. Primarily they exist to meet the needs of their members, nearly all of whom are practising barristers. Since the majority of these practise in London, the Inns act as their working libraries. Stock is for reference use only, though special arrangements may be made to take material into court if it is not readily available elsewhere. Like many other special libraries, they give emphasis to assistance to readers, and since information is frequently required at short notice there is need for assistance with speed – the user cannot wait until next week if the case is being heard tomorrow!

The second group of users served is that of the embryo barrister, *ie*, the student studying for his Bar examinations. For such users the Inn libraries provide a place for study where, because of their reference nature, all of the standard works, reports, statutes, etc. are always to hand. There is no attempt, however, as in other libraries serving students, to make special provision of student texts and cram books.

In addition to the above may be mentioned another class of user, best described as the general public. Because of the unique nature of these libraries, members of the public have not infrequently to resort to them for information not available elsewhere. Any assistance given to such users must obviously depend on the staff time left after the Inns' own members have been adequately provided for.

Law Societies

Law Society libraries perform similar functions for solicitors to those performed by Inn libraries for members of the Bar, *ie*, the provision of information and reference facilities for practitioners and assistance to students with their studies. However, whereas there are four major Inn libraries, only the Law Society in London possesses a comparable collection. The development of a significant library was in fact one of the purposes behind the creation of the Law Society in 1825 and one was founded in 1828 on the same London site on which it stands at the present day. Like the libraries of the four Inns, its holdings are both significant in size (now standing at over 80,000 volumes) and cosmopolitan in coverage – but the emphasis today is on current legal materials of value to the practising solicitor.

In addition to the main Law Society in London, which – unlike the Inns – handles a large variety of postal, telephone and telex enquiries from provincial members, there are a number of local law society libraries of varying size and quality of service. Most aim to provide local solicitors with at least a basic reference and information service, but few in fact have either the stock or the staff to perform these functions adequately. Perhaps the largest and most active provincial law society library is that at Birmingham, with a stock of 53,000 volumes; it also has the distinction of being the oldest law society library in the country – being founded in 1818 – and contains much rare and valuable early legal material.

Scotland

In Scotland, the Faculty of Advocates governs the senior branch of the profession; Scottish solicitors come under the aegis of the Law Society of Scotland, but they may also belong to any one of twenty-eight curiously named societies for law agents – the two most famous of which are the Society of Writers to Her Majesty's Signet and the Royal Faculty of Procurators.

Scottish professional law libraries have tended, for a variety of reasons, to accumulate more general collections than similar libraries in England. The original Advocates' Library, which was founded in Edinburgh in 1682 and enjoyed copyright privileges, was presented to the nation by the Faculty in 1925 and became the National Library of Scotland. The law books were retained to form the nucleus of the present library (which now totals over 66,000 volumes) and all British legal publications received by the National Library under the Copyright provisions are deposited in the Advocates' Library. In one sense, therefore, the library could be said to be the national law library for Scotland.

The Signet Library in Edinburgh, founded in 1722, is very much a general library containing but a basic working collection of English and Scots law which is included in the figure of 118,500 volumes quoted by Breem.[1] It is open only to members and their apprentices. The library of the Royal Faculty of Procurators in Glasgow dates back to the seventeenth century and is open to university teachers as well as to members of the Faculty and their staffs. It operates a branch library at the Sheriff's Court in the City for the use of sheriffs and judges.

Other parts of the United Kingdom

In Northern Ireland, judges and members of the profession have access to the Law Faculty Library of Queen's University. The Isle of Man Law Society specializes in Manx Law and is available to judges and practitioners on the island. The Channel Islands have a small law library in the Societé de Gens de Droit, use of which is restricted to members of the Society.

[1] Breem, W. W. S. Professional law libraries of Great Britain. *Law Library Journal*, vol. 64, 1971, pp. 278–90.

Republic of Ireland

In the Irish Republic, King's Inns serves a similar function for the Irish Bar as is performed by the English Inns of Court. Its origins are as old as its English counterparts, but the library can be traced back only to 1787. Of its present stock of over 110,000 volumes, approximately half are on legal topics, with English and Irish law predominating. Its facilities are extended to members of the Honourable Society of King's Inns (including students, barristers and judges) and these include the right to borrow material. Like its counterparts in the United Kingdom, it is housed in premises – in Dublin – which reflect the glories and splendours of a bygone age. The Incorporated Law Society of Ireland, also situated in Dublin, is similar in function to the Law Society in London, though in terms of size its Library holdings compare unfavourably with those of the latter.

COURT LIBRARIES

Apart from the libraries of their professional institutions, barristers also have access to legal material in some of the courts in which they practise. These court libraries vary considerably in their provision; some courts in fact have none. The Supreme Court of Judicature for England and Wales – consisting of the Court of Appeal and the High Court of Judicature – sits at the Royal Courts of Justice in the Strand, London, and it is here that court library provision is most comprehensive.

The Bar Library in the Royal Courts was founded in 1883 as a joint venture by the four Inns of Court and was intended as a reference library for members of the Bar of all the Inns having business in the courts. The library is managed by a joint committee of the four Inns and the cost of books, binding, salaries and overheads (*eg*, lighting, heating, etc.) is shared by the Inns and the Lord Chancellor's Department. The library contains well over 40,000 volumes, mainly on English law and its function is to provide the practising barrister with the reference material necessary for the proper presentation of his case in court. Judges also use the material held by the library in their deliberations. Of unique interest is its collection of typescript copies of unpublished judgments of the Court of Appeal. Most of the items in stock are loanable for use in court.

In addition to the Bar Library there are several smaller libraries throughout the Law Courts in the Strand and these are housed in the various courts, the largest being in the Appeal Courts. The administration of these libraries is in the hands of the Librarian of the Bar Library, but the expense of maintenance is borne entirely by the Treasury.

The Probate Library and the Supreme Court Library are also housed in the Royal Courts of Justice, in premises opened in 1968. Together they contain over 40,000 volumes. The Probate Library is a subscription library, all of whose members are barristers. Subscribers may borrow material and the library is under the control of the Librarian of the Bar Library. The Supreme Court Library is intended for the use of the judges, who may borrow material. Members of the Bar may use it for reference only.

In London, other court libraries are to be found (1) in the Central Criminal Court at the Old Bailey, which serves a similar purpose to the Bar Library, but on a smaller scale; (2) the Judicial Committee of the Privy Council, with over 15,000 volumes, available only to members of their Lordships' Board and to barristers engaged in cases before the Board; (3) the House of Lords which, in its judicial capacity is the highest court of appeal for all cases from the courts of England, Wales and Northern Ireland and also for civil appeals from the Scottish courts (see also page 50).

Outside London, library provision in the courts is very sparse. The Lord Chancellor's Office maintains small basic collections in the Crown and County courts for the use of judges, but there is no provision for the Bar as in the Royal Courts of Justice. Barristers therefore have to rely on their own personal resources for legal material or on the bar libraries established in some Crown Court centres by the local public library service.

In other parts of the British Isles, court libraries are as undeveloped as they are in English centres outside London. Provision in the courts themselves is minimal, judges and practitioners being dependent on their professional bodies for other than basic source material.

PUBLIC LIBRARIES

Most public libraries in the United Kingdom contain a certain amount of legal material both for the general public and for the legal staff employed by the local authority (although the latter often have their own working collection in the appropriate department). Some of the best collections are, as one might expect, in the larger municipal reference libraries, such as the Guildhall Library in the City of London and in provincial cities such as Liverpool. Worthwhile collections of monographic material are also to be found in those libraries responsible for law in the various local regional and national co-operative acquisition schemes (*eg*, under the Metropolitan subject specialization scheme, Hammersmith Central Library is responsible for acquiring all English legal texts).

Some public libraries are also responsible for the provision of libraries to serve the courts in their areas. The first public library to provide such a service was Leeds. There, a law library is stocked and staffed by the public library service and is situated in the building housing most of the courts in that city. Although in theory 'public', the law library there is, in effect, mainly for judges and barristers practising in that area. While the courts are sitting they alone have access to the library – although solicitors attending the courts are also allowed to use it. A basic working collection of English legal materials is held and this is for reference use within the library, though items may be taken into court if required there. During recesses, barristers and solicitors practising in Leeds may borrow material for use in their chambers or offices. Public access to stock is restricted to evening, week-end and vacation use, and then only for consultation in the City Reference Library.

Similar provision has been made for the courts in a number of other cities. Birmingham and Sheffield are noteworthy examples.

GOVERNMENT LAW LIBRARIES

Unlike some other countries, the United Kingdom does not possess a major government law library. All official libraries, however, have some legal connotations in that their primary function is to serve the various organs of state. Hence, official documents and basic legal materials in their specialist field of interest are to be found within their collections. For example, the library of the Board of Inland Revenue contains material on taxation law; the Department of Trade and Industry maintains a major reference library on commercial law; the Foreign and Commonwealth Office Library has special collections on international law, community law and the law of Commonwealth countries – including a virtually complete set of all Commonwealth legislation; the Home Office Library is particularly strong on criminal law and has a special collection of penal codes and codes of criminal procedure of overseas countries.

There are, however, two government libraries, albeit small ones, devoted specifically to law – the Law Commission Library and the library of the Treasury Solicitor's Department.

The Law Commission for England and Wales and a similar body for Scotland were established by statute in 1965 'to take and keep under review all the law with which they are respectively concerned, with a view to its systematic development and reform, including in particular the codification of such law, the elimination of anomolies, the repeal of obsolete and unnecessary enactments, the reduction of the number of separate enactments and generally the simplification and modernization of the law'. The English Law Commission established a library almost immediately in London with the aim of building up a collection geared to the current work of the parent body and ultimately to house an important collection of law reform material obtained from other legal systems as well as our own. It now contains over 16,000 volumes, mainly on English law – though general social science materials form a not insignificant part of the stock (for it is impossible to consider reforms in the law without studying the social background to the particular subject under consideration). Starting, as it did, from scratch the library was not hamstrung by procedures from the past and it is interesting to note that it was the first British library to adopt the *Classification Scheme for Law Books* devised by E. M. Moys (see page 568). The library of the Scottish Law Commission is similar in scope to its English cousin, but smaller in size (with approximately 7,000 volumes).

The office of Treasury Solicitor dates back to at least 1655 and his department provides a legal service for government departments not possessing their own legal sections. The library acts as a working library for the legal staff of the department and numbers over 10,000 volumes. It has the distinction of being one of the few law libraries to produce a printed catalogue in recent years (*Catalogue of the Legal Library of the Treasury Solicitor.* 2nd edition, 1967).

Government departmental libraries were set up to serve the staffs of those particular departments and are therefore not open to the public in the sense that the national libraries are. Most government libraries, however, are prepared to admit research workers and others who have a special interest in their holdings.

ACADEMIC LAW LIBRARIES

Though the practitioners' libraries previously described possess unique, rare and valuable material and are housed in buildings which, if they are not particularly practical, at least have character, the most rapidly expanding sector of the law library network today is to be found in our institutions of higher education.

From their earliest days, the Inns of Court had been teaching institutions; but their staple subject had been English law for practitioners. Civil law was outside their field of interest, but as early as the thirteenth century, Roman law (upon which civil law is based) was being taught as a subject in the two ancient universities, *ie*, Oxford and Cambridge. It was not, however, until the time of Henry VIII that such teaching was organized on a proper footing with the foundation of chairs of civil law at those institutions in 1538. The common law continued to be excluded from their curricula, however, until 1753 when Blackstone, who was a Fellow of All Souls, gave the first of a series of formal lectures at Oxford on the subject. This was originally a private venture, but thanks to the generosity of Viner – who left the proceeds of his *Abridgement* and other monies to the University – a chair in common law was endowed there in 1758, and Blackstone became the first Vinerian Professor. From then until his resignation in 1765 he delivered lectures which were later to form the basis of his famous *Commentaries*; but after his resignation the teaching of common law at Oxford again fell into abeyance. In the early nineteenth century attempts were again made to initiate courses in common law in the universities. Thus in 1800 the Downing Professorship of the Laws of England was founded at Cambridge, but it was not until the foundation of University College, London, in 1826 that the first modern university law school appeared in this country. A chair of law was also established at King's College, London, in 1831. It was not, however, until the second half of the century that law teaching as we now know it took firm root in our universities, when several courses were established and new professorial chairs installed at the above mentioned institutions. By 1908, with the growth of civic universities, there were eight law faculties in England and Wales. But most were relatively small and even by 1938 there were only 1,500 undergraduate students reading law in this country. By 1970, however, there were over 5,000 and the number continues to grow.

At the present time there are 34 universities and 15 non-university institutions (mainly polytechnics) in England and Wales offering undergraduate courses in law; and in each of these institutions there is a law library (either as a separate entity or as part of the parent institution's library), providing not only collections of legal materials but also – of equal importance – places in which to study.

Academic law libraries number three particular groups among their users; undergraduates, who need access to the basic materials required for their first degree course – multiple copies of these are often needed to provide adequately for the numbers of students involved; postgraduate students, who require virtually everything available in their specialist fields of study; and the teaching staff, whose needs are usually similar to those of the postgraduates, and who need in addition to be kept abreast of the latest developments in the law in general, as well as in their own particular subject fields.

Standards of provision

Alone among law libraries in the United Kingdom, the users of those in academic institutions have been sufficiently concerned with the services provided for them to have devised what they feel to be suitable standards of provision to support courses at both undergraduate and postgraduate level. The Society of Public Teachers of Law (the professional association representing lecturers in law in British universities) issued its first *Statement of proposed minimum library holdings for law libraries in England and Wales* in September 1958 as a result of the deficiencies revealed by a survey conducted the previous year. This *Statement* had no binding authority, but since it gave law faculties a standard to aim at, it has been a major factor in bringing about the expansion of university law libraries in the United Kingdom. (It is doubtful whether similar standards would have been so readily accepted if proposed by librarians!)

Apart from stock, the *Statement* dealt with staff, seating accommodation, finance and other matters which are discussed elsewhere in this *Manual*. As a result of several years' experience, and because of the need to take into account material other than that from the United Kingdom (in particular from the Commonwealth and the United States) after the coverage of many university law courses was widened, and because of the further need to reassess their multiple copy requirements as the number of students increased, a revised *Statement* was issued in December 1970.[1] This too was welcomed by librarians as well as teachers as a means of improving library facilities. However, on one point, namely that of multiple provision, sufficient law libraries expressed concern for the BIALL to undertake a survey in an attempt to assess their members' feelings on the subject. As a result of the findings of the survey, the Association expressed the opinion that whilst the provision of multiple copies was desirable in theory, this would place a very heavy burden on law library budgets. Librarians disagreed on the extent of duplication needed and, even had funds been available for early implementation of the survey's findings, several libraries would have severe space problems.

In terms of holdings, academic law libraries vary considerably, both in size and coverage. The SPTL *Standards* suggest a

[1] Society of Public Teachers of Law. Statement of minimum holdings . . . *Journal of the Society of Public Teachers of Law*, n. s., vol. 11, 1970–1, pp. 90–103.

basic minimum stock for all university law libraries in the
United Kingdom, but most have holdings well in excess of this.
Way's paper indicates that nine had a stock of over 15,000
volumes as long ago as 1968 and there has been a considerable
increase since that date.[1] A large percentage of the stock in
most of these libraries is for reference only, being composed of
reports, statutes, volumes of periodicals and basic reference
volumes. Duplication of the textbooks provided is common in
order to meet users' requirements.

Although most university law libraries have moved or are
moving towards standardization in terms of the SPTL minimum
holdings, there is still a wide variety of approaches in terms of
services and organization in the different institutions.

One of the main differences is that of relationships with the
main university library; or perhaps to put it in simpler terms
the problem of centralization versus decentralization or
departmental versus central libraries. Librarians tend to come
down on the side of centralization (*ie*, that the law library be an
integral part of the main university library, since it is then far
easier to organize and staff) but law teachers favour decentralization, as has been made quite plain by the SPTL on
more than one occasion (*ie*, in their evidence to the Parry
Committee[2] and in the preamble to their minimum holdings
list). They stress that law books, reports, etc., are essential
teaching and learning tools to the law student and teacher in
the same way that laboratory equipment and materials is
essential in science teaching. Because of this the law library
should be within the Faculty building rather than with the
main library. While not disputing this, it would be easier to
accept if legal literature formed a compact self-contained unit.
At one time it undoubtedly did, but today this is no longer the
case, as the SPTL itself admits in the same preamble. Law is now
more and more becoming an interdisciplinary subject. To quote
the SPTL document, 'There is an increasing tendency for
lawyers to draw on more general literature relating to the
specifically legal areas of study. The relationship between

[1] Way, D. J. University Law Libraries of Great Britain. *Law Library
Journal*, vol. 64, 1971, pp. 291–301.
[2] Great Britain. University Grants Committee. Report of the Committee
on Libraries. HMSO, 1967.

criminal law and criminology is obvious, but social and economic literature is also relied on by teachers in other subjects; for instance, the details of urban sociology in relation to certain aspects of land law, political science in relation to constitutional and administrative law, and philosophy in relation to jurisprudence.' The case for independent law libraries is therefore becoming harder to justify and with universities facing increasing costs, especially on their libraries, it will no doubt become even more difficult in the future to justify duplicate provision of non-legal material in the faculties. Perhaps the compromise solution is to provide basic undergraduate reference libraries in the law faculty with the major part of the law stock in the main university library alongside the other subjects. This is a topic which will no doubt occupy the minds of many teachers and librarians over the next few years, but there is certainly no evidence to prove that the user suffers from centralization or particularly benefits from decentralization. As yet, the case on either side remains unproven.

Educating the user

Another topic of current interest in academic law libraries – though certainly not a contentious issue, as was the previous one – is that of training or educating the user in the use of the law library and its holdings. Lawyers, in whatever branch of the profession they may practise, need to possess a knowledge of legal information sources, and there seems no better time to provide such knowledge than during their undergraduate days. It is thus now common practice for university law libraries – usually in conjunction with their Faculty or Department – to provide instruction in the use of the library and legal literature early on during university law courses. Various methods of instruction have been or are being used, *eg*, lectures, practical projects, tape/slide presentations, tape-recorded self-instruction sessions, etc. Whichever method is used, however, there is no doubt that such instruction should form an integral part of every undergraduate law course and therefore that academic law librarians should regard this as one of the most significant duties which they can perform for their users.

England and Wales

Of all the academic law libraries in the United Kingdom, three stand out in terms of their collections and facilities; namely the Bodleian Law Library at the University of Oxford, the Squire Law Library at the University of Cambridge, and the Institute of Advanced Legal Studies at London University.

The Bodleian Law Library is the largest law library in the United Kingdom (and probably in the Commonwealth) and is housed in fine premises opened in 1964. It is administratively part of the main Bodleian Library and thus receives all law books deposited there under the provisions of the Copyright Act; because of this provision, its stock is entirely for reference use only. Its holdings are now in excess of 135,000 volumes and apart from English law it is particularly rich in legal materials from the Commonwealth and the United States of America.

The Squire Law Library, in contrast to the Bodleian, is a faculty library and is thus independent of the main university library. It does however have a special arrangement with the latter in that law books received there under the Copyright Act are deposited in the Squire unless they are deemed of interest to readers other than lawyers. In practice, this excludes books on borderline subjects, *eg*, legal history, constitutional law, etc., and in 1964 it was estimated that books so deposited amounted to but 10 to 20 per cent of the total acquisitions. Like the Bodleian, its holdings are for reference and, though English law predominates, its stock is rich in foreign legal material.

Although there are a number of significant collections of legal material in the various libraries within the University of London (*eg*, University College, King's College, British Library of Political and Economic Science, etc.) among which there is a marked measure of co-operative provision, the library of the Institute of Advanced Legal Studies is by far the most significant. The Institute itself is unique in that it is solely for postgraduate students (the University in fact possesses a number of such institutes in various subject fields). It was set up in 1947 and – assisted by grants from such bodies as the Ford and Nuffield Foundations for special collections of American and Commonwealth material – it has built up its holdings to over 100,000 volumes. In 1969, together with the Middle Temple Library, it was designated by the Foundation for Overseas Libraries of American Law as one of the two centres in London which would receive material with a view to establishing special collections in American Law.

The Institute is perhaps best known to law librarians for its bibliographical activities. It is, in fact, the only organization in the United Kingdom that has carried out an organized programme of bibliographical publications, and it has produced over the years a number of unique lists which have proved invaluable to the profession, the most generally useful of such tools being its *Union list of legal periodicals* which is currently in its third edition. Other publications which have proved of great value include a *List of legal research topics . . .*, which gives details of theses accepted for higher degrees in law in United Kingdom universities, and a *List of official committees, commissions and other bodies concerned with the reform of the law*, whose title is self-explanatory and which appears in new editions from time to time. Last – but by no means least – among its bibliographical activities is the compilation (in co-operation with the American Association of Law Librarians) of the *Index of Foreign Legal Periodicals*. After being housed for nearly thirty years in a building which was far from adequate, the Institute library moved to more adequate and new premises in 1975.

Much of what has been said above in relation to university law libraries is also applicable to law libraries and collections in polytechnics, which are somewhat similar institutions of higher education. Several of these offer first degrees in law and to support these courses have collections of legal material. Since the polytechnics are relatively new bodies in comparison with universities – the first one only being established in 1970 – their collections are at present relatively small, but in most cases those offering law degrees are making every effort to increase their holdings so as to reach the standards set by the SPTL.

Other parts of the British Isles

Academic libraries in other parts of the British Isles closely resemble those in England and Wales. Where there is a law faculty there is a collection of legal material either in a separate library, as in Edinburgh University, or as part of the main library, as at the University of Strathclyde. In the Republic of Ireland, the most comprehensive legal collection exists at Trinity College, Dublin, which has legal deposit privileges in similar manner to the universities of Oxford and Cambridge.

LEGISLATIVE LIBRARIES

In most countries, the libraries of the legislature – as the main law making body in the land – have extensive holdings of law literature. In the United States, for example, the largest law library in that country is the Law Library of Congress. While no legislative body within the British Isles can boast of such a collection, each does contain within its library a significant amount of legal material, for legal information is obviously of great importance to those responsible for making our law – namely the members of the legislative body concerned. While the Stormont in Northern Ireland, the Dáil in the Irish Republic and their counterparts in the Isle of Man and the Channel Islands possess libraries for their respective members which contain – among other subjects – material on law, the two most significant legislative libraries are those of the British House of Commons and the House of Lords. The former provides for Members of Parliament a working law library, *ie,* current editions of the more important text and reference books on all major aspects of English and Scots law, together with reports, statutes and other such material relevant to those countries. This and similar material on the law of the European Communities is exploited by a highly sophisticated information service. The law collection in the Lords is far more comprehensive than in the Commons since the Lords of Appeal, sitting in the House, form the highest court in the land and the library is in effect their court library.

MISCELLANEOUS LAW LIBRARIES

Apart from the major groups of law libraries described above, there exist a number of others worthy of note.

For example, there is a small number of libraries within firms of solicitors. In the United States such private law libraries, as they are called, are commonplace, as many law practices are sufficiently large to justify the establishment of libraries to service the various partners within the firm. Until recent years, solicitors' practices in the United Kingdom have tended to be small, but nowadays there are several large groups and some have found it worthwhile to set up their own libraries so as to provide the legal staff with the information resources relevant to the needs of their job (*ie*, reports, statutes, practice books, etc.) and in some cases a librarian has been appointed to exploit this material on the lines of similar services in industrial libraries.

A unique library within the United Kingdom is the Law Notes Lending Library – unique in that it is one of the very few serious commercial lending libraries left in the country and that it is the only one devoted to law books (perhaps the Probate Library in the Royal Courts of Justice could also be regarded as a commercial library, but it has a very restricted clientele and therefore can best be regarded as a type of society library). The advantages of such a library include: no restriction on membership (unlike most of the other libraries we have mentioned) other than payment of the requisite subscription; all material is available for loan (many law libraries are for reference use only); books may be kept out indefinitely, provided the subscription has not expired (most normal libraries impose some restriction on the period of loan); the ability to borrow new books very shortly after they have been published, etc. The advantage of this type of library service to students and practitioners remote from other law libraries needs no emphasizing; but the service is also of value to practitioners who wish to supplement their own libraries or to borrow material not loaned by their Inn or Law Society library. Even other libraries can find that a subscription is a useful way of supplementing their own collections. That such a fee-paying library manages to survive successfully in this day of free library services is indicative of its usefulness to the community, legal or otherwise.

The last group of libraries worthy of note comprises the small number of specialized institutes and associations some of which are attached to universities (*eg*, the Institute of Criminology at Cambridge or the Centre for European Governmental Studies at the University of Edinburgh), others being independent bodies such as the British Institute of International and Comparative Law. Though small, such libraries usually have comprehensive collections in their field of interest and because of the narrowness of their subject range are usually able to exploit this much more successfully than the larger and more general law libraries.

PROFESSIONAL ASSOCIATIONS FOR LAW LIBRARIANS

Though, as we noted above, law libraries have existed in the United Kingdom for many centuries, law librarians until very recent years have never formed a cohesive professional group in comparison with – say – medical librarians. This failure is probably the result of two separate factors. Firstly, in the past the majority of librarians responsible for organizing law libraries, whatever their size, were not professionally qualified and thus remained outside the main organization for practising librarians – the Library Association. Secondly, those staff in law libraries who possessed qualifications were but a very tiny minority indeed within the Library Association and never formed a special interest group as did, for example, school or hospital librarians. Aslib, the other body in the United Kingdom concerned with libraries and librarians was, until recent years, directed almost entirely towards the fields of science and technology; and although it did, unlike the Library Association, welcome professionally unqualified staff into its ranks, law was not a subject in which it showed much interest.

In 1968, as part of its programme of post-professional courses, the Department of Librarianship of Leeds College of Commerce (now Leeds Polytechnic) organized a week-long Workshop on law librarianship – the first course specifically on the subject to be organized in the United Kingdom. This had the effect of bringing together, either as participants or lecturers, over thirty law library staff from all parts of the British Isles. It was out of this gathering that, in just over a year (*ie*, in 1969) the British and Irish Association of Law Librarians was formed. That there was a need for such a body to represent the particular interests of law librarians is obvious from the Association's growth over the first six years of the existence. It now contains representatives from every type of law library – large and small – and from the legal bookselling and publishing trade. The aims of the Association as noted in its constitution are 'to provide a forum for meetings of all interested in law library work, to hold conferences and discussions on bibliographical questions affecting law libraries, to promote their better administration, to promote whatever may tend to the improvement of the status of law librarians, to encourage legal bibliographical study and research, to publish information of service or interest to the members of the Association, and to support and co-operate with any other organizations or activities which tend to benefit the members or objects of the Association'.

Membership is open 'to any practising law librarian, government document or inter-governmental document librarian, lecturer in law librarianship, or any person who has held such a post for a minimum and consecutive period of five years in the United Kingdom, the Isle of Man, the Channel Islands and the Republic of Ireland'. Institutional membership is available to any institutional or professional library in the United Kingdom, Isle of Man, Channel Islands and Republic of Ireland; while any person not eligible for either of the above categories may become an Associate member.

Since its inception, the Association has been active in pursuing most of its stated aims, its activities being largely undertaken by various standing and sub-committees, for example on acquisitions, cataloguing and classification, education, etc. It has, by way of example, organized a number of seminars and training courses on various aspects of law librarianship (*eg*, training the library user); a scheme for the exchange of duplicate materials has been established; representations have been made to the British Library with a view to improving its provision of legal material; a thesaurus of English legal terms is projected.

Its Publications Sub-Committee has produced a number of items, not the least significant of which is the Association's journal, *The Law Librarian* – one of the few English-language journals on law librarianship in the world. Its pages carry not only notes of the Association's activities, but also papers of bibliographical, historical and current interest to law librarians, as well as book reviews. Bibliographical tools of various types are envisaged, the first of which was a bibliography on *Community Law*, one of the first comprehensive guides to the legal literature of the European Community to be published in the United Kingdom. This present *Manual* is another example of the Association's interest in producing tools of value to the law librarian.

In 1970, its first annual conference was held at Liverpool University. This set the pattern for future events, which are held at different locations throughout the British Isles. Each covers a specific theme (*eg*, The administration of justice, Scots and Community Law) and selected papers are later published in *The Law Librarian*. Speakers have included librarians, representatives of the leading law publishing houses, as well as distinguished academics and legal practitioners. Special meetings supplement these annual gatherings.

These numerous activities are organized and directed by the members themselves, who also provide the Association's only source of income through their annual subscriptions. The day-to-day affairs of the Association are managed by an elected committee of five members, assisted by elected officers, one of whom is appointed chairman for the year, as well as by co-opted members.

Although relatively young, the Association has already made its mark on the law library scene in the United Kingdom. It does not, however, exist in isolation and there is liaison between it and other bodies with similar interests, such as the American Association of Law Libraries, the International Association of Law Libraries, the Library Association, and non-library bodies such as the Society of Public Teachers of Law and the Association of Law Teachers.

In addition to their membership of the BIALL, many British law librarians are members of the International Association of Law Libraries, a body – as its name implies – which is concerned with bringing together law librarians from all parts of the world. While such a body cannot – because of its wide geographical scatter – conduct many activities which members can attend, it does attempt to unite law librarians in two particular ways. Firstly, by the publication of a journal carrying information from numerous contributors and countries of interest to law librarians (*eg*, bibliographic articles, descriptions of libraries, problems of techniques, such as indexing, reviews of new books, etc.). Although published for many years in typescript format as the *Bulletin of the IALL*, a new series – published and printed by C. F. Müller of Karlsruhe – appeared in 1973 under the title of the *International Journal of Law Libraries*. The Association's second way of bringing law librarians together is by the organizing of courses on law librarianship at biennial intervals. These are held in different member countries in turn and each covers the law of the host country. The courses are intended for law librarians from countries other than the host and the five courses held to date have all been successful in achieving this aim.

In such ways, the IALL serves to remind law librarians in whatever country they may practise of the trends and developments, both technical and bibliographical, taking place throughout the world. At a time when the law is becoming more international in outlook this is indeed a most valuable service.

LAW LIBRARIES OVERSEAS

This survey has of necessity been confined to the law libraries of the British Isles, since any attempt to do adequate justice to law libraries in other countries would require a chapter many times the size of this present one (though for the benefit of readers a bibliography of recent references to law libraries in other countries is appended). As will be obvious from the above account, the pattern of the law libraries described is influenced by two factors, namely the structure of the legal profession and the system of education and training for the law. Many common law countries, therefore, possess a pattern of law libraries similar to our own, the most important collections being those in the universities or held by the various professional bodies. No English-speaking country possesses a library comparable to our British Library Lending Division, but on the other hand we do not yet have the benefits of a national law library on the lines of the Law Library of Congress, which is perhaps the most comprehensive law library in the world. The possibility of creating such a valuable resource in the British Isles was envisaged by the compilers of the document noted above, *Provision for law in the British Library*. Until that day arrives, users of legal literature will continue to patronize the facilities described above, which have developed over the years in answer to the changing and developing needs of the subject which they serve.

FURTHER READING

NATIONAL LIBRARIES

Great Britain. National Libraries Committee. *Report*. HMSO, 1969. (Cmnd. 4028) (ISBN 0 10 140280 5) (The Dainton report).
British and Irish Association of Law Librarians. Provision for law in the British Library. *Law Librarian*, vol. 5, no. 2, 1974, pp. 25–6.
Allardyce, A. What can law libraries borrow direct from NCL? *Law Librarian*, vol. 3, no. 2, 1972, pp. 23–5.
Barr, K. P. Legal material at NLL. *Law Librarian*, vol. 1, no. 3, 1970, pp. 35 and 43.

SOCIETY LIBRARIES

Breem, W. W. S. Professional Law Libraries of Great Britain. *Law Library Journal*, vol. 64, 1971, pp. 278–90.
Breem, W. W. S. A Sketch of the Inner Temple Library. *Law Library Journal*, vol. 64, 1971, pp. 5–12.
Richardson, F. P. The Law Society Library. *Law Librarian*, vol. 1, no. 2, 1970, pp. 15–19.
Ballantyne, G. H. The Signet Library, Edinburgh. *Law Librarian*, vol. 2, no. 1, 1971, pp. 3–5.
Neylon, M. J. King's Inns Library, Dublin. *Law Librarian*, vol. 4, no. 1, 1973, pp. 3–4.

COURT LIBRARIES

British and Irish Association of Law Librarians. Court libraries: memorandum from BIALL to the Lord Chancellor's Office. *Law Librarian*, vol. 6, no. 2, 1975, pp. 22–4.

GOVERNMENT LAW LIBRARIES

Gibson, D. B. The Home Office Library. *Law Librarian*, vol. 3, no. 3, 1972, pp. 36–9.

Mullis, A. A. The Law Commission Library. *Bulletin of the Circle of State Librarians*, vol. 17, 1969, pp. 8–11.

Wormald, J. H. The Legal Section of the Foreign and Commonwealth Office Library. *Law Librarian*, vol. 3, no. 1, 1972, p. 3.

ACADEMIC LAW LIBRARIES

Great Britain. University Grants Committee. *Report of the Committee on Libraries*. HMSO, 1967.

Way, D. J. University Law Libraries of Great Britain. *Law Library Journal*, vol. 64, 1971, pp. 291–301.

Smith, J. C. Law Libraries in Universities and Colleges. *Law Librarian*, vol. 2, no. 2, 1971, pp. 21–3.

Blake, D. M. The Harding Law Library, University of Birmingham. *Law Librarian*, vol. 3, no. 2, 1972, pp. 19–22.

Fifoot, E. R. S. University of Edinburgh: the Law Library and the library of the Centre of European Governmental Studies. *Law Librarian*, vol. 4, no. 2, 1973, pp. 19–20.

Hoyle, J. L. Southampton University Library. Part 1: the law collection. *Law Librarian*, vol. 2, no. 2, 1971, p. 19.

Way, D. J. The Liverpool University Law Library. *Law Librarian*, vol. 1, no. 1, 1970, pp. 3–4.

LEGISLATIVE LIBRARIES

Menhennet, D. The Library of the House of Commons. *Law Librarian*, vol. 1, no. 3, 1970, pp. 31–4.

PROFESSIONAL ASSOCIATIONS FOR LAW LIBRARIANS

Breem, W. W. S. The British and Irish Association of Law Librarians. *International Journal of Law Libraries*, vol. 1, no. 2, 1973, pp. 76–8.

Dahlmanns, G. J. The International Association of Law Libraries: an interim account. *Bulletin of the International Association of Law Libraries*, no. 28, June 1972, pp. 7–12.

FOREIGN LAW LIBRARIES

International Association of Law Libraries. *European law libraries guide*. . . . ed. E. M. Moys. Morgan-Grampian, 1971 (ISBN 0 900865 75 X).

Brian, R. F. Australian Law Libraries 1971. *Law Librarian*, vol. 2, no. 3, 1971, pp. 35–6.

Greenstein, L. J. The Specialized Nature of South African Law Libraries. *South African Libraries*, vol. 39, no. 2, 1971, pp. 86–9.

Kenyon, C. W. Library of Congress Law Library. *Law Library Journal*, vol. 67, no. 2, 1974, pp. 276–82.

Kreuzer, K. F. Law Libraries and Law Collections in the Federal Republic of Germany. *Law Librarian*, vol. 2, no. 3, 1971, pp. 39–42.

Oluwakuyide, A. The Law Libraries of Nigeria: a reflection. *International Journal of Law Libraries*, vol. 1, no. 2, 1973, pp. 85–8.

Peletier, W. M. Law Libraries in the Netherlands. *Law Librarian*, vol. 2, no. 3, 1971, pp. 37–8.

Scott, M. Law Libraries in Canada. *Law Library Journal*, vol. 64, no. 3, 1971, pp. 314–22.

Schwerin, K. Law Libraries and Foreign Law Collections in the USA. *International and Comparative Law Quarterly*, April, 1962, pp. 537–67.

2. Legal Systems and Legal Literature

PROFESSOR W. R. CORNISH, LL.B, BCL
London School of Economics and Political Science

The unsuspecting foreign visitor who enquires about the legal system of the United Kingdom is generally non-plussed by the answer. Justice, he is told, is separately administered in England and Wales, in Scotland and in Northern Ireland. Each has its own system of courts and the law applied in them differs in many important respects. To add to our foreigner's confusion, if he looks beyond the United Kingdom he will discover the separate legal systems of the Isle of Man and the Channel Islands.

No sooner has he learnt to regard them all as distinct, than he will have his attention drawn to their many similarities. He will learn, for instance, that the United Kingdom Parliament has legislative authority over all these territories; that the comparatively advanced state of English case-law on many subjects makes it frequently an exemplar in the other jurisdictions; that a host of similar attitudes have been bred out of a common approach to the role of judges and lawyers. The long historical association of the territories, for all its difficulties, has produced many unifying characteristics in fundamental legal matters. These similarities, indeed, make it sensible to link the legal system of the Irish Republic with the others so far mentioned, despite the severance of that state from the United Kingdom in 1922. For Ireland, like the many countries that once were British colonies but have now attained sovereign independence, developed legal institutions that closely resembled the English model. Accordingly she shares with England, Wales and Northern Ireland, as well as with many countries of the British Commonwealth and the United States, a 'common law' legal system, as distinct from the 'Romanist' (or 'civil law'), 'Scandinavian' and 'socialist' systems of different parts of Europe (see page 86). The term 'common law' has a number of different usages. Here it is used to distinguish the family of legal systems deriving from England. We shall also see that it is used to describe the rules of law developed by the judges as opposed to legislation. Sometimes, according to context, 'common law' has a more specific historical sense: it refers to judge-made law developed in the former courts of the common law, as distinct from the rules of equity developed in the Court of Chancery (see page 75). So too 'civil law' has distinct meanings. Here it identifies the family of legal systems where the influence of Roman law has been strong. But 'civil law' or 'civil proceedings' are terms which also distinguish, in any legal system, private rights of action for compensation and other redress from 'criminal law' or 'criminal proceedings', which are concerned with the infliction of punishment in the name of the state.

This chapter, which outlines the principal characteristics of the six legal systems of the British islands, tries to emphasize the interplay of differences and similarities between them. To attempt such a comparison in any depth would be beyond the scope of this *Manual*. Much of what follows is conceived as a very general sketch, though some matters are dealt with in more detail in later chapters. Apart from this the reader must be referred to the more complete accounts of the different systems in the works listed in the chapter bibliography (see page 90).

Our attention will largely be concentrated upon two matters: the various structures of courts that exist to deal with civil actions and criminal prosecutions in the six jurisdictions, and the sources from which is derived the law applied in those courts. By 'sources of law' is meant those repositories of legal rules to which lawyers (and in particular, judges) turn in order to discover what the law is. We can at once say that there are two main sources of law in modern times – legislation and case-law – though we shall see the former influence of other sources, such as the Institutional writers in Scotland. To begin this investigation, we look at the development of the courts and make some preliminary observations about the law that is applied in them. Then certain basic characteristics of some or all of the six systems will be elaborated in more detail: the role of trial by jury, the organization of the legal profession and legal education, and the distinction between common law and equity. With this background, something more about the sources of law can be said in the last main section of the chapter.

EVOLUTION OF THE COURTS

We shall see that until the nineteenth century, the decisions of the judges formed the one regular source from which the general principles of English law were fashioned. And because the early judges and lawyers in Ireland were all trained in England the same principles were carried there. In both places there developed the twin branches of law that we know as common law and equity. (See page 75.) This characteristic is still shared by the legal systems of England and Wales, Northern Ireland and the Irish Republic, and these legal systems will therefore be treated together as a group distinct from the systems of Scotland, the Channel Islands and the Isle of Man. For, in the latter group, English common law and equity were not a direct model, important though English case law may now be as a course from which legal rules may be generated.

England, Wales and Ireland

Let us start with a simplified picture of the court system operating in England and Wales today. The principal courts which hear civil actions may be represented thus:

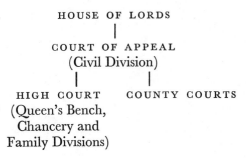

HOUSE OF LORDS

COURT OF APPEAL
(Civil Division)

HIGH COURT   COUNTY COURTS
(Queen's Bench,
Chancery and
Family Divisions)

Most civil actions are tried in one of the divisions of the High Court or else in a County Court. County Courts may hear actions involving amounts up to certain monetary limits. The

High Court has no such limits imposed upon it, but a litigant who prefers the High Court when he might have sued in the County Court may find himself penalized in costs. In this way the cases are divided up with reasonable flexibility. In addition, certain civil matters may be tried in other general courts: thus magistrates' courts have jurisdiction over certain important family and tenancy matters. Moreover, many disputes of a non-criminal character are handled by specially-created tribunals – disputes, for example, over national insurance benefits, fair rents, planning and restrictive practices.[1]

From the decision reached at the trial there is a two-tier system of appeals: first to the Court of Appeal, and from there to the House of Lords.[2] This structure was largely erected when the administration of justice was modernized by the Judicature Acts 1873–5, and the separation between the courts of common law and equity was abandoned.

A diagram of the courts dealing with criminal cases is rather more elaborate:

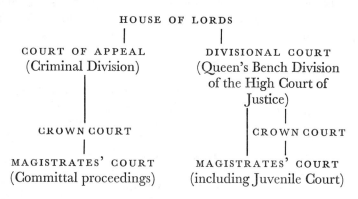

HOUSE OF LORDS

COURT OF APPEAL
(Criminal Division)

DIVISIONAL COURT
(Queen's Bench Division
of the High Court of
Justice)

CROWN COURT

CROWN COURT

MAGISTRATES' COURT
(Committal proceedings)

MAGISTRATES' COURT
(including Juvenile Court)

The criminal courts were not included in the Judicature Acts 1873–5 and their present structure has been built up more gradually. The basic division in the system is between cases which are tried on indictment by judge and jury in a Crown Court and those disposed of summarily in a magistrates' court. Again a fairly flexible system exists to determine whether a

---

[1] From most of these tribunals some right of appeal exists, either to another special tribunal or person, or to the general courts.

[2] In limited circumstances, it is now possible to appeal directly to the House of Lords, 'leap-frogging' over the Court of Appeal.

particular case goes to a higher court or a magistrates' court. Factors that *may* be taken into account include the intrinsic seriousness of the offence, the seriousness of the particular charge and the preference of the accused for one or other mode of trial.

A case that is tried on indictment may be the subject of an appeal by a convicted defendant to the Court of Appeal and then, in certain limited circumstances, to the House of Lords.[1] If a matter of law is involved in a case tried summarily there are certain rights of appeal by either side to a Divisional Court of the High Court and then to the House of Lords. Alternatively, a defendant who is convicted after pleading not guilty has a right to have his case completely retried in a Crown Court, sitting without a jury.

The pattern has been to divide cases into two groups according to their seriousness. Then, whether they are tried at the superior or the inferior level, there is the possibility of a two-tier appeal. The upper tier is constituted by a single court, the House of Lords, which is thus able to give the most authoritative rulings on legal questions that can be obtained from a court. It is also the supreme court of appeal for Northern Ireland and, in civil matters, for Scotland, so that on questions where the same law applies in these places the Lords may lay down a consistent rule for all three jurisdictions. (See also page 81.)

Edward I's conquest of Wales determined that no distinctive legal system would evolve in the principality. For a long period there were separate Welsh courts, but English influence was always strong and they were absorbed into the English judicial system in the nineteenth century. Henry II's conquest of Ireland, though more nominal in fact, led to the introduction of English common law and legal institutions which eventually, in the early seventeenth century, entirely superseded the native Irish Brehon law. An Irish Parliament developed from the late thirteenth century, but much English legislation came to apply directly or indirectly to Ireland. Though subordinate to Westminster this body was given greater independence in 1782, only to be abolished by Pitt's Act of Union 1800. Direct

---

[1] The prosecution has also recently acquired the right to have a question of law reviewed on appeal, but the result cannot affect the acquitted defendant.

rule was to rankle as one of the deepest and most persistent grievances in all the troubled Anglo-Irish relations that followed. The ultimate decision to partition the country not only created a separate state in the south, but created a subordinate parliament for the six counties of Ulster that became Northern Ireland. This Parliament at Stormont continued to exercise legislative power in most spheres of domestic government until the imposition of direct rule from Westminster in 1972.

Because the Irish courts had come so closely to resemble those of England the new system of the Judicature Acts was applied to them, the House of Lords constituting the final appellate court from the Irish Court of Appeal. In Northern Ireland after partition, the court structure retained its existing form: trial courts and the first tier of appeal courts were local; the House of Lords, sitting at Westminster, constituted the second tier. In detail, however, the structure varies somewhat from that of England. It may be thus represented (in simple form):

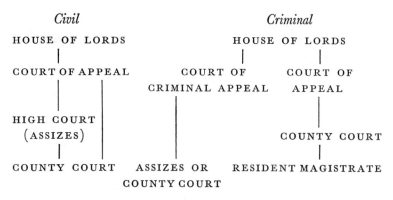

In particular, it should be noted that the right of appeal from the County Court to the High Court in civil matters may involve a complete rehearing.

Events in Southern Ireland stand witness to the capacity of a basic legal structure to survive the most bitter political conflict. Given the intensity of anti-British feeling that brought about the creation of the Irish Free State, it was not surprising that both the system of courts and the common law applied in them came under heavy fire. In the period of 'the troubles', Sinn Fein, or Dáil, courts were set up in competition with the existing courts to administer law based on Irish custom, Roman or continental jurisprudence – any source other than English law. However, they scarcely survived the creation of the Free State under its Constitution of 1922.

The established judicial system was reconstituted in 1924, the Irish Supreme Court becoming the ultimate court of appeal from the High Court. The reorganization involved the creation, for the first time, of a Court of Criminal Appeal (seven years in advance of the equivalent court in Northern Ireland). District courts replaced the petty sessions of justices of the peace and resident magistrates, and circuit courts amalgamated the work of county courts and county quarter sessions. An appeal may be made from the county court, by way of complete rehearing, to a visiting judge of assize; and from him or directly from the county court, on a question of law, to a Divisional Court of the Supreme Court. Attempts were made, notably by Gavan Duffy, judge and then President of the High Court, to loosen the ties of English precedents and to allow the selection of rules appropriate to the conditions of the new state. But on the whole, the attitude of the judges proved conservative. Such was the respect for the English system of case-law, that even single decisions of the House of Lords before 1922 were held to bind the Supreme Court.

One casualty in the partition of Ireland was the High Court of Appeal for Ireland. Created by the Government of Ireland Act 1920, it was intended as an appeal court for both north and south. When the Canadian and Australian federations were created as independent dominions they were each given a federal superior court that could have a unifying effect over the law of the different provinces or states. The High Court of Appeal was an attempt to provide a similar body for the two Irelands. But such an experiment could not survive in a political atmosphere of such hostility and the court sat for only a year before the creation of the Free State.

In many important matters the courts in both parts of Ireland, as in England and Wales, continue to work on very similar lines. The rules which determine whether a civil or criminal case shall be tried in the superior or the inferior

3

jurisdiction, and the rules which specify the grounds on which an appeal may be brought, though they may have grown apart in matters of detail, have retained the same general character. A lawyer trained in one of the systems can go to the others with the expectation (though no certainty) that similar principles of this nature will apply. This is the sense in which a family relationship survives between them. If he were to raise such a question in the context of (say) the French or Swedish legal systems, he could make no guess as to what the immediate answer or its ramifications might be. He would have to turn to an expert in the national law.

Scotland

By contrast with the close dependence of Irish common law upon that of England, the foundations of Scots law remain distinct. When the two kingdoms were joined by the accession of James I to the English throne, Scots law had already left behind its dark age. The re-discovery and interpretation of Roman law sources that had swept western Europe during the Renaissance had taken root in Scotland.

In England the native common law was too strong a growth to give much place to such foreign seed, and the difference became a means of marking Scots independence in legal matters. During the seventeenth century Scotland kept her own Parliament, but the Act of Union 1707 left Scotland without even a subordinate legislature equivalent to the Irish Parliament. At a time when statute was still only an occasional source of general law, the Romanist reception proved an ample buffer against any widespread penetration of English legal notions. Scots lawyers brought back to their homeland the learning of their student days in the great continental schools of law, particularly in France and the Low Countries. With time their own institutional writers emulated the European masters and provided the Romanized Scots law with texts that were treated in the courts as being of high authority.

It was therefore not until the rapid economic and social change of the nineteenth century, when law had to be made on an unprecedented scale, that English influences became more pronounced. In the first place statute became a substantial source of law. By no means all enactments applying to England were extended to Scotland and many acts were passed to deal with exclusively Scottish matters. None the less many were common to the two countries. (The same was true of Ireland during the years of direct rule.) Secondly, the jurisdiction of the House of Lords, as the final court of appeal in civil matters, which it had asserted immediately after the Act of Union, began to acquire increasing importance. While the modern form of the judicial body in the Lords allows for the appointment of Scots and Northern Irish, as well as English, Law Lords, there was, particularly in the early nineteenth century, a tendency to treat the concepts of Scots law as though they were simply English transplants. The cavalier disregard which English judges have from time to time shown for the nuances of Scots doctrine continues to rankle.

Thirdly, the Scots tradition of studying law on the continent changed as codification spread through Europe. Legal education became less international and more directed towards the interpretation of a particular national text. The era of Romanist influence in Scotland thus drew to a close. The Scottish judges began to attach increasing importance to judicial precedents, a source of law so dear to the hearts of their English counterparts.

Civil and criminal jurisdiction in Scotland today may be represented (in simplified form) thus:

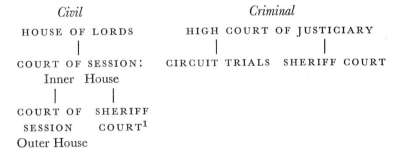

Civil	*Criminal*
HOUSE OF LORDS	HIGH COURT OF JUSTICIARY
COURT OF SESSION: Inner House	CIRCUIT TRIALS SHERIFF COURT
COURT OF SESSION SHERIFF COURT[1]	
Outer House	

While the system for trying civil cases bears some resemblance

[1] Unlike the English county courts, the sheriff is under no monetary limits in the civil cases that he hears. If a case is heard by the sheriff an appeal may first be taken to the sheriff-principal.

to the English, the criminal system is more distinctive. At the trial stage the cases tried 'in solemn form' with a jury are not sent to a different court from those tried summarily. Trials on circuit and some cases in the sheriff court are tried by jury, while the sheriffs also have an extensive summary jurisdiction. All summary trials are heard in the sheriff court. Moreover, there is only one tier for appeals. The House of Lords does not deal in criminal appeals from Scotland.

Channel Islands

The islands came to the English Crown as part of the Duchy of Normandy and remained English after the last of the French possessions had been given up. Their constitutional status is peculiar, being shared only with the Isle of Man. The two territories form no part of the United Kingdom, and they send no representatives to the United Kingdom Parliament. Parliament does have legislative competence over them which is superior to that of the local legislative bodies – the States of Jersey, Guernsey and Alderney, the Chief Pleas of Sark and the Tynwald of the Isle of Man. In this the islands resemble British colonies, such as Hong Kong and the Gilbert and Ellice Islands.

Yet there are important respects, particularly in matters such as citizenship, in which the islands are accorded a special status by British legislation. Moreover, there exist special procedures that are in practice followed before United Kingdom legislation, when it applies to the territories, is brought into effect there. Committees of the Privy Council for the affairs of the Channel Islands and the Isle of Man help ensure that a working relationship on the matter is maintained. The constitutional understanding is that the Channel Islands have autonomy over matters of domestic government (including taxation) and legislation from Westminster would be applied there only with the assent of the local legislatures. The degree of independence of the Isle of Man is not so great, since, for instance, certain matters relating to the police and the civil service are reserved to the United Kingdom government, which is accordingly represented by a Lieutenant-Governor invested with active executive duties.

The history of the Channel Islands has left its stamp upon their legal system, for the applicable common law remains that of the Duchy of Normandy. The sources in which that law is set down, however, are very imperfect. They comprise the late thirteenth-century *Grand Coutumier du Pays et Duché de Normandie*, together with the *Coutume Reformée* of 1585. In addition, there were codifications of the laws of Guernsey (1583) and Jersey (1771) which were given legislative force, and certain expositions of the law that acquired the status of important legal authorities. Yet the problem of ascertaining principles of the Norman customary law as it applies particularly to rights over land in the Channel Islands has remained a considerable problem.

The chief courts of the Islands are the Royal Courts of Jersey and Guernsey. In addition there is the Court of Alderney and the Court of the Seneschal in Sark, from which appeal may lie to the Royal Court of Guernsey. As well as the Bailiff who acts as judge in each of the Royal Courts, substantial use is made of jurats, their number depending on whether the court is sitting as a civil court of first instance, a criminal court of trial, or an appellate court. Above both Royal Courts there is a Court of Appeal with civil and criminal jurisdiction. An additional tier in the structure is provided by the possibility of appealing to the Judicial Committee of the Privy Council. The Judicial Committee may be composed of Privy Councillors from the Commonwealth with judicial experience as well as of British Lords of Appeal in Ordinary (appointed to hear appeals to the House of Lords). But normally the latter predominate upon the Committee, when they do not entirely make it up. So as final courts of appeal, the House of Lords and the Judicial Committee are generally homogeneous in character, while remaining distinct in form.

The Isle of Man

The legal system of the island is discussed together with those of Scotland and the Channel Islands out of respect for the Manx tradition that the system preserves its distinct origins. The island indeed had Viking and Scots rulers before passing to the English Crown. From 1406, it acquired greater stability of government than it had previously enjoyed when Henry IV granted its administration to the Stanleys as Lords of Man and the Isles. Not until 1765 and 1828 did the Crown, under statutory authority, purchase the feudal rights of its grantees. The feudal relationships that developed in the customary law of the Isle of Man were transmitted largely by oral tradition, though some were embodied in statutes of the local legislature, Tynwald. They continue to determine certain basic rules of the land law, but otherwise the law, so far as it is not to be found in statutes of Westminster or Tynwald, is mostly taken from English judicial precedents. The absorption of English common law, while not so complete as in Ireland, went to the extent of recognizing the special characteristics of English equity. The common law of the Isle of Man thus may be placed between that of England and Ireland on the one hand and that of Scotland and the Channel Islands on the other.

The fact that a Judicature Act was passed in 1883 to bring together the administration of law and equity in the island is one indication of the extent of English influence. Another is to be found in the composition of the present courts. The island's High Court consists of two judges called deemsters, who sit separately to try civil and serious criminal matters. From the deemster an appeal lies first to the Judge of Appeal (a Queen's Counsel of the English Bar) who sits together with the other deemster. From them, as with the Channel Islands, a second appeal is possible to the Judicial Committee of the Privy Council. Each deemster may sit as the Court of General Gaol Delivery in criminal cases, with appeal to a court consisting of all three judges. Summary trials are conducted by the High Bailiff and justices of the peace.

SOME BASIC CHARACTERISTICS

So far our discussion has scarcely touched upon English legal history, though we have indicated something of the evolution of the other five systems. The omission has been deliberate. There are aspects of the English story that tell a great deal about the distinctive character of common law systems today. Accordingly they deserve separate treatment. As we turn now to discuss three of them, we shall find that the most interesting comparisons lie with Scots law, providing as it does the most developed contrast within the British islands.

Trial by jury

The jury system has done much to determine the characteristic form of litigation in common law jurisdictions. As an institution it has displayed a remarkable capacity for adaptation. The first jurors who appeared in judicial proceedings reached their verdicts on their own knowledge of local affairs. Gradually, however, as society became more complex, witnesses were introduced to give evidence in court to the jurors. Eventually the principle became that the jurors were to decide only upon what they learnt from witnesses at court. The trial (or petty) jury first became popular in England during the thirteenth century, when it was used as a substitute for methods of trial – for instance, by battle or ordeal – which appealed for divine revelation of justice. A century later the jury system spread to Scotland where it acquired certain distinctive characteristics.[1] It did not, however, as in the English common law courts, acquire a dominant position in the trial of civil actions; as though to mark the resurgence of English influence, the civil jury was specifically reintroduced in 1815 by legislation.

In the Middle Ages, the English judges found that unpaid, local jurors could be used for the rapid despatch of justice at a time when judicial manpower was short. Developments in France and elsewhere in Europe provide a contrast of long-lasting importance. There monarchs looked to their royal judges to conduct their own investigations as the means of determining the truth of matters in dispute. Justice became *inquisitorial* and so an embodiment of royal power that was easily abused. Though juries proved capable of corruption, the system proved to have a certain resilience against the naked

[1] Scots juries in criminal cases have fifteen members and may reach a verdict by a bare majority; the verdict may be guilty, not guilty or not proven. English juries are twelve and had until very recently to return a unanimous verdict; now they may discount a small minority (*eg*, 10–2). The not proven verdict is not recognized in English law. In civil cases a Scots jury numbers twelve (Court of Session) or seven (Sheriff Court); in Northern Ireland and Eire the seven-man civil jury is also used,

misuse of the judicial process. To eighteenth-century liberals trial by jury stood as a bulwark of liberty, discouraging governments from mounting mere show trials of their political opponents.

Our interest, however, is not so much in the constitutional role of this form of 'government by rotation'. The presence of the jury did much to shape the nature of the trial process, civil and criminal. Of necessity a trial became accusatorial, short and oral. By *accusatorial* is meant a process in which one side is obliged to make out his accusation against the other by putting forward his own evidence. The judge is a mere arbitrator, securing orderly procedure and informing the jury of the relevant law. He bears no responsibility for investigating the issue raised before him. The evidence of witnesses is principally tested by the opponent's cross-examination. The need for brevity, dictated by the jury's limited capacity to understand, remember and evaluate oral evidence, led to the development of severe and technical rules for the exclusion of irrelevant and unduly prejudicial evidence. In civil process, the jury was also a cause of the important procedure of pleading. One purpose of this procedure was to fine down the cause between the parties so that the jury would only be concerned with facts really in dispute. The heavy reliance on oral evidence at the trial – essential when there could be no certainty that the jurors would be literate – came thus to be counterbalanced by elaborate written preliminaries. These proved vital to the formation of common law principle in England, for it was the form in which judges permitted parties to express their pleadings that determined the content of the law.

With time the contents of the pleadings gave place to reported judgments as sources of the law. But for a long period of English legal history the judges in the common law courts were shaping the law so that it could be both understood and applied in a reasonable fashion by jurors who had no legal training or experience. That flavour has remained characteristic of so much of our law. For instance, the judges have laid a duty upon all persons to take such care as would a reasonable man to avoid harm to others. They mean by the term 'reasonable man' the collective good sense of the twelve jurors in the jury-box. Today the amount and complexity of litigation and the need to secure conformity in similar cases have led to the virtual replacement of juries in civil cases by judges sitting alone. Yet it will be long before the characteristic forms which the jury gave to both the substantive law and the court procedures of English common law will be lost.

How different legal process could become without jury trial is illustrated not only by the inquisitorial systems of Continental Europe, but even by the English court of Chancery with its jurisdiction in equity. Chancery did not use juries and when it determined questions of fact for itself it relied upon documents where possible, even reducing the testimony of witnesses to written form by having them separately examined under oath.[1] The absence of a short, conclusive trial as a culminating focus to litigation contributed to the notorious dilatoriness and expense of Chancery proceedings in the time of Dickens.

The legal profession and legal education

Where a legal system depended upon the judges themselves to enquire into disputes, it was likely that a large body of judges would be built up. Indeed, in continental systems, judgeship became a lifetime's occupation. A young lawyer chose between entering the service of the state as a junior judge (expecting then to climb the judicial tree) and going into private practice.

In the various parts of Britain, the royal courts were able to operate with remarkably few judges. This was possible partly because of the limited role of the judge sitting with a jury, but partly also because of the extensive use that came to be made of another kind of unpaid lay judge – the justice of the peace.[2] The justices sat at their quarter sessions with a jury to dispose of serious criminal charges, as well as dealing with many matters of local administration. Increasingly they were given power to

---

[1] The procedures followed in trying Chancery actions were brought closer to those of the common law in the reforms of the mid-nineteenth century which culminated in the Judicature Acts 1873–5.

[2] While the justice of the peace flourished in the social organization of pre-industrial England, in Scotland he failed to gain the same wide powers in face of the well-established sheriffs. In Ireland, the lack of a landlord class to fill the position led to the evolution of the resident magistrates.

sit in petty sessions to try minor crimes, and from this has developed the modern notion of summary criminal trial.

It thus remained practicable to draw the royal judges from the ranks of the senior advocates practising before the courts. The progress from bar to bench, so characteristic of the British systems, had many consequences. It was an important factor in determining how work should be divided between the two sections of private practice (barristers and solicitors in England and Ireland; advocates and solicitors in Scotland).[1] It created a close rapport between judges and the advocates who appeared before them. This working relationship helped support the high degree of respect that has come to be shown to British judges.

Their special position is in its turn closely associated with the fact that, in England, preservation and development of the law was kept within the grasp of the practising lawyers. The precedents set by judges and stored up by practitioners were the sources of law that weighed with later courts. Not for the judges in England the great deference shown by their continental counterparts for the teaching of doctrine by the great professors of the universities. As we have already seen, the inbred English profession showed little interest for the Renaissance revival of Roman Law principle. Even the Scots lawyers, who for more than two centuries learned so much from the Dutch and other schools of jurisprudence, did not establish a system of legal education that in the nineteenth century could give the teachers of law in the Scots universities the status of their French or German counterparts.

In England the training of lawyers had always been regarded as a craft skill to be learnt from practitioners rather than an academic science to be studied at a distance. To this tradition

---

[1] The division of legal practice into two branches is neither unique to common law systems, nor, as events in the United States and elsewhere demonstrate, is it necessary to the efficient functioning of the profession. Where it is maintained within the common-law world, the dividing line gives the advocate a specialist function in litigation in the higher courts, with which is associated the giving of opinions on difficult matters of law. The advocate is not directly employed by the client but is engaged by the client's solicitor. This gives to members of the bar a certain aloofness; a close-knit fraternity lightens the tasks of maintaining professional standards and selecting judges.

Scotland returned in the nineteenth century. That century did, indeed, see the roots of legal studies beginning to extend in the universities of both countries and in Ireland. Today a degree in law has become a well-recognized route to the practice of the law. But, save in Scotland, it is neither a necessary nor a sufficient professional qualification. A person may become a legal practitioner purely by taking the examinations set by the relevant professional bodies and completing the prescribed period of practical training. The graduate is merely given exemption from all or part of the academic side of these requirements.

Common law and equity

We have already made passing reference to the distinction between common law and equity, which is so basic to the legal history of England. It is a division that must be further elucidated, not only for its past importance, but also because it retains its significance today in major fields of civil law, such as property and contract.

In the centuries after the Norman Conquest three courts – Exchequer, Common Pleas and King's Bench – came to be treated as distinct from the Curia Regis. The legal principles recognized and enforced by them were in this context the 'common law'. However, it remained possible to petition the king himself, as the fountain of justice, for redress against a wrong. In the later Middle Ages he deputed the hearing of these petitions to his Chancellor, who granted relief in 'equity' beyond that available in the courts of common law. Numerous causes contributed to the popularity of this equitable jurisdiction in Chancery. With time it lost its discretionary character and hardened into a body of rules that supplemented or qualified the common law in settled ways.

For instance, the common law courts could, in most cases, only order the payment of money by way of relief to a successful plaintiff. But in equity it was possible to obtain such orders as an injunction against a course of conduct, or specific performance requiring a contract to be carried out. Common law required a borrower of money to repay on the exact day due, if he did not wish entirely to forfeit land that he had transferred to the lender by way of mortgage security. Equity gave the borrower more time to pay. Above all, equity developed that distinctive conception of property ownership known as the trust. The person who owned property (in the sense that the common law courts would recognize him as owner) might become the trustee of it for another. Equity declared that the latter should be treated as the beneficial owner. His right to whatever benefits the property produced would be recognized and enforced in a court of equity. In its modern form, the trust was first developed to accommodate the elaborate property arrangements of the landed aristocracy. But it was also adapted to such varied purposes as the organization of joint-stock companies, the administration of charities, and the property holdings of trade unions.[1]

The presence of equity beside common law is perhaps the most distinctive characteristic of the developed legal system of England and one that was implanted in its direct descendants – in Ireland, the American colonies and other British possessions that had no recognized legal system of their own.

One evident difference in Scots legal history is the absence at any stage of a separate court administering its own distinctive forms of equitable relief. Yet principles have developed in Scots law which have been justified by reference to reason, fairness, natural justice and which have been referred to as 'equitable'.[2] The Court of Session today administers both common law and equity and there is a family resemblance between principles developed in the English Court of Chancery and Scots equity. In particular, the trust concept took root in Scots law and proved there an equally useful formula in matters of property.

THE SOURCES OF LAW

English common law and equity, as we have now seen, were

---

[1] However, most companies are today organized under a different legal scheme prescribed by the Companies Acts; charities (though not trade unions) may adopt a corporate form of this kind, or they may still use the trust.

[2] In addition the Court of Session has a special equitable jurisdiction, the *nobile officium*.

built over many centuries by a small central band of judges who worked with, and were drawn from, a compact body of advocates. At the dawn of the nineteenth century most of this law related to civil rights and touched the lives of only the thin strata of propertied classes. The law they needed could be wrought slowly by the pragmatic, practical technique of judicial precedent. This English tradition was strong enough to exert an increasing influence upon the separate system of Scots law. But with growing speed of economic and social change, the requirements of government and the need for new law were too pressing to leave most of the work to the judges. Legislation emerged in fact, as already it was in principle, the dominant source of law. Accordingly it is with legislation – the enactments of Parliament, the subordinate legislatures and other governmental bodies furnished with legislative power – that we turn first in discussing the different sources of law.

Legislation

The great constitutional struggles between the Stuarts and their Parliaments determined where the ultimate power of government should lie. The first principle upon which the Revolution of 1688 was founded was that Acts of Parliament – enactments passed in due form by King, Lords and Commons – were law beyond challenge. Subordinate legislatures, such as those of the Isle of Man, the Channel Islands and the colonies, can today pass valid enactments only within the powers allowed them by United Kingdom legislation. In those former colonies that have acquired dominion status or become republics under written constitutions, the legislatures must ensure that their ordinary legislation complies with the higher dictates of the constitution. In all such cases, an enactment which exceeds the limits of the legislature's power can be declared void by the courts: it is *ultra vires*. The Republic of Ireland is the obvious example for our purposes, but the same is true of the Dominion of Canada, the Commonwealth of Australia and the United States of America.

But courts in Britain have had no such power in relation to the statutes of Parliament – for Parliament is sovereign. All a court may do is to interpret the meaning of an Act in relation to a case before it. The principles upon which the judges approach this task of interpretation are by now elaborate. There have been instances where judges have given a meaning to the words of a statute which prevents it achieving its purpose. The judicial coach-and-horses of interpretation may leave behind only the crumbling frame of a statute. But the United Kingdom Parliament may always make a further attempt to express its will more clearly. By contrast, the Supreme Court of Ireland is entitled to say, once and for all, that a legislature may not pass a statute of a given character; its constitutional power has a significance of a wholly different order.

As nineteenth-century legislation on poor relief, education, public health, factories, pollution, police, prisons and so forth, swelled the pages of the statute book, new bodies, both central and local, were given power to carry the legislation into execution. Nor were the powers of these organs of government confined to administration. With growing frequency they became entitled to add details to the legislation itself under powers delegated by Parliament. What was novel was not the concept of such *delegated legislation* but the extent to which it came to be used. Because the bodies who exercised delegated legislative powers – ministries, local councils, and many others – can legislate only within the scope accorded them by Parliament, the courts may not only interpret the meaning, but may consider the validity, of their enactments.

Acts of Parliament and delegated legislation (sometimes referred to as 'subsidiary', 'subordinate' or 'secondary' legislation) thus form the most compelling source of law. If a statutory rule lays down a clear prescription for a particular situation, it prevails over any rule of case-law that may be at variance with it. Judges have no qualifying power to say when and where the legislation is not to apply.

So much for the accepted legislative forms. But when the United Kingdom and the Irish Republic joined the European Economic Communities novel constitutional questions were raised. The law of the Communities – the treaties and the regulations, directives and decisions of the Community organs – became a source of law in both countries. In particular, some treaty provisions and regulations made by the Council of

Ministers or the European Commission are 'directly applicable'. They confer rights and impose duties upon individuals, without the need for national legislation, which are enforceable in national courts. It is the opinion of the European Court of Justice that Community law prevails over inconsistent national law. But it remains an open question whether national courts will take this view when after a Community enactment there is passed a national statute that is beyond question inconsistent with it. In Ireland, moreover, there is the question whether community law can prevail over the constitution. To these questions no clear answers can be returned until they are raised in the courts. One thing, however, is sure: the highest judicial organ of the Communities, the European Court of Justice, has no power to declare any national legislation void. In this sense, at least, the sovereignty of the legislatures continues.

Judicial precedent

In nineteenth-century Europe, the movement to express the most general and basic legal principles in the form of a code progressed rapidly. Many governments, in support of their own legitimacy or in order to express a sense of national identity, promoted codes of civil, criminal, commercial and procedural law. Britain, which, in the person of Jeremy Bentham, had produced the foremost advocate of the cause of codification, nevertheless did not follow suit. The survival of both English and Scots law within the United Kingdom presented a difficulty, but a relatively minor one. The chief opposition to codification in England undoubtedly arose from the entrenched faith of the legal profession in the virtues of case-law, that is, in principles developed from the decisions of judges on the law applicable to the cases before them. Bentham objected vehemently to the obscurity of precedent – a form of law, as he saw it, capable of extraction only by those trained in the mystery of the lawyer's craft. To its protagonists, however, precedent allowed the law to remain flexible – capable of being adapted to fit unanticipated circumstances and changed social conditions in a manner often impossible within the set phrases of a code. The development of common law and equity in

England by means of judicial decision already had a long history and the technique was gaining importance in Scotland as continental influences receded. The close-knit profession of England, in particular, was consistently hostile towards plans to codify the criminal law and no serious attempts to codify either the law of contract or tort were ever made. Only in certain branches of commercial and property law were substantially complete statements of the law in legislative form achieved. Case-law has thus remained a vital source of fundamental principle in all the legal systems of the British islands and the many 'common-law' systems overseas.

The law-making content of a case is defined by the principle of *stare decisis* (let the decision stand). The essence of this conception may be stated thus: the decision of a court in a single case may be enough to settle that a general rule has the force of law and must be applied by judges to the determination of comparable cases. But there are two basic qualifications: first, it is only the *ratio decidendi* (the reason for deciding) that has this legally binding effect, and second, the decision of a particular court can only bind lower courts in the same hierarchy and, in some instances, the court itself.

In England, quite elaborate rules were laid down by each appellate court concerning the conditions in which that court would be bound by its own previous decisions. In 1966, however, the House of Lords abandoned its rule that it was always bound by its own precedents. Today it is only the Court of Appeal which, unless certain conditions are fulfilled, regards itself as bound by its earlier decisions. Even in that court, the senior member (Lord Denning, Master of the Rolls) has declared that so constricting a principle should be abandoned. Scots and Irish courts have always been reluctant to lay down general rules of this character, though the Court of Appeal of Northern Ireland has said that it follows the same principle as the English Court of Appeal.

Ratio decidendi is a notion of some subtlety. It is best understood by beginners as the principle of law upon which a judge relies in order to reach his judgment. In particular, the *ratio decidendi* is to be distinguished from *obiter dicta* – remarks made by judges about principles of law that are not directly relevant in deciding the issues before them. A court is never obliged to apply *obiter dicta* from earlier decisions, though it may do so. The *dicta* of the foremost judges do indeed carry considerable weight. But they never constitute more than persuasive precedents.

By careful manipulation, it is often possible for a later court to avoid applying a precedent that it dislikes. It may perhaps find the precedent to be *dictum* rather than *ratio* and for that reason not binding. It may find that there is something about the facts of the case before it that makes the *ratio decidendi* of the precedent inapplicable; the earlier case is then said to be *distinguished*. The rule that a contract is complete upon posting an acceptance would be restrictively distinguished if a judge said that it only applied when the acceptance was expected to be by post, and not, for instance, by telephone. The court may even find that the principle set forth in the precedent was put in terms that were unduly wide for the subject-matter in hand: this process of reasoning is known as *restrictive distinguishing*. Suppose the precedent lays down that a contract is formed when a letter accepting an offer is put in the post. That rule would be distinguished by a judge who said that it is not enough to hand the letter to a postman instead of posting it in the normal way. It is not unknown for a court to dispose of an apparently binding precedent which it thinks incorrect by saying that it was a decision reached only in relation to the particular facts before it. Since facts very rarely repeat themselves exactly, this disposes of the precedent. But so cavalier a technique has been not unfairly described as 'distinguishing out of existence'. All these possibilities, imaginatively used, can allow a desirable fluidity in the development of the law. In the wrong hands they open the gateway to legal indeterminacy on a grand scale.

A precedent can never be more than persuasive upon a higher court in the same hierarchy or any court in a different hierarchy. The British islands provide no less than six separate hierarchies of courts, three (England and Wales, Scotland, Northern Ireland) culminating in the House of Lords,[1] two in

---

[1] It has never been finally determined whether a decision of the House of Lords in an appeal from England binds the courts in Scotland (where there is no acknowledged difference in Scots law) or in Northern Ireland. If the precedent is not technically binding, it will in any case be highly persuasive.

the Judicial Committee of the Privy Council, and the Irish system in the Supreme Court of the Republic. A decision of the English Court of Appeal can bind neither the House of Lords nor the Court of Session in Scotland. The precedent would constitute persuasive authority. The House of Lords might choose to *overrule* it as wrongly decided. The Court of Session, not belonging to the same set of courts, could not declare it wrong in this fashion; but it could choose *not to follow* it. In either case, the later court would doubtless look for a sufficient reason before departing from the precedent. This, however, is merely to recognize that, as far as possible, it is desirable to preserve the continuity and certainty of the law.

Compared with legislation, case-law is difficult material to conserve and make available to lawyers. It has become possible to apply *stare decisis* with increasing rigidity over the past century because the methods of reporting judicial decisions have become more substantial and more careful. Even at the end of the eighteenth century the standards of the private reporters in England were frequently slap-dash, and it was still very much a novelty for reports to be made of judicial pronouncements out on the assize circuits, as opposed to those of the full benches sitting at Westminster.

In the nineteenth century reporting rapidly improved in accuracy and the range of courts covered was broadened. By the time that the Incorporated Council of Law Reporting was established in 1865 to publish semi-official case-reports of the superior courts of common law and equity a full report had reached its usual modern form. (For a fuller account of the history of law reporting, see Chapters 4 and 6.)

While a case in *The Law Reports* has special authority in that it will have been checked by the judge or judges involved, many additional series of reports, general and specialized, flourish today and may be cited in court.

In Scotland improvements in reporting follow a roughly parallel path. As early as 1705, however, the Faculty of Advocates (the professional bar organization) intervened by appointing its own reporter. This practice developed into the various series reporting the decisions of the Court of Session. Since 1907 referred to simply as *Session Cases*, these are now the responsibility of the Scottish Council of Law Reporting and are also checked by the judges. In Ireland the growth of law reporting was slower but equivalent series of modern reports now exist.

In the different jurisdictions a law report generally conforms to a standard pattern. A subject heading list is followed by an epitome of the facts and the decision in the case. This is known as the head-note. Then comes a full statement of the facts at issue, and often a summary of the arguments presented by counsel. The judgment or judgments delivered by the court follow, and finally there is a report of the order made to express the result of the judgment.

Especially in the appeal courts, where the judges are regularly preoccupied with general principles of law, British judgments have in modern times acquired two important characteristics. One is that they are written in a relatively free and discursive style; they have none of the rigid formalism that so limits the scope of, for instance, a French judgment and stands as an impediment to the formation of general principle out of a particular decision. The other is that the discussion generally concentrates upon the previous case-law and other legal sources. This pre-occupation with 'authority' is part of a tradition that is opposed to the overt discussion of the practical consequences that will ensue if one rule rather than another is adopted. In the United States the courts have been much readier to air such issues of policy in their judgments. This is one reason why particular precedents have not acquired such compulsive force in that country. English judges have long presented judgments stating the law as though they had an inevitable quality about them generated by an abstract sense of right.[1] It would be wrong to suggest that our judges have no concern with the consequences of their judgments, just as it would be misleading to suppose that most of them acknowledge a higher moral order, such as a system of natural law, from which particular rules are to be deduced. But their

---

[1] English common lawyers, led by Coke and Blackstone, have been partial to the notion that in laying down precedents the judges do not make, but only declare, the law. Whatever the reality of such a theory, when the royal courts were first making general rules out of established local customs, it is today rarely treated as more than a convenient fiction that 'explains' why a novel precedent applies to the very case in which it is laid down.

'authority-dominated' form of reasoning, together with the standing that is accorded even to isolated precedents, are but part of a larger phenomenon. Both contribute to the legal profession's own conception of the high and independent constitutional position of the judges. They contribute to that sense of distance that is thought to breed a respect for the law and its institutions amongst the lay public.

Texts and other legal writings

In many legal systems, the treatises and commentaries of legal scholars are treated by their courts as significant sources of law. The most authoritative writers may well be given greater weight by the courts than the decisions of judges, at least until a whole line of judicial precedent has been built up. This has been a characteristic, for instance, of the European states affected by the revival of Roman law. Thus, during its Romanist reception, Scots law was significantly developed and consolidated by the works of her own institutional writers. Today, on civil matters the works of Craig, Stair, Bankton, Erskine and Bell, and on matters of criminal law, those of Mackenzie and Hume, are universally conceded a special status, and in default of other authority would be treated as settling the law. English law has had its commentators, most notably Coke and Blackstone, whose writings have exerted considerable influence in their time upon the courts. Today, their interest is chiefly historical. More recent writers have not been accorded by judges a status that can compare with that of a clearly-expressed judicial decision. Writings may be cited in court to show what the law is, but it is unlikely that they will be given much weight unless the law to be extracted from statutory or case-law sources is contradictory, confusing or non-existent.

We may distinguish three kinds of legal writing. The first is the textbook prepared as a statement of what the law is for the use of legal practitioners. The widest-ranging of these is *Halsbury's Laws of England*, but almost every subject has at least one practitioner's text devoted to it. The tendency is for these works to be written and edited by practising lawyers. The second is the introductory textbook, designed primarily for students of the law. The third, the critical commentary upon an aspect of the law, has been a product particularly of the expansion of academic legal education in the universities. Here the tendency is for authors, whether they produce books or write articles or notes in legal periodicals, to have some connection with law teaching. Of course these three kinds of writing are not mutually exclusive categories. A few practitioners' texts, for example, have a critical and speculative tone; and many books written primarily for the instruction of students contain much that is purely descriptive of the existing law. It can safely be said that, when courts do look to legal writings for legal authority, their preference is for works of the first kind. It is not often in Britain that one sees the judicial imagination being fired by the critical analysis of an academic article. Even when such writings are referred to, the ideas expressed in them acquire status as a legal authority at secondhand – that is, because a judge expresses his approval of them in a judgment.

Custom

For the sake of completeness, it must be said that custom has a recognized place as a source of law, though today it is much less important than formerly. Much of what became the 'common law' of the whole territory amounted to a generalization of the custom of localities. But there remains the possibility that a purely local custom, constituting a variation in the general law, may be treated as the applicable rule in that locality. The custom must be both definite and certain, fair and reasonable, and of substantial antiquity.[1] The only circumstances in which such a custom is at all likely to arise today is in connection with local land rights. The use of custom as a source of law in this way needs to be distinguished from the role that trade practices and similar evidence may be given to explain what is meant in an ambiguous situation. By this means it may be possible to prove that 'a dozen' means 'thirteen' in a baker's contract. But no question of varying an

[1] In English and Irish law the custom must have existed 'from time immemorial' – an elaborate concept. In Scots law the custom does not have to be shown to have existed for any particular period.

otherwise applicable rule of law is involved; merely the explanation of what was meant in a particular agreement.

COMMON LAW AND CIVIL LAW

At the outset, we drew a distinction between 'common law' and 'Romanist' or 'civil' legal systems, as well as others. These are broad groupings of national legal systems which suggest no more than a family likeness. But just as bone structure is often more important than superficial markings to a zoologist, so also with the investigator of legal institutions.

The traditions and techniques that developed in the English legal system were not merely influential in other parts of the British Islands. Wherever the British settlers colonized unoccupied territory without an established legal order they took with them English common law and so much of the existing statute law as was appropriate to the new environment. In this way, a legal system was built in most of the American colonies which subsequently became parts of the United States, in all of Canada save Quebec, in Australia and New Zealand, and in the British colonies in East and West Africa.

By contrast, territories which became British by cession or conquest kept their own law unless and until altered by legislation. Thus in the Indian sub-continent, the regimes of Hindu and Mohammedan law were, during the nineteenth century, supplemented by statutory codes of criminal law, criminal procedure and evidence, contract and land law. There too, the judges were able to develop a law of tort based largely on principles of English common law. In South Africa and Ceylon, the inherited legal system, Roman-Dutch law, derived from earlier European colonization. In both countries, English influences arrived piecemeal by statutory change and the influence of practitioners, rather in the way that Scots law acquired English inflexions. To some extent the same has occurred in the French system of Quebec, though its separate character was strengthened by the adoption of the *Code Napoléon* shortly before the Canadian federation came into being.

The 'common law' family of legal systems now has two main branches, those of the various United States and those of countries that are or have been members of the British Commonwealth. The two centuries which now separate us from the Declaration of Independence have seen the growth of many important differences between the two. The protection of individual rights guaranteed by the Constitution of the United States, for instance, has had a profound influence there. But many foundations remain common: basic concepts of substantive law, attitudes to judicial precedent as a source of law, relationships between bench and practising profession – all the matters, indeed, which we have already seen to be most characteristic of the common law of England.

We have been able to glean from the course of events in Scotland some measure of the character shared by so many legal systems of Western Europe. In the sixteenth century, Roman law, as it had come to be interpreted by medieval scholars, began to be 'received' into them in addition to, or in place of, local customs. This meant that, in varying degrees, the common principles derived from this single source were adapted into the law of many kingdoms and republics scattered over the map of Europe. The reception of Roman law was much fostered by the teaching of the great university schools of law, whose international influence remained very considerable until the nineteenth century. Hence these 'civil law' systems, as they are often called, are also known to comparative lawyers as 'Romanist'.

The incorporation of law into national codes in these countries has in modern times made the influence of Roman law less direct. But it has left a pronounced mark upon many of the codes of European nations. And, as we have said already, the tradition has survived of placing considerable value upon scholarly commentaries as a source of law rather than upon the decisions of judges, at least when those decisions have not built up into an established line of authority. This difference is marked in the form which each takes. The scholarly treatise or commentary is expository in style, the judgment tends to be formal and elliptical; and accordingly it may be less useful as a source of general principle. Equally, while the regular study of common law in the English universities has mainly developed over the last century, the reporting of judgments in civil law countries has grown only over much the same period. As this suggests, the methods of common law and civil law are growing together. In France, for instance, decisions of the highest court, the Cour de Cassation, have a force not dissimilar to that of appellate courts in England. The differences that remain tend to be not so much of technique as of the substance of the law.

FOR THE FUTURE

In less than two centuries Britain and Ireland have changed from an agricultural to a largely urban, industrial society. In that time all institutions of government, including the legal system, have undergone many reforms. But much also has been allowed to stand unaltered. How much can perhaps be suggested if, in conclusion, we mention three novel ways in which the law and its services are now beginning to be changed.

Jeremy Bentham not only believed in a complete codification of the law. He thought that the code should be kept under constant review and he devised institutional procedures by which those who administered the law in the courts might forward suggestions for revision of the Codes. At various times since there has been pressure for a permanent body concerned with law reform. This has often taken the form of a plea for a Ministry of Justice in which could be centred the present responsibilities of various central departments of matters of legal administration and substantive law, as well as developing a section specifically concerned with law reform. For long this desire was met by a response typical of the British system: part-time bodies, composed of judges, practitioners and law teachers, were set up to report on desirable reforms. In addition, there were many *ad hoc* enquiries. Inevitably progress was slow and unsystematic. But the situation at last changed in 1965 when the English and Scottish Law Commissions were set up 'to take and keep under review all the law with which they are respectively concerned with a view to its systematic development and reform'. Already they have been responsible for many desirable changes, most extensively in the field of family law. The English Law Commission is also well advanced in a modern project to codify the criminal law. Since reform of this kind must need be by legislation, the more that the law commissions achieve, the more law takes statutory form. Increasingly the judge's role in law-making is that of interpreting legislation. If a defect in a statute emerges, the machinery for correction is now more efficient than it was, though the great difficulty of finding Parliamentary time for amendments makes it less than perfect.

The self-regarding character of English law has been apparent in much that has been said already. There have, of course, been occasions when English lawyers have looked to Western Europe for inspiration in dealing with particular problems, but compared with the development of Scots law the degree of foreign influence has hitherto been slight. But membership of the European Communities, if it does solidify into a permanent relationship, will produce a flow of legal ideas from (and to) Continental Europe on a scale previously unknown. Not only is a great deal of Community law now directly applicable on the particular matters of economic regulation with which the Communities are currently concerned, but there are projects completed or on foot for European and Community patents and trade marks and European companies. It is likely that in the commercial sphere there will be other attempts to harmonize the national laws of the member states. More fundamental still, native conceptions of judicial control of administrative bodies and public policy in relation to contracts may well with time be affected.

Let us end, however, not with law-making but with its application. So much of the law that is administered in the ordinary courts has, in the past, been devised for the needs of litigants who could afford to go there. The problem of making courts truly accessible to the community as a whole – a problem common to most legal systems – has, since the Second World War, been attacked with increasing vigour. In 1949, statutes covering England and Wales and Scotland made provision for state-aided legal assistance, both in and out of court, for those unable to afford it, on a much more substantial basis than ever before. These Acts have gradually been extended to cover more and more types of proceedings, though legal aid is still not available to secure representation before tribunals. Ways of providing cheap and simple redress have recently been introduced, and the opportunities for obtaining free advice from a solicitor have increased not only within the legal assistance scheme but by the development of neighbourhood law centres and legal services at citizens advice bureaux. In an age when the complexities of ordinary life are constantly growing, it is clear that the legal system must continue these first developments towards providing a real and usable service to the community. For without access justice has no meaning.

FURTHER READING

LEGAL SYSTEMS

England

Archer, P. *The Queen's Courts.* 2nd edition. Penguin, 1964.

Baker, J. H. *An Introduction to English Legal History.* Butterworth, 1971 (ISBN 0 406 55500 1).

De Smith, S. A. *Constitutional and Administrative Law.* 2nd edition. Penguin, 1973 (ISBN 0 14 080223 1).

Jackson, R. M. *The Machinery of Justice in England.* 6th edition. Cambridge University Press, 1972 (ISBN 0 521 08644 2).

Milsom, S. F. C. *Historical Foundations of the Common Law.* Butterworth, 1969 (ISBN 0 406 62500 x).

Phillips, O. H. *A First Book of English Law.* 6th edition. Sweet and Maxwell, 1970 (ISBN 0 421 13270 1).

Williams, G. L. *The Proof of Guilt.* 3rd edition. Stevens, 1963.

Wilson, G. P. *Cases and Materials on the English Legal System.* Sweet and Maxwell, 1973 (ISBN 0 421 14970 1).

Zander, M. *Cases and Materials on the English Legal System.* Weidenfeld and Nicolson, 1973 (ISBN 0 297 99547 2).

Scotland

Smith, T. B. Scotland. *In* Keeton, G. W. and Lloyd, D. *The British Commonwealth: The United Kingdom.* Stevens, 1955. Vol. 1, pt. 2.

Walker, D. M. *The Scottish Legal System.* 3rd edition. Green, 1969 (ISBN 0 414 00508 2).

Ireland

Calvert, H. *Constitutional Law in Northern Ireland.* Stevens, 1968 (ISBN 0 420 42230 7).

Donaldson, A. G. *Some comparative aspects of Irish law*. Durham, North Carolina, Duke University Press, 1957 (*Duke University Commonwealth Studies Center Publication no. 3*).

Channel Islands

Sheridan, L. A. Channel Islands. *In* Keeton, G. W. and Lloyd, D. *The British Commonwealth: The United Kingdom*. Stevens, 1965. Vol. 1, pt. 2.

Isle of Man

Holland, D. C. The Isle of Man. *In* Keeton, G. W. and Lloyd, D. *The British Commonwealth: The United Kingdom*. Stevens, 1955. Vol. 1, pt. 1.

JURIES

Cornish, W. R. *The Jury*. Allen Lane, 1968 (ISBN 0 7139 0076 8).
Devlin, Lord. *Trial by Jury*. New edition. Stevens, 1970 (ISBN 0 420 43490 9).
Willock, I. D. *Origins and Development of the Jury in Scotland*. Edinburgh, Stair Society, 1966 (ISBN 0 902292 98 6).

LEGAL PROFESSION

Abel-Smith, B. and Stevens, R. B. *Lawyers and the Courts*. Heinemann Educational, 1970 (ISBN 0 435 32003 3).
Megarry, R. E. *The Lawyer and Litigant in England*. Stevens, 1962 (*Hamlyn lectures*) (ISBN 0 420 37030 7).
Zander, M. *Lawyers and the Public Interest*. Weidenfeld and Nicolson, 1968 (ISBN 0 297 17605 6).

COMPARATIVE

Lawson, F. H. *A Common Lawyer Looks at the Civil Law*. Oxford University Press, 1955.
Yiannopoulos, A. N. *Civil Law in the Modern World*. Baton Rouge, La., Louisiana State University Press, 1965 (ISBN 0 8071 0841 3).

Part II   Legal Literature, Bibliography and Research

3. Primary Sources: Legislation

D. J. WAY, MA, FLA
Sub-Librarian, University of Liverpool (Faculty of Law)

The whole body of legislative materials of the United Kingdom, excluding subordinate legislation (see page 120), is often referred to conveniently as The Statute Book or, more concisely still, The Statutes. Individual items from the Statute Book are also referred to sometimes as Statutes or, more frequently, as Acts of Parliament. Unlike the legislative materials of many other countries, our Statute Book has grown over a period of several centuries without any overall plan, and hence is a body of exceptional size and complexity. We find, for example, that the current edition of the *Chronological Table of the Statutes* still begins with the Statute of Merton, 1235, and even after the recent extensive programme of law revision several sections of Magna Carta still remain on the Statute Book. The whole Statute Book in fact consists of specific Acts on specific topics, enacted by Parliament to remedy specific grievances, and often themselves amended by other Acts within a further twelve months.

PARLIAMENTARY BILLS

In considering this mass of material, we should start where it all begins, in Parliament. It is common knowledge that a new government is brought into power by a general election every four or five years with a mandate to bring into effect a certain programme, usually contained in a party manifesto published just before the election. Upon the new government taking office after the election, and again each year at the beginning of the new parliamentary session, it announces its legislative programme in the Queen's speech, which is indeed read by the Queen, but is of course drafted by the Cabinet. Then comes the first stage in legislation, which is the publication of parliamentary bills embodying the measures forecast in the Queen's

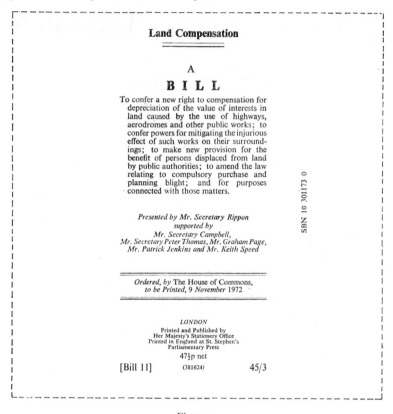

Land Compensation

A
B I L L

To confer a new right to compensation for
depreciation of the value of interests in
land caused by the use of highways,
aerodromes and other public works; to
confer powers for mitigating the injurious
effect of such works on their surround-
ings; to make new provision for the
benefit of persons displaced from land
by public authorities; to amend the law
relating to compulsory purchase and
planning blight; and for purposes
connected with those matters.

Presented by Mr. Secretary Rippon
supported by
Mr. Secretary Campbell,
Mr. Secretary Peter Thomas, Mr. Graham Page,
Mr. Patrick Jenkins and Mr. Keith Speed

Ordered, by The House of Commons,
to be Printed, 9 November 1972

LONDON
Printed and Published by
Her Majesty's Stationery Office
Printed in England at St. Stephen's
Parliamentary Press
47½p net

[Bill 11]   (381624)   45/3

SBN 10 301173 0

Figure 1

speech. These Bills have to pass through both Houses of
Parliament by means of an agreed procedure, which usually
consists of three readings, a Committee stage and a Report
stage in each House, and then – somewhat later in the session
and often somewhat amended – they receive the Royal Assent
and so become Acts of Parliament.

Format of Bills

As law librarians, we are less concerned with the details of the
legislative process than with the appearance which Parliamentary Bills have when they arrive in the law library. By placing
a standing order with HMSO, it is possible to receive copies of

76	*Land Compensation*	

Sch. 2

Chapter	Short Title	Extent of Repeal
1971 c. 78.	The Town and Country Planning Act 1971.	Section 130(1), (2), (4) and (5). In section 193, in subsection (1)(c) the words " since the relevant date " and subsection (3) except in relation to a blight notice served before the passing of this Act. In section 201(1)(b) the words " since the relevant date (within the meaning of section 193 of this Act) " except in relation to a blight notice served before the passing of this Act.
1972 c. 47.	The Housing Finance Act 1972.	Section 94.
1972 c. 52.	The Town and Country Planning (Scotland) Act 1972.	Section 120(5) and (6). In section 182, in subsection (1)(c) the words " since the relevant date " and subsection (3) except in relation to a blight notice served before the passing of this Act. In section 190(1)(b) the words " since the relevant date (within the meaning of section 182 of this Act) " except in relation to a blight notice served before the passing of this Act.

Figure 2

every Bill (except those of a personal or local nature) coming before either House of Parliament. These will include all amendments as and when tabled and all revised prints issued after amendments have been made during the later stages of the Bill. Alternatively, if so desired, selected Bills may be purchased individually.

The main parts of a Parliamentary Bill may be seen in the specimen, Fig. 1. Firstly, you will always find on the title page the date on which the Bill was ordered by the House of Commons to be printed, and you will also see the names of those by whom the Bill is proposed. You are thus enabled to keep your Bills in correct date order, by distinguishing between earlier and later prints of the same Bill, which is useful when several bundles arrive together from HMSO. You can also distinguish – by looking at the names of the promoters – between government Bills and those proposed by back-bench Members of

4

Parliament or peers, which may be of far less importance. (Many private members' Bills never get beyond a first reading during the course of a parliamentary session, and are often presented only so as to focus public attention on a particular topic.) Another feature to note about Bills is that they nearly always contain an *Explanatory and Financial Memorandum,* which outlines briefly and in simple language the main purpose of the Bill and which also states the additional charge likely to be incurred by the public expenditure as a result of the Bill. This seems such an obvious insertion as to call for no particular comment, yet we shall find later that no Statute – once it is enacted – has any such explanatory memorandum.

Each Bill has a serial number for citation purposes in the lower left-hand corner of the title page, enclosed within square brackets in the case of versions presented to the House of Commons and within round brackets in the case of versions presented to the House of Lords. The serial number is different for each stage of the Bill, and progresses throughout the session, so that the later versions of the Bill have higher serial numbers than the earlier. If citing a version of a Bill by its serial number, the session should also be indicated, as a new sequence of serial numbers is started at the beginning of each session. The example, Fig. 1, may be cited as H.C. Bill 1972–3 [11].

Library uses of Bills

The amount of use made of Parliamentary Bills depends very much upon the type of law library concerned. In a practitioners' law library, it is the final form taken by the Act that is alone of interest. For a practising lawyer to read a Bill at an earlier stage, when details in it still remain to be amended, would only confuse him unnecessarily, and he will as a rule leave it alone until it becomes an Act. In an academic law library, on the other hand, the situation is different. An academic lawyer teaching students a particular branch of the law must be able to give them forewarning of impending changes in that branch, because if a Bill is already on its way through Parliament, then it will be enacted and so part of the law by the time the students are qualified. For the same reason, an academic lawyer beginning to write a textbook on a particular topic must know what changes in the law are likely to be made while his textbook is under way, so that they may be incorporated as far as possible into the completed work. Given also that some academic lawyers have been associated with the work of the Law Commission and other law reforming bodies, you will see that in a university law library there is likely to be quite a lively interest in and use of Parliamentary Bills.

Progress of Bills through Parliament

A query often received in law libraries is how far a particular Bill has gone on its way through Parliament. This may be answered by reference to the *Public Bill List*, which appears weekly while Parliament is sitting and which indicates the title of each Bill before the House of Commons and the present state of its progress. If the library does not subscribe to this list, then the enquirer may have to be referred to the section headed 'Parliament' in the monthly issues of *Current Law* or to the appropriate sections in the *New Law Journal* or *Solicitors' Journal*.

ACTS OF PARLIAMENT (THE STATUTES)

Queen's Printer's copies

Assuming now that our Bill has passed through all its stages in both Houses of Parliament, at the end of this process it receives the Royal Assent and so becomes an Act. As such, it will first appear in a paper copy published by HMSO, which is often known as a 'Queen's Printer's copy'. All new Acts are published by HMSO separately in this form, and unless the Act is of exceptional length and complexity, it should appear thus within a month of receiving Royal Assent. As with Bills, so with Acts, a standing order can be placed with HMSO, and a copy of each new Act received as published, or alternatively selected Acts may be purchased individually.

Parts of an Act

A quick glance at the illustrations shown (Figs 3–5) of a Queen's Printer's copy of an Act will indicate the main parts of a Statute, which may be referred to again during the course of the chapter. The Statute, unless very short, begins with the Arrangement of Sections, or table of contents. On the next page, there follows the short title ('Land Charges Act 1972' in the example shown); then we have the citation ('1972 Chapter 61'), the long title ('An Act to consolidate certain enactments . . . '), the date of Royal Assent (within square brackets), and the enacting formula ('Be it enacted . . . '). Sometimes in old Acts, there is also a preamble before the enacting formula, usually beginning with the word 'Whereas' and setting forth the mischief which the Act is intended to remedy; but this is rarely used today. Note that there is no explanatory memorandum, which is dropped from the Bill after it has been enacted.

The text of the Act follows, beginning with Section 1. As a matter of nomenclature, it should be noted that an Act has sections and sub-sections, whereas a Bill has clauses and sub-sections.

At the end of the Statute, we normally have a section dealing with 'Short title, commencement and extent'; often, there are also preceding sections on 'Interpretation' and on 'Consequential amendments, repeals, savings, etc.' Then follow the Schedules, which among other things prescribe forms to be used, furnish illustrations, and list consequential amendments in more detail. The Schedules also always contain a table of repeals, indicating which Acts or sections of Acts have been repealed by the new Act.

The official editions of the Statutes

The Queen's Printer's copies of the Statutes, because of their format, are not suitable for permanent preservation, but for this there is a choice of several bound series. The first to be mentioned, inevitably, is the official series, now known as *Statutes in force: official revised edition,* 1972–   . To explain the lay-out and working of this, it is necessary to go back a little. In 1868, as a result of various criticisms of the form of the Statute Book similar to those heard today, a Statute Law Committee was set up, and its labours resulted in *The Statutes Revised,* published in 18 volumes between 1870 and 1885. A second edition of this appeared between 1888 and 1901, with supplements issued in 1909 and 1928–9, and a third edition

Land Charges Act 1972

CHAPTER 61

ARRANGEMENT OF SECTIONS

Figure 3

c. 61   1

ELIZABETH II

Land Charges Act 1972

1972 CHAPTER 61

An Act to consolidate certain enactments relating to the registration of land charges and other instruments and matters affecting land.   [9th August 1972]

BE IT ENACTED by the Queen's most Excellent Majesty, by and with the advice and consent of the Lords Spiritual and Temporal, and Commons, in this present Parliament assembled, and by the authority of the same, as follows:—

Preliminary

1.—(1) The registrar shall continue to keep at the registry in The registers the prescribed manner the following registers, namely— and the index.

    (*a*) a register of land charges ;

    (*b*) a register of pending actions ;

    (*c*) a register of writs and orders affecting land ;

    (*d*) a register of deeds of arrangement affecting land ;

    (*e*) a register of annuities,

and shall also continue to keep there an index whereby all entries made in any of those registers can readily be traced.

(2) Every application to register shall be in the prescribed form and shall contain the prescribed particulars.

(3) Where any charge or other matter is registrable in more than one of the registers kept under this Act or is registrable in one or more of those registers and also in a register kept under the Land Charges Act 1925 (registers of local land charges), 1925 c. 22. it shall be sufficient if it is registered in one register, and if it is so registered the person entitled to the benefit of it shall not be prejudicially affected by the provisions of this Act or that Act applying to any other register.

Figure 4

appeared in 1951. This third edition consisted of 33 volumes (including one volume of Church Assembly Measures), and it was complete up to the last day of 1948, containing in chronological order all the public general statutes still in force wholly or partly at that date.

The authoritative nature of these editions was buttressed by Section 35(2) of the Interpretation Act 1889, which provides that any reference to an Act in a later Act 'shall, unless a contrary intention appears, be read as referring, in the case of statutes included in any revised edition of the statutes purporting to be printed by authority, to that edition'.

To supplement the official collected editions of the Statutes, an annual series of bound volumes called *Public General Acts and*

Land Charges Act 1972   **c. 61**   15

(4) The Land Charges Rules 1972 are hereby revoked.   S.I. 1972/50.

(5) In so far as any entry in a register or instrument made or other thing whatsoever done under any enactment repealed by this Act could have been made or done under a corresponding provision in this Act, it shall have effect as if made or done under that corresponding provision ; and for the purposes of this provision any entry in a register which under section 24 of the Land Charges Act 1925 had effect as if made under that Act 1925 c. 22. shall, so far as may be necessary for the continuity of the law, be treated as made under this Act.

(6) Any enactment or other document referring to an enactment repealed by this Act or to an enactment repealed by the Land Charges Act 1925 shall, as far as may be necessary for preserving its effect, be construed as referring, or as including a reference, to the corresponding enactment in this Act.

(7) Nothing in the foregoing provisions of this section shall be taken as prejudicing the operation of section 38 of the Interpretation Act 1889 (which relates to the effect of repeals). 1889 c. 63.

19.—(1) This Act may be cited as the Land Charges Act Short title, 1972. commencement and (2) This Act shall come into force on such day as the Lord extent. Chancellor may by order made by statutory instrument appoint ; and different days may be so appointed for different purposes.

(3) This Act extends to England and Wales only.

Figure 5

Measures has been produced by HMSO. This series began as long ago as 1831, and each volume contains the full texts of the Statutes and Church Assembly Measures for each year, alphabetical and chronological lists of the Acts and Measures for the year, an alphabetical list only of the Local and Personal Acts for the year (since 1962), a table showing the effect of the year's legislation, a table of derivations of Consolidation Acts for the year (since 1967), and an index.

In addition to this, HMSO also issued annually a compilation called *Annotations to Acts*, containing gummed insertions to be pasted on to the pages of the official series of Statutes, and written directions for amendments and cancellations.

For the first few years after the issue of the 3rd edition of *The Statutes Revised*, this system worked reasonably well, but then criticism began to mount. Librarians especially found the insertion of all the amendments prescribed in *Annotations to Acts* exceedingly laborious, and many law libraries were years behind with this work. Mr Justice Scarman (in *Law reform*, Routledge, 1968) has described how by the close of the year 1965, 9,603 pages out of a total of 26,087 in the 32 volumes of *The Statutes Revised* (excluding *Church Assembly Measures*) had been cancelled, and how many of the remaining pages were 'physically disfigured by amendments, annotation slips and erasures'. At the same time, various people began to ask whether the Statutes could not be kept up to date by some new method. An example was Trevor Aldridge in an article called 'Consolidation without tears' (*Solicitors' Journal*, vol. 109, 1965, p. 762). Aldridge rightly considered that *Annotations to Acts* imposed far too heavy a burden on the subscriber, and he concluded: 'What is needed is a system whereby an Act, once amended, is officially republished in its altered form. This would be a Queen's Printer's copy, completely authoritative, and would provide a trouble-free way of establishing the up-to-date statutory position.'

Following these criticisms, the Statute Law Committee appointed a sub-committee early in 1967 'to consider what improvements should be made in the form and arrangement of the Statute Book, for example, (*a*) by the official publication of a loose-leaf edition of "Statutes Revised"; or (*b*) by the publication of an official edition, loose-leaf or otherwise, of

Acts arranged by subjects'. Members of the legal profession and other users of the statutes were asked to send in their comments to the Statute Law Committee. As a result of these deliberations, a new edition of *Statutes in force* started to appear during 1972, and is expected to continue appearing in instalments throughout the remainder of the decade. As compared with *The Statutes Revised*, quite a new principle of arrangement has been adopted. Instead of a series of bound volumes reprinting the statutes in chronological order, there are now a series of loose-leaf binders containing reprints of Acts as amended to stated dates, each Act being stapled so as to form a booklet and punched with holes ready for insertion in the binder. It will thus be possible to remove a repealed Act entirely from the binder, and to replace a heavily amended Act with a new booklet. At the same time, for those who require them, the annual volumes of the *Public General Acts* will continue to be produced as previously.

As Acts are going to be arranged in this edition in subject groups, it will be possible for specialist libraries or readers to order only the group or groups in which their interests lie. The Acts, or groups of Acts, can also be arranged within the binders to suit the readers' own requirements. A general law library, obviously, will need to order the whole set, which is likely to cost upwards of £1,000 at present prices.

One other interesting feature of the new edition is that magnetic tapes containing the texts of the Statutes will be made available, and can thus be used for information retrieval projects. (*Law Librarian*, vol. 3, 1972, p. 5; *New Law Journal*, vol. 122, 1972, p. 1143.)

Looking at the new edition of *Statutes in force* so far as it has appeared to date, it would appear that the Statute Law Committee have made a genuine effort to meet their critics. On the other hand, certain limitations still remain. The amount of annotation included with the text is limited compared with what there is in the commercial editions of the Statutes, and it is confined in general to footnotes giving the authority for printing the text as it is and to cross notes drawing attention to other provisions which affect the Act without amending it (for instance, where a section is applied with or without modifications in later Acts). There are also certain new difficulties inherent in this format, which are well summarized in a review by David M. Walker (*Scots Law Times*, 1973, pp. 14–16). For instance, it will be easy for unscrupulous readers to remove Acts from binders or to mislay them, and the need to incorporate written amendments is not entirely eliminated, merely reduced. So, although the *Statutes in force* will and must have a place in law libraries, the various other series of Statutes – to be described in the next section – will remain there also.

Proposals for reforming the official series of statutes still further have been made by the Statute Law Society, and may be studied in their two reports, *Statute law deficiencies*, 1970, and *Statute law : the key to clarity*, 1972. Since then, a Committee on the Preparation of Legislation, under the chairmanship of Sir David Renton, has been set up officially, and has reported. (Cmnd. 6053. 1975.)

Other collected editions of the Statutes

As alternatives to the official series of the Statutes, there are several series issued by commercial publishers, who are permitted to reprint them by arrangement with HMSO. Most of these series are annotated to a greater or lesser extent, so as to convey additional information not available in the official editions. A brief guide to the respective merits of the various series now follows.

Halsbury's Statutes of England

Halsbury's Statutes of England (3rd edition, Butterworth, 1968–72, 41 vols) is the most important privately issued series, and has several advantages in a law library over the official series. In the first place, it is complete as well as up-to-date, the new edition having been produced in four years (half the time estimated as necessary for the publication of the new official edition). Secondly, it is well annotated; the annotations usually follow each section of an Act, relating it to earlier legislation (stating, for example, whether it is a re-enactment), providing statutory definitions of terms used, giving cross-references where required, and mentioning any delegated legislation made under the authority of the section concerned. Thirdly, Halsbury has various time-saving arrangements for keeping up to date. Two loose-leaf volumes called the *Current statutes service* contain statutes for the current year, and are then replaced in due course by annual hardback continuation volumes. In addition, an annual cumulative supplement notes all amendments and repeals to Acts in the forty main volumes up to the end of the previous year, and a loose-leaf noter-up enables one to check more recent amendments or repeals. Arrangements are also to be made to reproduce European Community law of particular importance as part of the series. Finally, there is a bound volume containing tables of statutes and an index for volumes 1 to 40, thus enabling all Acts to be tracked down quickly in their respective volumes.

The order of statutes in Halsbury is by subject, rather than chronological. This is advantageous, in that Acts on the same subject are in the same volume, but there is a corresponding drawback in that certain Acts covering more than one subject are split rather inconveniently. For instance, the Finance Act 1968 is split between eleven headings, most of them in different volumes. Another drawback to Halsbury is that Acts applying to Scotland only are omitted, although Acts applying to Northern Ireland only are included. Volume 10 (Ecclesiastical Law) contains Church Assembly Measures (for a general discussion of Church Assembly Measures, see page 113), and volume 20 (London) contains a wide selection of London Local Acts, but in general Local Acts are not noted, apart from one or two provisions reproduced in volume 7 under Courts. (For a general discussion of Local Acts, see page 111.)

Current Law Statutes Annotated

Current Law Statutes Annotated is another publisher's series of current statutes only from 1948 onwards. The statutes first appear in several paper sections, which are replaced by a bound volume at the end of the year. The annotations are somewhat less detailed than those in Halsbury; but, unlike Halsbury, this series includes Acts of purely Scottish application. An accompanying *Current Law Statutes Citator and Index* now appears three times a year, and acts as a noter-up of amendments and repeals made during the current year.

Law Reports Statutes

The Law Reports Statutes, 1865 to date, are taken by a large number of law libraries, probably because they can be obtained on the same subscription as *The Law Reports*. They are not a wholly independent series, however, being in effect the Queen's Printer's copies reprinted under an Incorporated Council of Law Reporting imprint and with the same tables and indexes as *Public General Acts and Measures* at the end of the year. They are thus not annotated, and they have the further drawbacks (from the law librarian's point of view) that they are somewhat late in appearance and that they have to be bound by the subscriber.

Butterworths Annotated Legislation Service

Butterworths Annotated Legislation Service, 1947 to date, began as the continuation of a wartime loose-leaf series by the same publishers entitled *Butterworths Emergency Legislation Service Annotated*. The aim of the series is to provide practitioners with a working guide to those statutes which are of everyday importance. Hence, it is selective rather than comprehensive in its coverage; but it contains the most detailed annotations of any series for those Acts which it does cover. Each volume contains either one Act only, or a selection of a few Acts at a time, and many of the former have been reprinted as separate publications later. Every two years a cumulative index to the series is produced, and this indicates which Acts to date have been printed in the series and where they may be found.

Collections of statutes by subject

The collections of statutes described have all been general ones, covering the whole legislative field. There exist also, however, some very useful subject collections of statutes, which have been compiled for the law publishers. These include, for example, *Sweet and Maxwell's Property Statutes*, *Sweet and Maxwell's Family Law Statutes* and *Scots Mercantile Statutes*. Their main market is amongst law students, who are thus enabled to buy the statutes they most need in convenient format and at a reasonable price, but they also have their uses in law libraries.

Older statutes

All of the series of statutes mentioned so far have been current ones, suitable for tracing new or recent Acts, or older Acts still in force. Occasionally, however, it may be necessary to trace a nineteenth-century Act which has been repealed. Because it has been repealed, it will not be found in the third edition of *The Statutes Revised*, in *Statutes in force*, or in the latest edition of Halsbury. In this case, the best means of obtaining a copy of the Act concerned is through the earlier volumes of *Public General Acts and Measures*, a series which, as already indicated, commenced in 1831 (at first under the title *Public General Acts*). For all editions of the statutes during the period prior to 1800, see page 232.

Special types of statutes

So much for the main published series of statutes. It is useful, however, for a law librarian to know something about the subject matter with which he is dealing, and several aspects of the statutes are of interest. In the first place, the Public General Acts divide into several types according to purpose. The largest class, and that requiring the least comment, consists of those described in an old term as 'remedial Acts', in the sense that they are passed in order to remedy defects in the existing law or defective social situations. Such, for example, are the numerous Landlord and Tenant Acts or Housing Acts that have been passed in recent years. Another class requiring no comment here consists of the Finance Acts and others concerned with raising revenue for the Government. Other types of Acts will be described briefly below.

Constitutional statutes

In some countries, constitutional laws form a special class of their own, and often require special procedures to be used for their amendment or repeal. This is not the case in the United Kingdom, where constitutional statutes go through Parliament on exactly the same basis as all other statutes. The differing situation in this respect in the Republic of Ireland is mentioned on page 131.

Codifying Acts

Codification of the law is a process which has been used in a number of other countries, for instance, in the case of the *Code Napoléon* in France or the German Civil Code. There has been no general codification in the United Kingdom, but there have been a number of codifying and consolidating Acts. To quote from an authoritative source, 'Codifying Acts are Acts passed to codify the existing law, both statutory and common law, *ie*, not merely to declare the law on some particular point, but to declare in the form of a code the whole of the law on a particular subject'. (Craies, W. F. *Craies on statute law.* 7th edition, 1971, p. 59). Examples often quoted of Codifying Acts are the Bills of Exchange Act 1882, the Partnership Act 1890, the Sale of Goods Act 1893, and the Marine Insurance Act 1906.

Consolidating Acts

Consolidating Acts, on the other hand, only consolidate the statute law on a subject, and do not necessarily affect the case law. Their object is to consolidate in one Act the provisions contained in a number of statutes, sometimes with minor amendments, so as to make the law more accessible to the practitioner. A number of consolidating statutes are passed each year now, a special procedure being used in Parliament to enable them to go through without debate. Examples include the Highways Act 1959, the Income and Corporation Taxes Act 1970, and the Road Traffic Act 1972.

Statute Law Revision Acts

Another type of Act consists of the Statute Law Revision Acts or Statute Law (Repeals) Acts, which represent a tidying up operation on the Statute Book. The first Statute Law Revision Act at present in the Statute Book was passed in 1861, and others have continued at intervals to the present day. Activity in this field has become more systematic since the inception of the Law Commission and Scottish Law Commission. These bodies have been specifically charged with, among other duties, a review of the law 'with a view to its systematic development and reform, including in particular the codification of such law,

the elimination of anomalies, the repeal of obsolete and unnecessary enactments, the reduction of the number of separate
enactments, and generally the simplification and modernization of the law'. (Law Commissions Act 1965, s. 3.)

Geographical extent of statutes

So far, apart from brief references, we have been dealing with
Acts covering the whole of the United Kingdom. Normally, in
the case of Public General Acts, there is a presumption that the
Act extends to the whole of the United Kingdom, unless stated
otherwise. Any statement to the contrary will appear in the last
section of any statute, which nearly always deals with the
matters of 'Short title, commencement and extent'. Here, the
word 'extent' means geographical extent, and the section will
specify whether any portions of the United Kingdom are
excluded. Thus, certain Acts, such as the Land Charges Act
1972, extend to England and Wales only, while others may
extend to Scotland only or to Northern Ireland only; or
alternatively, Scotland or Northern Ireland may be expressly
excluded from the operation of the Act. Acts applying to
Scotland or to Northern Ireland only are often identifiable as
such from their titles, as for instance, the Administration of
Justice (Scotland) Act 1972 or the Northern Ireland (Financial
Provisions) Act 1972. Normally, England and Wales are
treated as one unit, but occasionally there are separate provisions for Wales, as in the Local Government Act 1972, or
Acts applying to Wales only, such as the Welsh Language Act
1967.

The statute law of Scotland and of Northern Ireland are
dealt with in more detail in the Scottish and Irish sections on
pages 126 and 128 respectively.

Local and Personal Acts

All of the statutes referred to in the last section are public
general statutes, even though only extending to part of the
United Kingdom, but there is a parallel series of Local and
Personal Acts (known before 1948 as Local and Private Acts),
which must now be considered. These are Acts of Parliament,

the application of which is limited to certain localities or individuals, for instance, by enabling local authorities to prohibit certain activities in their areas. An example of a Local Act is the Isle of Wight Act 1971, which gave the local council some special measures of control for purposes of health and hygiene over large assemblies of persons in the open air. An example of a Personal Act is the Arundel Estate Act 1957, which disentailed the estate of the Duke of Norfolk. Personal Acts are now very rare, and there were none shown in the indexes between the Lucas Estate Act 1963 and the Wellington Estate Act 1972.

To make things more confusing, however, not every Act which is local or personal in its nature or application is a Local or Personal Act. Thus, the Maplin Development Act 1973, which provides for the reclamation from the sea of land for the establishment of the proposed third London airport, has appeared in the Public General series, although clearly local in its application. Similarly with Mr Speaker King's Retirement Act 1971, which was an Act of a personal nature providing a pension to the retired Speaker of the House of Commons. So a further point of distinction may be made, which is that Public General Acts arise from Bills proposed by the Government or (occasionally) by private Members of Parliament, whereas Local or Personal Acts in England and Wales arise through a different procedure by petition from the promoters, who may be a local authority, a nationalized industry or public utility, or (very occasionally) a private individual. Because Local Acts originate in this way, all copies of the proposals in the Bill stage have to be printed by the promoters, and hence are not available from HMSO.

Historically, the distinction between Public General and Public Local and Personal Acts was first made in 1798. For the complicated history of their classification since that date, reference should be made to *Craies on statute law*, 7th edition, 1971, pp. 55–8, or, more briefly, *Halsbury's Laws of England*, 3rd edition, vol. 36, footnote (b) on p. 364.

All the Local and Personal Acts (previously Local and Private Acts) have been published by HMSO since 1924. Before that date, as shown in the works referred to in the preceding paragraph, there were some exceptions as regards Private Acts.

HMSO also publishes an annual table and index to the Local and Personal Acts, and it is possible to obtain all the Local and Personal Acts for the year on standing order as they come out. Few libraries in fact do obtain them all, so that a full collection of these Acts going back into the nineteenth century is extremely valuable. As we have already seen, there is also an alphabetical list of Local and Personal Acts of the year in the preliminaries to the volume of the Public General Acts and Measures for each year.

Two useful retrospective indexes to the Local and Personal Acts have been produced by HMSO, a main index covering the years 1801 to 1947 and a supplementary index covering the years 1948 to 1966. The main index is a classified subject index of all Local and Personal Acts during the period, broad subject headings being used such as Railways, Canals, Enclosures, and so on. The supplement has a similar arrangement, with only slight modifications to the subject headings used, and also contains separate alphabetical and chronological lists of all Local and Personal Acts passed during the nineteen years that it covers (a feature not contained in the main volume). Some repeals are shown in the entries in the main index, but not exhaustively, so that it is necessary to refer to the Acts themselves for certainty in this respect. At the same time, the indexes are a useful starting point in tracing Acts referring to a particular locality, and will at least suffice to give adequate references for inter-library loan, should the Acts required not be in your own library.

Church Assembly Measures

Another form of legislation, that it is convenient to mention here, are the Church Assembly Measures (known as General Synod Measures from 1972 onwards). Since the beginning of 1920, the National Assembly of the Church of England has been able to legislate for the Church, subject to the approval of the Ecclesiastical Committee of Parliament, under the terms of the Church of England Assembly (Powers) Act 1919. These Measures, as they are called, have the same binding force on the laity of the Church as statutes, and they are printed in the same volumes as the Public General Acts. There is also a volume of

Church Assembly Measures Revised, which appears at the close of the series of *The Statutes Revised*, 3rd edition. For further details about ecclesiastical law, see page 365.

Citation of statutes

Having described the various series of statutes, our next task is to discuss the problems which the law librarian is likely to encounter when using statutory material. One of the most important of these is the citation of statutes. This arises because statutes are frequently cited in the official manner in references that you may be given, and in fact you might even be required to find statutes identified only by their citation.

Citation by regnal year

Any statute, or Act of Parliament, then, may be cited by its short title and calendar year, which is in fact the way in which it is commonly referred to in normal speech. Alternatively, it may be cited more precisely in the official way, but this form of citation differs according to whether the Act was passed before or after the last day of 1962. Any Act passed before the close of 1962 should be cited by its regnal year and chapter number. Thus, the Highways Act 1959 is cited officially as 7 & 8 Eliz. 2 c. 25. This means that it was the 25th Act to receive the Royal Assent during the parliamentary session taking place in the seventh and eighth years of the present reign. The regnal year and the parliamentary session almost never coincide, and both differ from the calendar year. The regnal year begins always on the date of the monarch's accession, which is 6 February in the case of the present Queen, whereas the parliamentary session normally runs from about the last week in October or first week in November. On account of the commencement of the parliamentary session in November, we find that chapter numbers of a few statutes at the extreme end of the calendar year (that is, the beginning of the new session) are lower than those earlier in the calendar year. Thus, to return to the year 1959, the closing Act of the session 7 & 8 Eliz. 2 was the Legitimacy Act 1959 (7 & 8 Eliz. 2 c. 73), which received Royal Assent on 29 July 1959. The next Act in the Statute Book, Mr Speaker Morrison's

Retirement Act, received Royal Assent on 17 December 1959, and is cited as 8 Eliz. 2 c. 1.

Sometimes, it should be noted, the parliamentary session ends before its time, owing to an election, and then there is a much longer second sequence of Acts at the end of the year. For instance, in 1955, Parliament was dissolved for a General Election on 6 May, so closing the parliamentary session 3 & 4 Eliz. 2. The new Parliament assembled on 9 June, and 22 Public General Acts passed by it before the close of the year 1955 appear in the Statute Book, under the heading 4 Eliz. 2. The session, which became known as 4 & 5 Eliz. 2 as soon as the anniversary date of the Queen's accession on 6 February was passed, lasted until November 1956, so was considerably longer than a normal calendar year.

A further complication arises in the case of volumes of the Public General Acts prior to 1940. Each volume before that date contained all the Acts of a parliamentary session, not of a calendar year, so that the short second sequence of Acts at the end of a calendar year went in effect into the volume for the following year. One well-known example, which is often difficult to locate on this account, is the Public Order Act 1936. This Act was Chapter 6 of the parliamentary session 1 Edw. 8 & 1 Geo. 6, and it received Royal Assent on 18 December 1936. Because it came at the beginning of the new parliamentary session, it was included in the volume of the Public General Acts for 1937, not 1936. Another example where this practice had an odd effect is a volume of the Public General Statutes which runs over three calendar years, from 1914 to 1916, as it covers a parliamentary session extending from November 1914 to January 1916. It is thus most important, in the case of Acts passed before 1940, to have the citation to hand, in case difficulties such as these should arise.

Citation by calendar year

These complications were all brought to an end by the Acts of Parliament Numbering and Citation Act 1962 (10 & 11 Eliz. 2 c. 34), which laid down that the chapter numbers assigned to Acts of Parliament passed in the year 1963 and subsequently should be assigned by reference to the calendar year and not the session in which they were passed. This brings Britain into line with other Commonwealth countries and makes the whole method of citing statutes much easier to understand and to follow. The sequence of chapter numbers is now continuous throughout the whole calendar year, regardless of parliamentary session. Thus, the last Act of the parliamentary session 18 & 19 Eliz. 2 was the Indecent Advertisements (Amendment) Act 1970, which received Royal Assent on 29 May 1970 and is cited as 1970 c. 47; and the first Act of the new session of Parliament after the General Election was the Appropriation (No. 2) Act 1970, which is cited as 1970 c. 48. It should be noted also that many pre-1963 statutes are now being cited by calendar year retrospectively in official publications, although this is not obligatory.

Citation of Local and Personal Acts, and Church Assembly Measures

There are special methods of citing Local Acts, Personal Acts and Church Assembly Measures. Local and Personal Acts up to the end of 1962 were cited, like Public General Acts, by their regnal year and chapter number. The chapter numbers, however, ran in a different sequence from those of the Public General Acts, and so the citation was by means of a roman numeral in the case of Local Acts and by an italicized arabic numeral in the case of the few Personal Acts that remain. For instance, whereas the citation 7 & 8 Eliz. 2 c. 25 referred to the Highways Act 1959, as already mentioned, the corresponding roman numeral citation 7 & 8 Eliz. 2 c. xxv refers to the North Devon Water Act 1959, which of course is in the local series. After 1962, Local Acts are cited, like Public General Acts, by year and chapter number, but again the chapter number is in roman numerals. For example, whereas the Finance Act 1972 was 1972 c. 41, on the other hand the citation 1972 c. xli refers to the Liverpool Corporation Act 1972 in the local series. The one and only Personal Act passed in 1972, the Wellington Estate Act 1972, is cited as 1972 c. *1*.

Church Assembly Measures are cited similarly, with regnal year up to 1962 and calendar year since 1962, but with numbers instead of chapters. Thus, the Truro Cathedral Measure 1959 was 7 & 8 Eliz. 2 No. 1, and the Sharing of Church Buildings Measure 1970 was 1970 No. 2.

Coming into force of statutes

Another topic, on which library queries also arise, is the coming into force of statutes. The layman may think that an Act of Parliament automatically comes into force as soon as it is passed, but in fact the position is not quite so simple as that. Originally, it was deemed that an Act of Parliament came into operation on the first day of the parliamentary session in which it was passed. This legal fiction was found to involve some injustice, since it meant that Acts passed late in the session might be retrospective for several months in their operation. Accordingly, the Acts of Parliament (Commencement) Act 1793, which is still in force, provided that the Clerk of Parliament should endorse on every Act the date on which it received Royal Assent, and that this endorsement should be taken to be part of the Act and should be the date of its commencement where no other date was provided within the Act itself. If a date is provided within the Act, it will usually be found in the last section of the Act, which as mentioned on page 100 nearly always deals with the matters of short title, commencement and extent. (Occasionally this rule is broken, as in the Land Commission Act 1967, in which commencement was dealt with in Section 1 – so be prepared always for exceptions.)

On being asked whether and when an Act has come into operation, therefore, we should look first of all for the date of Royal Assent, which is to be found within square brackets at the beginning of the Act after the long title, (see Fig. 4). If nothing else is said about commencement at the beginning or end of the Act, then the date of Royal Assent may be regarded as the date that the Act comes into force. The two dates normally coincide in the case of short Acts or of Acts with few complications. An example is the Island of Rockall Act 1972, which specifically states, 'As from the date of the passing of this Act, the Island of Rockall . . . shall be incorporated into that part of the United Kingdom known as Scotland . . . ' Here, the date of Royal Assent is given as 10 February 1972.

Next, we find a number of Acts, usually of moderate length, which come into force after a short fixed period, often one month. An example is the Local Employment Act 1972, where Section 23(2) states, 'This Act shall come into force at the expiration of the period of one month beginning with the day on which it is passed'. The date of Royal Assent for this Act was 10 February 1972 (the same day as for the Island of Rockall Act), so that it may be regarded as coming into force on 10 March 1972.

A third class of Acts are those that provide the real difficulty. These are usually Acts of considerable length and complexity, and because of this administrative machinery has to be set up, and it is left to the Minister concerned to prescribe by order when the various sections of the Act shall come into force. An example is the Industrial Relations Act 1971, the closing section of which states that 'This Act shall come into operation on such day as the Secretary of State may appoint by order made by statutory instrument, and different days may be so appointed . . . ' This means that none of the Act came into force on the day on which it received Royal Assent (5 August 1971), but that it started to come into force subsequently by means of a series of commencement orders. These orders form part of the Statutory Instruments series (see page 120).

A useful summary of the date of commencement of statutes is to be found near the beginning of each monthly issue of *Current Law*, for which see page 164. (For Northern Ireland statutes reference should be made to the title 'Northern Ireland'.) Some Acts in fact take many years to come fully into operation. An instance is the Legal Aid and Advice Act 1949, of which the latest commencement order, the Legal Aid and Advice Act 1949 (Commencement No. 13) Order, appeared as late as 1973. One Act at least of recent years, the Offices Act 1960, never came into operation, as the regulations making it operative were never made before it was repealed!

Determining whether statutes are still in force

Having ascertained whether our statute has come into force, the next thing to do logically is to find out whether it is still in force, and many queries may centre round this point. Here, it is necessary to consult one of the indexes to the Statutes.

Chronological table of the Statutes

The *Chronological Table of the Statutes* is the best work to use for a quick-reference answer. It is published in July each year, and goes up to the end of the preceding year. It lists all the Public General Acts from 1235 onwards section by section, showing which sections have been repealed (and by what authority) and which have been amended in any way by subsequent legislation. Acts still wholly or partially in force have their titles printed in heavy type, while Acts now wholly repealed have their titles printed in italic type.

Index to the Statutes in force

The *Index to the Statutes in force,* which similarly appears each year (with a longer delay), is a research tool rather than a quick-reference guide. Its function is to index all the public general statute law still in force at the end of a given year under detailed subject headings.

Keeping up to date

As always, there is an awkward gap for the last few months, where the indexes leave off. The table of *Effect of legislation,* compiled for the annual volumes of the *Public General Acts and Measures,* helps a little, as this appears in March each year, four months ahead of the *Chronological Table of the Statutes,* which is in fact revised with its aid (*Law Librarian,* vol. 1, 1970, p. 8). The table of *Effect of legislation* lists in chronological order all Acts repealed or amended by Acts passed during the last preceding year. Alternatives which can be used are the annual cumulative supplement to *Halsbury's Statutes* and the loose-leaf noter-up to Halsbury, which appear more promptly still.

If it is suspected that an amendment to an old Act has been made by a statute passed in the current year, then even these aids will not suffice, and as a last resource reference may have to be made to *Current Law* (see page 164), or to the latest Queen's Printer's copies of the Acts themselves.

Searching for statutory material

The beginner to law librarianship should not be put off too much by the complicated nature of statutory material. Many enquiries will be quite easy, and will be simply requests for a specific Act or part of an Act. If the year and title of the Act have been quoted correctly, it will then be quite easy to find it.

Alternatively, the enquirer may think that there has been a new Act on such and such a subject, and it will then be a case of taking the latest material first and working your way backwards – and also of consulting digests such as *Current Law* (see page 164). If you are short of statutes for a particular year, it is always worth remembering that many legal textbooks are little more than reprints of the Acts on their subjects, with some annotations, and so you can if necessary fall back on these, where you know that the subject fits. It is also important in this connection not to forget the loose-leaf encyclopedias, which are described on page 199. Providing that you use all your sources intelligently, you should always be able to find a copy of the Act that you want in some form or other.

SUBORDINATE LEGISLATION

At the beginning of the chapter, a brief reference was made to the division of United Kingdom legislative materials into statutes and subordinate legislation. The latter category, to quote *Halsbury's Laws of England* (3rd edition, vol. 36, page 476), is 'legislation made by a person or body other than the Sovereign in Parliament by virtue of powers conferred either by statute or by legislation which is itself made under statutory powers'. To continue from Halsbury, 'it is frequently referred to as delegated legislation in the former case and sub-delegated legislation in the latter'.

From the law librarian's point of view, it is sufficient to know that any items referred to as Orders, Regulations, Rules, Schemes, Directions or Warrants are likely to be subordinate legislation, and that far and away the greater part of these will be found nowadays in the *Statutory Instruments* series. This series was set up under the authority of the Statutory Instruments Act 1946, which replaced the old term 'Statutory Rule' by the new term 'Statutory Instrument', and which laid down the procedure as regards publication, numbering and citation of Statutory Instruments.

Statutory Instruments

Statutory Instruments exist to deal with matters too detailed to be included in an Act of Parliament, and they also have the advantage that they can be revoked or amended at short notice by the Minister concerned, in order to meet changing circumstances. Like the Acts of Parliament themselves, Statutory Instruments cover every field of activity, and range from local or routine orders dealing with rights of way or Customs and Excise, to quite important items, such as the various Matrimonial Causes Rules. A large proportion of new legislation delegates power to the Minister to make orders covering the application of the Act concerned. For instance, the *70 miles per hour Speed Limit (England) Order 1967* (S.I. 1967 No. 1040) was made by the then Minister of Transport under the Road Traffic Act 1962, section 13(2), and continued indefinitely the maximum speed limit of 70 mph originally imposed for limited periods by a series of *70 miles per hour (Temporary Speed Limit) (England) Orders*. Again, an important series of orders has been made by the Treasury and other ministries under the Counter-Inflation Act 1973 (1973 c. 9), of which the most noteworthy is the *Counter-Inflation (Price and Pay Code) Order 1973* (S.I. 1973 No. 658), containing the text of the Price and Pay Code. These are examples of Statutory Instruments with wide and far-reaching effects, which may often need to be referred to in a law library.

Orders, regulations and rules are all contained in the Statutory Instruments series. The Donoughmore Report (Committee on Ministers' Powers, 1932) (Cmd. 4060), tried to distinguish between these terms, not very successfully. The difference between regulations and orders thus remains rather vague, but on the other hand the term 'Rules' has been restricted to those instruments appertaining to procedural matters, as for instance, the *Rules of the Supreme Court* or the *County Court Rules*.

An Order in Council is the highest form of subordinate legislation, and is made at a meeting of the Privy Council presided over by the Queen. Orders in Council are normally used for the matters remaining within the royal prerogative, such as the constitutions of dependent territories. They are usually printed in the annual volumes of the *Statutory Instruments*, although they are not numbered in the *Statutory Instruments* series. Occasionally, there are lapses. Thus, the *Territorial*

Waters Order in Council 1964 was printed in full in the *London Gazette*, but was not reprinted in the *Statutory Instruments* series until the final volume of 1965, because it was not brought to the editor's attention till then. Hence, it is necessary to subscribe to the *London Gazette* as well as to the *Statutory Instruments* series to be absolutely certain that you have complete coverage of all this type of material.

One or two more mundane regulations, also, have from time to time missed inclusion in the *Statutory Instruments* series or its predecessor the *Statutory Rules and Orders* series, whether through accident or design. Two noteworthy absentees, which are both still in force, are the Electricity Supply Regulations 1937 and the Children Act (Appeal Tribunal) Rules 1949. Fortunately, both are referred to in the series *Halsbury's Statutory Instruments* (described on page 123), and both may be obtained from HMSO.

Publication of Statutory Instruments

Like the statutes, the Statutory Instruments are first of all published individually in loose-paper copies by HMSO, and then in annual volumes. These now appear in three parts a year (bound as six volumes) and exclude only those instruments which are of a purely local character and those which have already been revoked by the end of the same year. The annual volumes were arranged by subject up to the end of 1960, but since then the instruments contained in them have been arranged chronologically in their order of registration, so enabling the volumes to be published more promptly. Each part contains a list of instruments published in that part, a table showing modifications to legislation, and an index. The final part for the year also contains a fuller table of modifications and index, a numerical list for the whole year, and also a classified list of local instruments with reference particulars.

The official edition of the Statutory Instruments

A collected official edition exists of *The Statutory Rules & Orders and Statutory Instruments revised to December 31, 1948.* The arrangement within the volumes is by subject, while the index volume contains a numerical table in chronological order. A new collected edition is needed very badly, since, not only have many rules and orders or instruments contained in the 1948 edition already been revoked or amended, but also many of the annual volumes published since 1948 are now out of print. It is unlikely, however, that any new edition will be provided, at least before the completion of the more pressing project of *Statutes in force.*

Halsbury's Statutory Instruments

Fortunately, there also exists a privately issued series of Statutory Instruments, namely, *Halsbury's Statutory Instruments* published by Butterworths. The volumes in this series are constantly being replaced by up-to-date re-issues, and in addition there is the loose-leaf service volume, which contains the latest material. The series is arranged by subject, so that all the references to all the Statutory Instruments on a given subject are set out in the form of a table at one point, usually at the beginning of the section dealing with that subject. Unfortunately, many of the instruments are only printed in Halsbury in an abbreviated form, so that it can in no sense be regarded as a full substitute for the official series. It is, however, a useful adjunct to it, since you can use it to look up the outline of a particular instrument quickly under its subject, obtain the correct citation, and then refer with the aid of this to the fuller version in the official volume. One other point to remember when using *Halsbury's Statutory Instruments* – always look in the service volume as well as in the subject volume, in order to take in the latest developments.

Other sources

Other sources of Statutory Instruments on the subjects covered include the various loose-leaf encyclopedias, which will be described more fully in Chapter 5. For instance, in a search for the latest *Motor Vehicle (Construction and Use) Regulations*, it might be quicker to look them up in the loose-leaf *Encyclopedia of road traffic law and practice* rather than in the official *Statutory Instruments* series, because there the possible field of search is so much narrower. The same will apply to any of the other subjects covered by this series.

Citation of Statutory Instruments

Citation of Statutory Instruments is regulated by section 2 of the Statutory Instruments Act 1946, and is very much simpler than that of statutes. They are referred to either by title, or by year and running number. Thus, the *Motor Vehicles (Variation of Speed Limit) Regulations 1973* are referred to by that title, and can be cited as S.I. 1973 No. 747. As shown in Fig. 6, this citation is always indicated prominently at the head of the front cover of the Statutory Instrument concerned.

There is also a secondary series number used in the headings of Statutory Instruments of certain restricted classes. These classes include commencement orders (indicated with a 'C'), instruments relating to fees or procedure in courts in England and Wales (indicated with an 'L'), instruments which apply to Scotland only (indicated with an 'S'), and instruments which apply to Northern Ireland only (indicated with 'N.I.'). Thus, the *County Court (Amendment) Rules 1973* have the heading '1973 No. 345 (L.6)', indicating that they were the sixth instrument relating to fees or procedure to be issued during the year. These series numbers are of interest, but are not of great practical importance – it is the main part of the citation that matters. Similarly, departmental reference marks printed on the bottom right hand corners of some instruments may be ignored by librarians outside those departments.

The date when a Statutory Instrument comes into force is always indicated prominently at the beginning (see Fig. 6), and at its close there is always an explanatory note indicating its general purport. It only remains to add that there have been a number of complaints in the legal press in recent years about the dilatory publishing of Statutory Instruments (for instance, *New Law Journal*, vol. 120, 1970, p. 1053), and this – where it exists – has added to the difficulties experienced by law librarians.

Indexes and tables of Statutory Instruments

As with statutes, so with Statutory Instruments, HMSO has published a number of reference indexes and tables in order to help their users.

The *Index to Government Orders in force* is published every two years, and is for Statutory Instruments the equivalent to the

---

STATUTORY INSTRUMENTS

1973 No. 747

ROAD TRAFFIC
The Motor Vehicles (Variation of Speed Limits) Regulations 1973

Made - - - -	*28th March* 1973
Laid before Parliament	*29th March* 1973
Coming into Operation	*1st May* 1973

The Secretary of State for the Environment, in exercise of powers conferred by section 78(2) of the Road Traffic Regulation Act 1967(a), and now vested in him (b), and of all other enabling powers, and after consultation with representative organisations in accordance with section 107(2) of that Act, hereby makes the following Regulations:—

1.—(1) These Regulations may be cited as the Motor Vehicles (Variation of Speed Limits) Regulations 1973 and shall come into operation on the fifteenth day following the day they are approved by Parliament.

(2) In these Regulations "the Act" means the Road Traffic Regulation Act 1967.

(3) The Interpretation Act 1889(c) shall apply for the interpretation of these Regulations as it applies for the interpretation of an Act of Parliament, and as if for the purposes of section 38 of that Act these Regulations were an Act of Parliament and the Regulations revoked by Regulation 3 of these Regulations were an Act of Parliament thereby repealed.

2. The provisions of Schedule 5 to the Act (which specifies the limits of speed for vehicles of certain classes) shall be varied in the manner set out in the Schedule to these Regulations and shall have effect as so varied.

3. The Motor Vehicles (Variation of Speed Limits) Regulations 1971(d) are hereby revoked.

Signed by authority of the Secretary of State.

28th March 1973.

John Peyton,
Minister for Transport Industries,
Department of the Environment.

(a) 1967 c. 76.
(c) 1889 c. 63.

(b) S.I. 1970/1681 (1970 III, p. 5551).
(d) 1971/602 (1971 I, p. 1594).

[D.O.E. 11480]

Figure 6

Index to the Statutes in force. The main sequence gives under subject headings particulars of the statutory powers under which all instruments are made and lists of the instruments made in exercise of those powers, thus in effect acting as an alphabetical subject index to the series. A subsidiary sequence gives a chronological table of statutes with references to subject headings in the main sequence, thus enabling one to trace instruments made under a particular section of a particular Act.

The *Table of Government orders* is the equivalent to the *Chronological Table of the Statutes.* This appears annually, and lists all the general Statutory Rules and Orders and Statutory Instruments in chronological and numerical order from 1671 to date, showing which of them have been revoked or amended, and by what. Where an instrument has been amended, particulars are given of the affected article or section.

HMSO also publishes separate monthly and annual *Lists of Statutory Instruments,* giving under subject headings the names and numbers of the latest instruments.

By-laws

It is convenient here to add a mention of local authority by-laws. These, too, are subordinate legislation of a kind, although they are not often thought of as such. By-laws generally comprehend such matters as good behaviour in public places and good rule and governance, and are made by the local council and confirmed by the Minister responsible at the time for local government (at present, the Department of the Environment in England or the Welsh Office in Wales, formerly the Ministry of Local Government and Planning). Under section 236(8) of the Local Government Act 1972, by-laws normally have to be printed and supplied on request to enquirers for a small fee. The best source, from which to enquire about the by-laws of a particular area, is naturally the local authority concerned, either through its administrative offices, or through its public library service.

SCOTLAND

Statutes

As mentioned above, in the section on 'Geographical extent of statutes' (see page 111), Acts referring specifically to Scotland have been included in the United Kingdom series for each regnal year since the Act of Union in 1707. In addition, several collections have been compiled during this period of Scottish Acts only.

In 1848, the Edinburgh publishing firm of William Blackwood and Sons commenced annual publication of *The public general statutes affecting Scotland*. The need for a comprehensive set of Scottish statutes from 1707 to 1847 was met by the same firm in 1876, when three volumes covering that period were issued. The annual volumes, known as *Blackwood's Acts*, continued for a century, save one year, terminating in 1947 with the Acts for 1946.

At the end of the nineteenth century another Edinburgh publishing firm, William Green, which specialized in law, commenced publication of *The Scots Statutes Revised*. This set contained all the Acts applicable to Scotland still in force in 1900. From 1901, Green also brought out an annual volume of statutes pertaining to Scotland, parallel to the Blackwood series. These continued until 1948, when they were replaced by *Scottish current law statutes*, which have since been issued annually. The difference between the two sets published by Green is accounted for by the inclusion of all United Kingdom statutes in the later set, as distinct from those affecting Scotland only. The *Scottish current law statutes* are essentially similar to *Current law statutes*, except that they also contain the Acts of Sederunt and Adjournal (see below).

A very useful practical tool for solicitors and law librarians which largely comprises statutes is the *Parliament House Book* published annually by Green since 1824. This covers most questions of law likely to arise from day to day and has the double advantage of assembling Acts, Statutory Instruments and other relevant material on one topic together, while it is always up to date. Four of the sections, including mercantile law, conveyancing, and what may be broadly termed family law, are issued separately for the convenience of those specializing in these subjects.

There are a few other types of legislation peculiar to Scotland which require to be mentioned. Local and personal bills may be introduced under the Private Legislation Procedure

(Scotland) Act 1936; under this, any private individual or local authority desirous of obtaining an Act applies to the Secretary of State for Scotland for a provisional order. Subject to the need for a local enquiry to meet objections, if any, the order is issued and a Confirmation Bill is introduced into Parliament, which upon passing is placed on the Statute Book.

Subordinate legislation

Acts of Sederunt are rules passed by the Court of Session, in modern times relating exclusively to procedure in that court and the Sheriff Courts. Various codifying Acts of Sederunt have been issued, the latest in 1965 known officially as *Rules of the Court of Session*, or more familiarly as *Rules of Court*. An Act of Adjournal is one passed by the High Court of Justiciary for regulating procedure in that court and in the inferior criminal courts. It should be noted that the *Rules of Court* appear in the *Parliament House Book* each year, brought up to date, and that this section is now issued separately. Other subordinate legislation in Scotland takes the same form as elsewhere in Britain, *ie*, through Statutory Instruments. Orders of a local nature are not printed by HMSO, and to check these it is necessary to consult *The Edinburgh Gazette*, issued twice weekly.

IRELAND

At the beginning of the period covered by this chapter, the separate Parliaments of Ireland and of Great Britain were merged as the Parliament of the United Kingdom, which came into existence on the first day of 1801. This legislated for the whole of Ireland, as for Great Britain also, up to 1921, when the Government of Ireland Act 1920 came into effect. Thereafter the ways of North and South in Ireland diverged, and must be dealt with separately.

Northern Ireland

Statutes

From 1921 to 1972, the Parliament of Northern Ireland (often known colloquially as 'Stormont') legislated on matters within its competence as laid down in the Government of Ireland Act 1920. Its Bills and Acts were issued on the Westminster pattern by HMSO Belfast. In 1956, a collected edition was published with the title *The Statutes Revised, Northern Ireland*; this included all legislation passed up to the close of 1950 and still in force in Northern Ireland at the close of 1954. Annual volumes of Northern Ireland statutes have been issued since 1921, and there are also a *Chronological Table* and an *Index to the Statutes in force*. Tables in the annual volumes may be used for years not yet covered by these last two works.

When the Parliament of Northern Ireland was dissolved in March 1972, the province passed under direct rule from Westminster. Legislation applying to Northern Ireland only was then passed by Orders in Council, issued as a sub-series of the United Kingdom *Statutory Instruments* series. Thus, as well as having its S.I. number, each order has an additional number relating to Northern Ireland only. These orders are included in the annual volume of the Northern Ireland statutes for 1972, and are not published in the annual volumes of United Kingdom Statutory Instruments.

During direct rule, Bills were replaced by Draft Orders in Council, the first stage of which was a Proposal for a Draft. The Proposals were issued by HMSO Belfast, while the Drafts were published by HMSO London. The Drafts and the Orders in Council were all recorded in the British *Daily Lists* of government publications and also in the Northern Ireland monthly and annual lists.

The new Northern Ireland Assembly came into being in July 1973 and until its prorogation in May 1974 had passed four 'measures'. These were published singly by HMSO Belfast. At the time of writing, government is again by direct rule from Westminster and legislation has reverted to the pattern described above.

Further information as to the constitutional situation in Northern Ireland may be obtained from the various papers, which have been issued from time to time by the Northern Ireland Office. The Northern Ireland section of *Current Law* contains the most rapidly published information after the primary sources and is a useful starting point for references. A clear exposition of new development is also given under the

5

heading 'Northern Ireland' in the *Current Survey* section of the quarterly journal *Public Law*. The title 'Constitutional Law' in volume 8 of the 4th edition of *Halsbury's Laws of England* contains a summary of the situation in Northern Ireland as at 15 May 1974, that is, just before the prorogation of the Northern Ireland Assembly.

Subordinate legislation

Statutory Rules and Orders have been published singly, and subsequently in annual volumes, by HMSO Belfast since 1922. They first appear in the *Belfast Gazette*. This procedure was not altered by direct rule. Rules and orders are noted in *Current Law* under 'Northern Ireland', and they have a periodic *Index to the Statutory Rules and Orders of Northern Ireland*, published every three years.

Citation

Generally speaking, citation is similar to that in England, sometimes with an indication of origin in the form (N.I.) or (Northern Ireland). The position of the words 'Northern Ireland' in the title enables one to distinguish between a Westminster Statute applying to Northern Ireland, *eg*, the Criminal Appeal (Northern Ireland) Act 1968, and a Northern Ireland Statute, *eg*, the Criminal Procedure Act (Northern Ireland) 1951. Since 1943, earlier than at Westminster, Northern Ireland statutes have been cited by calendar year and chapter number.

A full citation of a Statutory Rule and Order would be, for example, The Children (Performances) Regulations (Northern Ireland), 1971 (S.R. & O. (N.I.) 1971 No. 25, p. 146). They can be cited briefly by number and calendar year.

For full details regarding citation, one should refer to the *Manual of legal citations, Part 1, The British Isles* (1959), at pp. 32–5 under 'Ireland'.

Republic of Ireland

Statutes

The present legislative body (since 1922) is the Oireachtas, or parliament, which consists of the Dáil (lower house) and the Senate. Bills and Acts are published in a pattern not unlike Westminster's, statutes appearing singly and in annual volumes. There have been various consolidated indexes, the current one published in 1970 covering the period 1922–68. Annual volumes contain tables of the effect of legislation, and tables of latest collective citations.

Subordinate legislation

Orders were published as *Statutory Rules and Orders* until 1947, and annual volumes had running numbers. (Sets of collected orders appeared as follows: volumes 1–23, 1922–38, index volume 24; volumes 25–34, 1939–45, index volume 35; volumes 36–9, 1946–7, index volume 40.) From 1948, they have been called *Statutory Instruments*. Annual bound volumes are published about eight years after the printing of the individual instruments. Index volumes, non-cumulative, were published in 1962, 1965 and 1973, covering the periods 1948–1960, 1961–3 and 1964–70 respectively.

Citation

All Acts are published in Irish and English, and to distinguish the English form of Acts of the Oireachtas from Westminster Acts, the abbreviation (R.I.) may be used after the short title and date. Acts are cited by serial numbers instead of chapter numbers, for instance, the Higher Education Authority Act 1971, which is cited as No. 22 of 1971 or 22/1971. For full details, including the citation of Acts of the Irish Parliament before 1801, reference may be made to Part I of the *Manual of Legal Citations* already mentioned.

Statutory Instruments may be cited by the abbreviation S.I. and a number, and also by the short title, for instance, the Restriction of Imports (Fertilisers from East Germany) Order 1967 (S.I. (R.I.) No. 254 of 1967) or (S.I. (R.I.) 1967 No. 254). Since 1958, pagination is not continuous, so that there can be no full reference to volume and page numbers as previously.

Constitution

The Republic has a written constitution, enacted in 1937 by

plebiscite, to replace the original one of 1922. Amendments to the constitution require a referendum, for example that on entry to the European Communities which was held in 1972.

The most accessible account of the legal bibliography of the Channel Islands and the Isle of Man is contained in *A Bibliographical Guide to the Law of the United Kingdom, the Channel Islands and the Isle of Man*, 2nd edition, Institute of Advanced Legal Studies, 1973, edited by A. G. Chloros, from which are taken the extracts cited below. The statutory materials of the three main islands can best be considered separately.

Jersey

'Legislation is normally effected at the present time by the States, but an Act passed by the States requires confirmation by the Sovereign in Council before it can acquire the force of law. Such legislation is published in a series of "Recueils des Lois" commencing in 1771.' (Chloros, p. 232.) The series of *Recueils des lois* from 1771 to 1936 were republished in seven volumes in 1957–69. Since then, the series has been continued in annual volumes published by the States' Greffe, described as *Orders in Council, laws, etc.* on the title page and as *Recueil des lois* on the spine. Since 1968, apart from the spine title, they have been wholly in English.

There is also a separate series of *Regulations and orders*, commencing in 1939 and appearing annually. These correspond to the *Statutory Instruments* series on the mainland.

Guernsey

The principal legislative series in Guernsey is the *Ordinances of the States*, Volume 1 to date, 1533/1800 to date, printed by the *Guernsey Herald*. The spine title is *Recueil d'ordonnances*. These are usually published triennially.

The subsidiary legislative series for Guernsey has the title *Orders in Council, and other matters of general interest registered on the records of the Island of Guernsey*, and commences with Volume 1,

1803–   . The spine title is *Ordres en Conseil.* It is usually
biennial or triennial.
Both these Guernsey series appear wholly in English.

THE ISLE OF MAN

'The Isle of Man is governed by an ancient legislature known as
Tynwald ... The Manx legislature is empowered to enact
statutes concerning matters not transcending the frontiers of the
Island. Legislation in relation to certain matters falling outside
this category is normally enacted by the Parliament at Westminster and extended to the Isle of Man.' (Chloros, p. 237.)
    The revised edition of *Statutes of the Isle of Man,* commencing
from the year 1417, was published at Douglas in 1883, and 'is
supplemented by annual volumes entitled *Acts of Tynwald.*
Periodically these annual volumes are revised and incorporated
in the series of Statutes'. (Chloros, p. 242.) There is also an
Index to Statutes of the Isle of Man, in operation on the 6th July 1957,
published at Douglas in 1959.

FURTHER READING

GENERAL

There are two recent guides to government publications as a whole
written for librarians:

Ollé, J. G. H. *An Introduction to British Government Publications.* 2nd edi-
    tion. Association of Assistant Librarians, 1973 (ISBN 0 900092 20 3).
Pemberton, J. E. *British Official Publications.* 2nd edition. Oxford,
    Pergamon Press, 1974 (ISBN 0 08 017797 2).

Mr Pemberton has also published a useful series of articles in *Library
World,* two of which deal with legislation:

Loose-leaf statutes. *Library World,* vol. 71, 1969–70, pp. 72–4.
Delegated legislation. *Library World,* vol. 72, 1970–71, pp. 158–60.

Parliamentary procedure

Two standard books on constitutional law give an outline of
parliamentary procedure:

Phillips, O. H. *Constitutional and Administrative Law.* 5th edition.
    Sweet and Maxwell, 1973 (ISBN 0 421 15470 5).

Wade, E. C. S. and Phillips, G. C. *Constitutional Law.* 8th edition. Longmans, 1970 (ISBN 0 582 48823 0).

Other scholarly books cover the same ground at a more popular level:

Hanson, A. H. and Crick, B. *The Commons in Transition.* Collins, 1970 (ISBN 0 00 632373 1).

Hanson, A. H. and Walles, M. *Governing Britain.* Collins, 1970 (ISBN 0 00 632374 x).

Walkland, S. A. *The Legislative Process in Great Britain.* Allen and Unwin, 1968 (ISBN 0 04 320060 5).

Primary legislation

The ramifications of statute law are dealt with in detail in:

Craies, W. F. *Craies on Statute Law.* 7th edition. Sweet and Maxwell, 1971 (ISBN 0 421 14510 2). See especially Chapter 4: Classification of statutes.

Great Britain. Parliament. House of Commons. Library. *Acts of Parliament: some distinctions in their nature and numbering.* HMSO, 1955 (*Document* no. 1).

Halsbury's Laws of England. 3rd edition. Vol. 36. Butterworth, 1961. See especially 'Statutes', starting at p. 361, and 'Subordinate legislation', starting at p. 476.

Walker, R. J. and Walker, M. G. *The English Legal System.* 3rd edition. Butterworth, 1972 (ISBN 0 406 67752 2). See especially 'The legal and literary sources of English law', pp. 93–120.

A useful list of editions of the statutes is in:

Guide to Law Reports and statutes. 4th edition. Sweet and Maxwell, 1962 (ISBN 0 421 03090 0).

Discussion about statute law reform has been extensive in the last few years, and many articles on the subject have appeared in legal periodicals. These can be located via the periodical indexes. Some books and pamphlets on the subject are:

Great Britain. Law Commission for England and Wales *and* Great Britain. Scottish law commission. *The Interpretation of Statutes.* HMSO, 1969 (HC 256, 1968–9) (Law Com. no. 21) (Scot. Law Com. no. 11) (ISBN 0 10 225669 1).

Great Britain. Law Commission for England and Wales. *Second Programme on Consolidation and Statute Law Revision.* HMSO, 1971 (HC 338, 1970–1) (Law Com. no. 44) (ISBN 0 10 233871 x).

Scarman, Sir L. *Law Reform: the new pattern.* Routledge and Kegan Paul, 1968 (*Lindsay memorial lecture*) (ISBN 0 7100 6250 8).

Statute Law Society. *Statute Law Deficiencies.* Sweet and Maxwell, 1970 (ISBN 0 420 43290 6).
Statute Law Society. *Statute Law: the key to clarity.* Sweet and Maxwell, 1972 (ISBN 0 421 17580 x).

Subordinate legislation

Subordinate legislation is described in some of the general works already listed and in:

Great Britain. Committee on Ministers' Powers. *Report.* HMSO, 1932 (Cmd. 4060). Chairman: Lord Donoughmore.
Great Britain. Parliament. House of Commons. Library. *Access to Subordinate Legislation.* HMSO, 1963 (*Document* no. 5).
Great Britain. Parliament. Joint Committee on Delegated Legislation. *Report.* HMSO, 1972 (HL 184, 1971–2) (HC 475, 1971–2) (ISBN 0 10 247572 5).

The work of publishing the statutes and statutory instruments and preparing their indexes is described in:

Lyons, A. B. The Statutory Publications Office, past, present and future. *Law Librarian,* vol. 1, 1970, pp. 5–8, 20–1 and 27.

NORTHERN IRELAND

The standard work is:

Calvert, H. *Constitutional Law in Northern Ireland: a study in regional government.* Stevens, 1968 (ISBN 0 420 42230 7).

For a more recent assessment see:

Palley, C. *The Evolution, Disintegration and Possible Reconstruction of the Northern Ireland constitution.* Barry Rose, 1972 (ISBN 0 900500 55 7); also published in *Anglo-American Law Review,* vol. 1, 1972.

REPUBLIC OF IRELAND

A useful textbook, although now a little dated:

Kelly, J. M. *Fundamental Rights in the Irish Law and Constitution.* 2nd edition. Dublin, Figgis, 1967.

4. Primary Sources: Law Reports

W. W. S. BREEM
Librarian to the Honourable Society of the Inner Temple

The purpose of a modern law report has been defined as 'the production of an adequate record of a judicial decision upon a point of law in a case heard in open court, for subsequent citation as a precedent'. A law report then records only the issues and the facts considered necessary to the decision of the court. As of necessity there is a difference between the reporting of a case heard in a lower court as against one heard on appeal. In the lower court it is the duty of the judge to ascertain the facts if these are in dispute; and it is the reporter's obligation to provide a concisely edited transcript of only a part of the hearing. All irrelevancies, all repetitious matter is excised. In cases on appeal there is as a rule no dispute over the facts; the dispute concerns the effect of the law as applied to that particular situation. Then, it is the reporter's obligation to provide a transcript which is a contracted representation of the court's proceedings.

The report becomes a legal instrument of great precision. It records the decision of the court from which principles may be inferred, and from the mass of collective and related decisions emerges the corpus of judicial law known as case-law.

COMPOSITION OF A REPORT

A report is composed of a number of well-defined parts as follows:

1. The title. This is normally the surnames of the parties (see also page 157), together with the date of the hearing, the name of the court and the name or names of the judges presiding.

2. The catch words. These are placed below the title. The first is usually a legal term, such as 'Tort', but not always and it forms the index head to the head-note. It is also employed subsequently as the key word in the digest. It will be of wider meaning than the remaining catch words, since it is the practice of a reporter to go from the general to the particular.

3. The head-note. This is not a précis of the report but a digest of the law contained in it. Head-notes are either factual or propositional, the former being more common than the latter. Brevity is the hall mark of a good head-note. The best contain the material facts, the conclusion, and the proposition to be drawn from them.

4. The list of cases referred to in the judgment and cited in argument.

5. Arguments of counsel. These may or may not be quoted; seldom in cases reported in the lower courts, occasionally in cases reported on appeal.

6. The judgment. In reports of cases on appeal more than one judgment may be recorded, but the reporter will take care to ensure that those parts of the second or other judgments which merely cover the same ground are excised.

Other information included will be the names of counsel and solicitors concerned and, as required the *holding*, the points of law which are held, and the *per curiam*, a statement of law not considered essential, a list of cases referred to in the judgment and cited in argument and, lastly, the name of the reporter who has reported the case.

Citation in court

The authority which renders a report citable in court is the signature of the reporter, who alone must accept responsibility for its accuracy. This authority, long accepted, found formal recognition in 1889 when Lord Esher, delivering judgment, said, 'We will accept *The Times Law Reports* because they are reports by barristers who put their names to their reports.' A barrister, however, may not vouch a report solely on the basis of having read a transcript of the judgment and if he does so he abuses the privilege accorded him as a law reporter.

Reports from the superior courts of Ireland, the Commonwealth and the United States of America may be cited and, though not binding, are entitled to the utmost respect.

The superior courts in England are obliged to follow a unanimous decision of the Court of Session of Scotland on a statute equally applicable to England and Scotland.

When multiple reporting of a case occurs there is a recognized though largely unwritten order of precedence which governs the choice of series to be selected for citation purposes. The pre-eminence of *The Law Reports* was reinforced by the Law Reporting Committee who in 1940 recommended that 'the general rule of exclusive citation of a Report in the "Law Reports" should be enforced'. *The All England Law Reports* follow in order of selection. Other series fall naturally into order, much depending upon the case and the court in which it will be heard. If a suitable case cannot be found in any series it may be necessary to turn elsewhere:

1. to *The Times* newspaper reports. It should be noticed that these are of necessity résumés compiled at speed and should never be regarded as an adequate substitute for a proper law report. Although not appearing above the printed signature or initials of their authors, they are generally understood to be compiled by barristers-at-law and are acceptable to the superior courts.

2. to legal journals. These may contain the only reports on points of practice and are acceptable to the superior courts as well as the Court of Appeal.

3. to quasi-legal journals of repute, such as *The Estates Gazette*. Cases reported therein have been cited in the High Court since the 1940s, usually with approval and on occasion in the Court of Appeal.

4. to other legal publications. Notes of cases in *Current Law* have from time to time been cited in the Court of Appeal.

Cases are occasionally reported long after being decided, usually those heard before the House of Lords, or as a result of a brief note made *ex. rel.* a member of the Bar and printed in a journal, subsequently cited, thus requiring insertion in an official series of reports. Such belated reports are normally full reports.

MODERN REPORTS: 1865 TO DATE

Official

The Law Reports of the Incorporated Council of Law Reporting for England and Wales date from 1865 and are issued in monthly parts which usually obtain publication eight to ten weeks after the conclusion of the period covered. Though a bound-volume service is not available, the Council will handle the binding of subscribers' copies. Additionally, uncut copies are available for those subscribers who prefer to bind their own. The service also includes the issue of a weekly series as well as annual indexes, a table of cases judicially noticed, and digests to the main series. For details of the statutes series issued by the Council see page 108.

Originally *The Law Reports* were divided into eleven sets covering all the superior courts of the day. Changes in the number of sets issued took place thereafter, corresponding with the changes in the organization of the courts. The first series of eleven sets runs from 1865 to 1875, the second series of six sets runs from 1876 to 1890, and the third series from 1891 to date, containing four sets: the Appeal Cases (of the House of Lords and of the Privy Council), Queen's and King's Bench Division, Chancery Division and Probate Division (reconstituted as the Family Division from 1972). Subsequently the restrictive practices cases were issued as an additional set, but closed after seven volumes. Thereafter cases will be found in the *Industrial Court Reports* now *Industrial Cases Reports*, 1975– , a new series issued by the Council, but not as a part of their main series.

The recorded decision includes the arguments of counsel. The Queen's Bench Division reports now include admiralty, commercial, Court of Appeal criminal division, Court of Appeal civil division and divisional court cases.

The unique authority of the series lies in the fact that the reported decisions are read by the judiciary prior to publication; a privilege shared only, and then not consistently, by two other series, the *Law Journal Reports* (now defunct) and *The Reports of Patent, Design and Trade Mark Cases*.

The weekly series, known as *The Weekly Notes*, was designed as a holding series to provide for full publication with the least possible delay. To achieve this the arguments of counsel were not included. This series contained many reports of temporary concern, not subsequently printed in the main series. *The Weekly Notes* in eighty-seven volumes ran from 1866 to 1952, when it was curtailed, to be continued by *The Weekly Law Reports* which, while serving the same function, offers a superior service. The weekly issue consists of two parts. Part one contains decisions of points of minor or transitory interest which do not merit reprinting in the main series; part two contains reports of major concern worth reprinting, after revision, with the addition of counsels' arguments. Each issue contains a cumulative table of cases and an index of the subject matter. Annual cumulative indexes are also issued.

Commercial

The commercial publishing of law reports did not effectively commence until the nineteenth century, when legal journalism began to proliferate.

Some series commenced their existence independently of the journal with which they were associated and maintained their independence until they ceased publication; others began their existence as an integral part of the journal in which they were published, only to obtain independent publication at a subsequent date. Others again were independent one moment and merged the next. It was common practice to issue reports as a section at the back of a journal, but with a separate title page, and sometimes, though not always, a separate pagination. In some instances, through the need to keep the bound volume of the journal to a manageable size, the reports, if there were sufficient, might be pulled out by the subscriber to form physically a separate and apparently independent series, yet with others this justification has never arisen. Bibliographically speaking therefore, the history and status of commercial reports is confusing in the extreme, a subject for continuous debate between cataloguers, reflecting not only the varied policy decisions and commercial fortune of publishers, but also the fortuitous actions of librarians when faced with arbitrary changes in policy, size of format and physical bulk.

Only the more important series of general reports require notice below.

The Law Journal newspaper commenced existence as a monthly and issued reports of cases in the King's Bench and Chancery, 1803–6. In 1806 it ceased publication, but the reports were re-issued in three volumes under the name of the editor, J. P. Smith. *The Law Journal Reports* were recommenced independently in 1822 and the first series lasted till 1831; the new series followed in 1832, ran to 118 volumes and was discontinued in 1949, when it was technically incorporated with *The All England Law Reports* (All ER) which had commenced thirteen years previously.

The Jurist, a weekly periodical containing reports in all the courts commenced publication in 1837 and continued till 1866, when it became defunct partially as the result of the publication of *The Law Reports*.

The Law Times, a weekly newspaper, commenced in 1843, including in its pages what is now known as the old series of *The Law Times Reports*. The latter began an independent existence in 1859, ran to 177 volumes and ceased publication in 1947, when it was technically incorporated with All ER. Volumes 1 to 11 of the new series had a second title page on which they were termed 'The Law Reporter', while volumes 12 to 23 (issued monthly) had altered titles and were headlined as 'Bar Reports, vols. 1–12'. Volume two ends with page 320, contains a title page and table of cases, but lacks an index. General indexes were issued in twelve volumes, covering volumes 1 to 120 only.

The Weekly Reporter was established in 1852 as a journal containing reports. It effectively ceased any independent existence when in 1906 the reports were incorporated within *The Solicitors' Journal and Reporter*, lasting thus until 1927.

The New Reports, a weekly, established in November 1862, became a casualty as a result of the emergence of *The Law Reports* and ceased publication in 1865, six volumes only being issued.

The Times newspaper had published reports in their daily issues prior to 1885, when publication of *The Times Law Reports* commenced. These were issued weekly and at first merely reprinted condensed reports which had appeared in the newspaper. Subsequently, verbatim transcripts of the judgments were recorded. By the end of 1952 sixty-eight volumes had been published. The series ceased in 1953 by arrangement with the Incorporated Council of Law Reporting, upon the commencement of *The Weekly Law Reports*. Three digests were issued, covering the years 1884–95, 1895–1900 and 1900–5.

670   All England Law Reports   [1973] 1 All ER

Fakes v Taylor Woodrow Construction Ltd   *a*

COURT OF APPEAL, CIVIL DIVISION
LORD DENNING MR, MEGAW LJ AND SIR GORDON WILLMER
2nd, 3rd NOVEMBER 1972

Arbitration – Stay of court proceedings – Refusal of stay – Grounds for refusal – Insolvency of plaintiff – Availability of legal aid in court proceedings – Insolvency alleged to have been caused by defendant's breach of contract – Plaintiff unable to afford arbitration proceedings by reason of insolvency – Reasonable grounds for believing that insolvency caused by defendant's breach – Effect of granting stay a denial of justice to plaintiff.   *b*

Arbitration – Stay of court proceedings – Legal aid – Relevance – Legal aid not available in arbitration proceedings – Rights of person receiving legal aid not to affect rights or liabilities of other parties or principles on which court's discretion normally exercised – Plaintiff insolvent – Plaintiff granted legal aid for court proceedings – Application by defendant for stay – Defendant having no right to stay – No principles on which court's discretion exercised – Court not precluded from refusing stay on ground plaintiff having legal aid for court proceedings but unable to afford arbitration proceedings – Legal Aid and Advice Act 1949, s 1 (7) (b).   *c*   *d*

The plaintiff carried on business as a plumbing contractor. He was engaged by the defendants under sub-contracts made in 1967 and 1969 to carry out plumbing work on building sites where the defendants were the main contractors. The sub-contracts contained an arbitration clause which provided that any dispute, question or difference arising between the contractor and the sub-contractor in connection with the sub-contract 'shall be referred to arbitration'. The plaintiff carried out a great deal of work under the sub-contracts. He alleged, however, that because of breaches of contract by the defendants in delaying his work and in failing to pay him sums due at the times when payment should have been made, he was made insolvent and his business was ruined. It appeared that in 1970 the plaintiff was sued to judgment by various creditors and that he was in consequence without means. In May 1971 the plaintiff obtained a full certificate for legal aid to bring an action against the defendants. A writ was issued in February 1972 and a statement of claim was delivered in March 1972 alleging breaches of contract and claiming over £80,000 from the defendants for moneys due under the sub-contracts and as damages for the delay in paying the sums due. The defendants denied breach of contract. They took out a summons to stay the action on the ground of the arbitration clause in the sub-contracts; they wished to take the dispute to arbitration. The plaintiff resisted the summons on the ground that legal aid was not available for an arbitration and because of his insolvency he had not got the means to go to arbitration; he alleged that if he was forced to go to arbitration it was tantamount to losing the claim. The judge in chambers ordered the action to be stayed. The plaintiff appealed against the stay. There was before the court an affidavit sworn by the defendants and an affidavit in reply sworn by the plaintiff. The defendants admitted they had sought a stay because, believing the claim to be ill-founded and that the plaintiff could not afford to take the case to arbitration, it was the quickest way to stop the claim.   *e*   *f*   *g*   *h*

Held (Megaw LJ dissenting) – The appeal would be allowed for the following reasons—
   (i) although in general the poverty or insolvency of a plaintiff would not *per se* justify the court in refusing a stay, that rule was not applicable in circumstances where the plaintiff showed that there were grounds sufficient to raise a triable issue that his insolvency had been caused by the defendant's breach of contract; the plaintiff was not required to establish a prima facie case that the insolvency had been caused by the   *j*

Figure 1

Delay in the issue of the monthly parts of *The Law Reports* and dissatisfaction with the service offered by *The Weekly Notes* were two of the reasons that lay behind the publication of what may with justice be termed the most popular and satisfactory series of general reports yet issued commercially.

The All England Law Reports commenced in 1936 and are

issued in weekly parts, the aim being to print cases as soon as possible after decision (see Fig. 1). The majority, still, are published within four weeks of judgment being given. The arguments of counsel are not usually reported and the judgments are not always quoted. The reports so printed include not only cases involving fresh principles of law but also those illustrating the application of established principles to modern circumstances. The House of Lords, the Court of Appeal, and all divisions of the High Court are fully covered, as well as Privy Council cases which are of wide interest or concern English law. Many cases are included that are not subsequently to be found elsewhere. A digest of cases reported in each part appears on the cover of the weekly issue. Formerly, a monthly table was issued which showed whether any section of Halsbury had been affected by a reported case since the last supplement issued. The head-notes are now followed by references to *Halsbury's Laws, The English and Empire Digest, Halsbury's Statutes,* and *Halsbury's Statutory Instruments.* Thus the background of relevant law may be traced. Each weekly issue contains a noter-up for details of which see page 169. A two-volume consolidated index for 1936–65 has been issued, replacing former consolidations. The first volume contains an alphabetical list of cases, a consolidated table of cases and enactments judicially considered, and an alphabetical list of words and phrases judicially considered. The second volume is the subject index. An annual supplementary cumulative index is also issued, containing an alphabetical list of cases reported from 1966, also a table of cases reported in the All ER and *The All England Law Reports Reprint,* for details of which see page 148. Tables of enactments and of words and phrases, both judicially considered, are also included.

Specialist series

Certain series deal solely with limited topics, or record cases heard before courts not normally covered by the series of general law reports noticed above.

Topics covered by series still in progress include admiralty and shipping (*Lloyd's Law Reports,* 1919–), banking (*Legal Decisions affecting Bankers,* 1879–), licensing (*Brewing Trade*

Review Licensing Law Reports, 1913–), patents (*Reports of Patent, Design and Trade Mark Cases*, 1884–), property (*Property and Compensation Reports*, 1949–), rating (*Rating and Valuation Reporter*, 1961–) and taxation (*The Annotated Tax Cases*, 1922–). Other series and reports now closed have dealt with such varied topics as bankruptcy, building, copyright, friendly societies, registration, weights and measures, and workmen's compensation.

Magistrates' courts are covered by the *Local Government Reports* (formerly *Knight's Local Government and Magisterial Cases*) 1903– , county courts were reported by the *Law Journal Newspaper County Court Reports* (formerly the *LJCC* Reporter) 1912–47, while the Court of Criminal Appeal was recorded by *Cox's Criminal Cases*, 1843–1948, and by *The Criminal Appeal Reports*, 1908 to date.

The reports of cases heard before certain special courts now defunct but of concern primarily to legal historians will generally be found in the publications of learned societies, either national or local. Such courts include forest courts, palatine courts, quarter sessions, seignorial courts (manor courts, courts baron and courts leet), the Star Chamber and coroners' courts.

Cases on special subjects will also be found in practitioners' treatises. These are usually compressed versions of cases reported elsewhere, but gathered together to illustrate the author's argument or theme. The second volume of Chitty's *Bills of Exchange*, 1834, is devoted to such cases; Elmes' *Ecclesiastical and Civil Dilapidations*, 1929, has an appendix of cases; Montagu's *Law of Set-Off*, 1828, also contains an appendix of cases. Contemporary treatises continue this practice.

THE NOMINATE REPORTS: 1571–1865

The long run of reports called 'nominate', but better known to practising lawyers as simply 'the old reports', has a publishing history that covers 328 years, during which time over 260 separate series, many running into numerous editions, were issued. For 248 of these years the reports were published as collections, the date of issue bearing little or no relationship to the period spanned by the cases gathered within a volume. The nominate reports extend from 1220 for a case in the exchequer to 1881 for a case dealing with canals.

Though the majority of the reports published between 1571–1704 were issued in French (later editions often having English translations) a number were in English, Hobart's of 1641 being the earliest. The last in French was by Lutwyche in 1704. Thereafter all were in English.

Of the many reports issued only four require notice here: three for their role in developing the potentialities of law reporting; the fourth for its unparalleled influence upon the course of English law.

Reporting proper commenced with *Les commentaires, ou les reports de dyuers cases* . . . by Edmund Plowden. First published in 1571, they cover cases heard 1550–71 in the courts of King's Bench, Common Pleas and Exchequer. This was Part one. Part two, covering cases heard 1571–80 was issued in 1579, according to the title page.

Plowden's reports, the first to be issued, remain a model of the art of reporting. They contain the arguments of counsel and the opinions of the judges. Plowden reported nothing at second hand, often submitted his drafts to the judiciary, and included in the final script only what was essential to his purpose. His reports ran into a number of editions and if his success encouraged others to try likewise, few cared to emulate the principles that led to it.

Sir Edward Coke's reports, often cited simply as 'The Reports', cover Queen's Bench cases, 1572–1616. Parts one to eleven were issued 1600–15, while the final two parts appeared posthumously, 1656–9. An English translation of the whole appeared in 1658, while numerous editions of the various parts followed, as well as abridgments and tables prepared by other writers.

Technically the reports are poorly structured. The first eleven parts contain approximately 500 cases, but it is often difficult to know precisely where fact ends and comment begins, for the work is as much a commentary upon the law as a series of reported cases. Coke's learning was prodigious, but is here ill-digested and ill-arranged. None of this matters. The author's reputation was such that his reports were cited more than any other series and acquired immense authority, for they stated the principles of the law and did much to shape the legal system of his time.

Burrow's reports of cases in the King's Bench cover the period 1756–72 and were issued in five volumes, 1776–80. There were four subsequent English editions, the last being in 1812.

Then as now it was customary for the judiciary to deliver oral opinions. Burrow did not write shorthand and his reports could not be based on official transcripts, these not then being taken. He was a careful note-taker, however, and any loss in accuracy was minimized, for he took pains to heed the sense rather than the words. His reports are lucid as to style and orderly in arrangement; the results of painstaking editing. He took care to ensure that each report was preceded by a statement of the case. This, being by the reporter, set out the facts and issues in a form that separated it from the opinion of the court, which then followed. Burrow would seem to have been among the first to realize the importance of clear divisions being required between the facts, the arguments of counsel, and the judgment of the court. And he invented the head-note.

As the volume of business before the courts increased, the need developed for the regular reporting of important judicial decisions which should be published without undue delay. This need was initially met by Durnford and East, whose *Term reports of cases in the King's Bench* span the years 1785–1800 and were first published as a set of eight volumes, 1787–1800; though original publication took the form of parts issued at the end of the legal term covered. Their example was to be followed by other reporters in other courts.

Dissatisfaction with the private reporting system was to develop however. The multiplicity of reports requiring purchase, their growing cost and increasing delays in publication – these were among the contributing factors that led to a demand for the Bar to set up its own reporting system. This it did in 1865, when the Council of Law Reporting in England and Wales was established. As a result, the private reporting system died, only to be replaced by the commercial publisher.

Collections

As a result of publishing practice, the great majority of reports printed prior to the middle of the eighteenth century were issued in quarto- or folio-size volumes. Those which did not merit numerous printings seldom or never obtained publication in octavo format. Complete collections of nominate reports in original editions lack uniformity of size, prove awkward of shelf arrangement and are costly of space. Their indexing is also often inadequate and the dates on title pages, showing coverage of the cases contained therein, are usually inaccurate.

Two major reprints exist:

The Revised Reports (1786–1866), edited by Sir Frederick Pollock, was issued in 152 volumes, 1891–1920. It is a selected republication only of those reports issued between 1785 and 1866 of the superior courts of common law and equity which were considered at the time of publication to be of value still to the profession. Also included are Irish reports held to be authoritative in the English courts and reports of the Admiralty Court and the Privy Council. In general, criminal cases are excluded. The editorial work is not inconsiderable: references have been added to later relevant decisions, the head-notes revised and obsolete matter omitted, whilst each volume's preface constitutes a guide to the leading cases contained therein. A table of cases in one volume and an index-digest in two volumes is also included. To facilitate use, the names of the relevant reporters are to be found on the spine of the appropriate volumes. The series contains two interesting curiosities. The data on the spine of volume 51 records the names of reporters whose cases will not be found within that volume, though this may be because the reporters in question are the authors of collateral reports, that is of cases which may be found elsewhere. This explanation cannot, however, explain the listing of Murphy and Hurlstone's reports of cases in the Exchequer, these not being collateral. Potton's index volume to the series indicates on the title page that it lists 'the cases retained and (from vol. 90 to vol. 149, *c.* 1851–66) those omitted from the Revised Reports'. Tables of cases omitted are rare in legal publishing.

The English Reports reprint, 1220–1865, was issued in 178 volumes, 1900–32 and is in general a straight reprint in which the original footnotes are given. Notes in square brackets have been inserted, as required, above the head-notes, giving references to Mews' *Digest of English Case Law,* while in some instances editorial notes in square brackets have been added. Where pages of the original have been omitted this is usually stated and editorial notes indicate those decisions affected by subsequent legislation. Volume 12 records that references to Mews will be given by titles and sub-titles and that notes will be recorded at the conclusion instead of the commencement of cases. The reprint contains over 100,000 cases, representative of 265 separate series of reports. The whole includes a two-volume index of cases, and citations are recorded as they appear in the original reports. A table was also printed listing the nominate reports included in the series, keying them to the volume(s) in which they are to be located. Collateral reports in Admiralty and Ecclesiastical courts, Common Pleas, Exchequer and King's Bench are excluded, together with those in bail and bankruptcy courts.

A photographic reprint of *The English Reports,* in 178 volumes, commenced in 1974 and is in progress.

The only revised collection of modern times is *The All England Law Reports Reprint.* This consists of thirty-six volumes containing selected cases from the period 1558–1935, chosen for their present-day value to the legal profession. Up-to-date head-notes and annotations are provided, references to *Halsbury's Laws of England* being given where necessary. The work contains approximately four to five thousand cases. The first eight volumes cover the nominate reports. The later volumes include material selected from *The Law Times Reports.* Publication commenced in 1957 and was concluded in 1968. Coupled with this are the *Extension Volumes,* issued 1968–71 and covering the period 1861–1935. This, a parallel series, consists of sixteen volumes and contains some 2,000 cases, many drawn from *The Law Reports* which have been relied upon extensively as important precedents, especially in the Australian courts.

OTHER REPORTS

Unpublished cases

Under this head are noticed four major collections, three of which consist of documents relating to cases, individually issued in the first instance for the sole benefit of the courts concerned, and subsequently made available only to selected libraries. Not all the cases concerned are necessarily to be found reported elsewhere, and in any event the material recorded provides a valuable supplement to the condensed reports of the law reports.

The proceedings in peerage cases, also known as peerage claims and heard before the House of Lords, consist of a series of separate prints, the earliest of which dates from the eighteenth century. Initially unbound, these are available as collections, in whole or in part, in a number of the older libraries, such as the Inns of Court, the British Library and other public libraries. The cases include the claimant's statement of proofs, and documentary evidence such as pedigrees, together with appendices containing miscellaneous evidential documents. The best collection is almost certainly that in the House of Lords Library, for details of which see Bond, M. F., *Guide to the Records of Parliament*, 1971, at p. 163.

The reporting of cases heard by the House of Lords was not permitted till *c.* 1812. As a result, the nominate reporters, whose earliest HL case is dated 1694, provide an inadequate coverage and there are reporting gaps between 1801–11 and 1822–6. As from 1865 cases appear regularly in *The Law Reports*. Printed texts of material relating to cases are available in a number of libraries as special collections, dating from the 1660s onwards. Today the papers for each individually printed case include the case(s) for the appellant(s) and for the respondent(s), an appendix containing a record of the previous proceedings and relevant documents, and the judgment.

The reporting of cases on appeal to the Privy Council effectively commenced when Acton's reports for 1809–11 were issued in 1811–12. The printing of earlier cases for the period 1243–1783 did not commence till 1834. As from 1865 cases appear regularly in *The Law Reports*. In 1833 the judicial committee of the Privy Council was re-organized and individually printed cases were made available to selected libraries as from the 1840s. The material contained within each individually printed case is similar to that contained in the Lords' appeals. At least twenty per cent of the cases in this collection have not been reported in any series of law reports published in the United Kingdom or the Commonwealth.

Up to 1950, decisions of the civil division of the Court of Appeal were not officially recorded. In April 1951, the Lord Chancellor directed that an official note of all judgments in the court should be made, a copy to be filed in the Inns of Court Bar Library in the Royal Courts of Justice (see also pages 152 and 160). The typed documents are approved by the judiciary prior to filing and are available to those concerned. These transcripts are the property of the Treasury and may not be photo-copied. Manual copying either in whole or in part is also not permitted.

Notes of cases

Summary reports and notes on cases may be located in many legal periodicals. Maxwell and Brown's *List of British and Colonial Law Reports and Legal Periodicals*, 1937, lists 168 such titles, of which forty contain reports of cases. This list is now known not to have been complete at the time of compilation. While a supplement to the work, issued in 1946, adds another twenty-one titles to the list, this only partially rectifies the many omissions. Though the majority of these have ceased publication, numerous new titles have appeared in the decades since 1937.

In the early nineteenth century the reporting of cases in periodicals was, in general, the work of barristers engaged on the staffs of the periodicals concerned, many of which sponsored their own separate series of reports. Today the tendency, amongst a number of leading periodicals anyway, is to report in note form, and with due acknowledgment, cases that have been reported elsewhere.

Tax case notes will be found in *Accountancy* and *The Certified Accountant*, as well as other taxation and accountancy periodicals. *The Chartered Auctioneer and Estate Agent*, *The Chartered Secretary*, the *Journal of the Institute of Bankers* and *Land and*

Property contain summary reports under the headings Tax case notes, Legal decisions, Legal notes, Legal notes for bankers and Law reports respectively.

The Criminal Law Review contains a case and comment section which includes abbreviated notes on cases heard before the Court of Appeal and, as from 1973, courts-martial cases which previously were seldom officially noticed in legal literature. *The Journal of Criminal Law* has in its time noted police court cases, quarter sessions and the Court of Criminal Appeal. More recently its range was widened to include assizes, the divisional court, the Privy Council and cases heard before Scots and Irish courts.

The Law Journal contained a weekly review of cases on appeal and in the High Court; continued as *The New Law Journal* in 1965–6, the section entitled The Practitioner contains a digest of reported cases. Reported cases will also be found in *Law Notes*, *The Law Society's Gazette* and *The Law Times*.

The Secretary contains legal notes on company winding-up, exchange control, income tax and allied matters.

For journals containing notes of tribunals' cases, see page 156.

Not all the notes of cases commented upon are signed nor do all acknowledge their source of origin.

Judgments and opinions

A number of the nominate reports confined their reporting to cases heard by a single judge, and other nominate reports are based on the notes of a particular judge. Alternatively, a judge's decisions may be collected and published in order to prove or consolidate his reputation. That they record cases of importance is supplementary to this purpose. Evans' *Decisions of Lord Mansfield*, 1803, and Birkenhead's *Judgments*, 1923, compiled by the author, are cases in point.

Counsel's opinions have also been published; the material usually being drawn from the notebooks and papers of deceased barristers. Burton's *Cases with opinions of eminent counsel*, 1719, and Chalmers' *Opinions of eminent lawyers*, 1814, being notable examples. Opinions, however, are not a part of any court proceedings and must not be so regarded.

Unreported cases

No statutory obligation exists as regards the reporting of cases heard before the law courts and none is published under government authority, excepting only the *Reports of Tax Cases* and *Reports of Patent, Design and Trade Mark Cases*, which are issued by the relevant government departments concerned and are official publications. It is axiomatic, therefore, that only cases of general legal interest are reported in any of the established series of law reports. Of concern will be such cases as those which extend the law, modify it or break new ground.

Cases otherwise unreported may on occasion be found in treatises, usually in a compressed form. The second volume of Hudson's *Building and engineering contracts*, 1914, contains a number. Some fifty-one unpublished cases will be found in Duke's *Law of charitable uses*, 1805, while Sugden's *Law of property*, 1849, contains over 600 cases heard in the House of Lords, 1814–48, a period not covered by any other reporter. Challis' *Real property*, 1911, Hudson's *Compensation*, 1905, and Jones and Proudfoot's *Notes on hire purchase law*, 1937, include such cases also. Others may be located in *Current Law*. These latter usually relate to negligence and damages and are of interest as a guide to the damages awarded by the courts. Additionally, in *Current Law* will be found summary notes of decisions of the Court of Appeal (civil division) which have not yet been reported elsewhere but whose transcripts are available in the Bar Library. The summary contains a brief outline of the facts, the date of judgment and the case name. A cumulative list of all cases on appeal whose transcripts have been so lodged appears in *Current Law* at the back of the monthly case citator.

Other cases possessing a transitory interest may be noted briefly in both legal and quasi-legal periodicals. Their location can be difficult, since they are not always recorded in the relevant annual indexes, while cumulative indexes are rarely issued, if at all.

National newspapers often report cases of 'national interest' as news items, not all of which necessarily justify the attention of the law reporter. These, whether civil or criminal, can usually be traced through the files of the appropriate newspaper. *The Times Index* may, for the purpose of locating a case about which imprecise information has been supplied, be of use as a general index to the major national newspapers. Of these it may be noticed that the news reports of proceedings in both *The Times* and the *Evening Standard* are usually the most comprehensive; and whilst the standard of reporting in both is usually held to be reliable, news reports' transcripts are never an adequate substitute for an official transcript. For cases of local interest only, reference should be made to the files of newspapers covering the area in which the case was heard, the incident took place, or the parties resided. Similarly, cases of no legal concern that yet may become *causes célèbres* may be subsequently published in book form, as noted on pages 185–6. See also page 150 for details of unpublished civil judgments of the Court of Appeal. Excepting the latter, it must be emphasized that printed reports of proceedings, whether in newspapers or book form, are not law reports. Nor may a shorthand-writer's transcript be so regarded.

If an unreported case cannot be located anywhere in print, then recourse must be made to the official shorthand-writer's notes of the proceedings. As a general rule, the major firms of shorthand-writers have a franchise in respect of the proceedings in particular courts and their addresses may be located in the *Law List*. Transcripts may be obtained upon payment of a fee. In causes held in London, application should be made to Room 392 in the Royal Courts of Justice; in causes heard outside, to the official shorthand-writers attached to the court. Transcripts of hearings before the industrial court may be obtained from the Central Office of Industrial Tribunals. Transcripts of judgments in the Court of Appeal are obtainable from the Association of Shorthand Writers.

It was only after 1908 that the employment of official shorthand-writers was commenced in all divisions of the high court, as well as the criminal courts, following the practice already obtaining in the divorce courts. And not until after 1936 did this practice spread to include the Supreme Court.

On 2 October 1968 the Mechanical Recording Department was established in the Royal Courts of Justice and records the proceedings in thirty-seven such courts, as well as some nineteen county courts. Transcripts are only available to the parties and those immediately professionally concerned, or to others upon the recommendation of one of the solicitors in the case. The time taken to produce a transcript is variable; it may range from overnight to several months.

Official shorthand notes are taken in every action or proceeding heard in the Queen's Bench or Chancery Division which is tried or heard with witnesses and in every cause in the Admiralty courts, unless the judge directs otherwise. It is rare however for everything uttered in the court to be noted by the official writers. Certainly in criminal proceedings it is the duty of judge, counsel and court officers to ensure that the evidence and summing up is properly recorded, and if no shorthand-writer is present, care must be taken to ensure that an unchallengeable note is made. Yet if proceedings are noted by the shorthand-writer, the opening or closing addresses may be omitted at the discretion of the judge. In the divisional court in bankruptcy shorthand notes on a motion of appeal are taken only upon a successful application by one or both of the parties concerned, who must then bear the costs; whilst in the county court shorthand notes are not taken officially, it being the duty of counsel to take a note of a judgment and make it available in all cases likely to go on appeal. The proceedings in magistrates' courts are also not recorded by official shorthand-writers.

Transcripts are not always accurate as to detail. The speaker may err and his mistake be recorded, but no correction noted. Alternatively, the shorthand-writer may hear incorrectly what has been said and thus report it. The judge's summing-up in the NBT publication of the trial of Mrs Maybrick (1889) contains a number of mistakes in dates, besides misquoting the quantity of arsenic in the body.

The availability of transcripts is the prerogative of the Lord Chancellor's department, which may impose restrictions in the public interest. In practice this power is seldom exercised; almost never in the case of civil proceedings (with the exception of certain divorce actions and others involving minors) and only occasionally in criminal proceedings – the trial of Stephen Ward (1963) being a case in point.

It can be seen therefore that it is not always possible to obtain a written report of the proceedings of any case that is not officially reported in a law report. Nor, if such a report is obtainable, will it necessarily be a verbatim report of the entire proceedings.

ADMINISTRATIVE TRIBUNALS

Tribunals may be designated as boards, commissioners, committees, referees, tribunals or umpires. As quasi-judicial bodies exercising some of the functions of courts of law, though outside the conventional legal system, they have existed in their modern form ever since the establishment of the Railway and Canal Commission in the second quarter of the nineteenth century. Reports of proceedings under the Conciliation (Trades Disputes) Act 1896, were issued in sixteen volumes between 1896–1920. The First World War increased the number of tribunals, courts being established to deal with matters of compensation, munitions, and military service. *Civil Service Arbitration Board Awards* were published between 1917–19 and *Industrial Court Awards*, issued in over fifty volumes, cover the period 1919 to date. Tribunals did not multiply significantly, however, until after 1945. Their creation since has been an acknowledgment by government of the social obligations of a highly complex, industrial society.

At the present time some fifty separate authorities are in existence which between them authorize the activities of some 2,000 actual tribunals or courts. These authorities vary considerably in function and purpose. The Commons Commissioners operate a single tribunal whose jurisdiction covers England and Wales; rent tribunals, however, operate on a limited area basis and may be established in any area where it is deemed that the Furnished House (Rent Control) Act, 1946, shall apply. All tribunals operate under statutory authority and while only some are required to have lawyer chairmen preference is almost always given to the appointment of qualified lawyers as chairmen. The subject fields of tribunals are bewildering in their variety and attempts to classify them into neat divisions and classes are rarely successful. They may deal with agriculture, rents and criminal injuries on the one hand or mental health, performing rights and immigration on the other.

Tribunals are under no obligation to issue reports of their

proceedings and decisions, though in fact a number do so. They are not bound by the rules of procedure that govern courts of law and are not bound by precedent. They do not make decisions that affect the substantive law of the land, and such decisions cannot in any way be compared with those of courts of law. As a result, little useful purpose is served by publishing their decisions. Indeed, as in the case of domestic tribunals set up by professional bodies (though not all) publication may prove harmful to those appearing before them and thereby nullify the purpose for which they exist. Finally, it must be stressed that administrative decisions are not 'of authority', and the decisions of a tribunal may not be cited before the superior courts of record.

Of those tribunals whose function appears to warrant the publication of their decisions, some are issued as cyclo-styled paper parts or sheets, others are printed. Some, printed and published through the agency of HMSO, are available for public sale. Others may be obtained upon application by interested parties or those professionally concerned, either through purchase or presentation. Others again may be reported, by arrangement, in a legal periodical or a commercial series of law reports.

Information concerning availability is hard to come by. The *Annual Report* of the Council of Tribunals lists those with which it is concerned but not their addresses, which may change with frequency. And, while it notes the statutory authority under which the tribunal is to be established, the date of this is not necessarily the date upon which the tribunal commences its duties. A difference of five or six years may elapse before the one follows the other. Those decisions printed by HMSO may be located by reference to HMSO official publication lists; the existence of others not so printed may be located by searching *Current Law*, appropriate legal and quasi-legal journals, and specialist law reports. And the existence of others may become known only by chance.

The British Journal of Administrative Law, 1954–8 contains a section entitled Administrative Law Reports which records the decisions of some eleven major tribunals. This series ceased when the journal was merged with *Public Law*.

In 1974 the first volume in a new annual series, *Lands*

Tribunal Cases was published, reprinting reports that have appeared in the *Local Government Review*.

For detailed information on the nature and function of tribunals reference must be made to works on administrative law.

CITATIONS AND REFERENCES

Almost all law reports are known either by the name of the reporter(s) or editor(s), as in the case of the nominate reports issued before 1865 in England (see page 144), or by their title, as is the case with most post-1865 reports in the United Kingdom (see page 139). In practice all such reports are referred to in print by their citation. This is always an abbreviation of the name of the reporter(s) or of the title.

Cases

In general, citations of judicial decisions contain five elements, usually written in the following order: the name of the case, *ie*, that of the party or parties concerned; the date of the decision; the volume number of the relevant report; the name of the report, usually tersely abbreviated; and the page number of the volume at which the case is reported.

Name

A case is always cited by the surnames of the parties given at the head of the report, the Christian names being omitted. Thus: *Smith v. Jones*, the versus being abbreviated. In speech, however, the profession will refer to the case as 'Smith and Jones'. In actions where there are a number of plaintiffs and/or defendants, the names of all parties except the one first mentioned on either side are omitted and the case printed thus, *Smith et al v. Jones et al* will be cited as *Smith v. Jones*.

In the instance of either party possessing a title of honour or an official designation which is recorded at the head of the report, this will be included in the citation. Thus *Leicester (Earl of) v. Wells-next-the-Sea Urban District Council* or *R. v. Recorder of Oxford*.

In criminal actions where the prosecution is conducted by or against the Crown, *R* is the abbreviation employed for 'Rex', 'Regina', 'Regem' or 'Reginam'. Thus *R. v. Smith, Brown v. R.* Again in speech the case will be referred to as 'The King against Smith' or 'Brown against the Queen'. In some criminal prosecutions, however, the action is brought by the Director of Public Prosecutions who, since 1920, has represented the Crown in appeals to the House of Lords. So a case commenced as *R. v. Brown* in the lower court becomes *Brown v. Director of Public Prosecutions* when on appeal.

In instances where the Crown is a party to civil litigation, English is preferred to Latin and the case will be referred to as *The King v. Smith,* or *Brown v. The Queen,* whilst in civil appeals the names of the parties as recorded in the lower court are often reversed in the House of Lords.

The names of corporations and other bodies are given in full, the definite article alone being omitted. Thus *Rhokana Corporation, Ltd v. Inland Revenue Commissioners.* In Admiralty cases involving shipping, the ship becomes a party even though the action is in fact brought or defended by its owners, and then the definite article is retained. Thus *The 'Midhurst' v. The 'Lake Atlin'.*

Special forms of citation, however, are used in certain types of proceedings, as follows:

1. Where a particular estate, person or matter forms the matter to which proceedings relate, particularly in Chancery and bankruptcy cases, *eg: Warren in re Wheeler v. Mills* (the trustee in bankruptcy), the phrase 'in *re*' meaning 'in the matter of'. For citation purposes the title may be shortened to *Re Wheeler.*

2. Where a person voluntarily intervenes in proceedings in the Family Division; *eg: Thompson otherwise Hulton v. Thompson (Causton intervening)* may be shortened to *Thompson (orse Hulton) v. Thompson.*

But where the phrases 'In the estate of' and 'In the goods of' appear in clear they are not abbreviated. Yet *'In bonis'* meaning 'In the goods of' may be abbreviated as *in b. Jones.*

3. Where an application is made by a person who is not a party to the proceedings but who has an interest in the matter which entitles him to make an application; *eg: Regina v. Criminal Injuries Compensation Board, Ex parte Reinisch,* the phrase

Ex parte meaning 'on the application of' may be abbreviated, as in *Ex. p. Reinisch.*

4. Where anonymity is permitted, as in certain actions such as annulments of marriage, the names of the parties are suppressed and initials only used; thus: *B v. B.*

5. Where, as in the early nominate reports, the reporter has titled the case by its popular title, either the name of the party or even the subject, it must be so cited; thus: *Brown's Case*, or *The Case of Heresy.*

Date of decision

In certain nominate reports and some more modern reports the date is omitted from the citation. Where this is given in a modern citation it will usually be within round brackets; thus: *Steadman v. Arden* (1846) 15 M & W 587. In *The Law Reports* and certain other series, the date is given in square brackets; thus: *Welden v. Smith* [1924] A.C. 484. The date is almost always the date on which the decision is awarded and this need bear no relation to the date of the delivery of the judgment and thus the date of the actual hearing; thus: *Thomson v. Cremin* (1941) [1956] 1 WLR 103n indicates that judgment was given in 1941, but the decision was not awarded till fifteen years later.

Name of the report

There are conventional abbreviations for the majority of these and the best lists in print will be found in the works listed on page 161.

Volume and page number

Where the volume of a series is numbered consecutively, its number is always given; thus: 12 QBD. Not all series, however, are numbered, in which case the volume is identified by the year of coverage. The *Appeal Cases* series in *The Law Reports* are an example; *eg*: [1893] AC. The page number is normally that of the page on which the case commences; thus: 12 QBD 715. But where the reference is to a passage later in the text of the report it will read thus: 9 QBD 245 at 249; or 9 QBD 245, 249.

The court in which a case is heard is not normally cited. Exceptions, however, are made in respect of courts established or reconstituted since 1875, particularly the higher appellate courts, in which case the reference will end with the initial letters in capitals of the court concerned; *eg*: [1892] AC 105, HL.

Unreported cases are cited in the same manner as a reported case, but using such detail as may be available. Thus: *Haigh v. A. Lewis & Co.* (unreported) cited in *Dorber v. London Brick Co. Ltd.* [1974] I.C.R. 270 at 271. *Walton on the Naze U.D.C. v. T. J. Moran* (1905) as reported in Hudson, *Law of Building Contracts* (1914) II, 376. *Bastile Properties Ltd. & Another v. Cooper* (1966) *The Times*, October 6.

Cases available only in transcripts held in the Bar Library are sometimes cited as follows (particularly in textbooks): *Dean v. Woods* (1953, C.A.; unreported; Bar Library, no. 203). But the serial number allotted is both domestic and impermanent and should not be so employed. It is not of aid in locating the case in question.

For the usual form of citation in regard to court rolls see page 244.

Reports

England and Wales

Little uniformity in the citation of legal sources exists, though attempts have been made in recent years to establish standard forms of abbreviations for, in particular, law reports. Volumes sometimes print the citation which it is hoped will be used for the reference to the reports. This was not always the case, however, while authors of treatises have, throughout the centuries contrived to construct their own citations, paying little heed to the form adopted by others. This individuality of approach has meant (and still means) that a legal citation may have an abbreviated form that may be any one of a number of variants. This variation of form can be so violent that the reader may recognize the abbreviation in one form and fail completely to do so when confronted with it in another form. As a result, this diversity can cause extreme difficulty over tracing a much needed reference and may prove expensive of staff time.

The best treatises will contain lists of abbreviations of reports referred to in the main text and these should be consulted first in any case of difficulty. More general lists will be found in the standard law lexicons, particularly in Osborn's *Concise Law Dictionary* and Stroud's *Judicial Dictionary*. Excellent lists will also be found in the following:

Bouvier, J. *Law Dictionary and Concise Encyclopaedia*, 8th edition, 1914, 2 volumes. This contains a list of both English and American abbreviations.

Soule, C. C. and Rogers, W. T. *Legal Abbreviations, being citations of American, English, colonial and foreign law textbooks and reports*, 1911.

Sturgess, H. A. C. and Hewitt, A. R. *Dictionary of Legal Terms, Statutory Definitions and Citations*, 2nd edition, 1940. This contains abbreviations of the reports of the United Kingdom and Empire.

Price, M. O. and Bitner, H. *Effective Legal Research*, 2nd edition, 1953, claims to contain the most complete list of abbreviations in Anglo-American law. This is to be preferred to the 1963 edition which contains an abridged list designed for students.

English and Empire Digest, 2nd edition, 1950–70, 56 volumes. The cumulative supplements and continuation volumes provide an up-to-date series of lists covering United Kingdom, Irish and Commonwealth abbreviations.

Sweet and Maxwell *Guide to Law Reports and Statutes*, 4th edition, 1962. This contains a list of abbreviations covering United Kingdom, Irish and Commonwealth law reports, with dated denoting the period covered by the reports.

Where to look for your law, 14th edition, 1962. This contains the best basic list of United Kingdom and Irish law report abbreviations, with dates denoting the period covered by the reports.

University of London. Institute of Advanced Legal Studies. *Manual of Legal Citations, Part 1, The British Isles*, 1959. This contains the best exposition in print on the subject of citations and has abbreviation lists for United Kingdom and Irish reports.

6

These various lists, however, suffer from a number of common defects. Their alphabetical arrangements are variable and not always consistent with their own chosen plan, and, regardless of dates of publication, each is likely to contain some references that are not to be found in the others. In addition, none has attempted to give more than one form of an abbreviation for a specific report. As a result, it may often be necessary to consult more than one list before the required abbreviation is identified, if at all.

Scotland

Scottish cases are cited in a style similar to English cases. In verbal citation the form employed is Smith *against* Jones. A married woman, though, is named in the heading to the report by both her names, the maiden preceding the married name. In citing the case her maiden name is omitted.

Ireland

Irish cases are also cited in the same style as English cases, but the abbreviations may, for the sake of clarity, often be followed by 'Ireland' in brackets, shortened thus: (Ir.). In the Republic, the state prosecutes in the name of the people, thus: *The People (Attorney General) v. O'Donoghue.*

Channel Islands

Cases to be found in *Judgments of the Royal Court of Jersey* 1950– , are to be cited JJ followed by the page number. Cases will also be found in *Table des décisions de la cour royale de Jersey* for the period 1885– , the reference being given by date, series and page.

Isle of Man

Cases are cited in the same style as English cases.

DIGESTS AND INDEXES

Digests aim at recording reported cases in such a manner as to provide a ready guide to the case law on a given topic. The reports are presented in a highly compressed form and the notes on them seek to provide an abstract of the legal principles which may be inferred from them. Cases are usually arranged under titles, alphabetically ordered, according to their subject matter; the order of presentation of the cases normally being a chronological one. Digested cases, however, are not an adequate substitute for the reports themselves.

Digests may be general, aiming to record all the cases in all the courts, or limited, confining themselves to a particular series of reports, branch of the law or merely to cases that have been judicially noticed. For the latter see page 166.

Among the earliest digests must be noticed those abridgments which included the cases of the nominate reporters. Henry Rolle's *Un Abridgment des plusieurs cases et resolutions del common Ley*, 1668, was written in Law French, runs to some 1,700 pages, and in it the case law is abridged under alphabetical heads divided into sub-titles. The work is still cited from time to time. *A General Abridgment of Cases in Equity*, by a Gentleman of the Middle Temple, 1732–56, ran to five editions and aimed to contain all equity cases then in print. Charles Petersdorff's *Practical and Elementary Abridgment of Cases in the Courts of King's Bench, Common Pleas, Exchequer, and at Nisi Prius*, 15 volumes, 1825–30, was the first to approximate to a modern digest, containing as it did a series of catch-words or phrases under each title. Supplementary volumes were subsequently issued.

Of early modern general digests the first was Fisher's *Digest of Reported Cases*, 1756–1870, issued in five volumes 1870. Continuation volumes were added to 1879. The continued history of the work, credited to T. W. Chitty and J. Mews, is bibliographically confusing. It is sufficient to say that Mews was the *de facto* author of the new edition of Fisher, issued in seven volumes in 1884 and known as Fisher's *Common Law Digest*, that he issued annual digest volumes up to 1897, and that the first edition of Mews' *Digest of English Case Law*, in 16 volumes, appeared in 1898. A second edition followed in 1925 and was kept up-to-date by annual volumes to 1970, when it ceased publication. The original edition of Mews contained over 30,000 references to decided cases, but editorial policy precluded the inclusion of 'every case that ever has been reported'.

The English and Empire Digest was first issued in 49 volumes, 1919–32 and a second replacement edition, the 'blue band' re-issue, now being superseded by a 'green band' re-issue, was published in 56 volumes, 1950–70. The scheme of arrangement and classification is, in so far as is possible, modelled on *Halsbury's Laws of England*, for which it was designed to become a companion work. This digest purports to be a comprehensive digest of every case reported from early times and claims to contain over three-quarters of a million cases, principally English, together with cases from the courts of Scotland, Ireland, Canada, Australia, New Zealand, India and other countries of the Commonwealth and South Africa. The titles are arranged alphabetically and the cases under them are, in general, presented in chronological order, each section of cases being keyed to both *Halsbury's Laws* and *Statutes*. The work is kept up-to-date by annual cumulative supplements, each volume containing its own table of cases and index. Consolidated indexes have been issued for 1951–60, 1961–70 and 1971–3, and will continue to appear.

The Law Reports' Digest of Cases was first issued in 1892 in three volumes covering the period 1865–90, volume 1 being the index volume to the cases. Later supplements appeared at ten-yearly intervals till 1931. The Second World War caused a break in publication and the last supplement to be issued covered the period 1931–50 and was issued in 1952 (see Fig. 2). Since then consolidated indexes have been published covering cases printed 1951–73. As from 1912, the digest widened its scope to include other series of standard English reports, both general and special, as well as *Indian Appeals* and Scots reports, but until 1947 excluded all references to All ER.

The monthly issues of *Current Law* also digest selected cases in some thirty series, either reports or notes in journals; emphasis being given to *The Weekly Law Reports* and *The All England Law Reports*. In these digests the *ratio decidendi* is extracted from the decisions and set out in a separate paragraph. Cases from specialist series are more compressed, giving only the facts and the decision. In addition, reported case-notes of decisions in county courts and crown courts, not otherwise reported, are printed from time to time, while persuasive cases from reports and journals published in the Commonwealth, Scotland,

S

SALE OF GOODS.

Agreement to buy motor spirit—" Quantity : " Requirements up to but not exceeding 45,000 " Imperial gallons per week "—" Price : 6¾d. " per gallon ex wharf . . . plus petrol tax . . . " —Alleged underpayment—Buyers' plea that supplies were taken under subsequent verbal agreement which provided for reduction in price to 2d. per gallon, buyers to pay 2⅜d. per gallon and to be refunded the additional ⅜d. per gallon " when there is a rise in prices or " conditions improve "—Obligations of buyers under original agreement—Claim by buyers to refund under verbal agreement—Award that sellers' claim failed and that buyers were entitled to a refund.

Held, that the buyers were not obliged by the original agreement to take any fixed, or any, quantity of spirit unless they chose, and that therefore the sellers' claim in respect of alleged underpayment failed ; and that the buyers were not entitled to any refund (there was no rise in prices or improvement of conditions when the arbitrators were appointed, and any consideration of a subsequent improvement was outside their jurisdiction).   CORY BROS. & CO. *v.* UNIVERSE PETROLEUM CO.

Roche J. 46 Ll. L. Rep. 309

Article ordered by trade name—Composition of article.

A buyer ordering an article by its trade name must be taken to have ordered it as it was manufactured at the date of giving the order, whatever its composition may have been at some previous time.   HARRIS & SONS *v.* PLYMOUTH VARNISH AND COLOUR CO.

Branson J. 49 T. L. R. 521; 38 Com. Cas. 316

Auction — Lot knocked down to bidder — Entry of name in catalogue by auctioneer conducting sale—Note or memorandum—Action for purchase price—Sale of Goods Act, 1893 (56 & 57 Vict., c. 71), s. 4.

WILSON & SONS *v.* PIKE

C. A. [1948] W. N. 263 ; [1948] 2 All E. R. 267 ; 64 T. L. R. 566

Auction—Passing of property—Misrepresentation by purchaser as to his identity—Sale of Goods Act, 1893 (56 & 57 Vict., c. 71), ss. 18, 28, 39.

At an auction sale motor vehicles were sold to a man who was the highest bidder. After the sale, the purchaser made misrepresentations as to his identity to the auctioneer. Believing these misrepresentations the auctioneer allowed

SALE OF GOODS—*continued.*

the purchaser to take delivery of the vehicles and accepted in payment a cheque accompanied by the purchaser's certificate to the effect that the property in the vehicles would not pass to him until his cheque had been honoured. The purchaser sold one of the motor vehicles to the third party who in turn sold it to the defendant. The purchaser's cheque was dishonoured. The auctioneer brought this action to recover from the defendant the motor vehicle or its value :—

Held (1.) That this was not a case of larceny by a trick so as to prevent the property from passing to the purchaser.

(2.) That the property so passed on the fall of the hammer and there was no effective condition that it should not so pass until the cheque had been honoured.

(3.) That, the property having passed on the fall of the hammer, it was not possible for the purchaser, merely by signing such a certificate, to divest himself of the property and to revest it in the vendor.   DENNANT *v.* SKINNER AND COLLOM

Hallett J. [1948] 2 K. B. 164 ; [1948] 2 All E. R. 29 ; [1948] L. J. R. 1576

Breach—Agreement by plaintiffs to purchase from defendants " softwood goods of fair specifi- " cation over the season 1930 "—" Buyers shall " also have the option of entering into a contract " with sellers for the purchase of 100,000 stand- " ards for delivery during 1931. Such contract to " stipulate that whatever the conditions are, " buyers shall obtain the goods on conditions and " at prices which show to them a reduction of " 5 per cent. on the f. o. b. value of the official " price list at any time ruling during 1931 "— Option exercised—Failure of defendants to implement contract — Construction — Enforceability—Whether amounting to an agreement complete in itself or to an agreement that at a future date an agreement would be completed— Measure of damages.

Held, that the option having been exercised, such agreement was complete and binding in itself and was not dependent on any future agreement for its validity ; as to damages, that the defendants having withheld material from which the learned judge might more accurately assess the damages, the defendants could not complain of his Lordship's assessment upon such material as he had before him.

Appeal allowed.   Judgment of MacKinnon J. restored.   HILLAS & CO. *v.* ARCOS

H. L. (E.) 43 Ll. L. Rep. 359 ; 38 Com. Cas. 23 ; 147 L. T. 503 C. A. 40 Ll. L. Rep. 307; 36 Com. Cas. 353

Figure 2

Ireland, South Africa and the United States may also appear. All the latest cases authentically reported, even though not yet appearing in print in a series, are summarized in a special section at the back of each issue, as well as being referred to in the text. The decisions of a number of tribunals are also digested. The indexes to the monthly parts are cumulative but cases are best located by reference to the relevant topic, all topics being alphabetically ordered in the main text.

Tables of cases will be found also in the annual *Current Law Year Book*, usually issued each April and in the *Current Law Consolidation*, 1947–51 as well as the later *Master Volumes*, issued every five years as supplements to the Consolidation.

Certain series of law reports issued by or in conjunction with journals have issued digests in annual form as a part of their published proceedings. Among commercial series *Lloyds Law Reports* issue decennial digests.

NOTING-UP

In most series of modern reports, at the end of the preliminary matter that precedes the first or only judgment of each recorded case, there will be found a list of references to cases in other series of reports, usually currently published and which have been referred to (*ie*, judicially noticed in the judgment(s) that follow(s)). The case in which the reference is found (or cited) is known as the annotating case and the case referred to is known as the annotated case. The different expressions used to describe the effect of the annotating case have particular meanings and the terms most commonly used to describe these are as follows:

Affirmed (affd.), applied (appld.), approved (apprd.), considered (consd.), disapproved (disap.), distinguished (distd.), doubted (dbtd.), explained (expld.), extended (extd.), followed (folld.), not followed (n.f.), overruled (overd.), referred (refd.), reversed (revsd.). These terms are defined in appropriate legal dictionaries.

There exists in the United Kingdom no central index or citation system in published form for the recall of those cases that have been judicially noticed. Such a system would enable a lawyer to locate with facility all leading cases relevant to the case-law of the topics requiring his attention. Failing this, recourse must be made to a number of works whose inclusion of a citation system is, with one exception, incidental to their primary function.

Early works that attempted to meet this need require notice in passing. Dale and Lehmann's *Digest of Cases overruled, not followed, disapproved,* [etc.] from 1756 to 1886, 1887, was superseded by Woods and Ritchie's *Digest of Cases overruled, approved* [etc.] 3 volumes, 1907. The 30,000 cases were arranged under alphabetical topics and extracts from the more important judgments included. Talbot and Fort's *Index of Cases Judicially Noticed* was issued in 1891, ran to three editions and recorded in the last edition all cases cited in judgments published 1865–1905. Its arrangement was inferior to that of Woods and Ritchie. More ambitious in scope was Campbell's *Ruling Cases,* issued in 27 volumes, 1894–1908 and containing American notes by I. Brown.

In Mews' *Digest,* volume 23 contained an *Index of Cases Judicially Noticed.* This included cases noticed in 1926 and a citation search would commence with this volume, continue through the cumulative supplements for 1925–35, 1936–45, and then the twenty-four annual volumes to 1970.

The Law Reports Digest may similarly be consulted, but the cases digested are not earlier than 1865, though cases referred to may, of course, be of earlier date.

The most profitable digest for citation searches is undoubtedly *The English and Empire Digest.* The location of the case in question in the table of cases will give a reference to the appropriate volume in which the case is digested. The digest of the case is followed by the relevant citations which indicate how the case has been annotated in later cases. Reference should then be made to the later supplements where, under the same reference number as was given to the case in the original volume, will be found any later cases, together with digests of additional relevant cases.

It must be noticed however that a given case may be digested under more than one head and it must be looked for, in the first instance, under the head most appropriate to the searcher's requirements.

The *Current Law Citator,* issued annually since 1947, includes not only a statute citator but also a case citator. This lists in strict alphabetical order every English case reported since 1947; every case of whatever date which has been judicially considered in a case reported since 1947, giving also the reference to the paragraph in which the amending case or statute is digested in the CLYB; every case of whatever date which has been the subject of an article or substantial case-note in any of the legal periodicals covered by *Current Law* since 1947; and every Scots, Irish, Commonwealth or South African case similarly digested in *Current Law* since 1947. It also gives full references to every English case reported since 1947. The monthly parts of *Current Law* also contain a case citator section at the commencement of the part. If digested during the current year, the name of the case is printed in standard type; if written about or judicially considered, it is printed in italics; if the case is going to appeal it is marked with an asterisk.

Individual series of law reports such as *The Law Reports* and All ER issue tables of cases judicially considered, and these may also be of value as a means of ascertaining the status of a case.

LOCATION OF CASES

No central index to cases exists. The nearest approximation to such an index is that to *The English and Empire Digest* which claims to contain every English case reported from early times to the present day, with additional cases from the courts of Scotland, Ireland and the Commonwealth. Similarly, the *Current Law Citator* claims to list every English case reported since 1947. In both the lists are alphabetical.

If the correct citation is known there is rarely any problem, except that of identifying the relevant series of reports. It is possible, however, that a printed reference may be inaccurate, owing to typographical errors or poor proof-reading, in which case, if there is certainty as to the series, it may be advisable to examine alternative combinations of pages and volume numbers, or years.

Difficulty usually arises only when inadequate information is available.

If the name of a case is known but not its date or any citation, it may be traced:

1. by using the index volumes to *The English and Empire Digest* (if before 1930);
2. through the indexes to the supplements to the same digest (if after 1919);
3. through the *Current Law Citator*. Should these not yield results, indexes to the other digests may be consulted in the same manner. If still not located, it is likely to be a recent case not covered by the latest volume of the major digests. In this instance:
4. by consulting the *Current Law Consolidation* and then the subsequent *Current Law Year Books*.

If the name of a case and the report in which it appears is known but not its date, then trace it in the index volume of the appropriate series. *The All England Law Reports* have a consolidated index for all cases in the series since 1936, and there is an annual consolidated index to *The Law Reports* and *The Weekly Law Reports*, issued since 1953.

If the date of a modern case is known, but not its name, then trace it:
1. through Mews' *Digest of English Case Law* (if after 1924);
or
2. through *Current Law* (if after 1947).

If the date of a case and/or its name but not its citation is known (and it is before 1865), then it may be traced through the index volumes to *The English Reports*.

But if the case is prior to 1865 and is not listed in the index to *The English Reports* then, provided the date, name and type of case is known (*eg*, King's Bench or Admiralty) reference should be made to Maxwell and Brown's *List of British and Colonial Law Reports and Legal Periodicals* 1937. In this work reports are arranged chronologically by dates of coverage under courts and subjects, *ie*, Admiralty and taxation.

If none of the above methods proves successful, it is likely that the case has not been reported in any established series of reports and it should be treated as an unreported case, for which see page 152.

SCOTTISH REPORTS

The influences that shaped the development of Scottish law

reporting do not, as may be expected, mirror that of their English counterpart. Apparent similarities must not be explored too closely. There are no convenient cut-off dates marking changes in its history. In some important respects Scotland was ahead in ideas, in others merely different.

One major variant requires notice. The doctrine of the precedent as a means of influencing the course of Scots law did not begin to burgeon until the last half of the eighteenth century. Up to that time, and later, decided cases imposed no obligation upon the judiciary; they might influence but were not authoritative.

Modern reports

Official

The *Court of Session Cases* report the actions of the supreme civil court of Scotland and commenced publication in 1821. Initially they were a result of private enterprise and the first five series, each separately numbered, are often referred to and are sometimes better known by the name of the principal reporter for each series: Shaw, Dunlop, Macpherson, Rettie and Fraser. Volume 10 (1847–8) of the second series began to include cases in other courts, such as the Teind Court, and Court of Exchequer; volume 13 (1850–1) began to include House of Lords cases with a separate pagination, while volume 1 (1873–4) of the fourth series began to include justiciary (criminal) cases, the latter also separately paginated.

In 1907 responsibility for publication of the session cases was assumed by the Faculty of Advocates, who in turn handed this over to the Scottish Council of Law Reporting in 1957. Now, the *Session Cases* are published in parts throughout the year and include lands valuation appeal decisions in addition to those of courts already mentioned.

As a result of the separate pagination, the justiciary cases as from 1917 are occasionally to be found separately bound, generally five years to a volume and having their own distinctive citation are often regarded as a separate series. The House of Lords appeals appearing in the *Session Cases*, also with a separate pagination and an equally distinctive citation are similarly regarded. They are, however, rarely bound separately owing to the paucity of the material. Neither the Lords nor justiciary cases are accorded the dignity of a title page. This is reserved for the session cases alone.

It is usual for the recorded decisions to be submitted to the judiciary for correction and approval prior to printing. As a result, the series is held to be of the highest authority and the accuracy of its reporters is rarely if ever questioned.

The *Session Notes* were issued weekly 1925–48 under the authority of the Faculty of Advocates. They contained notes of cases decided in the court of session, court of justiciary and the House of Lords, and effectively provided an interim service whilst publication of the relevant part of the *Session Cases* was awaited. Not all such notes however were subsequently followed by full reports in the *Session Cases* and publication was discontinued, their purpose being already adequately met by the Notes of Recent Decisions to be found in *The Scots Law Times*, noted below.

Commercial

Commercial publication of reports had commenced in the nineteenth century. *The Law Chronicle* which appeared in five volumes, 1829–34, contained reports of appeals from Scottish courts as well as Dean and Anderson's reports. Of particular importance were the *Scottish Jurist*, 46 volumes, 1829–73 and the *Scottish Law Reporter*, 61 volumes, 1865–1924, the latter thereafter incorporated with *The Scots Law Times*. The former contained session, justiciary, teind and Lords cases from its commencement and, at its conclusion, was also reporting decisions reached by the railway and canal commission, the valuation appeal court, provisional order committees and the Privy Council.

The Scottish Law Review commenced publication in 1885 and was issued monthly. It contained reports of decisions in the sheriff courts from 1885 to 1963 as well as notes of English cases held to be of relevance. The former have their own citation and are occasionally to be found separately bound. From 1913 to 1963 (when it ceased publication) a supplement contained decisions of the Scottish land court.

With the demise of the *Scottish Jurist* and the *Scottish Law Review* only one main commercial series remains in progress.

The Scots Law Times Reports are issued within the weekly parts of *The Scots Law Times* but with a separate pagination. The make-up of the SLT is a complicated one and the various series of reports to be found within its published parts form such an integral part of this publication that its composition demands elucidation. Each has its own separate title page and pagination.

The Scots Law Times commenced publication in 1893–4 and the first two volumes contained brief signed notes under the heading 'Reports' of cases heard in the court of session, House of Lords and sheriff court. As from volume 3 (1895–6) *Scots Law Times Reports* appeared in the journal, entitled volume 3, 1895–6, with their own separate title page and pagination. The SLTR covered Lords, justiciary and session cases. Volumes 1 to 16 only were numbered. As from 1909 the volume numbering was dropped and citation was by the year, two volumes of reports being issued each year until 1922, when reversion was made to a single volume of reports. In 1922 the SLT commenced the *Sheriff Court Reports*, while an index of cases and annual digest appeared at the back of the SLTR. In 1932 the SLT added another series, the SLT *Poor Law Reports*. This series continued till 1941, when it ceased. In 1946 the SLT started a new series *Notes of Recent Decisions*. Cases in the Notes are often expanded into full reports in subsequent issues. Again, in 1950, a further series commenced, the SLT *Lyon Court Reports*. This series lasted till 1959, was discontinued, and revived only once since in 1966. In 1964 the SLT *Scottish Land Court Reports* commenced and in 1971 the SLT started the *Lands Tribunal for Scotland Reports*.

Other reports

Selected Scottish appeals to the House of Lords will be found in the following English series of reports: the two volumes of Scotch and Divorce Appeals, 1866–75, in the first series of *The Law Reports* (see page 139) and, as from 1876 onwards in the *Appeal Cases* of the later series, *The All England Law Reports*, 1936 to date.

Decisions by the Scottish courts on such specialist matters as elections, income tax, and pensions are reported from time to time and may generally be located either in the series recorded above or in appropriate specialist reports whether English or Scottish. For example, important Scottish cases on commercial and maritime law are to be located in *Lloyd's Law Reports* (see page 143) but matters affecting local government will be found in the *County and Municipal Record*, 1903 to date. Likewise, Scottish tribunal decisions may be recorded in for example *Knights Industrial Reports* or appropriate government publications.

Early reports

The earliest reports were either notes made for personal use or notes of cases to be found in volumes of Practicks. Private reporting commences with a case of 1540, not printed however till 1741, and the authors of the majority of the early reports were judges, whose notes, made initially for private use, were seldom intended for publication.

Session reports

Of early reports the most important are the twenty-one private or original reports, separately printed, which cover cases in the court of session from 1621 to 1822, commencing with Durie's *Decisions of the Lords of Council and Session*, 1621–42, issued by Sir A. Gibson of Durie, and concluding with David Hume's *Decisions*, 1781–1822, issued in 1839. Other notable reporters in this group were Sir James Dalrymple, 1st Viscount Stair, and Henry Home, Lord Kames.

Durie's was the earliest volume of reports in any court to be printed. The professional reporter did not appear till 1705, when William Forbes was appointed by the Faculty of Advocates to report the decisions of the court of session and his only volume, covering cases heard 1705–13, appeared in 1714. Lacking judicial encouragement, this venture to produce a systematic official series was temporarily abandoned. The judiciary were hostile to the suggestion of allowing more than mere decisions to be published and Robert Bell, the first independent reporter, met with animosity and obstruction when he announced his intention of reporting without an official appointment. His *Cases decided in the Court of Session,* 1790–2 was published in 1794, the judges being denoted in the text only by letters. His reward was a summons to the robing room and the reproof of the judiciary. It was over a decade before they changed their views.

If the absence of the binding authority of a decided case had delayed over-long the arrival of the professional reporter, his continued activity until the first quarter of the twentieth century was due, perhaps, to the failure of the second attempt by the Faculty of Advocates at an official series. Their *Decisions,* 1752–1808, issued in fourteen volumes, 1760–1815, was entitled 'Old Faculty Reports', the cases being reported by a Committee of the Bar. A new series was subsequently issued, bringing the period of cases covered down to 1841. The composite set of twenty-one volumes is best known as the 'Faculty Collection', more familiarly the 'Faculty Collection folios' to distinguish them from the later octavo set, covering the period 1825–41. The delay in their production proved unpopular and the session case series initiated by Patrick Shaw and his colleagues in 1821, and continued without a break by his successors until 1908, was to result in their closure.

Justiciary reports

Also of importance as a group are the eleven reporters of criminal cases who recorded decisions in the Court of Justiciary for the period 1670–1916, broken by a gap, 1774–1818. They commence with John MacLaurin, Lord Dreghorn's *Arguments and Decisions,* 1670–1773, issued 1774, and close with Adam's *Justiciary Cases,* 1893–1916, issued in seven volumes. Collections of early cases, principally of concern to legal historians, have been published by the Scottish History Society and the Stair Society. For collections of criminal trials refer to Trials at page 185. As from 1874, commencing with the fourth series, edited by Rettie, justiciary cases have been reported in the annual volumes of *Session Cases,* which are noticed above.

House of Lords' Appeals

The reporting of Lords' decisions in Scottish appeals commenced with Robertson's *Reports of Cases on appeal from Scotland, decided in the house of peers from 1707–27,* issued 1807. It continued in private hands till 1879, when Paterson published in two volumes his *Cases on appeal from Scotland in the House of Lords,* 1851–73. This was in fact a revision of reports that had already appeared in the *Scottish Jurist.* Of this group of ten reporters, Macqueen's *Reports* alone were subsequently reprinted in the *English Reports.* Certain English nominate reports recording English House of Lords cases also contain Scottish appeals, for details of which see Leadbetter, J. S. The printed Law Reports, in *Sources and Literature of Scots Law,* Stair Society 1, 1936, pp. 57–8.

Collections : 1540–1816

The majority of the early cases were reprinted in two major collections, which also printed for the first time a number of important manuscript series. Kames and Woodhouselee's *Decisions of the Court of Session,* abridged in the form of a dictionary, covered the period 1540–1796 and was issued in five volumes, 1741–1804. More comprehensive was Morison's *Decisions, Court of Session* [1540–1808] *in the form of a Dictionary,* issued in twenty-two volumes, 1801–15. The dictionary contains some reports earlier than 1540, taken from Balfour's *Practicks*; volumes 20 and 21 are a synopsis or digest of the cases recorded; volume 22 has supplemental matter; and two appendixes were subsequently added, the first containing decisions reported whilst the work was in progress. A supplement in five volumes by Brown was subsequently issued adding material omitted by Morison. For the location of material (the arrangement in Brown differs, the cases being arranged chronologically under each reporter) reference should be made to Tait's *Index,* 1823, which alone provides an adequate key as well as a full account of the complicated bibliographical make-up of Morison's work.

The most modern collection to date, noted here for convenience, is the *Scots Revised Reports,* a re-issue of many Scots decisions prior to 1873, published in forty-five volumes, 1898–1908. It is selective, drawing upon Morison's *Dictionary,* the Faculty's *Decisions,* Appeals to the House of Lords, the first three series of *Session Cases* and cases reported in the *Scottish Jurist*.

A microfilm edition of *Scottish Law Reports*, reproducing over 300 volumes, and a near complete collection of the early reports was issued in 1973–4.

Digests and indexes

The purpose and construction of Scottish law digests is so similar to that of their English counterparts (see page 162) as to require no elucidation.

Because of the order of their arrangement a number of the early published works noticed above at page 175 are sometimes treated as being digests of case law. They are not so regarded here.

A number of the earlier digests are still of value, but since there is a lack of uniformity in the style of headings used, searches must often be made under a variety of headings in order to locate the required material. Brown's *Synopsis of decisions in the court of session, including House of Lords appeals, 1540–1827* was issued in four volumes, 1827–9. This work covers all the cases in Morison's *Dictionary*, Brown's *Supplement*, the reported decisions of Elchies, Hailes and Bell, and the first four volumes also of the Faculty of Advocates' *Decisions* down to 1827. Bell's *Compendium of decisions of the court of session from 1803 33*, was issued in two volumes in 1841–2. Shaw's *Digest of cases decided*, issued [1869] was a consolidation of two previous digests and included cases decided in the supreme courts, 1800–68 and on appeal by the House of Lords, 1726–1868. It was in three volumes and included criminal cases under the heading Crime.

There are two major modern digests. The first is the Faculty of Advocates' *Digest* (a continuation of Shaw), covering 1868–1922 and issued in six volumes, 1924–6, which was continued up to 1950 by three supplementary volumes, and thereafter by annual parts. It includes all cases reported in the *Session Cases*, excluding sheriff court decisions, the *Scottish Law Reporter*, the *Scots Law Times* and the *Justiciary Reports*. The titles are arranged alphabetically, criminal cases being grouped under justiciary. The second is *The Scots Digest*, first published in four volumes, 1908–12 and digesting cases in the Lords from 1707 and in the supreme courts, 1800–73. A second series was issued in two volumes in 1905 and continuations appeared thereafter. The 1946 volume for the period 1937–44 covers *Session Cases, Session Notes,* the *Scots Law Times,* the *Scottish Law Reporter* and *Justiciary Cases.*

It should be noted that the last part-issue of the *Faculty Digest* (publication of which was assumed by the Scottish Council of Law Reporting after 1957) covers the year 1963 and was issued in 1967. A decennial continuation has been projected. The last part-issue of *The Scots Digest* for 1946–7 was issued in 1948. Both are unofficially supplemented by the Scottish edition of *Current Law.*

Digests, usually annual, will be found in the *Scots Law Times Reports* and the *Scottish Law Reporter.* Occasionally consolidations are issued. *The Digest of Sheriff Court Cases reported in SLT* covered the period 1893–1943 while the *Scottish Law Reporter Digest,* issued in 1898, digested nearly 1,300 cases reported in the first thirty-two volumes of the *Scottish Law Reporter,* 1865–95.

A selection of Scottish cases are digested in English publications such as Mews' *Digest of English Case-Law* and footnote references will be found in *The English and Empire Digest.*

The best quick reference guide to modern cases however must remain the Scottish edition of *Current Law.* Those sections applicable to the United Kingdom give an identical coverage to that in the English edition (see page 164), but the section giving material information applicable to Scotland contains references to cases reported in all the major series of Scottish law reports. Indexes to monthly parts are cumulative, but cases are best located by reference to the relevant topic, all topics being alphabetically ordered in the main text.

Tables of cases will be found also in the annual *Current Law Year Book,* which contains a special Scottish section, but for convenience these are general to the whole volume. Master volumes are issued quinquennially, giving coverage over the previous five years.

Noting-up

The general principle regarding the noting-up of cases is

identical with that for English material (see page 166). No
Scots digests specifically concerned with cases judicially noticed
have been published, however. Reference must be made to the
indexes of appropriate digests and to the *Scottish Current Law
Citator*, whose case citator is divided into two separate sections,
each arranged in alphabetical order. The first section relates to
English cases and the second to cases reported in Scotland,
together with cases of whatever date which have been judicially
considered in the Scottish courts during the period under
review. It is thus possible to trace the history of any case of
whatever date which has been judicially considered since 1948.

IRISH REPORTS

Republic of Ireland (Eire)

The Irish Reports, which now record the decisions of the High
Court, the Court of Criminal Appeal and the Supreme Court
of Eire, commenced publication in 1894. Until 1926, two
volumes were issued per year, the first covering the Chancery,
the second the King's Bench division. Initially the courts
reported included the Court of Appeal, High Court of Justice,
Court of Bankruptcy and Irish Land Commission. In 1898 for
bankruptcy was substituted crown cases reserved, and in 1923
(after independence) the reports covered the courts of the Irish
Free State and Northern Ireland. As from 1925, reporting was
confined to the Irish Free State alone, cases on appeal in the
then new supreme court being first recorded in volume 1 for
that year, criminal appeals appearing in volume 2. Land
Commission cases have not been reported since 1968. Now,
The Irish Reports are issued quarterly, though two parts are
frequently combined in one, and there are unavoidable
publication delays. Unlike the *Session Cases*, the volumes contain a single pagination system. A verbatim reprint for the
period 1894–1912 was issued in twelve volumes, 1913–15.

 The Irish Law Times and Solicitors Journal, issued weekly,
commenced publication in 1867 and initially reported cases
appeared in the miscellaneous part of the journal in the form of
weekly notes of cases, these being supplied by the reporters of
the Council of Law Reporting in Ireland. As from volume 5

(1871), a supplement with a separate title page and its own pagination was issued, entitled the *Irish Law Times Reports*. Notes of cases, however, continued to appear in the journal. Initially the ILTR included reports of cases in the Supreme Court of Judicature, bankruptcy and the county courts.

The Irish Jurist commenced publication in 1849. After seven volumes a new series, volumes 8 to 18, 1855–66, was issued. Volume 19, pt. 1 is said to have been issued also. Both series contained reports of decisions in all the courts. Between 1901–5, appeared *The New Irish Jurist and Local Government Review*, which contained the NIJ and LG *Reports* for 1900–5. *The Irish Jurist* was re-born in 1935, initially issued monthly and then quarterly. The periodical and law report sections were separately paginated and thirty-one volumes were issued, 1935–1965. A new series commenced in 1966 and continues. Both series contain reports of decisions in all the courts.

Northern Ireland

The Northern Ireland Law Reports commenced publication in 1925 under the authority of the newly-established Incorporated Council of Law Reporting for Northern Ireland. Prior to 1925, relevant cases appeared in *The Irish Reports*, as noticed above. The reports are issued in quarterly parts and cover cases in the High Court of Justice and Court of Appeal in Northern Ireland. As from 1970, cases on appeal therefrom in the House of Lords have been included. An *Index to Cases Decided in the courts of Northern Ireland and reported during the period 1921 to 1970*, edited by D. F. Greer and B. A. Childs, was published in 1975.

The *Northern Ireland Legal Quarterly* commenced publication in 1936 and the first part issued contained notes on case-law. As from the second part of volume 1, this title was changed to 'a survey of recent case-law'. As from volume 15 (volume 1 NS) the *Quarterly* was published from the Law Faculty, Queen's University and acquired a title page, a table of cases noted, a section entitled 'notes of cases', and a digest of unreported NI cases, the latter being dropped from volume 16. It should be noticed that in the later volumes the notes of cases section contains digests of special tribunal decisions as well as digests of unreported cases.

Selected appeals to the House of Lords will be found in the *Appeal Cases* of *The Law Reports* as well as in NILR.

The courts of Northern Ireland, while respecting the decisions of the English courts, are not bound by them, though they are bound by decisions of the House of Lords as the supreme court of appeal. Pre-1921 Irish decisions are said by some to be binding, particularly in the case of decisions of the Court of Appeal, and are at least accorded the same respect as English decisions below the House of Lords. Decisions of the courts of Eire are, naturally, not binding on Northern Ireland, but would in certain circumstances (*eg*, when interpreting the statutes in force in Northern Ireland) be treated with the utmost respect.

Earlier reports

Law reporting in Ireland did not effectively commence until the last quarter of the eighteenth century, though the earliest reporter would seem to have been Sir John Davies, whose *Le primer report des cases et matters en Ley . . . en les courts del roy en Ireland*, covering cases 1604–12, was issued in 1615. These are reprinted in ER volume 80. Exchequer cases were first reported by Howard in 1760; he was also the first to report Chancery cases in 1772 in a work entitled *Rules and Practice of the High Court of Chancery*. The nineteenth century saw a considerable increase in private reporting and some fifty reporters (or pairs of reporters) produced over one hundred volumes of reports during this period. Of later reporters Fitzgibbon was the most prolific. His *Irish Land Reports*, 1895–1920, in twenty-five volumes, 1895–1920 was issued almost concurrently with his *Irish Local Government Orders and Legal Decisions*, 1899–1919, in seventeen volumes, 1899–1919.

The earliest attempt to record cases in all the courts was the product of commercial enterprise. *The Law Recorder, containing reports of cases in the courts of law and equity*, 1827–31, a weekly publication, was issued in five volumes, 1828–32; a new series, 1833–8, in six volumes followed, issued 1833–8.

In 1839 were published two series, both covering the period 1838–50 in thirteen volumes and issued 1839–52. The first, *Irish Law Reports*, reported cases in the Queen's Bench, Common

Pleas and Exchequer; the second, *Irish Equity Reports*, cases in Chancery, Rolls court and Equity Exchequer. Both were subtitled 'Third Series of The Law Recorder'. These were followed by the *Irish Chancery Reports*, 1850–66, in seventeen volumes, 1852–67, and the *Irish Common Law Reports*, 1849–66, also in seventeen volumes, 1852–67.

In 1867 was established the Council of Law Reporting in Ireland. The *Irish Reports* were then first issued, publication following the pattern of their English equivalent. Initially there were two main series, the *Common Law Series* and the *Equity Series* covering decisions reported 1867–78 in eleven volumes each. In addition, a volume of registry appeals was published in 1879. This series was continued by *The Law Reports (Ireland)*, 1878–93, issued in thirty-two volumes, 1879–93, which in turn was to be continued by *The Irish Reports*, 1894– , already noticed above.

Collections

No reprint collection devoted solely to Irish reports has yet been produced in volume form, though a selection of Irish reports held to be authoritative may be located in *The Revised Reports* (see page 147).

A micro-film edition of the earlier reports is in the course of preparation. This aims to include the series in Maxwell and Brown to 1900 and the main series to 1894.

Digests and Indexes

The purpose and construction of Irish law digests is identical with that of their English counterparts (see page 162) and require no additional exposition.

The earliest digest would seem to have been Finlay's *Digested index to all Irish reported cases in law and equity from the earliest period*, issued in 1830. This also included cases dealing with ecclesiastical and criminal law and a variety of original cases from authentic sources. Thereafter, numerous digests, analytical and otherwise were published, few aiming to be all inclusive and the majority fated to be superseded when rationalization of law reporting took place. Kinahan's *Digested index to the reports of . . . courts of equity in Ireland,* issued 1830 requires notice because it included cases upon appeals from Ireland to be found in the English Reports. Similarly, Millin's *Digest* of reported cases relating to petty sessions between 1875–98 is useful, since it contains seventeen unreported cases.

The first inclusive digest and one which remains unsuperseded was Brunker's *Digest of Cases Superior and other Courts of Common Law and Court of Admiralty from Sir J. Davies reports to the present time.* This was issued in 1865.

In 1879 was issued the first *Digest of Cases* published by the Incorporated Council of Law Reporting for Ireland and covering the period 1867–77. Two extension volumes were issued, the first in 1890, covering 1867–88, the second in 1899 covering 1867–93. In 1899 another digest was issued for the period 1894–8 and digests have continued to be issued to date covering consecutive periods of time, not always decennially. The most recent, issued in 1974, covers the period 1959–70. In 1921 the *Digest of Cases,* by arrangement included also cases printed in the *Irish Law Times* and *New Irish Jurist* (subsequently the *Irish Jurist*), while as from 1930 the *Digest of Cases* has also included, by arrangement, the *Northern Ireland Law Reports.* It is now therefore a digest to all reported cases in the geographical area of Ireland.

The *Irish Jurist* digest, edited by Blackham in 1852, digested cases in volumes 11–13 of the *Irish Law Reports,* the first volume of the new series and volumes 2–4 of the *Irish Jurist.*

The *Irish Law Times Digest of Cases,* compiled by Stubbs, covering cases reported in the *Irish Law Times Reports* and the *Irish Law Times and Solicitors Journal* for the period 1867–1903, was published 1895–1905 in two volumes, and as with the 'official' *Digest of Cases* noted above, employed the same system of arrangement as that which was adopted by the Incorporated Council of Law Reporting of England and Wales.

As with Scottish cases, a selection of Irish cases, usually those of a persuasive nature, are digested in English publications such as *The English and Empire Digest.*

The English *Current Law* (see page 164) contains a section on Northern Ireland, but also contains references to cases of a persuasive nature reported in *The Irish Jurist, The Irish Law*

Times and *The Irish Reports*, as well as *Northern Ireland Land Tribunal Decisions* and *Northern Ireland Law Reports*.

Tables of cases will be found also in the annual *Current Law Year Book* and in the annual notices of the IR and NILR.

Noting-up

The general principle regarding the noting-up of cases is identical with that for English material. Reference should be made to the indexes of the appropriate digests noticed above, as well as to the *English and Empire Digest* (see page 164).

The Current Law Citator should also be consulted. This contains every Irish decision of a persuasive nature digested in *Current Law* since 1947.

THE CHANNEL ISLANDS

Jersey

The principal court is the Royal Court of Jersey whose more recent decisions will be found published in *Judgments of the Royal Court of Jersey and of the Court of Appeal of Jersey*, 1950– . These are issued in part-form; the two most recent volumes cover 1950–66 and 1967–9 respectively. There were no printed reports prior to 1950, but a classified summary of decisions has been issued since 1885, entitled *Table des décisions de la Cour Royale*, 1885– , issued in ten volumes, 1896– .

Appeals lie to the Privy Council and a number of decisions relative to Jersey will be found in *Ordres du conseil et pièces analogues enregistrés à Jersey*, edited by H. M. Godfray and A. Messeroy, 1536–1867, issued in six volumes, 1897–1906.

Guernsey

In 1814 was published *Causes heard and determined at St Peter Port in the Island of Guernsey before . . . His Majesty's Commissioners, 16 October to 20 December, 1607*. With this exception no reports of decisions have been printed.

In 1961 a Court of Appeal was set up to obviate the necessity of carrying appeals to the Privy Council, though such access still remains if needed.

THE ISLE OF MAN

The principal civil court is the High Court of Justice, which includes Chancery and Common Law divisions, together with a Court of Appeal. The principal criminal court is the Court of General Gaol Delivery. Appeals in civil and criminal cases lie to the Privy Council's Judicial Committee.

No law reports are published, but indexed records are maintained in the General Registry at Douglas and cases may be located also in the Island's newspapers. In 1948, there was published Farrant's *Digest of Manx cases heard and decided during the period, 1925–47*. The more important decisions on appeal will be found in the relevant series of English law reports.

Early cases, however, may be found in Talbot's *Manorial Roll of the Isle of Man*, issued 1924 and covering the period 1511–15, and in Bluett's *The Advocate's Notebook, being notes and minutes of cases heard before the judicial tribunals of the Isle of Man*, 1847.

TRIALS

Under this head come verbatim reports of the proceedings of actions in the civil and criminal courts. These by definition cannot be classed as law reports. The printed transcripts have normally been abridged, but will include counsel's opening and closing speeches, examinations-in-chief and cross-examination of witnesses, concluding with the judgment or sentence of the court. Being verbatim reports they are of value to practising lawyers, legal historians and students of advocacy. But they are not to be confused with works about trials which are narrative accounts, subjectively written, usually more concerned with the crime or cause of action than the trial itself. Dependent upon their importance, such cases may or may not be found reported elsewhere. It is unfortunate that there exists in print no adequate bibliography of this material.

Civil

Reports of civil actions are usually issued as individual works.

Publication (at its height in the eighteenth and nineteenth centuries) may be general or private. It may originate at the instigation of one of the interested parties; a legal journalist may be concerned to draw attention to the state of the law; or an editor be commissioned to record an historic event. The proceedings in the case of the *City of Manchester v. Manchester Palace of Varieties*, heard in the High Court of Chivalry in 1954 and published by the Heraldry Society, are an example.

Criminal

Reports of criminal actions, issued either in collections or as individual works, far outweigh civil actions, since public demand inevitably encourages the promotion of private gain. Criminal pamphlets and broadsides, allegedly relating the life, trial and execution of notorious criminals had been printed as early as the time of Elizabeth I. Enduring through the seventeenth and eighteenth centuries, they influenced the compilation of a number of remarkable works, some of which are noticed below. Attention however must first be given to the availability of official material.

The principal judicial records relating to the higher criminal jurisdiction are held in manuscript by the House of Lords' Record Office.

For printed records relating to proceedings in impeachment, reference should be made to the *Journals of the House of Lords*, 1621–1806. This run also contains related documents such as articles of impeachment, answers of the accused, and petitions and orders. For evidential documents, 1617–1795, not printed, reference must be made to the original manuscripts. The judgments, 1621–1806 are included in the *Journals* and reprinted in various collections of state trials as noted below.

For records of proceedings relating to the trials of peers, reference must again be made to the *Journals of the House of Lords*, 1678–1935. These also contain related records – petitions, 1641–1776, orders of the House, 1641–1935, writs of certiorari and commissions appointing the Lord High Steward, 1678–1935, indictments and inquisitions for the same period, and miscellaneous petitions and orders, 1641–1935. For recognizances of witnesses, not printed, reference must be made to the original manuscripts. The proceedings of peerage trials were ordered to be printed in 1693. For accounts of trials to 1776, see the various collections of state trials as noted below. For trials from 1841 reference should be made to the House of Lords sessional papers. It should be noted that the privilege of peers to be tried by the Lords was abolished by statute in 1948.

Though numerous works with titles which include the wording State Trials have been published, the term is most commonly used with reference to the collection initially edited by Thomas Salmon and issued in 1719. Of this work four editions were published, the last by Francis Hargrave. The best-known edition, based on Hargrave, is that credited to the two Howells: *Complete Collection of State Trials and Proceedings for High Treason*, edited by T. B. Howell and T. J. Howell, 33 volumes, 1809–26. This includes cases from 1163 to 1820. In fact, the first twelve volumes were edited by W. Cobbett, who is seldom credited except by professional bibliographers. This edition was continued by a new series in eight volumes, covering 1820–58 and issued 1888–98. In general, the trials record the prosecutions of notable English, Scottish and Irish personages, are of historic as well as legal interest and deal not only with impeachments, treason, sedition and other criminal matters, but also with cases of constitutional and public concern. The cases are chronologically arranged. Not all are strictly verbatim reports, the earliest ones being based on chronicles, histories and records. The proved reliability of the work, however, has given it a semi-official status and it is so regarded.

The Old Bailey Session Papers, 1729–1834, issued in seventy-six volumes, 1730–1834, were continued by the *Central Criminal Court Session Papers*, 1834–1913, issued in 158 volumes, 1834–1913. Together these remarkable series illustrate the work of the court and of criminal justice over a period of 140 years.

Of commercial publications the following require special notice: the *Notable British Trials* series, comprising eighty-four volumes under the general editorship of J. H. Hodge and issued 1905–59. Each volume deals with an individual action and the series (unnumbered) covers cases heard 1586–1953. The majority are criminal, but some civil actions are included. The series incorporates the *Notable Scottish Trials*, originally a separate series, of which a number of volumes were issued, distinguished by their own series title and a distinctive green binding. Later editions of the Scottish series were re-issued in the NBT format. A supplementary series under the same general editorship was issued after 1945, dealing with selected *War Crimes Trials* held under British jurisdiction and published in nine volumes, 1948–52. For detailed information relating to these and other war crimes trials reference should be made to the *History of the United Nations War Crimes Commission*, compiled by the Commission, issued by HMSO in 1948. This details the trials held, names of defendants, the courts' decisions and dates of sentences, as required.

In general, individually issued and commercially-backed reports of proceedings contain introductory essays of variable length and quality. Often, though not in the NBT, the verbatim passages are of the briefest and are linked by editorial commentaries.

For information on published criminal cases, refer to Sir J. Cummings' *Contribution towards a Bibliography dealing with Crime and Cognate Subjects*, 1935. The section entitled 'criminal trials' does not unfortunately differentiate between commentaries and transcripts. For summary details of newsworthy crimes and trials, refer to the relevant annual volume of *Whitaker's Almanack*; for details on published English, Scottish and Irish trials and causes, refer also to the subject indexes in the relevant volumes of Sweet and Maxwell's *Legal Bibliography*.

FURTHER READING

LAW REPORTING

Burrow, R. Law Reporting. *Law Quarterly Review*, vol. 58, no. 1, 1942, pp. 96–106.
Goodhart, A. L. Reporting the Law. *Law Quarterly Review*, vol. 55, no. 1, 1939, pp. 29–34. A reasoned attack by a distinguished jurist upon the current system of reporting.
Great Britain. Lord Chancellor's Office. *Report of the Lord Chancellor's Committee on Law Reporting*. HMSO, 1940.
Lindley, Lord. History of the Law Reports. *Law Quarterly Review*, vol. 1, no. 2, 1885, pp. 137–49. A review of Daniel, in which the author formulates principles of contemporary law reporting.

Mews, J. The Present System of Law Reporting. *Law Quarterly Review*, vol. 9, no. 2, 1893, pp. 179–87.

Moran, C. G. *Heralds of the Law*. Stevens, 1948. The best work on the responsibilities of the reporter and the composition of a modern report.

Mechanical Recording

Great Britain. Lord Chancellor's Office. *Report of a Working Party on Recording Court Proceedings*. HMSO, 1972 (SBN 11 390157 7).

MODERN REPORTS

Daniel, W. T. S. *History and Origin of the Law Reports*. Clones, 1884, reprint Wildy, 1968.

Pollock, F. English Law Reporting. *Law Quarterly Review*, vol. 19, no. 4, 1903, pp. 451–60. A critical assessment of *The Law Reports*.

NOMINATE REPORTS

Abbott, L. W. *Law Reporting in England, 1485–1585*. University of London, Athlone Press, 1973 (*University of London legal series, 10*) (ISBN 0 485 13410 1).

Holdsworth, W. S. *History of English Law*, various editions. Methuen, 1936–72, 17 vols. Vols. 5, pp. 355–78 and 6, pp. 531–73 and 617–19 (1485–1700) contain an assessment of the reports, with accounts of the reporters; vol. 12 (1701–1875) deals with reports and abridgments at pp. 101–78; vol. 13 (1701–1875) contains a section on the courts, with special reference to tribunals at pp. 181–7, and a section on the reports at pp. 424–43, with a list of authorized reporters at pp. 427–31; vol. 15 (1832–75) at pp. 248–75 deals with reports, abridgments, digests, indexes and collections of cases.

Pollock, F. *First Book of Jurisprudence*. 6th edition. Macmillan, 1929. Chapter 5 deals with the history of the reports, and Chapter 6 with the relation of one judicial decision to another.

Veeder, V. V. The English Reports. *Harvard Law Review*, vol. 15, 1901–2, pp. 1–25 (reprinted in *Select Essays in Anglo-American Legal History*, compiled by a Committee of the Association of American Law Schools, vol. 2, Boston, Mass., Little, Brown, 1908, pp. 123–68).

Wallace, J. W. *The Reporters*. 4th edition [by] F. F. Head, Boston, Mass., Soule and Bugbee, 1882. Gives bibliographical data, with critical assessments of the reporters to the time of George III.

Winfield, P. H. *Chief Sources of English Legal History*. Cambridge, Mass., Harvard University Press, 1925, reprinted 1962. Chapter 7,

'Case Law', contains a valuable assessment of some of the early reporters.

ADMINISTRATIVE TRIBUNALS

Way, D. J. Tribunals: an Outline of the Literature. *Law Librarian*, vol. 3, no. 1, 1972, pp. 10–14.

SCOTTISH REPORTS

[Hannay, R.] *Letter to the dean of the Faculty of Advocates relative to a plan which has been proposed for reporting the decisions of the court of session.* Edinburgh, Bell and Bradfute, 1823.

[Hannay, R.] *Address to the Right Hon. Lord President Hope and to members of the college of justice on the method of collecting and reporting decisions.* Edinburgh, David Brown, 1821.

Leadbetter, J. S. The printed law reports. In *Sources and Literature of Scots Law.* Edinburgh, Stair Society, 1936. *Stair Society*, 1, pp. 57–8.

Smith, T. B. *Scotland.* In Keeton, G. W. and Lloyd, D. *The British Commonwealth: The United Kingdom*, vol. 11. Stevens, 1962. Appendix D contains a detailed list of case reports. This work is identical with the author's *A Short Commentary on the Law of Scotland.* Green, 1962.

Tait, W. *Index to decisions, Court of Session, in the original collections and in Morison's Dictionary of decisions.* Edinburgh, William Tait, 1823. Contains 30 pages of valuable notes on reporters and reporting in Scotland.

Walker, D. M. *The Scottish Legal System.* 3rd edition. Edinburgh, Green, 1969 (ISBN 0 414 00508 2). Chapter 11, Repositories of the law, at pages 437–46, is especially valuable.

IRISH REPORTS

O'Higgins, P. *Bibliography of Periodical Literature Relating to Irish Law.* Northern Ireland Legal Quarterly Inc., Belfast, 1966; and supp. 1974. Contains a section on law reports and reporting in Ireland. There is no legal literature of any substance on Irish law reports and reporting.

TRIALS

Bond, M. F. *Guide to the Records of Parliament.* HMSO, 1971 (ISBN 0 11 700351 4). Invaluable for information on original material.

Langan, P. St J. Irish material in the State Trials. *Northern Ireland Law Quarterly*, vol. 18, 1967, pp. 428–36; vol. 19, 1968, pp. 48–53, 189–97, 299–309.

5. Secondary Sources

D. J. WAY, MA, FLA
Sub-Librarian, University of Liverpool (Faculty of Law)

D. J. WAY, MA, FLA
Sub-Librarian, University of Liverpool (Faculty of Law)

TEXTBOOKS

The place of textbooks in legal literature

The distinction between a textbook and a primary source is well defined in a popular work for law students: 'A textbook differs from a statute or a law report in that it is not an original literary source of law. Textbooks, even if of the highest author-ity, contain only opinions as to the state of the law. In short they are descriptive rather than creative.' (Walker, R. J. and Walker, M. G. *The English Legal System*, 3rd edition, 1972, p. 144).

There are, however, two types of textbooks, viewed as sources of law. The first type are the so-called 'books of authority', the last of which is generally agreed to be Black-stone's *Commentaries on the Laws of England* in the mid-eighteenth century, and the second type are modern textbooks. Most of the books of authority were written by judges, and many of them appeared before law reporting had been fully developed; they are therefore accorded intrinsic authority in their own right. They are described in more detail on pages 248–9. A modern textbook, on the other hand, to quote Walker and Walker again (p. 144), 'is not a source of law and is only of use in that it indicates where a direct source, such as a statute or a law report, may be found'.

Judicial attitudes to textbooks

The judicial attitude to textbooks has been illustrated most clearly in recent years in the case *Cordell v. Second Clanfield Properties Ltd*, in Mr Justice Megarry's judgment reported at [1969] 2 Ch. 9. Counsel had quoted to Mr Justice Megarry a passage from his own book (Megarry, R. E. and Wade, H. W. R. *The Law of Real Property*, 3rd edition, 1966), written before he became a judge. After making the point that words in a book written or subscribed to by an author who was or became a judge had the same value as words written by any other reputable author, neither more nor less, Mr Justice Megarry continued: 'I would, therefore, give credit to the words of any reputable author in book or article as expressing tenable and arguable ideas, as fertilizers of thought, and as conveniently expressing the fruits of research in print, often in apt and persuasive language. But I would do no more than that, and in particular I would expose those views to the testing and refining process of argument. Today, as of old, by good disputing shall the law be well known.'

It has been pointed out by legal writers that judges have not hesitated on several occasions to set aside statements in long-established textbooks, where they felt that these were inaccurate. To take only one example, the House of Lords in *R. v. Button and Swain* [1966] A.C. 591, drew attention to errors in Archbold's *Pleading, Evidence and Practice in Criminal Cases* and in Russell on *Crimes and Misdemeanors*, both standard works. On the other hand, there have been many more occasions on which statements in textbooks have been approved by the courts, and in particular the old practice that a living author must not be cited in court is no longer valid. Both Walker and Walker (p. 148) and Hood Phillips (*A First Book of English Law*, 6th edition, 1970, pp. 227–30) give several examples of cases in which statements by both textbook writers and the writers of articles in legal periodicals have been accepted by the courts in their own lifetime. Indeed, the law is changing so rapidly at present that it would be strange if a dead author were to be preferred to a living one.

Some features of legal textbooks

Practitioners' books and students' books

In general, legal textbooks are published at two levels – there are practitioners' books and students' books. The two levels are distinguished very obviously by their depth of treatment of the subject, and hence by their size and price. There is also a less obvious internal distinction. Practitioners' books are intended for reference and for consultation, rather than for continuous reading. Students' books, on the other hand, are meant for continuous reading, and are likely to contain much clearer statements of principle. The distinction is well set out by Lord Denning (then Sir Alfred Denning) in a review of Winfield's *Textbook of the Law of Tort* in the *Law Quarterly Review*, vol. 63, 1947, p. 516. It can, however, easily become blurred. Gibson's *Conveyancing*, for example, is regarded primarily as a students' textbook, and it has appeared as such on lists issued by the Council of Legal Education and the College of Law; but it is also sufficiently detailed to be referred to by many practitioners in their early years.

As regards external appearance, practitioners' books, which are intended to last four or five years with the aid of supplements, are normally still bound in hardback. Students' textbooks on the other hand have become almost exclusively paperback during the past few years, only sufficient hardback copies being bound to meet the expected sale to libraries.

Authorship

As already mentioned, it was the practice at one time that a living author could not be cited in court, and perhaps it is on this account that so many legal textbooks still bear the names of their original authors, even though these may have long since been dead and gone. For instance, the original author of Woodfall's *Law of Landlord and Tenant*, now in its 27th edition, died as long ago as 1806. In contrast, however, it is becoming increasingly usual nowadays for new legal authors to write under their own names and even to usurp the place of past favourites. Thus, Lushington's *Law of Affiliation and Bastardy* was replaced by Chislett's *Affiliation Proceedings*, and Burnett's *Elements of Conveyancing* by Bowman and Tyler's *Elements of Conveyancing*, a deliberate decision being made by the publisher in each case to make a new start rather than to continue with extra editions of an already existing work.

The credentials of the author – that is, stating whether he is a barrister or a solicitor – normally appear on the title page.

Books by authors with only academic qualifications are unlikely to commend themselves to practitioners.

The preface

The preface of a legal textbook always repays investigation. In the case of a completely new title, the author will use the preface to say what he is trying to do, while in a new edition of an old title, he will mention in it what has been excised or replaced and what has been retained, and will often summarize briefly the main changes in the subject of the book since the last edition. At the end of the preface, or immediately following it, there is usually the all-important statement giving the date up to which all new developments in the law have been covered by the book. This is naturally more important than the date on the title page, since there is always a certain lapse of time between completion of the work and publication.

The tables of cases and statutes

A textbook should always have full tables of cases and statutes, and nothing so much marks off the second rank of law publishers as their tendency to economize in this respect. A table of statutes may either be alphabetical or chronological, but ideally should always give the correct citations of the Acts concerned, as well as their short titles. A table of cases ideally should give, not only the title of the case and the page reference to it in the textbook, but also the full reference back to where it is reported in the original. A table of abbreviations is also often desirable, especially for textbooks which cite cases from unfamiliar law reports belonging to other jurisdictions.

Arrangements for keeping textbooks up-to-date

Keeping a work up-to-date is as important from the point of view of the author or publisher as from that of the librarian, since, once a work has lost its freshness, sales will drop and the stocks remaining in the publisher's hands will lose their value. There are several methods that a publisher may use, in order to keep up-to-date.

7

New editions

The publisher may, first of all, print new editions of his works much more frequently, possibly putting them on an annual basis. This can be done where changes in the law are frequent and continuous, so that sufficient copies can be sold of each edition to make the exercise worthwhile. Examples that come to mind are the various practice books (see page 202). A standard students' textbook that has also started to come out annually is *Revenue Law*, by Barry Pinson, published by Sweet and Maxwell (one edition a year from the 4th edition 1970 onwards). Revenue law is a subject that is constantly changing with each year's Finance Act and at the same time this particular book is prescribed reading for The Law Society's examinations on the subject, so that a new edition each year is economically possible.

Supplements

For practitioners' books as a whole, new editions each year are not economically possible. They represent a much larger investment to their purchasers than students' books, since the price of many of them (due to inflation) now runs into double figures in pounds. Also, whereas there is a new generation of students to study revenue law each year, the market for new editions of practitioners' books only changes and grows slowly. Hence, the most favoured method of keeping practitioners' books up-to-date is to issue a paperback supplement, which is only a fraction of the price of the original hardback volume. A space for insertion of the supplement is often left at the end of the volume, so that the two may be carried together as one unit. The supplement is arranged with chapter or key numbers similar to those in the original volume, so that reference to it for new developments may be quickly made. Supplements of many textbooks now appear on an annual basis; each issue is cumulative, so that the earlier supplement may be discarded on receiving the later one. For the checking and ordering of supplements, see page 492.

Loose-leaf format

In some subjects, even the method of issuing an annual paper-

back supplement is not sufficient to keep a book adequately up-
to-date. In these cases, the legal publishers have taken to issuing
whole works in a loose-leaf form, which can then be kept up-to-
date by periodically inserting and discarding pages according
to the instructions supplied. Usually fresh sets of pages with
instructions are sent out three or four times a year for this type
of work, occasionally (as with De Voil's *Value Added Tax*)
rather more frequently. These loose-leaf works comprise a
special genre of textbook (see page 199). For the servicing of
loose-leaf books, see page 487.

Special types of books

Encyclopedias

Encyclopedic works covering the whole of the law of England
in a single volume or series of volumes are nothing new, and they
can be traced back historically to the first abridgments (see
page 247). The outstanding representative today of the legal
encyclopedia is *Halsbury's Laws of England*, which has entered
its fourth edition. This work owed its origin to Stanley Shaw
Bond, of Messrs Butterworth's, who conceived the idea of a
collection of writings covering the whole range of English law
by the best legal minds of the day, with the Lord Chancellor as
editor-in-chief. By great pertinacity, he persuaded the then
Lord Chancellor, Lord Halsbury, to lend his name to the
project, and the volumes of the first edition started to appear in
1907.

The fourth edition of Halsbury, following the same basic
pattern, started to appear in 1973, and the full work of 56
volumes is expected to be complete within nine years. Again
the then Lord Chancellor, Lord Hailsham, agreed to be editor-
in-chief. As in previous editions, the whole of the law will be
covered, subjects which are likely to develop a great deal in the
near future (such as European Community law) being relega-
ted to the later volumes. Again, as in previous editions,
elaborate arrangements are being made for keeping up-to-date,
including an annual cumulative supplement, a monthly current
service issue, interim indexes, and replacement of individual
outdated volumes, if this seems necessary. A good description

of the planning and early progress of the fourth edition may be read in the *Law Society's Gazette*, vol. 70, 1973, p. 1839.

Halsbury's Laws of England is encyclopedic in scope, but in its internal arrangement it contains fewer and therefore broader subject headings than the conventional non-legal encyclopedia. In the fourth edition, for instance, the list of subjects begins with the new title *Administrative Law*. There are copious references to authorities after each paragraph, and the work is so comprehensive that it has been said that a legal office could if necessary function on Halsbury alone, which is more than could be said for any other single work. Fig. 1 shows a sample page from the fourth edition.

In the law library, Halsbury fills a key position. It plays a useful role for the librarian as the first port of call for any legal enquiry, of which the precise subject is not immediately apparent. Halsbury is especially useful to the novice law librarian, in suggesting to him the headings under which he should look for further information on any subject requested, and can thus help out in areas where the subject index of the law library may be deficient.

One other general legal encyclopedia, namely, Green's *Encyclopaedia of the Laws of Scotland*, is described on page 211.

Precedent books

In law libraries frequented by practitioners, precedent books are among the most used items. A lawyer who has, for example, to prepare a conveyance or a will does not have to draft the wording out of his head afresh each time. Instead, he can take a standard form from the book, and if necessary adapt it to the circumstances of the particular case. Requests for precedents can therefore arise quite often in practitioners' law libraries; some may be easy to find, while others may need a considerable amount of research. It is of course possible that there may be no particular precedent at all for the situation that the enquirer has in mind, but naturally every possible source must be checked before one can come to that conclusion. The following are some of the main collections of precedents, that can be tried in such an enquiry.

The Encyclopaedia of Forms and Precedents, 4th edition, 1964–73,

1. INTRODUCTION

(1) SCOPE AND NATURE OF THE SUBJECT

1. Scope. For the purposes of this work, administrative law[1] is understood to mean the law relating to the discharge of functions of a public nature in government and administration. It includes[2] functions of public authorities and officers and of special tribunals[3], judicial review of the exercise of those functions, the civil liability and legal protection of those purporting to exercise them and aspects of the means whereby extra-judicial redress may be obtainable at the instance of persons aggrieved.

1 For at least half a century after the publication of Dicey's Law of the Constitution (1st Edn) (1885), the term "administrative law" was identified with *droit administratif*, a separate body of rules relating to administrative authorities and officials, applied in special administrative courts. As thus defined, administrative law did not exist in England: see Dicey's Law of the Constitution (10th Edn) 330. See also *Re Grosvenor Hotel, London (No. 2)* [1965] Ch 1210 at 1261, [1964] 3 All ER 354 at 372, CA, per Salmon LJ; but see *Ridge v Baldwin* [1964] AC 40 at 72, [1963] 2 All ER 66 at 76, HL, per Lord Reid ("We do not have a developed system of administrative law—perhaps because until fairly recently we did not need it"), and *Breen v Amalgamated Engineering Union* [1971] 2 QB 175 at 189, [1971] 1 All ER 1148 at 1153, CA, per Lord Denning MR (". . . there have been important developments in the last twenty-two years which have transformed the situation. It may truly now be said that we have a developed system of administrative law").
2 Particular aspects of administrative law will be considered in more detail in other titles: see e.g. COMPULSORY ACQUISITION; CONSTITUTIONAL LAW; CROWN PROCEEDINGS; EDUCATION; EMPLOYMENT; HOUSING; LOCAL GOVERNMENT; LONDON GOVERNMENT; NATIONAL HEALTH; STATUTES; TOWN AND COUNTRY PLANNING.
3 Some special statutory tribunals dealing with private law relationships between landlord and tenant (agricultural land tribunals (see AGRICULTURE, paras. 1720-1724, post), rent assessment committees, rent tribunals (see LANDLORD AND TENANT)) are commonly styled "administrative" tribunals.

2. The principle of legality. The exercise of governmental authority directly affecting individual interests must rest on legitimate foundations[1]. For example, powers exercised by the Crown, its ministers and central government departments must be derived, directly or indirectly[2], from statute, common law or the royal prerogative[3]; and the ambit of those powers is determinable by the courts save insofar as their jurisdiction has been excluded by unambiguous statutory language[4]. The Executive does not enjoy a general or inherent rule-making or regulatory power, except in relation to the internal functioning of the central administrative hierarchy[5], though ministerial announcements[6] and departmental circulars[7] intended to influence or direct the conduct of public affairs in matters affecting individual interests are not uncommon[8]. Nor, in general, can state necessity be relied on to support the existence of a power or duty[9], or to justify deviations from lawful authority[10]. Moreover, in the absence of express statutory authority, public duties cannot normally be waived or dispensed with by administrative action for the benefit of members of the public[11].

1 This proposition is one aspect of the doctrine of the rule of law: see CONSTITUTIONAL LAW.
2 Indirectly, in the case of statutory instruments, byelaws and other subordinate legislation. As to statutory instruments generally, see STATUTES. As to the power of local authorities to make bye-laws, see LOCAL GOVERNMENT.
3 See CONSTITUTIONAL LAW.
4 As to ouster of jurisdiction, see para. 22, post.
5 See, however, *R v Criminal Injuries Compensation Board, ex parte Lain* [1967] 2 QB 864, [1967] 2 All ER 770, DC, where the court was prepared to accord legal redress to a person aggrieved by

Figure 1

known familiarly as the *Encyclopaedia*, contains 24 volumes in all. Of these, two volumes each are devoted to company law, landlord and tenant, and sale of land. Other topics in which the *Encyclopaedia* is strong, and which may be the subject of frequent enquiries, include agency documents, goodwill, service contracts, and wills.

The *Encyclopaedia* does not cover litigation, and this is taken care of by the parallel work, *Atkin's Encyclopaedia of Court Forms in Civil Proceedings*, 2nd edition, 1961–73, known familiarly as 'Atkin'. It may be noted that some titles already seen in the *Encyclopaedia* recur in Atkin, for instance, companies or landlord and tenant. Whereas the precedents in the *Encyclopaedia* include the original draft agreements under the respective subject headings, those in Atkin cover situations where litigation has intruded. For instance, the landlord and tenant section of the *Encyclopaedia* contains numerous specimen leases, whereas this section in Atkin contains actions for breach of agreement for a lease. The heading for divorce in Atkin has been especially well used, and the volume on divorce was re-issued in 1969.

There are many other precedent books covering smaller and more specialized fields than these two giant works, which naturally cannot all be described in detail. Quite apart from books with the word 'precedent' in the title, precedents on specific subjects can often be found in textbooks on those subjects. Sometimes, the precedents may be hidden away in an appendix, but are none the less useful. Examples that come to mind, for instance, are *Terrell on the Law of Patents*, and Potter and Monroe's *Tax Planning*. In assessing the usefulness of a legal textbook, therefore, a factor to be taken into account is the presence or otherwise of an appendix of precedents relating to the subject.

Some journals also include precedents. *The Conveyancer*, a journal published six times a year, was especially noted for its section on precedents, which included a high proportion of unusual precedents. For instance, it was at one time the first place in which one could find precedents on such new topics as the sale of flats or the sale of industrial know-how. More recently, these precedents have been taken out of the body of the journal and transferred to a separate loose-leaf publication (of the type described in the next section), called *Precedents for the Conveyancer*.

The *New Law Journal* also publishes precedents from time to time on its 'Practitioner' pages, and these are indexed at the end of each year's set of issues. These precedents, like those formerly contained in *The Conveyancer,* enable the practitioner to keep abreast of new situations not yet provided for in the textbooks. For instance, the *New Law Journal* published promptly a set of the forms prescribed for use in the National Industrial Relations Court under the Industrial Relations Act 1971.

Loose-leaf encyclopedias

Loose-leaf encyclopedias, which have already been mentioned briefly on page 195, are now sufficiently numerous to warrant inclusion as a separate class of work. *Simon's Taxes,* previously *Simon's Income Tax,* was one of the first textbooks to go partly loose-leaf, no doubt because revenue law is especially susceptible to frequent and unpredictable changes. Since then, Messrs Sweet and Maxwell in particular have adopted this type of work with enthusiasm and have published a whole range of loose-leaf encyclopedias in the *Local government library* series, covering not only revenue law, but also housing law, road traffic law, town and country planning, compulsory purchase and compensation, highways, factories and offices, public health, and labour relations.

Each encyclopedia contains all the Acts, Statutory Instruments and ministerial circulars relating to its subjects. To take one example, the *Encyclopedia of the Law of Town and Country Planning* contains five parts in its three volumes. These parts contain respectively a general statement of the law relating to town and country planning, statutes pre-1968 (so far as they are still in force), statutes post-1967, rules and orders (*ie,* Statutory Instruments relating to the subject), ministerial circulars, and decisions of selected planning appeals. Each of these parts is preceded by a complete list of contents, and there is an index to the whole work in each of the three volumes.

The releases containing new material to be inserted in the various loose-leaf encyclopedias in most cases come out three or four times a year. Examples are shown in Figs. 2 and 3 of two of the sheets of instructions accompanying these releases. Usually, the instructions simply provide, as the examples show,

SIMON'S TAXES—THIRD EDITION
Issue 13

To facilitate filing, the number of pages has been kept to the minimum necessary. We want you to have the maximum benefit from your set of Simon's Taxes so in your interests as well as our own we ask you to follow these instructions carefully.

SUBSCRIBERS ARE REMINDED ALWAYS TO REFER TO THE SERVICE SHEETS AT THE FRONT OF EACH VOLUME.

If issues have not been received, or pages are missing, write to Subscription Records Dept., Butterworths, 88 Kingsway, London WC2B 6AB, or telephone Mr. Peters 01-405 6900 ext. 346.

In the event of filing difficulty only, telephone Editorial Dept., 01 405 6900 ext. 305.

FILING INSTRUCTIONS

For method of operating binder, see pages 999-1000.

Before filing, ensure that page 1 in each volume is marked "*Issue* 12"; if not, file all previous issues in correct order.

Use the list which follows, otherwise you may fail to remove certain pages, and you may insert pages in the wrong place.

Page numbers are printed at the bottom of every page; ignore article numbers.

	REMOVE Number of old leaves	INSERT Number of new leaves		REMOVE Number of old leaves	INSERT Number of new leaves
Volume A			**Volume C—***contd.*		
pages			447–448	1	1
1–2	1	1	891–892	1	1
21–100	8	9	897·1–900	2	2
507–508	1. ·	1	919–930	1	1
	10			32	
Volume B					
pages			**Volume D**		
1–2	1	1	pages		
21–100	13	13	1–2	1	1
411–412	1	1	21–100	4	4
431–440	2	2	175–178	2	2
561–564	2	3	367–368	1	1
573–580	1	1	813–820	3	4
	20			11	
Volume C					
pages			**Volume E**		
1–2	1	1	pages		
21–100	15	16	1–2	1	1
429–440	11	14	21–100	16	16

Figure 2

	Destroy Old Pages	Insert New Pages
Pt. 3—Specific Employments		
	3077	3077
	3153–3154/3	3153–3154/3
	3415–3416 3421–3422	3415–3416 3421–3422
	3555–3592	3555–3592
Do not destroy *p. 3626/1*	3625–3626* *3626/3–3631 3643–3644 3666/1–3671 3681–3682	3625–3626 3626/3–3631 3643–3644 3666/1–3671 3681–3682
	3703	3703
Pt. 4—Rules and Orders		
	4001–4002 4005–4006 4047–4048	4001–4002 4005–4006 4047–4048
	4257–4258 4293	4257–4258 4293–4305
Pt. 5—Wages Councils		
	5001–5006 5015–5018 5035–5036 5073–5076 5089–5994	5001–5006 5015–5017 5035–5036 5073–5075 5089–5994
Pt. 6—Industrial Training		
	6005–6102	6005–6102
Pt. 7—Cases		
	7077 7096/1–7096/2	7077 7096/1–7096/2
	7100/101	7100/101
	7309	7309–7310
	7471	7471
	7555	7555–7556
	7792/5	7792/5
	7831	7831
	8000/1	

[Release 16: 27-i-75.]

Figure 3

for the insertion of new pages and taking out of the corresponding old pages; the latter are then to be destroyed after checking, as provided for in the instructions. One or two loose-leaf works issued by HMSO include further complications; here, there are occasionally little slips to be gummed in where it is deemed inappropriate to issue a whole new page, and occasionally there are also instructions for annotations to be written in by hand. The commercial publishers have fortunately omitted these additional refinements.

The advantages of loose-leaf encyclopedias are obvious, as are the disadvantages. If they are kept up-to-date, they often provide the most recent material available on their respective subjects. Their arrangement is usually so clear that it is often easier to trace Acts and Statutory Instruments on a subject through its loose-leaf encyclopedia (if it has one), than through the official publications described in Chapter 3. The compensating disadvantage of loose-leaf works is the amount of staff time swallowed up in their periodic servicing.

A good article on loose-leaf publications, which incidentally shows that the problem is an international one, is 'Publications à feuilles mobiles' by H. R. W. Gokkel in the *International Association of Law Libraries Bulletin*, no. 26, May 1971, page 3.

Practice books

Practice books form another sub-division under the general heading of textbooks, and like precedent books are used especially in law libraries devoted to the needs of practitioners. They usually appear annually, or alternatively have frequent supplements, and their purpose is to keep their users up-to-date in the practice of the courts.

The most important work of this genre is the *Supreme Court Practice*, sometimes known as the 'White Book', which now appears every three years, with a cumulative supplement every six months during the period in between editions. The *Supreme Court Practice* (formerly the *Annual Practice*) contains not only the revised text of the Rules of the Supreme Court, but also the prescribed forms, orders relating to court fees and stamps, practice directions, and other rules and orders sufficient to enable the practitioner to find his way through court procedure.

The *County Court Practice*, known sometimes as the 'Green

book', is the corresponding work for county court practice and procedure, and this appears annually.

Stone's Justices' Manual appears annually in three volumes, and contains a selection of the Acts most likely to be referred to in magistrates' courts, such as the Road Traffic Acts, the Betting, Gaming and Lotteries Act, and so on. A selection of relevant Statutory Instruments is included in an appendix. Because of the nature of its contents, Stone is one of the few law books suitable for use in a public reference library, since it covers those sections of the law that impinge most directly on the layman.

Paterson's Licensing Acts, which also appears annually, is devoted specifically to the needs of practitioners attending licensing sessions.

Finally, Archbold's *Pleading, Evidence and Practice in Criminal Cases* (38th edition, 1973), known more briefly as Archbold's *Criminal Pleading*, is the most comprehensive work on criminal practice. A new edition appears every three or four years, and in addition a cumulative supplement appears three times a year, and there is also a noter-up service.

Casebooks

So far, all the various types of books described have been devoted to the needs of practitioners. Casebooks, on the other hand, are designed especially to meet the needs of students and are more important in academic law libraries.

Although the so-called 'casebook' method of teaching law students originated in universities in America, casebooks as such have been published over a long period in this country, and owe nothing in their origin to transatlantic influence. The first edition of Smith's *Leading Cases*, for example, appeared as long ago as 1837. It would be true to say, however, that the use of casebooks has expanded in recent years, and university law faculties now generally expect their students to buy their own copies of these for their main subjects. The chief justification of the casebook is that the head-notes and the most relevant extracts from a whole series of reports can be placed together in one volume, together with comments by the editor, so enabling the students to have the materials which they need constantly to hand. Although ideally students should always pursue their references in the original reports, time in a university year is limited and the use of the casebook enables them to short-circuit this process – and, incidentally, also saves wear and tear on the original volumes of the reports in the library.

Publishers' series of casebooks are issued by Messrs Butterworth, Messrs Sweet and Maxwell, and by the Cambridge University Press. Although the general pattern of all of these is as described above, the proportion of a case that is reproduced can vary a great deal according to publishing policy and the decision of the individual editor. The most detailed casebooks are naturally the best to stock from the library point of view, but also the most expensive. It may be noted in this connection that the *Cambridge legal case book series*, published by Cambridge University Press, tends to include other materials than cases where appropriate, such as extracts from statutes and from White Papers.

Some casebooks are more abbreviated still. Instead of giving extracts from the originals, they merely give brief summaries by the editor of the cases concerned. These are essentially 'sweat books' for students, and are of little use from the point of view of libraries. Examples of this type of casebook include the *Cracknell's Law students' companion series* published by Messrs Butterworth and the *Concise college casenotes series* published by Messrs Sweet and Maxwell.

AUDIO-VISUAL MATERIALS

Legal textbooks are still based uncompromisingly on the printed word, and the use of audio-visual materials has been restricted to a few tentative experiments. One of these was the publication in 1970 of *The New Law of Estate Duty* by G. S. A. Wheatcroft. This was an audiotext live recording consisting of four double-sided long-playing records, accompanied by a sheet of instructions and a booklet. The last named contained examples and illustrations, and an outline of the course. This experiment met with some interest at the time, but does not seem to have caught on. The two main snags with this type of material, as was pointed out at the time in reviews in legal journals (*New Law Journal*, vol. 120, 1970, p. 931; *Solicitors' Journal*, vol. 114, 1970, p. 750), are the awkwardness of having to play back in order to go over specific points in the text again, and the difficulty of providing supplementation in this format. While, therefore, law librarians have accepted the use of photocopying and of microfilm as new techniques of making wanted materials available in their libraries, it is doubtful whether at present audio-visual materials have a similar role. For their use as a means of giving instruction to students in the use of the library, see page 459.

PERIODICALS

Periodicals rank after textbooks as an important secondary source of legal information. As with other subjects, so with law, periodicals are used for current professional news and as a means of disseminating the latest information well ahead of its appearance in book form. Additionally, some periodicals contain law reports, albeit abbreviated ones, which means that they have a continuing value.

Types of periodicals, by readership

Legal periodicals are best studied in connection with the audience at which they are aimed. Four types of audience are involved, namely, academic lawyers, practising lawyers, law students, and law librarians, and it will be seen that each group attracts different journals.

Academic lawyers

The main periodicals of interest to academic lawyers are the *Law Quarterly Review*, the *Modern Law Review* (published six times a year) and the *Cambridge Law Journal* (published twice a year). These appear relatively infrequently compared to practitioners' journals, and they contain long articles in depth and shorter notes on selected topics, but relatively little up-to-the-minute news. All have good book review sections, the usefulness of which is vitiated (for law librarians) by the fact that the books reviewed have often been published for a year or more before the reviews appear. Each of these journals covers the whole legal field, although there is a tendency for the *Modern Law Review* to concentrate more on socio-legal topics (for instance, it always contains a section headed 'Reports of Committees', with reviews of current White Papers), while the *Law Quarterly Review* is stronger in articles on legal history.

Also worthy of mention are the journals of the two professional associations for law teachers, namely, the *Journal of the Society of Public Teachers of Law* and *The Law Teacher*. Each of these has had to tread a careful balance between being just another legal journal on the one hand and being mainly a journal of teaching methods on the other hand. *The Law Teacher* has in fact been criticized at one stage by some of its readers for paying insufficient attention to the latter type of material (vol. 5, 1971, p. 226). The *Journal of the Society of Public Teachers of Law* has perhaps coped more successfully with this problem, and has also contained from time to time a number of features of especial interest to law librarians – for instance, it was chosen by the Society as the medium for publishing its *Statement of minimum library holdings for law libraries in England and Wales* (vol. 13, new series, no. 4, July 1975, p. 332).

Practising lawyers

The main periodicals of interest to practising lawyers are the *New Law Journal, Solicitors' Journal* and *Law Society's Gazette*, which all appear weekly. The type of information contained in all three of these follows a similar pattern. Each leads with editorial comments on current legal topics, and all contain articles on new legislation and other subjects (with a practising rather than an academic audience in mind), correspondence, book reviews, news about the profession, and practice sections.

The contents of these practice sections repay special investigation, as they contain useful reference aids. The *New Law Journal*, for instance, devotes the central section of each weekly issue to Practitioner pages printed on yellow paper. These contain details of the progress of parliamentary bills, appointed days for statutes, new Statutory Instruments, a digest of notes of reported cases, and from time to time new specimen precedents. (See Fig. 4.) In the *Solicitors' Journal*, there are somewhat similar pages with features headed Notes of Cases, Westminster and Whitehall, Points in Practice, Practice Directions and Notes and News. The *Law Society's Gazette* duplicates much of the same type of information in its practice pages, but in

NEW LAW JOURNAL, November 8, 1973   1013

The Practitioner

Practice in Direction–Admiralty Registrar 1014; Statutory Instruments 1014; Small Claims Forms 1015; Case Notes 1017; Precedent 1019.

H.M. LAND REGISTRY

Registration of Title Order 1973

An Order in Council, entitled The Registration of Title Order 1973 [SI 1973/1764] has been made extending the system of compulsory registration of title on sale of land to the whole of certain metropolitan and non-metropolitan districts which will come into existence on April 1, 1974 and which would otherwise be only partially subject thereto. The effect of the Order will be that compulsory registration will operate throughout the districts set out in the first column below as from the dates shown in the second column.

District	Date
Bolton	January 1, 1974
Bury	January 1, 1974
Coventry	March 1, 1974
Dudley	March 1, 1974
Kirklees	March 1, 1974
Leeds	March 1, 1974
Manchester	January 1, 1974
Middlesbrough	January 1, 1974
Newcastle upon Tyne	January 1, 1974
Northampton	January 1, 1974
Nottingham	January 1, 1974
Norwich	January 1, 1974
Oldham	January 1, 1974
Plymouth	January 1, 1974
Rochdale	January 1, 1974
St. Helens	March 1, 1974
Salford	January 1, 1974
Sheffield	March 1, 1974
Solihull	March 1, 1974
South Tyneside	January 1, 1974
Stockport	January 1, 1974
Sunderland	January 1, 1974
Tameside	January 1, 1974
Trafford	January 1, 1974
Walsall	January 1, 1974
Windsor & Maidenhead	January 1, 1974
Wirral	March 1, 1974

Throughout the above-mentioned districts conveyances on sale of freehold land, leases for not less than 40 years, assignments on sale of leasehold land having not less than 40 years to run, made in each case on and after the relevant date set out above, must be registered within two months of the date of the instrument.

The above-mentioned Order, which refers to the areas by their current descriptions, should be consulted for full details of the areas to which compulsory registration is being applied. The district land registries which serve each area are indicated in Explanatory Leaflet No. 9, which is updated as necessary.

Enquiries should be addressed to Theodore B.F. Ruoff, Esq., C.B., C.B.E., Chief Land Registrar, H.M. Land Registry, Lincoln's Inn Fields, London WC2A 3PH (Telephone 01-405 3488).

REVENUE LAW

Capital Duty —Letters· of Allotment

It has long been a recognised practice where, in the case of a rights issue, provisional letters of allotment are issued or where, in other cases, consideration shares are issued in the form of renounceable letters of allotment, that delivery of the return of allotments to the Registrar of Companies under section 52(1), Companies Act 1948 may be deferred until a reasonable time after the last day for renouncing the shares.

However, under the provisions of Part V, Finance Act 1973, capital duty is payable on a return of allotments in the case of the rights issue within one month of receipt of acceptances and in the other cases within one month of the allotment of the shares. In default a fine is payable.

The following procedure has therefore been agreed with the Registrar of Companies: in order to avoid incurring a fine under section 47(7), Finance Act 1973, companies may deliver to the Registrar of Companies within one month of the relevant date a return of allotments on form PUC 2 (or PUC 3, if appropriate) accompanied by the remittance in respect of capital duty, the reverse of such form being noted to the effect that details of the allotments will be delivered after expiry of the renunciation period: such later notification should be made as soon as possible on a continuation form PUC 2 (or PUC 3) cross-referenced with the original return.

October 25, 1973

Progress of Bills

Biological Weapons Bill [HC]: to prohibit the development, production, acquisition and possession of certain biological agents and toxins and of biological weapons: first reading in HC: October 31, 1973.

Channel Tunnel (Initial Finance) Bill [HC]: to make financial provision in relation to preliminary work on or in connection with the construction of a railway tunnel system under the English Channel: first reading in HC: October 31, 1973.

Charlwood and Horley Bill [HC]: to transfer parts of the new parishes of Charlwood and Horley to the new county of Surrey and for connected purposes: first reading in HC: October 31, 1973.

Cinematograph and Indecent Displays Bill [HC]: to amend the Cinematograph Acts 1909 and 1952 and, so far as it relates to things done in the course of a cinematographic exhibition, section 1 of the Obscene Publications Act 1959; to make fresh provision with respect to the display, advertisement or distribution of indecent matter and to the use of machines for the viewing of indecent pictures; and for purposes connected with those matters: first reading in HC: October 31, 1973.

Horticulture (Special Payments) Bill [HC]: to authorise payments out of moneys provided by Parliament to assist certain commercial growers of horticultural

P.ccxciii

Figure 4

addition it contains a feature headed Professional News, which gives details of such things as administrative changes in The Law Society, arrangements for the issue of practising certificates, admissions of new solicitors, and disciplinary proceedings under the Solicitors' Acts.

In addition to these three journals, which cover the whole legal field, there are also a large number of other journals of a more specialized nature, catering for practitioners in particular areas. These are too numerous to be detailed here, and may be found listed in the legal bibliographies.

Law students

All of the periodicals already described can and do contain articles and features of interest to law students from time to time. Nevertheless, there are two journals aimed specially at a student audience. The first of these is *Law Notes*, which is published monthly by the College of Law. This contains items similar to those in many of the journals already mentioned, such as current topics, case notes, new statutes, book reviews, and so on, but it is written throughout in a simpler and more concise style. Many practitioners, it may be noted, continue to take *Law Notes* as a refresher, even after they have qualified.

More recently, Messrs Sweet and Maxwell have started to publish the *Students' Law Reporter* three times a year, and copies of this are distributed to university law faculties throughout the country. It contains a full selection of case notes of recent cases.

The *Law Society's Gazette* contains a section headed Trainee Solicitors in most weeks' issues, and this is usually the first source of information for any changes in the Training Regulations of The Law Society, that is, the regulations dealing with the education and training of articled clerks.

Law librarians

Periodicals aimed especially at law librarians are naturally much fewer in number than those aimed at either academic lawyers or practitioners. The only British journal in this field is the *Law Librarian* (published three times a year), which began to appear as recently as 1970. English-language journals for law librarians published abroad include the *Law Library Journal* from America (published quarterly) and the *International Journal of Law Libraries* (published three times a year), which replaced the *International Association of Law Libraries Bulletin* from the beginning of 1973.

However, although there are at present only three easily accessible journals aimed especially at law librarians, in a sense all legal journals are of potential interest to law librarians, and this leads to a consideration of the use and function of periodicals in the law library.

Use and function of periodicals in the law library

The first use of periodicals from the point of view of the law librarian is in keeping abreast of his subject. The publishers' notices and book reviews contained in periodicals are an important aid to book selection, see page 485. At the same time, by scanning quickly the more important periodicals as they come in, the law librarian can keep in touch with current topics and developments, so that he is less likely to be at a loss when some new and unexpected query arrives on his desk.

Secondly, the practice sections of current periodicals form an invaluable quick reference aid. The type of material to be found in these sections has already been indicated. Although of course *Current Law* (see page 164) is normally the first source of information to which any law librarian goes, there is always a gap of two to six weeks (according to the time of the month), which is not covered by the last issue of *Current Law*. The latest issues of the weekly periodicals fill this gap and bring coverage of any particular query right up to date.

Thirdly, the articles in the periodicals form a source of reference to both students and practitioners, and, as has already been mentioned, may provide information on subjects which are too new or too specialized to have been written about in books. To take one example, an article in the *Solicitors' Journal* entitled 'Buying that castle in Spain' (vol. 117, no. 25, 22 June 1973, p. 455) gives useful information not easily obtainable elsewhere about the formalities necessary before a solicitor can buy property for a client wishing to settle in Spain. Again, an article in the *Law Society's Gazette* on 'Tape recordings as evidence' (vol. 69, no. 14, 12 April 1972, p. 297) has been similarly referred to in the absence of other material. Articles such as these will be a continuous source of reference over a longer period than the material in the practice sections of the journals, and hence obviously the need for maintaining back files of periodicals in law libraries.

In order to exploit periodicals fully, a knowledge of how the main periodical indexes work is clearly necessary, and for this the reader should refer to page 391.

MINOR SOURCES

Conferences and symposia

The proceedings of conferences and symposia on legal topics appear from time to time. The majority of them are in the field of comparative law, and those organized by the British Institute of International and Comparative Law have been especially noteworthy in this respect. In the field of domestic law, there has been less activity.

Theses and dissertations

About thirty-five to fifty legal theses and dissertations each year are listed in the *Index to theses accepted for higher degrees in the universities of Great Britain and Ireland,* which is published annually by Aslib. As might be expected, there is a bias towards the subjects of international law, comparative law and juris-prudence. Strictly speaking, theses, although they are now being listed, are unpublished works, requiring permission from the author and sometimes also from the university concerned before they may be consulted. Only about half a dozen legal theses a year out of those listed eventually see the full light of day by being published in the normal way, though it should be added that among these is some work of considerable quality.

SCOTLAND

Textbooks

The position of textbooks in Scottish law is similar to that in England: 'The function of the textbook is to collect and present in logical form a statement, of the rules of law on a given topic, drawn from the authoritative sources, the relevant statutes and scattered cases, and to suggest their cumulative effect and how they appear to the author to apply in different circumstances . . . Textbooks are, in general, therefore, only secondary authorities and useful in so far as they completely and accurately present rules laid down in the primary authorities, *ie*, the statutes and cases, on any topic.' (Walker, D. M., *The Scottish Legal System*, 3rd edition. Green, 1969, p. 293.) There are likewise books of authority in Scotland, known as the institutional writings, the best known being Viscount Stair, *The Institutions of the Law of Scotland*, 1681. These are described on page 250.

The actual number of textbooks dealing with Scots law is very much smaller than in England. This is largely because of the economics of law publishing, which make it difficult for a legal title to be a success commercially. Thus there are several successful books issued many years ago which normally would have gone through a number of editions, but which still await revision. On the other hand, some have been kept up-to-date, notably Gloag, W. M. and Henderson, R. C., *Introduction to the Law of Scotland*, which in 1968 reached its 7th edition. A recent textbook of high standard is Walker, D. M., *Principles of Scottish Private Law*, 1970, 2 volumes. An encouraging development in the last decade has been the establishment of the Scottish Universities' Law Institute, the avowed purpose of which is to 'encourage, stimulate and advance the scientific study of the law of Scotland'. To this end the Institute is endeavouring to restate the main branches of the law in some fifteen to twenty separate treatises. By early 1974 ten of these volumes had been published, and others were in hand.

The *Encyclopaedia of the Laws of Scotland* more familiarly known as *Green's Encyclopaedia*, was first issued in fourteen volumes between 1896–1904, and was followed by the 2nd edition, in twelve volumes, from 1904–14. After the First World War the need for revision was evident, and a 3rd edition in sixteen volumes appeared between 1926–35; a supplementary volume in two parts was published in 1949–51, with an appendix in 1952. The 3rd edition's consultative editor was Viscount Dunedin, and although, as he points out in his preface, the *Encyclopaedia* was by no means replaced by *Halsbury's Laws of England* (see page 195), the 2nd edition of which was then appearing, the fact remains that the Scottish work did not achieve the reputation gained by Halsbury. Although still consulted for authoritative information, the *Encyclopaedia* is now considerably out of date.

Complementary to the *Encyclopaedia*, and also published by Green, is the *Encyclopaedia of Scottish Legal Styles*, issued in ten volumes between 1935–40. This was well received, as it attempted to be exhaustive in its coverage of legal precedents and styles in Scotland. Like its companion, however, it is badly in need of revision. Other, more specialized, style books include Maclaren, J. A., *Bill Chamber Practice*, 1916, and Dobie, W. J., *Sheriff Court Styles*, 1951.

The only current practice book in Scotland, which has already been mentioned on page 127 as it includes certain statutes, is the *Parliament House Book*. This is published annually, now in two volumes, and amongst its diverse contents are sections on practice in the Courts of Session and Justiciary, and in the Sheriff and lower courts.

Periodicals

Those periodicals published in Scotland may conveniently be considered under a single heading, as they are few in number. The only independent journal which is general in its scope is the *Scots Law Times*, first issued in 1893, and which for most of its existence has appeared in several sequences, the two chief ones being *News* and *Reports*. The *Scottish Law Review*, also general in its coverage, was published regularly from 1885–1963, and included *Sheriff Court Reports* as an appendix (now in *Scots Law Times*). Following the setting up of the Law Society of Scotland in 1949, the Society's *Journal* has appeared monthly since 1956 and as well as Society news and events, etc., it features articles, commentaries, reviews, and similar matter. A sister periodical is the *Scottish Law Gazette*, published quarterly since 1933. This is intended for circulation among members of the Scottish Law Agents Society, but is of limited value to the law librarian.

The sole Scottish journal aimed at an academic audience is the *Juridical Review*. Sub-titled when it first appeared in 1889 as a *Journal of legal and political science*, in 1956 this became *The Law Journal of the Scottish Universities* (from 1968 the second definite article was dropped). This was as a result of an arrangement between Green, the publishers, and the then four Scottish University law faculties, which wished to have a journal but which saw little point in producing a rival title. It should be noted, for citation purposes, that the first series, from 1889–1955, was numbered volumes 1–67, but that the fresh series begun in 1956 is unnumbered.

A convenient summary of current British legal periodicals and indexes appears in Walker, D. M., *The Scottish Legal System*, 3rd edition, 1969, p. 461.

IRELAND

Textbooks

The status of textbooks in Irish courts is the same as in England. See Delany, *Administration of Justice in Ireland*, 4th edition, page 11.

So far as the publishing of legal works is concerned, the Republic of Ireland (or Eire) is in a similar position to Scotland, the number of copies sold being too small to make it a really attractive commercial proposition. In Northern Ireland, the problem is if anything more acute, but many English textbooks and works of reference are used in areas where the law is the same or similar. This also happens in the Republic, but to a lesser extent. Adaptation by way of supplement sometimes helps to bridge the gap; for example Dowrick, F. E. *Notes on the Irish law of contract*, is an Irish supplement to Cheshire, G. E. and Fifoot, C. H. S., *Law of Contract*, 3rd edition and covers the law of the Republic, while the Irish supplement to Challis, H. W., *Law of Real Property*, 3rd edition, covers both jurisdictions. A supplement may be available for one or two editions of the main work only, for example Keeton, G. W. and Sheridan, L. A. S., *Law of Trusts* (8th and 9th editions). The extent of the coverage of a textbook is not always clear from the title; for example the same authors' *Equity* covers both the United Kingdom and the Irish Republic, as does Green, A. W., *Bibliography of British Legal Education*, despite appearances to the contrary. Where Ireland is included in the title, it is often necessary to inspect the volume to see if it applies to both sides of the border; for example, Delany, V. T. H., *The Law Relating to Charities in Ireland* (which does) and Bartholomew, P. C., *The Irish Judiciary* (which does not). The lot of the Irish legal bibliographer is not a happy one.

For bibliographies of textbooks, see Chapter 10.

In the field of encyclopedias there are no specifically Irish works. The *English and Empire Digest* cites Irish cases where it is considered useful, but coverage is not extensive.

Practice books

For the Republic of Ireland, the main source is Rules of the Superior Courts, 1962 (S.I. 72 of 1962), amended by the Superior Courts Rules Committee from time to time, new rules being published as Statutory Instruments. The Committee on Court Practice and Procedure under the chairmanship of Mr Justice Walsh has published some nineteen reports to date, covering such topics as the jurisdiction and practice of the Supreme Court, liability for professional negligence, on-the-spot fines, interest on judgment debts, and desertion and maintenance.

In Northern Ireland, the Rules of the Supreme Court were published in 1936 (S.R. & O. 1936 No. 7) and are up-dated by further rules from time to time.

Periodicals

The only weekly legal periodical in Ireland is the *Irish Law Times and Solicitors' Journal*, which is chiefly a practitioner's periodical. So too is the monthly *Gazette of the Incorporated Law Society* of Ireland. There is also the *Irish Jurist*; a new series since 1966 is published twice a year.

Since 9 May 1974 the *New Law Journal* has been publishing a fortnightly supplement entitled the Irish Practitioner, in the form of an inset on green pages. It is described as a 'fortnightly news service especially designed for the Irish Legal Profession, both North and South of the border', but appears so far to cover the Republic only.

Under the heading Northern Ireland, *Current Law* provides a much-needed source of information and references.

The *Northern Ireland Legal Quarterly* (1936–) has been published from the Law Faculty, Queen's University since 1964. It was published until 1961 by the Incorporated Law Society of Northern Ireland. None appeared in 1962–3. The

Gazette of the Incorporated Law Society of Northern Ireland is currently appearing twice a year. Most of these periodicals are indexed in the *Index to Legal Periodicals*, but for Irish material and articles by Irish legal writers, O'Higgins, P., *A bibliography of periodical literature relating to Irish Law*, 1966, and supplement 1973, is invaluable, as both legal and non-legal journals have been used as source material.

FURTHER READING

Legal textbooks and periodicals have been much less written about than either the statutes or the law reports. The two best short accounts, which have already been referred to in the text, are:

Phillips, O. H. *A First Book of English Law*. 6th edition. Sweet and Maxwell, 1970 (ISBN 0 421 13270 1). See especially Chapter 14, Books of Authority, pp. 222–43.
Walker, R. J. and Walker, M. G. *The English Legal System*. 3rd edition. Butterworth, 1972 (ISBN 0 406 67752 2). See especially Chapter 8, Textbooks, pp. 144–8.

Chapters 1 and 6, in particular, of the symposium below contain material of considerable interest. (Chapter 6 has been reprinted in *The Law Librarian*, vol. 5, 1974, pp. 21–4 and 41–3):

Sweet and Maxwell. *Then and now, 1799–1974: commemorating 175 years of law bookselling and publishing*. Sweet and Maxwell, 1974 (ISBN 0 421 20490 7).

6. Historical Sources

W. W. S. BREEM
Librarian to the Honourable Society of the Inner Temple

It is the purpose of this chapter to deal, however briefly, with almost all classes of legal materials prior to 1800.

A sound general knowledge of historical source material is essential to a proper understanding of legal bibliography. Legal scholars still find medieval and post-renaissance records the most fruitful amongst which to conduct their researches, whilst the common law system's dependence upon precedent ensures the practising lawyer's continued concern with the written words and decisions of his predecessors. Though the doctrine exists still that legal memory is limited, being fixed at the year 1189, the fact remains that, in 1922, the presiding judge at the Old Bailey found it necessary to make reference to the laws of Ine, a West Saxon king who reigned c. AD 688–725; whilst in the second half of the twentieth century both counsel and judiciary have had occasion to consult the medieval Year Books in the course of high court actions. No law book can be said to be useless merely because it is old.

The advent of the photographic reprint and of microfilm has made potentially available to all law libraries not only the rare law books of yesterday, but also early manuscripts and record documents. An understanding of ancient records is therefore no longer the prerogative of the archivist.

Of the satellite subjects listed by Winfield as essential aids to legal historical research, a knowledge of chronology is among the most important for the successful location of data in early material. In England until the thirteenth century the Christian year commenced on 25 December, but in the fourteenth century the practice of dating the year from 25 March became generally accepted. In 1752 the Legal Year was ordered to commence on 1 January 1753. During the period of change preceding this order official records written between 1 January and 24 March often bear a double date: thus February 1671 or 1671–2. The top figure refers to the old year and the lower figure to the new year. The regnal year, which involves dating the year from the commencement of a sovereign's reign, did not become fully approved till 1189. From then on all government documents and private charters are so dated. Thus, the year 1 of Richard III's reign covers the period 26 June 1483 to 25 June 1484. The most accessible table of regnal years will be found in Sweet and Maxwell's *Guide to Law Reports and Statutes*, 1962. But in this and similar tables the year is calculated according to present reckoning, though all dates between 1 January and 25 March belong by the old reckoning to one year earlier. Thus, Edward IV's reign may be said to have commenced either on 4 March 1460 or 4 March 1461; both versions being correct. The four law terms owe their origins to the timing of church festivals, the dictates of Canon Law and the economic demands of medieval agricultural society. In 1831 the dates of the terms were defined by legislation as follows: Hilary Term (11 to 31 January); Paschal (Easter) Term (15 April to 8 May); Trinity Term (22 May to 12 June); Michaelmas Term (1 October to 25 November). A Bill intended to reduce the terms from four to three failed during the 1870 session. Parliamentary sessions are the chronological units of parliamentary business and the principal divisions into which the life of a parliament is divided. A session commences the day Parliament is opened and ends the day it is prorogued or dissolved. For a list of parliaments, 1242–1832 refer to the *Handbook of British Chronology*, edited by F. M. Powicke and E. B. Fryde, 1961, pp. 492–544.

Prior to the Conquest, legal documents were written in either Anglo-Saxon or Latin. But under the Normans Latin became the official language for the writing of records of administrative and judicial proceedings. After 1166, Anglo-French began to be used in the courts, and became the technical language of the legal profession both for speech and writing, but had become hopelessly corrupted by the first quarter of the sixteenth century. In 1650 an Act (subsequently nullified at the Restoration) was passed which required all judicial reports, resolutions and law books to be translated into English. Though Anglo-French or Law French, as it is also known, was employed as late even as the eighteenth century, it did not recover its former popularity. In 1731 an Act was passed making English the official language of the law, though a later amendment permitted technical phrases such as *quare impedit* to remain untranslated. The records of the courts of common law, however, though not those of equity proceedings were, except during the Interregnum, written in Latin until 1733.

In Wales, despite the Conquest by Edward I, the native tongue remained dominant till 1536, when English became the official language for all legal and government business. In 1967, however, the Welsh Language Act decreed that within the borders of Wales Welsh should have equal legal validity with English.

ARCHIVES AND MANUSCRIPTS

Sir Edward Coke defined a record as 'a memorial or remembrance in rolls of parchment of the proceedings and acts of a Court of Justice', but this definition was perhaps always too narrow. Certainly the term record has a wider meaning now and may be interpreted as including any document that is specially created as being authentic evidence of a matter of legal importance. Such a definition indicates that legal records are likely to be found in almost any place where manuscripts are deposited.

The distinction between public and private records was not finally clarified until 1838, when the Public Record Office of England and Wales, which now contains three-quarters of all public records, was founded. In general, public records are concerned with the business of the Crown and those public records which have never been officially out of official custody are accorded an authority as evidence in court that is denied all other records. Those which are held to be 'not of record' must first be proved by the testimony of experts before their content matter is acceptable. In the Middle Ages and in many series of records continued into modern times the language of the records is almost always either Latin or French.

Legal manuscripts of varying degrees of importance will be found in repositories as variable as public record offices, universities or family muniment rooms. Ownership therefore may be public, corporate or private and personal. Many collections still have been listed only briefly, if at all; some, of outstanding importance and in private hands, are not accessible even upon application; while the printed catalogues or calendars of others vary considerably as to treatment, accuracy and completeness.

Among major repositories the PRO is pre-eminent. It contains legal records dating from the twelfth century and Parliamentary records prior to 1497. The Scottish Record Office (HM General Register House, Edinburgh) has a continuous history since the thirteenth century and under the Treaty of Union preserves the older public records. The PRO, Belfast, and the Irish Record Office, Dublin, cover Irish affairs, particularly since 1922, while the House of Lords Record Office contains all Parliamentary records post-1497. The British Library contains perhaps the richest collection of legal manuscripts, as opposed to purely legal records, but much material of importance will also be found in the National Libraries of Scotland and Ireland, the Bodleian Library, Oxford, the University Libraries of Cambridge and Edinburgh, as well as Trinity College Library, Dublin and the Library of Queen's University, Belfast. Of the Inns of Court libraries, Lincoln's Inn, possesses the works of Sir Matthew Hale and Serjeant Maynard, while the Inner Temple contains the Petyt Collection.

County Record Offices were not established till 1924. Their holdings normally include records of the courts of quarter session and of petty sessions; in general these commence *c.* 1590.

Despite the apparent riches of the past, few lawyers today leave working records to posterity, the scripts of treatises excepted. The professional writings of a barrister in chambers are the property of the solicitor who engages him – carbon copies of typescript opinions, for example, are rarely made – and such documents must be sought in the archives of solicitors' firms. Notebooks, if preserved, may be located in family muniments.

For details of materials held, reference must be made to the published guides and catalogues of the institutions concerned, the best collection of these being held at London University's Institute for Historical Research.

PRINTED SOURCE COLLECTIONS

Record Commission Publications

In 1800 the Record Commission of Great Britain was established and between 1802–69 issued fifty-six publications concerning the records of England, Wales and Scotland. These included ancient laws, calendars, documents, fine and oblate rolls, parliamentary writs, pipe rolls, records of parliament, and statutes of the realm, together with Acts of the Parliament of Scotland and other important Scottish record material and *writs*. A high proportion of the material has, in consequence, considerable legal interest. The volumes were published in *record* type, a pioneer effort to reproduce by conventional letterpress, specially made, a near facsimile of the original manuscript.

The Commissioners' publications were not issued as a numbered series and for an easily obtainable list of their issued works see *Government Publications Sectional List* – no. 24. A fuller, bibliographically annotated list is in Mullins, E. L. C. *Texts and Calendars. An Analytical Guide to Serial Publications*, 1958, p. 3.

After 1837 the Commission was allowed to lapse and upon the establishment of the PRO the work of continuing publication of state records became the function of the Master of the Rolls.

The Irish Record Commission, established 1810, was dissolved in 1830. A list of publications issued or planned by the Commissioners will be found in Mullins at p. 14. For an account of the Commission, see volume 1 of Morrin, J. *Calendar of the Patent and Close Rolls*, 1861–3, 3 volumes.

For details of record publications relating to Scotland and Wales, see Gouldesbrough, P., Krupp, A. P. and Lewis, I., *Handlist of Scottish and Welsh Record Publications*, 1954. This list excludes official publications, for which refer to GPSL – no. 24, and Mullins noted above.

Rolls Series

This series of chronicles and memorials of Great Britain and Ireland during the Middle Ages was published under the official title of *Rerum Britannicarum medii aevi scriptores* by direction of the Master of the Rolls. Modelled on Pertz's *Monumenta Germaniae historica*, it consists of ninety-nine numbered publications in 251 volumes and was issued between 1858 and 1911, each chronicle or compilation of documents being treated as an individual work and edited by a commissioned specialist. The material includes calendars of state papers such as the close and patent rolls, cartularies, charters and year books, as well as parliamentary records. Most of the prominent chroniclers are included, so that the series covers the principal medieval sources of history. A number of works contain both texts and translations and their introductions are valuable for the bibliographical information contained therein concerning the manuscripts consulted. For a complete list of titles issued, see GPSL – no. 24. A fuller bibliographically annotated list is in Mullins.

Calendars of State Papers

In 1854 the State Paper Office and the Record Office were amalgamated and two years later the still-continuing series of calendars was commenced.

The various series include Chancery Records such as the charter rolls, patent rolls, close rolls and liberate rolls, treaty rolls, inquisitions post mortem and chancery warrants, Exchequer Records such as the memoranda rolls, judicial records such as the Curia Regis rolls and ancient deeds (particularly conveyances of land), state papers domestic, foreign and colonial; also documents preserved in foreign archives of Brussels, Simancas, Venice, Vienna and elsewhere relating to the history of Great Britain and Ireland. Calendars of state papers relating to Scotland and Ireland are also included.

Since the commencement of the calendars, over 800 volumes have been published. It is a measure of the richness of this material that only a minority of these series has yet been completed.

The calendars are issued in octavo-size volumes and are, generally speaking, in the language of the original, though in certain instances translations have been effected. Their purpose is to provide catalogues of the series of documents they record and to give summary notes of the contents of each item.

The documents so calendared relate to those held in the principal state secretariat offices from the first quarter of the sixteenth century onwards, excepting only the Chancery, Exchequer and judicial records of the Curia Regis which pre-date this period. A summary list of titles and volumes published to date will be found in GPSL – no. 24. A fuller bibliographically annotated list is in Mullins.

Historical Manuscripts Commission Reports

The reports of the Royal Commission on Historical Manuscripts commenced in 1870. The purpose of the Commission, established in 1869, was 'to enquire what papers and manuscripts belonging to private families and institutions are extant which would be of utility in the illustration of history, constitutional law, science and general literature, and to which possessors would be willing to give access'. The Commissioner's administration is centred in the PRO. To date it has reported on the mss of over 600 private owners and institutions, while its published reports on collections now exceeds 250 volumes. These are listed in detail in GPSL – no. 17. This indicates reprinted volumes still available. Historical manuscripts of the House of Lords 1450–1693 were also noted during the Commission's early years.

The reports of the Commission are of three kinds: the Commissioners' Reports to the Crown; Inspectors' Reports to the Commissioners; Reports of the Secretary to the Commissioners.

The Commissioners' Reports are statements of business during the period under review. It is the Inspectors' Reports which contain the essential data on the collections examined. All reports, however, published up to 1920 were issued as *Parliamentary Papers*.

There are three major guides to the location of material, each of which offers slightly varying data. There is the official *Guide to the Reports*, a series divided into two parts. Part I is topographical, the first volume covering reports 1870–1911. A second volume, covering reports 1911–57, is in the press. Part II is an index of persons; two volumes cover 1870–1911 and three the period 1911–57. Mullins contains a detailed list of reports issued, with notes on the contents of calendars. The index to this work includes persons and places referred to in the reports. Gross's *Sources and Literature of English History*, 1915 at p. 692

contains a list of reports with keyed references to their location in *Parliamentary Papers*, also an index of repositories holding medieval manuscripts. The complicated publishing history and technical composition of the reports may cause difficulties, and so the best brief location guide to collections will be found in GPSL – no. 17. This also contains a brief bibliographical statement and a valuable note on the correct citation of references to the collections reported upon.

Rolls of Parliament

These are the most important early records of Parliament and it is to these that the legal historian or practising lawyer must turn if he wishes to see the original authorized text of any statute from 1 Richard III onwards. Until the sixteenth century the rolls also recorded procedural matters relating to both Houses, but these were afterwards recorded in separate minute books, for details of which, see below under *Journals* of the Lords and Commons. In 1849 manuscript enrolment ceased, to be replaced by the deposit of acts printed on vellum.

In 1776 the rolls were ordered to be printed and publication was effected, certainly by 1783, of *Rotuli Parliamentorum* (n.d.) in six volumes, covering the period 1278–1503. A supplementary volume was afterwards issued to supply deficiencies in the Lords *Journals* and, in 1832, an analytical index. The text of this edition was drawn from uncollated transcripts, not the originals. For details of rolls subsequently published but excluded from this edition, refer to Mullins at pp. 10–11 (item 1.47), p. 268 (item 33.37), p. 270 (item 33.51); and see also *Records of the Parliament at Westminster*, edited F. W. Maitland, 1893, which contains the rolls of 1305.

Journals of the Lords and Commons

At first kept in manuscript, the journals have been printed more or less contemporaneously since 1762 (Commons) and 1819 (Lords). A record of the proceedings of the two Houses, they constitute the collection of precedents by which present-day parliamentary procedure is governed. They are of value therefore to constitutional historians and are the only authoritative source through which failed bills (sometimes referred to as acts) may be traced, or early statutes dated.

The Lords journals date from 1510. The early journals are in Latin, but entries in English appear in the sixteenth century. The manuscript series was concluded in 1830, to be continued for record purposes by a printed journal bound in vellum and kept on deposit in the Victoria Tower. The printed edition, 1510 to date, was first ordered in 1767 and consists of over 200 volumes. From 1820 onwards each sessional volume contains an index. General indexes have also been issued. These cover varying groups of volumes up to 1863. Thereafter indexes are issued decennially.

Of importance is the material relating to judicial powers, exercised since the eighteenth century by Parliament. These include proceedings on original causes, 1621–93, and cases of privilege, of which approximately 700 were heard between 1660 and 1853. Such cases range from the privilege of a peer to have freedom from arrest (except on certain charges) to actions which involve contempt of the House by its members or strangers. For details of record material relating to impeachments and trials of peers, appeal cases and cases in error, see page 185. For details of notes of proceedings and draft journals readily available in print and which include data edited out of the final journals, refer to Mullins at p. 253 (item 31.103), p. 258 (item 32.24), p. 269 (item 33.42) and p. 274 (item 33.83).

The Commons journals date from 1547; none, however, is extant for the period 1581–1603. Refer to D'Ewes, Sir S. *Journals*, 1682, which contains extracts from their contents, and Neale, J. E., Commons journals of the Tudor period. TRHS, fourth series, vol. 3, 1920, pp. 136–70. Those for 1801–33 were destroyed in the fire of 1834 and the series in manuscript does not extend beyond 1800 as a result. Unlike the Lords' archive copies, no printed edition is kept for record purposes, though HLRO keep a printed set on file. The printed edition, 1547 to date was first ordered in 1742 and consists of over 200 volumes, each provided with an index. The quality of the early printed transcripts is variable but their accuracy from 1642 onwards is held to be much improved. Volumes of general indexes have been issued, covering varying groups of volumes to 1900. Thereafter indexes are issued decennially.

The material recorded may be of particular concern to legal researchers. The progress of each bill is noted in detail, for, in regard to certain specific amendments the text may be set out in full. Similarly, where accounts and papers are presented these are recorded. In the seventeenth and eighteenth centuries the texts of many such papers were noted in full, while between 1801–34 the texts of the more important were printed in full in the appendix to the journal. Thereafter this practice was abandoned and all such papers ordered to be printed will be found in *Parliamentary Papers*. For details of notes of proceedings and draft journals readily available in print and which include data edited out of the final journals, refer to Mullins at p. 243 (item 31.33), p. 250 (item 31.81) and p. 255 (item 32.6).

Parliamentary Debates

The debates are invaluable as source material for the genesis of a statute. Through them may be traced the original purpose of a bill and the intentions of its sponsors. Its reception by both Houses and the climate of political opinion, reflecting the social views of the age, which may require its modification may also be discovered. In addition, the debates are useful as biographical records, for through them much may be learned concerning the parliamentary career of a member.

Prior to 1803 the reporting of debates was held to be a breach of privilege, though up to 1682 (in the Commons) and to 1714 (in the Lords) notes of speeches were recorded in the journals upon occasion. Despite this ban, unofficial reporting did take place in the seventeenth and eighteenth centuries and reports of speeches may be located in a variety of apparently unlikely publications. *The Gentleman's Magazine* reported debates from 1733–46, 1749 and 1752–3 and includes the reports by Samuel Johnson for 1740–2. Periodical cumulative indexes were issued. *The Annual Register* contains the reports of debates after 1762 and has importance because of Edmund Burke's connection with it.

Newspaper reporting of debates began in 1768 and a number carried accounts of parliamentary proceedings, notably: the *London Daily Post and General Advertiser* (afterwards the *Public Advertiser*) which contained the 'Letters of Junius'; and *The Daily Universal Register* (afterwards *The Times*).

Numerous collections of early proceedings have been published. Of these the most comprehensive is *The Parliamentary History of England from the Norman Conquest* in 1066 to 1803, edited by W. Cobbett and [after 1812] T. C. Hansard, 36 volumes, 1806–20. Volumes 1–12 are entitled 'Cobbett's Parliamentary History of England', continued by T. C. Hansard as *The Parliamentary History of England*. This is now held to be the most reliable source for material on debates, particularly in the eighteenth century.

For the continuation of the debates as published by Hansard reference must be made to page 259.

Calendars of Manuscripts of the House of Lords

Calendars of the Lords manuscripts, dating from 1450 to 1693 will be located in HMCR, notably series 1–8 and series 17, which contains thirteen volumes. Of concern to legal historians will be volume 7, which includes papers relating to the Act of Uniformity, the Regicides, and the Act of Indemnity; volume 9, which has material relating to the Test Act, Habeus Corpus Act, and the Statute of Frauds; volume 10, which includes the Exclusion Bill; and volume 11, which has material concerning the Bill of Rights. In general, they contain material relating to *Parliamentary Papers* (Lords and Commons) 1531–1714, judicial records such as papers on appeal and cases in error, and failed bills of the House of Lords.

As from 1900, the series was continued as House of Lords Papers and the first, or volume 14, in continuation of the old series, is entitled Manuscripts of the House of Lords, 1693–5, New Series, volume 1, 1900. The series to date totals eleven volumes in the new series, or twenty-four altogether, and covers the manuscripts up to the first quarter of the eighteenth century. The entire series is listed, with brief notes on the parliamentary material, in Bond, M. F. *Guide to the Records of Parliament*, 1971, pp. 8–10.

Societies' publications

There are over eighty learned societies in England and Wales alone and these may be classified as either national or local, dependent upon their aims and interests. Such societies, financed by private subscription, usually issue quarterly, annual or occasional publications devoted to the issue of previously unpublished manuscript material, edited transcripts of the same, or the re-issue of early printed texts. Alternatively their publications may consist of articles of original scholarship. Much depends upon the nature and purpose of the society.

Almost all publish a certain quantity of material that may be of concern to the legal historian. The Royal Historical Society, founded in 1868 and which in 1897 absorbed the Camden Society, itself founded in 1831, has established a reputation for being 'the principal organization representing English historical scholarship'. Their combined publications number over 250 volumes and include important records relating to parliamentary and constitutional law. The Pipe Roll Society, formed in 1883, has issued to date some forty volumes dealing with the records of the Court of Exchequer: pipe rolls, feet of fines, ancient charters and the Herefordshire Domesday. Local societies generally publish the assize rolls and quarter session records relevant to their geographical interests. The importance of society publications, therefore, as of the official collections noted above, lies in the fact that printed texts of the material issued by them may not easily be found elsewhere, if at all.

A number of societies, however, deserve special mention; their concern being wholly with legal materials of historic importance.

The Ames Foundation, established in the United States, requires notice since its publications relate wholly to English legal interests. It was founded in 1910 'for the purpose of continuing the advancement of legal knowledge and aiding the improvement of the law'. Seven volumes have been published, 1914– , and these consist of four volumes of year-books, two bibliographies of law books and a volume of proceedings before JPs in the fourteenth and fifteenth centuries.

The Selden Society was founded in 1888, largely at the instigation of F. W. Maitland, to encourage the study and advance the knowledge of the history of English law. A prime purpose was the publication of volumes of previously unpublished Year Books. While all publications are numbered in sequence, the Year Books have a secondary series of sub-numbers. Other material issued includes plea rolls, eyre rolls, select cases in Chancery, court of Admiralty, court of Requests, court of King's bench, and Exchequer chamber, select charters and early treatises, as well as source material for historical studies of the Inns of Court and legal education. Publication commenced in 1888 and over ninety volumes have been issued to date. The texts of works in Latin and French are often given with English translations.

The Manorial Society was founded to publish material on the manorial and allied courts and twelve monographs were issued 1906–23.

The best general guide to the works of the learned societies of England and Wales remains Mullins, which contains full bibliographical details relating to each volume published. Those concerned with the Selden Society should refer to the *General Guide to the Society's Publications*, compiled by A. K. R. Kiralfy and G. H. Jones, 1960. This gives detailed and indexed summaries of the contents of the introductions to the seventy-nine volumes then published.

The Stair Society was founded in order to encourage the study and learning of Scots law. Publication commenced in 1936 and continues, over twenty-seven volumes having been issued to date. These include justiciary cases, treatises, the writings of influential jurists and volumes of miscellany.

Other Scottish societies whose publications include a proportion of legal materials are the Bannatyne Club, the New Spalding Club, the Scottish Burgh Record Society, the Scottish Historical Society, and the Scottish Record Society. Details of materials published will be found in Terry, C. S. *A Catalogue of the Publications of Scottish historical and kindred clubs and societies and of the volume relating to Scottish history by HM Stationery Office*, 1780–1908, 1909. This work is continued by Matheson, C. *A Catalogue of the Publications of Scottish historical and kindred clubs and societies . . . including the reports of the Royal Commission on Historical MSS*, 1908–27, 1928.

Irish societies issuing occasional legal materials include the Royal Society of Antiquaries of Ireland, the Irish Archaeological Society and the Royal Irish Academy.

Also to be noticed are the Manx Society, who issued publications, 1859–95, and the Société Jersiaise pour l'Etude de l'Histoire, whose publications commenced in 1876.

LEGISLATION

Anglo-Saxon and Welsh

Anglo-Saxon legislation was originally preserved in the form of oral traditions and customs. The earliest recorded laws – enactments or dooms made by King and Witan – did not appear until the coming of St Augustine. The laws now extant cover the period *c*. 601–1020, but there is a gap of two centuries, *c*. 695–890, and there are various additions in private compilations of the eleventh and twelfth centuries. The dooms are not complete statements for they omit much customary law, *ie*, that which was undisputed or common knowledge.

The principal manuscript source material, which is not contemporary but dates from the eleventh century or later, is preserved in the Cottonian and Harleian collections at the British Library, at Corpus Christi, Cambridge, and at the Bodleian.

The most accessible printed edition of the dooms and one which contains most of the private compilations is *Ancient Laws and Institutes of England*, edited B. Thorp, 2 volumes, 1840.

This includes at pp. 300–3, De Institutis Lundoniae, which contains enactments relating to London gate tolls; at pp. 352–7 an ordinance concerning the Dunsaete, a law issued by Edgar (924–40); at pp. 426–30, Pseudo-Cnuts constitutiones de Foresta, a forgery compiled *c*. 1184 which expounds the administration and judicature of the forest temp. Henry II; at pp. 442–62, Leges Edwardi confessoris, compiled *c*. 1130–5, in which English institutions are described as they were prior to 1066 and temp. Henry I; at pp. 466–87, Leges Willelmi Conquestoris, which professes to contain the laws in the time of Edward the Confessor and promulgated by William I; and at pp. 497–631, Leges Henrici primi, which contain the coronation charter of Henry I.

The earliest Welsh laws are contained in a code promulgated by Howel Dda, *c*. 943–50 and ordered in three recensions: the Venedotian Code adopted for north Wales, the Dimetian Code for south Wales and the Gwentian Code for south-east Wales. The legal system formulated by these codes continued till the conquest by Edward I. The texts of these codes with Latin translations are printed in *Ancient Laws and Institutes of Wales*, edited by A. Owen, 2 volumes, 1841.

Magna Carta

There is no original of this charter to the terms of which King John gave his assent: 'in the meadow called Ronimede between Windsor and Staines on the fifteenth day of June in the seventeenth year of our reign.'

The nearest approximation to an original is a parchment containing preliminary draft terms and commences: 'Ista sunt capitula quae Barones petunt et dominus Rex concedit.' It contains articles or heads of agreement in forty unnumbered paragraphs, is cited as 'Additional MSS 4838', bears the King's seal and is held at the British Library.

Four copies of the charter are extant: two in the British Library. One cited as 'Cotton, charters, xiii, 31a', damaged by fire, is in part illegible and bears the mark of the King's seal; the second is cited as 'Cotton, Augustus II 106'. The third and fourth are in Lincoln and Salisbury cathedrals. The first two have corrections or omissions added at the foot of the text. The third and fourth incorporate these corrections in the body of the text. As to size, the Salisbury copy is seventeen inches by fourteen, running to approximately eighty lines.

It is most probable that the copy sealed on 15 June 1215 was in fact sealed on 19 June and antedated to the fifteenth, the day on which the King and Barons agreed the draft terms 'which served as a warrant to the Chancery for drawing it up and sealing it'. The text was not enrolled for eighty years, probably 'because there was no fitting roll for such an unprecedented document, which, though in form a charter, was really a statute, or even a legal code, whose proper place was in the Royal Treasury'. It was to be added to the Statute Roll some years after its re-affirmation in 1297, so that the Charter of the Statute Roll is not that of John, but of Henry III in modified form.

Early printed editions bearing 'Magna Carta' in their titles proliferated, from Pynson's edition of 1508 to Wight's edition of 1618. Unfortunately, all these reproduced the text of Edward I's Inspeximus of Henry III's re-issue of 1225; not the Charter of John. The earliest reliable edition in print is Blackstone, Sir W. *Magna Charta and Charta de Foresta*, 1759. This contains an account of the several originals and of the alterations made from the first granting to their final establishment in 1300. The other reproduction of note is contained in *Statutes of the Realm*.

For an assessment of the most notable of the many commentaries, reference should be made to McKechnie, W. S. *Magna Carta*, 1914 at pp. 165–82.

Proclamations

From early medieval times the proclamation, a prerogative instrument of the Crown, was employed for two main purposes: firstly to call attention to and enforce thereby the observation of an existing enactment; or secondly to announce formally an executive act. The use of proclamations as legislative instruments was undoubtedly at its height in early medieval society and decreased correspondingly through the centuries as the means of communication improved and the Royal Authority was diminished by the expanding powers of Parliament.

Writs of proclamation are recorded on the close rolls, patent rolls and the rolls of Parliament. (The last entry on the statute roll is that of 7 Henry V, 1414.) In Tudor times the entry on the patent roll is irregular, but as from 1600 entry is almost always the rule. Proclamations, however, were not so entered during the period of the Civil Wars; but from James II to the death of Queen Anne enrolment is regular and complete. Because of the often transitory nature of their contents few libraries hold anything like a complete collection of printed proclamations. A list of those issued prior to 1641 is contained in Pollard, A. W. and Redgrave, G. R. *Short-Title Catalogue of Books Printed, 1475–1640*, 1926 at nos. 7761–9175. The location of proclamations may also be effected by reference to *Tudor and Stuart Proclamations, 1485–1714*, calendared by R. Steel, 2 volumes, 1926. This contains a detailed bibliographical history for the period covered and lists at pp. xliv–xlviii the thirty-three principal collections held in England, Scotland and Ireland. Sweet and Maxwell's *Legal*

Bibliography, volume 1, 1955 at p. 549 lists four volumes of contemporary collections issued between 1550 and 1618.

Statutes

Original sources

The modern definition of a statute as being a legislative act of the Crown, established since the time of Henry VII, was meaningless to medieval lawyers, for whom no theory existed regarding the division of power between executive, legislative or judicial bodies. Prior to the fourteenth century there was no clear distinction between statutes and ordinances and the terminology for early laws varied accordingly: an assize under Henry II, Richard and John, a provision under Henry III, and a statute under Edward I. The term enactment might cover a bargain or contract, a grant of land, a peace treaty, a proclamation or a writ.

Though the Statute Book commences with the Provision of Merton, 1236, a law passed in the absence of the Commons, the earliest statute rolls commence in 1278, cover the period 6 Edward I to 8 Edward IV (1468), contain the enrolments of statutes of public concern, and are held by the PRO. This series is incomplete; gaps exist for the periods 1431–45 and 1468–89, so reference must be made to texts held in the Exchequer. From 1483 statutes were enrolled in their final form in the parliament rolls but a gap exists for 1483–97. The parliament rolls, classified by HLRO as original acts, run from 1497 to 1850, omitting legislation passed 1642–9, for which see Interregnum below. The texts are in manuscript and the handwriting is English. As from 1849, original acts are printed on vellum; duplicates being placed on deposit at the PRO. The term 'parliament roll' is not to be confused with those records described under Rolls of Parliament above. These – Rotuli Parliamentorum – cover the period 1290–1503, include some statutes omitted from the statute rolls and are invaluable for purposes of verification. The final edited and printed texts of Acts prior to 1713 will be located in *Statutes of the Realm* (see page 234). For final texts of Acts, 1714–1797 reference must be made to the appropriate sessional volumes of public Acts. Since 1798 the final texts of all Acts will be found printed in the appropriate sessional volumes. The later collections, known as *Statutes at Large*, contain slightly abbreviated texts of Acts from 1235.

Public Acts

Sessional volumes of public Acts were first officially printed by Machlinia in 1483 and have been issued regularly ever since. Till 1793 the type used was 'black letter' and those volumes printed in this manner are highly regarded, being composed direct from the original Act. Few complete or incomplete sets for the sixteenth and seventeenth centuries are held outside the libraries of the Lords and Commons. Acts for the Commonwealth are excluded from this series.

The first printed collection was *Nova Statuta I Edward III to XXII Edward IV*, a folio edition attributed to Machlinia and printed *c.* 1484. Numerous other editions by various printers followed, including Berthelet's ambitious printing venture, *In this Volume are contained the Statutes Made and Established from the time of Kynge Henry the thirde unto the fyrste yere of King Henry the viii.* This, issued in two editions in 1543, was the first attempt at a complete collection from Magna Carta to date. By 1600 close on 300 editions by differing printers had been issued, the great majority being unauthorized, incomplete and with suspect texts.

Few later editions are free of the criticisms noted above, but the following require notice, since it is upon one or other of these that the majority of law libraries base their own collections which are then continued by the sessional volumes of the eighteenth and nineteenth centuries. The first is *Statutes at Large from Magna Charta to the Union 41 George III (1800)* by T. E. Tomlins and J. Raithby, 10 volumes, quarto, 1811 or 20 volumes, octavo, 1811. The text for the period to 7 George II is based both on Ruffhead's edition of 1786–1800 and on Cay's proofs for an earlier edition by Cay and Ruffhead, issued 1758–1773; for the period 7 George II to 10 George III it is based on Ruffhead, as well as Hawkins' edition of 1734–58; and for the period 10 George III it is based on the King's Printers' copy. Local and personal acts were omitted from this edition, the titles only being printed. The second is *Statutes at Large from Magna Charta to 1761*, by D. Pickering [continued to 1806], 46 volumes, 1762–1807. Pickering's edition, which contains the same matter as Cay, also omits the texts of local and personal acts. Both Tomlins, and Raithby and Pickering, were continued by a King's Printers' edition. For informative notes on the collected editions of the statutes reference should be made to Sweet and Maxwell's *Guide*, p. 11.

The Statutes of the Realm is the authoritative edition for use when reference is required to statutes prior to 1714, but is known to be imperfect and where doubt arises only the parliament and statute rolls will suffice. *The Statutes of the Realm* [1225–1713] *printed from Original and Authentic Manuscripts*, edited by A. Luders [and others], 9 volumes in 10, 1810–22, was published by the Record Commissioners, indexes being subsequently issued. It contains a copy of all statutes in force or repealed from the Statute of Merton to 1713, including the 'Statutes of Uncertain Date' (for details of which see below) and excluding only the period of the Commonwealth. A parallel translation is provided of all early statutes not in English. The historical introduction to volume 1, which is reprinted in part in *Select Essays in Anglo-American Legal History*, by various authors, volume 2, 1908 at pp. 169–208, is bibliographically valuable.

Abridgments

In legal bibliography the terms abridgment, digest and encyclopedia are often interchangeable, the terminology in use at a given time owing more to fashion than to science. For those relating to the Year Books see page 247, and to case-law, see page 163.

The earliest printed abridgment, and one relating to statutes, was the *Abbreviamentum Statutorum*, printed *c*. 1481 by Lettou and Machlinia. Written in French, and arranged in alphabetical order, it covered statutes issued to 1455. Others followed, notably *The Statutes: Prohemium*, J. Rastell, issued in 1519. This offered transcripts in English and contained the texts of certain acts not included in *Statutes at Large*. It is distinguished by the scrupulous care with which the text was edited. Abridgments of sessional acts also commenced publication in the early sixteenth century, while the first abridgment of statues wholly or partly in force was edited by F. Pulton and issued in 1606.

One of the first attempts to produce an abridgment of the

general law was William Sheppard's *Epitome*, of 1656, subsequently re-issued as the *Grand Abridgment* in 1675. Principally
a recension of Coke's *Institutes*, though re-arranged under
alphabetical heads, it was, because written in English, popular
in its day. More memorable abridgments, however, were to
follow. Matthew Bacon's *New Abridgment of the Law* was issued
in 1736–66, ran to seven editions and is still consulted. Of this
work Winfield wrote: 'he did better what Sheppard had failed
to do . . . combine an exposition of the law with a digest of it.'
Charles Viner's *General Abridgment of Law and Equity* proved
itself a monumental work. Written in Law French over a period
of fifty years, it was finally published in English by the author
between 1742–53. It runs to 23 folio volumes, and though the
sub-headings lack the clarity of Bacon's, it remains indispensable as a work of reference for historians. A second edition,
a supplement and an index were to follow and prove its worth.
John Comyns' *Digest of the Laws of England* was published
between 1762–7 and was to run to five editions. Similar in
construction to Bacon's, it has a more elaborate arrangement of
divisions and sub-divisions and is admirably indexed.

Subsequent attempts to encapsule the law into a single work
were to be corporate rather than individual.

Private, Local and Personal Acts

Until 1798 acts were classified as being either public or private,
the latter term being used ostensibly to describe an act not held
to be of general application.

Acts of a private or local nature were not enscribed on the
statute rolls but were normally recorded on the parliament
rolls: the Exchequer series, 1290–1322 and Chancery series,
1327–1850. From 1593 to 1757 the texts of private acts, first
recorded on the parliament rolls *c.* 1500, were omitted, titles
alone being listed. Since such acts originated as private petitions, reference for the original texts, thirteenth to sixteenth
centuries, must be made to: the Chancery records, the Parliamentary and council proceedings (exchequer) and the ancient
petitions, in the PRO. For details of the 'original' texts of private
acts for the seventeenth century, see Bond page 99. Private
bills (printed) 1705 to date are held by HLRO, but the texts are
not necessarily true copies of the final acts.

No private act was officially printed until 1815, though private printing commenced in 1705, generally for local private use. Acts of a private or local nature appeared occasionally in the early printed sessional volumes of (public) statutes, and were so printed until 1539. Subsequent availability of titles and/or texts is as follows: sessional volumes of public acts, 1660–1752 contain titles of 'Local and Personal Acts declared Public' in one series with the public acts; from 1753 to 1797 the sessional volumes contain 'Local and Personal Acts declared Public', numbered in one series after the public acts; from 1798 to 1814 the sessional volumes contain 'Local and Personal Acts declared Public', numbered separately. Local and personal acts declared 'Public' are to be judicially noticed, but while judges must take notice of all public acts, this duty does not extend to a private act, which must always be produced in evidence. Private acts are listed in the sessional volumes of (public) acts, but in company with local and personal acts were not collected into a separate series in volume form until 1869.

As a result of lack of availability few, except the older libraries, possess even partially complete runs of these acts. The most complete is in HLRO as follows:

Sessional volumes of collected local and personal acts, 1798–1875; a series of collected separate prints.

Sessional volumes of collected local acts, 1876 to date, in continuation of the above.

Sessional volumes of collected private acts, 1815 to date; a series of printed texts of private acts not included in the above two series, such as enclosure, tithe and estate acts.

Certain private acts such as divorce, name and naturalization acts can only be located by reference to the original record copies in HLRO.

Two early guides to location require notice. First, the *Analytical Table of the Private Statutes*, 1727–1834 by G. Bramwell, 2 volumes, 1813–35. This is arranged chronologically, alphabetically and also according to subject matter. Second, Salt's *Index to Titles*, of 1863. This covers the period Anne to George I inclusive, deals with 2,231 acts, and was issued privately in three parts. The list in *Statutes at Large* gives the full title of all private acts after 1509 and House of Commons sessional paper 399 of 1914 lists completely the special class known as inclosure acts.

Commencement, Duration and Citation

Until 1793, when under 33 Geo. III c. 13 it became obligatory to endorse the date of royal assent upon an act, no date was fixed for the coming into force of an act. Unless otherwise specified, an act came into force on the first day of the parliamentary session in which it was passed, irrespective of the fact that royal assent was still wanting. This rule arose from the convenient fiction that the whole session lasted but one day.

The only effective means of dating the making of an act is by following its progress through the Lords journals which, until 1752, record the year of grace as commencing on 25 March (old calendar) not 1 January (new calendar) as now.

Unlike Scottish acts English statutes do not lapse through non usage.

Difficulty in the location or identification of early statutes may be avoided if it is remembered that the modern system of citation, superimposed upon the entire statute book, may create problems, especially when references occur that use a different style. None should arise when the act in question is one passed in a session that lies wholly within the regnal year and is the only session in that year.

But if two sessions lie wholly within a single regnal year it is necessary to distinguish acts as 'statute I' and 'statute II'. Thus 13 Charles II, stat. I, c. 1. and 13 Charles II, stat. II, c. 1. are not at all the same act. Again, a double citation is used if acts are passed in a session that covers two regnal years; thus 13 & 14 Charles II, c. 23.

Sir Cecil Carr in his article, Citation of Statutes in *Cambridge Legal Essays*, 1926, recommended in the interests of uniformity that it was desirable to cite acts down to 1713 as in *Statutes of the Realm*. The *Chronological Table of the Statutes* shows the variants between citations in *Statutes of the Realm* and Ruffhead's *Statutes at Large*.

Statutes of Uncertain Date

This is the term given to a group of statutes believed by Maitland to be apocryphal (see Maitland, F. W. *Collected Papers*, 1911, volume 2 at p. 39). They were included in *Statutes of the Realm* between Edward II and Edward III on the grounds that they were issued in the last year of Edward II's reign. For a list of these statutes, forty-four in number, see Holdsworth, W. S. *History of English Law*, volume 2, 1936, p. 604. Now, some are considered to be tracts from law treatises, some administrative measures, some ordinances, others rules relating to court procedure. Only a minority is held to be statutes.

The Interregnum: 1649–60

The last act to receive Charles I's assent was 1640 (16 Cha. I) c. 37. But it was not until January 1649 that Parliament assumed sovereignty. During the Interregnum a considerable body of legislation was passed by Parliament but, for historical reasons, little original material has survived. For original source material reference must be made to the Lords journals and the *Book of Orders and Ordinances*, 1640–95, 30 volumes, both held in HLRO. Each contain textual variations in readings and both are essential for comparative purposes.

The term 'ordinance' was adopted to signify a declaration of the two Houses of Parliament, authorized without the sanction of the King. For political reasons the legislation thus passed, 1642–60 alternated in terminology between 'ordinance' and 'act' six times. During this period enactments were always issued separately, not in sessional volumes. Few complete sets have survived.

Under authority contemporary collections, not always complete, were compiled; the most notable being those by E. Husband, issued in 1642 and 1646, and that by Henry Scobell, printed in 1658.

The most accessible edition is *Acts and Ordinances of the Interregnum*, 1642–60, edited by C. H. Firth and R. S. Rait, 3 volumes, 1911. The less important matter omitted belongs almost entirely to the period 1642–9. The Introduction, pp. III–XXXVIII, in volume 3 contains a full bibliographical statement on the legislative publications of the period.

Scotland

In Scotland, owing to the almost total lack of extant records, the sources of customary law are a matter for conjecture, though

Anglo-Saxon as well as Celtic influences are discernible. For the period between 410 and the introduction of feudal law by David I reference should be made to the *Ancient Laws and Institutes of Ireland* (see page 241) and the *Ancient Laws and Institutes of Wales* (see page 230), as well as to the following: *Ancient Laws and Customs of the Burghs of Scotland*, by C. Innes, 2 volumes, 1868–1910. *Scottish Burgh Record Society Publications*, volumes 1 and 2.

The law of Scotland has developed from a wide variety of sources, absorbing the influence of Mosaic and Roman, French, Dutch and Canon as well as English law. Differing sources and histories created differing systems which the Union has served to emphasize rather than efface. Indeed, owing to the Union with England in 1707 there is more emphasis on the historical aspect of statute law in Scotland, in which country it falls naturally into three parts. The first period lasts until 1424, when James I held his first Parliament after his years of captivity in England; the second covers the period 1424 to 1707; while the third continues from 1707 to date.

In general, original source material will be found in the acts and decrees and the *Acta Dominorum* held in manuscript in the General Register House, together with the Acts of Sederunt which, while nominally regulating the procedure of the supreme tribunal – the Court of Session – were often held to be of wider application.

The earliest extant statutory records consist of six rolls for the period 1292–3, 1368–9 and 1388–9; no original parliamentary records previous to 1466 surviving in any quantity. Printed acts relating to this lost period are based principally on transcripts of varying degrees of authenticity and reliability, and for information on which see Cooper, Lord, Early Scottish Statutes revisited, *Juridical Review*, volume 64, 1952, pp. 197–203.

For a detailed introduction to the period 1124–1423 refer to the introduction by Cosmo Innes in volume 1 of *Acts of the Parliament of Scotland*, noted below.

In 1960 there was published the first in a projected series of eight volumes entitled *Regesta Regum Scottorum*, 1153–1424. This set aims to bring together in one collection all the authenticated royal documents of Scotland for the period, with scholarly introductions to each volume.

Sessional laws were first issued in printed form in 1565 (printing being introduced into Scotland in 1507) but were not issued with such apparent regularity as English sessional legislation, since the early Scottish parliaments met infrequently. For details of these, see Sweet and Maxwell's *Legal Bibliography*, volume 5, 1957. After 1707, the last official Scottish edition of sessional acts was entitled *British Acts from 6 Anne to 12 George III*, 30 volumes in 33, 1718–72. This was in fact a binder's title, but is now so known. Subsequently those statutes referring specifically to Scotland were issued as part of the set of British sessional acts for each regnal year.

The earliest collection of note was the *Actis and Constitutionis of the Realme of Scotland* covering the period 1424–1564 and issued in 1566. This was the third and most important of the eight collections in the series known as the Black Acts because of their black-letter type. Another version, *The Lavves and Actes of Parliament*, collected by J. Skene and covering the period 1424–1597, was published in 1597. Known as Skene's Acts, it has been criticized for its textual errors. A later collection, much cited in the courts was *The Lavves and Acts of Parliament*, collected by Sir T. Murray, of Glendook, and printed in 1681. A reprint of Skene with seventeenth-century acts added, it was best known simply as Glendook's Acts. The inadequacy of these collections was to result in the publication of *The Acts of the Parliaments of Scotland*, 1124–1707, edited by T. Thomson and C. Innes, 12 volumes in 13, 1814–75. Volumes 5 and 6, being unsatisfactory, were replaced in 1870 and 1870–2 respectively. Volume 1 was published with interpolated material resulting in six separate paginations. Re-paginated copies in limited quantity were available under restriction, while the general index contains directions for re-paginating volume 1. Issued under the direction of the Record Commission, this remains the authoritative edition for Scottish statutes to 1707.

Scottish statutes, unlike English statutes, could fall into desuetude, either in whole or in part, and this doctrine is still held to apply to statutes promulgated prior to 1707. It is thought that the United Kingdom Parliament has power to repeal pre-1707 acts, subject to certain restrictions imposed by the Treaty of 1707.

Acts passed by the Parliament of Scotland prior to 1707 are

cited by the calendar year and chapter serial number. The serial number, however, varies between the two most commonly cited editions: the Record Commission edition of 1814–1875 and Murray of Glendook's edition of 1681.

Digest Practicks

The term Practick means a precedent but not necessarily a binding precedent. The Practicks may be divided into two classes: those known as Decision Practicks (for details of which see page 173); and those known as Digest Practicks. The latter were later in composition but included not only notes of decisions but also excerpts from statutes and the 'auld lawes', as well as much early material drawn from the registers. They were thus digests or encyclopedias of the law, not dissimilar to English abridgments and exercised a considerable influence on the institutional writers (see below). In general, the later Practicks were ordered alphabetically, their contents grouped under subject heads. James Balfour's Practicks, issued 1754 but written *c.* 1580, included supreme court decisions, aimed to cover the whole field of law and was based wholly on practice. It was to be recognized as 'a work of undoubted authority'. Robert Spotiswoode's *Practicks*, issued in 1706, is noted for its accuracy and is still much cited in court. Thomas Hope was the author of two works: firstly the *Minor Practicks*, written prior to 1634 and first issued in 1726 which is, in content, a treatise on different legal topics and so belies its title; and secondly the *Major Practicks*, not printed till 1937–8 by the Stair Society. It is a major work on seventeenth-century Scots law still virtually unknown to the profession.

Ireland

The earliest known Irish law is found in two major codes, the Senchus Mor, a code of legal usages compiled perhaps in the ninth or tenth century and dealing with civil law, and the Book of Aicill, a survey of the criminal law, both codes having a continuing influence till the end of the fifteenth century. Their texts will be found in *Ancient Laws and Institutes of Ireland*, edited by W. N. Hancock and A. G. Richey, 6 volumes, 1865–1901.

Volumes 1–3 contain the Senchus Mor, volume 3 also containing the Book of Aicill; volumes 4–5 contain the Brehon law tracts, and volume 6 contains a glossary to the other volumes. The text is in Irish with an English translation. This edition is held to be unreliable.

While certain early English statutes were enforceable in Ireland as early as the last quarter of the thirteenth century, the Irish Parliament in Dublin, established in the same period, was subservient to the Parliament in London, and was principally concerned with ratifying such English statutes as could be held to be applicable to Ireland. In 1495 under Poynings' Law, 10 Hen. VII c. 22 (Ir.) it was held that all English statutes of general application should apply to Ireland. In 1782 the Irish Parliament achieved independence until self-abolition in 1800, when the new United Kingdom was formed.

The earliest extant Irish legislation dates from 1278. For published statute rolls see *Statutes and Ordinances and Acts of the Parliament of Ireland, King John to [22 Edward IV]*, edited by H. F. Berry and J. F. Morissey, 4 volumes, 1907–39. Issued under the direction of the Irish Record Office, these contain transcripts with English translations of the Latin and French texts.

The confused history of the English conquest is reflected in the uncertainty that exists concerning full bibliographical details about sessional publications. The earliest recorded are the *Statuta, Ordinationes, Acta et Provisiones*, covering the period 1584–5 and issued by C. Barker sometime after 1585. No Parliament thereafter was summoned for twenty-seven years, while not till 1603 did English authority reign supreme. Parliaments were held intermittently between 1559 and 1713, only eleven being summoned, but were thereafter held regularly, with lapses of not more than twelve months between each, until 1800. Sessional laws are recorded for the period 1634–1800 and for details of these see Sweet and Maxwell: *Legal Bibliography*, volume 4, 1957 at p. 89. Until 1782 sessional laws are in general re-enactments of such statutes already in force in England, but which could suitably be held applicable to Ireland.

The first collection of statutes was printed by Tottell in 1572 and covered the period 10 Hen. VI to 14 Eliz. I. Other collections were subsequently published, the principal and most accurate being *Statutes at Large passed in Parliaments held in Ireland*, 1310–1767, issued in nine folio volumes in Dublin between 1765–69. A later collection, not however titled *Statutes at Large*, was published between 1786 and 1801 in twenty volumes and covered the years 1310 to 1800.

The Channel Islands and the Isle of Man

In Jersey the common law stems directly from the customary law of the ancient Duchy and the leading authority on this law remains a work compiled in, probably, the thirteenth century. Numerous extant editions were printed in the years between *c*. 1483 and 1578, but the 'authorized' text normally cited in the Royal Court remains *Le Grand Coustumier du pays et duché de Normandie*, composées par Guillaume le Rouillé d'Alencon, 1539. An annotated edition of this work was issued in 1831 by W. L. de Gruchy, which gives both Latin and French texts but this has not superseded a much earlier work: Terrien, G. *Commentaires du Droit Civil*, 1574. The principal authority for the maintenance of customary law will be found in Privy Council decisions (see page 183). Reference must also be made to the sixteenth-century *Coutume Réformée de Normandie* which expounds the Norman law of that period. There are a number of commentaries upon this work, the most notable being Bérault's *Coutume réformée* of 1614, Godefroy's *Commentaires* of 1626 and Pesnelle's *Coutume* of 1704.

Legislation has customarily been enacted by the States, the central legislative body. Refer to *Lois et règlements*, 1771 to date; part of the text of the early volumes is in French and the binder's title reads 'Recueil des Lois'.

In Guernsey the civil law of the island is based in part only upon the 'Ancienne Coutume de Normandie' and, as a result, the principal authority for citation in court remains the commentary by Terrien, noted above. Similarly reference must be made to the *Coutume Réformée* and, in particular, the commentaries most frequently cited in court. These are by Bérault, also noted above, and Basnage, H. *La coutume réformée du paiis et duché de Normandie*, 2 volumes, 1678–81. For legislation prior to 1800 reference must be made to *Recueil D'Ordonnances de la Cour Royale de L'Isle de Guernsey*, covering the period 1533–1932 and issued in six volumes between 1852–1933; also to *Actes des Etats*, covering the period 1605–1845 and issued in eight volumes between 1851–1938.

In the Isle of Man legislation has always been enacted by the Tynwald, a legislature that dates from the time of the Norse Kings, who conquered the island in the ninth century. Except for Briscoe, C., *Statute Laws of the Isle of Man*, 1797, the bulk of Manx legislation is available only in post-1800 works, for which see page 133.

REPORTS OF CASES

Plea Rolls

The extant medieval records of the early superior courts are best known by the term 'plea rolls', which describes their form and function. Their genealogy is confusing owing to the complicated history of their classification and arrangement, but the historical origin of some dates from the last quarter of the twelfth century. Among the most important are the curia regis rolls of the courts *coram rege* and *de banco*, later the King's Bench and Common Pleas. The plea rolls contain a succinct summary of each case, recording the place and date of trial, the names of the parties, the nature of the proceedings and the judgment awarded.

In 1884 Sir Paul Vinogradoff discovered a collection of cases drawn from the plea rolls. This was subsequently published as *Bracton's Notebook*, edited by F. W. Maitland, 3 volumes, 1887. It contains approximately 2,000 cases and provided the raw material upon which Bracton drew for his celebrated treatise, *De Legibus*, noted below. The value of the plea rolls to the historian lies in the data they record, omitted by the Year Books (see below).

At least forty volumes of select pleas have been printed since the nineteenth century – by the Record Commission, the Pipe Roll Society and others, principally the Selden Society. For details of these refer to Sweet and Maxwell: *Legal Bibliography*, volume 1, 1955, pp. 70–74.

References to printed decisions are made as to the page of a treatise in the normal manner, thus: Select Cases in the Court of King's Bench (S.S. 1936–9) ii, 415.

Year Books

These are the 'law reports' of English medieval society. They differ from the modern concept of reporting in that they are not simply factual and objective, but highly subjective. As a result, they are invaluable to both legal and social historians, whilst their language, for speeches are reported verbatim, provide an untapped source for the philologist. Written in Law French, they run in an almost unbroken sequence from the reign of Edward I to Richard III and thereafter intermittently to 27 Hen. VIII, when they end. Excepting the plea rolls, they are the only extant accounts of legal doctrine as laid down by judges of the fourteenth and fifteenth centuries and, being contemporary reports are of the utmost value. The reason for their compilation – whether as notes for students or as aids for practitioners – is still obscure; a topic for scholarly disputation.

A considerable quantity of manuscripts is still extant, though few are originals and the majority are to be located in libraries at Oxford and Cambridge and in London. No complete list of these exists, though attempts have been made at compilation, *eg*, Nicholson, J. *Register of Manuscripts of Year Books Extant*, 1956. Nicholson, though useful, is incomplete and occasionally inaccurate in defining ownership, whilst Abbott, L. W. *Law Reporting in England*, 1485–1585, 1973, pp. 257–305 lists Year Books for the period in question.

Numerous printed editions exist. A number were first issued by William de Machlinia, *c*. 1481; Richard Pynson printed fifty editions of various terms; while Richard Tottell, to whom 225 editions are attributed, commenced printing these in 1553.

The 'standard' edition is Maynard's. This may be entitled *Year Books; or Reports in the following reigns* [1 *Edward II to 27 Henry VIII*], *with notes to Brooke and Fitzherbert's Abridgments* [edited by Sir J. Maynard] 11 parts, 1678–80. The language is Law French, the volumes are folio size, the print is black-letter, and each part has a table of the principal matters. Two parts are usually bound together, but the parts are not numbered and only part one contains matter not previously printed. The coverage of the regnal years is incomplete.

Other editions require notice:

First: the Rolls Series edition, edited by A. J. Horwood and

L. O. Pike in twenty volumes between 1863–1911 and covering the years 20–22, 30–35 Edward I and 11–20 Edward III. This was made up of previously unpublished material and is notable in that the reports are compared with the original plea roll entries.

Second: the Selden Society, issued as part of that society's publications and edited by F. W. Maitland and others. Over twenty-five volumes of Year Books not previously printed have been issued and a modern English translation is given against the original text.

Both editions are equipped with extensive and informative introductions.

The black-letter editions of the Year Books omit any identification of the speaker and this is best rectified by reference to Foss, E. *The Judges of England*, 9 volumes, 1848–64.

Cases are cited by the regnal years and the law term in which the plea was heard, and the number of the plea is also given.

Abbreviations are commonly used. Thus, YB 11 Hen. 6; Hil. pl. 10; or Pasch. pl. 1. Where references contain a capital A or B this is usually to Maynard's edition. In this, the A at the head of the page indicates where the recto of the earlier folio (edition) begins; the B, halfway down, indicates where the verso of the earlier folio (edition) commences. With the modern editions reference is made thus: (RS) and (SS).

Excepting reprints, the last Year Book to be printed covered part of 1535–6 and was issued by Myddylton before 1547. Thereafter, though Year Books in manuscript continued to be produced, and some are extant for the later years of Henry VIII, none was published. Their eclipse was due not to the advent of printing but to other causes; a change in the style of reporting which, in Plowden's hands, was to prove immensely successful; the needs of authors to protect their reputation in an age lacking the certainties offered by a copyright act; the commercial advantage to be gained by both author and publisher through a personalization of the reporting; and a growing realization that the year-book format no longer met satisfactorily the changing needs of the profession. Their language had fallen into desuetude and their emphasis upon the arguments leading to the formulation of the issue in a case lost its value as a result of the change from oral to written pleadings. Legal interest was developing a concern with the decisions themselves. The period 1556–71 is a period of curious if expectant silence, but at the end of it the birth of law reporting took place (see page 144).

Abridgments

The order of arrangement in the Year Books was chronological and, side notes apart, it was difficult to locate the desired information in the mass of material available in manuscript and print. Abridgments digesting the essential under suitable heads were needed and provided. Statham's *Epitome*, of *c.* 1490, and the *Abridgment of the Book of Assizes*, of *c.* 1509, deserve mention. The latter is known to modern bibliographers as *Liber Assisarium*, but is not to be confused with the title of the same name in the Year Book series. Two major works, however, require special notice, since their authors did much to enhance the art of the abridger. The first is Sir Anthony Fitzherbert's *La Graunde Abridgment*, issued by Rastell in 1516 in three volumes. This records 14,039 cases under 260 titles alphabetically arranged. Invaluable as an epitome of case law, it is noted for its accuracy and its system of arrangement, while its structure established a pattern for future writers. Robert Brooke's *La Graunde Abridgment* was published by Tottell in 1573 in two volumes. Based on Fitzherbert, it records over 20,000 cases under 404 titles and abridges the Year Books of Henry VII and Henry VIII. Both works include matter not contained in the Year Books.

It must be noted that the term 'case' covers notes, opinions and points drawn from cases.

TREATISES

England

The early treatise was either an exposition upon a statute or collection of like statutes, designed to illuminate a particular branch of the law, or it was a book of practice to inform the lawyer as to the necessary expertise required for the conduct of his craft. Treatises were books on the law rather than books about the law – though there were exceptions – and they were written by practitioners for practitioners, rarely for the edification of the student.

In general, such treatises could not be regarded as literary sources of law for they contained only opinions as to the state of the law, not the law itself; thus they were not books of authority and could not be cited in court. But a rule was formulated which made permissible the citing in argument of the works of dead authors, though not those living. In practice, only a minority of works acquired a prestige that made them acceptable to the justiciary almost without question.

The construction of early treatises is at variance with that of the modern textbook, which assumed its present shape in the nineteenth century. They were descriptive rather than creative and the amount of exposition was at first very small. The realization that principles might be deduced from cases, and the cases in turn cited, was slow to develop, so that it is often hard to know where fact ends and comment begins. Systematic exposition was uncommon, texts lacked coherence and authors enjoyed digressions, too often uncritical of material cannibalized from other writers. Intellectual discipline was wanting. The lack of copyright protection did not help. New editions were likely to be edited by printers who altered texts unhindered; while a lack of uniformity in spelling, combined with indifferent proof reading, did little to assist the establishment of standards for accurate texts and references.

The earliest treatise on English common law was written in the twelfth century by Ranulph de Glanvil. Compiled in Latin between 1187–9, his *Tractatus de legibus* was printed by Tottell *c.* 1554 and 'presents a vivid image of the importance of land law and of procedure in mediaeval England'.

In the thirteenth century a number of anonymous tracts were circulated dealing with procedure, as well as the earliest extant manuscript of the *Registrum Brevium* or Register of Writs afterwards printed in 1531. In the middle of the century a great work was written describing the law and practice of the King's courts and of the judicial commissions: Bracton, H. de, *De Legibus et consuetudinibus Angliae*, printed by Tottell in 1569. Bracton contains 500 references to decided cases, fathered a number of epitomes, and remains a monument to medieval jurisprudence.

The first law book to be printed was a masterpiece: Thomas Littleton's *Tenures*, printed by Lettou and Machlinia, *c.* 1481. It was in French, but an English translation was issued before 1538. By 1628, eighty-two editions or variants of editions had been printed. Justly praised for its brevity and lucidity, it remains still a model of the art of treatise writing.

Works published between 1475–1603 include formula books, precedents of pleading (known then as 'books of entries'), readings of the Inns of Court and tracts containing selections of writs. There were works for lay judges dealing with the functions of justices of the peace, manorial courts, courts baron and courts leet, as well as books on special topics such as Admiralty and the law merchant. Others dealt with special jurisdictions such as the palatinates of Chester, Durham and Lancaster.

In 1628, Edward Coke had published the *First Part of the Institutes of the Lawes of England; or a Commentarie upon Littleton.* Three further parts followed, the last being printed in 1644. Coke surveyed the entire field of law and restated it for his age, but he did more; he asserted the supremacy of the law with an authority that was overwhelming and which remains undiminished to this day.

The seventeenth century also saw notable works by Heneage Finch, Francis Bacon, John Selden and Matthew Hale, as well as a stream of treatises by lesser men in response to the growing complexities of the law.

The eighteenth century saw a technical improvement in the standard of treatise writing and the volume of output increased though, with the exception of Gilbert, writers individually were less prolific and their work undistinguished. Yet the age produced a classic work aimed originally at academics not practitioners: William Blackstone's *Commentaries on the Laws of England,* issued in four volumes, 1765–9. Notable for its learning, its clarity and its style it ran into thirteen editions before 1800 and is still cited as a book of authority.

For select lists of notable treatise writers refer to the following: *Bibliography of British History,* Tudor Period, 1485–1603, editor, C. Read, 1959, and the companion volume for the Stuart Period, 1603–1714, editor, M. F. Keeler, 1970.

Scotland

The earliest treatises are the 'Buikes of the Auld Lawes' written before 1500. The first is the *Regiam Majestatem*, a collection of medieval royal and feudal laws with other treatises added, two-thirds of the whole consisting of Glanville's *Tractatus*, suitably modified. The second is the *Quoniam Attachiamenta*, a series of 'statutes' attributed to early kings. Both works are anonymous, deal with court procedure, and were published together in 1597 under the title of the former. Skene's edition of 1609, issued in both Latin and Scottish remains the authoritative edition.

It is impossible to offer a precise definition of an institutional writer. It is perhaps sufficient to say of those under review that their work, owing much, perhaps, to the influence of Roman Law writings, have a scope and depth not to be found in even the best of treatises, and all are held to be of high authority. Thomas Craig, author of the *Jus Feudale* published in 1655, was the first. He has been described as 'the first systematic writer on Scots law' and his work remains the standard authority on feudal law; a disquisition of enormous learning which in form provided a model for his successors. James Dalrymple, Viscount Stair, issued his *Institutions of the Law of Scotland* in 1681. It ran to five editions, of which the last two are those now normally cited. Stair was a great scholar, a profound thinker and a fine judge. His intellect was formidable and it did not fail him as a writer. His *Institutions*, which did so much to create the Scottish legal system, is one of the great legal books of the world. George Mackenzie's *Institutions*, 1694, was a slighter work which ran to eight editions and is still consulted, while Andrew McDouall, Lord Bankton's *Institute*, issued 1751–3 in three volumes, is a comparative work designed for the instruction of Scottish and English lawyers. John Erskine's *Institute* was published posthumously in 1773 and ran to seven editions, while his *Principles*, an epitome of the former, two volumes in one, issued in 1754, ran into twenty-one editions. These were academic works, the latter designed for students.

Major treatises on the criminal law were written by Mackenzie and Baron David Hume in the seventeenth and eighteenth centuries respectively. The latter's work has been highly regarded. Hume's *Lectures* were subsequently published by the Stair Society in six volumes between 1939–58 and are now regarded as of quasi-institutional authority.

For notes on select treatises, refer to the *Bibliography of British History*, noticed above.

Ireland

The enforcement of English law upon Ireland till 1782 sterilized the production of major treatises, since it was primarily to English textbooks that the profession of necessity turned for guidance. The output of treatises was inevitably small and though the publications of the eighteenth century more than doubled those of the seventeenth, the range of topics dealt with was not dissimilar. Works on practice and procedure, the duties of justices of the peace and petty constables, landlord and tenant, master and servant, and the corn law appeared in equal proportion with treatises on sovereignty and the constitution, as well as tracts touching upon religious problems.

For a detailed list of treatises see Sweet and Maxwell: *Legal Bibliography*, volume 4, *Irish Law to 1956*, 1957.

The Channel Islands and Isle of Man

Since in the Channel Islands customary law is dominant, there is little treatise material available except the commentaries already noted above. The principal treatises date from the seventeenth century but were not printed till much later: Poingdestre, J. *Les lois et Coutumes*, 1928 and Le Geyt, P. *Les Manuscrits sur la Constitution*, 1846–7 both relate to Jersey, the latter being held by the Privy Council in 1846 to be the authoritative work. For Guernsey, see Dicey, T. *Historical Account of Guernsey*, 1751.

Treatises on the Isle of Man are equally sparse. Its early history may be studied in Ross, A. *Mona, or the History, Laws and Constitutions of the Isle of Man, c.* 1744, and in Oswald, H. R. *Vestigia Insulae Manniae Antiquiora*, 1860, dealing with similar topics.

FURTHER READING

GENERAL WORKS

An Introductory Survey of the Sources and Literature of Scots Law, by various authors [editor, H. McKechnie]. Stair Society, Edinburgh, 1936 (*Stair Society*, 1).

Ball, J. T. *Historical review of the legislative system operative in Ireland, 1172–1800*. 3rd edition. Longman, Green, 1891.

Holdsworth, W. S. *Sources and Literature of English Law*. Clarendon Press, Oxford, 1925. The early chapters dealing with the Statutes, the Year Books, the Reports and Abridgments, the Register of Writs, Text Books and Books of Authority are the most valuable for the librarian.

Holdsworth, W. S. *History of English Law*. Various editions. Methuen, 1936–72, 17 vols. (ISBN 0 431 05160 4, etc.); see especially vols. 4 and 6 (1485–1700), pp. 313 and 312–13 respectively, on chief abridgments of the statutes; vol. 2 (449–1485), pp. 525–56 for the Year Books; vol. 5 (1485–1700), pp. 378–412 on literature of the common law, pp. 460–72 on the writings of Edward Coke; vol. 6 (1485–1700), pp. 574–613 and 614–16 on law books; vol. 12 (1701–1875), pp. 331–43 on treatises; vol. 13 (1701–85) on law books.

Plucknett, T. F. T. *Early English Legal Literature*, Cambridge University Press, 1958. (*Cambridge Studies in English Legal History*) (ISBN 0 521 05966 6).

Winfield, P. H. *Chief Sources of English Legal History*. Cambridge, Mass., Harvard University Press, 1925, reprinted 1962.

Chronology

Powicke, F. M. and Fryde, E. B. *Handbook of British Chronology*. 2nd edition. Royal Historical Society, 1961, pp. 141–55. (*Royal Historical Society guides and handbooks*, 2) (ISBN 0 901050 17 2).

Handbook of Dates for Students of English History, editor C. R. Cheney. Royal Historical Society, 1945. (*Royal Historical Society guides and handbooks*, 4).

Poole, R. L. *Medieval reckonings of time*. Society for Promoting Christian Knowledge, 1918. (*Helps for students of history*, 3).

Legal Language

Latham, R. E. Coping with Medieval Latin. *Amateur Historian*, vol. 1, 1952–4, pp. 331–3. The *Amateur Historian* changed its title to the *Local Historian* with vol. 8, no. 1 (1968).

Luders, A. *Essay on the use of the French language in our ancient laws.* Privately printed, 1807.

Menger, L. E. *The Anglo-Norman Dialect.* New York, 1904.

Pollock, F. *First Books of Jurisprudence.* 6th edition. Macmillan, 1929. Contains information at pp. 299–302 on reading Law French.

ARCHIVES AND MANUSCRIPTS

Baker, J. H. Unprinted Sources of English Legal History. *Law Library Journal,* vol. 64, no. 3, 1971, pp. 302–13.

Bond, M. F. The Formation of the Archives of Parliament, 1497–1691. *Journal of the Society of Archivists,* vol. 1, 1957, pp. 151–8.

Denholm-Young, N. *Handwriting in England and Wales.* 2nd edition. Cardiff, University of Wales Press, 1964.

Galbraith, V. H. *An Introduction to the Use of the Public Records.* Oxford University Press, 1934. (ISBN 0 19 821221 6).

Galbraith, V. H. *Studies in the Public Records.* Nelson, 1948.

Jenkinson, Sir H. *A Manual of Archive Administration.* 2nd edition. Lund Humphries, 1937, reprinted 1965 (ISBN 0 85331 072 6).

Le Hardy, W. How to read 16th and 17th century handwriting. *Amateur Historian,* vol. 1, 1952–4, pp. 146–54.

Livingstone, M. *Guide to the Public Records of Scotland in HM General Register House.* Edinburgh, HMSO, 1905. A supplementary list of accessions to 1946 is contained in *Scottish Historical Review,* vol. 24, no. 101, 1947.

Madan, F. *Books in Manuscript: a short introduction to their study and use.* 2nd edition, 1920.

Maitland Thompson, J. *The Public Records of Scotland.* (Rhind lectures). Glasgow, 1922.

Paton, H. M. *The Scottish Records, their value and history.* Edinburgh, Historical Association of Scotland, 1933.

PRINTED SOURCE COLLECTIONS

Aspinall, A. The reporting and publishing of the House of Commons Debates, 1771–1834. In Pares, R. and Taylor, A. J. P. *Essays presented to Sir Lewis Namier.* Macmillan, 1956, pp. 227–57.

Cobb, H. S. *The journals, minutes and committee books of the House of Lords.* House of Lords Record Office, 1957. (*House of Lords Record Office memorandum,* 13).

Knowles, M. D. The Rolls Series. *Royal Historical Society Transactions,* 5th series, vol. 11, 1961, pp. 137–59.

Menhennet, D. *The Journals of the House of Commons: a bibliographical and historical guide.* HMSO, 1971. (*House of Commons library documents,* 7) (ISBN 0 10 831070 1).

Neale, J. E. The Commons Journals of the Tudor Period. *Transactions of the Royal Historical Society*, 4th series, vol. 3, 1920, pp. 136–70.

LEGISLATION

Bond, M. F. *Acts of Parliament: some notes on the original acts preserved at the House of Lords, their use and interpretation.* British Record Association, 1958.

Edwards, Sir G. The historical study of the Welsh law books. *Royal Historical Society Transactions*, 5th series, vol. 12, 1962, pp. 141–55.

United Kingdom Record Commission: an historical survey of ancient English statutes. In *Select essays in Anglo-American legal history*, compiled by a committee of the Association of American Law Schools. Boston, Mass., Little, Brown, 1908. Vol. 2, pp. 169–205.

Beale, J. H. The early English statutes. *Harvard Law Review*, vol. 35, 1922, pp. 519–38.

REPORTS OF CASES

Bolland, W. C. *The Year Books.* Cambridge University Press, 1921.

Bolland, W. C. *Manual of Year Book Studies.* Cambridge University Press, 1925. *(Cambridge studies in English legal history)*.

Holdsworth, W. S. The Year Books. In *Select essays in Anglo-American legal history*, compiled by a committee of the Association of American Law Schools. Boston, Mass., Little, Brown, 1908. Vol. 2, pp. 96–122.

Simpson, A. W. B. The circulation of year books in the fifteenth century. *Law Quarterly Review*, vol. 73, no. 4, 1957, pp. 492–3.

7. Official Publications

Part 1: Government Official Publications

E. J. MILLER, BA, FSA, FRHIST.S
Formerly Head, Official Publications Library, British
Library

Official publications – books, pamphlets and other documents
issued by a government, whether those of a sovereign state or of
the component parts of a federation, are of particular value to a
law librarian. Some are the fundamental documents, the laws,
decrees and so on, on which the legal system of any country
is based, which are described in Chapter 3. Others are the
results of enquiries or research into numerous aspects of our
complex civilization, covering a wide range of secondary
material in many different fields. They provide, in an easily
accessible and often predigested form, a high proportion of the
information needed by lawyers or other users of a law library.
Official publications are, on the whole, relatively cheap and
easy to obtain, whether, as in many countries from a central
governmental publishing agency, such as the Stationery Office,
or directly from a ministry or other issuing body. Governments
may, or indeed do, publish almost anything, from laws to
novels and patriotic songs, from scholarly art histories to hints
for the do-it-yourself enthusiast.

But for the law librarian, however, it is publications within
the following subject areas which are most likely to be of
interest (though it should always be remembered that almost
any government publication may be found useful at one time or
another): crime; economics; education; housing; immigration; industrial relations; law; local government; public
health; statistics, general; and taxation.

We are concerned here only with British and Irish official
publications and specifically, at the moment, with those
covering just England and Wales or Great Britain as a whole.
Official publications relating solely to other parts of the United
Kingdom and the Republic of Ireland will be dealt with below.

Of the numerous and ever-proliferating number of government departments and similar organizations now to be found in this country, there are certain whose publications will be of special value to the law librarian. Such are the Department of Education and Science, the Department of Health and Social Security and the Department of Trade and Industry, together with their various predecessors; the Home Office, the Board of Inland Revenue; the Lord Chamberlain's Department; the minor legal departments; the Scottish and Welsh Offices and the Treasury. Two further departments whose publications may be of less immediate value, but which, nevertheless, are of considerable importance, especially when dealing with questions of historic interest, are the former Colonial and Foreign Offices and their successor, the Foreign and Commonwealth Office.

TYPES OF OFFICIAL PUBLICATIONS

Parliamentary publications

There is a widespread group of publications of great value to the law librarian which are issued, not formally by a specific department, but under the authority of Parliament itself and which are, in general, concerned with matters likely to be subject to early legislation. Of these the most important are first those presented to Parliament, not under the authority of a specific act, but by command of Her Majesty on the initiative of the responsible minister and known therefore as Command papers. Second is that large group of papers, for the most part ordered to be printed by either House and entitled sessional papers of the House of Lords or of the House of Commons. Until 1921 a very large number of departmental reports and similar publications were issued as Parliamentary papers. The following year, and subsequently, their number was greatly reduced, the papers in question being issued directly by the department concerned. Even so, the last bound set to be issued, that for 1969–70, amounts to no less than twenty-nine volumes.

Command papers

Command papers, which have now been appearing in more or less their present form for well over two hundred years, are issued either to expound government policy or to disseminate information which the government considers should be laid before Parliament and made known to the general public. The reports of Royal Commissions, Departmental Committees and other publications of a like nature are now normally therefore issued as Command papers. Recent examples are the *Report of the Departmental Committee on Liquor Licensing*, Cmnd. 5154 (the Erroll Report); that of the *Departmental Committee on Section 2 of the Official Secrets Act of 1911*, Cmnd. 5104 (the Franks Report); that of the *Committee to consider Legal Proceedings to deal with Terrorist Activities in Northern Ireland*, Cmnd. 5185 (the Diplock Report) and the *Northern Ireland Constitutional Proposals*, Cmnd. 5259. It will be seen that many commissions and committees, as well as their reports, are popularly known by the name of their chairmen. It is essential, therefore, that law libraries have a card catalogue, or similar device, arranged under the chairmen's names for quick reference. Some useful published guides are mentioned in the bibliography.

Command papers are numbered in four consecutive sequences. From 1833 to 1869 such papers bore only a plain number, 1–4,222, the numbers not actually appearing on the papers themselves until 1839. From 1870 to 1899 the sequence went from C.1–C.9,500, followed from 1900 to 1918 by Cd. 1–9,239; from 1919 to 1956 Cmd. 1–9,998 and subsequently the current sequence of Cmnd. 1 onwards from November 1956 to the present day.

Sessional papers

Sessional papers are, for the most part, those laid before either House by an order of that House or by a minister under the authority of an Act of Parliament. Whilst not now so numerous as in the nineteenth century, when much information was furnished by government in the form of returns to addresses moved by members of either House, sessional papers still cover a wide variety of subjects. Examples of recent papers are the Report of the Monopolies Commission on breakfast cereals (1972–3 no. 2); that of the Law Commission on family property (1972–3 no. 274); the report under the Import Duties Act, 1958 and so on.

9

Another broad class consists of rules, orders-in-council and similar regulations made by ministers, whilst reports of standing or *ad hoc* committees of either House, such as that of the Committee on Expenditure or that on the Nationalized Industries are likewise issued as sessional papers. Not all such papers, however, are printed, though the majority now are. If printed by order of the House of Lords or of Commons, they rank as sessional papers proper and are given a distinctive numeration within each session. Some reports, presented in pursuance of a statute, are issued directly by the Stationery Office.

Green papers

These constitute a new type of official publications, which may be either Parliamentary or non-Parliamentary and which were first introduced in 1967. Their green covers are designed as a visual contrast to the traditional 'white papers' and 'blue books', though the latter themselves, more often than not, now appear with covers of many colours. Green papers contain tentative proposals involving frequently a change in government policy and are intended primarily to serve as a basis of discussion. Usually the Green paper is followed subsequently by a further paper, normally a Command paper, which makes known the Government's final decisions. Occasionally, as a result of the criticism aroused, the original proposals are abandoned and no further paper appears.

Examples of Green papers are: *National Health Service. The Administrative structure of the medical and related services in England and Wales*, issued by the Ministry of Health in July 1968; *Proposals for a Tax-Credit System*, issued by the Treasury and the Department of Health and Social Security as Cmnd. 5116 in October 1972 and *The Channel Tunnel Project*, issued by the Department of the Environment as Cmnd. 5256 in March 1973.

Journals and proceedings

Among other publications issued under the authority of Parliament and of interest to law librarians are the *Journals* of both Houses, the day-to-day transactions in summarized form, essential for tracing the legislative history of any bill and, in earlier centuries, containing moreover a large number of papers and other documents now likely to be issued as Parliamentary or even as departmental publications. The proceedings of both Houses, popularly known as *Hansard*, 1803–   , can likewise be of considerable importance to the law librarian, as can also be, in special circumstances, other Parliamentary publications, such as *Votes*, 1689–   , *Notices of Motions*, 1849–   , and so on.

Gazettes

Gazettes are another form of official publications best treated separately. Three are now published within the United Kingdom: the *London Gazette*, 1665–   , the *Edinburgh Gazette*, 1793–   , and the *Belfast Gazette*, 1921–   . The oldest of these is of course the *London Gazette*, published continuously since November 1665, being then known as the *Oxford Gazette*, the Court having moved to that city to avoid the plague.

The *Edinburgh Gazette*, after a short-lived, semi-official existence at the beginning of the eighteenth century, has appeared from 1793 to the present day. The *Belfast Gazette* commenced in June 1921 and still continues, despite direct rule, whilst the *Dublin Gazette*, which had been issued since the early eighteenth century ceased as such on 27 January 1922, being succeeded by the *Iris Ofigiúil*, 1922–   , the gazette of the Irish Free State, afterwards the Republic of Ireland. Since we are at the moment dealing with material relating to England only the *London Gazette* will here be discussed in detail. The others, of course, contain similar material, relating to their respective countries.

The *London Gazette* now contains much miscellaneous information of value to law librarians. Such are notices issued by departments under the authority of various acts; other official notices; companies struck off the Register of Companies and similar material grouped together under the heading State Intelligence and Public Notices. Also to be found in the *Gazette* are various other notices of a legal or commercial nature, such as de-registry of chapels, petitions for the compulsory winding up of companies; changes of name and other personal advertisements. Up to approximately the middle of the eighteenth century, the *Gazette* contained a large amount of general news, in particular foreign news, but with the growth of the commercial press, this has become restricted to the publication of naval and military dispatches and other announcements of a purely public nature.

Departmental publications

The remaining, and now by far the largest class of government publications, consists of those issued directly by the major departments of state and numerous other statutory authorities. Many are published by HM Stationery Office, although a growing number, with the rapid increase of fringe organizations, are published by the relevant body itself. Certain of the major departments are now likewise undertaking their own publishing. Some of these publications may be obtained through HMSO and are listed in their catalogues, even though not published by that organization, but, unfortunately, many now are not. A thorough account of those not listed in HMSO catalogues and how they may be obtained will be found in the revised Chapter 17 of the second edition of Pemberton's *British Official Publications*, 2nd edition, 1974.

Of other official publications, often of a restricted nature and intended, for the most part, for a limited circulation only, it is not necessary to speak, since they are primarily of an archival nature and will not normally be made available for scholars until after an interval of at least thirty years.

SOME USEFUL SERIAL PUBLICATIONS

Within these special fields which the law librarian is most likely to have to deal with, there are a certain number of serial publications which may well prove of especial value. For instance, in the complex area of crime and criminology, the various statistical publications issued by the Home Office are of outstanding importance. Examples of these are: *The Report of Her Majesty's Chief Inspector of Constabulary*, 1879–   and the *Criminal Statistics, England and Wales*, 1857–   . Other studies sponsored by the Home Office cover a wide range of social problems. Questions on economics and finance may be answered by such publications as the *Bank of England Quarterly Bulletin*, 1960– , *The Bank of England Report and Accounts*, 1948– or their *Banking Statistics*, 1972– . The Treasury, as might be expected, produces several important serials, such as the *Economic Progress Report*, 1970– or the annual *Financial Statement and Budget Report*, 1880– . *Economic Trends*, 1953– and *Financial Statistics*, 1963– , both published by the Central Statistical Office, will likewise prove useful.

There are numerous publications of value in the field of education, whilst the vexed subject of immigration is covered by several Home Office publications, as well as those issued by the Community Relations Commission. The reports of the various nationalized industries are of obvious importance, as are other publications on trade and industry. The Department of Employment and the Departments of Trade and of Industry, produce a number of useful serials, such as the *Annual Report of HM Chief Inspector of Factories* and the *British Labour Statistics Year Book*, both issued by the Department of Employment and *Trade and Industry* (*incorporating the Board of Trade Journal*), issued by the Department of Trade. It should always be remembered that a number of such serials have been published by the predecessors of the present departments for many years, often continuously from the middle of the nineteenth century onwards. Many were and sometimes continue to be Parliamentary papers and details of them may be found in the various indexes to Parliamentary papers mentioned below.

The important field of local government and such largely municipal activities as housing, welfare, public health and so on are dealt with in various serials now produced by the Department of the Environment, the Department of Health and Social Security and the Medical Research Council. Amongst them are the Department of the Environment's *Housing and Construction Statistics*; the *Annual Report* and the *Statistical and Research Report Series*, issued by the Department of Health and Social Security and the *Special Report Series*, issued by the Medical Research Council. *Studies on Medical and Population Subjects*, now issued by the Office of Population, Censuses and Surveys, likewise contains much valuable material.

There are also a number of general statistical publications

which the law librarian may well find extremely useful. Such are the *Annual Abstract of Statistics*, 1840–   and *Studies in Official Statistics*, 1949– , both from the Central Statistical Office and the many statistical and other publications produced by the Office of Population, Censuses and Surveys. Finally there are a number of publications on taxation and related matters, including the Board of Inland Revenue's *A Digest and Index of Tax Cases*, of which seven editions have now appeared, together with numerous supplements and their *Tax Case Appeals to the High Court*, 1938– . Details of all such serials and of many more will be found in the *Check List of British Official Serial Publications*, issued annually by the Official Publications Library, formerly the State Paper Room of the British Library and described more fully on page 268.

Legal publications have scarcely been mentioned, nor have treaties and similar agreements with foreign powers. Both these very important classes of official publications are fully dealt with elsewhere in the *Manual*.

BIBLIOGRAPHIES, INDEXES AND GUIDES

Stationery Office lists

The indexes which will probably be most frequently consulted by the law librarian are those published by HMSO. These consist of daily, monthly and annual editions, together with a consolidated index published every five years, of which the most recent to appear is that covering the five years 1966–70. The daily is probably less likely to be consulted than the monthly and annual compilations, but, being arranged on the same principle, it should present no difficulty if use has to be made of it. The weekly list is confined to publications of interest primarily to Local Authorities and is not generally distributed.

All these lists contain not only all publications issued by the Stationery Office, whether Parliamentary or non-Parliamentary, but also a large number described as 'sold but not published by HMSO'. These consist partly of publications of the United Nations, UNESCO and other international bodies (see also page 294), partly of the publications of certain museums and art galleries, such as the British Museum or the National

Gallery and those of organizations such as the British Tourist Authority, the Design Centre and other quasi-official bodies which undertake their own publishing. The Annual Catalogue does not, however, contain publications of international organizations, a list of these being issued as a separate pamphlet. As mentioned above, there is, however, a growing tendency for many departments to issue their own publications, which do not, therefore, appear in the Stationery Office lists. This means that there is now no longer a single bibliographical source for virtually all official publications. It is all too clear that both librarians and research workers will be increasingly adversely affected by this new development.

Each monthly Stationery Office catalogue is divided into three principal sections, the first being Parliamentary publications. These consist of House of Lords and House of Commons Papers, Bills and Debates, the Papers and Bills in their sessional numerical order. Command papers follow, likewise in numerical order, whilst Public, General and Local Acts conclude this section.

The next major division is a classified list, containing both Parliamentary and non-Parliamentary material, but excluding Bills, Acts, Debates and Church Assembly measures. Publications are arranged in alphabetical order of the issuing organization. For example, a list may start with the Agricultural Research Council and end with the Welsh Office. Organizations whose publications are sold, though not published, by HMSO are now included in the same alphabetical sequence. Each entry consists of a short title, author if any, International Standard Book Number, size, pagination and price. Some extensive series are grouped together, whilst publications of sub-departments and divisions are listed under the parent department. Thus the Social Survey Division of the Office of Population, Censuses and Surveys is arranged alphabetically within the main heading.

The third major division is that of Periodicals, sub-divided into Parliamentary and non-Parliamentary publications and arranged alphabetically. The list concludes, in the case of the annual edition, with an ISBN index and a comprehensive general index in both the monthly and annual editions. It is here that any enquirer would normally begin his search.

All HMSO publications may be obtained directly or by post from the various government bookshops in London, Edinburgh, Cardiff, Manchester, Bristol, Birmingham and Belfast or from appointed booksellers elsewhere in the United Kingdom, the Republic of Ireland and overseas.

Supplementary lists which may be of assistance are *Forthcoming Government Publications* (a monthly news sheet, issued gratis), and the *List of Non-Parliamentary Publications sent for Press* (weekly – also gratis). HMSO also publishes a useful illustrated free brochure: *HMSO – the British Government Publisher*, describing not only the Stationery Office's own activities, but also how to trace and obtain their publications and guidance on official publications not obtainable from them.

Another publication of great potential use to librarians is the series of index cards, giving full details of all HMSO publications on library cards, enabling special indexes to be readily compiled and the various *Sectional Lists*. These, of which there are now some forty available, are catalogues of all non-Parliamentary publications and a few important Parliamentary ones arranged according to the issuing department or group of departments. List no. 3, for instance, covers publications of the former Department of Trade and Industry; List 32 those of the Treasury and allied departments. Sectional lists are of particular value in enabling the enquirer to see at a glance all material currently available in any particular field.

Indexes to Parliamentary papers

The principal indexes to Parliamentary papers are those each covering a fifty-year period and which, between them, run from 1801 to 1949. An index is published to the papers of each Parliamentary session and there are decennial cumulative alphabetical indexes, of which the last so far issued is that for 1950 to 1958–9. All such indexes are primarily guides to the bound set of Parliamentary papers published by the Stationery Office. There is normally a delay of some four to five years before these appear. Current papers may, of course, be traced from the various HMSO lists.

As an example of the use of the fifty-year indexes, let us take the most recent, that published in 1960 and covering all Bills,

Reports and Papers printed by order of the House of Commons, together with all Command papers issued from 1900 to the end of the session 1948–9. These consist of over 40,000 individual papers, contained in nearly 2,700 volumes. The index is divided alphabetically into subject headings which give details of all papers on that particular subject. Every heading, unless very small or just a cross-reference, is sub-divided into three sections, a traditional arrangement derived from the original grouping of papers first devised by Speaker Abbot (Lord Colchester) in the early nineteenth century. These are *Bills; Reports of Committees and Commissions* and *Accounts and Papers*. Although, on the whole, a satisfactory method, at least for the arrangement of the papers in the bound set, it has the disadvantage, as far as the index is concerned, of separating papers on the same subject, but of a different type. Thus the report of a departmental committee, a paper or a bill on any particular subject may be widely separated within the same heading. Care should always therefore be taken not to overlook a paper, especially in a large and complex heading. It usually pays to read right through the whole heading in case one has overlooked anything of value.

In all major headings will be found many sub-divisions. Thus *Land–Landlord and Tenant, Sub-Division III, Reports of Commissioners* is again divided into eleven further sub-divisions, ranging from *Acquisitions and Valuation* to *Titles, Inclosures, etc.* Many such sub-division headings are based on the short title of the relevant paper, others are purely descriptive.

To look up a paper the enquirer should first turn to the heading covering the subject in which he is interested. This may take a little time as some of the headings used are not immediately obvious. Having selected an appropriate heading, and knowing presumably that his paper is neither a bill nor the report of a committee on a bill, but unsure whether it is a report of Commissioners or an Account or Paper, he would be well advised to look at all entries in the relevant sections. A list of headings will be found arranged in alphabetical order at the head of each sub-division. Let us take as an example the heading *Criminal Law, Justice and Procedure*. The enquirer wishes to trace the report of the Committee on alterations in Criminal Procedure (indictable offences), 1921. He searches for it under the main heading Criminal Law and finds it under Section III 2 *Criminal Procedure*. The reference given is 1923. Cmd. 1813.X.273. If he has access to a bound set of Parliamentary papers this reference will enable him to find his paper straight away, together with the additional information that it is a Command paper, number Cmd. 1813. The report will be found in volume 10 of the collected papers for the 1923 session and is on page 273. All bound volumes of Parliamentary papers are given a continuous pagination throughout and it is this which is always quoted in the index. A particular note should be taken of the numerous cross-references to be found in these indexes, either to alternative forms of headings, *eg*, 'Mails, see Post Office', or 'Notaries, Public, see Solicitors', or those leading to individual papers, dealing, say, with a particular person, event or ship. Also extremely useful are the lists of alternative headings which are to be found at the end of all but the smallest entries. Often they are such that even an experienced researcher might well have overlooked them and will provide the answer to many a query hitherto thought insoluble.

Should, however, as sometimes happens, an enquirer know no more than the mere command number, possibly from an abbreviated reference, any such paper may yet be traced.

If the date of the session is even approximately known it may be found from the numerical list of Command papers published in every sessional index. If no precise date is known, but the paper is thought to be recent, a search through the Annual Stationery Office lists will quickly find it. These, as has already been said, give a list of Command papers in numerical order, published during that year. If the paper is, however, of an older date, recourse should be had, if it is available, to *A Numerical Finding List of British Command Papers, published 1833–1961–2*, compiled by E. di Roma and J. A. Rosenthal. This gives all Command papers in numerical order within the five series so far issued. Alongside each number is given the year, volume and page, making the retrieval of any paper remarkably easy.

Also of considerable help and possibly more readily available, is the *Concordance of Command Papers, 1833–1968*, to be found in J. E. Pemberton's *British Official Publications*, 2nd edition, 1974. This gives what command numbers are contained within each year and from this one may turn to the relevant sessional index to trace the actual paper.

For sessional papers the procedure is more straightforward. These are numbered only for each session and, unlike Command papers, do not form a continuous series. It is therefore most unlikely that any reference will fail to give the session concerned and the paper can be found immediately by consulting the numerical list of sessional papers to be found in every sessional index.

The indexes of the House of Lords papers are of limited use, as scarcely any library possesses anything like a complete set. Only one general index has so far been issued covering the period 1801 to 1859, and all entries in it refer merely to the complete set in the House of Lords itself. A microfilm edition of all Lords papers from 1805–59 has now been published and an edition in photographic facsimile of all earlier Lords papers from 1641 to 1805 is now also being issued by the same firm. Many of these papers are extremely rare, a number being represented by a single surviving copy, perhaps no longer even to be found in this country. Their importance, especially for the legal historian, can scarcely be exaggerated and almost every class of enquirer will benefit from the papers contained in these collections.

Indexes to the earlier series of Commons papers also exist both to *Reports from Committees of the House of Commons*, the so-called 'First Series' of papers, which covers the period 1715–1802 and to *Parliamentary Papers printed by order of the House of Commons from the year 1731 to 1800* (the Abbot collection). This latter collection has now been likewise issued on microfiche. An extremely comprehensive list of Commons papers from 1701 to 1750 has been compiled by Sheila Lambert and was published in 1968. This list covers all bills, reports and accounts and papers printed during this period, including papers not printed separately, but of which the text may be found in the *Journals* of the House of Commons and demonstrates the very wide range of eighteenth-century Parliamentary printing.

Other official indexes

Another publication which law librarians may frequently wish to consult is the *Check List of British Official Serial Publications* issued by the Official Publications Library, British Library, and already briefly mentioned. This consists of an alphabetical list of current serials, revised annually and includes both those published by HMSO and by individual departments. The check list also contains lists of new and changed official bodies – always a potential source of confusion – and of discontinued and changed titles.

A group of special indexes invaluable to the law librarian are those more specifically in the legal field but which often have a general application. Such, for example, are the *Chronological Table of the Statutes*; the *Index to Government Orders*; the *Index to the Statutes*; the *Index to Local and Personal Acts* and similar publications. They are more fully described on pages 118–19 and 113.

Unofficial breviates and guides

There are also, of course, such excellent guides and handbooks covering this complex subject as those published, for instance, by Professor and Mrs Ford, by John Pemberton and M. F. Bond, which almost all law librarians will find essential and of which details will be found in the bibliography on page 294. All these various lists and indexes should enable the law librarian to solve the majority of questions with which he may be faced in the field of official publications.

SCOTLAND

In essence, there is little difference between official publications in Scotland and those issued in other countries in Britain. There is a separate office of Her Majesty's Stationery Office in Edinburgh, the function of which is 'to publish officially for Scottish Departments and to sell government publications to the public and bookselling trade' (Royal Commission on Scottish Affairs, 1953, volume III, p. 163).

The administration of central government in Scotland is centred on the Scottish Office, the headquarters of which in Scotland is St Andrew's House in Edinburgh. This houses several departments and it is through these that the Secretary of State for Scotland administers affairs in that country; each department has a small liaison staff in London, located at Dover House. Full details of these and other government departments may be found in Milne, Sir D. *The Scottish Office and other Scottish Government Departments*, 1957; and *Scottish Administration*: a handbook prepared by the Scottish Office, revised edition, 1967. Other useful titles include McLarty, M. R., ed., *A Sourcebook and History of Administrative Law in Scotland*, 1956 – this has nineteen descriptive chapters and includes bibliographies at the end of each; while Chapters 2–5 of Kellas, J. G. *The Scottish Political System*, 1973, provide relevant information.

The same system of government publications applies equally in Scotland as elsewhere, *ie*, through Command papers, Green papers, departmental publications, etc. These are issued, for example, where Scotland, or parts of it, are treated separately for reasons of geography, special local conditions, etc., and include such subjects as crofting conditions, salmon and other fisheries, local government reform, and so on. Where Scots law differs from English law, there are numerous parliamentary papers, including the *Report of the Scottish Law Commission* (formerly the Scottish Law Reform Committee) from 1957 to date; and separate reports on such subjects as licensing laws, marriage and divorce, the Scottish Courts, conveyancing, land tenure, etc. Most of the Scottish government departments publish reports, among the more prolific being the Scottish Development Department and the Scottish Education Department. These may be traced in the daily, monthly or annual lists of government publications referred to on page 262, or in the sectional lists. There are no separate official indexes to Scottish government publications.

The *Edinburgh Gazette*, mentioned on page 259, appears twice weekly, and since January 1973 has been accompanied by a *Company Law Official Notifications Supplement* to comply with EEC regulations. The *Gazette* itself largely comprises notices of companies' liquidations; sequestrations, meeting of creditors, etc.; and what is termed 'state intelligence', *eg*, information relating to the Post Office, the Privy Council Office, road traffic regulations, notices under the Town and Country Planning Acts, and so on.

Some annual Scottish serial publications of use to the law

librarian include the separate volumes on *Criminal Statistics* and *Judicial Statistics*, while the Law Society of Scotland draws up each year the *Report on the Legal Aid Scheme*. The *Scottish Land Court Report*, and in particular, its separate *Appendix*, contains a mine of information, while the report of the Crofters Commission is a related document. For general details of Scotland's population, the publications of the Registrar General of Scotland, together with the various census volumes, are full of useful statistics.

NORTHERN IRELAND

The publications of the Northern Ireland government for the period 1921–March 1972 closely resemble those of the British government and were published by HMSO, Belfast. During the months of direct rule, from April 1972 until the end of 1973, Departmental publications continued as usual, but Parliamentary publications either ceased entirely or were replaced in various ways which will be described later. After the restoration of partial self-government several entirely new ones appeared, but since the return to direct rule in May 1974 it is impossible to forecast the form of future publications.

Parliamentary publications

During the years 1921–72 Parliamentary publications (including Bills and Acts – see page 128) consisted of the same groups as their British counterparts with the following minor differences. Command papers, being fewer in number than the British, have had only one series of numbers. Cmd 1–568 appeared during the period in question. Sessional papers fell into two sections, House of Commons papers and Senate papers. While in Britain a new sequence of House of Commons and House of Lords papers begins each session, the Northern Ireland papers have had a continuous sequence from their inception. Between 1921 and 1972, 2,201 House of Commons papers appeared and twenty Senate papers. Only one Green paper, *The future development of the Parliament and government*, was produced as a Parliamentary publication under the former Northern Ireland government. It was published as Cmd 560 in 1971. The other Green paper issued during the period, *The*

Administrative structure of the health and personal social services, appeared in 1969 as a non-Parliamentary publication.

The Northern Ireland House of Commons also had its *Notices of motion* and both houses had their *Journals* and, most important, their *Debates*. These appeared daily and later were cumulated into a sessional volume or volumes each with its own index.

Departmental publications

The Departmental publications of Northern Ireland are few by comparison with those in Britain. There are some statistical publications, such as the *Digest of statistics* prepared by the Ministry of Finance and the *Census of production* and *Census of population*, issued respectively by the Ministry of Commerce and the Registrar-General. Some reports in the fields of education, agriculture, commerce and law were sponsored by the ministries concerned. Of special interest to members of the legal profession are *Operation of juvenile courts : report by the Northern Ireland Child Welfare Council,* 1960 ; *Joint Working Party on the Enforcement of Judgments, Orders and Decrees of the Courts . . . report to the Ministry of Home Affairs,* chairman: A. E. Anderson, 1965, and *Survey of the land law of Northern Ireland* by a working party of the Faculty of Law, Queen's University, Belfast: report to the Director of Law Reform for Northern Ireland, 1971. All these are published by HMSO and are recorded in their monthly and annual lists.

Some Ministries and other bodies themselves publish material. The Ministry of Agriculture produces its *Annual report on research and technical work,* the General Certificate of Education Committee issues examination papers and examination results. Other Ministries put out mimeographed reports and documents such as the *Review of the linen industry* issued by the Ministry of Commerce. A very small proportion of the printed publications and none of the mimeographed material is recorded in the HMSO annual or monthly lists of publications. Some may be included in the useful bibliographies contained in the *Ulster Yearbook.* Apart from this there is really no means of finding out about departmental material other than by making a direct approach to the Ministry concerned.

Indexes, guides and bibliographies

Items published by HMSO are first recorded in *Monthly Lists* which eventually cumulate into Annual Lists. These, unlike their British counterparts, have no alphabetical index. For the periods 1921–37 and 1938–47 there have been two cumulated catalogues, each with an alphabetical index.

There are no guides to the publications of the Northern Ireland government but, as already mentioned, the bibliographies relating to each chapter in the *Ulster Yearbook* are a valuable indication of what has been produced. Happily, a new work on Parliamentary publications has just been produced by Arthur Maltby: *The Government of Northern Ireland, 1921–1972: a catalogue and a breviate of Parliamentary papers,* 1974, which should prove an invaluable tool for those wishing to use Northern Ireland publications. The main purpose of the book is, of course, to provide summaries of the Parliamentary papers. This means that the enquirer may not need to refer to the original paper, as the summary may give him all the information he requires. This is particularly helpful to those interested in legal matters, as the papers are arranged in subject groups, including a section on law. There is an excellent title and key-word index, as well as an index of authors and chairmen. By means of these it should be possible to track down any desired Parliamentary publication.

Statistical material such as *Criminal statistics* may be traced through the *List of Principal Statistical Series and Publications* issued by the British Central Statistical Office. This guide lists British publications, many of which include figures for Northern Ireland, and also mentions the relevant Northern Ireland publications.

Recent developments

The greatest changes which took place in the publications of Northern Ireland during 1972 and 1973 were in relation to legislative material (see page 129). Command papers continued as usual, being issued by command of the Secretary of State instead of by command of the Governor. Many of these were annual reports of government departments and other special reports on current events, such as the Scarman enquiry:

Violence and civil disturbances in Northern Ireland which appeared as
Cmd 566.

House of Commons and Senate papers were, of course, discontinued, but many reports which had formerly been issued as
House of Commons papers appeared as departmental papers.

Parliamentary material such as *Notices of motion, Journals* and
Debates naturally ceased with the disappearance of the Stormont
Parliament, but after the election of the Northern Ireland
Assembly official reports began to appear from July 1973. Later
some Assembly papers were issued.

Departmental publications survived the period of direct rule
and will doubtless continue from 1974. However, as the functions of the former Ministries have been taken over by departments and as some functions have been re-allocated among the
departments the content and titles of some of the publications is
bound to change, but it is to be hoped that there will be a
measure of continuity.

THE REPUBLIC OF IRELAND

Historical background

For the period 1310 to 1800, see page 241. After the Act of
Union 1800, Westminster became the parliament for the United
Kingdom of Great Britain and Ireland until 1920, the majority
of official publications relating to Ireland being issued in
London. They can be traced in the various ways suggested
above. For statutes and bills, see page 130.

Sinn Fein members elected in the United Kingdom general
election of 1918 formed the unofficial 'First Dáil' (Parliament),
which met twelve times between 1919 and 1921. The Government of Ireland Act 1920 provided for the creation of the two
States of Northern Ireland and Southern Ireland. Elections
were accordingly held in 1921. Southern leaders treated the
election for the House of Commons of Southern Ireland as an
election for a 'Second Dáil'. A settlement with Britain was
finally reached and led to the Irish Free State Constitution Act
1922.

The change in status from Free State to Republic in 1948
necessitated no change in the style or nature of official papers.

The following documents, published or re-printed by the Stationery Office at various dates, are still in print: *Minutes of proceedings of the first Parliament of the Republic of Ireland, 1919–21*; *Official report: Debate on the treaty between Great Britain and Ireland signed in London on the 6th December, 1921*; *Official report: August 1921, February–June 1922 with index* [Includes index to the two volumes cited above]; *Private sessions of Second Dáil*; *Minutes of proceedings 18 August 1921 to 14 September 1921* and *Report of debates 14 December 1921 to 6 January 1922.*

Publications from 1922 onwards

The official languages of the State are English and Irish. In practice, with very few exceptions, only those publications which relate to the Irish language are issued in that language.

Oireachtas publications

This term indicates the records and proceedings of Parliament but does not include papers presented to or laid before the Oireachtas. These publications are:

> Acts and Bills
> Debates (both Houses)
> Reports of Committees (both Houses)
> Joint Committee Reports
> Divisions (both Houses)
> Proceedings (both Houses)
> Dáil Éireann Questions
> Seanad Éireann Orders of the Day

Debates are issued in daily unrevised parts. Bound volumes are issued approximately three years later, and each is indexed and contains a list of Ministers and Deputies (Dáil Éireann) or Senators (Seanad Éireann). There are five consolidated indexes covering the debates of the Dáil from 1922 to 1954, and two of the Seanad covering the period 1922–48.

Committees, whether of the whole Oireachtas or of the Dáil or of the Seanad, have usually been assigned the task of examining bills, accounts or some aspect of the internal workings of Parliament. Their number is small; their function is more analytical than investigative; they deal with specific issues rather than general policies.

Analysis can become investigation as was demonstrated by the recent report of the Committee of Public Accounts into Northern Ireland relief expenditure. In the course of this particular inquiry the constitutional powers of Committees to call witnesses and demand information were tested and found wanting.

Other Oireachtas publications record divisions and list the agenda and order of business in the Houses. They are thus of a very technical nature.

Departmental papers

The volume and nature of departmental papers – and the departmental structure itself – have altered little in the past fifty years.

Departmental papers are of two kinds, policy papers and information papers. The former cover a wide variety of subjects. Investigations into social and economic problems may be published by a department or may appear as the results of the deliberations of a Commission of Inquiry. In fifty years some 250 such reports have been issued. Their number has tended to fall. Between 1922 and 1925 thirty Reports of Commissioners were published, between 1967 and 1970 there were only thirteen. Many of the early reports with their voluminous minutes are still of considerable importance, for example, the *Commission of Inquiry into the Resources and Industries of Ireland, 1920–2.*

In the context of a relatively small number of policy papers, annual and other departmental serials take on an added importance. Some of these papers continue nineteenth-century British serials – for example, *Report of the Irish Land Commissioners.* In many cases they not only offer invaluable statistical data but also chart changing government and public attitudes where no formal report provides an obvious landmark.

Information papers number annually some 200 items and are of three kinds: Administrative, Statistical, and Scientific and Cultural.

Documents in the administrative class form the largest single category of departmental papers. They range from the minutiae of child health service school cards to the highly important *Estimates* and *Appropriation accounts*.

Among the statistical serials issued by the Central Statistics Office – an Agency of the Department of Finance – are : *Trade Statistics of Ireland, Annual Report on Vital Statistics, Statistical abstract of Ireland.* Departmental annuals contain statistics as appropriate.

Scientific and cultural papers are dominated by general literature in Irish – books produced as part of the government's efforts to foster the Irish language. Other items include *Irish Fisheries Investigations*.

The small number of information papers may be attributed in part to the existence of State sponsored bodies with ambitious publishing programmes. Amongst these are An Foras Taluntais (Agricultural Institute) and An Foras Forbartha (National Institute for Physical Planning and Construction Research). Some departments issue reports in addition to those published by the Stationery Office. The only major departmental series with a comprehensive index is the *Treaty Series* of the Department of Foreign Affairs.

Stationery Office indexes

Government publications for the week ending the previous Wednesday are first listed in the Friday issue of the bi-weekly *Iris Oifigiúil*, the official gazette. An off-print is available from the Stationery Office.

Three-monthly indexes are published in duplicated typescript form and are available about two months after each quarter. An annual index entitled *Annual catalogue of government publications* is published.

Nine consolidated lists have been published covering the period 1922–66, generally every three to five years. Bills and general literature in Irish are omitted from these lists. Statutory Instruments do not appear on the 1951–5 or 1956–60 lists. Bibliographical details are minimal, only whether Oireachtas or Stationery Office, order number, short title, price and postage charge.

Unofficial indexes

A select list of the reports of enquiries . . . 1922–72 by Professor and Mrs Ford was published in 1974. Emphasis is to be on policy documents, the style and criteria of selection to be those made familiar by the various select lists of British government publications by the same authors.

How to obtain Irish official publications

Ireland has not ratified the UNESCO conventions concerning the international exchange of publication and the exchange of official publications and government documents between States. There is no national exchange centre and although government departments may enter into exchange agreements with corresponding departments of other countries, general exchange agreements may be ruled out. Publications may be purchased from the Government Publications Sale Office, GPO Arcade, Dublin 1.

Sets of Oireachtas publications (excluding bound volumes of Acts and Debates) may be obtained by annual subscription.

The *Iris Oifigiúil* and several statistical series are also available by subscription. All other items must be ordered from the Stationery Office lists. There are no standing order or deposit account systems. Irish official papers are cheap and few in number. The annual cost of a complete collection is under £80. Once the practical difficulties of ordering are overcome (perhaps by ordering every three months) there are considerable advantages to be gained from buying everything or almost everything.

Part 2: Publications of International Organizations

K. O. PARSONS, MA
Assistant Librarian (Law), British Library of Political and Economic Science

PUBLICATION PATTERNS

International organizations are so numerous and diverse that it would be impossible within the space available to describe the publications of each individually and in turn, even if the description were confined, as it must be, to legal publications and those of legal interest. Instead, an attempt will be made to identify categories of publication common to a large number of organizations, or at least to the more important ones, and to illustrate these with examples. Special emphasis will be placed on the United Nations, as the largest and perhaps the most active organization in the legal sphere, but the specialized agencies and larger regional bodies will also receive attention. For bibliographical details of the publications of the UN and other international organizations, see the lists and catalogues issued by the organization concerned, or the section on International Organizations in the HMSO catalogue.

Documents and sales publications

The terms 'documents' and 'publications' require defining more exactly, since they have a somewhat specialized meaning in the context of international organizations. It is convenient to take the UN system as a model since it is here that the differences between categories has the greatest practical importance, and the practice of other organizations can best be understood by reference to that of the UN.

The three basic categories of UN 'publications' are mimeographed documents, official records, and sales publications. They are not mutually exclusive, but each contains some material not found in either of the other two. The mimeographed documents are the basic material in that most of the items in the other two categories are first issued as documents. These are identified by symbols consisting of letters and figures, separated by oblique strokes, which express the relationship of the document to one of the main organs of the UN, and frequently also to a subsidiary body. Thus General Assembly documents symbols begin with the letter A/, Security Council documents with S/. The letter C denotes Committee, CN Commission, AC *Ad Hoc* Committee, SC Sub-Committee, etc. The symbol used for the International Law Commission is A/CN.4, and for the Human Rights Commission E/CN.4. Various descriptive sub-series symbols may follow, *eg*, /PV for verbatim plenary records of meetings and SR for summary records. For a list of such symbols, see UN document ST/LIB/ SER.B/5.

Whereas mimeographed documents are produced primarily for delegations and the Secretariat, sales publications are usually printed books intended for a wider public. Most such publications carry on the inside front cover or on the back of the title-page a box containing a sales number, consisting of the year of publication, the category number of the work in Roman numerals and the number of the work in this particular category issued during the year. Roman numerals I to XVII are used to denote subject groups, but with the changes in UN activities over the years some groups have become superfluous and others overcrowded. This is especially true of class II, Economics, which has had to be further sub-divided by capital letters, on a geographical or subject basis.

BASIC GENERAL PUBLICATIONS

Constitutional documents

Examples of such documents are the Charter of the UN and the Statute of the International Court of Justice. Most organizations have published such texts, either singly or as part of a larger collection of administrative and procedural rules and regulations. Examples of this approach are afforded by FAO, in its *Basic Texts*, and WHO, with its *Basic Documents*. The UN has also issued separately the texts of the definitive instruments of two of its principal legal sub-organs – the International Law Commission and the Administrative Tribunal.

Official records

The publishing programme of an international organization often follows or is closely related to its organizational structure. Official records, especially, depend directly on the hierarchy of organs which has produced them. Their function is to provide an authoritative account for permanent reference of the proceedings and decisions of the principal policy-making organs of the organization. The degree of detail with which this is done will vary according to the importance of the body concerned and the requirements of its members for documentation. The complex and much used record system of the United Nations will serve as an example.

The UN official records consist of reports of plenary meetings of the main organs, with papers produced for consideration by them, reports of subordinate bodies or officers submitted to them and resolutions that they have arrived at. Thus for the General Assembly there is a series of verbatim reports of proceedings of the Assembly itself and also (this is unique to the Assembly) summary records of its six main committees and sessional *ad hoc* committees. These first appear as mimeographed documents to which a symbol is assigned, but are subsequently re-published in corrected, edited versions as printed fascicles numbered in sequence of meetings and each dealing with a particular item on the sessional agenda. Once the issuance of these fascicles has been completed, three prefatory fascicles are issued, containing respectively a contents list of the volume together with the agenda, a list of delegations and a check-list of documents. Another volume will contain annexes of documents considered at the session, and another supplements comprising, in addition to resolutions adopted at the session, the annual reports of the Secretary-General, the Councils and other bodies. Volumes are grouped by annual sessions, which are numbered consecutively from the first session held in 1945, and both the meetings and their corresponding fascicles follow an uninterrupted numerical sequence from the earliest days of the organization.

The other main organs of the UN follow a similar pattern to that of the General Assembly in their official records, though they do not issue reports of meetings for their committees or commissions. For the Security Council, whose records are arranged according to a numbered sequence of years rather than sessions, there are verbatim records of plenary meetings, supplements containing essential documents and an annual fascicle of Resolutions and Decisions. For each session of the Economic and Social Council there are summary reports of plenary meetings, annexes of essential documents and supplements containing reports and resolutions.

Most official records have a prior and much earlier existence as mimeographed documents which are therefore essential for current research. Moreover, it is the document symbols which are more often cited in non-UN references, though this difficulty may be overcome by consultation of the re-publication lists in UNDI (the *United Nations Documents Index*) and footnote references in the documents. The official records, however, are well-produced, final, corrected versions, without the numerous minor documents.

For research, as for quick reference, the printed *Indexes to Proceedings* issued in the Dag Hammarskjöld Library's *Bibliographical Series* are equally important. They are issued sessionally or annually for the UN's main organs and provide not only a subject key to the proceedings covered, but also lists of meetings, agenda items and documents arranged by symbols. In addition, they enable the attitude of a delegation to all matters raised in debate to be followed by providing a separate index of speeches arranged in alphabetical order of countries, sub-divided by subjects and speakers.

For the official records of an organization other than the UN one may take the Council of Europe. These report the proceedings, etc. of the two main organs of the Council – the Consultative Assembly and the Committee of Ministers. There is a series of *Official Reports of Debates* of the Assembly, being a verbatim record of speeches made at each sitting, together with other series of Documents, Texts Adopted, Orders of the Day and Minutes. The *Statutory Reports* of the Committee of Ministers are included in the volumes of Documents after being issued separately for some years.

Official languages

For reasons of economy and practical convenience international organizations can use only a very few languages for their proceedings and publications and not all of those to the same extent. Thus the UN has five official languages – English, French, Spanish, Russian and Chinese – but of these, only the first three are regularly used. Where several languages are used there may be separate, unilingual editions in each language, as is normally the practice with the UN, or a single bilingual edition, as with the *Records of Proceedings* of the Council of

Europe. Since English is normally one of the official languages of all major organizations (though not, until British accession in 1973, of the European Communities) few problems arise for librarians in English-speaking countries. Some specialist monographs may, however, be obtainable only in the original language of composition and publication.

Manuals of practice and procedure

Manuals of practice are issued by large organizations to assist member States and their representatives to understand the organization's constitution and its working. The larger and more complex the organization, the more elaborate such manuals tend to be. The *Repertory of United Nations Practice* was first issued in 1955, in five volumes, and has required several further multi-volume supplements. In the *Repertory* each article of the Charter is followed by a summary of the decisions of main UN organs concerning it, which, with other material, is arranged and presented so as to bring out and elucidate practical questions of interpretation and application. For each Article there is an introduction, a general survey and an analytical summary of practice. Only important decisions relevant to Charter problems are analysed. The Supplements are not cumulative but must be read together with the main work.

The *Repertoire of the Practice of the Security Council* performs a similar function in relation to the Security Council. Material evidence has been selected, digested, arranged and analysed under appropriate headings. The original work, covering the period 1946–51, appeared in 1954 and has been followed by several supplements. The procedural rules and practice of other UN organs are described in a series of individual handbooks.

Similar publications for other organizations are less numerous and complex. ICAO has a series of documents containing rules of procedure for its various main organs, whilst FAO includes such material in its *Basic Texts*, and the Council of Europe in its *Procedure and Practice*.

LEGAL PUBLICATIONS

International legislation

Official records are probably more important to the student of international affairs than to the international lawyer, with the exception of the resolutions of the UN General Assembly, for which something of the force of law has been claimed. Other classes of material have a more direct legal interest.

Of these, the UN and other Treaty Series are described on page 339. Related to these but more diffuse in character are those publications which contain the record of the exercise by an organization of what may be described as its quasi-legislative function. Some organizations are supervising repositories of basic multi-lateral agreements in their special field, which are renewed as needed by amendments which, once formally adopted and promulgated by the organization, are legally binding upon its member states, signatories to the original agreement. An outstanding example is the International Civil Aviation Organization which administers the Chicago Convention of 1944 on International Civil Aviation. Annexes to the Convention are revised at intervals by amendments adopted by the Council of the Organization. Revised editions of the Annexes are then published in a series of *International Standards and Recommended Practices*.

Another example is provided by the General Agreement on Tariffs and Trade. The secretariat, which takes its name from the agreement it services, issues a series entitled *Basic Instruments and Selected Documents*, which comprises the General Agreement and numerous supplements, with protocols for amendments and accessions, rectifications of schedules, etc. A similar activity of the International Labour Organization results in the publication of the *International Labour Code*, a systematic arrangement of the Conventions and Recommendations adopted by the International Conference. Another UN specialized agency, the World Health Organization, does comparable work within its own speciality by the formulation and promulgation of *International Health Regulations*, eg, as adopted in 1969 by the 22nd World Health Assembly.

Surveys of legislation

Several organizations issue periodical surveys of legislation in their special field. Outstanding among them is the ILO's *Legislative Series*, published continuously since 1919. This is a selection of the more important texts in the fields of labour and social security legislation. English texts are issued separately at intervals and may be arranged at will. With a subject index and a chronological list under countries, these then form an annual volume. In 1969 a consolidated *Chronological Index of Laws and Regulations 1919–67* was issued, including, as do the annual indexes, not only the laws reproduced but also others of international interest. A *General Subject Index 1919–1968*, in which texts are classified by subject and country, appeared in 1970.

A similar service is provided in its own sphere of interest by FAO with its *Food and Agriculture Legislation*, which is a selection of full or summary texts or titles of food and agricultural laws and regulations of international significance. It has appeared at quarterly or half-yearly intervals since 1952. The contents of each issue are arranged in a classified order, with a chronological index by country and a list of official sources. Another legislative digest of more restricted scope produced by the same organization is its *Current Food Additives Legislation*, issued at irregular intervals since 1957 under the joint FAO/WHO programme on non-nutritive additives and pesticide residues.

WHO's *International Digest of Health Legislation* contains a selection of health laws and regulations, a bibliographical section and occasional studies in comparative health legislation. In effect, it continues the section 'Lois et règlements sanitaires' of the *Bulletin mensuel de l'Office international d'Hygiène publique*, which was published from 1909 to 1946. Both the *Digest* and FAO's *Food and Agriculture Legislation* are compiled from official texts deposited with the respective organizations by their member states in fulfilment of constitutional obligations.

Specialist legal organizations

Most of the organizations mentioned, though doing some legal work, are not exclusively legal in character. There are, however, a few specialist legal organizations less well known to the general public. Prominent among them is The Hague Conference on Private International Law, which has been meeting at intervals since 1893, to discuss and draft conventions on many subjects from family law to maritime law. It has a permanent office at The Hague, where the Staatsdrukkerij publishes its *Actes et Documents*. Also inter-governmental in character, though working in the more specialized field of copyright, patents and trade-marks, are the International Union for the Protection of Literary Works and the International Union for the Protection of Industrial Property, now amalgamated in the World Intellectual Property Organization.

Among non-governmental legal organizations one of the best known in recent years, though a relative newcomer, has been the International Commission of Jurists. In addition to its regular *Review*, the Commission has issued Reports on some highly topical and controversial matters, such as the rule of law in various countries, and has published reports of several conferences. By contrast, two long-established bodies – the Institut de Droit International and the International Law Association – have worked steadily for a century, debating and drafting improvements to international law, both public and private. Many of the texts thus produced have found their way into national legislation or international conventions or have been widely adopted in practice. Their principal publications are the proceedings, including documents, etc., of their biennial conferences – issued by the Institut as its *Annuaire* 1876–   , and by the Association as its *Reports of Conferences*, 1873–   .

Specialist legal sub-organs

Several of the major inter-governmental organizations have a subordinate functional organ – a commission or committee, with supporting secretariat – to do the organization's legal work. Whereas the League had no standing committee in charge of legal questions, the UN has the Sixth Committee of the General Assembly, formally named the Legal Committee. This is, however, a political body composed of diplomats rather than lawyers. Hence the creation of the International Law Commission, consisting of eminent international lawyers, with a Statute of its own regulating its constitution and functions. The main task of this Commission is to carry out the work assigned to the General Assembly by Article 13 (1)(a) of the Charter, *viz.* 'to initiate studies and make recommendations for the purpose of . . . (a) encouraging the progressive development of international law and its codification'.

The material records of the Commission's work are initially mimeographed documents in the UN series A/CN/. The most important of these, however, are subsequently re-issued with corrections and editorial changes in the two-volume *Yearbook of the International Law Commission*. This has been published sessionally since 1949, volume 1 containing summary records of sessional meetings and volume 2 the sessional documents and the Commission's report to the General Assembly. Since the Commission's work consists mostly of drafting the texts of codes or conventions with explanatory commentaries, or of making reports on matters specifically referred to it by the Assembly, the final outcome of its labours is to be seen either in the proceedings and final acts of conferences specifically convened to discuss the drafts or in *Resolutions* of the General Assembly arising from the reports submitted to it. A subordinate function of the Commission, described in its Statute as 'the making more readily available the evidence of customary international law', is also reflected, though to a lesser extent, in its output of reports and documents.

Legal sub-organs in other organizations are of less general importance than the International Law Commission. The closest parallel to it is the Inter-American Council of Jurists working within the Organization of American States. Its periodic meetings are reported in a series of *Proceedings*, and between sessions a permanent committee – the Inter-American Juridical Committee – undertakes preparatory work and special studies. In other organizations, such as ICAO, these functions are carried out by a Legal Committee supported by a branch of the secretariat and publishing, typically, a series of *Minutes* and *Documents*.

Legal conferences

Of particular legal interest are the proceedings of conferences called by organizations to achieve international agreement on various legal problems. Such publications resemble official records and may be so called. They may be quasi-legislative in nature in that their Final Act may enshrine a Convention binding on member states. Such conferences are normally occasional meetings called *ad hoc*, however, unlike the regular meetings of main organs, and also, like the second UN Conference on the Law of the Sea, they do not necessarily result in an agreed Convention.

Outstanding among these publications are the records of certain major UN conferences – those on the Law of the Sea (Geneva 1958 and 1960), on Diplomatic Relations (Vienna 1961), Consular Relations (Vienna 1963), and on the Law of Treaties (Vienna 1968–9). The official records are broadly similar, comprising preparatory documents, summary records of plenary meetings and of committee meetings, with the Final Act, and annexes containing the Convention and any protocols or resolutions.

Large legal conferences are rarely called by more specialized organizations. An example is the Conference on Private International Air Law, held by ICAO in Rome in 1952. This Conference adopted an important multilateral agreement – the Rome Convention on Damages Caused by Foreign Aircraft to Third Parties on the Surface, the text of which is to be found in the Proceedings published by ICAO and in the UN *Treaty Series*.

Several organizations hold conferences which are general as to subject, but organized on a regional basis; the object being to achieve a measure of de-centralization. WHO is notable here, also the ILO with its regularly recurring Asian and European, etc., regional conferences, and ICAO with its European Civil Aviation Conference.

MISCELLANEOUS PUBLICATIONS

Monographic series

Most of the larger organizations, in addition to their regular series of official records and other serials – legislative, statistical, etc. – also publish occasional monographs by individual authors or groups of authors. These writings are usually commissioned from consultants, who may prepare them in close association with the secretariat.

Those organizations which are large publishers may divide their monographs into subject series. Thus FAO has various series entitled *Agricultural Studies, Agricultural Development Papers, Nutritional Studies,* etc. Most organizations do not publish enough legal works to form a separate series. FAO is an exception, however, with its *Legislative Series,* and the International Atomic Energy Agency (IAEA) is another, with its *Legal Series.* More often, legal publications appear *hors série,* or as one of a large miscellaneous monographic series, such as the ILO's *Studies and Reports.*

The UN series *International Law,* which is Class V of its Sales Publications, is not restricted to monographs but includes many legal publications which form serials of their own, *eg,* the annual volumes of the *Yearbook of the International Law Commission* and the volumes of *Reports of International Arbitral Awards,* both of which are allotted numbers in Class V according to the year of publication. The UN also issues works of an undoubted legal character in classes other than Class V. This is true especially of comparative studies and other works which are not strictly international law, several of which have appeared in Class II, Economics, Class IV, Social Questions, Class X, International Administration and Class XIV, Human Rights.

The legal monographs published by international organizations are often comparative surveys of the law on a given subject in a number of countries. Thus FAO's *Principles of Land Consolidation Legislation,* by P. Moral-Lopez, 1962, is described in the organization's catalogue as follows: 'Dealing with 31 countries, this study in comparative law analyses and compares the most representative legislative techniques on various aspects of land consolidation.' WHO has published several texts with the sub-title 'A survey of existing legislation', dealing, *inter alia,* with pharmaceutical advertising, abortion laws and the use of human tissues and organs for therapeutic purposes. Similar collections of national legislative texts have also been made by the UN on subjects as diverse as the régime of the high seas, nationality, and the conclusion of treaties.

Sponsored publications

Some organizations, especially UNESCO and the Council of Europe, have issued many works through commercial publishers. Legal publications form only a small proportion of UNESCO's output, but in the field of copyright, its principal legal interest, it has published either directly, as with the *Copyright Bulletin*, a quarterly review issued since 1948 in various forms, or in an unusual form of collaboration with government departments of two member states. The loose-leaf collection, *Copyright Laws and Treaties of the World*, is compiled by UNESCO in co-operation with the Copyright Office of the United States of America and the Industrial Property Department of the Department of Trade and Industry of the United Kingdom. Legal publications issued under the auspices of the Council of Europe are more numerous, especially in the field of human rights. Thus two important series emanating from the Registry of the European Court of Human Rights – Series A, *Judgments and Decisions*; and Series B, *Pleadings, Oral Arguments and Documents* are published by Carl Heymanns Verlag of Cologne. Martinus Nijhoff of The Hague has issued, since 1959, the *Yearbook of the European Convention on Human Rights*, containing basic texts, selected documents and decisions of the Commission. Editions Administratives, of Heule in Belgium, has published a bilingual English-French *Digest of Case Law relating to the European Convention on Human Rights 1955–1967*. Nijhoff again has published annually since 1955 the *European Yearbook*, providing a conspectus of the problems of European integration and organization.

Technical assistance reports

A numerous class of documents of a distinctive character are the reports produced in the course of the technical assistance activities of inter-governmental organizations. These are usually written by consultant experts or staff members sent to under-developed countries in pursuance of an agreement between the government of the country and the organization. The reports are made to the government concerned in the first place and are confidential, but many are subsequently cleared for wider distribution and may be obtained from the organization concerned. Some organizations include them in their

10

bibliographical serials, *eg*, FAO in its *Quarterly List of Publications and Main Documents*. Very few are of legal interest, though governments sometimes seek advice on the drafting of legislation, *eg*, from ILO on industrial relations or from FAO on agricultural co-operation.

Serials

International organizations are considerable publishers of periodicals and annuals. A related activity of periodical indexing is carried out by the UN Library at Geneva in its *Monthly List of Selected Articles*, covering political, legal, economic, financial and other questions of the day. Both the Geneva and the New York Libraries issue monthly accessions lists, variously entitled, as do some of the larger specialized agencies.

REFERENCE AND BIBLIOGRAPHICAL PUBLICATIONS

Reference works

The compilation of data, especially statistical data, on a world-wide basis, is a feature of the work of most inter-governmental organizations, and is consequently reflected in a considerable output of statistical publications, usually of a serial nature. Directories are also produced, often with the help of unofficial bodies in a specialized field. An example is the *European Law Libraries Guide* 1971, prepared by the International Association of Law Libraries under the auspices of the Council of Europe.

The Yearbooks published by the UN itself and by several of its organs may also be considered reference works in that they usually report on and describe the work done during the year and reproduce essential documents. In addition to the *UN Yearbook* proper, there is also the *Yearbook of the International Law Commission* and the *Yearbook of Human Rights*, issued by the Commission of Human Rights. Another *UN Yearbook* is that published by the UN Commission on International Trade Law, a relative newcomer among major UN organs, whose purpose is the progressive harmonization and unification of the law of international trade.

Bibliographical aids

General

The bibliographical activity of inter-governmental organizations may take two forms – subject bibliographies in their own special field, or the recording of their own output of publications and documents. The Dag Hammarskjöld Library's *Bibliographical Series* includes both classes of work – from a bibliography on industrialization in under-developed countries to the indexes of proceedings of the main UN organs. Other forms of bibliographical activity include a style manual for the secretariat and the series of topical lists entitled *Current Issues*.

Bibliographies of strictly legal interest prepared by international organizations are relatively infrequent. Among the most useful is UNESCO's *A Register of Legal Documentation in the World*, 2nd edition, 1957, in its series Documentation in the Social Sciences. By 'legal documentation' is meant 'sources of law', and under each country or group of countries, in alphabetical order, we find such headings as 'Constitution, codes, legislation, law reports', etc.

A useful aid to comparative law studies is the *Bibliography of Translations of Codes of Private Law in Member States* compiled by the Council of Europe in co-operation with The Hague Conference on Private International Law and published in 1967. Of interest to the international lawyer is the *Bibliography of the International Court*, prepared by the Library of the Court and published annually as a separate fascicle, though until 1964–5 it appeared as part of the Court's *Yearbook*. It contains bibliographical references of interest in connection with the Court received by the Registry during the previous year.

UN document indexes

The *United Nations Documents Index* was a monthly publication which listed, described and indexed all documents and publications of the UN – except internal or restricted material – and also all printed publications of the International Court. Each issue had three sections: (1) a checklist of UN documents and publications arranged by symbol and described bibliographically; (2) a second section comprising three lists – (*a*) a list of documents by symbol only with indication of the various language editions and of their availability, (*b*) a list of mimeographed documents republished in the Official Records and elsewhere, (*c*) a list of sales publications; (3) the third section was a combined author-subject index to the documents described in the checklist, arranged alphabetically and printed on yellow paper in a separate and separable fascicle. From volume 14 (1963) onwards the monthly issues were cumulated annually in two separate cumulations – the Cumulative Checklist and the Cumulative Index. In addition to providing a consolidated version of the monthly indexes the latter volume also contained (*a*) a consolidated list by symbol of all documents and publications issued by the UN and the International Court during the year; (*b*) a consolidated list of re-published documents; (*c*) a consolidated list of sales publications, together with lists of new document series symbols and of depository libraries and UN Information Centres.

To cope with the increased flow of documents, etc. a computer-assisted indexing programme (UNDEX) has been set up within the UN's Documentation Division. Eight standard series are produced, but only those three intended for use outside the Secretariat will be described here. Series A is a Subject Index consisting of three elements: (1) a list of document symbols, (2) a list of terms describing the type of document, *eg*, report, resolution, meeting record, etc., (3) a list of subject terms describing the contents of the document. These three lists are arranged in parallel columns on the page, with the subject terms on the left in alphabetical order. Series B, the Country Index, uses the lists of subject terms and of symbols with a list of names of countries and of types of action. The country column appears on the left of the page. Series C is a List of Documents Issued, arranged by symbol, and is still produced by conventional methods.

When UNDEX achieves full coverage and regularity of publication it is intended that it should replace UNDI.

Catalogues

Whilst no other organization approaches the UN in the range and thoroughness of its bibliographic activity, virtually all of them provide some sort of guide to their publications. The usual practice is to issue current lists annually and then every few years a consolidated, classified list with indexes. Thus the UN offers a quarterly check-list, a list for the whole period 1945–71, and an elaborate descriptive catalogue for 1945–66. There are also special catalogues of Official Records and of the UN's periodicals. UNESCO's full-scale catalogue for 1946–59, arranged according to the Universal Decimal Classification, appeared in 1962, and has been followed by two supplements similarly produced.

The ILO Library has a good deal of bibliographic work to its credit in the series *Bibliographical Contributions*. These include mimeographed catalogues of all printed documents issued from 1919 to 1950 in English and French and a *Subject Guide to Publications of the International Labour Office 1919–1964*, issued in 1967.

A somewhat different method is followed by the Council of Europe, which issues its *Catalogue of Publications* annually in revised form, including free as well as sales items. By contrast, the OECD prefers a biennial classified catalogue.

PRACTICAL ASPECTS

Availability and distribution

Publications of inter-governmental organizations are made available to the public (or not) according to a pattern which is most fully developed and therefore most readily described in relation to the UN. Sales publications, official records and various periodicals are, of course, intended for the public, but mimeographed documents are the subject of various distinctions. The distribution classification categories of UN documents are as follows : (*a*) general, for full circulation ; (*b*) limited, mostly provisional documents which later become 'general' ; (*c*) restricted, ie, confidential and not for public circulation.

Documents and publications made generally available may be distributed either (*a*) by sale from authorized distributors and from the UN Sales Sections in Geneva and New York ; (*b*) free of charge (to member states, other organizations, etc.) ; (*c*) by deposit in reference collections accessible to the public.

The sales agent in the United Kingdom for most organizations is HMSO, which lists available publications in a supplement to its Catalogue. Some organizations, *eg*, the ILO, distribute their publications through Branch Offices in different countries. In countries of large area or population there are likely to be several depository libraries, some acting for several organizations. No organization is obliged to appoint depository libraries, and many, such as the ILO, IBRD, etc., have not done so, though they may nevertheless distribute some of their publications on a free or exchange basis.

Reference method

To identify a publication of an inter-governmental organization, consult the organization's own catalogue, or HMSO *International organizations and overseas agencies publications : supplement to Government publications*, 1955 to date.

To identify a UN document or publication consult UNDI, 1950 to date, or UNDEX, 1971 to date.

FURTHER READING

NATIONAL GOVERNMENTS

Abraham, L. A. and Hawtrey, S. C. *A Parliamentary Dictionary.* 3rd edition. Butterworth, 1970 (ISBN 0 406 10101 9).

Adam, M. I. *Guide to the Principal Parliamentary Papers relating to the Dominions, 1812–1911.* Edinburgh, London, Oliver and Boyd, 1913.

Bond, M. F. *Guide to the Records of Parliament.* HMSO, 1971 (ISBN 0 11 700351 4).

Ford, P. and Ford, G. *A Breviate of Parliamentary Papers, 1900–1916.* Oxford, Blackwell, 1957.

Ford, P. and Ford, G. *A Breviate of Parliamentary Papers, 1917–1939.* Revised edition. Shannon, Irish University Press, 1969. *Southampton University Studies in Parliamentary Papers* (ISBN 0 7165 0576 2).

Ford, P. and Ford, G. *A Breviate of Parliamentary Papers, 1940–1954.* Oxford, Blackwell, 1962.

Ford, P. and Ford, G. *A Guide to Parliamentary Papers.* New edition. Oxford, Blackwell, 1956.

Ford, P. and Ford, G. *Select List of British Parliamentary Papers,*

1833–1899. Revised edition. Shannon, Irish University Press, 1969 (ISBN 0 7165 0574 6).

Ford, P. *Select List of British Parliamentary Papers, 1955–1964.* Shannon, Irish University Press, 1970. *Southampton University Studies in Parliamentary Papers* (ISBN 0 7165 0884 2).

Gabioné, B. L. *A finding list of British Royal Commission reports: 1860 to 1935.* Cambridge, Mass., Harvard University Press, 1935.

Great Britain. HM Stationery Office. *Royal Commissions, 1937–1972.* Revised edition. HMSO, 1973. *Sectional list, 59.*

Great Britain. Interdepartmental Committee on Social and Economic Research. *Guides to Official Sources*, no. 1–6. HMSO, 1948–61.

Great Britain. Treasury. *Official Publications.* HMSO, 1958. A guide to the various types of publication produced by Parliament or the government.

Handover, P. M. *A History of the London Gazette, 1665–1965.* HMSO, 1965.

Kemp, B. *Votes and Standing Orders of the House of Commons: the beginning.* HMSO, 1971. *House of Commons Library document,* 8 (ISBN 0 10 831080 9).

Lambert, S. *List of House of Commons Sessional Papers, 1701–1750.* Swift (P. and D.), 1968. (*List and Index Society, Special series,* 1.)

Mallaber, K. A. The sale catalogues of British government publications, 1836–1965. *Journal of Librarianship,* vol. 5, no. 4, 1973, pp. 116–31.

Marshallsay, D. *British Government Publications. A mainly alphabetical guide.* Southampton, University of Southampton, 1970. *Southampton University Library occasional paper,* 2. (ISBN 0 85432 029 x).

Menhennet, D. *The Journals of the House of Commons: a bibliographical and historical guide.* HMSO, 1971. *House of Commons Library document,* 7 (ISBN 0 10 831070 1).

Morgan, A. M. *British Government Publications: an index to chairmen and authors, 1941–1966.* Library Association, 1969 (ISBN 0 85365 121 3).

Ollé, J. G. H. *An Introduction to British Government Publications.* 2nd edition. Association of Assistant Librarians, 1973 (ISBN 0 900092 20 3).

Parsons, K. A. C. *A Checklist of the British Parliamentary Papers, bound set, 1801–1950.* Cambridge University Library, 1958.

Pemberton, J. E. *British Official Publications.* 2nd edition. Oxford, Pergamon Press, 1974 (ISBN 0 08 017797 2).

Rodgers, F. *Serial Publications in the British Parliamentary Papers, 1900–1968: a bibliography.* Library Association, 1971 (ISBN 0 85365 494 8).

Roma, E. di and Rosenthal, J. D. *Numerical list of British Command*

Papers, 1833–1961/62. New York, New York Public Library and Arno Press, 1967 (ISBN 0 817104 505 2).

Staveley, R. and Piggott, M. *Government Information and the Research Worker.* 2nd edition. Library Association, 1965.

Wilding, N. and Laundy, P. *An Encyclopaedia of Parliament.* 2nd edition. Cassell, 1958.

INTERNATIONAL PUBLICATIONS

Auburn, F. M. United Nations documentation and international law. *Law Librarian*, vol. 4, no. 3, December 1973, pp. 37–9.

Aufricht, H. *Guide to League of Nations publications: a bibliographical survey of the work of the League, 1920–1947.* New York, Columbia University Press, 1951 (ISBN 0 404 00418 0).

Brimmer, B. *A guide to the use of United Nations documents, including reference to the Specialized Agencies and special U.N. bodies.* Dobbs Ferry, New York, Oceana, 1962 (ISBN 0 379 00035 0).

Evans, L. H. and Vamberry, J. T. Documents and publications of contemporary international governmental organizations. *Law Library Journal*, vol. 64, no. 3, 1971, pp. 338–62.

Schermers, H. G. *International institutional law.* Leiden, Sijthoff, 1972. 2 vols.

UN. Dag Hammarskjöld Library. *List of United Nations document series symbols.* New York, UN, 1965 (65.I.6) (*Bibliographical series no. 5/rev. 1*).

UN. Office of Public Information. *Everyman's United Nations . . .* 8th edition. New York, UN, 1968 (E.67.I.5).

UN. Sales Section. *Catalogue: United Nations publications.* New York, UN, 1967 (ST/CS/SER.J/9).

UN. Secretariat. *Instructions for depository libraries receiving United Nations material.* New York, UN, 1968 (ST/LIB/13/Rev.1).

UN. Secretariat. *List of depository libraries receiving United Nations material.* New York, UN, 1970 (ST/LIB/12/Rev.4).

Van Panhuys, H. F. *International organisation and integration: a collection of the texts of documents relating to the United Nations, its related agencies and regional international organisations.* New York, Humanities Press, 1968.

Winton, H. N. M. *Publications of the United Nations system.* New York, Bowker, 1972 (ISBN 0 8352 0597 5).

Yearbook of international organizations, 1948—Brussels, Union of International Associations (ISSN IX 0084-3814).

8. Foreign Law

W. A. STEINER, ll.m, ma, ala
Librarian, Institute of Advanced Legal Studies (University of London)

This chapter is concerned with the legal literature of a large number of jurisdictions. It is neither necessary nor possible to discuss the literature of each of them, and some generalization will be inevitable. It will be convenient to begin with the literature of comparative law and that dealing with more than one jurisdiction or a group of jurisdictions, and then to discuss groups of jurisdictions as follows: the Commonwealth, the United States of America, the civil law jurisdictions, the European Communities. Within the Commonwealth and civil law groups, common features will be dealt with first, with a description of the special features of individual jurisdictions where needed.

COMPARATIVE LAW

It is necessary to distinguish the literature of comparative law properly so called, as will be explained below, from the literature covering the law of several jurisdictions without comparative treatment. The distinction is essential, although there are works which straddle both categories.

The literature of comparative law, properly so called, consists of several types of work. There are first of all, general works on the principles and methods of comparative study. The pioneer work in Britain was Gutteridge, H. C. *Comparative Law*, 1949. Among other scholars who have written books on this topic in recent years are Ancel, Constantinesco, David, Derrett, Rotondi, Schnitzer, Zweigert, Kötz and Rheinstein.

Books of this type tend to be primarily academic; the publications which will be discussed in the following paragraphs vary from primarily academic treatises to works which are intended mainly for use in practice, though no clear distinction can be drawn.

We must now turn to the numerous works which treat comparatively, either the law of a given jurisdiction in general, *eg,* Amos, M. S. and Walton, F. P. *Introduction to French Law,* 1967; Cohn, E. J. *Manual of German Law,* 1968–71, or a given topic in the law of an individual jurisdiction, *eg,* Brown, L. N. and Garner, J. F. *French Administrative Law;* 1973, David, R. *Les contrats en droit anglais,* 1973, or a single topic on a multi-jurisdictional basis. Examples are Nagel, H. *Die Grundzüge des Beweisrechts im europäischen Zivilprozess,* 1967; Ommeslaghe, P, van *Régime des sociétés en droit comparé,* 1960; Szászy, I. *International Civil Procedure : a comparative study,* 1967.

Special mention must be made of the *Continental Legal History series,* 1912–28, and of the *International Encyclopedia of Comparative Law,* 1971–   , which is now in course of publication. It contains brief surveys of the legal systems of all jurisdictions, and a large number of essays on individual topics on a multijurisdictional basis. Constitutional, administrative and criminal law are, in general, excluded.

A great deal of the literature of comparative law is to be found in contributions to Festschriften and similar collections. Very few libraries can afford to catalogue these analytically, but indexes exist. German Festschriften, which are very numerous, from 1945 to 1966 are indexed in Dau, H. *Bibliographie juristischer Festschriften und Festschriftenbeiträge 1945–61 : Deutschland-Schweiz-Österreich,* 1962 (with supplement 1962–6, 1967). They are now regularly indexed in the *International Journal of Law Libraries.* Contributions to collections are indexed or listed in the bibliographical sections of some periodicals, in the general legal bibliographies such as the *Annual Legal Bibliography* and the *Karlsruher juristische Bibliographie,* and a selection of collections is indexed in the *Index to Foreign Legal Periodicals,* beginning with 1963. Contributions in English are indexed in Szladits, C. *Bibliography on Foreign and Comparative Law : books and articles in English,* 1955–   . A bibliography of all legal Festschriften from 1868 to 1968, though not an index of contributions, is: Roberts, L. M. *A Bibliography of legal Festschriften,* 1972.

Valuable material is to be found in the proceedings of international conferences, notably the reports (general and national) to the International Congresses of Comparative Law which are held every four years. There are many general periodicals, such as : *American Journal of Comparative Law*, 1952–   ; *Annuario di diritto comparato e di studi legislativi*, 1927–   ; *Boletín mexicano de derecho comparado*, 1948–   ; *International and Comparative Law Quarterly*, 1952–   ; *Revue internationale de droit compare*, 1872–   ; *Rabels Zeitschrift für ausländisches und internationales Privatrecht*, 1927–   .

There are some periodicals which deal with the comparative aspects of one or more single topics, *eg*, the *Revue internationale de droit pénal*, 1924–   or the *Rivista di diritto internazionale e comparato del lavoro*, 1953–   .

It should not be forgotten that the conflict of laws lends itself particularly to comparative treatment, and to a considerable extent demands it. The most important specialized periodicals must therefore be referred to here insofar as they have not yet been mentioned : both those dealing with the conflict of laws only, such as *Revue critique de droit international privé*, 1905–   ; *Rivista di diritto internazionale privato e processuale*, 1965–   , and those which cover both public international law and the conflict of laws, such as the *British Yearbook of International Law*, 1920–   , and *Comunicazioni e studi*, 1942–   .

Unification of law

A matter of special interest to comparative lawyers is the unification and harmonization of law. This is a matter of importance in federal states, *eg*, the United States, and was also of great importance in some of the successor states of the Austro-Hungarian monarchy which were composed of parts in which different legal systems had been in force before 1918, *eg*, Poland and Yugoslavia. Here it is proposed to discuss international unification and harmonization. With the exception of the European Communities (see page 326), where special considerations apply, the matters which lend themselves most readily to unification are branches of commercial law and cognate matters. Apart from regional unification, *eg*, uniform Benelux laws and uniform laws in the Nordic countries, most unification has been the work of the Rome Institute for the Unification of Private Law, which was established in 1928, and of numerous international organizations, such as the Inter-governmental Maritime Consultative Organization, or The Hague Conference on Private International Law, or of *ad hoc* international conferences. Uniform laws have been brought into being by means of conventions concluded at conferences or under the auspices of the organizations mentioned. A great deal of primary and secondary material can be found in the publications and documents of the Rome Institute, in particular *Unification of Law : yearbook*, 1948–71, *Uniform Law Cases*, 1956–71 (a collection of decisions of national courts applying and interpreting uniform laws), both of which have been superseded by the *Uniform Law Review*, 1973– . The pre-war documents of the Institute were often mimeographed; they were reproduced on microfilm, together with those up to 1965, by Oceana Publications in 1967. Other sources are the acts and documents of The Hague Conference on Private International Law, the various treaty series containing the conventions themselves, reprints of texts in the periodicals mentioned above, and Zweigert, K. and Kropholler, J., eds. *Sources of International Uniform Law*, 1971–3, 3 volumes, 1: private and commercial law; 2: transport law; 3: law of copyright, competition and industrial property. Further references are: Harvard Law School Library *Index to proceedings and documents of the International Institute for the Unification of Private Law 1928–1965*, 1967, and the *Digest of legal activities of international organizations and other institutions*, compiled by the International Institute. This is a very substantial loose-leaf publication and contains comprehensive information about the law-making activities of international organizations, etc. Many of these tend towards unification or at least harmonization of laws or establishing international standards.

Reception

A matter of great interest to comparative lawyers are the instances in which whole codes of one country have been adopted or substantially adopted by another country. This is a process of respectable antiquity, if we include the reception of Roman law, which admittedly was not codified, in the later Middle Ages and the early post-Medieval period. The Code Napoléon was either taken over or closely followed by the civil codes of some of the countries which formed or had formed part of Napoleon's empire. One of the best-known cases is that of the wholesale introduction of the Swiss civil code into Turkey.

COLLECTIONS FROM SEVERAL JURISDICTIONS

Primary materials

There is a considerable body of literature giving information on the law of more than one jurisdiction, both primary texts (mostly legislation) and doctrinal writing. The texts appear frequently in translation. Some periodical collections of texts cover potentially all subjects, *eg*, the *Boletín de legislación extranjera* or the *Documentation juridique étrangère*, which contains texts as well as secondary material. A series of monographs on topics of interest to international lawyers is the UN *Legislative Series*. Most collections, however, are restricted to one topic or a group of related topics. Examples are the periodical ILO *Legislative Series*, which covers labour law and social security; Blaustein, A. P. and Flanz, G. H. *Constitutions of Countries*, 1971–   ; Peaslee, A. J., ed. *Constitutions of Nations*, 1965–70; Makarov, A. N., comp. *Quellen des internationalen Privatrechts*, 1954–60; Ancel, M. and Marx, Y., eds. *Les codes pénaux européens*; or series of monographs, such as *Aktiengesetze der Gegenwart*, the *American series of foreign penal codes*.

It must always be borne in mind that material of this type is scattered through periodicals, *eg*, an English translation of the Swiss criminal code is to be found in the *Journal of Criminal Law and Criminology*, volume 30, no. 1, May–June 1939, supplement, and that there are periodicals which exist wholly or partly for the purpose of publishing this type of material, *eg*, *Copyright*, 1965–   . Collections of this nature of decisions of courts are rarer, but they exist; examples are the ILO *Survey of Decisions on Labour Law*, 1925–38, some series on very specialized topics such as air law, and the *Uniform Law Cases* mentioned above, which are now incorporated in the *Uniform Law Review*.

Secondary materials

There is a good deal of secondary literature, *ie*, not containing the texts themselves. Some of this is global in its coverage and not restricted to any one subject or group of subjects. Periodical publications of this type are, *eg*, the *Annuaire de législation française et étrangère*, 1872–   or the *Bulletin of Legal Developments*, 1966– , which is much more summary. Some collections are restricted as to subject, *eg*, *Income Taxes outside the United Kingdom*, or Metzger, E. and others *Das ausländische Strafrecht der Gegenwart*, 1955–62, or Pinner, H. L. *World Unfair Competition law*, 1965. Examples of works on a single narrow topic, consisting of reports on the position in individual jurisdictions with comparative sections are several works published by the Max-Planck-Institut für ausländisches öffentliches Recht und Völkerrecht, *eg*, *Judicial Protection against the Executive*, 1969–71.

Bibliographies

For bibliographical information reference may be made to the following: general bibliographies are: Besterman, T. *Law and International Law: a bibliography of bibliographies*, 1971; *Annual Legal Bibliography*, 1961–   (supplemented by the monthly *Current Legal Bibliography*); this lists American and foreign books and articles; *Index to Legal Periodicals*, 1908– ; this indexes articles, book reviews and case notes in legal periodicals published in the United States, the United Kingdom, Canada, Australia, New Zealand; *Index to Foreign Legal Periodicals*, 1960– ; this indexes articles and book reviews in periodicals in languages other than English, and in periodicals in English on international and comparative law, and periodicals in English published in English-speaking countries other than those covered by the *Index to Legal Periodicals*; *Karlsruher juristische Bibliographie*, 1965– ; this lists books and articles in German and, selectively, books and articles in other languages; American Association of Law Schools *Law Books Recommended for Libraries*, 1967– ; a very comprehensive list of books covering all subjects and jurisdictions; *A Bibliography on Foreign and Comparative Law: books and articles in English*, 1955– ; this work, which covers all jurisdictions with the exception of Anglo-American law, is continued by supplements which are, from time to time, cumulated; in between supplements it is up-dated by lists in the *American Journal of Comparative Law*. More specialized bibliographies are: Gilissen, J., ed. *Introduction*

bibliographique à l'histoire du droit et à la ethnologie juridique, 1963– .
Council of Europe *Bibliography of Translations of Codes of private
law of member countries of the Council of Europe and of The Hague
Conference on Private International Law*, 1967; this lists translations into English, French and German and is not confined to
codes; it lists translations of individual acts on civil and commercial law and cognate matters, *eg*, of copyright acts. Hart-
mann, J. *Bibliographie der Übersetzungen von Gesetzestexten : deutsch-
englisch-französisch-spanisch*, 1971; this lists translations of laws of
undivided Germany, the German Federal Republic, France, the
United Kingdom and the United States. The activities of international organizations in the field of law-making which are of
particular interest from the point of view of international
unification are described in: *Digest of legal activities of international organizations and other institutions*, mentioned above.
Bibliographical information in the field of comparative law in
its wider sense is to be found in the periodicals which have been
listed, and in a number of law library catalogues and union
catalogues. Among the former, the following will be found
helpful: Columbia University in the City of New York. Law
Library *Dictionary Catalog*, 1969 with supplement 1973; Marke,
J. J., ed. *Catalog of the Law Collection at New York University with
selected annotations*, 1953; University of Cambridge. Squire Law
Library *Catalogue*, 1974–5. Among the latter the following
should be mentioned: University of London. Institute of
Advanced Legal Studies: *Union list of Legal Periodicals*, 1968;
Zeitschriftenverzeichnis der juristischen Max-Planck-Institute, 1969.

A work which gives a great deal of useful information about
the legal systems of all jurisdictions is the *Register of Legal
Documentation in the World*, 1957. It contains information about
basic laws, collections of legislation and of law reports, legal
periodicals, and chief centres of legal research. Unfortunately,
it is now out-of-date, but it has been up-dated in respect of most
African countries by Vanderlinden, J. *An introduction to the
Sources of contemporary African laws: independent sub-Saharian
Africa*, 1975. The International Association of Legal Science, a
body which functions under the auspices of UNESCO and which
is responsible for the *Register*, has sponsored a series of bibliographical guides to the law of numerous countries, which are
described on page 386.

THE COMMONWEALTH

It is necessary to distinguish clearly the body of law which governs the relations between the members of the Commonwealth, including the relations between the United Kingdom and other members, *ie*, the constitutional law of the Commonwealth, on the one hand, and the internal laws of the member states, on the other hand.

Relations between members of the Commonwealth in general

As a result of the movement towards independence of individual territories, the relations between the United Kingdom and the other members of the Commonwealth have changed considerably over the whole period of its existence, and they are still in a state of flux. The principal sources in this field are certain United Kingdom statutes, *eg*, the Colonial Laws Validity Act 1865, and the Statute of Westminster 1931. There is some case-law, and reference must be made to some official papers; these include the proceedings and reports of the Imperial (Commonwealth) conferences, and some documents which deal with the affairs of a single jurisdiction, but have become of wider importance, *eg*, the Durham report of 1839 (H.C. 1839 xvii.1). Many modern documents, laws and others, are reprinted in Mansergh, N., ed. *Documents and Speeches on British Commonwealth Affairs*, 1953. Increasingly, international law is becoming relevant to inter-Commonwealth relations, and the number of treaties which are applicable is growing. The most important secondary literature are Roberts-Wray, Sir K. *Commonwealth and Colonial Law*, 1966, and the works on this topic by S. A. de Smith and those by Sir Ivor Jennings, in particular his *Constitutional Laws of the Commonwealth*, 3rd edition, volume 1, *The Monarchies*, 1957. The works by A. B. Keith are now largely of historical interest. Some information is to be found in most works on United Kingdom constitutional law. On the international law aspect of Commonwealth relations, see Fawcett, J. E. S. *The British Commonwealth in International Law*, 1963.

Relations between the United Kingdom and individual countries, including their constitutional provisions

The relations between the individual members of the Commonwealth, on the one hand, and the United Kingdom, or the Crown, or whatever expression be used, on the other, are governed by a wide variety of instruments, the character of which depends largely on the degree of independence of any given jurisdiction. These instruments tend to contain also the constitutions of given jurisdictions. If a sufficient degree of independence has been reached, some of the instruments may be statutes or other kinds of legislation of the jurisdictions themselves (see below). In other cases, the relevant instruments are legislation of the United Kingdom. These may be Acts of Parliament, or Statutory Rules and Orders (now Statutory Instruments), or instruments made under the prerogative powers of the Crown. Nothing further need be said about statutes (see page 99). Other instruments may be letters patent, orders in council, instructions to governors or, occasionally, charters. Any of these may be made by virtue of authority conferred by statute, or by virtue of the prerogative. If they are made under statutory authority, they are Statutory Instruments (formerly Statutory Rules and Orders); these have been published as such from the time when regular publication of S.R. & O.s started. Prerogative instruments are printed in an appendix to the S.I.s (S.R. & O.s) for the year in which they are made. In addition, they can usually be found in any revised or consolidated edition of the legislation of the jurisdiction in question if they were in force at the operative date of the revision or consolidation. An alternative source is the *London Gazette*, and if all else fails, it is worth consulting the Foreign and Commonwealth Office.

In many cases, reports of constitutional conferences or other official reports are of relevance; these are normally published as Command papers. As for secondary literature, reference should be made to the *British Commonwealth series*: Keeton, G. W., ed. *The British Commonwealth: the development of its laws and constitutions*, 1952–67.

Municipal law of individual jurisdictions : general

Though variations occur and though some jurisdictions, in particular the federations, will require individual treatment, general patterns exist, in particular in the field of legislation; in the absence of indications to the contrary, the remarks which follow are of general application.

Something must be said about special features of individual jurisdictions. The legal systems of most British and former British jurisdictions overseas are based on the English common law, but those of Rhodesia and Sri Lanka are based on Roman-Dutch law, and the law of Quebec is French in origin. Rhodesia has native courts as well as its ordinary law courts. The role played by Hindu law in India, and by Islamic law as well as Chinese customary law and African customary law in many jurisdictions must not be lost sight of (see also page 372–4).

Legislation

All legislation, both primary and secondary, is published as enacted. This is sometimes done by publishing each piece of legislation separately as in the United Kingdom, or in a government gazette. In the latter case, legislation may appear in the body of the gazette or in an appendix, in which case legislation is conveniently separate from other contents. In most jurisdictions, annual or sessional volumes of legislation are published, but sometimes this is not done or it is done with delays of up to several years. If in such cases it is not desired to preserve the gazette, it may be possible to extract the legislation and bind it. From time to time, at intervals which vary enormously from one jurisdiction to the other, all legislation in force at a given date is printed in the form of revised or consolidated legislation. Principal and secondary legislation may be published in the same publication, if revised at the same time, or they may be published separately. Great variety exists in the methods of up-dating such revisions or consolidations. It may be simply done by means of subsequent annual or sessional volumes of legislation, or by special supplements. Increasingly, too, revisions, etc. are published in loose-leaf form.

In dependent jurisdictions, the terms ordinances, proclamations or King's (Queen's) regulations were or are used for principal legislation, and terms such as orders, rules, regulations, proclamations, are used for secondary legislation; in independent jurisdictions, the terms acts and statutes tend to be used. It is obvious that in federations, there are both federal principal and subsidiary legislation, and principal and subsidiary legislation of the component units of the federations.

In certain jurisdictions, particularly some of those the law of which is based on the civil law, codes exist, which are part of the statute law of the jurisdiction in question, but are published on their own as well as forming part of revised legislation and, if appropriate, of annual (sessional) volumes. If published separately, such codes may be up-dated by supplements or by frequent re-publication. They may be published with or without annotations. Examples of codes are the civil codes of Quebec or of the Seychelles or, within the area of the common law, the criminal code of Canada. Mention may be made here of a source of information on future legislation: the *List of government commissions, committees and other bodies concerned with the reform of the law,* published at intervals by the Institute of Advanced Legal Studies; this list gives, as far as possible, for each body, the terms of reference, the names of the members, the programme of work and publications issued or, in some cases, details of reports not published.

Law reports

The vast majority of jurisdictions within the Commonwealth have law reports which are basically modelled on the English ones, and from the point of view of both processing and reference work are handled in a similar way. In the smaller jurisdictions there is often only one series, or several series which follow one another, with or without gaps. In the larger jurisdictions there tends to be a multiplicity of reports and special features of some individual jurisdictions will be noted below. It is worth remembering that there are some series which cover more than one jurisdiction, eg, the *African law reports,* 1964– (several parallel series).

Digests

There are a number of digests covering individual jurisdictions, some of which will be noted below, but selected cases from all Commonwealth countries are to be found digested in the *English and Empire digest* (see page 164).

Serial publications

Mention should be made of two annual publications, *viz*, the *Annual Survey of Commonwealth law*, 1965– , and the *Annual Survey of African law*, 1967– . No discussion of Commonwealth periodicals in general is called for; those published in Canada, Australia and New Zealand are indexed in the ILP; a selection of those published in the other members of the Commonwealth in the IFLP.

Textbooks

In general, textbooks on the law of the British overseas jurisdictions follow the pattern of English legal textbooks. Information on them, and in particular on new publications, can be found in the *Cumulative Book Index*, the *Law Book Guide*, 1973– ; *Law Books in Print*, 1971 (coverage to the end of 1969) and its supplement: *Law Books Published*, 1969– , and in the lists issued by Butterworth and by Sweet and Maxwell, both in their periodicals and separately, and in the national bibliographies of Commonwealth countries in so far as they are published.

Bibliographies

Some of the bibliographies mentioned in Chapter 10 contain information on the Commonwealth; particulars of law reports will also be found in Maxwell, W. H. and Brown, C. R., comps. *A complete list of British and colonial law reports and legal periodicals, etc.*, 1937.

Canada

Canada is a federation and has both Dominion and Provincial law courts. Some series of law reports cover both Dominion and Provincial courts, *eg*, the *Dominion Law Reports*, 1912– , some cover Dominion courts only, *eg*, the *Canada Federal Court Reports*, 1971– , some cover the courts of single Provinces, and there are some series of regional reports, covering the courts of several Provinces, *eg*, the *Maritime Provinces Reports*, 1929–68, and the *Western Weekly Reports*, 1912– . Ontario and Quebec have large numbers of series of older reports.

There are digests covering the whole of Canadian law, *eg*, the *Canadian Abridgment*, 2nd edition, 1966– , supplemented by *Canadian Current Law*, 1948– , some digests covering individual Provinces, and two regional digests, *viz*, the *Canadian Encyclopedic Digest (Western edition)*, 2nd edition, 1956– , and the *Canadian encyclopedic digest (Ontario)*, 2nd edition, 1949– . The former covers the Western Provinces, the latter Ontario and the Eastern Maritime Provinces. The *Canadian Abridgment* is complete in respect of the common law Provinces, but contains only cases of general interest from Quebec.

Halsbury's Laws of England; 3rd edition: Canadian converter, 1965–75, 9 volumes, supports its statements by reference to Canadian statute and case-law.

Australia and New Zealand

Australia is a federation; in addition to the States, there are some Commonwealth territories, *eg*, the Northern Territory. Some of them have become independent, *eg*, Papua and New Guinea. Some series of law reports contain the decisions of Commonwealth and State courts, *eg*, the *Australian Law Journal reports*, 1958– , or the *Australian Bankruptcy Cases*, 1928– , some contain those of Commonwealth courts and of other courts when exercising federal jurisdiction, *eg*, the *Federal law reports*, 1956– , some those of individual States.

There are several State digests in addition to the *Australian Digest*, 2nd edition, 1963– which covers all Australian jurisdictions.

There is an *Australian and New Zealand commentary on Halsbury's Laws of England, 4th edition*, 1974– .

India

India is a federation, consisting of States and several Union territories. There has been considerable revision of State boundaries as well as amalgamation and division of States.

India has some codes within the usual meaning of that term, but the so-called State codes, *eg*, Madras code, are really revised editions of statutes.

Among the multiplicity of Indian law reports attention should be drawn to the *Indian Law Reports*, which have been published from 1876 in numerous parallel series, corresponding to the several high courts. Political changes, as reflected in changes in the number and territorial jurisdiction of these courts, have affected these series correspondingly.

Malaysia

Before the Second World War, Malaya consisted of three categories of constituent parts: the Unfederated Malay States (Johore, Kedah, Kelantan, Perlis, Trengganu) which had no constitutional ties among themselves; the Federated Malay States (Negri Sembilan, Pahang, Perak, Selangor) which were federated among themselves, as well as forming part of Malaya; and the Straits Settlements (Malacca, Penang, Singapore), which were also linked among themselves. After periods as Malayan Union and Federation of Malaya, the area has become the Federation of Malaysia. All the former Unfederated and Federated Malay States form part of it as well as Malacca and Penang. Singapore has left the Federation, but Sabah (formerly British North Borneo) and Sarawak have joined it.

It is a feature of the Federation, as well as of the former Federated Malay States, that federal and State legislation have sometimes been published together and sometimes separately, and that the legislation of all the constituent units has sometimes been included in one publication without federal legislation.

West Indies

There have been several constitutional arrangements linking all or some of the territories in the West Indies. It is worth noting that some of them are comprised within two groups: the Leeward Islands (Antigua; St Christopher, Nevis and Anguilla; Montserrat; the British Virgin Islands) and the Windward Islands (Dominica; Grenada; St Lucia; St Vincent). In addition to material covering the whole of the West Indies and to material relating to individual territories, there is legislation for the Leeward Islands and there are law reports for the Windward Islands as groups.

Nigeria

Independent Nigeria was established as a federation, consisting of the Federal Territory of Lagos and the Eastern, Northern, Western and (later) Mid-West Regions. In 1967, the country was reorganized: Lagos became Lagos State; the Western and Mid-West Regions became States almost unchanged; the Eastern Region was divided into the South Eastern, Rivers and East Central States; and the Northern Region was divided into six new states – North Western, North Central, Kano, North Eastern, Benue – Plateau and Kwara.

UNITED STATES OF AMERICA

The United States of America are a federation. The respective legislative powers of the federal authorities and of the individual states are clearly distinguished, and there are two separate systems of courts, *viz*, federal and state courts. The unwritten common law which the British settlers took to North America forms the basis of the American legal system except in so far as it has been modified or replaced by statute law. An exception is Louisiana which has a legal system based on the civil law.

The legal literature of the United States is so vast and complex that the standard bibliographical manuals such as Hicks, F. C. *Materials and Methods of Legal Research*, 1942; Pollack, E. H. *Fundamentals of Legal Research*, 1973; Price, M. O. and Bitner, H. *Effective Legal Research*, 1969; Roalfe, W. R. *How to Find the Law and Legal Writing*, 1965, are works of several hundred pages. For detailed information reference must be made to them or to other bibliographical manuals. In these lines it will be possible to highlight only the most important types of American legal literature, without giving detailed instruction in their use. This would be difficult to grasp without the actual books; these usually provide their own instructions.

It is worth stating that although there are many law publishers in the United States, there are two firms which, between them, dominate the production of legislation and conventional law reports, digests and encyclopedias: the West Publishing Co. and the Lawyers' Co-operative Publishing Co. The publications of each are keyed so as to be compatible with other publications of the same firm.

Constitutions

Each of the states has its own constitution, but the most important single piece of legislation in the United States is the federal constitution, including the amendments to it, which controls all other legislation and judicial law-making. It is one of the most important – perhaps the most important – part of the jurisdiction of the Supreme Court to judge the constitutionality of laws. The constitution can be found in the collections of federal legislation, annotated and unannotated, and also generally in the compiled or revised editions of state legislation, annotated and unannotated. The latter also always contain the constitution of the state in question. The leading edition of the federal constitution is the annotated edition published by the Library of Congress: *The Constitution of the United States of America: analysis and interpretation*, 1964. Other annotated versions are those contained in the *U.S. Code Annotated* and *Federal Code Annotated*. A collection of state constitutions is Columbia University. Legislative Drafting Research Fund. *Constitutions of the United States, national and state*, 2nd edition, 1974–   ; with index digest.

Federal legislation

Primary legislation

The most usual form of primary legislation is the statute or act of Congress. As in the United Kingdom, there are public and private laws. Joint resolutions of both Houses of Congress have the force of legislation. Federal statutes are issued as enacted in the form of 'slip laws', *ie*, in individual pamphlets. These are replaced by the volumes of the *Statutes at large*, each of which formerly covered the legislation of a whole Congress, but now that of a single session. These contain public and private acts and other matters, such as treaties (until 1950), presidential proclamations, and joint resolutions (of both Houses of Congress). There have been two editions of revised statutes. The public laws of each year are reprinted in the supplementary services to the *U.S. Code Annotated* and to the *United States Code Service* (see below).

For practical purposes, the compiled editions of federal legislation are of great importance. There is first the *United States Code*, an official edition which contains only texts of legislation. The legislation contained in it is the legislation in force; it is arranged by subject, in so-called titles. There have been several editions: it is kept up to date by annual supplements until a new edition is required.

The *U.S. Code* forms the basis of two annotated editions, *viz*, the *U.S. Code Annotated* and the *United States Code Service*, formerly *Federal Code Annotated*. American lawyers find it essential to have one of the two annotated editions available. Each of them contains full annotations and is kept up to date by pocket supplements, supplementary volumes and replacement volumes. Each has a supplementary service which consists of annual volumes and pamphlets issued during the year. That of the *U.S. Code Annotated* is the *U.S. Code Congressional and Administrative News*. This contains the public laws, legislative histories of the laws published, which are of great importance in the United States, as well as presidential proclamations, executive orders, and reorganization plans. The service linked to the former *Federal Code Annotated* was the *Federal Code Annotated Public Laws and Administrative Material*. It is now called *United States Code Service*, like its parent publication. It contains the public laws, proclamations, executive orders and some other documents. Many public laws have popular names by which they are known. Apart from tables in some of the publications referred to, attention should be drawn to *Acts and Cases by Popular Names* published as one of the *Shepard's Citations*.

Secondary legislation

The most important categories of secondary legislation are rules made by various administrative agencies, and manifestations of the President's law-making power. The most important of these are presidential proclamations, executive orders and reorganization plans (affecting government departments). Proclamations and executive orders are, strictly speaking, not always subordinate legislation because some of them are made by virtue of powers which are analogous to the royal prerogative. They are, however, published in the same way as genuinely subordinate legislation. Presidential proclamations, executive orders and reorganization plans as well as rules made by agencies are first published in the *Federal Register,* which began publication in 1936 and is published five times a week. They are subsequently incorporated in the *Code of Federal Regulations,* which is a subject arrangement of rules, etc. in force, rather analogous to the *U.S. Code.* It is supplemented by the *Government Organization Manual,* an annual publication which shows the structure of the federal government. Proclamations and executive orders are also printed in the *U.S. Code Congressional and Administrative News* and in the *United States Code Service.*

State Legislation

The constitutions of the individual states have been referred to above. The way the statutes of the states are published varies from state to state, but a general pattern can be discerned. In many cases there are slip laws, and laws are published as enacted as part of the commercially produced annotated editions of legislation. They are published officially in sessional volumes, and there are usually both official compiled editions and commercially produced annotated editions. The former contain the texts of laws in force arranged by subject, rather on the model of the *U.S. Code,* the latter contain the same material with annotations and other ancillary material. Up-dating takes various forms, but the annotated editions are usually up-dated by pocket parts, supplementary and replacement volumes, depending to some extent on the volume and character of the legislation of any given year.

Uniform laws

The diversity of the laws of the individual states can produce serious inconveniences in some branches of the law, particularly those affecting matters of commerce. To eliminate, or at the very least to mitigate, these inconveniences, the Commissioners on Uniform State Laws were appointed in 1892. They are responsible for drawing up model laws; these have no legal force, but they can be, and in many cases have been adopted by individual states. This means that they have been incorporated into the statute law of each adopting state, and form part of its laws. The best-known example is the Uniform Commercial Code, which has superseded several uniform laws on commercial matters. The uniform laws are published conveniently in the *Uniform Laws Annotated ; master edition*, 1968– , a publication which shows how the uniform laws have been interpreted by the various states. Information about the work of the Commissioners and about proposed uniform laws can be found in *Handbook of the National Conference of Commissioners on Uniform State Laws and proceedings of the annual conference*, 1892– . The American Law Institute (see below) has also produced some models of laws which might be adopted by states, *eg*, a model penal code.

Congressional documents and other government publications

Congress produces a very large body of documents; some of these, *eg*, certain committee hearings, form part of individual legislative histories, but the range and variety of documents is enormous. Details can be found in Schmeckebier, L. F. and Eastin, R. B. *Government Publications and Their Use*, 1969, and it is worth noting that the British Library of Political and Economic Science is a library of deposit for US federal government publications, both congressional and departmental.

Law reports

The Supreme Court

Each judgment of the Court is printed in a separate pamphlet when it is delivered. These pamphlets are replaced by bound volumes of which there are several each year. The expression 'October term . . . ' means the whole judicial year beginning in October. The first ninety volumes of the *Reports of the Supreme*

Court are usually cited by the name of the reporter, *eg*, Dallas, Cranch, rather than as ' ... U.S.', although they were retrospectively given consecutive numbers; from volume 91 (1875), reference is simply ' ... U.S.'. There are two unofficial editions, both of which have annotations, though they differ from one another. One is the *Lawyers' edition of the Supreme Court Reports* published by the Lawyers' Co-operative Publishing Co. and covering the whole series, the other one the *Supreme Court Reporter*, a unit of the *National Reporter System*, from 106 U.S. (1882).

Lower federal courts

The decisions of the lower federal courts before 1880 were reported in a multiplicity of reports; for practical purposes, they are now to be found in the *Federal Cases 1789–1880*, 1894–7. The arrangement of the cases, with some exceptions, is alphabetical. From 1880 onwards, the lower federal courts have been reported in the *Federal Reporter, Federal Supplement* and *Federal Rules Decisions*, all three of which form part of the *National Reporter System* (see below). Coverage is as follows: *Federal Reporter*, 1880–   : courts of appeals, U.S. Court of Customs and Patent Appeals (for patent cases), United States Emergency Court of Appeals, District of Columbia Court of Appeals, and (1880–1932) U.S. district courts and the tax cases of the U.S. Court of Claims. *Federal Supplement*, 1932–   : U.S. district courts and tax cases of the U.S. Court of Claims. *Federal Rules Decisions*, 1940–   : decisions interpreting the federal rules of civil and criminal procedure not reported elsewhere.

There are also a number of specialized federal courts, *eg*, Court of Claims, Court of Customs and Patent Appeals. The decisions of these are reported in series published by the Government Printing Office, and the decisions of some of them appear in the *Federal Reporter* or *Federal Supplement*, as explained. Cases in the lower federal courts are selectively reprinted in the *American Law Reports Annotated (federal)*.

State reports

All states have official reports which report at least the decisions of their supreme courts (whatever their designation). Most states, *eg*, New York, have a variety of reports, partly unofficial, cited by the names of the reporters. It is true to say that all these are rarely encountered in Britain; the Middle Temple Library is known to have a comprehensive collection of them for the period before the inception of the *National Reporter System*. Outside the United States, the decisions of the state courts are usually encountered in the form of the regional reports which form the *National Reporter System*, which began publication about 1880. Each series reports the decisions of the courts of a group of states. The volumes contain a reprint of the reports in the official editions (where they exist) as well as reports of other cases with tables, references and head-notes which are original to the *National Reporter System*. The decisions are those of the supreme courts of the states and of intermediate courts of appeal though coverage varies from state to state. There are two series which are confined to the decisions of single states: the *New York Supplement*, which contains also cases of New York courts not printed in the *North-Eastern Reporter*, and the *California Reporter*, which contains also cases not found in the *Pacific Reporter*. All the series, except for the *California Reporter*, are now in their second series (Pacific 2nd, etc.).

Specialized reports

In addition to the general reports discussed so far, there are a number of specialized reports which report cases on a single subject irrespective of jurisdiction, *eg*, the *American Maritime Cases*, 1923– . A further group which must be mentioned are the various loose-leaf series on specific subjects, called topical law reports, many published by the Commerce Clearing House, *eg*, the *Standard Federal Tax Reporter*.

Since many decisions of state courts are mainly of local interest, selective reprints of those which are of general interest have been published over many years, at first without annotations, but over the years with increasingly detailed annotations. The earlier series, known as the Trinity series, were: *American Decisions*, to 1886, 100 volumes; *American Reports*, 1869–87, 60 volumes; *American State Reports*, 1887–1911, 104 volumes. Other annotated series were: *Lawyers' Reports Annotated*, 1888–1918,

146 volumes; *American and English Annotated Cases*, 1906–11, 21 volumes; *American Annotated Cases*, 1912–18, 32 volumes. All these were replaced from 1918 by the *American Law Reports Annotated*. In these the notes are very elaborate, and the series is completed by a very complex apparatus of auxiliary volumes of indexes, tables, digests, etc. Important federal cases were added from 1918 until 1969, when the *American Law Reports (federal)* began publication.

Virtually all commercially published series (other than those which are loose-leaf) publish advance opinions, usually in monthly issues, which are superseded by the bound volumes. The official series, on the other hand, are often supplemented by individual decisions in pamphlet form, issued at once; some of them, however, issue advance sheets in the same way as the commercial series.

Digests

The wealth of American case-law requires a formidable apparatus of ancillary material such as indexes, tables, citators and digests, in order to make proper use of the available law reports. It is not necessary to describe here these various items in detail, since difficulties are normally elucidated in the volumes in question themselves, but some idea must be given of what is available. Some form of digest is usually included in the volumes of the reports themselves, but there are separate digest series. The most important is the *American Digest System*. This digests all American reported cases from 1658. The century edition covers the years 1658–1896. From then onwards, the digest is being cumulated every ten years into decennial digests. During each ten-year period, pamphlets are issued monthly and cumulated into bound volumes, which are superseded by the volumes of the decennial digest when published. The last completed decennial digest is the seventh.

The pamphlets of the *General Digest* are up-dated further by the digests contained in the advance sheets of the various series of reports, or at any rate of those within the *National Reporter System*.

Apart from the *American Digest System*, the following digests which cover only part of reported case-law should be mentioned:

1. Covering decisions of the Supreme Court: *Digest of the United States Supreme Court Reports* to fit in with the Lawyers' edition of the Supreme Court reports; and the *United States Supreme Court Digest* to fit in with the *Supreme Court Reporter* in the *National Reporter System.*

2. Digests covering decisions of federal courts including the Supreme Court: *Federal Digest* and its continuation, the *Modern Federal Practice Digest.* The latter covers cases from 1939.

3. Digests to the reports of one or more states: there are digests to each of the units of the *National Reporter System,* and in many cases digests to the reports of the decisions of the courts of single states.

Mention may be made here of *Words and Phrases,* a dictionary of all words and phrases judicially defined by American courts.

Court rules

Rules of court and rules of the administrative agencies are made by the courts and agencies themselves; those of the lower federal courts must not be inconsistent with the general rules made for them by the Supreme Court, and those of state courts must not be inconsistent with the legislation of the state. The rules of court of most courts are printed in the appropriate series of law reports; those of the Supreme Court are to be found in the *U.S. Code,* and those of administrative agencies affecting the exercise of their judicial or quasi-judicial functions in the *Code of Federal Regulations.*

Citators

The complexity of American law makes it essential to check the subsequent history of any case or piece of legislation cited. This is done by the use of the so-called citators. There are various aids of this nature, often included in volumes of reports, digests, etc., but the best-known and most comprehensive set are *Shepard's Citations.* There are numerous sets of *Shepard's* state citators to cover the reports and laws of practically all states, and each unit of the *National Reporter System* is matched by a set of *Shepard's.* These regional *Shepard's* are case citators only. In addition, there is *Shepard's United States Citations* (case and statute editions) which covers the decisions of the Supreme Court, the *Constitution,* the *U.S. Code* and the *Statutes at large.* State legislation must be 'shepardized' in the state *Shepard's.* A rather more specialized set is *Shepard's Law Review Citations,* which shows citations of articles in court. The *Index to Legal Periodicals* lists all cases which have been the subject of notes in law reviews and gives references to the notes.

Secondary sources

Attorneys-general's opinions

The opinions given by the federal and state Attorneys-general in their capacity of legal advisers to the executive branch of government are not sources of law in the same way as judgments of the courts. They are, however, weighty and considered opinions meant to be acted upon and therefore authoritative statements of the law expounded in them. The opinions of the federal Attorneys-general have been published in a series covering the period from the appointment of the first Attorney-general in 1789, and some opinions of state Attorneys-general have been published also.

Appellate briefs

The procedure in the appellate courts of the United States relies far more extensively on written briefs than is the case in England. These set out, in the United States, both the facts and the law with arguments. They are distributed to a certain number of libraries and while no library in this country, as far as is known, has a collection of American appellate briefs their existence should be noted.

Legal encyclopedias

There are two major legal encyclopedias in the United States, namely *Corpus Juris Secundum,* 106 volumes, published by the West Publishing Company, and *American Jurisprudence,* 67 volumes, now in process of being superseded by *American Jurisprudence Second,* which at 73 volumes is still incomplete, published by the Lawyers' Co-operative Publishing Co. Each of these is keyed to the various series of law reports, digests, etc., published by its publisher. Each of them sets out to be a complete statement of American law as developed by the decisions of the courts. Each set is being kept up to date by replacement volumes where necessary and by pocket supplements, and each is equipped with its own apparatus of indexes, etc.

Restatements

The multiplicity of jurisdictions in the United States has made it essential that the principles of the common law should be restated in a form which should be recognized as authoritative on a nation-wide basis. This task is being performed by the American Law Institute, which has been producing the so-called *Restatements* over many years. Each subject is in the hands of one or more reporters, who are always among the leading authorities on the topic in question. The procedure is that successive tentative drafts are produced which are considered by the Institute at its annual meetings. When a text has been finally approved it is published in book form. Revision continues even of the subjects on which *Restatements* have been published and in a number of cases a second *Restatement* has been published to supersede the first. The topics dealt with tend to be the traditional common law subjects, which means private and commercial law rather than public law, though there is one *Restatement of the Foreign Relations Law of the United States*. There is a general index and also the *Restatement in the Courts*, which gives references to cases in which the *Restatements* have been judicially considered. The present list of published *Restatements* is: contracts, judgments, property, restitution, security; *Second Restatement*: agency, conflict of laws, foreign relations law, torts, trusts.

Periodicals

Writing for and editing law journals is part of American legal education and most law schools, therefore, publish at least one law review, edited by senior students. The number of reviews is consequently very large. It is not necessary to discuss them in detail. Many of them have case-notes which are valuable for research. The book review sections are often very

11

short. In recent years an increasing number of law schools have begun to publish specialized, as distinct from general, law reviews; many of these are devoted to international law, but there are also other specialities, *eg*, environmental law. All American law reviews are indexed in the *Index to Legal Periodicals*, 1908– and its predecessor, the *Index to Legal Periodical Literature*, 1886–1937 by L. E. Jones and F. E. Chipman, the first volume of which covers the period to the end of 1886. American periodicals on foreign and international law are, in many cases, also indexed in the *Index to Foreign Legal Periodicals*, 1960– . Articles of legal interest in periodicals not indexed in these two indexes are indexed in the *Index to Periodical Articles related to Law*, 1960– .

Treatises and textbooks

One characteristic feature of the American law book scene is the large number of casebooks; this is a direct consequence of the American teaching method. For a number of years casebooks have tended to develop into books containing 'cases and materials'. At the other end of the scale there are the major treatises, works on specific branches of the law which are comprehensive and detailed in their coverage, run into many volumes, and are recognized as standard authorities on their subjects. Examples are Williston or Corbin on Contract, or Wigmore on Evidence. All these works are normally kept up-to-date by cumulative annual pocket supplements. In so far as they are on the traditional common law subjects, they are relevant authority in the common law jurisdictions outside the United States. Some of them are now published in loose-leaf form. Information on them can be found in the *Cumulative Book Index*, *Law Books in Print* and its supplement, the *Law Book Guide*, *Law books recommended for libraries*, as well as book reviews and information from publishers. Attention should be drawn to the book appraisals which are published regularly in the *Law Library Journal*.

In addition to the bibliographies on American law referred to above, the following work will be found useful: Andrews, J. L. and others *The Law in the United States of America : a selective bibliographical guide*, 1966.

CIVIL LAW JURISDICTIONS

The jurisdictions, the legal literature of which has to be described in this section, are a somewhat heterogeneous collection. It is impossible within the framework of this chapter to describe the literature of each in detail and, as with the British Commonwealth, an attempt will be made to describe elements common to all or a large number of them, with some indication of the features of individual jurisdictions. The jurisdictions in question are Continental Europe, both the countries with a Western-style legal system and the countries of Eastern Europe, the Asian and African countries outside the Commonwealth, and the countries of Latin America. The legal systems of most of these countries are what are technically known as civil law systems, *ie*, they are either based on Roman law or they are at least influenced by it. The legal systems of the Republic of South Africa, as well as those of Rhodesia and Sri Lanka, are based on Roman-Dutch law (see page 359), but have been influenced by English law. This is true of the style of their law reports which, in the case of South Africa, are bibliographically very complicated. This influence of Roman law varies from country to country or at least varies from one group of countries to another and, within the non-common law jurisdictions, groups can be distinguished; the laws of the Nordic countries form one family which is closer to English law than are the laws of the countries of French or German inspiration. As might be expected, the laws of the communist Eastern European countries have been strongly influenced by Soviet law.

It is true to say that in most civil law countries the law is codified. This means that the central areas of the law, such as private law, commercial law, civil procedure, criminal law and criminal procedure, are governed by codes. The term 'code' has, however, come to be used in a wider sense also; one speaks, for instance, of codes of social security, codes of navigation, etc. By this is meant that a branch of the law is governed by one statute which is applied in the same way as a code but covers, of course, a much narrower field of law than one of the traditional codes. It should be noted as a general feature also that, although the law of these countries is by and large statute law and not case-law in the common law sense, decisions of the courts are of very great importance. It is not possible to study the provisions of a code in isolation without reference to the decisions which have applied and interpreted them; and even in countries, the law of which is codified, there may be areas or branches of the law which are largely judge-made. An example is the law applicable to the judicial review of administrative acts in France. This is not only applied in the last resort by the Conseil d'Etat, but has largely been created by decisions of that court.

When dealing with a point of law arising in any of the jurisdictions in question, the first approach is to look at any relevant code; editions of other legislation are used essentially to supplement and up-date the provisions of any relevant code.

Codes and legislation

There are various methods of publishing codes. In the countries influenced by the French tradition composite editions of codes are often found. These are one-volume editions of the principal codes which are easy to carry: they tend to be re-issued very frequently or to be supplemented at frequent intervals. An example are the Italian *Cinque codici*. In addition, in most countries annotated and unannotated editions of single codes are published. The annotated editions vary enormously in size and detail. It is worth noting here that in Germany and the countries influenced by the German style of legal literature, *eg*, Austria and Switzerland, a distinction is drawn between commentaries and textbooks. Commentaries or annotated codes are works in which each section of a code is set out separately with annotations, whereas textbooks are systematic expositions. The commentaries vary in size from short one-volume commentaries, which tend to be published for all codes and major pieces of legislation, to the German *Grosskommentare*, which run to many large volumes. Among the most striking examples of these are the two Swiss standard commentaries on the civil code and code of obligations known as the *Zürcher Kommentar* and the *Berner Kommentar*. Each of these is being published piecemeal over a period of very many years with overlapping editions.

Mention must also be made of the Belgian type edition of the codes, *ie*, multi-volume editions of the codes and the legislation on cognate matters with notes.

Legislation other than codes tends to be published in official gazettes which are issued frequently, very often several times a week, and which contain both primary and secondary legislation. These gazettes have to be bound at the end of the year, together with the appropriate indexes, as they are not normally replaced by bound volumes on the English pattern. In some cases, *eg*, France, the gazette is not confined to legislation. The *Journal officiel* contains other material also. In many countries there are also unofficial editions of legislation, *eg*, the *Pasinomie* in Belgium and *Lex* in Italy. In France a great deal of legislation, but not all of it, is reprinted in the principal series of law reports, namely, the *Recueil Dalloz Sirey*; this was true of both its predecessor series.

Law reports

The way law reports are published depends inevitably on the judicial organization of a country and on the importance of judicial decisions in its law. In most countries decisions cannot only be found in the law reports properly so-called but also in legal periodicals, which must therefore not be left out of consideration. Often, there are separate series of reports for different courts, *eg*, in Germany and Austria the decisions of the Supreme Courts are reported in separate series (in the case of these two countries there are even two Supreme Court series covering civil and criminal matters respectively, as well as separate series for the supreme administrative and constitutional courts). A similar state of affairs prevails in France and Italy with the proviso, however, that there are general series which report decisions of all courts, such as the *Recueil Dalloz Sirey* in France and the *Giurisprudenza italiana* in Italy. In smaller countries or countries where for this or other reasons the volume of case-law is not as extensive, there tend to be fewer series of reports. The practice concerning the reporting of decisions of lower courts varies from country to country, but in France and Italy at any rate the decisions of lower courts are reported, and in Germany there is a separate series covering the courts of appeal. In addition to general series of reports there are collections which cover certain topics or areas of the law only, *eg*, a series reporting cases relating to the regulation of competition in Germany.

Periodicals

The number of legal periodicals in most countries is substantial. Some countries have national indexes of legal periodical literature, *eg*, the *Karlsruher juristische Bibliographie*, 1965–   ; and Napoletano, V., ed. *Dizionario bibliografico delle riviste giuridiche italiane, 1865–1954*; 1956 with supplements. In addition, a selection of the most important periodicals of all countries is indexed in the *Index to Foreign Legal Periodicals*.

Monographic literature

It has been pointed out that in the German-speaking countries a clear distinction is drawn between commentaries and textbooks and that the large commentary is possibly the most characteristic type of legal writing. In the countries of French inspiration the leading doctrinal works tend to be systematic treatises; these may follow the arrangement of the codes but they are systematic expositions and not commentaries. Commentaries on individual statutes do, of course, exist and also shorter commentaries on the codes.

Increasingly, textbooks have given way to loose-leaf services or treatises published in loose-leaf form for easy up-dating. This is a universal trend.

THE EUROPEAN COMMUNITIES

Scholars are not agreed on the precise nature of the European Communities, but this is a problem which it is not necessary to solve for the purposes of these remarks. There are, in fact, three European Communities, namely, the European Coal and Steel Community, which came into being in 1952; the European Economic Community (colloquially known as the Common Market) and the European Atomic Energy Community, both of which came into being in 1958. Each of them is an association of states which have combined for certain definite purposes by means of a treaty. Under each of the three treaties the parties enjoy certain rights and are liable to perform certain duties. The purposes for which the three Communities have been created are fairly similar and the parties in all three cases are identical. It has therefore been found convenient that the work of the Communities should be carried out by the same organs. When the European Economic Community and the European Atomic Energy Community were established they did not create a new Court of Justice, but the existing Court of Justice of the European Coal and Steel Community was turned into the Court of Justice of the European Communities. Similarly, the Common Assembly of the ECSC was enlarged to become the Assembly of the three Communities and was re-named the European Parliamentary Assembly. The so-called Merger treaty of 1966 which came into force on 1 July 1967 replaced the three existing Councils of Ministers by one Council of the three Communities, and the Commissions of the EEC and of Euratom, as well as the High Authority of the ECSC, by the single Commission of the European Communities.

These common organs exercise legislative, executive and judicial functions arising from the three treaties. They have the right to make laws or render judgments respectively, binding on the member countries and their nationals; the analogy with a federation is therefore sufficiently strong to warrant the same bibliographical treatment. In practice, the European Economic Community is now the most important of the three and has come to overshadow the other two. The term community law is sometimes loosely used to denote not only the law which is derived from the three treaties establishing the Communities and binding on the United Kingdom by virtue of the Treaty of accession but also the law, or at least certain portions of the law, of the member countries. The municipal law of the member countries must, however, be clearly distinguished from Community law properly so-called. The following remarks will be concerned with that law only unless the contrary is expressly stated.

Basic law

The basic law of the three Communities consists of the three treaties establishing them. These treaties were drawn up in the original four languages, *ie*, French, German, Dutch and Italian. The texts are to be found in the treaty series of the countries concerned, commentaries on the treaties, and the works mentioned below.

Of fundamental importance from the point of view of the United Kingdom is the Treaty of accession of 22 January 1972, which came into force on 1 January 1973. The United Kingdom is a member of the EEC and Euratom by virtue of this treaty, and of the ECSC by virtue of the *Decision of the Council of the European Communities concerning the accession of the Kingdom of Denmark, Ireland, the Kingdom of Norway and the United Kingdom of Great Britain and Northern Ireland to the European Coal and Steel Community*. Several unofficial translations of the founding treaties into English were issued before 1 January 1973, when the United Kingdom became a member of the Communities. All these translations were unsatisfactory in one way or another and they have now been superseded by the official translations issued in conjunction with the Treaty of accession: *Treaty concerning the accession of the Kingdom of Denmark, Ireland, the Kingdom of Norway and the United Kingdom of Great Britain and Northern Ireland to the European Economic Community and the European Atomic Energy Community including the Act concerning the conditions of accession and the adjustments to the treaties (with Final act) Brussels, 22 January 1972*, 1973 (Cmnd. 5179), (which includes the treaties establishing the European Economic Community and the European Atomic Energy Community). *Treaty establishing the European Coal and Steel Community, Paris, 18 April 1951*, 1972 (Cmnd. 5189), (includes the *Decision of the Council . . . concerning the accession . . . to the European Coal and Steel Community*). These do not show later amendments to the three basic treaties.

They are reprinted in *Sweet and Maxwell's European Community treaties, including the European Communities act 1972*, 1972, and in the *Encyclopaedia of European Economic Community Law*, 1973– , volume B.

A useful collection is *European Communities. Treaties establishing the European Communities; treaties amending these treaties; documents concerning the accession*, 1973.

In the course of the existence of the Communities, numerous treaties have been concluded, both by the member states among themselves on Community matters, the most important treaty being the Merger treaty mentioned earlier, and by the Communities with non-member states. Translations into English of all of these can be found in *European Communities, Treaties and related instruments*, 1972 and in the *Encyclopaedia of European Economic Community Law*, 1973– , volume B (European Community treaties). French versions of all these and of a large number of other instruments affecting the countries of Western Europe can be found in *Juris classeur, codes et lois: traités de l'Europe occidentale et textes d'application*, 1945– .

The Treaty of accession was given effect in the United Kingdom by the European Communities Act 1972, reprinted in *Sweet and Maxwell's European Community treaties, including the European Communities act 1972*, 1972; Wall, E. H. *European Communities act, 1972*, 1973, and together with other United Kingdom legislation of relevance to Community law, in the *Encyclopaedia of European Economic Community law*, volume A (United Kingdom sources).

Secondary legislation

The term secondary legislation when applied in a national context means Statutory Instruments in the United Kingdom and equivalent delegated legislation elsewhere. In the case of the European Communities, however, it means everything below the level of the treaties establishing the Communities. There are various kinds of such secondary legislation: regulations, directives, decisions, recommendations and opinions. The most important of these are the regulations, which are fully binding on the member countries; the other categories are not binding to the same extent, *eg*, member countries have a certain discretion in the way in which they give effect to directives. All the regulations and other instruments are published in the European Communities *Journal officiel*, 1958– . [From 1968 in two series: C. Communications et informations; L. Législation.] This continues the European Coal and Steel Community *Journal officiel*, 1952–8; it has always been published in all the official languages, which means that from 1 January 1973 there has also been an English edition. Before 1973 the Foreign and Commonwealth Office published the European

Communities regulations as follows: Great Britain Foreign and Commonwealth Office *European Economic Community regulations, 1958–68*, published 1962–8, *European Atomic Energy Community regulations, 1962–5*, and European Communities *Official Journal, Legislation*: English translation, 1969–72.

Official English translations of all secondary legislation in force on 1 January 1973 were published as follows: European Communities *Official Journal*: special edition (English), 1952–1972, 1972–3. This contains authentic texts of all secondary legislation in force on 1 January 1973, arranged chronologically. European Communities *Secondary Legislation 1952–72*, 1973–4 is a subject arrangement of the material contained in the preceding item. The texts are authentic and this edition replaces, therefore, the non-authentic version published in 1972 in 42 volumes. It is supplemented by European Communities *Secondary Legislation, 1952–72: Subject Index and Numerical List, 1973*, 1973. Many of the regulations and other items of secondary legislation are reprinted in the *Common Market Reporter*, 1965– , and many will be found in the *Encyclopaedia of European Community Law*, volume C (Community secondary legislation).

The authentic English versions of European Community secondary legislation list all items in force on 1 January 1973; for instruments which had ceased to be in force by that date it may be necessary to go back to the earlier volumes of the *Official Journal* or the translations published before 1973. Draft instruments are published in the *Official Journal*, series C: Information and notices, and those submitted to the European Parliament for advice or consultation are printed in the working papers of the Parliament.

Court of Justice and law reports

When the European Coal and Steel Community was established a court was set up in Luxembourg which, on the establishment of the other two Communities, was enlarged to be the Court of Justice of the European Communities. It has jurisdiction over the Communities and their organs and over the governments and nationals of member countries. It exists in order to enforce Community law and to control the exercise of powers conferred by the treaties and by secondary legislation. It also has jurisdiction to adjudicate on questions of Community law which might arise in a national court of one of the member countries and which that court refers to the Court of Justice. The decisions of the Court have been published in the four original official languages from 1954 (*Recueil de la jurisprudence de la Cour*) with an English edition from 1973. English translations of the decisions from 1961 have been published in the *Common Market Law Reports*. This series does not contain all the decisions of the Court of Justice but it does contain translations of some important judgments on questions of Community law rendered by national courts of member countries. This series has a *Restrictive Practices supplement* beginning with 1966. The decisions of the Court, up to and including 1960, in English translation, are contained in Valentine, D. G. *The Court of Justice of the European Communities*, 1965, volume 2. Some decisions are reprinted in the *Common Market Reporter*. Digests of the decisions of the Court of Justice and of decisions of national courts on points of Community law can be found in Eversen, H. and Sperl, H., eds. *Répertoire de la jurisprudence relative aux traités instituant les Communautés européennes, 1953–* , 1965– ; with annual supplements; and Dölle, H. and Zweigert, K., eds. *Rechtsprechungssammlung zum Europarecht*, 1966– ; the digests of individual cases in the latter are rather more extensive than is usual in a digest. The *European Law Digest*, 1973– digests legislation as well as the decisions of the Court of Justice and of national courts.

The rules of the court will be found in Court of Justice of the European Communities *Recueil de textes : organisation, compétences et procédure de la cour*, 1967. Further sources of information on judgments of the court and works on the court will be found in the lists at the end of the chapter.

The European Parliamentary Assembly

The European Parliament does not perform all the functions within the Communities that an ordinary parliament performs within a country. In particular, it is not the legislature, though it has to be consulted as part of the legislative process in respect of some categories of legislation. The Parliament has a variety of important powers nevertheless, and its documents are of importance. There are several classes of these, and the following must be mentioned: the minutes of proceedings, which are published in the *Official Journal*: series C; the verbatim record of the debates, which is published as an annex to the *Official Journal*: series C; the working papers of Parliament, which are published and contain *inter alia* the reports of the committees of Parliament and copies of the legislative proposals submitted to Parliament for consultation or advice.

Current information on the work of the Parliament is contained in European Parliament *Information*, 1967– . The standard work on the Parliament in English is Cocks, B. *The European Parliament : structure, procedure and practice*, 1973.

Digests, etc.

The obvious sources of information on the work of the Communities are their own documents, in particular the *General reports on the Activities* of ECSC 1953–67, EEC 1958–67, Euratom 1958–67, European Communities 1968– , and the *Bulletins* of ECSC 1956–67, EEC 1958–67, with supplements 1961–7, European Communities 1968– with supplements 1968– . The supplements contain many documents of great importance, *eg*, the Vedel report on the powers of the European Parliament. These official sources are complemented by two non-official surveys or digests: Lasalle, C. *Répertoire du droit des Communautés européennes*, 1967; and Dörsch, H. J. and Legros, H. *Les faits et les décisions de la Communauté économique européenne*, 1958–64, 1969, continued by a volume covering the years 1965–8, published in 1973.

Secondary literature

The secondary literature on Community law is growing rapidly and by now there is a great deal of it. There are not only commentaries and monographic works, as well as periodicals on Community law in general, but also a good deal of literature on those topics which are of relevance to the establishment of a common economic area. These are above all the regulation of competition, or rather the elimination of restrictions on competition, but also company law, the law relating to establishment, the law relating to agriculture, the law of social security, and tax law. It is not practicable, in this chapter, to deal with works on the municipal law of individual member countries of the Communities, nor even with works on topics relevant to Community law. It should be remembered that literature on the law of several jurisdictions was discussed on pages 301–3, that collections and digests of the decisions of the national courts of the member countries on points of Community law were discussed together with those of the decisions of the Court of Justice of the European Communities, and that the periodicals devoted to Community law inevitably deal with its national aspects, including its repercussions on municipal law.

FURTHER READING

COMPARATIVE LAW

David, R. and Brierley, J. E. C. *Major Legal Systems in the World Today: an introduction to the comparative study of law*. Stevens, 1968 (ISBN 0 420 41600 5).

Attention is drawn to the bibliographical sections of the leading periodicals in this field.

COMMONWEALTH

In addition to the works mentioned in this chapter and in Chapter 10, reference may be made to:

Hewitt, A. R. *Guide to resources for Commonwealth studies in London, Oxford and Cambridge, with bibliographical and other information*. Athlone Press, for Institute of Commonwealth Studies, 1957.

Index to Canadian Legal Periodical Literature, 1961– . Montreal, Canadian Association of Law Libraries.

Index to Indian Legal Periodicals, 1963– . New Delhi, Indian Law Institute (ISSN II 0019-4034).

Jain, H. C. *Indian Legal Materials: a bibliographical guide*. Bombay, Tripathi; Dobbs Ferry, New York, Oceana, 1970 (ISBN 0 379 00466 6).

UNITED STATES

Mayers, L. *The American Legal System: the administration of justice in the United States by judicial, administrative, military and arbitral tribunals.* Revised edition. New York, Harper and Row, 1964.

CIVIL LAW SYSTEMS

Attention is drawn to the bibliographical sections of the leading periodicals in each jurisdiction and the works mentioned in this chapter and in Chapter 10, in particular to the legal bibliographies published under the auspices of the International Association of Legal Science and to the Parker School guides to foreign law: France, Germany and Switzerland by Szladits; Italy by Grisoli; Belgium, Luxembourg and the Netherlands by Graulich and others.

Ryan, K. W. *An Introduction to the Civil Law.* Brisbane, Law Book Co. of Australasia [etc.], 1962.

Africa

Roberts, A. A. *A South African Legal Bibliography: being a bio-bibliographical survey and law-finder of the Roman and Roman-Dutch legal literature in Southern Africa.* Pretoria, The author, 1942.
Vanderlinden, J. *African Legal Bibliography . . . 1947–1966.* Brussels, Presses Universitaires de Bruxelles, 1972.

Latin America

US. Library of Congress. Law Library. Hispanic Law Division. *Index to Latin American Legislation, 1950–1960.* Boston, Mass., G. K. Hall, 1961. Supplements, 1961–70, 4 vols. (ISBN 0 8161 1020 4, etc.).
Wallach, K. *Union List of Basic Latin-American Legal Materials.* South Hackensack, New Jersey, Rothman, 1971 (*AALL Publications Series*, no. 10).

Eastern Europe

Sipkov, I. *Legal Sources and Bibliography of Bulgaria.* New York, Praeger, 1956.
Bohmer, A. *Legal Sources and Bibliography of Czechoslovakia.* New York, Praeger, 1959.
Kalnoki Bedo, A. and Torzsay-Biber, G. *Legal Sources and Bibliography of Hungary.* New York, Praeger, 1956.

Siekanowicz, P. *Legal Sources and Bibliography of Poland*. New York, Praeger, 1964.
Stoicoiu, V. *Legal Sources and Bibliography of Romania*. New York, Praeger, 1964.
Gjupanovich, F. and Adamovitch, A. *Legal Sources and Bibliography of Yugoslavia*. New York, Praeger, 1964.

USSR

Johnson, E. L. *An Introduction to the Soviet Legal System*. Methuen, 1969 (ISBN 0 416 13230 8).
Klesment, J. *Legal Sources and Bibliography of the Baltic States (Estonia, Latvia, Lithuania)*. New York, Praeger, 1963.
Mostecky, V. and Butler, W. E. *Soviet Legal Bibliography: a classified and annotated listing of books and serials published in the Soviet Union since 1917*. Cambridge, Mass., Harvard Law School Library, 1965.

Western Europe

Austria

Friedl, G. *Abkürzungs- und Zitierregeln der österreichischen Rechtssprache (AZR) samt Abkürzungsverzeichnis*. Vienna, Manz, 1970.

Benelux Countries

Bosly, H. *Répertoire bibliographique de droit belge 1919–1945*. Liège, Presses Universitaires de Liège, 1947. Supplements.
Sprudzs, A. *Benelux Abbreviations and Symbols: law and related subjects*. Dobbs Ferry, New York, Oceana, 1971 (ISBN 0 379 00120 9).

France

Grandin, A. *Bibliographie générale des sciences juridiques, politiques, économiques et sociales, de 1800 à 1925–1926*. Paris, Sirey, 1926. 3 vols. Supplements, 1927–1950. 19 vols.
Sprudzs, A. *Foreign Law Abbreviations: French*. Dobbs Ferry, New York, Oceana, 1968 (ISBN 0 379 00358 9).

Germany

Jahresfachkatalog Recht, Sozialwissenschaften, Wirtschaft, Steuern. Bd. 1– 1950– . Berlin, Elwert and Meurer. Generalregister, 1950– 1970/71. 3 vols.
Kirchner, H. *Abkürzungsverzeichnis der Rechtssprache*. 2nd edition. Berlin, de Gruyter, 1968.

Lansky, R. *Grundliteratur zur Rechtswissenschaft in allgemeinen und zum in der Bundesrepublik Deutschland geltenden Recht* . . . Hamburg, Arbeitsgemeinschaft für juristisches Bibliotheks- und Dokumentationswesen, 1974 (*Arbeitshefte* . . . nr. 1).

Italy

Cappelletti, M. *The Italian Legal System: an introduction.* Stanford, Calif., Stanford University Press, 1967.

Napoletano, V. *Dizionario bibliografico delle riviste giuridiche italiane su leggi vigenti (1864–1954).* Milan, Giuffrè, 1956. Supplements.

Sprudzs, A. *Italian Abbreviations and Symbols: law and related subjects.* Dobbs Ferry, New York, Oceana, 1969 (ISBN 0 379 00358 9).

Scandinavia

Danish Committee on Comparative Law. *Danish and Norwegian Law: a general survey.* Copenhagen, G. E. C. Gad, 1963.

Søndergaard, J. *Dansk juridisk bibliografi, 1950–1971.* Copenhagen, Juristforbundets Forlag, 1973 (ISBN 87 574 0120 9).

EUROPEAN COMMUNITIES

Churchill, R. R. European Community Law: a guide to sources and bibliography. *Law Librarian*, vol. 5, no. 1, 1974, pp. 6–8, 13.

Court of Justice of the European Communities. *Bibliographie de jurisprudence européenne.* Luxembourg, The Court, 1965. Supplements.

Court of Justice of the European Communities. *Publications juridiques concernant l'intégration européenne, 1952–1966.* Luxembourg, The Court, 1966. Supplements.

Hopkins, M. The legislative documentation of the European Communities. *Journal of Librarianship*, vol. 6, no. 3, July 1974, pp. 165–78.

Mathijsen, P. S. R. F. *A Guide to European Community Law.* Sweet and Maxwell, 1972 (ISBN 0 421 17690 3).

9. Other Systems of Law

Part 1: Public International Law

K. O. PARSONS, MA
Assistant Librarian (Law), British Library of Political and
Economic Science

SOURCES

This survey may begin with the statement in Article 38(1) of
the Statute of the International Court of Justice which is
generally accepted as defining the sources of international law.
The Article states that, 'The Court . . . shall apply: (a) international conventions . . . ; (b) international custom . . . ;
(c) the general principles of law recognised by civilised nations;
(d) . . . judicial decisions and the teachings of the most highly
qualified publicists, etc.'

We are concerned primarily with the published materials
recording four of the above sources, *viz*, treaties, custom,
judicial decisions and the teachings of publicists. The 'general
principles of law, etc.' are excluded as being expressed in
national rather than international legal literature. Private
international law, or conflict of laws, is also excluded as being
essentially a branch of municipal law, though with a foreign
element.

TREATIES

The published texts of international agreements are to be found
in various collections compiled according to differing principles.
The main distinction is between general collections, which aim
at comprehensiveness without distinction of states, and national
collections, which are limited to the treaties of a particular
state. A national collection may be of general interest if the
state concerned has long been active in international affairs.
Intermediate between these two categories is the regional
collection extending to a group of states, usually on the same
continent.

General collections : unofficial

General collections of treaties may be further divided into those compiled by named individual scholars (even though, perhaps, under royal or official patronage) and published commercially, and those more modern compilations of a wholly official, anonymous character. Probably the earliest private collection of importance is Dumont, J. *Corps Universel diplomatique de droit des gens*, etc. 1726–32, supplement 1739. European treaties since Charlemagne are reproduced in the language of the original text, with particulars of the source and often an extended title in French.

The next large collection, that known as Martens, is still an important source for the nineteenth century, extending in five series from 1760 to 1943. The *Recueil des principaux traités d'alliance, de paix*, etc. 1791–1801, supplement 1802–8, was originally compiled by G. F. de Martens. Subsequent collections appeared as the *Recueil général des traités* and then as the *Nouveau recueil général*, of which three series compiled by various hands were issued in continuation.

The only modern privately compiled and commercially published collection of comparable scope and magnitude is Parry, C., ed., *The consolidated Treaty Series*, published by Oceana from 1969 onwards. The purpose of this considerable undertaking is to make good the deficiencies in Dumont and Martens by providing the text, in its original language, of treaties concluded between the Peace of Munster in 1648 and 1918–20. For treaties whose original language is not English or French a contemporary translation into one of those languages is provided where such is available, and if not, a summary in English of the main provisions. Brief notes are also given on the source used and the subsequent history of the treaty. The desirability of using archival instead of secondary sources is admitted, but little hope held out that this will actually be possible in most cases. The claim advanced that the texts of treaties 'however familiar already' are presented 'in a format infinitely more legible and convenient than the original prints from which they are taken' is probably justified.

The reproduction of Martens' *Discours préliminaire* from volume 1 of his 1802 *Supplément* provides a helpful critical guide

to the earlier treaty collections. It is anticipated that the Series
will be complete by about 1976 in some one hundred or more
volumes. The arrangement is chronological, though material
discovered too late for inclusion in the earlier volumes will be
issued in supplements, together with indexes and additional
notes.

Contrasting with these comprehensive collections are those
which, though general as to states, are yet restricted in some
other respect, *eg*, as to the kind of treaties printed. A notable
example is Israel, F. L. *Major Peace Treaties of Modern History,
1648–1967*, 1967. This publication claims to be the first comprehensive collection of peace treaties to appear in English.
More than half of the treaties included date from the years after
1918. Another privately compiled collection devoted to a
special type of treaty is Hudson, M. O. *International Legislation
1931–49*, which is sufficiently described by its sub-title 'a collection of the texts of multipartite international instruments of
general interest, beginning with the Covenant of the League of
Nations'. The growing importance of the multipartite treaty
has been further demonstrated by the Harvard Law School
Library's *Index to Multi-lateral Treaties*, 1965, which lists such
agreements chronologically from the sixteenth century until
1963, with citations to their text.

General collections : official

The two great general collections of an official character are the
Treaty Series of the League of Nations and the United Nations.
The League's series was founded upon an obligation imposed on
member states by Article 18 of the Covenant to register their
treaties with the Secretariat, and upon an invitation to non-
members to do likewise. Four thousand eight hundred and
thirty-four international instruments were so registered and 205
volumes of the *Treaty Series* published between 1920 and 1946.
Texts were reproduced in the original, with translations in
English and French where required. Three indexes were provided – one chronological, one of general international agreements, and another of countries and subjects.

The Note by the Secretariat in volume 1 of the UN *Treaty
Series* clearly establishes the continuity of that series with the

League's series. Article 102 of the Charter, like Article 18 of the Covenant, requires member states to register their treaties with the Secretariat, whilst provision is also made for the 'filing and recording' of agreements made by the UN or the specialized agencies and of earlier agreements not registered with the League. Treaty texts are published in the original language with English and French translations where one of these languages is not the original. Separate annexes contain ratifications, accessions, etc.

Adequate and timely indexing is essential for so large a collection. The UN indexes are similar to those of the League, and include in all three sections volume and page and treaty number references. Unfortunately, these indexes are slow to appear and use of the latest volumes of the series is made more difficult in consequence. Before publication in the series, however, a treaty is listed in the monthly *Statement of treaties and international agreements*, 1946–   which also contains information on subsequent action in respect of treaties already registered, etc.

Other UN works on treaty law include *Multilateral treaties in respect of which the Secretary-General performs depository functions: list of signatures, ratifications, accessions, etc.*, an annual publication covering treaties concluded under the auspices of and deposited with the UN, its specialized agencies or the League. The record of state action is classified according to the subject of the treaty, and there is a separate annex of final clauses.

Also published by the UN are the *International Tax Agreements*, 1948–   , and the *Register of texts of conventions and other instruments concerning international trade law*, 1971–   , by the Commission on International Trade Law. The tax series gives up-to-date information, by means of supplements to loose-leaf volumes 8 and 9 of the collection, on the text and current status of double taxation conventions. Other publications of the UN on treaty law may be traced by reference to the heading 'Treaties, agreements and conventions' in the index to the 1967 *Catalogue of UN Publications*.

Regional collections

Although some of the earliest collections might be considered regional in that they are virtually confined to European states, it is better to regard them as general, since international law as it is normally understood was the product of European scholarship and diplomacy within the European state system. Truly regional collections made with a deliberately restrictive intention came later. Some outstanding examples are the compilations of Edward Hertslet in the nineteenth century, especially his *Map of Europe by Treaty 1814–1891*, 1875–91, recording those international instruments which had effected territorial and political changes, and *Map of Africa by Treaty*, 3rd edition, 1909.

Some of the regional inter-governmental organizations have compiled and published agreements between their members. The Council of Europe's *European Treaty Series* is limited, however, to agreements concluded under the auspices of the Council, mostly of a cultural, social or administrative character and some with explanatory reports. The Organization of American States has a series *Bilateral Treaty Developments in Latin America*, covering the years 1938 to 1955, whilst its *Manual of Inter-American Relations* provides a systematic classification of the treaties, declarations, etc. adopted at Inter-American conferences and meetings.

National collections

National collections of treaties are nowadays published regularly by the Foreign Office of the country concerned. In earlier times, however, they were the work of individual scholars and commercial publishers, though often with some degree of royal or official patronage or sponsorship. Only a few typical publications of selected countries can be mentioned here.

United Kingdom

Though preceded by Arthur Agard's *Calendar* in 1610 and by the manuscript collection of Sir Joseph Williamson in 1669 (now in the PRO), the first official compilation of English treaties is Thomas Rymer's *Foedera*, 1704–17, covering the period 1101–1654. Later years were covered by other eighteenth-century private collections, notably those of Darby (for 1648–1710); Chalmers, 1790; and that ascribed to Charles Jenkinson for the years 1648–1783.

Apart from a decade or so during the Napoleonic wars British treaties have probably received a more comprehensive published coverage than those of any other country until comparatively recent times. For this the Hertslets, Lewis and Edward, nineteenth-century librarians of the Foreign Office, are largely responsible. In addition to several special collections, some of which have already been mentioned, they commenced and carried on several major series, some of which are still continuing. Their *Commercial Treaties*, 1820–1925, extends to agreements concerning the slave trade and various private interests and was eventually absorbed into their larger collection *British and Foreign State Papers*, 1832–   . This covers, with some omissions, the period from 1812 onwards, and includes not only treaties of all kinds but also many other diplomatic papers, such as UN resolutions, conference documents, communiqués, statements, etc., some of foreign origin.

The current official series of United Kingdom treaties is the *Treaty Series*, prepared in the Foreign Office. It includes, besides treaties proper, many forms of international instruments – exchanges of notes, amending protocols, etc. These are published in the series only after ratification, which may follow several years after signature, though they may previously have been issued as Command papers. The *Treaty Series* forms a sub-series to the Command papers and every issue has both a Command paper number and a *Treaty Series* number, followed by the year of issue, for the series has a fresh numerical sequence every year. There is an annual index, cumulating every four years with numerical and subject sequences and separate lists of multi-lateral and bilateral treaties. During the year several lists of ratifications, accessions, withdrawals, etc. are issued.

Parry and Hopkins: *An Index of British Treaties 1101–1968*, 1970, provides a consolidated index to the *Treaty Series* and to treaties included in the League and UN series and to other official and semi-official collections. It consists of a chronological list of treaties with indexes – of multi-lateral and bilateral treaties by subject and of bilateral treaties also by country. Foreign collections, except for Martens, have been excluded, but agreements with African and Arab chiefs as in Aitchison's *Treaties . . . and Sunnuds* are covered. The *Treaty Series* itself included, until 1945, at least some of the agreements entered into by the Dominions in their own name with foreign states, but until 1965 agreements between the United Kingdom and other Commonwealth countries were excluded.

Other countries

Lack of space forbids description of other national collections except for a brief mention of the main US series. For the period 1776 to 1949 a consolidated official edition of English texts or translations by Charles I. Bevans will shortly be complete. Alternative sources are the collections of William M. Malloy for the period 1776–1937 and David Hunter Miller for 1776–1863. The sessional volumes of *U.S. Statutes at Large* also reproduced treaties from volume 8 (1776–1845) to volume 64 (1949).

Since 1945, US treaties have been currently and separately published in *Treaties and other International Acts Series* (TIAS). From 1950 onwards they have subsequently been incorporated in the annual bound volumes of *United States Treaties and other International Agreements* (UST). A useful annual index published by the State Department since 1950 is the list *Treaties in Force*, which has a classified arrangement with citations to the texts.

REPORTS OF CASES

General collections

Though the Statute of the International Court mentions judicial decisions only as 'subsidiary means for the determination of rules of law' their importance is growing, due partly to the development of regular law reporting.

Of the general collections, that with the widest coverage is the *International Law Reports*, 1929– , formerly the *Annual Digest of Public International Law Cases*. Coverage now extends retrospectively to 1919, volumes are numbered and consolidated tables and indexes have appeared for 1919–42, and for volumes 1–35 and 36–45. The present title was adopted in the volume for 1950 to mark the changed character of the series (beginning with the volume 1933–4) from a digest of decisions to full reports. Its scope is very wide, covering not only decisions of international courts of all kinds, but also decisions of national courts applying public international law. A classified arrangement has been adopted, and a standard form of presentation whereby a head-note is followed by a summary of the facts and of the findings of the court preceding the full text of the judgment in English.

Particular courts

Permanent Court of International Justice

The Permanent Court of International Justice issued six series of publications: A, *Judgments*; B, *Advisory Opinions*; C, *Acts and Documents relating to Judgments and Opinions*; D, *Acts and Documents concerning the organization of the court*; E, *Annual Reports*; F, *Indexes*.

Difficulties sometimes arise with the identification and retrieval of reports, etc. in series A, B and C owing to changes made in 1931. Series A and B were combined in a new series A/B, of which the fascicules could be collected into annual volumes. Previous fascicules in both series were re-numbered retrospectively in a single sequence which was continued unbroken into the new series A/B, the first fascicule of which became No. 40. In series C all volumes or parts were henceforward numbered consecutively instead of sessionally and previous issues re-numbered retrospectively. Thus No. 19 (in 5 volumes) of the old numbering, issued for the 19th session of the Court, is followed by No. 52 in the new numbering, and the apparent gap 20–51 in series C is not really a gap at all. Tables of the re-numbered series are in the 8th *Annual Report* of the Court, p. 309. A bibliography of official and unofficial publications on the Court formed a chapter in each of its *Annual Reports*. A convenient collection of the judgments, orders and advisory opinions only is Hudson, M. O. *World Court Reports 1922–1942*.

International Court of Justice

The publishing programme of the International Court of Justice comprises five series – *Reports of Judgments, Advisory Opinions and Orders,* issued in fascicules forming an annual volume with an index; *Pleadings, Oral Arguments, Documents* constituting the documentation for each case; *Acts and Documents concerning the Organization of the Court*, of which only two volumes have so far appeared, the *Yearbook*; and the *Bibliography*, until 1963–64 (No. 18) issued as a chapter in the *Yearbook* but since then published separately.

European regional courts

Other international tribunals whose jurisdiction the United Kingdom has accepted are the Court of Justice of the European Communities and the European Commission and Court of Human Rights.

The official reports for the Communities Court are the *Recueil de la Jurisprudence de la Cour*. This appears first in fascicules which, with index and tables, form an annual volume. There will be an English edition of this official series (including reports previously published), but already there is the unofficial English language series *Common Market Law Reports*, 1962– . This series now prints reports in the original language of the proceedings, as well as providing an English translation and a special supplement devoted to restrictive practices cases. English translations of judgments given before 1962 are available in volume 2 of D. G. Valentine's *Court of Justice of the European Communities*.

Another series in English is *Common Market Reports*, 1961 to date, published by Commerce Clearing House, of New York. The Court itself has issued in English a chronological *List of Judgments giving their Citations 1954–1972*.

The most important decisions of the European Commission and Court of Human Rights are published in French and English in the *Yearbook of the European Convention on Human Rights, 1955–* , which also contains various official texts relating to the Convention, decisions of the Committee of Ministers, reports of the Commission and national references to the Convention. Whilst the *Yearbook* is prepared by the Directorate of Human Rights of the Council of Europe and appears usually with some two years delay, the Commission itself prepares and issues, at more frequent though irregular intervals, a mimeographed series of *Collections of Decisions*.

National collections

Collections of cases on international law confined to one country are few, save in special fields, and relatively recent.

United Kingdom

The principal British series is *British International Law Cases*, 1964–73, edited by Clive Parry. Six volumes cover the years 1607–1950, with three supplementary volumes bringing the collection up to 1970. The purpose of the series is to provide, in the words of the sub-title, 'a collection of decisions of courts in the British Isles on points of international law'. Within its restricted geographical range the intention is to complement the *International Law Reports* by reproducing the earlier cases which were altogether outside the scope of the Lauterpachts' series and also by giving full reports of those which were only summarized in the *Annual Digest* between 1918 and 1950. Cases on private international law are excluded, and also prize cases unless of general interest. Coverage does not at present extend to war and neutrality or to the decisions of British courts overseas. The reports are in full and are arranged similarly to those in the *International Law Reports*. There is a cumulative index and table of cases in volume 9.

Other countries

A similar series, *American International Law Cases*, commenced under the editorship of the late Francis Deak, is intended to provide for the United States the same sort of retrospective coverage of public international law cases that Dr Parry's collection has provided for Britain. Reports of Federal and State court decisions from 1793 to 1968 will be reproduced in a classified arrangement under major branches of international law.

Arbitration cases

As an introduction to arbitrations there is available A. M. Stuyt's *Survey of international arbitrations, 1794–1970*, 1972, whilst a systematic, annotated digest is currently being compiled and edited by K. R. Simmonds and E. H. Cordeaux for Oceana.

There existed no regular series of reports until the International Court and the UN co-operated to launch *Reports of International Arbitral Awards*, 1948– . This aims to report only decisions rendered between states and chiefly those not hitherto published elsewhere. Consequently almost all the volumes so far issued have contained awards made since 1902. The text is in English or French, with editorial head-notes. There is as yet no cumulative index or table of cases.

The RIAA was preceded by several partial collections made by individual scholars, chiefly French or American, of which the more important are: Lafontaine, H. *Pasicrisie internationale. Histoire documentaire des arbitrages internationaux, 1794–1900,* 1902. La Pradelle, A. de and Politis, N. *Recueil des arbitrages internationaux, 1798–1875,* 1905–54. *Recueil général périodique et critique des decisions,* etc., 1934–8.

Two collections of more restricted scope are J. B. Moore's *History and digest of the international arbitrations to which the United States had been a party,* etc., 1898; and *International adjudications, ancient and modern. Modern Series, 1798–1817,* 1929–36.

The decisions of the Permanent Court of Arbitration at The Hague have been published in J. B. Scott's two series of *Hague Court Reports,* 1916–32.

War crimes trials

The International Military Tribunal at Nuremberg published its proceedings as *The trial of the major war criminals,* 1947–9. Of these forty-two volumes about half report the trials in English, two are indexes, and the remainder contain documentary evidence, in the original language. A smaller edition was published by HMSO, without the documentary annexes. The other Nuremberg trials, of twelve leading German soldiers and officials by US military courts, are recorded in the US official *Trials of War Criminals before the Nuernberg military tribunals under Control Council Law No. 10,* 1946–9.

A collection of trials of so-called 'minor' war criminals of various nationalities was selected and prepared by the United Nations War Crimes Commission and published by HMSO as *Law Reports of Trials of War Criminals,* 1945–9. This series provides not only reports but also legal comment, summaries and analyses, with annexes on municipal war crimes laws, and a final volume assessing the significance of the trials for international criminal law and the law of war.

Japanese war crimes trials are much less amply documented. The judgment of the Tokyo Tribunal has been published (15 ILR 1948), also the dissenting judgment of Justice R. B. Pal, Calcutta, 1953, and a subject index to the proceedings, Michigan, 1957. The proceedings themselves appear to be available only as mimeographed documents, one set of which is held by the British Library of Political and Economic Science.

Prize cases

Cases in prize, because of their distinctive character and importance to maritime law, have received separate treatment in the literature. English cases are nearly all available in three collections, of which the first is Roscoe's *Reports of Prize Cases*, 1905, which is intended to cover 'all the reported cases which remain of value' from the period 1745 to 1859. Cases arising from the First World War are reported in Trehern and Grant: *British and Colonial Prize Cases*, 1916–22, and in the ten volumes of *Lloyd's Reports of Prize Cases, First Series, 1915–24*. For the Second World War *Lloyd's Reports, Second Series, 1957*, should be consulted.

STATE PRACTICE

'International custom, as evidence of a general practice accepted as law' is recognized by the Statute of the ICJ as a source of international law. The evidence of custom may take many forms, chief of which are diplomatic correspondence; official instructions to diplomats and military commanders; acts of state, legislation and judicial decisions; and legal opinions. General practice is formed by the practice of individual states and in particular of those whose extensive international relationships have long been consciously guided by a respect for law. State practice is recorded in a number of important national digests. These are collections of documents and extracts, mostly official, arranged under recognized legal headings, and revealing the attitude of governments, etc. towards important international issues.

United Kingdom

For the United Kingdom there is the *British Digest of International Law*, 1965 to date, compiled principally from unprinted or confidential papers and reports of the Foreign Office. These, with papers from other departments, Command papers, judicial decisions, etc. have been welded together into a narrative, though with a minimum of editorial expression.

For the period before 1860 a major source is the Opinions of the King's or Queen's Advocates, of which, until 1969, only a few were published, chiefly in a selection edited by Lord McNair, *International Law Opinions, 1956*, the rest being accessible only in the Public Record Office. A reproduction series of the manuscripts of some 9,500 Opinions is now being published, *Law Officers' Opinions to the Foreign Office, 1793–1860*, 1970– .

Modern British practice in international law is covered by the British Institute of International and Comparative Law in a series currently issued twice yearly since 1963 and previously in its journal (1956–61). Much reliance is placed on Parliamentary statements with interpretative comment by the editor.

Other countries

The US digests are the most elaborate and consistent. They set out the official position on various issues by means of extracts from documents issued by Presidents and Secretaries of State, the opinions of Attorneys-General and the decisions of courts, federal and state, together with references to treaties, international awards, etc. Editors of the various series have been Francis Wharton, 1886, John Passett Moore, 1906, and Hackworth, 1940–44, whilst the current official *Digest* (not incorporating its predecessor) is that compiled by Marjorie Whiteman, 1963–73. The pattern of classified arrangement under chapter headings has been broadly adhered to by successive editors.

Another notable digest is that of France, Kiss, A. C. *Répertoire de la pratique française en matière de droit international public*, 1966–72.

Following a recommendation by the Council of Europe that

its member states prepare such digests, one has been commenced by Roberto Ago for Italy covering the period 1861–1942.

Two other digests, though not of state practice, may here be mentioned because of their importance for reference. Hambro, E. and Rovine, A. W. *The Case Law of the International Court*, summarizes under classified subject headings the work of both courts, including dissenting and separate opinions. *Répertoire des décisions et des documents de la procédure écrite et orale*, Guggenheim, P., is complementary in that it is primarily concerned with the pleadings and documents of each case.

SECONDARY SOURCES

Treatises

'The teachings of the most highly qualified publicists of the various nations' are expressly mentioned in the Statute of the ICJ as subsidiary sources of law. Their functions have been defined as being: (*a*) to provide useful evidence of what the law is; and (*b*) to influence the development of the law by speculations as to what it ought to be. Textbooks are numerous but only a few are authoritative statements of national interpretation. For the United Kingdom this must be Oppenheim's *International Law*, 1952–5, described as being 'as nearly official as anything of the kind can be'. Its recent editors – Lord McNair and Professor Sir Hersch Lauterpacht – have both been judges of the International Court.

The work of corresponding authority for the United States though now in need of revision is Hyde's *International Law chiefly as interpreted and applied by the United States*, 2nd edition, 1945.

Periodicals

As with treatises, the countries of major importance in international relations usually have at least one specialist periodical which is of more than usual authority. Thus in the United States there is the *American Journal of International Law*, in the United Kingdom the *International and Comparative Law Quarterly*, in France the *Revue Général de Droit International Public*, etc. These journals frequently publish, sometimes in a supplementary series, the texts of official documents – treaties, etc. – before they appear in the relevant national or international collections. The American Society of International Law, publishers of the Journal, also issue separately *International Legal Materials*, 1962– , a collection of current documents reproduced from the originals. The ICLQ also issues numerous supplements containing reports of meetings, monographs on topics of contemporary interest, etc.

Many countries now have a national year book on international law containing longer articles. The *British Yearbook of International Law*, 1920– , has a longer history than most, whilst those published in Australia, Canada, Germany, Japan, the Netherlands, etc., have all begun publication since the Second World War.

An annual of a different type and virtually unique in respect of both its composition and authority is the *Recueil des Cours*, 1923– , published by the Académie de Droit International at The Hague, containing lectures by leading international lawyers.

Reference works

There is no special encyclopedia of international law in English, but in German there is Strupp: *Wörterbuch des Völkerrechts*, 2nd edition, by Schlochauer, H. J., 1960–62. All the articles are in German, with an English contents list. In French there is the *Répertoire de droit international*, 1929–31, edited by Darras, La Pradelle and Niboyet. A new work is now appearing also entitled *Répertoire de droit international*, but forming part of the Dalloz Encyclopédie Juridique.

For a specialized dictionary of terminology there is the *Dictionnaire de la Terminologie du Droit International*, 1960. The text is in French, but a table in English provides a key to the French terms by which the articles are arranged.

There are many bibliographies, but none sufficiently comprehensive to be singled out for special mention. The nearest approach to full coverage is achieved by the catalogues of certain large libraries, in particular that of the Peace Palace at

The Hague. The *Catalogue de la Bibliothèque du Palais de la Paix*, 1916–66, is a classified catalogue with alphabetical and subject indexes covering acquisitions to 1952. Other catalogues have been issued more recently for the international law collections of the Harvard Law Library and the Squire Law Library, Cambridge.

REFERENCE METHOD

Cases, Opinions and Awards

(1) For a case, etc. decided since 1918, see the *International Law Reports – Consolidated Tables and Index*. Before 1933–4 a digest only is provided, though with a reference to the full report. After 1933–4 increasingly full reports appear.

(2) For the decision or opinion of an international court between 1922 and 1942, see first the *Permanent Court of International Justice: Publications. Series A or A-B*. Alternatively, see Hudson's *World Court Reports*.

(3) For the decision or opinion of an international court after 1946, see first the *International Court of Justice: Reports of Judgments*.

(4) For summaries of arbitral awards and references to full reports, see Stuyt, A. M. *Survey of international arbitrations, 1794–1970*. For awards made before 1900 see Lafontaine, *Pasicrisie Internationale* or Lapradelle and Politis, *Recueil des arbitrages internationaux*. For US arbitrations see Moore, *International arbitrations*, or his *International adjudications*.

A forthcoming general collection is Simmonds, K. R. and Cordeaux, E. H. *International arbitrations*.

For arbitrations at The Hague, see Scott, *Hague Court Reports*, series 1 and 2.

For awards made after 1900, see *Reports of International Arbitral awards*, volumes 1–11 for 1902–41; volume 12 onwards for 1942– .

(5) For decisions by national courts on points of international law, see the appropriate national series of reports. The following special collections are also useful – for Great Britain, Parry, Clive, *British International Law Cases*; for the United States, Deak, F. *American International Law Cases*.

(6) For leading cases, see the casebooks, especially Green, L. G. *International Law through the cases*, 3rd edition, 1970; also those by Bishop, W. W.; Briggs, H. W.; and Orfield, L. B. and Re, E. B.

Treaties

(1) See as follows according to year of treaty:
800–1739, Dumont and Rousset, *Corps universel diplomatique.*
1648–1918, Parry, *Consolidated Treaty Series*, or Martens, *Recueil des Traités* (for 1761–1943).
1918–1945, League of Nations: *Treaty Series*, or Martens.
1945 to date, United Nations: *Treaty Series.*

(2) For British treaties, see first Parry and Hopkins, *Index of British treaties 1108–1968* for references to texts.
The main collections are:
1066–1654 Rymer's *Foedera.*
1648–1794 Jenkinson, C. *Treaties of peace*, etc.
1812–1892 *British and Foreign State Papers.*
1892 to date *U.K. Treaty Series*, annually.

(3) For US treaties see as follows:
1776–1949, Bevans, C. I. *Treaties and other international acts of the U.S.A.*; or, *U.S. Statutes at Large.*
1950 to date, US Dept. of State: *U.S. Treaties and Other International Agreements*, annually.

(4) For treaties not in a general collection, see Myers, *Manual of Collections of Treaties*, 1922, for references to the older national collections.

(5) For multipartite treaties 1596–1963, see Harvard Law School Library: *Index to Multilateral Treaties*, 1965, for citations to texts.

Part 2: Roman Law and Roman-Dutch Law

I. M. SAINSBURY, BA, ALA
Law Librarian, University of Reading

Nowadays Roman law and Roman-Dutch law excite little

12

interest in Great Britain. Roman law did influence English legal developments slightly in medieval times and Scottish law to a greater extent from the seventeenth to the nineteenth century, but is now mostly of academic interest. Roman-Dutch law, on the other hand, still flourishes in Rhodesia, South Africa and Sri Lanka. Modern conditions have necessitated the introduction of legislation that has abrogated areas of Roman-Dutch law. Considerable areas remain, however, to which the legal solution is found by consulting the writings of the Dutch jurists of the sixteenth to the early nineteenth centuries and the subsequent case law based on them. On occasions, recourse is had to the original Roman text on which the Dutch jurists' writings are based.

ROMAN LAW

The literary sources of Roman law are generally divided into pre-Justinian sources and Justinian's work. Very few Roman law sources have survived independently of Justinian's codification, notwithstanding that a great volume of literature was produced during the classical period of Roman jurisprudence (from Augustus to the middle of the third century AD).

Pre-Justinian sources

A selection of *leges publicae*, praetorian edicts, *senatus consulta, constitutiones principum*, and the *interpretatio* of jurists, all sources of pre-Justinian Roman law, can be found in Bruns, C. G., and others, *Fontes juris Romani antiqui*, 1909–12; Girard, P. F. and Senn, F. *Textes de droit Romain publiés et annotés*, 1937 and *Fontes juris Romani anteiustiniani* (FIRA), 1940–3. Of course, there are many authors who have gathered together texts of one or more of the Roman law sources. Stephen L. Sass in his admirable article Research in Roman Law; a guide to the sources and their English translations. *Law Library Journal*, volume 56, no. 3, 1963, pp. 210–33, lists in detail many of these works, as he does for all other sources.

Juristic writings

The most important pre-Justinian source was the *interpretatio* of jurists. At first the jurists' opinions were only persuasive, but by the Law of Citations AD 426, the opinions of Papinianus, Gaius, Paulus, Ulpianus, and Modestinus became binding.

Three main juristic writings have survived independently. The Institutes of Gaius (*c.* AD 161) is an introductory elementary textbook arranged according to the tripartite classification of law: law of persons, law of things, and law of actions. This work which is known to have formed the basis of Justinian's Institutes provides the only evidence of classical law believed to be free from later alterations. FIRA and Girard include it and there are many editions with translations which will be mentioned later. Paulus's *Sententiae* and Ulpian's *Regulae* are the two other main works. Doubts exist about their authorship. Extracts from the first are included in the *Lex Romana Visigothorum* (AD 506). The *Regulae* is an abridgment made after AD 320 of Ulpian's *Liber singularis regularum*. Both texts are in FIRA and Girard.

Codes

In the post-classical period the independent jurist disappeared, giving way to the jurist who edited abridgments of the literature of classical jurists and produced compilations of imperial enactments. The *Codex Gregorianus* (*c.* AD 291) and the *Codex Hermogenianus* (*c.* AD 295) were the first compilations whose contents are only known from excerpts in other compilations. FIRA includes them. In AD 438, under the auspices of Theodosius II, an official compilation, the *Codex Theodosianus*, appeared, covering imperial enactments from AD 312 to 438. An early edition is Gothofredus, J. *Codex Theodosianus cum perpetuis commentariis*, 1665. Another important compilation is the *Fragmenta Vaticana* which contains fragments of the works of Papinian, Paul, and Ulpian, and of imperial enactments. It is reproduced in FIRA and Girard.

There is one important barbarian code, promulgated by the conquering Teutonic king Alaric II in the former Western Roman Empire. As with the two other barbarian codes, the *Lex Romana Visigothorum* reveals Roman works not otherwise preserved, containing excerpts from the three pre-Justinian codes and abridgments of Paulus's works and Gaius's *Institutes*. Extracts are found in FIRA and Girard.

Corpus Juris Civilis

All other Roman law sources pale before the great work of the Emperor Justinian, the *Corpus Juris Civilis*. Justinian's aim was the comprehensive compilation of Roman law. By consolidating both the statutes of his predecessors and his own as well as the writings of Roman jurists, Roman law was enabled first to conquer the European continent and then to influence the rest of the world. Although the commissions entrusted with this compilation were allowed to omit all that was obsolete and make such consolidations, deletions, and alterations as were necessary to obviate contradictions, the original form of the fragments was preserved.

Justinian's work comprises four parts, excluding the first Code (AD 529) which has not survived. The compilation of excerpts from Roman juristic literature began in 530 and ended in 533. The result was the *Digesta sive Pandectae Justiniani*, arranged in fifty books divided into 432 titles and sub-divided into 'laws' or fragments of varying length. Long fragments are further sub-divided into sections or paragraphs. Each fragment is an excerpt from one of the thirty-nine jurists and is preceded by an inscription giving the name of the author, the title of the work, and the number of the book (*eg*, Ulpian, first book ad Sabinium). The great bulk (95 per cent) of the Digest is taken from the jurists of the period AD 100 to 250, principally from Ulpian and Paul.

Tribonian, the head of the commission, and two law professors were entrusted with producing an official elementary textbook for students – the *Institutes*. This was also promulgated in 533 as *Imperatoris Iustiniani Institutiones*. A large part was borrowed from Gaius's *Institutes*. Other passages of classical institutional works and pieces of the compilers' own composition serve to give it a patchwork appearance. A new code was now necessary and appeared in 534 as *Codex repetitae praelectionis*. About half the Digest's size, it consists of twelve books and contains about 4,700 *constitutiones* dating from the reign of Hadrian. The last part of the *Corpus Juris Civilis* is the *Novellae* (Novels). Justinian continued to issue *novellae constitutiones* (new statutes) after the second code and intended to have an official compilation of them. This never came to fruition. Hence the collection of Novels in modern editions is derived from three unofficial or semi-official collections.

Dionysius Gothofredus was the first to comment on the *Corpus Juris Civilis* in the following order – Institutes, Digest, Code, Novels – in 1583. The most widely used and cited edition is the stereotype edition by P. Krueger, T. Mommsen, R. Schoell, and G. Kroll, last published in 1954.

Justinian's work had many defects. There were contradictory passages and a lack of logic. Excerpts were thrown together with little rewriting. One reason for this was no doubt the rush in which the work was completed. Yet these defects were to provide Roman law with unforeseen advantages. The revival of Roman law in the Middle Ages was due in no small measure to the fact that the *Corpus Juris* provided a boundless number of solutions; the contradictions and conflicts enabled the jurists to choose the solution that fitted their current needs.

Translations and commentaries

All the important Roman law sources have been translated. Often the translation is accompanied by a commentary on the text and on Roman legal institutions in general. Some earlier translations are now out of date because the best of the original texts were not used.

E. G. Hardy's *Six Roman laws*, 1911, is a bilingual work that contains six *leges publicae*, the *Lex Agraria* of 111 BC being the most important. There is a general introduction to each law and, as in most translations, a number of footnotes on technical or obscure points. F. de Zulueta's *The Institutes of Gaius*, 2 volumes, 1946–53, contains an excellent translation. Another bilingual work, with the Latin on the left and the translation on the right, it consists of the text with critical notes and the translation in the first volume and a commentary in the second volume. Other well-known translations are in Hunter, W. A. *A systematic and historical exposition of Roman law in the order of a code, embodying the Institutes of Gaius and the Institutes of Justinian*, 1903, and in Mears, T. L. *The Institutes of Gaius and Justinian, the Twelve Tables, and the CXVIIIth and CXVIIth Novels*, 1882. The latter work is also useful for its translation of the Twelve Tables, the most important of the *leges publicae*. Both of these works appeared before 1933 when three parchment sheets filling some lacunae in Gaius were discovered.

The most comprehensive translation of Roman law sources, including the *Corpus Juris Civilis*, is Scott, S. P. *The Civil Law*, 1932. It also contains translations of the Twelve Tables, the Institutes of Gaius, the Rules of Ulpian, the Opinions of Paul, the enactments of Justinian and the constitutions of Leo. Unfortunately, the best modern editions of the texts were not used and some highly technical Roman law terms were translated into uncertain English equivalents. However, it is still very useful for reference purposes and is the most easily accessible and convenient translation, having been recently reprinted by AMS Press. It is also the only complete translation of Justinian's enactments. Scott includes footnotes (not always reliable) on any point which he thinks the reader should know and gives references to other systems of law and the relevant sections on the particular point in question. Another significant monolingual translation is Monro, C. H. *The Digest of Justinian*, 1904–9, which covers the first fifteen books. In this work technical expressions are generally untranslated although Latin terms are sometimes interpreted. Monro believes that many *Digest* passages are difficult to comprehend or incomprehensible and, therefore, makes the English version just as obscure. There are countless works that translate particular *Digest* titles, usually with a commentary (see Sass, pp. 229–30). These often form special examination subjects for students. Justinian's *Institutes* has been separately translated by Hunter and Mears (see above) and by Lee, R. W. *The Elements of Roman Law with a Translation of the Institutes of Justinian*, 4th edition, 1956, and Moyle, J. B. *Imperatoris Iustiniani Institutionum libri quattuor*, 1912–13. Lee and Moyle are the most used by students.

There are many commentaries on Roman law that can be used to great advantage in answering queries. W. W. Buckland's *A Text Book of Roman law from Augustus to Justinian*, 3rd edition, 1964, is a detailed and comprehensive statement of the private law of the Roman Empire for the use of students. The first chapter on sources of laws in the Empire is very good, although confusing in places. B. Nicholas's *An Introduction to Roman law*, 1962, also has a very readable section on sources of Roman law and its influence. H. F. Jolowicz and B. Nicholas's *Historical*

Introduction to the Study of Roman law, 3rd edition, 1972, is an up-to-date work on the sources. The explanation of symbols used in citing Roman law sources, such as D.47.2.15.3, appears at the end of Sass's article (see page 354).

ROMAN-DUTCH LAW

Roman-Dutch law used to be the common law of the Dutch settlements, carried there by the Dutch trading companies. It was the system of law of the province of Holland from the middle of the fifteenth century until the adoption of the Napoleonic codification in 1809 and was based upon Germanic customary law. The Roman law of the *Corpus Juris Civilis*, as interpreted in the medieval law schools, was grafted onto it in the late fifteenth to seventeenth centuries, filling in gaps and making it a coherent whole. When the Cape of Good Hope, Ceylon (Sri Lanka) and part of Guiana (all Dutch settlements) passed under British control in 1806, 1796, and 1803 respectively, the old law was retained as the common law. This law was later extended to the Union of South Africa and Southern Rhodesia. Now it survives only in Rhodesia, South Africa and Sri Lanka. Legislation, judicial decisions, and customs have replaced much of this Roman-Dutch law. The influence of English law has also been strong.

Treatises

The sources of Roman-Dutch law are treatises, statute law, judicial decisions, opinions of jurists, and custom. The works of the Dutch jurists, written in Dutch and Latin, from the sixteenth to the early nineteenth century are authoritative in respect of the law to which they relate. There are conflicts among these writers which are resolved by the courts usually in a way that will satisfy modern needs. The most consulted writers are Groot (Grotius), Groenwegen, Van Leeuwen, Voet, Van Bijnkershoek, Van der Keessel and Van der Linden. One of the best editions of H. Grotius's *Inleidinge tot de Hollandsche Rechts-Geleerdheid* (Introduction to Dutch Jurisprudence) is that of 1895, which has notes by Fockema Andreae. This has been translated in Lee, R. W. *The Jurisprudence of Holland by Hugo*

Grotius, 1926–36, a bilingual work with the translation and textual, historical and linguistic notes in the first volume and a commentary in the second volume. Lee is concerned to answer the question as to what use can be made of Grotius in court and uses a number of writers who were commentators on Grotius – Groenwegen, Voet, Schorer, and Van der Keessel.

Groenwegen's main work is his *Tractatus de legibus abrogatis et inusitatis in Hollandia vicinisque regionibus*, 1649, part of which was translated by V. Sampson in 1908. S. Van Leeuwen is famous for two works – *Censura forensis* and *Het Roomsch Hollandsch Recht*. The best edition of the former is considered to be that of 1741 with de Haas's notes; of the latter, that of 1780 with Decker's notes, translated by J. G. Kotzé with additional notes, 1921–3. Juta published translations of *Censura forensis* from 1883 to 1896.

The writer who is probably best known and most consulted is Johannes Voet. There are many editions of his *Commentarius ad pandectas*; one of the best was edited by A. Drevon and A. Maurice, 1827–9. All the portions that have any particular relevance to the present law of South Africa, including Van der Linden's 1793 supplement, have been translated in Gane, P. *The Selective Voet*, 1955–8. Explanatory notes of recondite words and phrases are given, together with information on every reported case in which Voet's work has been judicially considered, showing how far his opinions have been accepted. This magnificent translation is well indexed and is kept up to date by cumulative supplements. There have also been translations of individual titles in Voet, most of which are listed in Roberts, A. A. *A Guide to Voet*, 1933.

Turning to the eighteenth-century jurists, C. Van Bijnkershoek's main work *Quaestionum juris privati libri quatuor* appeared in 1744. D. G. Van der Keessel's *Theses selectae juris Hollandici et Zelandici*, 1800, is a commentary on Grotius's *Introduction* and has been translated by C. A. Lorenz, 1901. Finally, there is J. Van der Linden's *Verhandeling over de judicieele practijcq*, 1794–8, first published in 1781. But his best known work is *Rechtsgeleerd, Practicaal, en Koopmans Handboek* (Institutes of the laws of Holland), 1806, translated by H. Juta, 1906, and G. T. Morice, 1922.

Other sources

The statute law of the States-General and of the States of Holland and West Friesland is in the *Groot Placaat-Boek*, 1658–1796. The Batavian statutes of the Governor-General of the East Indies are printed in *Nederlandsch-Indisch Plakaatboek*, ed. by Van der Chijs, J. A., 1885–1900.

Amongst the many published volumes of judicial decisions are Judge Johannes a Sande's *Decisiones Frisicae sive rerum in Suprema Frisiarum Curia judicatarum libri V*, 1635 (see also Lee, p. 19).

The collection of opinions of jurists which is most used is *Consultatien, Advysen en Advertissementen*, 1648–66, commonly known as *Hollandsche Consultatien*. Grotius's opinions have been translated and annotated by D. P. de Bruyn in *The Opinions of Grotius as contained in the Hollandsche Consultatien en advysen*, 1894. The opinions have been rearranged according to the juristic questions discussed and to the mode of treatment in Grotius's *Introduction*. Every important topic is annotated, with special reference to South African case and statute law.

Custom is important because it was by this means that Roman law entered Holland and as custom it continues to exist in the modern law.

Commentaries

A simple but detailed explanation of the origin, development, and reception of Roman-Dutch law can be found in Lee, R. W. *An introduction to Roman-Dutch law*, 5th edition, 1953, which is also a good elementary textbook, even if a little out of date. The most useful work is Maasdorp, A. F. S. *Institutes of South African Law*, 1968–72, which covers in a straightforward comprehensible manner the law of persons, property, contracts, delicts, and dissolution of obligations. It is intended mainly for practising lawyers and attempts to state the law as laid down in Voet, Grotius, Van Leeuwen, Van der Linden, Van der Keessel, and the notes of Schorer, but to elucidate, correct and up-date by reference to the statute law and judicial decisions of South Africa. A work based on Voet's *Commentary* is Nathan, M. *The Common Law of South Africa*, 1904–7. The effect of judicial decision and legislation is set out and at the end of each section reference is made to where that topic is found in Voet. Lastly, mention must be made of Wessels, J. W. *History of the Roman-Dutch law*, 1908, a useful reference work, and Roberts, A. A. *A South African Legal Bibliography*, 1942, which has an excellent introduction on Roman-Dutch law, lists all Roman and Roman-Dutch legal literature to be found in South Africa up to 1942, often giving notes about the authors, and contains a useful historical chart of Roman and Roman-Dutch jurists.

It must always be remembered that the old works are the authorities. Modern works do not make law but help the enquirer to find out what the law is. Roberts reminds us in his bibliography that the usual starting point in solving a problem are the works of Maasdorp or Lee or another modern textbook in the hope that there will be a reference to Voet or Van Leeuwen to open the door to even older authorities.

Part 3: Religious Laws

SHEILA M. DOYLE, BA, ALA
Assistant Librarian, University of Durham

Religious laws include both those legal systems which claim divine origin and those regulations which are made by religious bodies for the conduct of their spiritual and temporal affairs.

All religious bodies are bound by the general law of the land, so any of the normal legal sources may include material relating to them. General publications on comparative law are also of considerable value, for example *A Bibliography on foreign and comparative law books . . . in English*, 1955– , and periodicals such as the *International and Comparative Law Quarterly*, 1952– and the *American Journal of Comparative Law*, 1952– . Among introductions to comparative law, including religious systems, are *Introduction to Legal Systems*, edited by J. D. M. Derrett, 1968, which has chapters on Jewish, Islamic and Hindu law, and *Major Legal Systems in the world today*, by R. David and J. E. C. Brierley, 1968, which has sections on Muslim law and on the law of India. Both have useful select bibliographies.

General reference works, such as the *New Catholic Encyclopedia*, 1967, 15 volumes, are often of considerable assistance. Among general bibliographies, the catalogue of the School of Oriental and African Studies at London University is an invaluable source as regards Eastern legal systems. It was published in Boston, 1963, in 22 volumes, and is continued by supplements. Another major bibliography of Asian materials is D. E. Hall's *Union catalogue of Asian publications*, 1971, 4 volumes.

ROMAN CANON LAW

Medieval and early modern sources

Medieval canon law was based on a variety of materials, including bulls and other decrees issued by the Popes, the decretals, *ie*, rulings by Popes on questions brought to them for decision, and the decrees of church councils. In the year 1500 six major collections of these sources of canon law were brought together and issued by Jean Chappuis, of Paris, the most notable item in the collection being the *Decretum* of Gratian. Known as the *Corpus iuris canonici*, this collection became the definitive embodiment of canon law up to that date, and received the official sanction of the Roman Catholic Church in 1580. The modern standard edition is that of E. Friedberg, published in 1879–81, reprinted Graz, Akademische Druck- und Verlagsanstalt, 1955, 2 volumes.

For the period following the *Corpus*, the main sources of Roman canon law are the official acts of the Popes, the decrees of councils and the decisions of the Congregations – bodies entrusted with expounding the law in various fields. A. van Hove's *Prolegomena ad Codicem iuris canonici*, 2nd edition, 1945, is a wide-ranging and comprehensive guide to these materials.

Modern sources

By the second half of the nineteenth century, simplification was becoming necessary, and in 1917 the immense work of revision resulted in the *Codex iuris canonici* – the Code of canon law. A permanent Commission was set up for its interpretation. Subsequent papal legislation is promulgated in the *Acta*

Apostolicae Sedis, a publication which appears about once or twice a month. The rulings of the Commission for interpretation also appear in the *Acta*, as do the decisions of the Congregations. There are a number of commentaries on the Codex, of which the best known in English is that of T. L. Bouscaren and A. C. Ellis, 3rd revised edition, 1957, while T. L. Bouscaren and J. I. O'Connor: *Canon Law Digest*, 1954, is a compilation of decisions subsequent to the *Codex*. Both are published in Milwaukee by Bruce.

Under the authority of the Pope, bodies such as provincial councils and individual prelates have limited powers of local legislation. These laws are often to be found in the official organ of the diocese. There is no rule of precedent in Roman canon law, but the decisions of the appeal tribunal, the Rota, are a legitimate guide to inferior courts. They are published in annual volumes, ten years after the decisions have been made.

It is also appropriate to mention that the Roman Catholic Church, as an international organization, may enter into legal agreements with temporal governments. Concordats and conventions up to 1954 have been collected in the *Raccolta di concordati* of A. Mercati, 1954, and the texts of these agreements are also to be found in the appropriate volumes of the *Acta Apostolicae Sedis*.

Recent developments include the second Vatican Ecumenical Council, the Latin text of whose decrees was published in 1966 by the Vatican Press. Various translations are available. A Commission is also at work on a new edition of the Code, and publishes a biannual series of *Communicationes*, 1969– . The revised Code, however, is not likely to appear before the 1980s.

Secondary sources and bibliographies

Among numerous periodicals dealing with canon law, both in Latin and in the vernacular, *Ephemerides theologicae lovanienses*, issued by the Catholic University of Louvain, 1924– , is particularly worth mentioning for its bibliography and reviews. A listing of periodical articles published in the years 1918–34, compiled by G. Moschetti, appears in volume 14 of *Apollinaris*, pp. 121–45. In 1958, a further bibliographical aid was started, in the form of *Canon Law Abstracts*. A helpful introduction to the subject for laymen is *What is Canon Law?* by R. Metz, translated by M. Derrick, 1960.

THE LAW OF THE CHURCH OF ENGLAND

Primary sources

Legislation

Prior to the Reformation, the major sources of canon law in England were those common to the whole of western Christendom, as embodied in the *Corpus iuris canonici*, together with various enactments relating specifically to the application of canon law in England. At the Reformation, legislative authority over the English Church became vested in the King in Parliament, although the old canon law remained in force in so far as it was compatible with the general law of the land. Thus, much of the law of the Church of England derives its authority from statute. To some extent, however, the power of legislating was delegated to various other bodies. Thus the Convocations – *ie*, the assemblies of clergy – were empowered, subject to certain restrictions, to enact legislative canons. The canons of 1603 have, with minor exceptions, remained in force until the present century. They have now been replaced by the canons of 1969, including those promulgated in 1964. In this century, further delegation of legislative authority has taken place. In 1919, the Church Assembly was empowered, subject to Parliamentary consent, to pass Measures having the force of Acts of Parliament. More recently, the Assembly has been replaced by the General Synod, which has also taken over the power of the Convocations to make canons.

Synodical and Church Assembly Measures, and subordinate legislation enacted under them, are to be found included in the major collections of Acts of Parliament, both the official publications and private ones such as *Halsbury's Statutes* and *Statutory Instruments*. A volume entitled *Church Assembly Measures Revised* corresponds to the *Statutes Revised*. Liaison of the Synod with Parliament is conducted by a Legislative Committee in conjunction with an Ecclesiastical Committee of Parliament. The reports of the Committee are published by HMSO as Parliamentary papers. The Synod and the Assembly have also issued many non-legislative publications, such as minutes, reports, drafts of Measures, etc., which are available from the Church Information Office. Among publications of the Synod's Legal Advisory Commission and its predecessor, the Legal Board, are its *Opinions*, 5th edition, 1973, published in loose-leaf form. The acts and proceedings of the Convocations are published in the *Chronicle of the Convocation of Canterbury*, 1859–   , and the *York Journal of Convocation*, 1874–   , and a compilation edited by H. Riley and R. J. Graham and covering the period 1921–70 was issued in 1971 by SPCK.

Ecclesiastical courts and court reports

The system of ecclesiastical courts is governed by the Ecclesiastical Jurisdiction Measure, 1963, the effect of which is explained in E. G. Moore's *Introduction to English Canon Law*, pp. 125–48. Accounts of the situation prior to 1963 are to be found in the section on ecclesiastical law in *Halsbury's Laws of England*, 3rd edition, 1957, and in the report of the Archbishops' Commission on the Ecclesiastical Courts, published by SPCK in 1954.

Early reports of the ecclesiastical courts may be found in various series of reports, covered by volumes 161–7 of the *English Reports*. A full listing may be found in Sweet and Maxwell's *Guide to Law Reports and Statutes*, 4th edition, 1962. For the period 1865–75, ecclesiastical reports are to be found in the Admiralty series of the *Law Reports*, while from 1875 they are published with Probate, and subsequently with the Family Division. The ecclesiastical courts are also covered by such series as the *All England Reports*.

Secondary sources

Among outlines of English canon law, mainly intended for the non-lawyer, are Sir William Dale's *The Law of the Parish Church*, 4th edition, 1967, and E. G. Moore's *An Introduction to English Canon Law*, 1967. Dale's is a concise handbook, Moore's a more extended treatment. Practitioner's works include H. W. Cripps's *A Practical Treatise on the Law Relating to the Church and*

Clergy, 8th edition, 1937, and Sir Robert Phillimore's *Ecclesiastical law in the Church of England*, 2nd edition, 1895. A most helpful quick reference source is the Church of England *Year Book*, 1963– , which lists Church Assembly Measures passed since 1920, and has a legal appendix of short notes on various topics. The *Year Book* also contains information on the structure, personnel and activities of the churches of the Anglican communion in Wales, Ireland, Scotland and overseas. There are many useful references throughout the *Year Book* to further reading and sources of information. A clear account of the historical development of canon law in England from earliest times to the date of the report is the report of the Archbishops' Commission on Canon Law, 1947.

OTHER CHRISTIAN CHURCHES

Information on the doctrines and organization of the non-episcopal churches can be found in the *Free Church Directory*, 1965– , which has a short section of book reviews. In addition, many of the free churches and of the episcopal churches outside England produce their own yearbooks or similar publications. These vary in the amount and type of information they provide, but most give some account of the church's administrative structure. Often a church will publish a compilation of rules and regulations which the yearbook serves to up-date until such time as a new edition becomes necessary. For the most part, publications of this type are to be found recorded in general bibliographies, such as the *British National Bibliography*.

IRELAND

Catholic Church

Ireland is covered by the general sources of canon law, but specifically Irish rules can be found in the Maynooth Decrees, 1956. Since that date, the rules promulgated by individual bishops and issued to the clergy in their diocese can be found in such journals as *The Furrow*, 1950– . They will be incorporated in the next edition of the Maynooth Decrees. For information on the Catholic Church in Ireland there is also the *Irish Catholic Directory*, 1838– .

Church of Ireland, and other churches

As the Church of Ireland was disestablished in 1869, the statutes are not published in the *Public General Acts*, although the form and terminology of a parliamentary Act are retained. Legislation is passed by the General Synod, and statutes are found as an appendix in the *Journal* of the General Synod, published annually, 1911– . An index and chronological table of statutes are included. The latest edition of the Constitution of the Church of Ireland was published in 1972, in loose-leaf form for up-dating, and the *Church of Ireland Handbook*, by J. L. B. Deans, 1962, is a useful guide to the organization of the Church.

As regards the Presbyterian Church, *The Code : the Book of the Constitution and Government of the Presbyterian Church in Ireland* is published by the authority of the General Assembly. The latest edition is that of 1962, up-dated by loose-leaf amendments. *The Minutes of the Assembly and Presbyterian Directory* is published annually.

For the Methodist Church, the *Manual of the Laws and Discipline of the Methodist Church in Ireland*, 1935, has a supplement published in 1954. For laws since that date, reference should be made to the *Minutes* of the Conference, published annually, Dublin.

SCOTLAND

A most useful concise outline of the development and status of the canon law with particular reference to Scotland is to be found in D. M. Walker's *The Scottish Legal System*, 3rd edition, 1969, pp. 54–7. Until the Reformation, the Roman canon law formed an important part of the Scottish legal system, and subsequently, though canon law ceased to be widely studied, much of the canon law relating to family matters was absorbed into the general law. Since 1560, the Church of Scotland has been the principal church in Scotland, and its courts are legally constituted. Volumes 1 (1936, pp. 133–62, 183–92) and 20 (1958, pp. 363–73) of the publications of the Stair Society contain much information on the history of the canon law and church courts in Scotland, and provide detailed guidance as to the materials available for their study. Volume 20 (pp. 69–89) also contains a useful account of the canon law of marriage. Less specialized periodicals which carry relevant material include the *Juridical Review*, in which the articles by R. K. Hannay (Some questions regarding Scotland and the canon law, vol. 49, 1937, pp. 25–34) and T. M. Taylor (Church and state in Scotland, new series, volume 2, 1957, pp. 121–37) are especially worth consulting. The statutes of the Scottish Church, 1225–1559, have been issued as volume 54, new series, 1907, of the *Publications of the Scottish History Society*, 1887– , and since 1690 *The Principal Acts of the General Assembly* have appeared annually, while from 1895 the *Reports to the General Assembly* have been issued as companion volumes. Treatises include P. A. Lempriere's *Compendium of the Canon law for the use of . . . the Scottish Episcopal Church*, 1903, and J. T. Cox's *Practice and Procedure in the Church of Scotland*, 5th edition, 1964. The Episcopal Church in Scotland issued a *Code of Canons* in 1973. W. G. Black's *The Parochial Ecclesiastical law of Scotland*, 4th edition, 1928, is particularly informative regarding the Teind Court, which decided questions relating to teinds – the tenth part of the fruits of the land and labour assigned for the maintenance of the church and clergy.

JEWISH LAW

A useful guide as to where to start looking for information on legal and other Jewish literature is S. Shunami's *Bibliography of Jewish bibliographies*, 1965, while J. Fraenkel's *Guide to the Jewish libraries of the world*, 1959, gives some indication of the extensive collections to be found in this country and abroad. The *Encyclopaedia judaica*, 1972, 16 volumes, is an indispensable work for the study of Jewish culture, with extensive articles and valuable bibliographies on legal topics. At a popular level, P. Elman's *Introduction to Jewish Law*, 1958, is a clear outline with a short bibliography, while a series of articles by M. Elon in the *Israel Law Review* (see page 371) afford another helpful introduction. The *Journal of Jewish studies*, 1948– , carries some articles on legal topics, and a special issue for February 1974, was *Studies in Jewish Legal History in Honour of David Daube*, edited by B. S. Jenkinson.

Basic sources

Jewish law derives from a wide variety of sources. Of primary importance is the Torah – a term used narrowly to denote the Pentateuch and laws derived from it by exegesis, together with the oral law, though it can also refer to the law as a whole. This is supplemented by tradition, regulations and custom. The oldest important compilation of Jewish law is the Mishnah of Rabbi Judah ha-Nasi, written about AD 200, a modern English translation of which is that of H. Danby, 1933. To this was added, in course of time, the Gemara, or commentary of the Palestinian and Babylonian scholars. The Mishnah and Gemara combined constitute the Talmud. An English translation of the Babylonian Talmud, edited by I. Epstein has been published, 1935–48, 35 volumes. *The Student's Guide through the Talmud*, by Z. H. Chajes, 1960, and *Introduction to the Talmud and Midrash*, by H. L. Strack, 1931, are valuable introductions to this vast work. During the Middle Ages, further redaction of the mass of legal material deriving from the Talmud became necessary, and a number of codes were compiled, notably the *Mishneh Torah* of Moses Maimonides, of which an English translation is in process of publication (1949–   ), and the *Shulhan 'Arukh* of Joseph Caro, to which glosses were added by Moses Isserles.

A further important form of Jewish legal literature is the responsa – answers by rabbis to specific questions submitted to them. A comprehensive indexing project for this category of Jewish legal literature is in progress at the Hebrew University of Jerusalem. For English readers, S. B. Freehof's *The Responsa Literature*, 1955, is a useful introduction to the field, while the same author's *A Treasury of Responsa*, 1965, is a selection from the total literature. Both have been published in New York by Ktav. Freehof's *Reform Responsa*, 1960, is a selection of his own responsa on various current topics, re-published with *Recent Reform Responsa*, 1973.

Jewish law in Israel

Since the establishment of the state of Israel, Jewish legal thought has had an extensive influence on the development of the Israeli legal system, in which the rabbinic courts have jurisdiction to administer Jewish religious law in certain fields. An account of their work is to be found in an article by M. Chigier, entitled 'The rabbinical courts in the state of Israel' (*Israel Law Review*, volume 2, no. 2, 1967, pp. 147–81). The *Israel Law Review* is an essential periodical for the study of law in Israel, and carries notes on cases and book reviews. Another important journal is *Diné Israel*. Largely in Hebrew, it has some articles in English, as well as reviews and reports on current research and has absorbed Z. W. Falk's *Current bibliography of Hebrew Law and allied subjects*, 1966– . E. Livneh's *Israel Legal Bibliography*, 1963, with its 1965 supplement has little on specifically religious law, but is useful with regard to the Israeli legal system in general. Work in progress at the Hebrew University of Jerusalem includes a Talmudic encyclopedia, an English translation of which started to appear in 1969.

The Jews in Britain

For information on the legal status of the Jews in England at the present day, the section on ecclesiastical law in *Halsbury's Laws of England* should be consulted. The *Jews and the English Law*, by H. S. Q. Henriques, 1908, is an interesting, if not up to date, historical treatment of the topic. Bibliographies of Anglo-Jewish relations include J. Jacobs and L. Wolf's *Bibliotheca Anglo-Judaica*, 1888, and its successors, *Magna Bibliotheca Anglo-Judaica*, edited by C. Roth, 1937, and R. P. Lehmann's *Nova Bibliotheca Anglo-Judaica*, 1961, and *Anglo-Jewish Bibliography*, 1973, all published by the Jewish Historical Society of England.

INDIAN RELIGIOUS LAW

The history of Indian law falls into three main periods – the pre-British, the period of British administration and the period following independence in 1947. In all these phases it has been recognized by the ruling powers that in certain areas, such as family law, adherents of different religions should be permitted to follow their appropriate personal law based on religious principles. A valuable bibliographical guide to Indian legal materials is H. C. Jain's *Indian Legal Materials: a Bibliographical*

Guide, 1970. For information on periodical articles, *Index to Indian Legal Periodicals*, 1963– , should be consulted.

Ancient Hindu law

Hindu law derives ultimately from a large number of very ancient texts known as *srutis* – that which is revealed – and *smritis* – that which is remembered. The *srutis*, which include the four *vedas* and the *upanishads*, treat of a wide variety of religious and social topics in addition to the legal material that they contain. Among the *smritis*, however, is a class of works dealing specifically with *dharma* – righteousness – the *dharmaśāstras*. This term is also used to denote the 'science of righteousness' itself. The most important of the *dharmaśāstras* include those known by the names of Manu, Yājñavalkya and Nārada. Springing from the *dharmaśāstras* are numerous commentaries and digests known as *nibandhas*. Leading works in this class are the *Dāyabhāga*, a digest by Jimutavahana, which gives its name to the school general in Bengal, and the *Mitāksharā*, a commentary on Yājñavalkya by Vijñaneśvara, from which the other major school of Hindu law derives its name. The definitive work on the fundamental sources of Hindu law is P. V. Kane's *History of Dharmaśāstra*, 2nd edition, 1968– . R. Lingat's *The Classical Law of India*, 1973, is a shorter study which includes a bibliography.

Anglo-Hindu and modern Hindu law

During the British administration, Hindu law became modified by the application of British judicial principles, including precedent, and by the operation of statutes. Reference should be made to Jain's bibliography for a fuller listing of the appropriate reports and other publications than is possible here.

Since independence much of the Anglo-Indian Hindu law has been replaced by a series of enactments known as the Hindu Code, and many commentaries on these Acts have been published, including that annexed to Mulla's treatise. Practitioner's books on modern Hindu law include Sir Dinshah F. Mulla's *Principles of Hindu Law*, 13th edition, 1966, and N. R. Raghavachariar's *Hindu Law: Principles and Precedents*, 6th edition, 1970. J. D. M. Derrett's *Introduction to Modern Hindu Law*, 1963, is a useful work designed for the student. The same author's *Religion, Law and the State in India*, 1968, is a series of studies of the religious and social background.

Under the Hindu Code, Sikhs, Jains and Parsees are regarded as Hindus and are subject to Hindu law. The Code, however, gives legal recognition to customary usages in certain circumstances, and to this extent the law applicable to these groups may vary from the general norm. The *Sikh Courier* is the organ of the Sikh community in Britain, and occasionally carries articles relating to the social and legal status of the Sikhs in this country.

ISLAMIC LAW

Basic sources

The first source of Islamic law – the *Sharī'a* – is, of course, the *Qur'ān*, of which M. W. Pickthall's *The Meaning of the Glorious Koran*, 1930, is a widely accepted English translation. But there is, in fact, very little in the *Qur'ān* which is directly legal in character. This has led to considerable emphasis on the second source – the *sunna*, or practice of the Prophet as recorded in the *aḥādīth*, or traditions of his actions and words. Of the numerous collections of these traditions, those of Bukhārī, Muslim, Ibn Māja, Abū Dāwūd, Tirmidhī and Nasā'ī are regarded as particularly authoritative. M. Z. Siddiqi's *Ḥadith Literature*, 1961, is a study of this group of sources from an orthodox Muslim viewpoint. The law also derives from *ijmā'*, or the consensus of learned opinion, and *qiyās*, or analogical deduction from these primary sources.

This fourfold basis has been subject to many centuries of learned study and commentary, and each particular school or sub-school has its own authoritative books of *fiqh*, or legal science. The four main schools are the Ḥanafī, Mālikī, Shāfi'ī and Ḥanbalī, and there are numerous groups which are generally regarded as heterodox. Three texts of particular importance on the Indian sub-continent are the *Hedāya* and the *Fatāwa 'Ālamgīrī* (both Ḥanafī), and the *Sharā'i 'al-Islam*, which is a major text of the Ithnā 'Asharī Shiites. The former has been translated by C. H. Hamilton, while the two latter form the basis of volumes 1 and 2 respectively of N. B. F. Baillie's *Digest of Moohummudan law*, 1869–75, reprinted 1965, 2 volumes.

A detailed study of the first two centuries' development of Islamic law is J. Schacht's *The Origins of Muhammadan Jurisprudence*, 1950. The same author's *An Introduction to Islamic law*, 1964, has a historical section on Sunnī (orthodox) law, and a systematic section on the law of the Ḥanafī school. The bibliography is very extensive, and includes material relating to all schools. At a somewhat more popular level, an excellent account of the historical development of Islamic law is N. J. Coulson's *A History of Islamic Law*, 1964.

Anglo-Muhammadan and modern Islamic law

According to traditional Islamic legal theory, no new interpretation of the sources of law has been possible since the 'closing of the gate of interpretation' in the tenth Christian century. In India, however, the administration of Islamic law by the British judiciary brought about the development of an Anglo-Muhammadan system, in the same way that the Anglo-Hindu law already mentioned came into being. As with Anglo-Hindu law, reference should be made to Jain's bibliography. Treatises on Islamic law as practised in the Indian sub-continent include Sir Dinshah F. Mulla's *Principles of Mohomedan Law*, 17th edition, 1972, a leading practitioner's book, and A. A. A. Fyzee's *Outlines of Mohammadan Law*, 4th edition, 1974, an excellent introduction for students.

Elsewhere, the last century has seen a very extensive move towards meeting changed social conditions by means of legislation and other expedients. An account of these can be found in J. N. D. Anderson's *Islamic Law in the Modern World*, 1959, and numerous articles by the same author in various periodicals. A valuable bibliography on The Law in the Near and Middle East, by I. Azzam, has appeared in the *Law Library Journal*, volume 57, no. 3, 1964, pp. 234–40. For Africa, see J. N. D. Anderson's *Islamic Law in Africa*, 1955, reprinted 1970. The *Encyclopaedia of Islam*, 2nd edition, 1954– is an essential reference tool, with numerous articles on legal topics, while *Index Islamicus*, 1958– , is an important key to articles in periodicals and other composite works. General orientalist journals which carry articles on legal topics include *Muslim World*, 1911–   , and the *Bulletin* of the School of Oriental and African Studies at London University, first published in 1917.

FURTHER READING

PUBLIC INTERNATIONAL LAW

Council of Europe. *Publication of digests of state practice in the field of public international law*. Strasbourg, Council of Europe, 1971 (ISBN 0 11 981257 6).

Myers, D. P. *Manual of Collections of Treaties and of Collections Relating to Treaties*. New York, Burt Franklin, 1922 (ISBN 0 8337 2499 1).

Parry, C. *Sources and Evidence of International Law*. Manchester University Press, 1965 (*Melland Schill law series*) (ISBN 0 7190 0231 1).

Peace Palace. Library. *Selective bibliographies*. Leyden, Sijthoff, 1953–5. 3 vols.

Robinson, J. *International Law and Organization: general sources of information*. New York, Humanities Press, 1967.

Sprudzs, A. *Treaty sources in legal and political research – tools, techniques and problems: the conventional and the new*. Tucson, Arizona, University of Arizona Press, 1971 (*Institute of Government Research, University of Arizona, International Studies, no. 3*) (ISBN 0 8165 0292 7).

UN. Legal Department. Division for the development and codification of international law. *Laws and Practices Concerning the Conclusion of Treaties; with a selective bibliography on the law of treaties*. New York, UN, 1953 (1952.v.4) (*United Nations legislative series*). Bibliography, pp. 139–59.

UN. *Ways and means of making the evidence of customary international law more readily available*. Lake Success, New York, UN, 1949 (1949.v.6).

ROMAN LAW

Buckland, W. W. *A Text-book of Roman Law from Augustus to Justinian*. 3rd edition. Cambridge University Press, 1964 (ISBN 0 531 04360 3).

Jolowicz, H. F. and Nicholas, B. *Historical Introduction to the Study of Roman Law*. 3rd edition. Cambridge University Press, 1972 (ISBN 0 521 08253 6).

Kunkel, W. *An Introduction to Roman Legal and Constitutional History.* 2nd edition. Oxford, Clarendon Press, 1973 (ISBN 0 19 825317 6).

Leage, R. W. *Roman Private Law founded on the Institutes of Gaius and Justinian.* 3rd edition. Macmillan, 1961 (ISBN 0 333 05484 9).

Lee, R. W. *The Elements of Roman Law with a translation of the Institutes of Justinian.* 4th edition. Sweet and Maxwell, 1956 (ISBN 0 421 01780 5).

Nicholas, B. *An Introduction to Roman Law.* Oxford, Clarendon Press, 1962 (ISBN 0 19 876003 5) (*Clarendon law series*).

Sass, S. L. Research in Roman law; a guide to the sources and their English translations. *Law Library Journal*, vol. 56, no. 3, 1963, pp. 210–33.

ROMAN-DUTCH LAW

Lee, R. W. *An Introduction to Roman-Dutch Law.* 5th edition. Oxford, Clarendon Press, 1953 (ISBN 0 19 825129 7).

Nathan, M. *The Common Law of South Africa: a treatise based on Voet's Commentaries on the Pandects.* Grahamstown, African Book Co., Butterworth, 1904–7. 4 vols.

Wessels, J. W. *History of the Roman-Dutch Law.* Grahamstown, African Book Co., 1908.

RELIGIOUS LAWS

David, R. and Brierly, J. E. C. *Major Legal Systems in the World Today.* English edition. Stevens, 1968 (ISBN 0 420 41600 5).

Derrett, J. D. M. *An Introduction to Legal Systems.* Sweet and Maxwell, 1968 (ISBN 0 421 12940 9).

A Bibliography on Foreign and Comparative Law Books and Articles in English (Parker School of Foreign and Comparative Law) 1955– . Dobbs Ferry, New York, Oceana (ISSN US 0067-7329).

Roman Catholic Church

Catholic University of America. *New Catholic Encyclopedia.* New York, McGraw Hill, 1967. 15 vols. (ISBN 0 07 010235 x, etc.).

Hove, A. van. *Prolegomena ad Codicem iuris canonici.* Ed. 2. Mechelin, Dessain, 1945 (*Commentarium lovaniense in Codicem iuris canonici*, 1, i).

Metz, R. *What is Canon Law?* Tr. by M. Derrick. Burns and Oates, 1960 (*Faith and fact book*, 79) (ISBN 0 223 29330 x).

Church of England

Church of England. Archbishops' Commission on Canon Law. *The Canon Law of the Church of England.* SPCK, 1947.

Church of England. *Year Book*, 1963– Church Information Office (ISSN UK 0069-3987).

Dale, Sir William. *The Law of the Parish Church.* 4th edition. Butterworth, 1967 (ISBN 0 406 17400 8).

Moore, E. G. *An Introduction to English Canon Law.* Oxford University Press, 1967 (*Clarendon Law Series*) (ISBN 0 19 876009 4).

Church of Scotland

Cox, J. T. *Practice and Procedure in the Church of Scotland.* 5th edition. Edinburgh, Blackwood, 1964.

Jewish Law

Chajes, Z. H. *The Student's Guide through the Talmud*, tr . . . by J. Schachter. New York, Feldheim, 1960.

Elman, P. *An Introduction to Jewish Law.* New York, Lincolns-Praegar, 1958 (*Popular Jewish Library*, 11).

Elon, M. The Sources and Nature of Jewish Law. *Israel Law Review*, vol. 2, 1967, pp. 515–65; vol. 3, 1969, pp. 88–126, 416–57; vol. 4, 1969, pp. 80–140.

Encyclopaedia Judaica. Jerusalem, Keter, 1972. 16 vols.

Strack, H. L. *Introduction to the Talmud and Midrash.* Philadelphia, Jewish Publication Society, 1931, repr. New York, Atheneum, 1969 (*Temple book*, 10) (ISBN 0 689 70189 6).

India

Derrett, J. D. M. *Introduction to Modern Hindu Law.* Oxford University Press, 1963 (ISBN 0 19 635201 0).

Jain, H. C. *Indian Legal Materials: a bibliographical guide.* Bombay, Tripathi; Dobbs Ferry, New York, Oceana, 1970 (ISBN 0 379 00466 6).

Kane, P. V. *History of Dharmaśāstra.* 2nd edition. Poona, Bhandarkar Institute, 1968– (*Government Oriental Series*, B6).

Lingat, R. *The Classical Law of India*, tr. . . . by J. D. M. Derrett. Berkeley, University of California Press, 1973 (ISBN 0 520 01898 2).

Islamic Law

Azzam, I. The Law in the Near and Middle East: basic sources in

English. *Law Library Journal*, vol. 57, no. 3, August 1964, pp. 234–40.

Coulson, N. J. *A History of Islamic Law*. Edinburgh University Press, 1964 (*Islamic Surveys*, 2) (ISBN 0 85224 111 9).

Encyclopaedia of Islam. 2nd edition. Luzac, 1954– .

Fyzee, A. A. *Outlines of Muhammadon Law*. 4th edition. Oxford University Press, 1974 (ISBN 0 19 560378 3).

Pearson, J. D. *Index Islamicus*. Cambridge, Heffer, 1958– .

Schacht, J. *An Introduction to Islamic Law*. Oxford, Clarendon Press, 1964 (ISBN 0 19 825161 0).

10. Legal Bibliographies and Reference Books

R. G. LOGAN, LL.B, ALA and
BARBARA M. TEARLE, LLB, ALA

This chapter deals with a variety of reference books which assist the librarian in answering everyday enquiries from his readers. They include guides to legal literature, bibliographies, periodical indexes, union catalogues, lists of research, dictionaries, biographical dictionaries, and directories.

GUIDES TO LEGAL LITERATURE

Guides to legal literature describe the nature and purpose of the various types of law book and give instruction in their usage. They are concerned with teaching basic legal study methods.

There is no detailed guide to the use of English legal literature. The best introductory book to the study of law is Williams, G. L. *Learning the Law*, 9th edition, 1973, which is written in plain language and has brief sections on the literature. The pamphlet by Way, D. J. *The Student's Guide to Law Libraries*, 1967, is written for students for the professional examinations but rightly enjoys a wider readership. It has sections on the lay-out and contents of a law library and how to use the library's resources in tackling a legal problem.

A model guide to Australian legal literature is Campbell, E. and MacDougall, D. *Legal Research: materials and methods*, 1967. Although the emphasis is on Australian material, the basic legal materials of other common law jurisdictions are discussed. Included are chapters on law reports, digests, statutes, subordinate legislation, legal encyclopedias, treatises and dictionaries, legal periodicals, loose-leaf services, government publications, and non-legal materials. An appendix includes specimen pages from reports, digests and statutes.

There are several excellent American guides to legal literature. These are largely concerned with the intricacies of

United States materials, but some contain sections on English law. Examples are Hicks, F. C. *Materials and Methods of Legal Research*, 3rd edition, 1942; Pollack, E. H. *Fundamentals of Legal Research*, 4th edition, 1973; and Price, M. O. and Bitner, H. *Effective Legal Research*, 3rd edition, 1969. The latter is noteworthy for its precise analyses of the form and function of various types of legal reference works, such as digests, looseleaf services, citators and periodicals. The later editions are abridged and simplified, omitting some historical material and the bibliographical appendices, which included a lengthy table of Anglo-American legal periodicals. Thus the first edition published in 1953 is still useful.

Three guides to the literature of civil law jurisdictions have been published under the auspices of the Parker School of Foreign and Comparative Law at Columbia University. The titles are: Szladits, C. A. *Guide to Foreign Legal Materials: French, German, Swiss*, 1959; Grisoli, A. *Guide to Foreign Legal Materials: Italian*, 1965; and Graulich, P. *Guide to Foreign Legal Materials: Belgium, Netherlands, Luxembourg*, 1968. Under each national system there is an account of the sources of law, a bibliographic survey of the literature, and a list of legal abbreviations.

BIBLIOGRAPHIES

Bibliographies are systematic lists of books relating to a particular subject. Other items such as periodical articles or essays may be included. In evaluating a bibliography it is necessary to consider the extent of the coverage, the accuracy and detail of the entries, the logic of their arrangement, whether the entries are annotated, and the adequacy of the indexing. A good bibliography is of immense value in any library as a reference tool. It enables the reader to check quickly the details of a particular work or to discover what has been written upon a topic.

There are several types of bibliography relevant to law librarianship. They include general bibliographies of law books, national bibliographies, bibliographies of legal subjects, and printed law library catalogues.

General legal bibliographies

These fall into two categories, current and retrospective.

Current bibliographies are published periodically and list all books within the subject field as soon as possible after publication. They usually appear in unbound parts with regular bound cumulations. Retrospective bibliographies list items up to a certain date. Although supplements or revised editions may be published if the work is successful, they are not essential characteristics of such works.

Current

There is no British publication specifically devoted to current legal bibliography. However, the various American series provide adequate coverage of the British output.

Law Books in Print, first published in 1957, attempts to list all English language legal texts in print. The current cumulation, published in 1971, is the second and lists books in print at the end of 1969. The earlier cumulation, published in 1965, consists of two volumes with author and subject entries filed in one sequence. The 1969 cumulation has three volumes, the first arranged by author and title, the second by subject, and the third by publisher. The entries generally include author, title, date, pagination and price (in dollars). Primary materials, government publications and periodicals are omitted. Since 1970 *Law Books in Print* has been supplemented by *Law Books Published*. There were two issues in 1970 and since 1971 there have been three issues each year, the third one being cumulative. There are author/title and subject sequences. The latter now includes lists of new reprint and periodical titles.

A companion series is *Law Books in Review*, which commenced in January 1974. It is published quarterly and consists of short reviews of recent books. The entries are arranged by subject. Some British books are included, but it is unlikely that there will have been no prior reviews in British legal journals. *Law Books in Review* really mirrors discontent at the selective and laggardly book review policy of many American legal journals.

A recent rival to *Law Books in Print* is *Law Book Guide*, which began publication in 1973. The main entries are arranged alphabetically by author and include full cataloguing details. Other features are a subject sequence arranged by Library of Congress subject headings, an 'area studies' sequence which groups books by country or geographical area, and a title index. *Law Book Guide* is now published monthly with an annual cumulation. Retrospective cumulations have been prepared for 1969–71 and 1972. *Law Book Guide* has much to recommend it and will prove invaluable to libraries where detailed cataloguing is regarded as important, but it is more expensive than *Law Books in Print.*

Annual Legal Bibliography is a selected list of books and articles received by the Harvard Law School library. It is supplemented by *Current Legal Bibliography*, which has nine issues a year. However, *Annual Legal Bibliography* is more than just a cumulation, for it contains many additional items. It has a broad classified arrangement with subject and geographic indexes. It is very useful for a detailed subject search, but the lack of an author index is a considerable disadvantage.

Apart from the specialist series there are other sources which serve as current bibliographical tools. The monthly issues of *Current Law* (see page 164) list recent books, usually on the inside back cover. The *Current Law Year Book* cumulates these lists, which give details of author, title and price, but not publisher. Because the main legal publishers are few their annual catalogues are important bibliographies in their own right. The law catalogues of such houses as Butterworth, Sweet and Maxwell, and Oceana should be kept in that section of the library.

Retrospective

There are three such works which every law library should possess.

The first is Sweet and Maxwell's *A Legal Bibliography of the British Commonwealth of Nations*, 2nd edition, 1955–64, 7 volumes. Volumes 1 and 2 cover English law, including Wales, the Channel Islands and the Isle of Man, to 1800 and from 1801 to 1954; volume 3 covers Canadian and British-American colonial law to 1956; volume 4 Irish law to 1956; volume 5 Scottish law to 1956, together with a list of Roman law books in the English language; volume 6 the law of Australia, New Zealand, and their dependencies to 1958; and volume 7 the law of the British Commonwealth, excluding the United Kingdom, Australia,

New Zealand, Canada, India and Pakistan. A projected eighth volume on the law of India and Pakistan was not published. Volume I has a subject arrangement with an author index, but otherwise arrangement is by author with subject indexes. The entries are brief, usually including only author, title and date, but an attempt is made to list all known editions. Occasional entries are annotated, mostly in volume I.

The second retrospective work is Chloros, A. G. *A Bibliographical Guide to the Law of the United Kingdom, the Channel Islands and the Isle of Man*, 2nd edition, 1973. The first edition in 1956 was edited under the direction of F. H. Lawson. This volume, published by the Institute of Advanced Legal Studies, is one of the series sponsored by the International Association of Legal Science as aids to those studying legal systems other than their own. Nevertheless it fills a gap for British lawyers. There are chapters on all the major topics of English law, on other United Kingdom legal systems, including those of Scotland and Northern Ireland, and on international law, the Commonwealth, jurisprudence, Roman law and canon law. The second edition has an additional chapter on Common Market law. Each chapter is written by an expert in the field and has a commentary on the literature, followed by a select bibliography.

The third work is *Where to Look for Your Law*, 14th edition by C. W. Ringrose, 1962. This is a brief guide to law books, Command papers and law reports. The list of books is selective, but includes all those of any importance. The entries are arranged by author with a subject index, and give details of author, title, edition, date and price. The latter information is now woefully out of date, but in spite of this the 'yellow book' maintains its popularity as a guide to the leading texts. A new edition has been promised for many years but has yet to materialize.

The major work on legal systems other than common law jurisdictions is Szladits, C. A. *Bibliography on Foreign and Comparative Law*, 1955. Cumulated supplements have been published covering the years 1953–9, 1960–5 and 1966–71, and an interim supplement issued for 1972. Entries are restricted to English language items, but nevertheless coverage is extensive and includes periodical articles as well as books. The entries for

384 · *Manual of Law Librarianship*

books are annotated. The arrangement is by subject with an author index.

Information on the basic legal literature of different countries can be gleaned from Unesco's *A Register of Legal Documentation in the World*, 2nd edition, 1957, although it is now rather out-of-date. Under each country are listed legislation, law reports, centres of legal studies, periodicals, reference works and bibliographies. Many entries have short notes concerning their scope.

Another type of retrospective bibliography is the printed library catalogue, which is discussed on page 389.

National bibliographies

National bibliographies attempt to list all books published in one country or sometimes in one language. They fall into two categories: lists of books noted as they appear, and lists of books in print at a particular date. The law librarian may use national bibliographies to check details of books on peripheral and non-legal topics or as an alternative means of checking publishing details of law books. They are useful for tracing the author if only the title is known, or for discovering the correct form of author and title.

The *British National Bibliography* (BNB) began publication in 1950. It currently appears weekly with cumulations monthly, every four months and annually. Five cumulative indexes cover the period 1950–70. The entries are arranged by subject according to the Dewey Decimal Classification and give full cataloguing details. There are author/title and subject indexes. Coverage extends to most books published in Britain and includes works deposited with the British Library under the copyright regulations.

British Books in Print is published annually and lists books available from British publishers. It currently consists of two volumes containing author and title entries filed in one sequence. Entries are brief but give all the information required for book ordering. A useful feature is the very full directory of publishers' addresses.

An equivalent United States publication is *Books in Print*, which is also an annual. It consists of two volumes, one listing authors and the other titles. There is a semi-annual supplement.

Another series published in the United States is *Cumulative Book Index* (CBI), which purports to list all books published in the English language. It appears monthly (except July) with quarterly and annual cumulations. Six cumulations cover the period 1928–56 and biennial cumulations the period 1957–68. Author, title and subject entries are listed in one alphabetical sequence. The author entries are the most complete and give full publishing details.

Bibliographies of legal subjects

Law is not a field in which British bibliographers have been active. Their output compares unfavourably with that of other countries, notably the United States. There are several possible reasons for this. One is the comparatively small number of law research students. Another is the fact that most practising lawyers confine their reading to primary materials, standard texts and a few professional journals. A third reason is the almost universal preference of legal authors for footnote references to the exclusion of lists of works cited. Nevertheless, there are available many bibliographies of interest, and there is space here to cite only a few examples.

Dias, R. W. M. *A Bibliography of Jurisprudence*, 2nd edition, 1970, is arranged by subjects and lists book chapters and periodical articles. There are excellent annotations. Bland, D. S. *A Bibliography of the Inns of Court and Chancery*, 1965, includes manuscript sources as well as books and articles. Many entries have one line annotations. Green, A. W. *Bibliography on British Legal Education*, 1973, is curiously arranged and badly needs a subject index, but lists a wealth of material largely culled from British journals. Both the last two works include relevant items on law libraries.

Britain's successful negotiation for entry to the Common Market inspired two useful bibliographies. A brief introductory bibliographical guide to the legal system of the European Community is provided by the British Institute of International and Comparative Law, *Where to Find your Community Law*, 2nd edition, 1973, which includes primary and secondary materials. A more comprehensive list is the British and Irish Association of Law Librarians, *Community Law: a selection of*

13

publications, 1973, which also includes items on the relevant law of the six original member states. Both works have useful address lists.

Bibliographies of national legal systems are of particular interest. Titles in the series published at the instance of the International Association of Legal Science are listed on the last page of Chloros (see above). They include Andrews, J. L. and others, *The Law in the United States of America: a selective bibliographical guide*, 1965, which lists primary and secondary materials. Most entries have one line annotations. In the same series is the German Association of Comparative Law, *Bibliography of German Law*, 1964, with supplements covering the periods 1964–8 and 1969–73. Also worthy of mention under this heading are the bibliographical sections in the Parker School of Foreign and Comparative Law guides to foreign legal materials (see above).

Gilissen, J. *Introduction bibliographique à l'histoire du droit et à l'ethnologie juridique*, 6 volumes, 1963– , is a loose-leaf publication which lists readings in the legal history of many countries. Volume C includes sections on the British Isles (England, Wales, Scotland) and Ireland (Republic of Ireland and Northern Ireland).

International lawyers have always been well served by bibliographers. There is a good survey in Robinson, J. *International Law and Organization: general sources of information*, 1967. A useful acquisition for the law library in that it relates international law to the wider field of social science is Gould, W. L. and Barkun, M. *Social Science Literature: a bibliography for international law*, 1972.

Early law books

Surveys

Such works provide an introduction to the books and materials which make up the framework of legal history and place them in context. They assist the librarian in commenting upon the subject-matter or assessing the relative importance of a text.

Three scholarly surveys of early English legal literature have remarkably similar origins in that all are based on lecture series. The librarian will turn first to Winfield, P. H. *The Chief Sources of English Legal History*, 1925, which includes many bibliographical annotations within the text in addition to several chapter bibliographies. Although dated, the chapter on bibliographical guides is still useful. Other topics include statutes, public records, case-law, abridgments, textbooks and books of practice. A similar range of topics is covered by Holdsworth, W. S. *Sources and Literature of English Law*, 1925, but it lacks the annotations of Winfield. No guidance to further reading is given, but there are cross-references to his then incomplete *History of English Law* (see below). Plucknett, T. F. T. *Early English Legal Literature*, 1958, is narrower in scope but makes useful background reading, especially on Bracton.

Other sources of information include: Hicks, F. C. *Men and Books Famous in the Law*, 1921, on Cowell, Coke, Littleton and Blackstone; the Selden Society, *General guide to the Society's publications*, 1960, on the materials in volumes 1–79 of their series; and Cowley (see below) on abridgments and dictionaries.

Most English legal history texts comment upon the nature and importance of early legal literature. The standard work is Holdsworth, W. S. *History of English Law*, 17 volumes, various editions, 1903–72, which contains several detailed sections on law books. The final volume is the index. See also page 252.

Scottish legal historians are well served by the Stair Society, *An Introductory Survey of the Sources and Literature of Scots law*, 1936. This detailed work is divided into four major sections: native sources, non-native sources, indirect sources and special subjects. Each of the thirty-eight chapters includes a list of source material, commentary on the sources and literature, and a bibliography.

Bibliographies

A basic checklist is provided by *A Legal Bibliography of the British Commonwealth of Nations* (see above), but for the certain identification of a particular edition which the legal historian requires it is necessary to consult a descriptive bibliography.

Law books printed in England up to 1600 are covered by

Beale, J. H. *A Bibliography of Early English Law Books*, 1926. This is reinforced by Anderson, R. B. *A supplement to Beale's Bibliography*, 1943. The supplement contains additional entries and corrections, but does not extend the scope of the work beyond 1600. The entries in Beale are arranged in chapters listing statutes, decisions (Year Books, abridgments, reports) and treatises. Other features include a list of printers and their law books, illustrations of printers' devices, and a table of entries. The latter serves as a kind of index and records copies in selected libraries.

A more specialized work containing very detailed descriptions is Cowley, J. D. *Bibliography of Abridgements, Digests, Indexes and Dictionaries of English Law to the Year 1800*, 1932. The introduction is informative on the history and textual matter of the works included. The work is enhanced by the index, which includes references to the introduction, and the illustrations, mostly of title pages. Each entry in Cowley is followed by a list of locations.

Older legal bibliographies are now of more interest to legal historians than librarians, and copies are scarce. Bridgman, R. W. *Short View of Legal Bibliography*, 1807, is very selective but has detailed notes. Marvin, J. G. *Legal Bibliography*, 1847, is more complete, but omits editions not deemed to be of interest to American lawyers. The annotations frequently quote criticism by other writers. Soule, C. C. *Lawyers Reference Manual of Law Books*, 1883, is more helpful on reports than treatises.

Details of early law books may also be checked in the printed catalogues of older law libraries (see below).

Because books on or relevant to law formed quite a high proportion of early printing output, general bibliographies of early literature are helpful. For basic purposes the field is adequately covered by Pollard, A. W. and Redgrave, G. R. *A Short-Title Catalogue of Books printed in England, Scotland and Ireland and of English books printed abroad, 1475–1640*, 1926, and Wing, D. *Short-Title Catalogue of Books printed in England, Scotland, Ireland, Wales and British America and of English books printed in other countries, 1641–1700*, 3 volumes, 1945–51. They are commonly abbreviated to STC and Wing. Revised editions are in progress and the new volume 1 of Wing was published in 1973. Each entry is allotted an identifying number and gives

details of author, short title, printer, date and a selective list of
locations in major British and American libraries.

Law library catalogues

Printed library catalogues are useful for locating individual
copies of a book, for indicating the relative strength of a
particular library's stock, and for bibliographical purposes. The
great era of the printed catalogue was the period covering the
nineteenth and early twentieth centuries, when all the major
professional libraries were active. A comprehensive list may be
traced through *A Legal Bibliography of the British Commonwealth
of Nations*, especially for England (volume 1, p. 2) and Scotland
(volume 5, pp. 20–1). With the modern development of first
photocopying techniques and then computerized print-outs
there has been a resurgence of interest in the printed catalogue
(see pages 541 and 642).

The last of the great traditional English law library catalogues was *A Catalogue of the Printed Books in the Library of the
Honourable Society of the Middle Temple*, 3 volumes, 1914, compiled
by C. E. A. Bedwell. A supplement by H. A. C. Sturgess was
published in 1925. The first two volumes comprise an alphabetical author sequence and the third a subject index. Also
notable are catalogues of the libraries of Inner Temple,
Lincoln's Inn, Gray's Inn and the Law Society.

Far more up to date is the *University of Cambridge Squire Law
Library Catalogue*, 14 volumes, published in 1974. A catalogue
of the international law collection was published in advance in
1972 in four volumes, but all the entries are incorporated in the
main catalogue. This classified listing of more than 60,000
volumes in one of the major British law libraries was made
possible by computerization.

When dealing with Scottish catalogues it should be remembered that the great Scottish law libraries contained much
general literature. The catalogues fall into three categories:
those in which law books are not differentiated, those in which
law books are listed in a separate section, and those which
consist exclusively of law books. A good systematic example of
the last category is the *Catalogue of the Law Books in the Library of
the Society of Writers to Her Majesty's Signet in Scotland*, 1856,

compiled by W. Ivory. Examples of all three types may be found in the catalogues of the libraries of the Faculty of Advocates, the Society of Writers to HM Signet, the Society of Solicitors of the Supreme Court, and the Faculty of Procurators.

A useful United States item is Marke, J. J. *Catalog of the Law Collection at New York University*, 1953. This volume lists a good selection of titles, mainly on Anglo-American law, with annotations and critical quotes.

An example of a complete library catalogue produced by photo-reproduction of catalogue cards is the Columbia University, *Dictionary Catalog of the Columbia University Law Library*, 28 volumes, 1969. For those libraries which can afford it this provides an excellent comprehensive reference tool.

Bibliographies of legal bibliographies

The best way to keep up to date with what is available is to consult the relevant sections in the general current legal bibliographies and to scan the reviews in journals of law librarianship (see p. 208). Bibliographies published in periodicals are noted in the indexes to legal periodicals (see below).

A distinguished guide to work done up to the Second World War is provided by Friend, W. L. *Anglo-American Legal Bibliographies*, 1944. It contains a historical survey followed by an author list with critical notes. Coverage extends to important bibliographies in books and periodicals.

Besterman, T. *Law and International Law: a bibliography of bibliographies*, 1971, lists separately published bibliographies, including printed catalogues. The list is exhaustive, but the entries are not annotated and the arrangement, by broad subject or country and date of publication, makes them difficult to trace. There is no index. Coverage is world-wide and multilingual.

PERIODICALS

Directories

The most convenient directory of legal periodical titles is the *Union List of Legal Periodicals* (see below), which gives details of place, publisher and dates.

Legal Periodicals in English (formerly *Checklist of Anglo-American Legal Periodicals*) is a two volume loose-leaf service which lists the publisher and the dates, number of issues and pagination for each volume. It is incomplete on British journals and not all entries are kept up to date regularly. It is only of use in checking the completeness of back sets. It ceased in 1974.

The list of periodicals indexed in each issue of *Index to Legal Periodicals* (see below) includes details of price, frequency and publisher's address. Information on established periodicals indexed in the *Index to Foreign Legal Periodicals* is given in Blaustein, A. P. *Manual on Foreign Legal Periodicals and their Index*, 1962. The information includes date of commencement, frequency, language and topics covered, but not the publisher's address.

A comprehensive general directory of periodicals in print is Ulrich, C. F. *Ulrich's International Periodicals Directory*, 15th edition, 2 volumes, 1973–4. This gives details of date of first issue, frequency, price, publisher and circulation, and notes features such as book reviews and abstracts. The entries include some law reports, but many series are omitted. Also useful as a general directory is the *British Union Catalogue of Periodicals* (see below).

Indexes to articles

Indexes to periodical literature assist in tracing individual articles and in discovering what has been written upon a topic. Most periodicals, of course, have their own index to each volume, and some have cumulated indexes covering a number of volumes. An example is the *Law Quarterly Review* index to volumes 1–80. There are also indexes which cover a large number of periodicals.

The earliest in the field of law was the *Index to Legal Periodical Literature* (the 'Jones-Chipman index'), published in six volumes and covering the years 1803–1937. Coverage included the main Anglo-American legal journals of the time. The arrangement was alphabetically by subject, with an author index. The first three volumes, covering the period to 1907, are still invaluable, but the later volumes are less comprehensive than the *Index to Legal Periodicals*, which commenced in 1908. There are annual volumes for the years to 1925, since when the annual volumes have been cumulated triennially. At present the index is issued monthly (except in September) and cumulated quarterly, annually and triennially. It indexes about 350 periodicals published in the United States, Canada, Great Britain, Australia and New Zealand, which regularly publish legal content of high quality. It has a combined subject and author sequence, but the main entries are under subject and the author entries are merely cross-references. There have been separate tables indexing case-notes since 1917 and book reviews since 1940. One disadvantage of *Index to Legal Periodicals* is that items for inclusion are not selected just by quality but also by length. Excluded are articles of less than five ordinary pages, and case-notes and book reviews of less than two pages. The relatively compact style and format of British journals means that some worthwhile items are thereby not indexed. Nevertheless this fact should not obscure the merits of the index.

Since 1960 a complementary service has been provided by the *Index to Foreign Legal Periodicals*. 'Foreign' in this sense denotes the main journals dealing with international law, comparative law, and legal systems other than those with a common law basis. Coverage is world-wide and is not restricted to English language journals. Since 1963 the contents of selected volumes of legal essays and Festschriften have been indexed. The index is published quarterly, the fourth issue of each year being cumulative. The annual volumes are cumulated triennially. The index currently covers about 300 journals and indexes articles of at least four pages in length and book reviews of at least two and a half pages. The main sequence is arranged by subject, with sub-headings for countries under each term. Articles on the laws of a particular country may be traced through the geographical index. Other features are indexes of authors and book reviews.

Some articles on legal subjects published in non-legal journals may be traced through the *Index to Periodical Articles Related to Law*, which selectively indexes articles of research value which do not appear in *Index to Legal Periodicals* or *Index to Foreign Legal Periodicals*. It began in 1958 and a cumulation covers the first ten years. It is published quarterly and the fourth issue is normally cumulative, although this was not so in 1973 as a new five-year cumulation for the period 1968–73 is in preparation. The arrangement is by subject, with an author index. Another means of tracing relevant articles in non-legal journals is to make use of more general periodical indexes, such as the *British Humanities Index*.

It should be remembered that many bibliographies list articles in periodicals. Good examples are *Annual Legal Bibliography* and *Bibliography on Foreign and Comparative Law* (see above).

British periodical literature is indexed in *Current Law* (see page 164). In the monthly issues articles are listed at the end of the entries under each subject heading, but in the *Current Law Year Book* they are grouped by subject in a separate sequence. Details are given of the title and reference of the article, but the author's name is noted only in the monthly issues.

Indexes of legal periodical literature relating to individual nations are useful for any detailed research into those legal systems. Examples of regularly published indexes are *Index to Canadian Periodical Literature*, which began in 1966 but has produced a retrospective cumulation covering the period 1961–70, and *Current Australian and New Zealand Legal Literature Index*, which commenced in 1973. An excellent retrospective index is O'Higgins, P. *A Bibliography of Periodical Literature Relating to Irish Law*, 1966, which includes relevant items from non-Irish journals. A supplement was published in the autumn of 1974.

ABSTRACTS

Abstracts are publications which provide brief synopses of articles, essays, books and theses. The main purpose of each synopsis is to indicate the scope and level of the item rather than to give a critical review of the contents.

There is no abstracting service which satisfactorily covers British legal literature. We have no equivalent to the American *Legal Periodical Digest*, which began in 1928 and was published in loose-leaf form until it ceased in 1962. It abstracted selected articles in English language periodicals, but was mainly of interest to American lawyers.

Some subjects peripheral to law are well served by abstracting services. All aspects of sociology of law are covered by *Sociological Abstracts*, and criminal procedure and the administration of justice are covered in *Abstracts of Criminology and Penology* (formerly *Excerpta criminologica*).

UNION CATALOGUES

Union catalogues are catalogues in which each entry is followed by a list of participating libraries holding that item. It is customary to add details of a particular holding if it is incomplete. (See page 544 for methods of compiling union catalogues.) The primary function of such catalogues is to act as a location device, so that readers may be directed to items not held by their own libraries. They are indispensable to libraries operating an inter-library loan service (see page 471). They also have valuable secondary functions as subject bibliographies and as a means of checking the completeness of a particular library's stock.

British law librarians are well provided for in this field by the series of five union catalogues published by the Institute of Advanced Legal Studies. The most widely used is the *Union List of Legal Periodicals*, 3rd edition, 1968. Earlier editions of 1949 and 1957 had the title *A Survey of Legal Periodicals*. This lists 1,831 titles with the holdings of eighty-seven libraries, including several in Scotland and one in Northern Ireland. The entries are arranged alphabetically by title, with an index of countries of publication. The list includes nearly all periodicals taken by specialist law libraries in the United Kingdom and some titles for which no holding is recorded, but generally excludes law reports, legislation and non-legal periodicals. This is an essential tool for any law library.

The *Union List of Commonwealth and South African Law*, 2nd edition, 1963, is a location guide to legislation, law reports and digests held by fifty-one United Kingdom libraries. It is arranged alphabetically by country, with an index of countries and their states or provinces and a subject index to special series of law reports. The *Union List of United States Legal Literature*, 2nd edition, 1967, includes the holdings of nine libraries in London, Oxford and Cambridge. It covers federal and state legislation, federal and state reports, digests and special subject law reports. Treatises and periodicals are excluded. There is a comprehensive index. The *Union List of West European Legal Literature*, 1966, gives the holdings of eight libraries in London, Oxford and Cambridge. There are sections on general reference, countries and regional organizations. Under each country are listed treatises, law reports, legislation, periodicals and other serial publications. Except in the latter case, holdings before 1945 are largely excluded. There are general author and serial indexes as well as subject indexes under each section.

The *Union List of Air Law Literature*, 1956, lists 453 items with holdings in twenty-two libraries in London, Oxford and Cambridge. The list includes books and pamphlets, international conferences and treaties, international organizations, laws and regulations, and periodicals and reports. There is a subject index. A revised edition, expanded to include space law, was published in 1975.

No published list satisfactorily provides locations for United Kingdom law reports. In fact, the Institute of Advanced Legal Studies has prepared a *Union List of British and Irish Law Reports and Statutes in London Libraries* for private circulation amongst the co-operating libraries. It is a disappointment that there can be no plans at present to extend and publish this list, for paradoxically it is easier to locate Commonwealth, United States and Western European law reports than copies of the less important British series.

One general catalogue which includes law journals and reports is the *British Union Catalogue of Periodicals* (BUCOP), 4 volumes, 1955–8. Supplements cover the period to 1960 (2 volumes) and 1960–8. Since 1969 they have been published quarterly, with an annual cumulation. BUCOP tries to list all periodicals permanently filed in United Kingdom libraries, although the actual locations given are highly selective. It does provide some means of tracing sets of British law reports. The main entry is by the earliest title, which can be confusing. For example, *All England Law Reports* is filed as a supplement to *Law Journal*. The nominate reports prior to 1865 are excluded by the scope of the work.

Some bibliographies perform a secondary function as union catalogues. Thus in the field of early law books locations in selected libraries can be traced through STC, Wing, Beale and Cowley (see page 388).

LEGAL RESEARCH

Legal research is conducted for several purposes and at different levels. It may state the law as it is; provide facts to ascertain how the law is working; or suggest reform. It can be conducted in the universities and polytechnics for higher degrees or as the basis for future publications; on a regular basis by government departments and committees, in particular the Law Commission, the Scottish Law Commission, and the Northern Ireland Department of Law Reform; by *ad hoc* committees and commissions set up to investigate a particular subject, such as the Royal Commission on the Constitution, which has published background research papers as well as its report; and by independent bodies to further their own aims, such as the Statute Law Society.

Publication of the results of research is often by the sponsoring body. Some sponsors have easily identifiable series, such as the *Cambridge Studies in Criminology*. However, most theses for higher degrees are not published.

An attempt to list current research from all these sources for the whole of the British Isles is made in *Scientific Research in British Universities and Colleges*, volume 3. Its scope is wider than the academic world and covers work in progress in government departments and other institutions, although the law section is mainly concerned with universities and polytechnics. Indeed, there is no entry for either the Law Commission or the Scottish Law Commission in the current edition, but research commissioned from an academic source by these bodies is included. On the other hand, there are long entries for the Home Office Social Survey Department.

A more complete source for research in progress in government departments throughout the British Isles, and selectively for the Commonwealth, is the Institute of Advanced Legal Studies: *List of official committees, commissions and other bodies concerned with the reform of the law*, which is revised annually. Completed government legal research should be published as parliamentary or departmental publications and appear in the indexes to government publications described on page 262. Among the government publications sectional lists, the most useful for published government legal research are the *Home Office List*, the *Miscellaneous List* which includes the Lord Chancellor's Department and the Law Commission, the *Scottish Home and Health List*, and *Reports of Royal Commissions from 1937–72*, as these are often the starting point for law reform. The sectional lists are revised frequently.

Academic research in progress is listed regularly in both *Scientific Research in British Universities and Colleges*, volume 3, which covers thoroughly the research interests of academic staff, and IALS *List of Current Legal Research Topics*. Details of completed research can be found in IALS *List of Legal Research Topics Completed and Approved since about 1935*, 1961, and the supplement for 1961–6. Aslib *Index to Theses* has a law section but there are several classes of theses omitted, so that IALS's list is more complete. Aslib *Index to Theses* sets out the terms on which universities and colleges will lend or give access to theses, which is useful, as many are unpublished. Many universities publish annual lists of theses and dissertations prepared within their university and some lists, for example those published by Southampton University, contain abstracts. However, except for the universities which are strong in post-graduate law studies, the law entries in these lists are few.

Research, either in progress or completed, which has been sponsored by independent bodies, is not listed regularly, although details of some projects appear in *Scientific Research in British Universities and Colleges*, volume 3.

The research interests of a common law lawyer cannot be confined to the British Isles. For official government research and law reform in other common law jurisdictions, recourse can be made to IALS's annual *List of official committees, commissions and other bodies concerned with the reform of the law*. The Law Commission Library, *Law Reform Commissions and other bodies*, 1969, was based on the 1967 edition with additional information mainly on the United States of America. Unfortunately it has not been revised and so it has been overtaken by later editions of IALS's list, which widens in scope annually.

In the international field, Unidroit has compiled a massive loose-leaf *Digest of legal activities of international organizations and other institutions*, 1969, which has details of aims and research programmes of many international governmental and non-governmental bodies. The Council of Europe, *Exchange of Information on Research in European law*, lists research since 1971, mainly for higher degrees, in comparative European law from selected institutions, including some from the British Isles.

DICTIONARIES

It is essential for a law library to possess good English and bilingual dictionaries. They are needed for general language purposes and for precise definitions.

The *Oxford English Dictionary* is the authoritative source for definitions, etymology and examples of use of the English language, including legal terms. As such, it is always consulted by the courts when questions of interpretation of legal and non-legal words arise. However, for normal library use, the *Shorter Oxford English Dictionary*, 1959, is sufficient.

Legal dictionaries

English legal dictionaries have several characteristics, whether they deal with the whole range of law, or a special aspect. Unlike general language dictionaries where the entries are of one word, law dictionaries reflect the concepts, terms and institutions of the subject, which may be expressed in one or more words. When the terms and explanations are long, the dictionary resembles an alphabetically arranged digest. They may contain old Anglo-Saxon, Law French and Law Latin terms drawn from ancient deeds and charters, although there is a tendency to excise obsolete terms from new dictionaries or new editions of established dictionaries. The terminology of the law is constantly developing, so that it is important to know to what date a dictionary is current. The citation of the authority for a definition is necessary to understand its context and to assess its accuracy.

As well as exhibiting these characteristics, legal dictionaries fall into two categories, the explanatory and the interpreting dictionary.

Explanatory dictionaries

Historically, the development of legal dictionaries went through several stages.

The first legal dictionary to be published in England was *Expositiones terminorum legum anglorum* in 1527, better known in editions from 1624 as *Les termes de la ley*. Lists of difficult legal words already existed, but the novelty of this first dictionary was its alphabetical arrangement. It was intended for the use of students and contained contemporary legal terms with explanations in English. Later editions were larger than the first pocket-size ones, because they had words from the early word lists added. Altogether, it was used for over 300 years in twenty-nine editions.

The next dictionary to be published was Cowell, J. *The Interpreter*, in 1607, which differed from *Expositiones terminorum legum anglorum* in several respects. It included civil, canon and common law terms, and it cited authorities for its definitions. Later editions included antiquarian terms. The seventeenth-century legal dictionaries seem to have been either scholarly antiquarian compilations – Spellman, H. *Archaeologus*, 1626, and Blount, T. *Nomo-lexikon*, 1670; or inferior products, often intended for students – Leigh, E. *Philologicall Commentary*, 1652, and *The Law-French, Law-Latin Dictionary*, 1701. The additional characteristics from this period are the reference to authorities for definitions and the inclusion of many non-legal words. The latter characteristic occurred partly because general dictionaries were inadequate, and partly because, according to Cowell, the lawyer 'professeth true philosophy' and should understand any obscure word which he encounters.

A change in the nature of legal dictionaries can be seen in Jacob, G. *New-Law Dictionary*, 1729. He claims to include 'derivations and definitions of words and terms used in the law, likewise the whole law, with the practice thereof, collected and abstracted'. From Jacob onwards, the better legal dictionaries concentrated on legal terms. In the nature and length of their definitions they became almost digests of the law itself. This encyclopedic characteristic is most pronounced in Cunningham, T. *A New and Complete Law-dictionary*, 1764–5, and Marriot, W. *A New Law Dictionary*, 1798. In an abbreviated form, the encyclopedic law dictionary continued with Wharton, J. J. S. *Law Lexicon*; Sweet, C. *Dictionary of English Law*, 1882; Byrne, W. J. *Dictionary of English Law*, 1923, and Jowitt, W. *Dictionary of English Law*, 1959. The more recent of these encyclopedic dictionaries endeavour to reduce the number of obsolete terms, but Byrne, Wharton and Jowitt include those Anglo-Saxon, medieval Law French and Latin terms, which may still be used.

Of the dictionaries used today, Jowitt is the major one. The introduction states that it is not only a 'dictionary of legal terms' but also 'a compact encyclopedia of law and it may be used to get a quick, accurate summary of a topic and as an index to the whole of English law'. The terms range from concepts such as 'tort' to institutions such as the 'Law of Property Act 1925' and many historical words, *eg*, 'escuage' and 'brigbote' are included. The definitions contain etymology, present meaning and examples of use, arranged chronologically, with reference to the authority of statutes, cases, and the classic textbooks. The pocket-size dictionaries, Osborn, P. G. *The Concise Law Dictionary*, 5th edition, 1964, and Mozley, H. N. and Whiteley, G. C. *Law Dictionary*, 8th edition, 1970, are similar in scope, but only a fraction of the size of Jowitt. Their value for students lies in their concise, authoritative definitions and their more recent publication. New editions, although not published with the frequency of major textbooks, are produced occasionally, compiled from primary sources to take account of legal developments.

Interpreting dictionaries

The interpreting dictionaries work on a different principle from the explanatory category. They define ordinary and legal words and phrases in the context in which they have been used in the courts and in legislation. Legislation and judicial interpretation are continuous activities and the same words may be defined in different ways, depending upon their context. Therefore it is important to have up-to-date information on legislative and judicial definitions.

Stroud, F. *Judicial Dictionary of Words and Phrases Judicially Interpreted*, 1890, was the first interpreting dictionary to be published in England. The present edition, the fourth, 1971–4, refers to cases, statutes and textbooks for the authority for its definitions. Most of the citations are from English sources, but Scottish, Irish, Commonwealth and American cases are also cited. A similar work, *Words and Phrases Legally Defined*, 1969–70, is arranged alphabetically in broad subject headings with subdivisions for terms and jurisdictions (England, Scotland, Ireland, Canada, Australia and New Zealand). Its definitions quote directly from law reports and, to a lesser extent, from statutes and textbooks. In order to take developments into account, both Stroud and *Words and Phrases* have supplements.

For both retrospective and current judicial definitions, the indexes to law reports and legal encyclopedias can be used. Law report indexes are published frequently, so that they are up-to-date sources for judicial pronouncements. Most have alphabetically arranged 'words' or 'words and phrases' sections. In some, this section is part of the subject index (the *Law Reports* digests and indexes, *Lloyd's Law Reports Digest* and indexes, and *Current Law Year Book*); in others it is a separate sequence (*All England Law Reports Index*, *Halsbury's Laws of England*, volume 42, and *Halsbury's Statutes of England* index). The words and phrases list in *Halsbury's Statutes* is confined to statutory definitions. An earlier dictionary of statutory definitions, *Index to Statutory Definitions*, 2nd edition, compiled by the Office of the Parliamentary Counsel, is now so out of date as to be of little use.

Welsh legal dictionaries

Welsh legal dictionaries are of two distinct types: those of medieval Welsh terms (Lewis, T. *Glossary of Medieval Welsh Law*, 1913) now only of historical use; and those of today which attempt to provide a vocabulary of modern legal terms for use by Welsh speakers in the courts (Lewis, R. *Termau cyfraith, Welsh legal terms*, 1973).

Scottish legal dictionaries

In Scotland the first legal dictionary was Skene, J. *De verborum significatione*, 1597, which contained explanations, sources and examples of use of legal and some non-legal 'difficill wordes' drawn mainly from his *Regiam majestatem*, 1597, and previous legislation. The explanations, in English, of each term often occupy several pages. Although now over seventy-five years old, the last edition of Bell, R. *Dictionary and Digest of the Law of Scotland*, 1890, is still used. It displays the encyclopedic characteristic to a greater extent than any of the modern English legal dictionaries, *eg*, the entry for bankruptcy is explained under several sub-headings and takes up nine pages. The explanations refer to the institutional writers, legislation, cases and textbooks. Dalrymple, A. W. and Gibb, A. D. *A Dictionary of Words and Phrases Judicially Defined*, 1946, belongs to the interpreting category. It has judicial, not statutory, definitions from 1800 to 1944 and refers to the cases in which the terms were defined and, if relevant, the acts in which the words occur. Unlike many legal dictionaries, Dalrymple and Gibb contains a list of statutes and cases.

Others

Irish law has not produced any legal dictionaries of its own, although several English ones have also been published in Ireland.

Dictionaries of special legal subjects are most common in those areas of the law which have strong connections with other disciplines. Thus, there are subject dictionaries for parliamentary terms (Abraham, L. A. and Hawtry, S. C. *A Parliamentary Dictionary*, 3rd edition, 1970), commerce (Osborn, P. G. *Concise Commercial Dictionary*, 1966), and banking (*Thomson's Dictionary of Banking*, 11th edition, 1965). Some are straightforward defining dictionaries but others, *eg*, Abraham and Hawtry, contain long explanations providing a digest of the subject.

One result of the early use of Latin as the language of the law has been the growth of legal maxims, a summary of a principle of law described as 'the wisdom of many and the wit of one'. Translations appear in most legal dictionaries and in the second part of *Latin for Lawyers*, 3rd edition, 1960, but little explanation is given. For that, Broom, H. *A Selection of Legal Maxims*, 1939, must be used. Broom is not a dictionary although it has an alphabetical index of the 500–600 maxims which are collected, translated and explained with reference to cases, under ten headings dealing with different branches of the law.

Besides normal contents, some dictionaries have other useful information. Mozley and Whiteley and Byrne have tables of law report abbreviations. The latter also has a table of regnal years and an explanation of the difference between historical, legal and regnal years. Lewis, R. *Termau cyfraith* has forms of addressing the court in Welsh.

Foreign language dictionaries

General bilingual dictionaries complement legal bilingual dictionaries for foreign language legal work. Several – Harrap's *Standard French and English Dictionary*, 1948, and the *Cambridge Italian Dictionary*, 1962 – have a high reputation for the accuracy of their definitions of foreign legal terms. But law has a special terminology in every language and for legal purposes general dictionaries should be used with special caution.

Legal dictionaries

To use bilingual and multilingual legal dictionaries effectively, the user must have a good knowledge of both languages and legal systems. Great care is necessary as, even between two similar legal systems or the same language used in two jurisdictions, the same term can have different meanings. With two languages and two different legal systems the problems are greater. Many of the concepts of the civil law and common law systems differ although linguistically the words used appear to be the same, *eg*, 'domicile' in French and English law.

Several factors should be borne in mind when using bilingual dictionaries. The first is whether the English language part is biased towards English or American law. Quemner, Th. A. *Dictionnaire juridique*, 1953–5, indicates the appropriate jurisdiction in individual entries where necessary. The second is whether the definitions in each language are brief, one word translations themselves drawn from secondary sources such as other legal or general dictionaries, *eg*, Jéraute, J. *Vocabulaire français-anglais, anglais-français*, 1953, or whether the dictionary has been compiled from original sources, *eg*, Prischepenko, N. P. *Russian-English Law Dictionary*, 1969, whose preface claims that it was compiled from source material, although they are not quoted in the entries.

Adequate translation into the context of another legal system often requires long explanations. The dictionaries which attempt this thoroughly are often not dictionaries but glossaries of terms in special subjects. An example is the series of glossaries being published under the title *European Glossaries of Legal and Administrative Terminology*. These are small works containing only a few hundred terms in a special subject area such as the law of establishment, and each confined to two languages only out of a list that so far includes French, German, Italian and English. The terms in Anderson, R. J. B. and Deckers, R. J. *Selected French Legal Terms in European Treaties ; French/English,* 1972, no. 12 of the series, are taken from the French texts of European Communities and Council of Europe treaties. An explanation of their use in French law is given, followed by the English equivalent.

These glossaries also show that bilingual legal dictionaries are not confined to the whole field of law but may relate to special subject areas only. A particular subject area is that of legal abbreviations. Many bilingual legal dictionaries include abbreviations and some attempt to translate them into the other language. Of more use is Sprudz, A. *Foreign Law Abbreviations ; French,* 1967, and his other two lists for Italian and Benelux law. They expand the abbreviation in the original language, but make no attempt to translate into English. Although they cannot be classed as bilingual legal dictionaries, they are nevertheless aids in understanding a foreign legal text.

BIOGRAPHICAL SOURCES

Historical

General

Many lawyers appear in the *Dictionary of National Biography*. Its entries are long in comparison with the legal biographical dictionaries, but sometimes inaccurate on matters of detail, such as dates of admission or call for barristers. The entries end with references to sources and further biographies and are signed. A supplementary source of biographical information for those who died between 1851 and 1900 and are excluded from the *Dictionary of National Biography* is Boase, F. *Modern English Biography*, 1892–1921. Its subjects, chosen from a wider but lower section of society, are nevertheless notable or interesting people. A quick reference source, particularly useful for a person's official appointments, is *Who Was Who*.

Oxford and Cambridge were the only universities in England until the early nineteenth century. Their teaching of law was confined to the civil law until the 1850s, except for a short period when Blackstone gave his lectures at Oxford from 1753 to 1765. Thus the dictionaries of students at Oxford and Cambridge include only civilians up to 1850, but of course many students who subsequently became lawyers read other subjects. Oxford is covered by Emden, A. B. *A Biographical Register of the University of Oxford to AD 1500*, 1957, and a second volume for 1500–41 published in 1973; and Foster, J. *Alumni Oxonienses: the members of the University of Oxford, 1500–1714*, and a second series for 1715–1886. Emden's works, although relating to the earlier period, contain more information than Foster's. For Cambridge, Emden has prepared a similar *Biographical Register of the University of Cambridge to 1500*, 1963, and the later years are covered by Venn, J. *Alumni Cantabrigienses: a biographical list of all known students, graduates and holders of office . . . from the earliest times to 1900*, 1922–54. All give information on academic and subsequent careers quoting sources for the statements.

Biographical material in the form of books, essays or articles can be traced through the normal bibliographical tools. For articles, the heading 'biography' in the *Index to Legal Periodicals* is useful. *Biography Index* includes books, essays and extracts from newspapers as well as periodical articles. With both of these the bias is towards Americans and American publications, but items on British lawyers are included.

England

The historical biographical sources of information about lawyers, other than general sources, emanate almost entirely from the professional bodies.

The Inns of Court, which have been in existence since the fifteenth and sixteenth centuries, maintain, and have published, registers of their students. Foster, J. *The Register of admissions to*

Gray's Inn 1521–1889, 1889, and *Students admitted to the Inner Temple 1547–1660*, 1877, were both privately printed. For the other two Inns there are *Admission from AD 1420 to AD 1893*, 1896, for Lincoln's Inn, and Sturgess, H. A. C. *Register of admission to the Honourable Society of the Middle Temple from the fifteenth century to the year 1944*, 1949. All these lists are arranged in chronological order of admission. The amount of information varies, but generally only the student's name appears during the early period. Later, parents and place of origin were added. Several of the registers have been selectively annotated for publication with details of subsequent offices held and date of death.

More biographical information has been published by the Inner and Middle Temples about their prominent members. In addition to the type of information in the admission registers, further details of Benchers' legal careers can be found in *Masters of the Bench of the Honourable Society of the Inner Temple 1450–1883*, 1883, and its two supplements for the periods 1883–1900 and 1901–18. Although these books are arranged chronologically, the second supplement contains an alphabetical index to the three volumes. The Middle Temple has published two works with a large amount of biographical information about its members. The *Middle Temple Bench Book*, 2nd edition, 1937, is a chronological list with biographical notes of the Middle Temple Benchers from 1463–1937. It also has a list of all Masters of the Temple since the Reformation. By far the most detailed biographical source for any of the four Inns is Hutchinson, J. *A Catalogue of Notable Middle Templars*, 1922. It is the first source so far discussed to be arranged alphabetically. The entries, mostly taken from other published sources, cover career at the bar, on the bench, or in other walks of life, and the subject's publications. It includes such Middle Templars from 1501–1901 'as have been considered deserving of a place of record in any standard work of British biography' or who have achieved prominence in the 'British North American colonies'.

Several sources cover lawyers generally and those who have attained high judicial office in particular. Foster, J. *Men-at-the-Bar*, 1885, is an alphabetically arranged dictionary of 7000–8000 barristers alive in 1885. It gives extensive information on their lives and careers and, as in Hutchinson's book, includes those whose subsequent careers have not been in the law.

For the identification of judges a useful source is Foss, E. *Tabulae Curiales*, 1865. It shows the rank attained and the reign during which office was held since 1066. A separate regnal list shows the judges who sat in each court. In the biographical dictionary field, Foss, E. *Biographia Juridica*, 1870, includes all the judges of England from 1066 to 1870. His other biographical work, *The Judges of England*, 1848–64, is praised by Holdsworth for its 'solid quality of learning and accuracy', in contrast with the biographical works for the same period by Lord Campbell. Besides narrating the lives of the judges he also lists serjeants and QCs for the period.

Three different works collectively cover biographical sources for Lord Chancellors from 1066 to 1940. Campbell J. *The Lives of the Lord Chancellors*, 1845–69, takes them from 1066 to George IV's reign. Various sources note that, while readable, Campbell's work cannot be relied upon, but Heuston records his admiration for the work as a whole and only faults the later volumes. The history of the Lord Chancellors is continued in Atlay, J. B. *The Victorian Chancellors*, 1906–8, which covers Lords Lyndhurst to Herschell. Heuston, R. F. V. *Lives of the Lord Chancellors 1885–1940*, 1964, commences with Lords Halsbury and Herschell, who were included in the previous work, and finishes with Lord Caldecote. The last two works give a straightforward narrative account of the lives and careers of the Lord Chancellors with some assessment, against their political and legal backgrounds.

Scotland

In Scotland several of the professional societies have published their histories, which include some biographical information about their members. Grant, Sir F. J. *The Faculty of Advocates in Scotland 1532–1943*, 1944, and *The Society of Writers to His Majesty's Signet*, 1936, attempt to list all their members with genealogical and biographical notes.

Several books deal with Scottish lawyers who have held office. Omond, G. W. T. *The Lord Advocates of Scotland*, 1883 and 1914, gives 'historical sketches . . . , rather than a series of complete "lives", to trace the history of the office' from 1483 to 1880. For the judiciary, a biographical dictionary arranged in chronological order is available in Brunton, G. and Haig, D. *An Historical Account of the Senators of the College of Justice, from its Institution in MDXXXII,* 1849. The introduction relates its establishment and the development of the offices of Lord Chancellor, Lord President and the judges of the Court of Session. The biographical entries, of varying length, cover family, offices and political career. The lives of the Lord Chancellors from 1124 to 1708 are narrated, with reference to sources, in Cowan, S. *The Lord Chancellors of Scotland,* 1911, which has some assessment of the careers of the later ones. These sources emphasize the political more than the legal activities of their subjects.

Ireland

There are no biographical dictionaries of the Irish judiciary, but several collected biographies have been published. Ball, F. *The Judges in Ireland 1221–1921,* 1927, makes an original approach and is nearest in form to a biographical dictionary. The chapters deal with legal developments, but each group of chapters is followed by chronological lists and a catalogue of the judges of that period. The catalogue contains the type of information usually found in biographical dictionaries. Two works deal with the Irish Lord Chancellors, Burke, O. J. *The History of the Lord Chancellors of Ireland from AD 1186 to AD 1874,* 1879, and O'Flanagan, J. *The Lives of the Lord Chancellors,* 1870. Both are arranged chronologically and the latter has references to original sources, as well as quoting from them and from contemporaries of those whose lives he narrates.

Current

Legal practitioners

Legal practitioners in England and Wales are listed in the annual *Law List.* All the judicial officers from the House of Lords to coroners appear in the first section. There is no information about previous careers, but dates of appointment are given for some classes of judges. There is no alphabetical list of judges from all courts. The barristers' section is divided into several lists: QCs in alphabetical order showing the year of appointment and whether they are practising in England and Wales or not; barristers in an alphabetical sequence; lists of counsels' chambers for London and the provinces, with members of each chambers; circuit bar lists; and the Northern Ireland bar. The most recently appointed QCs appear at the front of the *Law List*, not in the main lists. The most informative is the alphabetical list of barristers. It shows all practising barristers, their qualifications, participation in the legal aid scheme, Inn and date of call, address and telephone number of chambers or office, circuit, and some oddments of information, usually about membership of overseas bars or legal appointments. Barristers not in practice may be included on request and their names are printed in italics.

Only those solicitors with current practising certificates are in the solicitors' section of the *Law List*. It is divided into several sequences to facilitate various approaches. The two principal lists are of firms in London arranged by postal address, and outside London arranged alphabetically by town. The entries give the names of the solicitors employed by the firm, its address, telephone and telex number. There are ancillary alphabetical lists of solicitors in London and outside London. Entries merely give an address sufficient for the employer to be traced in the main lists, where the solicitor will appear with such details as membership of the Law Society and any appointments he may hold.

The legal executives' section lists those members who are fellows of the Institute of Legal Executives. The only information about them is where and by whom they are employed.

Most of this information is repeated in the *Solicitor's Diary and Directory*, which is published in November and based on the *Law List* for the previous May, so that it is less up-to-date.

Scottish legal practitioners are listed similarly in the *Scottish Law Directory*. The solicitors' list, like the English one, is of certificated practitioners and is also classified by town with alphabetical lists of solicitors and of firms.

Judges, barristers and solicitors of Eire with solicitors for Northern Ireland are listed in the *Law Directory and Diary* published annually by the Incorporated Law Society of Ireland. Northern Ireland barristers are in the *Law List*;

Northern Ireland judges, barristers and solicitors are listed in small sections in the *Handbook of the Incorporated Law Society of Northern Ireland*, 1959. This is a loose-leaf publication with supplements, but unfortunately these are published infrequently, so that the lists are not up-to-date.

The legal profession of the Isle of Man consists of the judge of appeal, the deemsters, and the advocates of the Manx bar, who act both as barristers and solicitors. All appear in the *Law List* and the *Solicitors' Diary and Directory*.

The judges, advocates and solicitors of the Channel Islands and their London agents can also be found in the *Law List* in the international section, although not in the *Solicitors' Diary and Directory*.

Academic lawyers

Academic lawyers in the British Isles teach in universities and polytechnics. Many are barristers or solicitors, although this is not essential. If barristers, they may be listed in the appropriate professional directory; those who are solicitors are only listed if they hold current practising certificates. All academic staff are listed in the calendar of the university or polytechnic in which they teach. The amount of personal information in these calendars varies, but subjects taught and works published may be shown.

There are two associations to which academic lawyers may belong, the Society of Public Teachers of Law and the Association of Law Teachers, which cater for university and polytechnic teachers respectively. They both publish, for private circulation only, directories of their members with information on their qualifications, careers, teaching interests, and publications. The Society of Public Teachers of Law *Directory of Members* is published annually and also has a long list of associate members teaching overseas. The Association of Law Teachers *Directory of Members* is published occasionally and has less detail in its entries. Both directories list the officers of the associations.

For 1973–4 a new directory was published entitled the *Academic Who's Who*, which attempts to include all university teachers throughout the British Isles who have more than five years' teaching experience. The entries are based on returns to a questionnaire which sought similar information to that included in the *Directory of Members* of the SPTL. The *Academic Who's Who* does not attain complete coverage of all academic lawyers within its terms of reference. It appears in alternate years.

Others

Besides practice and teaching, many lawyers work in other fields, for example, central and local government, Parliament and industry. Several directories for these bodies include the legal staff. Civil service lawyers are listed under department or ministry in a section of the *Law List*. The senior grades are included in the *Civil Service Year Book*, the successor to the *British Imperial Calendar and Civil Service List*. It covers government departments in England and Wales, Scotland and Northern Ireland. Where the *British Imperial Calendar* concentrated on listing all civil servants above a certain grade, the *Civil Service Year Book* is more concerned to tabulate the structure and functions of the civil service and only gives the name of the senior person in charge of each function with an address and telephone enquiry number. Thus more information is given on the scope of the legal departments and less about their staff.

Only the chief legal officers in local government appear in such directories as the *Municipal Year Book*. From 1974 the *Law List* includes local authorities and nationalized industries with their legal employees in its lists of legal firms.

Lawyers who sit in Parliament are listed in the general directories of members, *Vacher's Parliamentary Companion*, and *Dod's Parliamentary Companion*. Vacher is merely a list of names, but Dod gives some biographical information including parliamentary career.

The general sources for current information about people, such as *Who's Who* and *Who's who, what's what and where in Ireland, 1973*, should not be overlooked. The latter is partly a biographical dictionary including entries for over 200 Irish lawyers from both Northern Ireland and Eire.

Foreign lawyers

Several directories are published in this country which include foreign lawyers. They are all selective and the only source for complete information about foreign legal practitioners is the directory for the country.

Kime's International Law List, Butterworth's Law List Commonwealth and International, and the *International Law List* have similar entries. They generally show the partners in a firm, their address, cable address, telephone and telex number. Often the languages in which the firm corresponds and the names of London agents are included. Several of the British directories already discussed have international sections of foreign lawyers and of British lawyers with a knowledge of foreign law.

ORGANIZATIONS

Courts

The same sources for England and Wales, Scotland and Ireland that list legal practitioners also list courts and officials, usually following the list of judges for each court. However, for England and Wales a directory solely concerned with courts is *Shaw's Directory of Courts in England and Wales.* It overlaps and complements the court information in the *Law List.* The *Law List* includes special courts such as the ecclesiastical courts, not found in *Shaw's Directory.* But *Shaw's Directory* has more information about crown, county and magistrates' courts, especially the names of judges, jurisdictions, days and times of sittings, court officers' addresses and telephone numbers. Although some of this information is in the *Law List, Shaw's Directory* brings together most of the factual information one might require about the major courts.

The judges and court officials of Scotland are listed in the *Scottish Law Directory* and volume 1 of the *Parliament House Book,* although the arrangement in the two books differs. The *Scottish Law Directory* gives the dates of circuit sittings of the High Court of Justiciary and the *Parliament House Book,* the sheriff court days.

Additional information about jurisdictional areas of courts is provided by Ordnance Survey maps and two indexes published by the Lord Chancellor's Department. The Ordnance Survey publishes a series showing Petty Sessional Areas in England and Wales on the scale 1 :100,000 superimposed on the administrative area series. A separate map for the London Metropolitan Police District outlines local government areas in red and judicial areas in blue. For London, there is also the *London County Courts Directory*, 9th edition, 1971, which lists in alphabetical order streets in the London postal area, giving the county court district in which they fall. A similar index of places, *County Court Districts (England and Wales)*, 11th edition, 1971, shows the county court districts and divisions into which any place in England and Wales falls.

Associations

There are many organizations of, or for, lawyers, or connected with the law. Some are official bodies, others, voluntary associations. They range from those connected with the legal profession, such as the Inns of Court, or formed for some general purpose, such as the International Bar Association, to those having a limited function, like the College of Law, the Howard League for Penal Reform or the Criminal Injuries Compensation Board. There are also many associations whose purpose is related to some aspect of law, such as the Association of Official Shorthand Writers.

Many are listed in the law lists already mentioned, in *Who's Who, what's what and where in Ireland*, 1973, and in the *Lawyer's Remembrancer*, which is valuable for the addresses of Law Society area secretaries for legal aid areas. Many voluntary associations, but not public offices or educational establishments, are listed in the *Directory of British Associations and Associations in Ireland*, Edition 4, 1973–4. Considerably more information is given than appears in the previous sources. The entries include the date of foundation of the association, its address, purpose, membership, annual conference and other meetings, and publications, with price and frequency.

Law libraries and librarians

Two problems arise for the potential user of a law library. The first is to locate specialized collections; and the other is to obtain admission to a library, as many leading law libraries belong to private societies.

The Library Association has published several regional guides to library resources in England and Wales and the Scottish Library Association has a similar guide for Scotland. The guides give the address, admission regulations and subject coverage of the libraries in the region and have detailed subject indexes through which not only the general legal library but also the specialized subject collection can be traced. These guides have the advantage of enabling the enquirer to conduct his search on an area basis, unlike *Aslib Directory*, whose law section is arranged alphabetically by town. A projected directory of British law libraries by the British and Irish Association of Law Librarians should achieve a wider coverage than the general guides.

The practice and study of law is increasingly international and information on overseas library resources may be needed. International Association of Law Libraries: *European Law Libraries Guide*, 1971, with its coverage of 522 of the major law libraries in eighteen countries is a starting point for tracing specialized collections. It follows the usual pattern of library directories in giving address, size, facilities and specializations.

Associations of law librarians have already been described in Chapter 1. Most associations publish a list of members and their official addresses. For this country the most important are the British and Irish Association of Law Librarians and the International Association of Law Libraries. The former publishes its membership list as one of the documents for its annual conference and the latter last published its list of members in *IALL Bulletin*, no. 29/30, 1972, pp. 59–79. Both associations keep the information up to date by membership news columns in their journals. Many British law librarians are members of the appropriate national Library Association and thus appear with their qualifications, posts and official addresses in the *Library Association Year Book*. Substantially more biographical information about selected librarians in libraries throughout the British Isles appears in *Who's Who in Librarianship and Information Science*, 2nd edition, 1972.

FURTHER READING

GENERAL

Daintree, D. Bibliographical aids and other reference works, encyclopedias, practice books, principle treatises. *International Association of Law Libraries Bulletin*, no. 28, 1968, pp. 10–27.

Lewis, P. R. *The Literature of the Social Sciences*. Library Association, 1960, pp. 142–63.

Walford, A. J. *Guide to Reference Material*. Volume 2: Social and historical sciences, philosophy and religion. 3rd edition. Library Association, 1975, pp. 180–213 (ISBN 0 85365 088 8).

Winchell, C. M. *Guide to Reference Books*. 8th edition. Chicago, American Library Association, 1967, pp. 429–41 (ISBN 0 8389 0034 8).

BIBLIOGRAPHIES

Collison, R. L. *Bibliographies: subject and national*. 3rd edition. Crosby Lockwood, 1968 (ISBN 0 258 96515 0) pp. 31–6.

Friend, W. L. *Anglo-American Legal Bibliographies*. Washington, D.C., Library of Congress, 1944.

Friend, W. L. Survey of Anglo-American Legal Bibliography. *Law Library Journal*, vol. 33, no. 1, 1940, pp. 1–18.

Logan, R. G. Bibliographical Guides to Early British Law Books. *Law Librarian*, vol. 4, no. 1, 1973, pp. 9–12.

Marke, J. J. Legal Literature. *Library Trends*, vol. 11, no. 3, 1963, pp. 244–58.

Price, M. O. Anglo-American Law. *Library Trends*, vol. 15, no. 4, 1967, pp. 616–27.

Way, D. J. Book Selection. *Law Librarian*, vol. 4, no. 2, 1973, pp. 25–7.

DICTIONARIES

Alness, Lord. Brocards. *In* Stair Society. *An introductory survey of the sources and literature of Scots law*. Edinburgh, Stair Society, 1936, pp. 282–8.

Cowley, J. D. *A bibliography of abridgments, digests, dictionaries and indexes of English law to the year 1800*. Quaritch, 1932, pp. lxxix–xciii.

Hicks, F. C. *Materials and Methods of Legal Research*. 3rd edition. Rochester, New York, Lawyers' Co-operative Publishing Co., 1942, pp. 244–9.

Holdsworth, Sir W. S. *History of English Law*. Various editions. Methuen, 1936–72. 17 volumes.

Sweet and Maxwell Ltd. *A Legal Bibliography of the British Commonwealth of Nations*. Sweet and Maxwell, 1955–64. 7 vols., see especially volumes 1, 2 and 5.

A bibliography on foreign and comparative law books and articles in English. Dobbs Ferry, New York, Oceana for the Parker School of Foreign and Comparative Law, 1955– (ISSN US 0067-7329).

Part III   Law Library Practice

11. Law Library Practice: General Principles

ELIZABETH M. MOYS, BA, FLA
Librarian, University of London Goldsmiths' College

This introductory chapter to the section of the volume dealing with law library practice covers policy and general administration. It could have been entitled 'What the chief librarian does', if it were not that in many law libraries the same individual is chief librarian and everything else. Most of the general administrative matters are common to a wide range of libraries. They are outlined here for the use of librarians in charge of small or medium-sized libraries, because practical information about library committees, estimates, etc., is not readily available elsewhere.

POLICY AND PLANNING

Function

The first necessity for the law librarian is to have a firm grasp of the reasons for the existence of his library and the policy he should endeavour to follow for both the immediate and the distant future. This should present little difficulty in a new library, but it sometimes happens that a long-established library has been allowed to develop from year to year with no clear statement of policy denoting the directions in which the library should be developing. The governing body may have been content to let matters drift to the point where the initial reason for the library's existence has been obscured.

Whatever the present situation may be, a sound basic policy for future expansion is essential. Every aspect of the library's purpose, function and services should be examined. For a sample policy statement, see page 444.

Services

One of the first considerations in planning a library service is the type of reader to be served. A public library must admit the general public, whereas a private society may limit admission strictly to its own members. Between these extremes, there are many possible policies. For example, most academic libraries admit members of other academic or research institutions, on proof of membership, on a broadly reciprocal basis. Libraries must frequently cater for several levels of user: undergraduate, postgraduate, academic, administrative, clerical and so on, each of whom has different information needs.

Few law libraries lend books on a large scale, as the major proportion of their stock consists of continuing series and there is a grave danger of the sets becoming defective. Not only do many issues of serials go out of print quickly, but also some multi-volume encyclopedic works can be purchased only as complete sets. Some libraries, including many of those serving professional associations, are private libraries, specifically constituted as reference libraries, and are therefore unable to lend books under any circumstances. The library of a firm of solicitors is likely to lend to members and employees but to no one else. Some libraries used by students allow borrowing of treatises, but not of primary materials. It is an almost invariable rule that volumes of legislation and law reports may never be removed from the library, with the occasional exception of their production in court or temporary removal for photocopying. The occasion, some years ago, when a volume of Tasmanian law reports was sent from a London academic library to a court in Cyprus by diplomatic bag, was an outstanding exception to this rule.

Purchasing policy in government departments is to provide multiple copies of basic treatises and particularly those on the special subjects covered by the various departments. As copies are held permanently in the offices of the officials concerned, the demand for loans is reduced.

Further discussion of admission and loan policies, and other services that may be provided by a law library appears on pages 447–51.

Centralization or decentralization

In large organizations, especially universities, the question of decentralization may arise. Most librarians, being largely divorced from the turmoil of departmental teaching problems and inter-departmental rivalries, see very clearly the educational advantages of a large central library to which all students may come. This provides an opportunity for some degree of cultural cross-fertilization. How much 'culture' actually rubs off on an engineer or how much scientific background is gained by a law student who strays from his usual route through the stacks is debatable, but at least a large central library offers more opportunities for broadening horizons than a series of faculty or departmental libraries.

On the other hand, the teacher (and frequently the student too) wants 'his' material close at hand for classes, moot rooms, laboratories, etc. The Wilson report on legal education revealed that 'three out of four law teachers are in favour of a separate law library under Faculty control in a self-contained Faculty building' (JSPTL, volume 9, 1966, p. 36). This opinion cannot be ignored, but in some of the newer universities, general academic opinion is in favour of a central library with few, if any, decentralized service points.

A forceful argument against decentralization is the increasingly interdisciplinary nature of law teaching. For example, students of criminology, sociology of law, jurisprudence and legal history all have to use non-legal texts as well as legal ones. In the reverse direction, legal texts may well be needed by historians, sociologists, economists, accountants and others. There is also the economic factor: a central library requires a smaller number of duplicate copies of frequently used volumes or basic reference works than the total number required by several faculty or departmental libraries.

In other organizations the predominant need is for instant information. Lawyers in a large government department, for example, may be scattered in several buildings, and small groups may be accommodated adjacent to the administrators they are to advise. The supply of basic treatises to individual offices has already been mentioned on page 420, but lawyers still need quick access to the primary materials in a library.

They cannot be expected to make a journey of anything up to half an hour for each consultation. Therefore, the ministry librarian must set up as many branch law libraries as are justified by the existence of scattered groups of lawyers, with the consequent duplication of primary materials, journals, etc.

Access to the books

Another basic question in planning a library service is the extent to which the books should be freely accessible to all readers. In most of the English-speaking world, open access is the general rule, with special collections of rare books, incunabula or manuscripts being available only on special application. Open access has the advantage that readers who know their way about the library can serve themselves for a good proportion of the time, leaving the library staff free to deal with the more difficult enquiries. Readers who are not in a hurry can also, in theory, browse along the shelves, finding new material to interest them.

On the other hand, open access requires a rational order among the books (see Chapter 15) which in turn requires more shelf-space than an arbitrary fixed location system, based on the sizes of the volumes (see also page 605). It also means that a little more time must be spent in producing shelf labels, notices, plans, printed guides, etc. (see page 460).

A modified form of closed access may be needed for a limited number of heavily used books, especially in academic libraries (see page 450).

Whichever methods of arrangement are used, good catalogues are essential (see Chapter 14).

GOVERNMENT

Most libraries operate under some form of committee government. A small law library probably comes directly under a general committee of the parent body (local law society, etc.), while a large law library, such as that of one of the Inns of Court, is likely to have a special library committee. Law libraries that are contained within large general libraries, such as those of universities or borough libraries, usually come under the central library committee of the university or local authority. The libraries of government departments do not normally function under a library committee, but under the usual civil service chain of command. The librarian reports to a senior administrator, who includes the library among several responsibilities. The Law Commission Library, which does have a committee, is an exception.

The conduct of individual readers is governed by the rules and regulations of the library, which are usually promulgated by the library committee.

Committees

The membership and powers of the library committee are matters over which the librarian rarely has much influence. In some cases, notably in public libraries, these matters are governed by legislation and, in others, such as universities and professional associations, by the constitution of the individual organization.

Membership

A university library committee used to be primarily a 'consumer body', made up largely of academic staff. More recently a student user element has been added. The University Librarian has usually been a full member and there is now a welcome trend towards greater 'worker representation': other members of the library staff, elected by their fellows. The users usually represent large groups, such as faculties. It is therefore probable that the Law Faculty will have one or two members only, and that the Law Librarian will have to convince the University Librarian of his case for or against a particular proposal, rather than having direct access to the University Library Committee himself. If there is a Law Faculty Library Committee, the Law Librarian should be a full member, and must be if he is to perform his functions properly.

Unfortunately, a professional association tends to be less willing than an academic body to give due recognition to the professional status of its library staff, for the chief librarian is rarely granted full membership of the library committee. In this respect, some firms of solicitors seem to have a better record. This type of inter-professional non-recognition, which is not confined to lawyers, and which is a result of administrative and social history, can arouse resentment on the part of the librarian who is highly qualified by reason of years of training and experience, and who may well be a nationally or internationally distinguished member of his profession and a scholar in his own right.

Functions and powers

One of the most important functions of any library committee is to act as a two-way channel of communication between the library users and the library staff. The committee of an academic library, for example, can plan the acquisitions policy needed to cope with changes in the syllabus, and every committee may have to deal with disciplinary matters and problems of security.

In general, a library committee's powers should, if legally possible, be confined to establishing broad lines of policy, making regulations, setting the amount of charges and fines, and *advising* the librarian on any other matter he brings before it. Committee members are usually busy people, and should not burden themselves with the minutiae of daily affairs. The librarian is employed to administer the library, within the policy framework established by the library committee, but cannot do so satisfactorily if he is subject to constant interference by the committee in matters which should not be its concern.

As an example of the problems that can arise: some committees of professional society libraries tend to keep such close control over book selection that the librarian finds difficulty in purchasing urgently needed new treatises between committee meetings. In such cases, it is highly desirable that discretion should be given to the librarian to make purchases valued up to a specified amount, without prior reference to the committee, and report them to the next meeting.

Complaints and suggestions, whether from committee members or others, should always be discussed with the librarian before being brought up at a committee meeting. It is both unjust and discourteous to the librarian for complaints or proposals, serious or trivial, to be raised for the first time during a committee meeting, thus giving him no opportunity to investigate and make an accurate reply. Many complaints either involve relatively minor errors (such as the misfiling of a card) which can be put right quickly by administrative action, or arise from misunderstandings which can be corrected with tact. Similarly, some proposals may seem ideal in theory but prove unworkable in practice. The committee's time is best reserved for matters involving new principles, such as problems arising from applications from Open University students for facilities that have not hitherto been available to them.

The committee secretary

Whether he is a voting member of the committee or not, the librarian will almost certainly be expected to act as committee secretary. He should maintain close liaison with the committee chairman, discussing the agenda with him in advance, and pointing out the items of greatest importance, including those where a decision is essential before a certain date. The secretary usually writes letters on behalf of the committee, but in some organizations it is traditional for the chairman to sign the more important letters.

It is always easier for a committee to make informed decisions if it has a memorandum before it, preferably circulated in advance with the agenda. Committee memoranda, and other supporting papers, should be written objectively, setting out all sides of the argument. Having done that conscientiously, the librarian may be allowed to indicate his own preference, but if in doubt about the propriety of doing so, he should consult the chairman.

A draft of the minutes should be written as soon as possible, certainly not more than a day or two after the meeting, before the details can fade from memory. It is better to begin with a detailed draft, gradually paring it down to the final text, rather than to try to work in the reverse direction. It is quite common for the librarian to show the final draft to the chairman before sending out official copies to the bulk of the members. The need for later amendments can usually be avoided in this way.

Regulations

Every library needs a clear and unambiguous code of regulations governing matters such as: admissions, loans, general discipline (*eg*, prohibition of smoking, bringing in bags, etc.), charges for photocopying or other services, and penalties for the breach of these regulations. Where substantial penalties are allowed, such as exclusion from the library, an appeal procedure must be formulated. If an appeal is made against a disciplinary decision, the librarian must, of course, be scrupulous in referring the appeal to higher authority.

It is advisable that governing regulations should be promulgated by the library committee. The librarian can find himself in embarrassing situations if he is (or is thought to be) both legislator and policeman. The committee, being both representative of wider interests and relatively anonymous, can wield more power and, if necessary, bear any opprobrium better than a single administrator.

Further consideration of library regulations is to be found on page 451.

FINANCE

The sources of library finance vary. A professional library will be financed largely from the general funds of, or subscriptions of the members to, the parent organization, together with income from any investments that may be earmarked for library purposes. These funds will almost always be private. Academic, public and government libraries are financed almost entirely from public funds, *ie*, taxation, central or local. Both may be liable to fluctuations, but tax-supported libraries are particularly vulnerable to cuts in public expenditure.

Occasionally, a library may be fortunate enough to receive unsolicited monetary gifts, though gifts in kind are more usual. Certain problems that may be involved in the receipt of gifts of books are discussed on page 488. It may be desirable to make an appeal to the members, or to a wider public, for funds to bring about a specially important development, such as the purchase of land for a new building. The chief librarian should endeavour to ensure that monetary gifts are made directly to the library rather than to the general funds of the parent organization.

Estimates

The librarian is usually expected to produce estimates for the cost of running the service, either on an annual or a quinquennial basis. The details of the estimating procedure will be laid down by the body served, but the main areas of expenditure that may have to be covered are:

books, periodicals and binding
consumable materials (*eg*, stationery, library forms, catalogue cards, printed publicity)
durable materials (*eg*, shelves, furniture, photocopying machines, microform readers)
building maintenance (*eg*, rent, rates, decoration, cleaning, security patrols)
staff salaries
capital expenditure (new buildings or major alterations)
insurance

Not every librarian will have to cover all of these.

Since a very high proportion of the stock of a law library is made up of serial publications, the subscriptions for which are rising even more rapidly than book prices, special care must be taken not to underestimate future costs. Some assistance can be gained from the lists of average prices published regularly in the *Library Association Record* and *The Bookseller*. If these figures are used, they must be interpreted with great care, as they may include or exclude certain types of material, such as pamphlets and law reports. It is probably more reliable to draw up lists of costs of a representative sample of the actual materials held. A librarian who has to buy a fair proportion of second-hand material can obtain help in estimating from second-hand catalogues or publications such as *Book Auction Records*.

Costs of stationery, printing, furniture and equipment can be gauged from suppliers' price lists. Most firms, hoping for a possible future sale, are happy to provide quotations or additional information.

Staff estimates must include, in addition to salaries, the

employer's contributions to National Insurance and super-annuation, holiday or other bonuses and any payroll-type of tax (such as the extinct SET) that may be in force, and any threshold agreement or other automatic increases that may be incurred.

Accounts records

Systems of handling invoices and payments vary according to the practice of individual organizations. The most likely procedure is that the librarian certifies invoices as correct and passes them to the central financial officer (chief accountant, bursar, etc.), who usually prefers to receive them in regular batches, often with a covering form setting out the fund numbers involved. The central office prepares and despatches cheques and keeps the official account records. For a large library, it is highly desirable that there should be regular meetings between the librarian and the chief accountant, or their representatives, to reconcile their records. It is very helpful if regular itemized statements are produced and sent to the library by the accounts office.

Whatever the system for despatching payments may be, every library, however small, must maintain its own detailed records of expenditure on books, serial publications and binding. An independent law library will do this for itself but, in some organizations, such as universities, the law library's ordering and accounting is likely to be performed by the central acquisitions department, with special columns set aside for legal items. The law librarian can expect to receive regular statements of account to enable him to guide the rate of ordering. However, he would be well advised to keep at least his own records of commitments, especially for subscriptions to serial publications, including legislation and law reports.

If a breakdown of figures is required, either by form (*eg*, law reports, journals, treatises) or by subject (*eg*, United Kingdom, Commonwealth, United States, international law) a printed analysis book with the appropriate number of columns should be used. Considerable staff time and temper may be saved by the use of an adding machine, which will also facilitate the production of frequent, perhaps monthly, statements of expenditure, thus easing the problems of keeping proper control over both the actual total and the monthly rate of expenditure.

Suppliers' statements of account should be checked against the library's account books. Any apparent discrepancies should be referred immediately to the supplier or the accounts office, as appropriate. If this is not done, the library may later receive urgent reminders or even final demands for sums that are not due.

Petty cash

The library should have a small petty cash float, for purposes such as postage (libraries commonly generate mail after the central post-room has closed); refunds of postage on inter-library loans or material received by exchange; operating a coin-operated photocopying machine for office purposes; and other small items. An appropriate record of all expenses, together with receipts where possible, should be kept for the accountant's and auditors' inspection.

Audits

Annual auditing of financial records is conducted in most organizations, but the degree to which the library is affected depends on where the responsibility for official book-keeping rests. Local authority auditors examining library accounts may be assisted by Department of the Environment officials. Government supported libraries may expect to receive occasional visits from the Exchequer and Audit Department. Private organizations' accounts are usually checked by outside commercial auditors.

Auditors may require the production of stock records, loan statistics, information on the steps taken to recover missing books and general security arrangements.

Value added tax

United Kingdom

If the organization is in a position to reclaim them, separate records of VAT charges should be maintained. At present, the following are zero-rated: books, pamphlets, newspapers, journals, maps and all covers, binders, etc. supplied and charged with them. Taxable items include: industrial and architectural plans and drawings, stationery, microforms and their hardware. Also taxable are services, such as postage, telephone, telex, and binding of individual books. Periodical binding (using pattern boards) is zero-rated.

Local authorities may reclaim the payments made by their libraries, while libraries financed by the University Grants Committee are given extra consideration during the allocation of funds. Other libraries, depending on the status of their organizations, may find no way of recovering the tax. Libraries providing and charging for services such as photocopying will generally be required to add the tax to these charges, and must account for this to HM Customs and Excise, if their total intake exceeds £5,000 a year (*ie*, few law libraries are likely to be affected).

Republic of Ireland

Exemption is allowed only on books and papers imported for review or as authors' complimentary copies, and all such packages must be clearly marked. All other transactions are taxed upon importation at 5·26 per cent, and the charges must be paid by the importer on delivery, otherwise parcels are returned at once to the sender. Items liable to tax include: books, pamphlets, newspapers, periodicals, trade literature of eight pages or more, maps and globes. Stationery of all kinds is exempt.

Repayment may be claimed if the transaction is non-commercial, for example, books and documents received in free exchange from academic, literary and other bodies; textbooks supplied free of charge to educational authorities; publications on loan for study or research; reports and supplements issued free of charge by learned bodies; books temporarily imported by library subscribers; free documentation relating to conferences. Claims for repayment, accompanied by full details and supporting evidence, should be made to the Revenue Commissioners in Dublin, from whom instructions and a guide may be obtained.

Discounts

Under the Net Book Agreement booksellers are not permitted to give discounts on new publications except under a library licence; or if the books have been in stock for more than a year and the publisher has refused to re-purchase them; or if the books were purchased second-hand and six months have elapsed since their original publication date.

Library licence

Any library which officially grants access, however limited, to the public, is entitled under the Net Book Agreement to apply for a library licence. This permits specified booksellers to give the library a discount, usually of 10 per cent, on net books. The librarian should obtain the booksellers' agreement in principle before applying to the Publishers' Association for the licence, naming the booksellers. A minimum of £100 should be spent with each supplier each year. Further booksellers may be added later, by written application to the PA, accompanied by the original licence. A notice must be prominently displayed, in or near the library entrance, inviting the public to enter and stating conditions for admission. Lists of libraries holding licences, by geographical areas, should also be exhibited in public libraries.

Libraries, educational or otherwise, which are privately owned and maintained, and any other libraries which do not or cannot permit public access, are not eligible for library licences.

Insurance

The librarian should ensure that both the fabric and the contents of the library are fully covered by insurance. An exception to this may be made for those government and local authority bodies where the cost of complete insurance would be higher than that of replacing actual losses. The chief accountant usually conducts the actual negotiations with the insurance company or brokers.

LIBRARY ADMINISTRATION

The chief librarian, whether of a one-man library or of a medium or large organization, is responsible to the authorities of his organization, to his readers and to his own staff for the proper running of the library. If he is to exercise this responsibility he must have the concomitant power and authority to do so. He should have, and be seen to have, a suitably high status within the organization. For example, he should be consulted in his own right before any changes are made that will affect the library, its services or its staff, and he should be the first person that any member of the organization considers when any bibliographic or information problem arises. Full use should be made of his knowledge and experience in skills ancillary to library work, such as publicity for a newly started journal or copyright deposit procedures for a professional handbook.

One principle that every librarian should remember is that no one is indispensable. Where there are several staff, the chief librarian must learn to delegate authority, especially when he is away from the library himself. One test of a good leader is that his organization can function quite well, on a day-to-day basis, without him. At all levels, it is highly desirable that at least two people should know how to perform any particular routine task. It can be disastrous, for example, if no one deals with the incoming serial publications for two or three weeks. In the same way, when the librarian is absent from a one-man library, for any reason, the library must shut down or risk disruption, unless arrangements have been made in advance for a relief librarian to be given at least an elementary training.

It is important that the law librarian should keep full records of his activities, decisions and plans. No one is completely safe from sudden illness or accident, and great difficulty will be experienced by the person taking over in an emergency if sufficient records are not available and their organization is not simple and clear. Various kinds of library records, and methods of maintaining them consistently, are discussed at appropriate points throughout this section of the volume.

Another factor, that may not be immediately obvious to a person who has not had a formal library school training, is that there is nearly always a choice of several good methods available for handling any library routine. For example, there are various alternative methods of recording loans to readers, each with its own group of advantages and disadvantages. In the abstract, it is impossible to say that any one of these is better than the others. Each librarian setting up or revising a lending service should examine a variety of issuing systems and decide for himself which best suits the circumstances of his particular library.

A general feature of specialist libraries is that they tend to grow. Sooner or later the informal methods, based on the close personal relationships and intimate atmosphere of a small library, become inadequate. It is then necessary to take a hard critical look at the library administration and amend the techniques used, or even substitute new ones. A larger library usually requires more formal arrangements. For example, additional forms may be needed for matters such as inter-library loans.

Internal organization

Large and medium-sized libraries have been traditionally arranged in departments based on library techniques: acquisitions, cataloguing, lending and reference. The first two are sometimes combined as technical services and the last two as readers' services. More recently in those university, polytechnic and public libraries that have appointed numbers of subject specialist librarians, subject divisions have taken over many of the functions previously covered by the technical departments. The most suitable areas for such treatment are : information and enquiry work, subject cataloguing and classification. Another function well suited to a subject specialist librarian is book selection, or at least advising both on new publications and on finding second-hand material. On the other hand, the actual ordering and accounting is best handled by a single central acquisitions department and it is usual to have a single service point for home loans in each library building.

Many law libraries, however, are administered by very few staff, each of whom carries responsibility for a variety of major duties. These librarians may thus enjoy a greater variety of tasks and gain fuller knowledge and experience in one post than their colleagues in larger organizations. On the other hand, in very small libraries, they may feel the lack of the stimulus that can be provided by working with other members of the library profession.

Personnel management

The chief librarian is responsible for ensuring that all members of staff are kept informed of developments, plans and decisions and are consulted, especially about the practical effects of all projected changes. In a small library, or a branch or department of a larger organization, it should be possible to hold occasional meetings of all the staff to pass information to them and to collect their opinions. The junior staff can often make very useful suggestions or constructive criticisms, based on their intimate knowledge of routine procedures and of readers' reactions to them. In a larger library, the chief librarian may be obliged by the needs of the service to restrict attendance at his staff meetings to senior staff or heads of departments, while in a very large library system, a staff bulletin may be found necessary. It is not possible to run a library by taking a vote on every problem, but a regular informal meeting, where each person feels that his opinion is taken into account before a decision is made, helps to maintain staff morale.

Once decisions have been taken on procedures and methods, they should be carried out consistently. Continuity of practice is a corner-stone of efficient library administration, and must be maintained by the succession of people who occupy each post. One of the best methods of ensuring consistency is the compilation and regular maintenance of a staff manual. This consists of written accounts, frequently illustrated with sample order forms, catalogue cards, etc., of all the regular routines in the library, in whatever degree of detail appears to be necessary. This applies to large and small libraries equally. The manual must be available for reference at any time, especially during the librarian's absence, and can be studied at greater length by new recruits, visiting library students, or temporary replacement librarians. In a large library, there may be a series of departmental manuals, rather than one large centralized volume.

Other personnel matters are discussed in Chapter 16.

Office organization

If the number of correspondence files is never likely to be large, they can be housed in a deep desk drawer fitted with runners to hold standard manilla filing pockets. Large collections should be kept in separate cabinets of filing drawers or in a lateral filing unit. All office furniture manufacturers make this type of equipment. The contents of the various files should be clearly indicated and a list of files, either in alphabetical order or arranged by a simple home-made classification (*eg*, booksellers, other libraries, staff matters, estimates, etc.) is helpful to a relief librarian or to the successor to a vacated post.

A policy decision should be taken regarding the normal period of time for the retention of letters and documents. This will depend, ultimately, upon the nature of their contents, since some matters, such as acquisition or possible disposal of materials, may be resurrected as much as twenty years later.

If regular information is required from users, a form is often the best method of obtaining the exact type and quantity of details needed. Forms may easily be filed for future reference and should always be as simple as circumstances permit. This does not necessarily mean that they should be as small as possible – a form that provides insufficient blank space for proper answers is tiresome to the reader and nearly useless to the librarian. Any experienced printer will be happy to advise on the design of printed forms, and an experienced typist should be trusted with the details of the layout of a form to be duplicated from typescript, once the objectives have been clearly explained.

In correspondence with booksellers, the librarian will often receive form letters, stating common situations, such as 'out of print' or 'not yet published'. In writing routine letters to firms, there is no objection to following the same principle and sending form letters, provided that full details of references, order numbers, invoice numbers, etc. are given. More important letters, however, may require meticulous drafting to ensure that no misunderstandings can arise. For example, a request to supply a costly item on approval, if not very clearly worded, could result in a demand for payment and refusal to accept return of goods 'ordered'.

Statistics

Library statistics are needed, both to tell the librarian what is actually happening, enabling him to take early note of new trends, and for use in reporting to the library's governing body and the general public. Figures can show not only the size and rate of growth of the book-stock, but also changes in costs, the growth of the catalogue, increases or decreases in the number of loans, inter-library loans, reservations, etc., changes in the number of people using the library at various times of the day, the volume of book losses, and rates of staff productivity. Among the uses of the information collected are: planning developments, including the need for additional shelving, catalogue drawers and so on; estimating insurance value and, in the event of a disaster, an insurance claim.

Collecting statistics need not be too burdensome if it is dealt with in frequent small doses. If the daily and weekly figures are cumulated regularly, the task of compiling statements for termly committee meetings or the annual report is less of a chore than adding long columns of figures at the last minute.

PUBLIC RELATIONS

No library can make adequate progress without financial and moral support from within its organization and, frequently, from outside as well. Good public relations are therefore an important consideration for the librarian. This is not a matter of advertising or high-powered publicity of the commercial/political variety, but rather of presenting facts in an interesting manner and of keeping the library in the public eye. In many ways the best form of publicity is good service, but this reaches only those people who already use the library. A good reputation is built up with difficulty and easily destroyed. One unfortunate incident can damage years of good and careful work.

The function of the library committee in public relations has been discussed on page 424. The committee is only one strand in the web of the library's relationships. Inside the parent organization are influential people: Benchers, professors, senior administrators, whose goodwill is needed for the promotion of costly new developments and, in a period of economic stringency, even for the finance needed to maintain existing services.

Publications

Library publications may take a variety of forms, both of content and method of production. Most publicly financed bodies and many private organizations are required to report to their public on their activities and expenditure. Libraries may also produce guides and bibliographical publications, such as accessions lists, subject bibliographies or catalogues.

Publications may be duplicated, photocopied or printed and bound. The production work may be carried out in the library or elsewhere in the organization, if the facilities are available. If the text is sufficiently important, it may be sent to a commercial printer. All library publications should be of high quality. It may seem expensive to use professional designers, but the resultant good impression may well justify the cost.

Most library publications are intended for circulation free of charge to staff, readers and possibly other librarians, but special bibliographies and catalogues may be produced for sale. It is not advisable to handle the sale of publications in the library, unless the parent organization possesses a professional sales department. Customers' orders may be incomplete or indecipherable, or bear a bewildering variety of complicated instructions for delivery and invoicing. Some prospective purchasers may consider that a telephone call or personal visit is sufficient and fail to supply a written order. Invoices must be made out and there may be different rates of discount to be allowed to members, booksellers or other categories of purchasers. The banking of remittances, especially if they come from several different foreign countries and in their local currencies, rather than sterling, causes further problems.

The considerable cost of running a sales organization must be taken into account when deciding whether to handle sales or to arrange for a commercial firm to publish the volume on the library's behalf. It should be remembered that complete and detailed records of all transactions will be **required** by the auditors.

Annual reports

An almost universal vehicle for discreet publicity is the library's annual report. Its primary purpose is to provide a factual record of the library's activities year by year, accompanied by statistics of the stock, loans, etc. The report is normally drafted by the librarian, adopted by the library committee and published, or passed to higher authority, as the committee's annual report. Consequently, the language of the report should be formal. Physical presentation of a law library report is also likely to be formal, although some illustrations may be included, especially if there has been a new building or extension during the year under review. It is usually acceptable for the committee's agreed policies or views on future problems to be aired, with a view to obtaining support, but the librarian should never use the annual report for giving his personal opinions.

Guides

Many libraries produce guides to their facilities. A guide written in simple language, well illustrated and attractively printed can be a good advertisement for the library, in addition to fulfilling its more obvious purpose. Library guiding and instruction is dealt with in more detail in Chapter 12.

Catalogues and bibliographies

The older law libraries, such as those of the Inns of Court, used to publish printed catalogues. Additions to stock are too rapid for this to be any longer a commercial proposition, but many libraries produce regular lists of newly acquired titles, usually in a duplicated typescript. A good up-to-date accessions list, especially from a library with specialist collections, can be very helpful to other libraries as a book selection tool, as well as keeping the library's own readers informed.

If the library compiles subject book-lists for individuals or groups, a file copy of each should be kept. Any of these lists may be useful later on as the basis for a new list, possibly for a wider public.

The compilation and use of union catalogues are discussed on pages 544 and 394 respectively. Occasionally, a union catalogue may be printed, as are those of the Institute of Advanced Legal Studies.

Exhibitions and displays

Publicity, in the form of posters, newspaper advertisements and circulars may be needed for any exhibitions and displays of library material that are mounted. Exhibitions themselves are a good form of publicity. For further discussion see page 461.

External relations

Most librarians enjoy showing visitors round and press on them copies of all available guides, book-lists and reports. Some libraries, particularly those of library schools, are delighted to receive other libraries' publications, which are used both as sources of information and as samples for study. The cultivation of good relations with library schools can also bring rewards when the library wishes to recruit good young professional staff, permanent or temporary. Library schools have also appreciated offers from some law libraries to receive either groups of students on organized visits or single students for field-work placings for about a month at a time.

Prospective visitors should be encouraged to make arrangements in advance, if possible, as unheralded arrivals can cause inconvenience and disappointment.

Librarians, in both their professional and personal capacities, should support their professional associations. These provide the opportunity for bringing librarians together to discuss aspects of their work and so provide a common pool of experience and knowledge in which all who are interested may share, for a deeper knowledge always comes from a free interchange of ideas. Individuals and libraries are both eligible for membership at the British and Irish Association of Law Librarians and of the International Association of Law Libraries, whose functions are described on pages 52–5.

Librarians should become acquainted with their local booksellers (whether ordering is done centrally or locally) whose expertise is at the library's disposal on request. The bookseller's service to the library is almost invariably improved with the establishment of personal contact and, in return, valuable assistance may be given by a librarian with specialist biblio-graphical knowledge.

Law publishers also value contacts with librarians. These can be furthered either with their travelling regional representatives or through attendance at BIALL conferences. A note or tele-phone call to head office is sure to produce a visit to the library. Additionally, law publishers value librarians' opinions of their publications and suggestions for fresh ventures.

LIBRARY CO-OPERATION

Librarians, by tradition and training are normally of a helpful disposition. At the same time, no library, however large and wealthy, can be self-sufficient. Both factors inevitably lead towards co-operation with other librarians. There is a network of formal and informal co-operation from which any library, large or small, general or special, can benefit, whether or not it is in a position to reciprocate. Any person, whether a 'librarian' in the professional sense or not, who is charged with looking after a law library, can ask for help and advice from the nearest large library service, public or university, or from any member of the BIALL. If the first librarian approached is not equipped to deal with a particular problem, he should be able to pass the enquiry to one who is. The addresses and telephone numbers of likely libraries can be found in the directories mentioned on page 414.

Library co-operation used to be thought of primarily in terms of inter-library loans (see pages 471–4). While the inter-lending system is being constantly extended and improved, there are several other areas of regular co-operation that may be relevant to a law library, such as: co-operative acquisitions, exchanges and storage (see pages 484–501); union catalogues (page 544); and mechanization projects (page 638).

LIBRARY RESEARCH

A list of major current library and information research projects is published annually in the LA's *Radicals Bulletin*. This does not include theses for Fellowship of the Library Association, though theses for higher degrees in librarianship are covered. Nor does it include work on bibliographies or union catalogues, or small informal projects being carried out in libraries. Details of LA thesis titles are published separately in the *Library Association Library and Information Bulletin*, from time to time.

Advice for librarians wishing to undertake research can be obtained from any of the library schools or from professional literature. Articles can be traced through *Library and Information Science Abstracts* or *Library Literature*.

FURTHER READING

GENERAL WORKS ON LIBRARY ADMINISTRATION

Handbook of Special Librarianship and Information Work. 4th edition. Aslib, 1975.
Astall, R. *Special Libraries and Information Bureaux.* Bingley, 1966.
Davinson, D. E. *Academic and Legal Deposit Libraries.* Bingley, 1965.
Smith, D. L. and Baxter, E. G. *College Library Administration in colleges of technology, art, commerce and further education.* Oxford University Press, 1965 (ISBN 0 19 859801 7).
Thompson, J. *An Introduction to University Library Administration.* 2nd edition. Bingley, 1974 (ISBN 0 85157 171 9).
Wilson, L. R. and Tauber, M. F. *University Library: the organization, administration and the functions of academic libraries.* 2nd edition. New York, Columbia University Press, 1956 (ISBN 0 231 02114 3).

LAW LIBRARY POLICY AND PLANNING

Bruno, J. M. Decentralization in academic libraries. *Library Trends,* vol. 19, 1971, pp. 311–17.
Price, M. O. The place of the law school library in library administration. *Journal of Legal Education,* vol. 13, 1960, pp. 230–8.
Ratcliffe, F. W. Problems of open access in large academic libraries. *Libri,* vol. 18, no. 2, 1968, pp. 95–111.
Roalfe, W. R. Centralized university library service and the law school. *Law Library Journal,* vol. 50, 1957, pp. 2–5.
Wilson, J. F. A survey of legal education in the United Kingdom. *Journal of the Society of Public Teachers of Law,* vol. 9, 1966, pp. 1–144.

GOVERNMENT

Corbett, E. V. *The Public Library and its Control*. Association of Assistant Librarians, 1962.

Guttsman, W. L. The government of university libraries in Britain. *Journal of Librarianship*, vol. 6, no. 3, July 1974, pp. 203–18.

Hewitt, A. R. *A summary of Public Library Law, England, Wales, Scotland and Northern Ireland*, 4th edition. Association of Assistant Librarians, 1965.

Stockham, K. A. *The Government and Control of Libraries*. Deutsch, 1968 (ISBN 0 233 96023 6).

FINANCE

Corbett, E. V. *Public Library Finance and Accountancy*. Library Association, 1960.

ADMINISTRATION

Finley, Elizabeth. *Manual of Procedures for Private Law Libraries*. Revised edition. South Hackensack, New Jersey, Rothman, 1966 (*AALL Publication series*, no. 8).

Jain, H. C. *Law Library Administration and Reference*. Delhi, Metropolitan Book Co., 1972.

Library Association. *Management for Librarians, based on a course of lectures . . . ed. J. Cloke*. Association of Assistant Librarians, 1968.

Lock, R. N. *Library Administration*. 3rd edition. Crosby Lockwood, 1973 (ISBN 0 258 96923 7).

Smith, G. C. K. and Schofield, J. L. Administrative effectiveness: times and costs of library operations. *Journal of Librarianship*, vol. 3, 1971, pp. 245–63.

Subject departmentalization

Crossley, C. A. The subject specialist librarian in an academic library. *Aslib Proceedings*, vol. 26, no. 6, June 1974, pp. 236–49.

Overington, M. A. *The subject departmentalized public library*. Library Association, 1969 (ISBN 0 85365 051 9).

Personnel management

Drucker, P. F. *The Practice of Management*. New edition. Pan Books, 1968 (ISBN 0 330 02031 5).

Newman, W. H. *Administrative Action*. 2nd edition. Pitman, 1964 (ISBN 0 273 40021 5).

PUBLIC RELATIONS

Angoff, A. *Public Relations for Libraries: essays in communications techniques.* Greenwood, 1973 (*Contributions in librarianship and information science,* no. 5) (ISBN 0 8371 6060 x).

Harrison, K. C. *Public Relations for Librarians.* Deutsch, 1973 (ISBN 0 233 95657 3).

Holman, W. R. *Library Publications.* San Francisco, Roger Beacham, 1965.

Raburn, J. Public relations for a special public. *Special Libraries,* vol. 60, 1969, pp. 647–50.

LIBRARY CO-OPERATION

Jefferson, G. *Library Co-operation.* Deutsch, 1966.

Vollans, R. *Library Co-operation in Great Britain.* National Central Library, 1952.

LIBRARY RESEARCH

Register of United Kingdom research in information science and librarianship. *Unesco Bulletin for Libraries,* vol. 28, no. 5, 1974, pp. 249–51.

12. Services for Readers

F. P. RICHARDSON, FLA
Librarian, The Law Society, London

F. P. RICHARDSON, FLA
Librarian, The Law Society, London

POLICIES AND FUNCTIONS

Fundamental to any definition of the purpose and function of a law library is the question of the range of its activities, in particular which jurisdictions it should endeavour to cover and with what degree of adequacy. The principles outlined on page 419 should be applied to produce a comprehensive statement, capable of expansion where necessary, within the framework of which the professional law librarian can be entrusted to develop and improve the quality of his library and all the various services it can offer to its readers.

The following definition of a statement of a law library's purpose and function can be taken as an illustration, in its simplest form. The words in square brackets give an indication of how the definition can be expanded or amended to enable it to cover almost any type of law library. The danger to be avoided is that the original statement should not be over explicit in the initial stage, thereby possibly excluding a vital expansion given a different set of circumstances which may well arise in the future, some years after a general policy has been agreed.

'Subject to financial limitations, the law library should aim to be a comprehensive reference [*and/or lending*] library in all branches of English [*here define other jurisdictions as necessary*] law and in selected branches of the law of other jurisdictions [*these may be defined if considered necessary*]. The dominant criterion should be usefulness to present and future members of [*here define the institution or other corporate body whom it is intended to serve*] as outlined in the bye-laws and/or rules and regulations presently in force'.

Given a simple statement of general policy as outlined above, the law librarian should be in a position to be able to organize and administer all the various services for his readers, many of which are referred to in this chapter, by correctly interpreting this policy, issuing directions to all the departments of the library and delegating responsibility within those directions to approved staff.

Some attempt must be made to define as specifically as possible the librarian's view of what is meant by 'Services for readers'. The verb 'to serve' may be interpreted in many ways, for example 'to attend or wait upon, to work for and obey'. Thus, the noun 'service' implies the condition or occupation of a servant or 'a working for another'. In the context of this book the term 'reader' will again have several connotations. Essentially, however, our reader is a person who at any given moment is engaged in the pursuit of some specialized knowledge for which he is using the law library. It follows therefore that the law librarian who is endeavouring to give service to his readers is himself engaged upon the task of working for the other person, in this instance the reader, his client, by trying to help him fulfil the particular task in hand.

Too much importance cannot be placed upon the initial point of contact between the librarian and his reader, no matter what type of law library is concerned. Ideally, no barrier or inhibition should mar this contact. The reader should be able to feel that he can communicate with the librarian at any given level of intelligence without impediment. This implies a very high degree of accessibility of the librarian to any given reader at any time and, ideally, ability on the part of the law librarian to enable him to switch from enquiry to enquiry in tune with the varying demands of his readers.

Limitations

Interpretation

The degree of training a law librarian receives has, of necessity, to be set at a very high level to enable him, ultimately, to reach the position of being of service to *all* his readers. Assuming a basic knowledge of, and training in, general librarianship, the law librarian must strive to superimpose upon this foundation the particular skills demanded by the type of law library in which he is working. For example, the academic approach of the university law lecturer may differ greatly from that of the legal practitioner in the courts. Although each may be looking up a similar point of case law, the degree of interpretation required by the practitioner may be far more detailed in practice than the general outline needed by the undergraduate whom the law lecturer is guiding. It may be necessary, therefore, for the librarian to grasp the context of a particular case sufficiently well to enable him to help the practitioner quickly and in sufficient detail to interpret a specific point of law (often from the head-note alone), whereas the law lecturer may be satisfied with the general principles of law contained in a particular case as outlined, for example, in a law report index.

Note the emphasis in the preceding paragraph on the word 'interpret' in relation to the particular reader concerned. It should be no part of the law librarian's task to attempt to interpret specific points of law, unless he happens also to be qualified by legal training to carry out this function. It follows from this that the prime function of the librarian in this field is to produce from his stock, quickly and efficiently, all material relevant to any particular enquiry to enable his reader to form his own opinion or judgment. This can be a difficult task when dealing with specific points of law. It presupposes that the librarian has an intimate knowledge of the material contained in his library and that the library is equipped, in sufficient detail, with the tools of his trade; that is, a comprehensive catalogue and a workable arrangement of the material on the shelves.

Bibliographical searching

It is often said that the librarian should not place himself in the position of doing his client's work for him. This is particularly true in law libraries, perhaps especially those attached to teaching establishments, where students, in particular, may seek to compensate their own inexperience and inadequacy by posing problems to the law librarian, which they themselves have been requested to solve by their tutors. Where an enquiry involves bibliographical searching for a specific item the principles outlined on pages 379 to 414 must always be borne in mind. Very often the reader himself will have inadequate information regarding an item simply because he has not ascertained for himself the specific details required.

In law librarianship, as in general reference work, library staff are frequently asked to supply bibliographical details of an author and title purporting to be a major work in a subject when, in reality, the information refers, for example, to a pamphlet or to an article in a legal journal. This is a common trap for inexperienced library assistants to fall into. It is very difficult to avoid. One of the best ways is for law librarians to familiarize themselves on a regular day-to-day basis with the contents of all legal journals. This may seem a mammoth task but, especially in libraries serving the legal practitioner, it is an absolutely essential process if complete coverage is desired. There are three or four regular weekly journals with which law librarians in this type of library will need to familiarize themselves – *Justice of the Peace*, *The Law Society's Gazette*, *New Law Journal* and *Solicitors' Journal*. In addition to these weeklies there are the monthlies and quarterlies, which are of especial assistance and necessity to the academic lawyer, as well as being of use to the legal practitioner. The contents of these types of periodical literature should be scanned regularly and diligently by the law librarian and his staff.

Bibliographic searching in the general sense of that term includes not only the scanning of the foregoing periodical literature but also being familiar with the contents of regularly produced bibliographies such as the *British National Bibliography*, as well as the various bibliographical guides to law literature described in Chapter 10.

TYPES OF SERVICE

Reference facilities

There exists a wide variety of circumstances, all of which will have a specific bearing upon the development of any particular law library. When dealing with libraries which supply only reference facilities it can be assumed that the librarian will be able to exercise a very firm control over all aspects of the library. It should be possible, even over an extended period of years, to develop a reference law library within the framework of its statement of purpose (see page 444) more easily than a library which has mixed lending and reference facilities. Policy should always be formulated so as to enable developments to take place within the previously agreed framework of the functions of the library.

The arrangement and control of the book-stock, together with other ancillary material, will reflect local pressures to a greater extent in a purely reference law library than in one with a dual function. First thoughts on this question of arrangement turn automatically to the way in which material is displayed upon open access or reserve stock shelves. The question of choosing a specific classification scheme is dealt with in Chapter 15. In the context of this chapter, where a broad outline of the law library's development from infancy to advanced stage has to be borne in mind, one of the first definitions to be decided is that of which jurisdiction(s) the law library should cover.

The physical arrangement of the book-stock on all types of shelves will depend to a large extent upon the use to be made of the contents of those shelves. Thus, whatever classification system is employed, particularly upon open shelves whose contents are available to the general readership, the degree of accessibility to both staff and readers will be a prime consideration when decisions are being made about the arrangement of material. If it is known, for example, that much of the work to be undertaken by staff and readers will be of a type where the use of textbook and case material will dominate, it would be foolish to locate the books of this type of stock at any great distance from either the general reading area or the main staff enclosures. To assist in the speedy identification of specific material the main catalogue should also be within easy reach of both staff and readers. Similarly with staff control points – these must be considered from both staff and readership point of view. There must be a sufficient number of staff points to enable readers to be able to identify members of staff and also to avoid undue delay in helping readers. The emphasis, from an idealistic point of view, must be on providing sufficient qualified staff to attend to the immediate needs of the readership, dependent, of course, upon the purpose of the library. In practice, it is often found necessary to strike a balance between the ideal and the practical. Economic factors in particular have a great bearing upon decisions regarding staff.

The depth of book-stock in any given category within a reference law library should be sufficient to cover not only known present day needs but also estimated future needs of the library clientele. Consideration must be given in the strictly reference type of law library to whether it serves solely practitioners or academics or a mixture of both types of lawyer. The practitioners' reference law library strives, within the limits of its jurisdictions, to remain as up-to-date and as comprehensive as possible, subject only to economic limitations. For example, it is often necessary for the law librarian serving the practitioner (whether he be solicitor or barrister) to be able to find out the state of the law within any given narrow field, often at a moment's notice. This means keeping up-to-date with each Statutory Instrument as it is published and also providing immediate access for his client to such items as official committee reports, enquiries, tribunals, etc., many of which are published as Command papers. Provision of the daily debates and decisions of both Houses of Parliament, together with advance information of their proceedings, will also be a fundamental necessity. Any information, no matter how published or where published, which has any bearing upon the current state of the law should be available to the librarian in his library when dealing with the practitioner.

The librarian in the academic law library will also strive for up-to-dateness but with a different emphasis. A great deal of his basic material will be in academic periodical form and his procedures for ensuring that these files are kept up-to-date must be as faultless as possible. While it will also be necessary for the academic librarian to stock most, if not all, government publications, there is not usually the urgency to supply up-to-date information quite as quickly as in the law library serving the practitioner. Both types of library will need to ensure that their book-stock, in all its aspects, is maintained in an efficient manner commensurate with limiting economic factors. (See also Chapter 13.)

Lending facilities

The most common type of law library in Great Britain provides both reference and lending facilities for its members. In this type of library the principles governing the reference section will not differ very much from those already discussed for the purely reference law library. The provision of a quick-reference section, situated preferably near the main staff enclosure to facilitate telephone enquiries, enables the law librarian to gather together in one place material which is not only legal but can cover the whole subject field. This is also a good place for a complete range of telephone directories with indexes and other purely directory material.

If both reference and lending materials are to be shelved within the same sequence of books some differentiating mark will need to be placed on the spines of those books which may be consulted only in the library. This will be needed for staff checking purposes as well as to help the reader. Depending upon the actual arrangement of the book-stock, many law librarians in a combined library prefer to shelve their reference material in completely separate sequences from the lending material. This has the disadvantage of separating known and like subjects, but from an administrative point of view it can be easier to oversee. Much will depend upon the functions of the institution to which the law library is attached as to the amount of book provision necessary. It will be a question of equating demand with both space and money. The economic factor will play the largest part in deciding ultimately what and how much material finds a place on the lending library shelves.

Restricted loans

Certain categories of books, notably those used by students in university and college law libraries, will have to be placed on restricted circulation and the lending regulations will need to be more strictly applied in relation to this type of book. The most used basic student texts and some of the legal treatises in constant demand by members of the teaching staff and students in this type of library very often need to be kept under constant supervision. To meet this limitation, a restricted book section, available for loan, is desirable. All copies of the above types of material are placed on its shelves when the books enter or return to the library. This has the disadvantage of denuding the main book shelves in the library, but is a prime means of ensuring supervision of material. All books in either type of library will need some form of identification mark, preferably visible from the outside, such as an ownership stamp on the top of the pages, and those volumes available for loan will have, at the very least, a date label inside the front cover or on the recto of the fly-leaf. Depending upon the method of recording issues it may be necessary to add, in addition, a book-card pocket, although many libraries now employ a combined date label and book-card pocket, thus saving at least one sticking-in operation.

RULES AND REGULATIONS

It is useful, and usual, for every law library, large or small, busy or not, to have in existence some form of rules and regulations. (For procedure for drawing up regulations see page 426.) The purpose of these is to impart information both to the readership and staff. Rules and regulations, as distinct from by-laws, do not often contain punitive measures, except possibly where fines are charged on overdue books or for mis-use of the library. The basic framework of any rules and regulations will discuss such matters as admission to the library (*ie*, who can use the various sections of the library), the borrowing regulations (*ie*, how many and what type of books can be borrowed or consulted), the procedure for borrowing and return of books, provision for the recall of overdue books from the lending section, photocopying and other photographic facilities, times of opening and miscellaneous rules governing the conduct of readers in the law library. The general principle to be adopted should be one of brevity commensurate with accuracy and having the purpose of making sure that the library can be used to the utmost advantage by the greatest number of its clientele.

The rules and regulations of a large university law library will of necessity need to be expanded and presented in far greater detail than, for example, those few rules necessary for the government of the library of a small private institution.

Discretion should always be available to the law librarian to interpret the rules governing his particular library in the spirit of co-operation with all users for the good government of the library. It should always be remembered that no set of rules and regulations will ever cover every contingency which may arise in the daily use of the library and that, ultimately, the law librarian should be left with the authority to ensure the proper conduct of the library.

Admission and registration

Some attention must now be paid to the differing types of readers using law libraries. Earlier in this chapter emphasis was placed upon the different approach to the services given by law libraries serving the academic and the practising lawyer. In discussing the different types of readership found in the library this broad division will have to be borne in mind, but too much emphasis should not be placed upon attempting definitions of types of readers. The law librarian will be aware in the normal course of his daily duties of differing approaches to subject enquiries by lawyers working in specific fields. The type of readership will be governed, initially, by the character of the institution any specific library is serving. This factor will also impose limitations upon who may or may not use the library. In general, law libraries tend to be very conservative and self-contained units. The membership will, in most cases, be restricted and, in the case of libraries belonging to recognized institutions, will be governed by the rules and regulations, and possibly also by by-laws, applicable to those bodies.

Some system of registration is desirable in all types of law library. This usually involves the reader completing a declaration on a form of application for membership of the library, such membership to be operative for a fixed period of time.

The regulations governing the admission of readers to a typical English university library can be used as an example of varying types of readership. In the first instance, all readers are usually required to register their membership and, in the case of senior members of some of the older universities especially, a statutory declaration may well have to be read and complied with. Most rules and regulations of the universities governing admission to the use of their libraries set out different procedures for degrees of seniority of members of the university who wish to register to use the library. Members of the University Court and of the University Council normally have no restrictions placed upon their membership, other than initial registration and possible compliance with any statutory declaration. Similarly, full-time and part-time members of university research and teaching staffs, as well as senior administrative staff of the university, are permitted to register at the library on appointment. Other members of a university staff are usually issued with some type of staff card, very often renewable annually, and similarly, may be required to register for use of the library on an annual basis. Research students registered at a university should be permitted to use the library during their period of research – other registered students of the university, whether full-time or part-time, may have the privilege of using the library during the time they are registered at the university.

Various other regulations, including in some cases written recommendations from Heads of Departments, are imposed by certain libraries. University librarians often have a wide range of discretion to admit to membership of the library readers who do not fall within the foregoing categories, such as for example, graduates of the university, staffs of constituent colleges, students and members of other universities and other 'outside' readers. Registration is usually followed by the issuing of some form of readers' card which acts as identification and which the library staff may demand for inspection at any time.

Libraries of private institutions are often included in by-laws governing the use of the institution's premises, particularly if the institution is incorporated by royal charter. Pursuant to these by-laws (which do, of course, have the force of law) rules and regulations for the conduct of the law library may be drawn up. There is usually a relevant rule governing the use of the library, confining this, very often, to members of the private institution. Many types of institution are governed by an elected council which, from time to time, may lay down additional conditions regarding the use of the law library and which often charges its librarian with the task of enforcing regulations. Sometimes he is given delegated authority regarding the admission of 'outsiders'. Being organized on a smaller scale, it is not very usual for the law libraries of such institutions to have to insist on any form of registration for the use of their reference services, although where lending services are concerned some degree of registration may be necessary, together with a card of identification.

Rules and regulations governing admission of readers to other types of law library, for example, the library of a solicitors' group practice or that of an industrial concern, can be based on simple local rules as demanded by local conditions. From the above notes it will be realized that where reference services only are provided the division of types of readership and their registration for the use of the law library is comparatively simple, but that some definite form of rule is necessary where registration for lending purposes is required.

Hours of opening

When deciding how long and how often a law library should be open to serve its membership two basic points will have to be borne constantly in mind – the needs of the readership and the ability of the library authority to provide adequate staff during whatever hours of opening are considered desirable.

In the simplest of cases, such as the library of, for example, a solicitors' group practice, the facilities of the library should be available at those times when it is most likely to be needed, that is in the main during normal commercial business hours. The library of a private institution whose membership, for example, is governed by the hours of opening of the law courts in a particular vicinity will need to be open both some time before the courts themselves are opened and for some time after they have closed. In a busy university or college law library, however, matters may have to be viewed in a slightly different light. Here the basic division is usually between full term time and vacation time, with special provision for weekends. Again, it may be necessary to have the facilities of the library available at all times to a particular section of the readership, but not necessarily to the whole clientele.

Any library committee discussing this complex question will need to try to consider the requirements of all the differing types of readership who may, in the future, wish to avail themselves of the facilities provided by the library. The rules and regulations setting out hours of opening of the law library will invariably state also on which particular days of the year the library will be closed (such as, for example, Sundays and Bank Holidays). It may also be necessary to make provision for the calling in of all book and other material at a particular time each year for the purpose of stock-taking. In any event, it is usual for the hours of opening and closing of the law library to be prominently displayed near all entrance points.

Library security

Librarians, no matter what type of library they control, frequently have to give much thought to the question of ensuring that the stock on their shelves is not depleted by theft. This can develop into a full-scale security problem in some of the busier types of library. Essentially, of course, it is all a question of staff supervision, but there are very few law libraries adequately designed or staffed to ensure that books or other materials cannot be taken out of the library without the loan being recorded.

One of the basic tenets of security is to ensure that all departments of the library, and all separate rooms where possible, can be adequately sealed during the hours that the library is not open. This means denying access in any way whatever, but principally by door or window. Very few librarians will be in a position of being able to fit burglar alarms to doors and windows, but certainly where special strong rooms are in being, containing rare or valuable material, serious thought must be given to some sort of alarm system. When law libraries are situated within larger buildings it is often possible to employ night security staff on regular patrol duties.

For the smaller, average law library, however, such methods cannot even be considered and here it is absolutely necessary that the library staff should be constantly aware of the possibility that much used reference material, and in some cases lending material, may be removed from the library in an unauthorized manner.

Most law libraries nowadays insist that umbrellas, briefcases and other impedimenta which might be used to conceal library material shall not be brought into the library. One of the essential factors to be borne in mind here is the provision of some sort of lockable storage equipment in an annexe to the library where clients may safely leave their belongings. Too often, readers are faced with prohibitive regulations, only to find that the library authority has not taken any steps to provide such safe accommodation. In all cases, however, it is usual for the library authority to disclaim any responsibility for lost property – this is unfortunate, but seems to be a general rule of life in all types of library.

In many busy law libraries stringent methods have to be employed to ensure that library book-stock and other materials remain available to all readers at all times. Many larger libraries now employ special security systems, very often concealing within the books and other materials a device, which, if a book is removed from the library in an illegitimate manner, will set off an alarm system to warn the library staff. This is achieved by using special electronic detectors at all exits from the library and readers are frequently warned, by means of notices, that to remove any book from the library without having its loan correctly recorded will set off alarm bells. Regulations often inform readers that if they remember to have loans correctly recorded, no difficulty should be experienced, but that if they do (inadvertently or not) set off the alarm they must stop immediately so that the reason can be determined.

Another advanced system of warning, not employed to any great extent as yet in this country, is the use of television cameras coupled with a central control point from which views of different sections of the library can be seen, with especial scrutiny of all exit points. The installation of such sophisticated equipment needs careful planning, as does the procedure involved should the equipment indicate that material was about to be removed from the law library in an unauthorized manner. A code of practice would need to be worked out ensuring that all correct legal procedures are effectively complied with.

REFERENCE METHOD

When dealing with a specific reference enquiry the law librarian needs to bear in mind basic principles of reference method employed in all types of library and then adapt these to the specialized field of law.

It may sometimes be thought that the easiest type of enquiry is that received from a client in person. It must be remembered, however, that many law librarians receive reference enquiries in other ways – through the post, by telex or, perhaps most frequently, by telephone. In any case, the first essential is to ensure that the person receiving the request is perfectly clear in his own mind as to the information specifically required. A good principle to work on is to concentrate one's mind on a single aspect of any problem, producing the required material, and then permitting the enquirer to expand from that stage. Far too often reference queries are made to seem complicated because the basic simple facts required are not elicited in the first instance. As an example of this, the complicated mass of material surrounding the Counter-Inflation Acts of 1972 and 1973 can be cited. Many enquiries on this subject could often be simplified into searching out one particular paragraph of these Acts and any subsequent secondary legislation embodied in Statutory Instruments. This presupposes that the law librarian is in a position to relate the reader's enquiry to specific paragraphs of particular Acts of Parliament, and is an example of the absolute necessity for the practising law librarian to be able to pin-point any enquiry. The only way to do this is for the law librarian himself to be familiar with the material in his library. Reference method is, in essence, the ability of the law librarian to interpret his own book-stock. It is a well-known fact that the lawyer will often require to surround himself with material from the shelves of the library (including, of course, case material) in order to elucidate one small but particular point of law. This illustrates, once again, the necessity for full comprehension of the book-stock.

Complicated reference queries can only be reduced to simple terms by the law librarian thoroughly understanding what his client is trying to do. If the reader is present in person when the enquiry is made it is absolutely essential that the full facts of each enquiry should be ascertained before accepting responsibility for trying to answer it. This is a basic tenet in all forms of reference work, but especially in law librarianship. Much staff time can be saved by a clear understanding of the problem. A great deal of library staff time is wasted in all types of reference library, perhaps especially in law libraries, by inexperienced assistants receiving enquiries from a client and not being trained to a sufficiently high degree to enable basic facts to be elicited in the first instance.

The following illustration of a subject enquiry form (Fig. 1) which can be adapted for use in all types of law library, is

Name and details of Library	SUBJECT ENQUIRY		
Name and address of ENQUIRER			
	Reply required by (date and time)		
Telephone/telex number			
		Initials	*Date*
ENQUIRY INDICATE (1) Sources of information already known (2) Level & amount of information required (3) Limitations, *eg*, languages, depth & period of search, etc.	RECEIVED		
	ACTION		
	ANSWERED		

Figure 1

based upon the form devised by the Library Association Reference, Special and Information Section. An article, 'A standard subject enquiry form', with further explanations, was published in *Library Association Record*, vol. 74, no. 2, 1972, pp. 23–4.

The obverse side of this form should be used for recording details of sources used in answering the enquiry, together with details of information collected.

Instruction in the use of the library

Many libraries, particularly those attached to the larger institutions, issue some form of printed guide to the use of the library, embodying most of the rules and regulations but written in a more discursive style. Basically, such guides are aimed at new readers and should be as informative as possible. In addition to stating the location of the law library, together with details of the senior staff, and the library's hours of opening, it is useful for such a guide to begin with a brief history of the library before detailing its present usefulness to the new reader. Such guides will also give an outline of the main stock of the library, together with its arrangement on the shelves, and will guide the client in varying detail, around the library, beginning with the main enquiries desk, at which the new reader will be able to obtain the necessary information about registration, tickets, etc. Reference will also be made to any classification scheme and, in some detail, how to use the catalogues and other guides to the contents of the library. Again, brief references will be made to photocopying, microforms and any other technical aids to the use of the library. It is also useful for such an elementary introduction to the law library to contain particulars of telephone and cloakroom facilities.

The law librarian must always bear in mind the necessity of having staff available to explain various aspects of the library's functions. It may be necessary, and in the case of law libraries attached, for example, to universities where there is a regular new intake of members it will be necessary, to provide facilities for the actual instruction of new readers in the efficient use of the library. Opinions differ as to when this form of instruction should take place – perhaps the best compromise is to provide more than one session of instruction, leaving a gap of one academic term in the case of university law libraries between the elementary and the more advanced instruction talk. In this connection the use of audio-visual aids can be very informative and useful. A simple film-strip accompanied by a good tape-recorded commentary can often take the place of a formal talk. A modern extension of this method is the provision of a taped cassette which a new reader can borrow and play back at his leisure. The Standing Committee on National and University

Libraries (Sconul) is active in the production of film-strips and their distribution between all types of library. A basic point to be emphasized again is the importance of marrying to the text a good well-spoken and understandable commentary which, whilst not being obtrusive, should be aimed at explaining in detail points portrayed by the camera on the film-strip.

Shelf guiding, floor plans, etc.

The principle to be remembered under this heading is that of the need to impart information to the new client of the law library, enabling him to find his way about the library without necessarily seeking the assistance of the staff.

Most law libraries follow a definite plan. This may or may not be based upon one of the recognized classification schemes, but in every type of law library it should be possible to produce some form of lay-out plan to be exhibited for the benefit of readers. Important points such as enquiry areas, issue desks, telephones, etc., should all be shown, as well as the actual information as to the arrangement of the book-stock.

Coupled with such a plan should be a system of shelf guiding. The most usual one is to indicate subject contents with notices placed at the head of each bay of shelves. Methods of indicating specific books on the shelves (by means of a call mark on the spines of the books) are dealt with on pages 575–6.

All forms of guiding and plans should be designed in a display type which is both clear and reasonably concise. Many libraries also issue printed leaflets or booklets describing the library and its facilities in detail (see page 438).

Publications and displays

In the field of publications it is both possible and, in many cases, desirable for all types of law libraries to make available to their readership information in the form of separate publications about specific areas of their book-stock. Where a library specializes, for example, in material of a particular jurisdiction which is not represented in many law libraries in the country, a publication outlining the holdings with annotations can be invaluable. The use of displays and exhibitions is not as usual in the majority of law libraries as in many other types of library. However, on occasion, a display of some part of the stock of the library can be very beneficial. Similarly, the law library can take part in general exhibitions put on by any larger authority to which it belongs.

The purpose of any display or exhibition can be seen as a simple means to extend the area to which the facilities offered by the library can be explained. Propaganda such as this may not be considered necessary, in which case the librarian need not consider participation, but it must always be remembered that it is the responsibility of the law librarian to project the image of his library in a favourable light, and this can be very useful, especially where the financing of the library is dependent upon outside sources and influences. This is a vital factor which should be constantly borne in mind by any librarian considering whether it is desirable to participate in any display or exhibition.

Selective dissemination of information

Many specialist libraries, including law libraries, now offer this form of service to important selected clients. Basically, SDI means that known interests are tabulated and any new material received into the library, or seen by library staff in publications, is speedily brought to the attention of the client.

To operate such a system effectively may mean employing specialist staff, although it is quite possible to use the services of law library assistants in this task. The essential need is that the members of staff employed in this way should be in a position to scan all material received into the library, including all periodical literature. This can be a very time consuming task.

If an extensive system of SDI is developed it will be necessary to ensure that no issue of any weekly, monthly, or quarterly periodical, or any other type of publication, received by the law library is missed.

To attain this end means compiling a card index of known interests of particular clients under their surname, preferably referring to a series of files in which the information passed on to the client can be recorded. For example, *The Law Society's Gazette* publishes at irregular intervals directions from the

Society's Council on a wide variety of diverse matters of specific interest to solicitors. It could be that a reader of the law library would wish to be kept informed of each of this type of announcement as it is published in the weekly issues of the *Gazette*. Thus, these issues will need to be scanned regularly, as published, and a note kept on the client's file of items noticed, together with details of when this information was notified. The introduction of photocopying facilities to most law libraries could be used, subject to the normal copyright legal requirements, to prepare a basic file of the actual material (see page 474).

All librarians considering commencement of SDI should be aware of the difficulties involved in keeping up-to-date, especially if the file of clients grows to any large degree. Members of the law library staff will need to be briefed as to individual requirements and some system of supervision will be needed on the part of the law librarian.

Microforms

An increasing amount of American law material is now being produced in various microforms, but at the time of writing the demand for English law material in microform has not been great enough to attract many publishers of this type of material to experiment in its production.

Initially the selling point of any publication in microform (whether it be microfilm, microfiche or any other specialist reduction process) is the great saving in shelf or storage space which the law library can make. Thus it can be shown that long runs of, for example, *The Times* newspaper can be disposed of in favour of a few short racks of microfilm storage space. This type of argument ignores the fact that expensive equipment is necessary to read such microforms and also that comprehensive indexes are not always provided. These may have to be produced by the law librarian in order to make long runs of microform material usable.

The reproduction in the form of a photocopy of material on microfilm or any other microform is, in 1974, a very costly process. Special machines are required which would need to be in use for many hours each day to justify costs in many cases.

It is also open to doubt, at present, whether, in fact, the English courts would accept a photocopy at second hand, as it were, taken from a microfilm of the original work.

Undoubtedly, however, in the future, when more English legal material becomes available in microform, this type of service will need to be supplied by, at least, many of the larger law libraries in this country. Generally speaking, therefore, although very few of the English law reports and other long runs of periodical legal literature are not as yet produced in microform, a rapid expansion of this type of material might have to be catered for in the next decade or two.

LENDING SYSTEMS

Many of the larger law libraries are as busy in their lending departments as a medium-sized branch library in a public library system. On the other hand, a small academic library providing both reference and lending facilities may issue only a few works each day. From this it will be seen that the choice of method to be used in recording the loan of each book is governed to a great extent by the busyness or otherwise of the library. Again, the law library may have to conform to methods used by a larger system of libraries; for example, the law department on a university campus may be physically separated from the main university library but as regards issue methods may have to conform to those in use in the larger library.

Basically, whatever system is adopted, an efficient lending procedure will yield a number of useful statistics and keep firm control of both the book-stock and the readership. There are thus three main characteristics of any system of loan procedure:

First, if a book from the lending section is not on the shelves it must be possible to trace who has it.

Second, from the arrangement within any issue procedure system it must be possible to trace when a particular book is due to be returned to the library.

Third, again from the arrangement, it must be possible to indicate easily those books the return of which is overdue.

Most efficient loan procedures will indicate the above three points easily but, in addition to these, certain types of library will need to have a closer recorded loan system which will indicate, *inter alia*, how many books a particular reader has on loan from the library at any one time, a record of what books any particular reader has borrowed during his membership of the law library and, in extreme cases, the identity of each reader who has borrowed any particular book during its lifetime. These last three points can only be covered, to any degree of detail, by an elaborate manuscript recording system or computerization, which will be outside the scope of the vast majority of practical law librarians (see page 648).

Issue methods

When deciding which loan procedure to adopt, the librarian must pay particular attention to the economic factors involved, especially staff availability (with which are linked the questions of time and money required for the operation).

Broadly speaking, the loan procedures in use in the majority of law libraries today can be classified into two groups. First, those in which the individual reader is registered and issued with a reader's ticket; and second, those where, after initial registration procedures, the reader makes a manuscript record, usually including his signature, in respect of every book borrowed. Where the law library is part of a very large system it may be necessary for borrowers to be registered at a central point and be issued with some form of reader's ticket which can then be taken along to the local borrowing point.

Where each borrower is issued with individual tickets (as in many public library systems throughout Great Britain) that library ticket is usually presented to a member of the law library staff in exchange for the loan of a specific book. For this system to be efficient it is necessary for each book to be recorded within the book-stock of the library and to have a separate individual identification mark, such as a running number, often prefixed by a class symbol in the form of letters (see page 555). The loan procedure is completed by marrying the book-card in the book with the reader's ticket, stamping the book with a date by which it is due for return, and filing the book-card and the reader's ticket behind the appropriate date-due-for-return indicator in one sequence by the afore-mentioned stock number. This system has the advantage of recording how many books have been issued on any one particular day and, because each day's issue is filed behind a specific date-card, will answer quite adequately all the criteria posed above.

When it is not thought necessary to go into the details described above, especially as regards preparation of the book-stock by means of a stock number etc., no reader's tickets are issued to borrowers and issue procedures are confined to manuscript entries at the lending library exit counter. The most usual form of book issue procedure not involving a reader's ticket or a great deal of individual book preparation is that which necessitates the completion of a separate form for each book issued. If this system is combined with the use of some method of completing a form in triplicate or quadruplicate, several records can be maintained referring to the issue of each particular book. Issue forms can be made up, for example, into packs of four, printed on no-carbon-required paper so that by writing on the top form a record is made on all four forms. It is essential that the reader completes the top copy using a writing instrument such as a ball-point pen to ensure a good bottom copy. The completed pack of forms, together with the book, is presented to a member of staff for checking and for having the date-due-for-return stamp impressed on the date label, which must be provided in every book available for loan.

It is essential that a member of staff checks each form to ensure that correct particulars have been entered and also that the declaration, which is usually printed on the top copy of the form, has been signed. This declaration can be full enough, if desired, to ensure that a borrower agrees to the rules and regulations in force at that time in the law library by appending his signature to the form, or, in its simplest form, the signature can denote that the borrower has taken the book from the library and has agreed to return it by the date due. This date by which the book is due for return can also be stamped on the form – in practice this is often accomplished by pre-dating the estimated number of packs being used each day. Once the borrower has taken the book from the library, the pack of forms can be split and filed in various sequences depending on how much statistical and other information the law librarian wishes to deduce from every book issued. This method of completing a slip in triplicate or quadruplicate can, if desired, answer all the questions posed earlier. Basically, however, one slip is filed usually in date order under the author or call mark of the individual book, and a second slip is filed under the reader's surname (to which the other slips are left attached, being available for use should any overdue procedure need to be set in motion, etc.). When the book is returned to the library the appropriate slips are withdrawn from each file and should be individually cancelled (most conveniently by using a stamp). It is at this stage that the slips can, if desired, be collated and filed to produce ultimate statistics regarding what books a particular reader has had over a period of time and to whom the loan of any particular book has been recorded.

For information on mechanized charging systems see page 648.

In assessing the type of loan recording procedure to be adopted in any particular law library, the librarian will have to bear in mind the difficulties inherent in each of the procedures set out above and balance all known factors, particularly with regard to staff time and finance, before ultimately deciding on any particular system.

Overdue books

Similar economic factors have to be borne in mind when devising any system for the recovery of overdue books lent from the library. Basically, because each loan recording system makes provision for a file of slips or cards in date-due-for-return order, any books which the loan record shows to be overdue will automatically project themselves to the attention of the librarian.

In a very busy lending law library detailed instructions will need to be issued to staff regarding the recall of overdue books. In the first instance this may take the form of a telephone call if the borrower is known to the library staff or, more usually, the despatch of an overdue notice in either letter or postcard form to the borrower requesting the urgent return of one of the library's books. This will result in the return of perhaps half of those overdue. It is normal in a public lending library system to send out two or three overdue notices, but, because of the narrow field in which the law librarian operates and because it is most important that he should endeavour to secure the return of all books as quickly as possible, many law librarians have found it expedient to send, not a second overdue notice, but an actual account invoice for the replacement value of the book in question, should it not be returned within a short period of time upon receipt of the first overdue notice. This procedure, although seeming drastic, is often very necessary where book-stock is kept out of circulation for any length of time by borrowers who ignore the first request to return overdue books.

The account system can very often be followed up by strict procedures as authorized by the rules and regulations or even by the by-laws of the law library authority. Once it becomes known that the librarian will chase overdue books in this manner and providing his authority is backed by a clear rule, regulation or by-law, little difficulty should be experienced in ensuring that lending copies of books from the shelves of the law library are kept in constant circulation or are available on the book shelves for loan purposes.

Fines

The question of whether or not to charge some form of fine for the non-return of material to the law library can be a vexed one. So much depends on the type of library involved and the relationship between library staff and the readership. For example, where the library is financed by subscriptions from members of an institution, even though it may be financed by only a small part of a general membership subscription, then the authority concerned cannot be too insistent in the matter of fining members for non-return of library books. On the other hand, where a very large and varied readership is concerned, such as in a busy university law library, conditions regarding loan and return of books approach those in being in a public lending library. Conditions of membership of the library will be different and the library authority will be able to introduce some system of fines for overdue books with greater ease.

Once again economic factors come into play. Set against the obviously desirable feature of the use of fines as a deterrent must be placed the practical factors which will govern the actual collection and recording of any monies paid. On one hand, a reader might insist on a receipt being given for every penny paid over in fines – on the other hand, another reader may cheerfully admit his fault and pay up without query. In either case, the library staff will have to be considered. Whatever system is adopted, it must be sufficiently easy to keep records and at the same time not place the library staff in a position where any one person's honesty can possibly be called into question. In a small law library to set up machinery to ensure all these points are adequately covered may not be worth the effort, when the actual cash involved is weighed against the staff-time (and its costing) it would take to collect this money.

In a very busy library with a varied readership the matter would be viewed in quite a different light. Here it could be tackled on the same basis as that of a branch lending library in a public library system. Tear-off receipts could be given for each amount and the amount of cash taken tallied at the end of each working day. Alternatively, with some modern systems of fines collection, it is not necessary for library staff to handle cash at all, other than the giving of change from a petty cash float, which can be checked at irregular intervals. This system is achieved by ensuring that the reader places the correct amount of money for each fine into a receptacle, often with a glass or perspex top, so that the amount paid can be checked as it is paid, and this receptacle is sealed and not handled in any way by the library staff, other than by the person responsible for accounting for cash received. A modern refinement of this system is similar to the one used for the collection of monies from public telephone boxes or parking meters where, in effect, once the box is placed in position the mere action of taking it away from its fixed position seals a shutter over the opening and the box can then be opened only by the use of a special key. By using a system such as this all responsibility for accounting for fines and other monies taken from readers at any library service point can be removed from the shoulders of the library staff. The cash collected can be counted and accounted for by a member of the authority's fiscal staff.

Summing up, the whole question of whether or not to charge any system of fines for the late return of material to the library has to be viewed in perspective, taking into account all relevant factors, not least the effect upon staff time involved.

Reservations

An important part of any law librarian's duties to his clients is the offering of a service which will ensure that any book required can be made available to any particular reader in the shortest possible time. This involves setting up procedures for tracing material, recalling it from other readers if necessary, and notification that the material required is available.

The most usual method of doing this is to provide pre-printed postcards upon which the reader can request specific material and, often on the obverse side, inscribe the name and postal address to which the card can eventually be despatched as notification of availability of the work required.

A specimen reservation card appears as Fig. 2.

The words FIRST CLASS MAIL should be printed at the top of the obverse side of this postcard.

A fee will usually be charged for this service and in assessing its size the law librarian should bear in mind all costs which might be incurred in tracing a specific request, not excluding that for current postal rates.

In 1974 many libraries in this country were charging a fee of

---

AUTHOR

Surname first, in BLOCK LETTERS

TITLE   EDITION

                               AND DATE

                                    Date as postmark

        This book is now available for collection from

        (*Name, address and telephone number of library*)

and will be held until closing time on ....

        Please bring this card and your reader's authority
when collecting the book, or notify the Library staff if you are
unable to call by the time stated.

(FOR LIBRARY USE ONLY)

Publisher   Price   Card received

Class/Call number   Stopped in issue

Figure 2

5p for each reservation request. Such a fee (of 5p) can be seen to be an uneconomic charge, when the regular increases in the rate for first class mail are taken into consideration; when this fee was fixed in most libraries the postal rate was 3p – by June 1975 it was 7p. Any future increases in the first class mail rate must be taken into account when assessing the charge for individual reservation cards. To this postal charge must be added the cost of a proportion of staff time taken up by all the different processes involved in servicing each individual card, *ie*, the initial checking, the searching and stopping of the book concerned, filing processes and the procedures for making the book ready for collection, including completion of the final card before posting. An attempt should be made to assess the cost of all these processes before arriving at an economic book reservation charge. Admittedly, many law libraries regard the book reservation system as a service and may therefore be prepared to subsidize each card in some way, but with stringent budgeting the general rule nowadays all subsidies must be fully documented and justified.

The various procedures within the library for satisfying an individual reservation will also embrace the checking of the original card before the reader leaves the library, the tracing by means of catalogues and classification schemes of a specific copy of that request, a filing system to retain the cards pending the return of any material on loan (this presupposes that the loan recording system is capable of being flagged in such a way that when material is returned to the library it can be speedily diverted to a special reservation section), coupled with staff availability to process material and ensure that clients receive postal notification as quickly as possible.

Many law libraries also have, within their bibliographical research sections, procedures for obtaining material not already in the stock of the library. Such a reader's request service can be coupled with the reservation system, although many librarians prefer to separate this service from the other. More rigid staff control is necessary for a reader's request service to ensure that specific details are recorded by a member of the staff before the reader leaves the library. Bibliographical details will need to be recorded at greater length and to this end a special reader's request form may need to be designed.

A specimen reader's request form appears as Fig. 3.

Name and details of Library			READER'S REQUEST		
Name & address of ENQUIRER					
Telephone/telex number					
AUTHOR Surname first, followed by forenames, in BLOCK LETTERS			Indicate if PHOTOCOPY will suffice YES/NO		
				Initials	*Date*
TITLE			RECEIVED		
			ACTION		
EDITION	DATE	PUBLISHER	ORDERED		
SOURCE OF INFORMATION			SUPPLIED		
Bibliographical details checked in			ANSWERED		

Figure 3

INTER-LIBRARY CO-OPERATION

In the context of this chapter two facets can be considered –
co-operation between law libraries on an inter-library loan
basis, and co-operation between nearby law libraries in the
somewhat wider field, by means of exchange of ideas and processes between neighbouring librarians. (See also page 440.)

It should be remembered that, for any system of inter-library loans of books or other materials to be viable, an essential element is that the librarians concerned must be prepared to make this a two-way process. One of the many reasons why it is difficult to start any system of inter-library lending of material is that so many law libraries are private concerns providing 'reference only' facilities for their own members. Many of the larger law libraries will belong to co-operative schemes between libraries within a given area and may even be members of the wider regional inter-library loan system which has been set up throughout Great Britain. Some law librarians tend to look upon this large scale system of loans purely from the point of view of what they can borrow from the system, rather than what they can offer to the system. Economic factors play a large part in this thinking, but for any system to work efficiently all co-operating libraries must be prepared to lend as much as, or more than, they borrow.

The regional inter-library systems are linked with the British Library Lending Division (BLLD) and the British Library Reference Division (BLRD). Membership of the BLLD brings many advantages to the smaller library, particularly when urgent photocopies of articles in otherwise sparsely located periodicals are required. BLLD is taking currently 44,000 periodicals in all subjects and languages, wherever published, and operates from these a direct lending and photocopying service. It has also a large number of 'dead' titles and considerable back runs. BLLD also acquires currently all worthwhile non-technical legal monographs in the English language (*ie*, works in the socio-legal and political-legal fields) and, in addition, British legal textbooks and treatises listed in the *British National Bibliography*. Loose-leaf practitioners' works requiring the insertion of revision pages are excepted from this policy, but other monographs with printed up-dating supplements are acquired. It should be noted that in the context of BLLD acquisitions policy the term 'worthwhile' should be interpreted to mean normally *excluding* undergraduate-level works and other low-level books, although some of these are acquired in response to demand. These measures, as far as English language monographs as well as periodicals in all languages are concerned, ensure a very adequate coverage of current output.

Older monographs and periodical back runs may not be so well covered. BLLD handles about 2,000,000 requests each year, in all fields.

As far as government publications are concerned, the policy of BLLD is to acquire the total HMSO output, together with the Irish University Press reprints and other reprints of nineteenth-century British parliamentary papers. Selected official publications from certain other English language sources and microform series are also acquired. These policies had been in force since 1962 at the National Central Library, which is now part of BLLD. American government publications and documents now published in microfiche by the Congressional Information Service are available for loan as fiche, including Congressional Committee hearings and reports. The American Statistical Index Library is available in the same format, thus covering all US Federal sources of statistical information.

The BLLD has greatly expanded its original NCL policies of ten or fifteen years ago and is gradually working towards completion of its aim to provide a centralized loan collection of periodicals and English language monographs, as well as microfilm and microfiche resources at the British Library Lending Division, housed at Boston Spa in Yorkshire, loans from which are available to libraries of any kind and size throughout the British Isles. This policy is developing in response to demand. BLLD can call on the reserves of BLRD for older periodicals and on several other libraries, including the other copyright libraries, for older material of all kinds.

Inter-library loan policy between neighbouring law libraries is dependent to a large extent upon co-operation between individual librarians and the policies of varying kinds of autonomous libraries. House rules of some libraries forbid the loan of any material, sometimes even to the members of those libraries. Where this is the case, individual librarians are prevented from taking part in any scheme. Membership of the BLLD is obviously advantageous in these circumstances.

In the law library field there are two private subscription lending libraries, membership of which can be of assistance to the smaller type of library. The principal lending service is that provided by the Law Notes Lending Library, 25 Chancery Lane, London WC2, where the varying subscription is directly related to the value of the books which can be borrowed at any one time. The H. K. Lewis Lending Library, 136 Gower Street, London WC1, is not so much used, perhaps, by law librarians, but for books in related fields it can be invaluable. Membership of such organizations as the Association of Special Libraries and Information Bureaux (Aslib) and The Library Association by individual law libraries can open up other fields in the area of inter-library co-operation.

PHOTOCOPYING AND THE LAW OF COPYRIGHT

The possession of some kind of copying facility is a necessary feature of any modern law library. The facility of being able to reproduce extracts from material held in the library is an essential one, if only for the amount of time which can thereby be saved over a period of years. The busy practitioner who visits his library to consult material not readily available in his own office or the law lecturer preparing to help a group of students are both examples of the type of person to whom photocopies are a valuable asset.

Equipment

When considering the type of equipment needed to produce copies legibly and efficiently certain basic criteria need to be examined if it is to be exactly suited to the requirements of the law library. Most of the photocopying equipment on the commercial market has been designed with the office manager in mind, and a large number of machines have curved printing surfaces which can cause damage to book bindings. It is not our purpose here to discuss in great detail the differences between wet and dry copiers or to attempt to assess the qualities of the different types of processes. Essentially, it is sufficient to ensure that the quality of the finished article, *ie*, the sheet of photocopy, together with an assessment of its durability and legibility, are the two cardinal principles which decide the type of photocopying machine which should be chosen.

One very important feature of any photocopying machine used by a library should be the size and position of the platen, *ie*, the surface on to which the material being copied has to be placed. A good deal of the photocopying work in the average law library has to be from book material. Much of this material will be rebound or individual copies of periodicals bound up into volumes. In many cases it is often found in practice that the inner edge of the spine of such bindings is drastically reduced by the rebinding process, with the result that it is not possible to lay the open book face downwards on the platen in a completely horizontal position. This often means that it is difficult to obtain a good image on the photocopy of the printed words in the spines of such material. The platen of any photocopying machine being used in a law library should have a completely flat glass surface extended to the very edge of the machine and should also have a drop away of at least twelve inches, thus being able to take a photocopy right to the edge of the glass platen. It is essential that when the book is opened at right angles and laid with its spine on the edge of the platen a good clean photocopy can be taken right into the spine of the book. Another consideration should be the size of the platen. It is suggested that this should be at least brief size (16″ × 14″) to enable as large an image as possible to be obtained, such as a complete page of a periodical like *The Law Society's Gazette* which, in 1974, had a page size of 15″ × 11″.

From the foregoing remarks it will be obvious that the choice of the correct photocopying machine to satisfy all the requirements of a busy law library can develop into a complicated task. The best way of deciding what sort of copying machine to acquire is to list the principle characteristics required and, by a process of elimination, settle for the best machine on the market which falls within the economic factors and finance available.

Copyright requirements

The operation of a photocopying machine in any library is governed by the law of copyright in force in the particular country where that library is situated. Law librarians should be aware of their responsibilities in this matter of copyright and should be quite clear just what can be photocopied, for whom, and under what conditions. It is very easy to transgress, perhaps unwittingly, the law of copyright when photocopying material in the library's stock.

It should be borne in mind that a substantial part of any copyright work has to be copied before an infringement occurs and even if a substantial part is copied, such copying may be permissible in England and Wales under current copyright laws as fair dealing for the purpose of research or private study. Section 7 of the Copyright Act 1956 and the Copyright (Libraries) Regulations 1957 (Statutory Instrument 1957/868) govern the right of certain types of libraries to make photocopies of copyright material. These regulations, issued by the Board of Trade initially, permit the library of any school, university, college or establishment of further education, any public library, any parliament library or that of any department of government, or any library which exists for the purpose of facilitating or encouraging the study of all or any of the following subjects, *ie*, religion, philosophy, science (including any natural or social science), technology, medicine, history, literature, languages, education, bibliography, fine arts, music or law, to make or supply a copy of certain copyright works under certain conditions. It should be noted that the special exceptions do not apply to any library established or conducted for profit.

Law librarians researching into the question of copyright should refer to the actual wording of the Copyright Act 1956, particularly Section 7. Briefly, libraries covered by the Board of Trade Regulations may make only single copies of any material protected by this Act. Similarly, a single copy of an article from a periodical publication may be supplied to anyone, provided that not more than one article is copied from any one publication. The person requesting the copy should be required to complete and sign the formal declaration and undertaking as set out in Statutory Instrument 1957/868 (see Fig. 4), thereby declaring that the copy is required 'for the purposes of research or private study'. The legal interpretation of this phrase sometimes causes difficulty, particularly, for example, when a busy practitioner or law lecturer requests copies from several publications in connection with urgent work. It should be no part of the law librarian's duties to attempt to expand the meaning of this phrase to cover any particular case posed by the person requesting the photocopies. Copies should be supplied only if the person requesting them is prepared to sign the

Copyright Act 1956
Form of Declaration and Undertaking
(s. i. 1957/868)

To: The Librarian,   Our Ref:..

Name and full
postal address   Your Ref: ....
of library.

1. I, (name in block capitals)...

of (firm) ....

(address) ....

....

                        Telephone: ....

hereby request you to make and supply to me a copy of

* ....

* ....

* ....

* ....

which I require for the purpose of research or private study.

2. I have not previously been supplied with a copy of
†the said article
†the said part of the said work } – by any librarian.

3. I undertake that if a copy is supplied to me in compliance with
the request made above, I will not use it except for the purposes
of research or private study.

‡Signature ....

Date ....

*   Here insert particulars of the article, or of the work of which a part
is to be supplied and particulars of that part, including page numbers.

†   Delete whichever is inappropriate.

‡   This must be the personal signature of the person making the request.
A stamped or typewritten signature, or the signature of an agent, is
NOT sufficient.

Figure 4

declaration without alteration or amendment. Failure to sign this declaration should automatically mean that photocopies cannot be supplied. Librarians are reminded that the ultimate responsibility for any contravention of the Copyright Act 1956, especially in respect of the making of photocopies from any material in their libraries subject to copyright, remains theirs alone.

The Regulations also refer to the matter of charging for the cost of the photocopies and to the undertaking on the declaration that the person requesting the photocopy has not previously been supplied with that particular photocopy by any librarian.

When dealing with photocopies from books or other printed material subject to copyright, the law librarian must also interpret the provisions of the Copyright Act 1956 which refer to the obtaining of permission from the copyright owner for the copy to be made. The practice of many libraries of including in the formal undertaking (as set out above) a section denoting that the person requiring the photocopy has obtained the permission of the copyright owner to the making of the copy should be used with discretion. The responsibility for obtaining permission of the copyright owner rests with the librarian and a declaration signed by the person requesting the photocopy that this permission has been obtained may not exonerate the librarian from this responsibility.

The interpretation of the fair dealing clause (section 6(i) of the Copyright Act 1956), can also be a matter on which legal opinions differ. Although this section states that 'no fair dealing with a literary . . . work for purposes of research or private study shall constitute an infringement of the copyright in the work' no satisfactory legal definition is made in the Act of the extent to which copyright works may be copied without infringement. Certainly, it is very difficult to interpret this clause in the context of the law librarian producing photocopies of copyright material for another person. The declaration by the Society of Authors and the Publishers' Association on this matter of fair dealing, made some ten years ago, seems to have no firm basis as a matter of law and, accordingly, should be treated as a rule-of-thumb measure. This declaration of 1965 stated limits which authors and publishers would not regard as unreasonable, in a general context, when dealing with the production of photocopies. The announcement dealt with what the Society and the Association regarded as not unfair in the matter of fair dealing when photocopying extracts from copyright works such as books, etc., *ie,* if a single copy is produced from a work still in copyright of a single extract not exceeding 4,000 words, or a series of extracts to a total of 8,000 words, of which no single extract exceeds 3,000 words, but the total amount photocopied must not exceed 10 per cent of the whole work. The practice seems to have developed, perhaps erroneously, over the years of regarding this statement as giving to librarians a general licence laying down limits within which material coming under the restrictions of the Copyright Act 1956 can be photocopied, provided all the other provisions of the Act as outlined in the previous paragraphs are strictly complied with. The main difficulties facing law librarians in this matter of photocopying material covered by copyright legislation, however, are the correct interpretation of the limitations imposed by the law, reconciliation of these limitations with the demands of readers for photocopies and the practical tasks of producing photocopies in an economic manner as speedily and as frequently as necessary.

A departmental committee was set up by the Minister for Trade and Consumer Affairs in August, 1973, to enquire into the law of copyright, under the chairmanship of Mr Justice Whitford. Under its terms of reference, this committee was asked to consider whether any changes were desirable in the present law relating to copyright, with special reference to the Copyright Act of 1956 and the Design Copyright Act of 1968, and also to suggest, in some detail, the format of any such changes.

The Copyright Act of 1956 is based upon the work of the previous committee in this field, set up some twenty years earlier than the Whitford committee. In spite of the fact that this Act was forward-looking when enacted, there have since been many technical developments which made a fresh look at the law of copyright essential. The increasing use of photocopying machines and tape recorders during recent years had produced the situation where many additional copies of copyright works were being produced without any recompense to the owners of the copyright. It should be realized, therefore, that some of the law outlined in this chapter may ultimately be changed and law librarians should ensure that any documents consulted on this subject are currently in force and up to date.

FURTHER READING

American Association of Law Libraries [Annual meeting, 1972]. General session on copyright, *Law Library Journal*, vol. 65, 1972, pp. 443–53.

American Library Association. Library Technology Project. *Study of Circulation Control Systems.* American Library Association, Chicago, 1961.

Brown, J. D. *Manual of Library Economy.* 7th edition. Deutsch, 1962.

Burkett, J. *Government and Related Library and Information Services in the U.K.* 3rd revised edition. Library Association, 1974 (ISBN 0 85365 127 2).

Burkett, J. *Industrial and Related Library and Information Services in the U.K.* 3rd edition. Library Association, 1972 (ISBN 0 85365 086 1).

Collison, R. L. *Library Assistance to Readers.* 5th edition. Crosby Lockwood, 1965 (*New librarianship series*).

Corbett, E. V. *An Introduction to Librarianship.* 2nd edition. James Clarke, 1969. Supplement, 1970 (ISBN 0 227 67502 9).

Geer, H. T. *Charging Systems.* Chicago, American Library Association, 1955.

Harrison, K. C. *Public Relations for Librarians.* Deutsch, 1973 (ISBN 0 233 95657 3).

Jefferson, G. *Library Co-operation.* Revised edition. Deutsch, 1968.

Katz, W. A. *Introduction to Reference Work.* New York, McGraw Hill, 1974. 2 vols (ISBN 0 07 033353 x, etc.).

Kaufman, P. *Libraries and Their Users: collected papers in library history.* Library Association, 1969 (ISBN 0 85365 171 x).

McDonald, Alice P. Circulation Procedures in Law Libraries. *Law Library Journal*, vol. 65, 1972, pp. 58–64.

Mason, D. *Document Reproduction in Libraries.* Association of Assistant Librarians, 1968 (ISBN 0 900092 01 7).

Ochal, Bethany. Microforms on Legal Subjects. *Law Library Journal*, vol. 65, 1972, pp. 65–8.

Williams, B. J. S. *Miniaturised Communications (a review of microforms).* Library Association, 1970 (ISBN 0 85365 112 4).

13. Acquisitions and Storage

DAPHNE A. PARNHAM
Sub-librarian, the Honourable Society of the Inner Temple

BOOK-STOCK POLICIES

Policy is mainly influenced by the type of library concerned and its scope of readership, yet all require certain classes of material: legislation, law reports, journals and major treatises. Expansion may be influenced by the following factors: the automatic growth of serial publications, which increases the stock held though not, except indirectly, its range; the physical size of the library area, which may dictate future purchase policy; specialized areas of interest resulting in the need to purchase new titles. Thus a library serving practitioners in taxation requires different publications in the field of reports, journals and treatises, from those purchased by one concerned with commercial or property law. Similarly, academic and educational libraries differ from those used by practising lawyers, government departments, or the general public.

Although the latest and most important books and recent issues of periodicals must be stocked, it is of greater value if the library can offer an additional service. The provision of superseded editions, early printed books and later works long out of print, complete sets of legislation, law reports and journals, and fringe publications, which practitioners or students cannot possess, will be of lasting value to readers. In all libraries, however, a good collection of bibliographical works relating to legal topics and the holdings of other libraries is advisable. Inevitably, enquiries may be made regarding publications not held, or topics not covered by one library. Information may thus be provided as to the details of publications and their possible location elsewhere. It is important to realize that the service offered by a library need not be confined to the material held.

16

Selection policy

New acquisitions are usually selected according to the general stock policy, and with consideration for readers' needs. The current state of budget allowances must always be remembered, as a large proportion of annual expenditure is permanently allocated to periodical materials, new editions and supplements. New publications may also be required within these fields. The resultant allocation for individual publications is usually small and great care must be exercised or funds may be used too rapidly; important publications appearing later in the financial year will not then receive consideration until the year following.

The author's intentions require careful examination, since his book may be written for practitioners or students of either branch of the legal profession, or of another profession; for schoolchildren, or the general public. Thus a work on doctors and the law may expound general legal problems for medical practitioners, or medico-legal problems for lawyers, or present an outline of the layman's rights. Nevertheless, simple expositions of subjects will often assist students, or practitioners working in unaccustomed legal fields, more readily than authoritative specialist works. If doubts arise regarding the possible duplication of items it is advisable to double-check, since off-prints of articles in journals, chapters from books, sections of encyclopedic works, and individual volumes from titled series may be published and advertised as separate works.

Opportunities to remedy deficiencies in important collections or series should not be lost, while decisions to purchase all subsequent editions of new works may be reversed if these prove inadequate or unpopular.

Whether librarians purchase books directly, or are required to submit titles to committees for consideration, detailed information should first be acquired through bibliographical searching (see page 484). Wherever possible, publications should be seen and examined. This may be achieved by visiting other libraries already holding these items, or by calling on suppliers. Alternatively, suppliers or publishers may be asked to send copies on approval, though not all will necessarily do so. This practice can, however, raise genuine difficulties, as alternative purchasers may not be found for books specially obtained and then rejected. Also, special care must be taken to ensure that these books are neither damaged in any way, nor retained for an indefinite period for further consideration. Such factors will affect eventual sale elsewhere and, therefore, the suppliers' willingness to accept returns. Additionally, should the library be situated beyond the supplier's delivery area, the constant rise in postage costs may prove a further deterrent.

Whether purchases are directed by the librarian's choice, the recommendation of an influential reader, or by the final decision of a committee, certain guidelines may prove valuable. The work of a well-known author or editor, and the productions of a specialist publisher, will always receive primary consideration. Yet it may be that the famous name has been lent to a publication which is mainly the work of other and less expert writers, while publishers occasionally produce books which are principally aimed at other markets. Consultation with an expert academic or practising lawyer can be of value in these instances. Committee members, while usually requiring full descriptions of works under consideration, and often their physical presence, may also prove individually knowledgeable about doubtful items.

Multiple copies

Additional copies of works in constant demand by readers should ideally be provided. The influencing factors of available shelf-space and finance may, however, make compromise a necessity. The SPTL recommendations,[1] regarding the ratio of copies required per number of students, give valuable guidance to educational libraries which must also provide for the diverse needs of academic staff. Libraries attached to government departments, and other organizations, such as law firms, are often responsible for supplying a particularly high ratio of copies to meet staff needs. Again, practice libraries which serve students studying for professional examinations must not only supply multiple copies of recommended syllabus reading, but standard practice treatises as well.

[1] Minimum Standards for Law Libraries . . . *Journal of the Society of Public Teachers of Law*, n.s., vol. 13, 1974–5, pp. 332–41.

Co-operative acquisition

Independent libraries often maintain independence only at the expense of stocking a wider range of material, particularly in regard to reference and bibliographical tools, than is needed in a library that is part of a complex. Co-operation between libraries regarding subject specialization or fringe materials is therefore advantageous, geographical conditions permitting. Duplication of materials may be minimized, and the total shelf-space available be fully exploited to hold the widest possible range of stock.

University library complexes gain when specialized legal departments are instituted. Material such as record publications (see page 220) may be located in the history library, while works concerned with the sociological aspects of law are likely to be held in the sociology library.

Government departmental libraries may assist each other, but while public and educational libraries may participate in local, regional or national loan schemes, these are not often acceptable to libraries which are privately owned and administered. These, of necessity, must be as self-sufficient as possible, and co-operate with each other if feasible, since loan schemes which impose a delay exceeding four hours in supplying titles are largely useless to legal practitioners.

Annual subscriptions, on a personal or group basis, may be advantageous. Organizations such as Law Notes Lending Library can prove invaluable to small units, while demands for historical record material could be supplied by the London Library; both offer postal services. Yet problems may arise regarding responsibility for items borrowed.

Outside London, local law societies offer facilities upon subscription, while many universities are willing to assist practitioners who wish to research materials not available in their local court or chambers libraries.

ORDERING PRACTICE

Bibliographical searching

It is advisable to watch constantly for the issue of new editions and other publications of interest. The weekly *Bookseller, Daily*

Lists of Government Publications, publishers' lists and advertisements all give current news. *Whitaker's Books of the Month,* the
twice-yearly export number of the *Bookseller,* and publishers'
advance catalogues forecast future issues, while the *British
National Bibliography, Whitaker's Cumulative Booklist,* publishers'
stock lists, and reviews in leading journals supply details of
recent and past publications. *British Books in Print* and *Paper-
backs in Print* annually list the availability of older items;
American and United Kingdom publications are represented
in the *Cumulative Book Index, Law Books in Print* and *Law Books
Published,* while [American] *Books in Print* and the *Publishers'
Trade List Annual* are also valuable. *Government Publications Lists*
in monthly and annual cumulations, together with the *International Organizations Supplements* and *Sectional Lists* give details
of all materials published and handled by HMSO. Lists of recent
textbooks are given in the monthly issues of *Current Law,* but
they do not include the names of publishers.

Information regarding older materials, especially early law
books, may be obtained from Sweet and Maxwell's *Legal
Bibliography,* printed catalogues of other libraries, Wing,
Pollard and Redgrave, and earlier volumes of the publications
already mentioned.

Reading lists supplied by law faculties, colleges and tutors
give basic references to titles required by students. The information given, however, is often dangerously brief, especially
in the case of multiple works by one author on one subject,
while titles seen in proof stage only, but not yet published, may
be recommended.

Law publishers do not generally conform to the accepted
principles of publication dates. These cannot be accurately
gauged as legislative changes may occur, or be awaited. Also
since a high proportion are commissioned from busy practice
and academic lawyers, the completion of these publications is
often influenced by pressure of work or its unexpected cessation.

Suggestions

It is always good policy to invite suggestions for unstocked titles
from readers and staff. Requests should be entered on forms (see
sample at Fig. 1) or in a special book. These requests may prove

```
pcl                              The Polytechnic of Central London Library

                SUGGESTION FOR PURCHASE

   Author(s)

   Title


   Publisher              Editor              Date

   Price                  Number of copies

   Suggested by

   Department                                 Date

   Catalogue       BBIP         PBIP          BNB
   Order file      BIP          TBIP

   Now available in the library
```

Figure 1

to be held but overlooked, already considered and rejected, outside the stock policy, minor students' aids, ephemera, or expensive works suiting one reader's purpose but of little general interest. Alternately, they may prove well worth consideration.

Suggestion books, if kept in a prominent place, have the advantage that readers may easily see if their suggestions have been accepted, but their disadvantage lies in the need for regular checking and copying of entries by staff.

Forms are portable and many types are available, some of which may additionally be utilized for orders and intake records. However, their direct use by readers may create problems of legibility. Publishing data will certainly have to be traced and added to all suggestions.

Ordering methods

Individual and block orders may be entered in duplicate books, on printed forms or on cards (see Fig. 2) and should each contain the maximum publication data. ISBNs and ISSNs may be used as identifying aids, but it is inadvisable to use them alone as extreme care must be taken to list the correct digits, though they may still be mis-read by the receiver. Also, they are some-

AUTHOR		PUBLISHER		LBY. CODE
TITLE, EDITION, DATE				NO. OF COPIES
BOOKSELLER		ORDER NUMBER		X FOR PB
PRICE	ACTUAL PRICE	REMARKS		NYP
				RP
DATE SENT TO BS	DATE BS SENT			BDG
				OP
ACCESSION NUMBER				OS
				OOA
CLASS NUMBER				R
				CAN

Figure 2

times mis-printed in catalogues and book lists. Confirmation orders for material supplied on approval must be equally precise, as this will assist the supplier to forward the correct invoices.

It is advisable that standing orders for future issues should be placed with initial orders for new publications. New editions, volumes and supplements may be frequent; individual ordering is usually time-consuming and may well create unnecessary delays. Some textbook and most loose-leaf supplements are available upon annual subscriptions and should be ordered accordingly (see page 492). Dependent upon the organization, suppliers' records of standing orders may be filed on cards, entered in books, or fed into computers, under either customers' names or publication references. A list may be maintained in the library of all publications on standing order, apart from periodicals (see page 490). This list should be checked, and imminent new issues noted while conducting bibliographical searching (see page 484), thus reducing the risk of omissions.

Blanket orders placed for all publications on a given subject may be treated similarly to standing orders. Arrangements should, however, be made with suppliers regarding the possibility of returning duplicated items since, for example, a lego-historical work may be supplied for both the legal and the historical collections within the same library.

Faculty members or library staff may, on occasions, purchase books on behalf of the library, preferably by prior arrangement with the librarian. These are usually second-hand items, publications available on special terms to certain individuals, or works published abroad. Receipt of all such material should be recorded and the purchasers reimbursed.

Suppliers (home and abroad)

The number of suppliers retained depends largely upon the range of material stocked. Specialist publishers, such as HMSO, Sweet and Maxwell, Butterworth, and Green, maintain bookshops and supply-services. Some specialist booksellers, such as Wildy and Sons, also stock second-hand titles, while a general bookseller may be retained to handle quick-reference works and other non-legal publications. The existence of nearby specialist suppliers is extremely advantageous, since they may be visited in order to examine new publications and discuss problems. Alternatively, more distant organizations may be utilized to satisfaction.

Publishers and suppliers abroad may offer large discounts to direct purchasers, but this fact should be weighed against the advantages offered by home agencies. Language difficulties will inevitably heighten the problems of ordering, errors and returns; individual post or freight charges are usually high, and not all accounts departments are equipped to handle complex foreign payments on a large scale.

The direct purchase of the publications of societies, institutes and similar bodies usually combines economy of cost with speed of delivery, but organizations may prefer to restrict their accounts commitments to a few major suppliers. A substantial discount may sometimes be obtained by joining the society as an institutional member.

GIFTS AND EXCHANGES

Donations may or may not prove suitable for inclusion in stock yet some cannot, in the interests of diplomacy, be declined.

Potential donors, once rebuffed, may be reluctant to offer more suitable items subsequently, so providing no restrictions are imposed regarding eventual disposal, it is often advantageous to accept unwanted materials in order to gain a few long-sought items. The conditions, if any, of living donors must be strictly observed, during their life-time at least, but those relating to bequests may have, rightly, to be observed in perpetuity.

Publications of readers known to be generous may be deleted from standing orders but, if not forthcoming, they must be re-ordered. The problems created by donations are frequently as great as their benefits, but discretion and tact should be exercised at all times, since many valuable collections have developed from the reluctant acceptance of a handful of apparently extraneous materials.

The receipt of donations should always be formally acknowledged in writing as a matter of courtesy. The details of items presented and retained should, for record purposes, be entered in a special index, together with the name, address and status of the donor. This index will, in future, supply useful information regarding past accessions. Items thus received should be marked with the donors' names and should be retained during their lifetime, as donors rightly enjoy visiting a library to see their gifts upon the shelves and show them to their friends.

Collections or items deposited on loan or permanent loan are often subject to conditions or restrictions. Since they are not part of the library's stock, they cannot be marked or catalogued as such, and are usually retained upon closed or limited access with a separate catalogue or index.

The exchange of duplicate or unwanted materials may be effected informally between two or more libraries, or more formally by subscribing to an organized scheme. In the latter a central authority usually acts as a clearing house for lists of items available, which are supplied by the offering libraries, and distributes them to all other subscribers. According to the system in use, requests may be made directly to the library concerned or to the central authority. Allocation is usually made to the first applicant, who arranges for collection or refunds expenses upon receipt of the books.

The British and Irish Association of Law Librarians started an experimental exchange scheme in 1972, based on the

Harding Law Library at the University of Birmingham. Probably the best-known exchange scheme in the British Isles is that operated by the British National Book Centre, a part of the British Library Lending Division at Boston Spa near Leeds. Both these systems charge modest subscriptions for the consolidated lists of material on offer which they circulate.

PERIODICALS

Law reports, journals and most legislative materials are mainly issued in individual parts which, after completion of a volume, are bound, or replaced by the publishers with bound volumes. Some, however, may be issued directly as volumes only.

New publications may be selected and purchased through the system governing new acquisitions, though careful judgment must be exercised before committing the library to additional annual claims upon its budget.

Subscription agents

Existing suppliers may be requested to handle all administrative matters relating to standing orders for periodicals. Alternatively, if the library's regular bookseller is not equipped to deal with the large number of titles involved, a separate agent should be sought for this purpose. Direct subscriptions to societies may include free receipt or reduced rates for their publications; additionally, it may prove economical to subscribe directly to publishers and organizations. Nevertheless, this practice may increase staff work, while agents can more easily arrange the return of erroneous or faulty copies, and make representations regarding missing parts. These advantages may well outweigh the cost of handling charges.

Visible indexes

The unusually large proportion of unbound material taken by most law libraries requires careful documentation. Day books, wherein items are recorded in order of receipt, are insufficient for all but the smallest library, and are scarcely adequate to supply rapid answers to complicated queries. Visible indexes, if maintained in detail, will supply immediate information upon the most proliferate of running series and the most

occasional of casual series. The indexes are usually housed in
metal cabinets, ledger-type holders or drums, but the size of the
collection, space and cost must influence the style and amount
of equipment selected. Figures 3 and 4 show both sides of a

YEAR							
JAN							
FEB							
MAR							
APR							
MAY							
JUNE							
JULY							
AUG							
SEPT							
OCT							
NOV·							
DEC							
INDEX							

FILED:
BOUND:

TITLE   pcl

Commence
typing here

In order that the Titles be VISIBLE they must be typed between the perforation and the light horizontal line which
is ½" above it—as close to the perforation as possible. After typing front and back, tear off perforated strip.

Figure 3

TITLE							
HOLDING							
PUBLISHER							
AGENT							
O/N AND DATE							
SUB PERIOD							
INVOICE No.							
DATE PASSED							
BINDER							
VOL. No.							
DATE SENT							
DATE RET.							
STYLE							

pcl

Figure 4

typical visible index card (reduced in size). Small coloured tabs are easily obtained for use with these cards to indicate matters such as: date due, material overdue, call-up sent, etc. Use of these tabs on the visible section of the card greatly facilitates the scanning of the drawer full of cards for action needed, such as calling up overdue issues.

SPECIAL TYPES OF MATERIAL

Supplements fall into two separate categories of publication. The first are issued as paper pamphlets, or bound volumes, up-dating textbooks and multi-volume works, on an occasional or annual basis. These may generally be treated as books, but those acquired upon subscription may be handled with periodicals. The other consists of supplementary or replacement sheets, supplied upon subscription to augment loose-leaf works (see page 194) and may also be included with periodicals.

Pamphlets may be ordered and treated as books, but those issued as parts of series may be placed upon standing order and entered in the periodicals index, if desired.

Out of print materials may be required to replace items lost or irretrievably damaged, to complete imperfect sets, or to expand collections. A list of works thus required, containing full bibliographical details, should be maintained and standing orders may be placed with specialist second-hand booksellers. When copies become available, and notification is given, prompt action should then be taken to confirm requirement, or they may be offered elsewhere. Catalogues of antiquarian and second-hand booksellers should be searched immediately upon receipt. It is advisable to telephone promptly for wanted items and, if they are still available, reservation may be requested and a confirmation order despatched. Additionally, the catalogues of reprint publishers may be checked, as many of these produce facsimiles of previously rare titles and editions.

Photocopies may also provide a solution to the acquisition problems of out-of-print books, pamphlets and periodical parts, also articles of interest and missing pages. These may be obtained from either the original publisher, or another library, but care must be taken regarding infringement of copyright (see page 475).

Microforms offer a currently widening coverage of many types of material, from single titles to long runs of periodicals. These may be otherwise unobtainable, but many are still available in book format. They are especially valuable, to libraries with acute space problems, in offering an alternative coverage on long runs of little-used series and newspaper collections, such as *The Times*. Additionally, subscriptions may be paid for some periodicals to be supplied in parts, as issued, and replaced by a microfilm upon completion.

Microforms are issued as films, fiches, cards and prints and are usually purchased directly from the producing organization. These may be repositories issuing material from their own archives, publishers, or other commercial concerns, many of which issue lists or catalogues of items thus available.

ACCESSIONING

Upon receipt, the contents of all packages should be carefully checked against delivery notes or invoices. Discrepancies should be noted, all relevant items recorded in the periodicals index, and new receipts checked against orders. Errors and omissions must be promptly followed up, duplicated materials set aside for return and invoices or statements of account passed on for attention (see page 428).

Accessions registers

Opinions vary as to the value of maintaining accessions registers. Some libraries record all items, others only selected ones. Many regard the practice as a duplication of work and feel that the catalogue provides sufficient record. If the practice is followed, the new accessions may be listed in books, on slips or on cards (see Fig. 5), either by chronological numbers allocated upon receipt, by authors, titles, subjects, classifications, ISBNs or ISSNs, as preferred. The required data should be entered on a slip or card which accompanies the book until processing is complete. Additional data may be added throughout, as required, prior to entry in the accessions register.

```
┌─────────────────────────────────────────────────────────────────────┐
│  Acc................................. Date added............................. Class ....................... │
│  Author......................................................................................... │
│  Title........................................................................................... │
│  ............................................................................................... │
│  Date........................Publisher.................................. Price............... │
│  Edition..................Vendor................................ Cost ................... │
│  Ordered ................Order No. .............................. Invoice No. ........ │
│  Binding................Withdrawn........................................ │
│  Remarks : .................................................................... │
│  ............................................................................................... │
│  180459                                              (2518)  │
└─────────────────────────────────────────────────────────────────────┘
```

Figure 5

Processing

Collating

Whenever possible all publications should be properly collated prior to stamping or marking. It is no longer feasible for publishers to undertake this, but they will always exchange faulty copies. This procedure is especially important since legal publications are consulted rather than read, many books and periodical parts go out of print rapidly, and replacement becomes difficult if not impossible should faults subsequently be discovered.

Collating is both tedious and time-consuming, and will only be properly performed by trained staff, who alone may be trusted to conduct this task to satisfaction. Each item should be carefully examined for physical damage, accuracy and completeness of make-up. Pagination sequences of new periodical parts should be checked against the preceding part before filing. If a discrepancy exists, but the text is complete, the paper cover may be annotated, thus anticipating readers' or bookbinder's queries. A paper-knife should be used on uncut pages and new or freshly bound books be eased open gently, from the centre outwards, to avoid cracking of bindings. This will render them more flexible and able to withstand heavier usage.

It is advisable to check new microforms upon receipt, especially if they have been made to order. Pages or even volumes may be omitted, while incorrect focusing will result in blurred prints. Faulty copies should be returned for replacement.

Stamping

The use of rubber, brass or embossing stamps to indicate ownership is advisable, particularly in libraries operating loan services. Such stamp impressions may be placed at intervals throughout the text, on the title-page and along the fore-edge. It is necessary to stamp all separate periodical parts, including prelims and indexes, upon receipt, otherwise doubts regarding their provenance may arise when they reach the bookbinders' premises.

Stamps for administrative purposes may also be employed, particularly accession stamps to record accession references, location marks, codes denoting suppliers and prices, together with initials of staff who have undertaken various processes on the volume. All stamps should be impressed neatly, care being taken not to mask any portion of the text, and to avoid page edges, which may be trimmed when re-binding takes place.

Side-stamps and tail-stamps bearing the library's insignia may be impressed upon the boards and spines respectively, this usually being undertaken by a professional bookbinder, while embossed stamping of pages or boards may be carried out on the premises, if the necessary equipment is held.

Bookplates and date labels

Bookplates bearing the library's name or insignia may be affixed inside the front boards, unless vital references have been printed there, when they are better placed on the front or reverse of the flyleaf. Lists of rules may be pasted inside the front boards, or on the flyleaf, while in lending libraries they can be printed at the head of date-sheets, which may then be inserted inside the front or back of volumes, together with card-holding pockets, if required. Labels, if necessary, regarding the availability of books for loan, or prohibition of their removal, may be placed inside the volumes or on the front boards.

Labelling methods

Class numbers or location marks may be placed on the spine as required. The following methods are in current use:

(1) hand-lettering in white or indelible ink,
(2) transfer-lettering, written manually with an electric stylus;
(3) adhesive labels, typed or written.

These methods are relatively cheap, and may be undertaken by anyone with a flair for art work, but care and practice is required to maintain maximum legibility. To ensure permanence and minimize torn labels and smudged lettering, all should be overlaid with transparent material.

(4) Embossed labels are quickly produced and clear to read, but may become detached eventually.

(5) An alternative is the American system of large-letter typing on special adhesive tape which is heat-sealed to the book. This method is slow, and the tape is only removable if re-heated, but a Canadian product may be used with the same equipment which does not require heat for sealing. This tape is thinner and may be overlaid with a fresh strip if alterations become necessary.

(6) The most permanent method is stamping with a hot iron on gold foil but this requires the expertise of a professional bookbinder.

If possible, all lettering should be placed at a given height above the base of the spine or, if impracticable, in the bottom left-hand corner of the front board. On books with narrow spines the lettering may have to run lengthwise and a decision as to whether it runs up or down should be made and permanently adhered to, since variation will create difficulties for readers and staff.

STORAGE

Since most law libraries must retain the bulk of their holdings in perpetuity, and since a large percentage of their stock is in constant demand, great attention must at all times be paid to the care and storage of materials (see also page 604). Books should be shelved according to the library's system and, if space permits, all stacks should contain one or two empty shelves to preclude excessive movement when interpolating. Books should never be laid flat on top of others on packed shelves. A minimum clearance of one inch between the head of the tallest book and the underside of the shelf above is essential. All shelves should be under- rather than over-filled, or damage to bindings will result. Books on partly-filled shelves require support, and shelving should be easily adjustable, since tall books should never be placed on their fore-edges. This form of stacking weakens bindings and makes location difficult.

Over-size books should be shelved in a separate sequence adjoining their section, or together in one sequence placed apart, in stacks with suitably spaced shelves. Elephant-size folios require extra deep shelves in narrow or partitioned stacks for upright filing. Alternatively, they may be placed flat upon specially designed separate shelves. All items filed outside the sequence of their section should bear an identifying symbol on their spines.

Storage temperature should average 55–65 degrees F. and humidity 55–65 per cent, or paper may become brittle and bindings, especially leather, will dry, crack and crumble. The necessity for reasonable working conditions, however, will require compromise in respect of items on open access. Light should be clear but diffused, as strong sunlight may render paper yellow and brittle, while binding dyes will fade. Excessive temperature changes and extreme dampness should be avoided. Volumes showing traces of bookworm should be isolated for treatment, and vermin discouraged by forbidding food to be eaten or left on the premises. Fire risk should be minimized by the enforcement of rules banning smoking, the igniting of matches or lighters, use of candles or any form of ignited lamps or heaters. Automatic heat detection equipment linked to alarm bells may be installed; immediate attention should be given to defects in all electrical installations, and CO_2 or *Sargom* fire fighting extinguishers be made readily available. These cause less damage to books than water or the contents of ordinary extinguishers.

Periodicals

If suitable storage racks (see below) are not available, or not considered feasible, individual parts of periodicals may be filed in loose binders, unless the parts are too thick or consist of single sheets, when boxes may be preferred. Specially blocked binders may be obtained from publishers or purchased through stationers. 'Cordex' or 'Easibinders' are frequently employed for this purpose; spring-back folders will hold single items or small collections of documents, and all will keep parts clean and relatively free from loss or damage.

If preferred, boxes may be employed to house all periodicals, and may be specially made to match the bound series volumes, but this method is expensive. Box-files with spring-clips, record cases with overlapping front covers, or transfer cases with hinged lids will protect little-used or infrequently published items from dust. However, spring-clips may damage paper, and hinged lids wear and break off. Open-topped boxes may suffice for popular and prolific series, and it is advisable to stock several basic sizes to accommodate a variety of publications.

Alternatively, periodicals may be piled flat on open shelves, but in this position they may become vulnerable to damage, especially if piled too high. Fuller protection is offered by cupboards with adjustable shelving, or steel shelving with adjustable vertical partitions for upright filing.

If space permits, the most recent issues may be displayed in special racks. Some are designed with hinged partitions covering a space which houses all previous parts. Current issues on display require the protection of transparent plastic or perspex holders.

Binders or boxes containing loose parts of current volumes are more easily located if they are shelved with the bound series. These may be together in one area, filed by title, accession or class number. Alternatively, they may be appended to their various subject sections.

Other materials

Supplements to textbooks, if size permits, may be fitted into slits inside the back boards, while stiff folders may be provided to protect the thicker ones. All current supplements must accompany the main works at all times.

Pamphlets may be stored in vertical cabinet files, by accession or class number; boxed and shelved in a separate section, or apportioned to their subject sections. If retained, it is advisable to have them bound, either as single items or in collected volumes.

Opinions may be filed by given numbers, key words, or subjects, according to cataloguing treatment, in boxes carefully labelled as to contents.

Press cuttings and articles from journals may be placed in envelopes and filed in cabinets, mounted upon sheets in ring-binders, or pasted into press-cutting books.

Newspaper files may be retained for set periods of time and then discarded, but are sometimes bound in volumes. The copies for general consultation may be held in weekly or monthly batches, on open racks, in large loose binders, or in clamping devices. Binding copies should be stored flat and never handled until bound.

Maps and plans may be stored flat within folders in large shallow drawers. Alternatively, they may be folded into outer covers or slip-cases, but this is not practical unless they are seldom used. The practices of rolling or storing upright on shelves are not recommended. Wherever possible, it is advisable to have maps linen-backed, and if large ones are to be folded and bound in a volume they should be cut and jointed by a bookbinder.

Photographs and illustrations may be mounted on light-weight card or thick paper, using photographic corners or cement for photographs, and starch-paste for other items. They should be stored flat to prevent buckling, but this may prove impractical. Small collections may be mounted in albums, filed in cabinets, or in transfer cases, unmounted items having first been placed in envelopes.

Manuscript materials require special care and, if valuable, should be housed in a fire- and burglar-proof strong room. Air conditioning to maintain an even 55–65 degrees F. temperature, and 55–65 per cent relative humidity, should be installed, but parchment and vellum require a higher relative humidity; daylight should be diffused or eliminated. Unbound manuscripts should be unfolded and stored in boxes lying flat, or mounted on guards into stout folders, which may then be filed in upright boxes. The filing order should duplicate the entries in their catalogue, usually by volume number within a titled or numbered class. Strict rules should be drawn up, printed, and adhered to, regarding the use of manuscripts for research purposes.

Microforms

Storage of films and microfilms requires stringent precautions. Older film stock is cellulose-nitrate based, inflammable, and subject to government regulations, but modern triacetate-based film materials are very slow-burning or non-inflammable and not subject to the regulations. Deterioration is very slow, but is hastened if fungi or bacteria attack the gelatin of the emulsion. Films should be stored in special rooms with a steady temperature within 60–80 degrees F. and an even relative humidity. A temperature of 85 degrees F. with 85 per cent humidity must be avoided, as encouraging the incubation rate of fungi and bacteria. Film becomes brittle in excessive dryness and heat, and condensation, forming mould, will result from extreme fluctuations of temperature. The British Standards Institution *Recommendations for the storage of microfilm* (BS 1153:1955) gives the official guide to storage. Microfilm, as a medium for permanent storage, has not been in existence long enough for precise certainty as to its average lifetime, and this will be further affected by the variability of standards in film stock and storage conditions. At the present stage of knowledge, archive films are currently given twenty-five years, though expected to outlive this; while fifty years is the limit laid down as a cautious maximum estimate.

Individual strips of film may be filed in transparent pockets attached to sheets inserted in loose-leaf binders and shelved. They may alternatively be inserted in specially prepared cards with apertures, and filed in standard card cabinets. Rolls of film wound on reels should be placed in metal boxes with loose-fitting lids, and stored flat in metal cabinets, the film resting on its edge. They should not be filed vertically, since it is damaging for the film to rest on its surface. Shelves with raised edges will prevent containers being dislodged. All films stored in open or loose boxes should be subject to the foregoing conditions, but if this is impossible they should be placed in closed, airtight boxes. Cardboard should never be used for storage, as it may exude damaging gases. Filing by accession numbers has much to recommend it, since numbers may be marked clearly and easily, but filing by the system used for books and other materials may be thought less confusing. The leading edge of the film can be marked with an electric stylus, the reel itself with white enamel, and the container with a gummed label to which may be added the title and a summary of contents.

Microfiches, cards and prints are not subject to the storage conditions for films. Fiches and cards, placed in individual opaque envelopes with the tops cut away in front to display headtitling, may be filed in card-index drawers or steel cabinets, but care must be taken with those microcards which bear photographic emulsion on one side only; these should be very tightly packed or they will curl. Vertical files or pamphlet cases will hold microprints adequately.

Co-operative storage

Apart from the natural progression of co-operative acquisition, storage on a co-operative basis mainly applies to reserve stocks and superseded materials. Several libraries may resolve to maintain one joint collection of these items, or divide the classes between them, housing the collection on the premises of one or more of the libraries concerned or elsewhere as required. Such a decision is only wisely made if the storage area is within easy reach of all these libraries, for services to readers will be seriously hampered if materials must be supplied by distant repositories.

The many and various libraries within the University of London maintain a co-operative depository library at Egham in Surrey, which has been in operation since 1961. About twelve libraries deposit books on the understanding that they will be entered in the depository's union catalogue and be available for loan to any other library in the country. Others are permitted to rent private storage space. The University Library operates a van delivery and collection service. Another example of a co-operative depository library is the Mid-West Inter-Library Center at Chicago, established in 1949.

REPAIRS AND BINDING

Print orders for legal publications are small and seldom repeated. Yet no law book ever becomes entirely out-dated; all remain of value for reference purposes by historians, academics and practitioners. It is therefore important that the utmost vigilance be observed to prevent damage to stock which has to last a lifetime.

Protection against natural hazards has been noted above (see page 496). Protection against human hazards, caused through wear and tear, is best effected initially by basic care on the part of staff and readers. Strict observation of regulations for the easing of books (page 494) and shelving conditions (page 497) will reduce strain upon bindings. Additionally, books should never be placed open and face-downwards on tables, piled open on top of one another, used as a writing pad or reading stand, nor closed upon any thick object substituting for a book mark. The marking of leaves in pencil or ink should be forbidden to all except staff authorized to make official annotations.

Repairs

In general, all repair work is best undertaken by professionally qualified craftsmen, but some minor repairs may be safely undertaken by experienced staff observing the limitations noted below.

Torn sheets may be repaired by using approved materials such as bookbinders' gummed paper, but care must be taken not to mask any portion of the text. Invisible repairs with tissue will not withstand heavy usage, and self-adhesive tapes are not recommended.

Loose pages or illustrations may be reinserted after a narrow application of paste along the inner edges.

Brittle paper, resulting from production faults or exposure to wrong conditions, must be laminated by an expert.

Water-soaked sections should be parted and each leaf

smoothed and dried by pressure. Subsequent re-sizing to remove stains, reassembly and rebinding is best undertaken professionally.

Ink may be removed by the application of a commercial ink remover, provided it is not indian ink, or that from a ball-point pen. Commercial products available for the removal of the latter are unsuitable for the treatment of paper.

Stains caused by mould and mildew may be removed by wiping with ethyl alcohol, provided the penetration is not deep, and the printed surface is avoided. The removal of oil, grease and 'foxing' should not be attempted.

Insects may be discouraged by the application, to all surfaces of boards and spines, of formaldehyde compounds combined with insecticides.

Ink lettering may be removed from spines by gentle rubbing with a damp cloth, or by scraping with a sharp knife. The latter, combined with an application of acetone, will remove letters made by an electric stylus.

Dirty leather bindings may be washed with saddle soap, but the protective salts must be restored thereafter by the application of a solution containing seven per cent potassium lactate.

All washed or little-used leather-bound books should be treated with recommended leather dressings at two-yearly intervals. Frequently consulted volumes will require only occasional treatment, since the human hand provides its own grease. The application of leather dressings keeps hinges supple, prevents major cracking, and retards the effects of use or atmospheric conditions, particularly on wrongly-tanned leather which absorbs sulphuric acid, thus causing eventual decay.

Vellum bindings do not absorb sulphuric acid, but require a temperature of 55–65 degrees F. with 60–70 per cent relative humidity, to prevent their becoming brittle and cracking. They may be cleaned with a damp sponge, dried quickly at room temperature, and given a sparing application of a leather dressing.

Torn microfilms should be heat-spliced, since old film stock will tear. Finger-marks on microforms should be treated with film-cleaning solution and wiped with a duster.

Queries and doubts regarding treatment of books or binding

should be raised with a bookbinder, while those relating to microforms should be taken to a photographic expert.

Binding

Binding or re-binding of any kind should be undertaken only by a professional bookbinder, and must be of the highest quality consistent with the financial resources available. True economy lies always in having an item well, not cheaply, bound.

Hand-bound books are almost always stronger and more durable than those bound by mechanical means. A leather-bound book will last longer than any other, and this style of binding is always to be recommended where cost is of secondary importance and permanence of a high order is required. Owing to a number of factors, amongst which a change in the process of tanning may be noted, the manufacture of durable leather is more variable than was formerly the case yet, if the use of approved leather is insisted upon, the problem of powdery decay will be minimized, if not eliminated. Buckram, however, is also extremely hard-wearing and, if leather can be afforded for books requiring extreme durability, provides an excellent substitute for those of lesser importance, which may correspondingly receive less use. Cloth is less durable and is best reserved for books of least importance. Synthetics such as rexine have proved as hard-wearing as buckram, but suffer from the major defect that it is impossible to stamp efficiently by hand the required lettering upon the spine.

There is a limit to the number of times a book may be re-bound, for its length of life is finally determined by the quality of the paper and its ability to withstand use. Under hard and continuous wear it may become pulpy or perhaps brittle, the sewing may give way under strain and the inside edges of the sheets become ragged. The book becomes tighter with each re-sewing until the print in the margins cannot be read except with difficulty, while the sewing thread finds no purchase in the paper. Repair work then becomes impossible and the book is rendered useless. It is important, therefore, that all law books, which perhaps receive more hard wear from readers than any other class of literature, should be bound as infrequently as possible, consistent with the need to protect their sheets.

Considerable variety exists as to the manner in which books may be bound. Spines may be flexible or hollow-backed, while raised bands and head-bands may be required; leather bindings may be decorated with blind or gold tooling, and coloured lettering pieces giving greater clarity on all binding materials. Split, matching or contrasting boards may be preferred, while plain, antique or marble end-papers may need reinforcement by linen guards. Whatever the choice, written instructions should accompany each item sent for binding or re-binding. They should be both precise and unambiguous and, subject to contrary advice from the bookbinder, their exact execution should be insisted upon. Law books or periodicals made up of different sections, each with its own pagination, may cause problems over re-assembly when the book or parts have been stripped for sewing. It is advisable in such instances to attach to the work a sheet enumerating the make-up of its contents, unless the bookbinder already holds a pattern-board giving exact guidance as to all requirements of make-up and binding. These are essential for periodical series, in order to ensure exact continuity of style. Orders may be entered in duplicate books, or upon printed cards or forms.

STOCK-TAKING

Stock should be checked with regularity, if possible, either completely or by sections. This practice, if performed systematically, is of value for obtaining the following data:

(1) Total number of volumes held. Comparisons with previous checks will then enable accurate figures to be compiled of the annual accession rate, from which in turn it may be possible to calculate future growth.

(2) Items missing and therefore requiring replacement.

(3) Items previously missing, but now unofficially returned.

(4) Mis-shelved items, formerly presumed lost.

(5) The current state of loan systems.

(6) An accurate survey of stationery possibly requiring fresh stocks, and equipment which may need repair or replacement.

Additionally, stock-taking provides an opportunity for the

accurate re-ordering of books by sections, and a close survey of those requiring repair or re-binding.

The most practical aids to efficient stock-taking are shelf-lists of classified or subject sections (see page 511).

Withdrawals and disposal

Superseded works and those rendered out-of-date by subsequent legislation can be misleading to the unwary reader. They should be withdrawn from open shelves and transferred to reserve storage. If these works are to be retained, location marks on the books, catalogue, subject and other indexes and guides require amendment. Duplicate copies will be rendered superfluous and may be discarded.

Libraries attached to law firms or government departments frequently offer copies to their general staff. Dependent upon policy, saleable items may be offered to specialist second-hand booksellers, or to libraries subscribing to duplicate exchange schemes (see page 489). Each book marked for disposal should bear a stamp officially authorizing this fact. Waste paper merchants will dispose of unwanted works upon request. These should first be broken to prevent unauthorized circulation of works bearing the library's stamp.

FURTHER READING

ACQUISITION

Astbury, R. *Libraries and the Book Trade*. Bingley, 1968 (ISBN 0 85157 009 7).

Bloomfield, B. C., ed. *Acquisition and Provision of Foreign Books by National and University Libraries in the United Kingdom*. Mansell, 1972 (ISBN 0 7201 0299 5).

Dewe, M. *Library Supply Agencies in Europe*. Library Association, 1968 (ISBN 0 83565 480 8).

Logan, R. G. Bibliographical Guides to Early British Law Books. *Law Librarian*, vol. 4, part 1, 1973, pp. 9–12.

Melcher, D. *Melcher on acquisition*. Chicago, American Library Association, 1971 (ISBN 0 8389 0108 5).

Spiller, D. *Book Selection*. Bingley, 1971 (ISBN 0 85157 112 3).

Way, D. J. Book Selection. *Law Librarian*, vol. 4, part 2, 1973, pp. 25–7.

Wulfkoetter, G. *Acquisition Work: process involved in building library collections.* Seattle, University of Washington Press, 1961 (ISBN 0 295 73701 8).

CARE OF BOOKS AND BINDING

Brown, L. A. *Notes on the care and cataloguing of old maps.* New York, Kennikat Press, 1941, re-issued 1971 (ISBN 0 8046 1319 2).

The Care of Books and Documents. Library Association, 1972. (*Library Association research publication*, 10.) (ISBN 0 85365 246 5).

Cockerell, D. *Bookbinding and the Care of Books.* 5th edition. Pitman, 1963 (ISBN 0 27340 365 6).

Cockerell, S. M. *The Repair of Books.* 2nd edition. Sheppard Press, 1960.

Horton, C. *Cleaning and Preserving Bindings and Related Materials.* 2nd edition. Chicago, American Library Association, 1969. (*Conservation of library materials – LTP publication*, 16.) (ISBN 0 83893 008 5).

Iiams, T. M. and Beckwith, T. D. Notes on the causes and prevention of foxing in books. *Library Quarterly*, vol. 5, no. 4, 1935, pp. 407–18.

Langwell, W. H. *The Conservation of Books and Documents.* Pitman, 1957.

Jenkinson, Sir H. *A Manual of Archive Administration.* 2nd edition. Lund Humphries, 1937, repr. 1965 (ISBN 0 85331 072 6).

Lydenberg, H. M. and Archer, J. *The Care and Repair of Books.* 4th edition. New York, Bowker, 1960.

Middleton, B. C. *The Restoration of Leather Bindings.* Chicago, American Library Association, 1972. (*Conservation of library materials – LTP publication*, 18.) (ISBN 0 83893 133 2).

Plenderleith, H. J. *Preservation of Leather Bookbindings.* British Museum, 1946, reprinted 1970 (ISBN 0 7141 0227 x).

Society of Archivists. Conservation Section Committee. *List of suppliers of materials used by record offices.* Southampton, Society of Archivists, 1973 (ISBN 0 902886 01 0).

United States. Library of Congress. Division of Manuscripts. *Notes on the care, cataloguing, calendaring and arranging of manuscripts.* 2nd edition. Washington, Government Printing Office, 1921.

MICROFORMS

Barnes, P. M. *Microfilming and the Archivist.* Public Record Office, 1973.

Celluloid and cinematographic film act, 1922. HMSO, 1922.

Davison, G. H. *Review of Equipment for Microtext.* Library Association, 1962. [Council for microphotography and document reproduction.]

Expanding use of microform in law libraries : proceedings – conference and seminar, 7 April 1973, New York University. Dobbs Ferry, New York, Trans-Media Publishing Co. Inc., 1973.

Microdoc. Vol. 1– , 1962– . Belfast, Microfilm association of Great Britain (ISSN UK 0026–2684).

Practice for the storage of microfilm. PH5.4. American Standards Association, 1957.

Houghton, S. M. *Legal Materials in Microform*: a complete bibliography. 2nd edition. Dobbs Ferry, New York, Oceana, 1973, for Law School Library, Brigham Young University. (*BYU Legal Research Series*, no. III.)

PERIODICALS

Davinson, D. E. *Periodicals Collection : its purpose and use in libraries.* Revised edition. Deutsch, 1969 (ISBN 0 233 95962 9).

Grenfell, D. *Periodicals and Serials : their treatment in special libraries.* 2nd edition. Aslib, 1965 (ISBN 0 85142 012 5).

Jacobs, R. M. Focal Point: a composite record for the control of periodicals using a visible signalling device. *Journal of Documentation*, vol. 6, part 4, 1950, pp. 213–28.

PROCESSING

Collison, R. L. *Treatment of special material in libraries.* 2nd edition. Aslib, 1955.

GENERAL

Handbook of special librarianship and information work. 4th edition. Aslib. 1975.

Smith, D. L. and Baxter, E. G. *College Library Administration.* Oxford University Press, 1965 (ISBN 0 19 859801 7).

14. Cataloguing and Indexing

ELIZABETH M. MOYS, BA, FLA
Librarian, University of London Goldsmiths' College

ELIZABETH M. MOYS, BA, FLA
Librarian, University of London Goldsmiths' College

PRINCIPLES OF BIBLIOGRAPHIC ORGANIZATION

This and the succeeding chapter are designed together to cover that part of library service which is called either, in terms of the techniques involved, bibliographic organization or, in terms of its purpose, information retrieval. The second chapter deals with the physical arrangement of the library's materials on the shelves, while the first chapter is concerned with the records created by the librarian to enable the reader to discover what the library's resources are and to find the information that he needs. The two operations involved, classification and cataloguing, are very closely linked (they are often performed by the same person, see page 540) and complement each other. Neither should be regarded as sufficient in itself; even less is either an end in itself. Together, they are intended to enable the reader (via the library staff, if necessary) to obtain the fullest and most efficient access to the information stored in the library.

It is obvious that a book can occupy only a single place on the shelves. The particular place allocated is usually related to the subject content of the book, however broadly the subject may be defined (see page 552), but in a few of the oldest libraries, the shelf position may be largely arbitrary. In any case, other important attributes of the books, such as their authorship, titles, editions, dates, illustrations, levels of treatment and their place in series of publications can be brought out better in catalogues, which can contain as many different entries for a book as are needed to convey all the useful information about it.

Without a good catalogue, a proportion of the information contained in the book-stock will be effectively lost, because no one will know of its existence. The basic functions of the library's catalogues are: to list the contents of the particular library; to provide information giving guidance to the reader in the selection of items most likely to suit his needs; and to tell the reader whereabouts those items are to be found within the library. It is occasionally claimed that catalogues are unnecessary because readers do not make full use of them. But, even in libraries where consultation of the catalogue by readers is rare, it is still an essential tool for the library staff, both for information retrieval and as a stock record.

Usefulness and consistency

An information retrieval service can be fully useful only if it is constructed according to a relevant system and is consistent within itself. The systems used must be suited both to the nature of the materials being recorded or organized and to the particular information needs of the library's users.

Once cataloguing and classification systems have been adopted, it is vital that they are applied with the utmost possible consistency. Accuracy is very important too, but it is probably true to say that, in practice, it is better to make a mistake consistently than to be sometimes accurate and sometimes mistaken within the same area. For example, the cataloguing rules in use may specify that House of Commons documents are to be entered under **Great Britain**. *Parliament. House of Commons*, but a cataloguer may mistakenly enter some under **Great Britain**. *House of Commons*. It matters less to the reader which heading is used than that *all* House of Commons documents should be entered under one or the other. If the entries are divided between the two headings, the usefulness of the catalogue has been seriously reduced.

To enable the cataloguer and classifier to achieve consistency, there are a number of well-tried devices, such as codes of cataloguing and filing rules and classification schemes. But the responsibility rests squarely on the librarian to ensure that all necessary steps are taken, including the compilation of authority files and staff working manuals for the individual library, as well as full annotation of all codes and schemes used.

Types of catalogues

The commonest form is the author catalogue. The term is often used somewhat loosely to include catalogues containing, in addition to author entries, various other alphabetical entries, other than those for subjects. It almost invariably means 'author and title catalogue'.

The other basic form is the subject catalogue, which is discussed on page 534.

Many libraries also maintain a shelf-list, with only one entry for each book, primarily for staff use. The entries are arranged strictly in shelf order, and the main functions of the list are to facilitate stock-taking (see page 505) and to determine class numbers for new acquisitions (see page 575).

Types of entry

Each item in a catalogue is either an entry containing information about a book or document or it is a reference to another part of the catalogue where information is to be found. In early catalogues, which were usually in manuscript or printed book form, it was quite common for each entry or reference to be individually compiled. As libraries grew and productivity had to be increased, librarians developed a new method of 'unit entries' which is still used in many British libraries. Some computerized catalogues may return to something resembling the older system (see page 642).

Unit entry principle

For each book, one entry is designated the main entry. The choice of main entry is made according to the code of cataloguing rules in use (see page 512) and the entry is made out with the full range of detail required. The main entry is reproduced in full for all other entries and their headings (for co-authors, editors, titles, series, forms, subjects and so on), are added above the main entry. For an example, see Fig. 5 on page 531. An entry thus created, consisting of the unit entry plus an added heading, is called an added entry.

References

When the name of an author or a subject could appear in several forms, for example **Clarke Hall**, *Sir* William or **Hall**, *Sir*

William Clarke, it is essential that one form is used for all entries and that a *see* reference is made from each of the other alternative forms, *eg*:

Hall, Sir William Clarke *see* Clarke Hall, Sir William

Another type of reference can be made, at the cataloguer's discretion, to link entries under one heading to entries under closely related headings. These *see also* references are essential in an alphabetical subject catalogue. In the author catalogue they are used, for example, to link entries for countries which have changed names, such as:

Ceylon *see also* Sri Lanka (for material published after 22 May 1972)

Sri Lanka *see also* Ceylon (for material published before 22 May 1972)

Analytical entries

If a volume consists of several distinct contributions, each with a separate author, title or subject, such as a Festschrift or a collection of conference papers, the cataloguer may consider it desirable to catalogue all or some of the individual contributions, as well as the whole volume. This is especially likely if the contributors are well-known writers or if the subject of the volume is a speciality of the library. Analytical entries can be limited to authors or titles or subjects, or made for any combination of them, as desired. For an example, see Fig. 8 on page 533.

CATALOGUING THEORIES AND CODES

In the English-speaking world, the first large catalogues, such as that of the Bodleian Library of 1674, entered books under the author's surname, unless his forename only was known. But the true origin of modern cataloguing was the British Museum *Rules for the compiling of the catalogue*, first published in 1841. During the next sixty years, the concept of author entry was developed and extended in several ways.

Authorship can be defined as the responsibility for a work's existence. For cataloguing purposes, it can be extended to encompass, for example, the composer of a musical work, an artist who produces illustrations or an editor who compiles a collection consisting of the work of several separate authors, of which this volume is an example. Authorship, in any of these senses, is sometimes shared between two or more individuals, often in such a way that it is impossible to say that any individual is the principal author.

With the growth of publications emanating from learned societies, government departments and other bodies, a concept of corporate authorship was developed. The only alternative to this would presumably have been to regard most of these materials as anonymous and enter them, like truly anonymous works, under title. In continental Europe, where the concept of corporate authorship is less acceptable, more emphasis has been placed on title entries.

Whether a library decides to base its catalogue on the authorship principle, or any other principle, authors and their works vary so enormously that a code of rules is essential to ensure consistent choice of the many alternatives available. The nature of the problems involved can best be demonstrated by reference to some of the leading codes published in English during this century.

Anglo-American Code, 1908[1]

This code was widely used for over forty years. Indeed, many libraries have not yet been able to undertake the expense of re-cataloguing by a later code. It is sometimes known as the AA code or the joint code. Rules 1–135 govern choice and form of entry, while rules 136–74 cover descriptive cataloguing. There were a number of disagreements between the British and American compilers, chiefly in cases where the British preferred the earliest form of changed names, while the Americans preferred the latest form.

There are rules for personal and corporate authorship and for title entry. The treatment of corporate authorship, including government publications, was probably the most controversial

[1] *Cataloguing rules, author and title entries,* compiled by committees of the Library Association and the American Library Association. English ed. Library Association, 1908, repr. frequently.

17

feature of the 1908 code. The corporate principle was accepted and attention was concentrated on the form the entries should take. An attempt was made to draw a distinction between 'societies' and 'institutions', according to organizations' degree of attachment to a particular place, usually a building, *eg*, a museum, school or hospital would be an institution, whereas a learned society or professional body would be a society. The rules provided for a number of exceptions.

For law librarians, one of the code's most interesting features is its use of form sub-headings under jurisdiction: *Statutes, Constitution, Charters* and *Treaties.* The compilers noted in rule 62 that entry of laws under the legislature 'offers an alternative which may be preferred by those who object to the sub-divisions suggested under the main rule on the ground that they introduce form or subject entries into the author catalogue. Libraries which have extensive collections of laws, particularly of foreign laws, will, however, find it simpler to follow the main rule. Attempts to arrange all legislative enactments of a country under the name of the legislative body or the ruling power, the names of which are in some countries subject to frequent changes, are likely to prove perplexing and unsatisfactory'.

ALA Code, 1949[1]

The disadvantages of the joint code, such as the inadequacy of the examples and the difficulty of applying it to new developments in publishing, made the question of revision urgent by the late 1930s. The same two library associations worked on revising the code before the war, but after 1939 the American Library Association went ahead alone. They produced a preliminary code in 1941 and a second, more permanent edition in 1949, containing 158 rules, with many sub-divisions, covering author and title entry only.

The volume marks the high point of the traditional enumerative method of compiling rules. The number of exceptions to general principles and basic rules are legion, making the code appear elaborate and sometimes arbitrary. The arrangement is

[1] American Library Association. Division of cataloging and classification. *A.L.A. cataloging rules for author and title entries.* 2nd edition. Chicago, American Library Association, 1949 (ISBN 0 8389 3003 4).

more logical than that of the 1908 code, many omissions are filled in, and there are more and better examples. The concept of corporate authorship was considerably developed, especially in the greatly expanded field of government publications. The use of form sub-headings for legal materials was retained, as was the distinction between societies and institutions.

Lubetzky and the Paris Principles

Seymour Lubetzky, acting as a consultant both to the Library of Congress and the American Library Association, strongly opposed some features of the 1908 and 1949 codes, notably the institution/society dichotomy and the form sub-headings. For corporate authors in general he proposed that entry under the corporate body should be restricted to 'communications purporting to be those of the corporate body and bearing the authority of that body', and that the form of entry should be the name of the body as it appears on its publications. He also argued that form sub-headings had no logical place in an author and title catalogue. If actual authorship is difficult to establish, as it is with much legislation and most treaties, a uniform title should be used, rather than a form entry. In his *Code of cataloging rules* (Chicago, ALA, 1960) Lubetzky showed how his attempt to return to first principles could reduce drastically the length and complexity of cataloguing codes.

A year later, an international conference on cataloguing principles was held in Paris under the auspices of the International Federation of Library Associations. Lubetzky's work was the basis of its discussions and the resulting 'Paris principles' were confined to author and title cataloguing (ICCP *Statement of principles adopted* . . . annotated ed. . . . by A. H. Chaplin and D. Anderson. Bingley, 1969).

The Paris principles cover the function and structure of the catalogue, kinds of entries and their functions, entry under personal and corporate authors, multiple authorship and title entry. They are broad principles, not the full framework for a code, but their great significance is that they are the result of international agreement (over fifty countries were represented).

For law libraries, one of the most significant results was principle 9.5: 'Constitutions, laws and treaties, and certain other works having similar characteristics, should be entered under the name of the appropriate state or other territorial authority, with formal or conventional titles indicating the nature of the material. Added entries for the actual titles should be made as needed.' The interpretation of this principle has varied, according to the aims of the commentator, from an absolute ban on form sub-headings through grudging toleration to full acceptance of them. Some of the leading writings on the very vexed question of form sub-headings are listed at the end of the chapter.

Anglo-American Cataloguing Rules, 1967[1]

Work on a new code was resumed in Britain in 1951 and co-operation between the British and American associations was soon renewed. On the American side, Lubetzky was editor from 1956 to 1962, and his influence can clearly be seen in AACR, though considerably blunted in places. The code was based on the Paris principles, more wholeheartedly so in the British edition than in the North American one. The history of the code and a full explanation of the reasons for the existence of two editions are to be found in Phillip Escreet's *Introduction to the Anglo-American Cataloguing Rules* (Deutsch, 1971).

The 1967 code contains rules for the selection of entry (Chapter One), form of heading (Chapters Two and Three), uniform titles (Chapter Four), references (Chapter Five), descriptive cataloguing (Chapters Six to Nine), and non-book materials (Chapters Ten to Fifteen), together with lists of abbreviations and notes on capitalization, punctuation, etc. In each case, general rules are stated first, followed by general exceptions and any special cases.

Among the special rules is a group for 'certain legal publications', rules 20–26, which are discussed in detail below.

AUTHOR AND TITLE ENTRIES FOR LEGAL MATERIALS

The summary below is based on the *Anglo-American Cataloguing*

[1] *Anglo-American cataloguing rules,* prepared by the American Library Association, the Library of Congress, the Library Association and the Canadian Library Association. British text. Library Association, 1967. (ISBN 0 85365 170 1).

Rules, 1967, and rule numbers given in the text refer to AACR, unless otherwise specified.

Secondary sources

Entry is normally made under the only author, or under the principal of several authors or, if no hierarchy is indicated, under the author named first on the title page (rules 1 and 3). Composite works and collections are entered under the name of the editor or under the title, depending on the importance of the editor's work and the existence of a collective title (rules 4 and 5). Rules 4 and 5 were amended in April 1975, so that all composite works are now to be entered under title. Works of unknown or uncertain authorship are entered under their titles (rule 2).

A work that has been revised by an editor other than the original author is usually entered under the original author (whether he was still alive at the time of publication or not), with an added entry for the editor (rule 14). This situation occurs very frequently with legal treatises, where title pages such as the following are common:

> Rayden's / Law and practice in / divorce and family matters / in the High Court, County Courts / and Magistrates' Courts / eleventh edition / editor in chief / Joseph Jackson / editors / C. F. Turner / Margaret Booth / E. W. Morris / consulting editor / W. D. S. Caird / London / Butterworths / 1971.

An unwary cataloguer may make the elementary mistake of entering this volume under Jackson, whereas the correct heading is Rayden. Law publishers usually print a list of earlier editions on the back of the title page, from which the original author's initials, if not his full first names, can be found.

Serial publications (other than primary materials) are usually entered under their titles. But serials such as annual reports, transactions and bulletins issued officially by a corporate body are entered under the name of the corporate body (rule 6).

Other rules which should be consulted include the general rules on the selection of added entries (33) and references (120), the collection of rules governing the forms of personal names

(40 to 58), and the headings for corporate bodies including governments and legal bodies (60 to 98).

Primary sources in general

Since 1908 at least, special rules have been devised for legal primary materials. From the cataloguing point of view, most modern volumes of legislation, law reports and treaties have, because of the nature of their contents, an official or quasi-official character, whether they are actually published by a government printer or a commercial publisher. A high proportion of primary materials are in serial form and require cataloguing only once, with an open entry (see page 528) in a law library, although general libraries may buy only some items from the series and need to catalogue each individually. In spite of all efforts to eliminate special cases from AACR, six or seven special rules (British or North American text) were eventually included. The practical implications of these rules are considered below, in the context of three series of recommendations, from the United States, Australia and Britain.

The American Association of Law Libraries' recommendations (*Law Library Journal*, vol. 48, 1955, pp. 3–39) submitted before the promulgation of the AACR, concerned amendment of the ALA code of 1949. Although a considerable number of non-American examples were given, the arguments were based almost exclusively on United States publishing practice and library problems, notably in the recommendations for delegated legislation, local laws and court rules. The document was based firmly on the retention of form sub-headings and, indeed, their extension to cover law reports.

The recommendations for the amendment of AACR produced by the Australian Law Librarians' Group in August 1971 (printed in Sydney by Butterworth's) were based on two main principles: fundamental opposition to form sub-headings, both in principle and because of the resultant scatter of legal entries; and a strong preference for dealing with legal materials under the general cataloguing rules, with special rules only for those that are so unlike other materials that special treatment is unavoidable.

The British and Irish Association of Law Librarians'

memorandum (*Law Librarian*, vol. 5, no. 1, April 1974, pp. 9–13) submitted to the LA Cataloguing Rules Committee in August 1973, was concerned primarily with the practical needs of law libraries and of members of the legal profession using them, although the needs of general libraries were also mentioned. It was also aimed at correcting the North American bias of the AACR, which is evident in both the content and the vocabulary of several of the special legal rules, even in the British edition.

There is much common ground in the results that would be achieved by adopting the Australian or British proposals, which are much closer to each other, though prepared entirely independently, than either is to the American document. But it must be mentioned that some law libraries, particularly if they have subject catalogues, do not include primary materials in their author catalogues at all.

Choice of jurisdiction

Most legislation, including constitutional documents, is entered under the name of the country or other jurisdiction concerned. In most cases, there is no problem of choice, as the jurisdiction that produced the document is identical to the one governed by it. But in a limited number of cases, one government produces a law, often a constitution, that applies to another government. For example, the British North America Act 1867 (30 & 31 Vict. c. 3) was the first of a long line of independence constitutions enacted by the United Kingdom Parliament.

Some means of linking these documents with the countries in which they are effective was necessary, and was provided in the 1908 code (rule 68) by the use of the sub-heading *Constitution*, so that the BNA Act, for example, was entered under **Canada**. *Constitution*. This provision was extended in the 1949 ALA code (rule 84.B) to cover all legislation passed by one parliament but intended to have effect in a dependency, with the usual subheading for legislation used with the name of the dependency. The rule has been further extended in AACR (rule 20.A) to cover any 'law or decree promulgated by a jurisdiction other than the one governed by it'.

But the question is not as simple as it may seem, especially in the United Kingdom. A number of acts of the United Kingdom Parliament at Westminster are specifically restricted to England and Wales or to Scotland or to Northern Ireland (see page 111). It would be intolerable to have current British legislation entered under several different jurisdictional headings. A second problem concerns the Local Acts of the United Kingdom parliament. AACR prints as an example the London County Council (General Powers) Act 1892, which is shown entered under **London** (*County*). *Laws, by-laws, etc.* The British committee registered a strong objection to this on the grounds that an act of the United Kingdom Parliament is binding on all citizens, although its intended effect may be largely or wholly limited in geographical extent. Indeed, one reason for the existence of a Local Act may be the need to authorize one local authority to perform stated actions outside its own normal jurisdictional area. A new wording was therefore proposed: 'If one jurisdiction enacts a law intended to form part of the law of a jurisdiction outside its own borders, enter under the jurisdiction governed by the law. (N.B. A Local Act of the United Kingdom Parliament is entered under the heading for United Kingdom legislation, not that of the local authority named in the title of the Act.)'

Arrangement within a jurisdiction

The 1967 AACR provides form sub-headings to be used with jurisdictions, for legislation, constitutions, charters and treaties and with the name of the court concerned for court rules. Both the Australian and British law librarians now oppose the use of form sub-headings on the practical grounds that if they are used, legal materials will inevitably be interfiled with other official publications emanating from a wide range of government departments, committees and other bodies. The resulting scatter of the records of basic legal documents is very unsatisfactory, especially for law libraries. The practical solution is both reasonably simple and theoretically pure: all such materials should be entered under the name of the jurisdiction with no sub-heading.

The British committee considered that it was very important to achieve a useful filing order, more useful than a single alphabetical sequence, for the scores or even hundreds of assorted titles that will accumulate under important jurisdictions. They proposed a system of what they called form filing titles: words or phrases inserted between the heading and the actual title of the document, fulfilling a function very similar to that of uniform titles used in filing literary or other works, but made up of conventional descriptions of legal forms, bearing some similarity in wording to the discarded form sub-headings. An example will demonstrate the difference:

> form sub-heading **Canada**. *Laws, statutes, etc.*
> form filing title **Canada**
> [Legislation. Individual laws]

The British memorandum includes a complete list of all form filing titles recommended, with guide numbers to help maintain the correct filing order and to assist with any mechanical filing routine (see page 530).

Legislation

The AACR contains four rules that deal with legislation:

> rule 20   Laws, etc.
> rule 21   Administrative regulations
> rule 22   Constitutions and charters
> rule 23   Court rules

Rule 20.A specifies three alternative form sub-headings for legislation: *Laws, statutes, etc.*, which is used for sovereign jurisdictions (nations, states of a federation, city-states, etc.); *Laws, by-laws, etc.*, which is used for Commonwealth local jurisdictions (counties, towns, etc.); and *Ordinances, local laws, etc.* for use with non-Commonwealth jurisdictions.

The British recommendation for sovereign jurisdictions was to substitute a filing title [Legislation] for the sub-heading *Laws, statutes, etc.*, with sub-divisions for closed collections, serial collections and individual laws. For local legislation, they recommended a single filing title, preferably [By-laws, etc.] or alternatively [Local laws].

Rule 20.B covers volumes containing legislation of more than one jurisdiction which, as the Australians pointed out, could be covered by rule 20.A coupled with the standard rules on shared authorship (3) and collections (5). Rule 20.C for legislative bills and drafts, specifies entry under personal or corporate author. According to rule 20.D, ancient, medieval and customary laws are to be entered under suitable uniform titles.

Although the titles of rules 20 and 21 suggest that they cover respectively primary and subsidiary legislation (see page 120) the distinction is not clearly drawn. The only publications unambiguously covered by rule 21 are special subject collections of subsidiary legislation (or primary and subsidiary legislation together) issued by government departments, which are to be entered under the department. This omits most of the volumes of secondary legislation likely to be encountered in a British or Irish library, especially both the closed and serial collections. Presumably they should be catalogued under rule 20, but this is not clearly stated.

For the main bulk of delegated legislation, the BIALL proposed entry under jurisdiction, with a group of filing titles, with the main element [Legislation – Subsidiary] being subdivided in the same way as primary legislation, by closed and serial collections and individual laws. Both the Australian and British groups recommended the abolition of rule 21.B, so that volumes containing both primary and secondary legislation would be catalogued under the rules for primary legislation.

Constitutions and charters

According to rule 22.A and B, constitutions and charters of political jurisdictions, the League of Nations and the United Nations are entered under the name of the jurisdiction or organization governed with the sub-heading *Constitution* or *Charter* as appropriate (*Covenant* for the League). Both the British and Australian committees preferred filing titles to sub-headings, the British being content with filing titles in English, while the Australians preferred the language of the country concerned, *eg* [Bundesverfassung] for West Germany.

Court rules

The rules governing procedure and allied matters in the courts of the United Kingdom are found in Statutory Instruments, *ie*, subsidiary legislation, drafted by special committees set up for the purpose. There seems to be no particular need for special rules for cataloguing this material, which most law libraries will also have in the convenient annotated form of *The Supreme Court Practice, County Court Practice*, etc., which can be catalogued by the normal rules.

The situation in the United States, with its multiplicity of legal jurisdictions, is far more complicated. Rule 23 in the North American text of AACR specifies a form sub-heading *Court rules* to be used with the jurisdiction and sub-divided by courts, *eg*, **Canada**. *Court rules. Supreme Court.* The Library Association Cataloguing Rules Committee, possibly under the misapprehension that there was more similarity than in fact exists between United Kingdom and United States practice in this area, decided to separate court rules from other delegated legislation and placed them, in the British version of rule 23, under the court governed, with a form sub-heading *Rules, eg,* **Canada**. *Supreme Court. Rules.* The same argument was followed by the Australian group. The BIALL considered that, if a special rule was needed because of variations in national practice, the American principle of entry under jurisdiction was better, and proposed filing titles accordingly.

Law reports

As explained in Chapters 2 and 4, law reports form the core of any British or Irish law library. Cataloguing codes, at least since 1908, have entered them under the court concerned, as if it was the author, unless the reports cover four or more courts, when they are entered under the title (26.A). Although the legal profession would probably fail to recognize court authorship of law reports, the cataloguing rule is based on the theory that law reports 'communicate the substantive results of a corporate activity' (Escreet, *Introduction to the Anglo-American Cataloguing Rules*, p. 108). In terms of cataloguing theory this is no doubt correct, and its application may be adequate for a general library which happens to hold one or two series of law reports. But for the legal profession, whose members are almost the sole users of this highly specialized form of publication, entries under the names of courts are almost totally irrelevant and useless. The law library user possesses the citation of a specific case, in one of the forms described in Chapter 4, and may not know what court was concerned or even, possibly, the jurisdiction. To locate an unfamiliar report, he requires a catalogue entry based either on the citation or on form. It is significant that all three law librarians' groups rejected entry under the names of courts.

The AALL examined the advantages and disadvantages of both author and form entry, including questions of logical arrangement and the scattering of entries, problems of reports covering several courts (as many of the most important series do) and the need for filing titles and subject entries. They proposed a new form sub-heading, *Law reports*, to be used with the jurisdiction, which was not accepted in AACR.

The British and Australian groups, though taking different routes, arrived at virtually identical results: enter law reports under the full form of the standard citation, *ie*, the reporter, for the older nominate reports, otherwise under title. This means, in effect, applying the original rules 4 and 6 to all law reports.

Digests and citators

Rule 26.B specifies entry for digests and citators under the compiler or editor, if named, otherwise under the title. The BIALL committee found this satisfactory, but the Australians pointed out that the same result would be achieved by using general rules 4 and 6. The Americans proposed that these materials should be entered under the jurisdiction with form sub-heading *Law reports*, with a further sub-heading *Digests* or *Citations*.

Single cases

Rule 26.C has nine sub-sections dealing with the proceedings, briefs, pleas, jury charges, decisions and other records relating to individual cases. Proceedings and general reports of a single case are entered under the name of one of the parties: the plaintiff in civil cases and the defendant in criminal cases. The rules for entering the various individual documents are based either on authorship or the name most closely associated with the case. A law library which holds such materials in any quantity is likely to collect them – and its readers are likely to look for them – by particular cases, rather than by the names of judges, barristers or others. The British committee recommended that all such documents should be catalogued under the heading for the case. If this is done, a law library would need only one entry for each case, in which the individual documents held could be listed as a contents note. It was also proposed that collections of an individual's judgments, pleas, etc., in a variety of cases should be entered under his name.

Treaties

Under rule 27.F, collections of treaties of one party with several other parties, such as the United Kingdom *Treaty Series*, are entered under the jurisdiction with the sub-heading *Treaties, etc*. The Australians recommended that they could be adequately catalogued under original rules 5 and 6, collections and serials.

Cataloguing individual treaties is more difficult. There are many kinds of treaties, varying according to the number and legal status of the parties. As with legislation, they cannot usefully be catalogued by the authorship principle. Under rule 25.A to C, single treaties are entered under the names of jurisdictions or international organizations, with the form sub-heading *Treaties, etc*. The jurisdiction for the main entry is selected according to a list of priorities in which the home jurisdiction and the country first mentioned on the title-page figure high up. This means that entries for a particular multi-partite treaty in libraries in different countries, or entries for editions published in different countries, will be made under a wide variety of jurisdictions.

The AACR method of categorizing treaties results in a lengthy and complicated rule. The British recommendation, also based on entry under jurisdiction, with suitable filing titles, used different categories, but is not substantially simpler. The Australian proposal was more radical: to enter each treaty under an accepted form of its name. This could be an attractive solution to a difficult problem, but could also cause considerable problems of filing and identification in a large collection of individual treaties.

So far, it seems, a satisfactory answer to the multifarious

problems of entering treaties in the author and title catalogue has yet to be found. Subject cataloguing of this material is considerably easier, and probably provides a more effective method of information retrieval.

DESCRIPTIVE CATALOGUING

The term 'descriptive cataloguing' is sometimes used to cover the whole process of compiling the entries for the main alphabetical catalogue, including the selection of headings according to a cataloguing code. Here it is confined to the compilation of the individual descriptive entry. The objects of the description are to identify the book, clearly distinguishing it from any similar works, including other editions of the same work, and to give other information which may assist the reader in the choice of material for his particular purposes. The first type of information forms the essential core of all entries, the second may vary considerably from library to library according to the cataloguer's assessment of his readers' needs. It is advisable to follow a code of rules, such as AACR rules 130 to 168 or the Library of Congress *Rules for descriptive cataloguing* (Washington, D.C., Government Printing Office, 1949, and Supplement, 1952).

The elements of an entry are: the heading, title statement, imprint, collation, call mark and notes. Figure 1 shows a conventional typed entry containing all these elements. The heading, whose selection is dealt with on pages 516–26, is usually typed in capitals (wholly or partly) or printed in bold type, so that it stands out clearly from the main body of the entry, for ease of finding and filing. The title statement, which includes the edition number (after the first edition) and the imprint (details of publisher and date) usually form a single paragraph. The collation, which contains details of the physical make up of the book, such as the number of pages, size, illustrations, maps, etc., usually forms a new paragraph, to which is sometimes added a series note. Other notes form another paragraph. The call mark (see page 575), which leads the reader to the subject section where the book is shelved, should have a prominent position in the entry. Some libraries type call marks in red to make them stand out.

```
KN 196.4

KAHN-FREUND, Otto

    Laws against strikes [by] Otto Kahn-
Freund & Bob Hepple. London, Fabian Society,
1972.

    [2], 61p. 22 cm (Fabian research series,
305; International comparisons in social
policy, 1)

    ISBN 0 7163 1305--7
```

Figure 1

Monographs

The title page is used as the basis of the entry. The title statement should be transcribed from it as exactly as possible.
Accepted variations from exact copying are: putting in second
position an explanatory sub-title that precedes the main
title; omitting the series title from the title statement and
placing it in the series note position; abbreviation of a very
long title, using the standard omission sign (. . .). Imprint
details are usually found on one or both sides of the title page.

It is very important that the edition number (except for the
first edition) should be included in the title statement. Care is
needed to distinguish between a mere reprint, re-issue, etc. of a
previous identical text, and a true new edition, with textual
changes of substance.

The amount of detail needed in the collation depends to a
considerable extent on the age and rarity of the volume. Early
printed books require painstaking detail of signatures and
pagination to help identify the exact edition or copy held. For
modern books, printed in thousands, the simple number of
volumes or pages is probably sufficient. Few law books contain
illustrations, but those there are should be noted in the collation.

Series notes can be useful, and for many official documents, such as Command papers, they are an essential feature of the item's identity. Other notes may be devised by the cataloguer giving any additional information required, for example: a list of contributors or special contents (such as papers in a particular case, see page 524); other pamphlets bound in the same cover as the one being catalogued; whether the book is written for academics, students or the general public. The International Standard Book Number should be noted, if it can be found, but a standard position for the note has not yet been agreed. (The Standard Book Numbering Agency produced an explanatory leaflet in 1967.)

Serial publications

Series, such as annual reports, which are to be entered under an author heading, take a form similar to that of monographs (Fig. 2).

```
KL 131.1

UNIVERSITY OF LONDON. Institute of Advanced
    Legal Studies.

    Annual report.  18th, 1st August, 1964
    [to] 31st July, 1965 -

    London, the Institute.
```

Figure 2

Series that are to be entered by title, with no heading, have a slightly different format (Fig. 3).

In either case, the details of the volumes held should be included, normally in the title statement. If the holding is too broken for this to be practical, the information should be given

K1.M6

MODERN law review. Vol. 1, 1937 -

   London, Stevens.

   Index to vols. 1-21, 1959.

Figure 3

in a note (extending, if necessary, onto a second card). Current continuations are usually indicated, as in Figs. 2 and 3, by an open entry. This should be closed when the series ceases publication or the library's subscription is cancelled. The International Standard Serial Number should be given if possible.

Use of filing titles

As explained on page 521, entries for primary materials are made, according to the main codes, using sub-headings in a similar manner to Fig. 2. If it is decided to use form filing titles, instead of form sub-headings, entry would be as in Figure 4.

A complete list of the form filing titles recommended by the BIALL follows. Main entries for law reports are not made in this form (see page 523). For the benefit of libraries that wish to have a record of law reports under jurisdiction in the author catalogue, thus completing the record of primary materials for each jurisdiction, the Sub-Committee produced an unpublished suggestion for added entries under jurisdiction with a form filing title. These optional added entries are marked with an asterisk in the list.

```
KF 23. H1

GREAT BRITAIN
    [Legislation. Collections. 1968]

    Halsbury's statutes of England. 3rd ed.
London, Butterworths, 1968-72.

    42 v.
    [Annual] statutes, 1968 -
    Tables and index to volumes 1-40
    Cumulative supplement 1973.
```

Figure 4

Sovereign jurisdictions :

1. [Constitution]
2. [Constitution. Amendments. Collections]
3. [Constitution. [x th] amendment, [date]]
4. [Legislation. Collections, [date]]
5. [Legislation. Collections – Serial]
6. [Legislation. Individual laws]
7. [Legislation. Indexes, etc.]
8. [Legislation – Codes. Collections, [date]]
9. [Legislation – Codes. Separate codes]
10. [Legislation – Subsidiary. Collections, [date]]
11. [Legislation – Subsidiary. Collections – Serial]
12. [Legislation – Subsidiary. Individual laws]
13. [Legislation – Subsidiary. Indexes, etc.]
14. [Treaty of establishment]
15. [Treaties. Collections, [inclusive dates]]
16. [Treaties. Collections, [subjects, A–Z]]
17. [Treaties. Multi-partite, [date]]
18. [Treaties. Bi-partite, [date]]
19. [Treaties. Bi-partite, [countries, A–Z], [date]]
20. [Treaties. Indexes, etc.]
21. [Court rules. Collections, [date]]
22. [Court rules. [Court(s), A–Z]]

*23. [Law reports. Collections, [inclusive dates]]
*24. [Law reports. Collections, [subjects, A–Z]]
*25. [Law reports. [Individual courts, A–Z], [inclusive dates]]
*26. [Law reports. Digests, etc.]

Local jurisdictions

1. [Charter]
2. [By-laws, etc.]

Other entries and references

If the unit entry principle has been adopted (see page 511) added entries are made, according to the cataloguing rules, by simply adding the appropriate heading above the unit entry (Fig. 5). If unit entries are not used, some form of reference is usually made.

```
KN 196.4

HEPPLE, Bob

KAHN-FREUND, Otto

    Laws against strikes [by] Otto Kahn-
Freund & Bob Hepple. London, Fabian Society,
1972.

    [2], 61p. 22 cm. (Fabian research series,
305; International comparisons in social
policy, 1)

    ISBN 0 7163 1305 7
```

Figure 5

A normal *see* reference from a form of heading not used to the selected form requires a single card in a format such as Figure 6.

References used instead of added entries are usually in a format somewhere between a *see* reference and a full entry.

```
FREUND, Otto Kahn-

    see KAHN-FREUND, Otto
```

Figure 6

A subject *see also* reference usually lists all relevant subjects on a single card (Fig. 7).

```
CRIMINAL PROCEDURE

    see also
    Appellate procedure      Juries
    Bail                     Law and fact
    Confession(Law)          Parole
    Criminal courts          Pleading
    Criminal law             Probation
    Evidence, Criminal       Psychology,Forensic
    Habeas corpus            Public defenders
    Indictments              Public prosecutors
    Instructions to juries
```

Figure 7

Entries for films, microfilms, slides, discs, tapes, etc., should be made in a format similar to that for books, with appropriate variations. Guidance can be had from the codes listed at the end of the chapter.

Analytical entries of any kind, author, title or subject, should give details of the article or chapter concerned, together with an abbreviated entry for the whole work in which it appears (Fig. 8).

```
KV 11

SCHWARZENBERGER, Georg

    European common law.

    in Current legal problems, 1973. London,
       Stevens, 1973. pp.114-130
       Shelved at K1.C9
```

Figure 8

Simplified cataloguing

Always provided that the entry contains the details essential for identification of the document catalogued (heading, title, edition, date) other details can be abbreviated or omitted. The saving in time and stationery is unlikely to be substantial, but the simpler entry may be easier for readers to absorb than a full one. As details of imprint and collation are needed by library staff, if not by readers, the shelf-list at least should have full entries.

Tracings

Sooner or later, the entries for a book will probably have to be removed from the catalogue, either for amendment or cancellation. To ensure that all entries will be traced and dealt with, it is usual to type a list of all entries for the book on the back of the master card, which can be either the main entry card or the shelf-list card. Printed cards from LC or BNB have the tracings printed at the bottom. Whatever physical form of catalogue a library has, it is strongly recommended that a master card file of tracings should be maintained. For example, the tracings on the back of the card printed as Fig. 1 on page 527 would be as Figure 9.

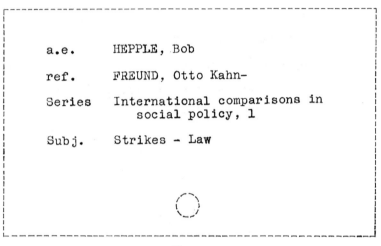

```
   a.e.      HEPPLE, Bob

   ref.      FREUND, Otto Kahn-

   Series    International comparisons in
                 social policy, 1

   Subj.     Strikes - Law
```

Figure 9

SUBJECT CATALOGUES AND INDEXES

Many librarians think that a good subject catalogue is the finest single research tool that a large library can possess. The compilation of a good subject catalogue is one of the most difficult tasks that a librarian can undertake. Another important factor is cost. It is not difficult to produce a fairly cheap subject list that is better than nothing, but whose value is so limited as to be scarcely worth the trouble. For the creation of a *good* subject catalogue, much time and patience is needed, and corners may not be cut.

There are two basic forms of subject catalogue, the alphabetical and the classified. The balance of advantage between the two is finely poised. A librarian who wishes to have the benefits of both systems, at least for his own use, may well

choose to have a public alphabetical catalogue supplemented
by a classified, and possibly expanded, shelf-list.

Classified catalogues

As the name suggests, a classified catalogue is arranged in class
order. For details of classification schemes, see Chapter 15.
There used to be a tendency in British libraries to compile a
simple classified sequence, with one card for each book, which
could be done with a minimum of time, effort and expense, and
to claim that the library had a classified catalogue. Any such
claims were false. The classified file is only half the catalogue,
the other half being an alphabetical subject index, which
enables users to find the class numbers for the subjects they
wish to investigate. For indexing methods see page 536.

The need for two separate sequences, one classified and one
alphabetical, demonstrates a disadvantage of the classified
catalogue. The reader frequently has to consult both sequences
before receiving any bibliographic information. The subject
index leads him, not directly to catalogue entries, but only to a
class number. Once he has reached the appropriate part of the
classified file, he should receive the benefits of a catalogue in a
useful systematic order, but these benefits can be only as good as
the classification scheme used. An unsuitable classification
scheme is unlikely to result in a first class classified catalogue.
But the catalogue has two great advantages over the classified
shelf arrangement of the books themselves: it can contain
several cards, at different class numbers, for each book; and the
cards are in place permanently, whereas many of the best books
are off the shelves most of the time.

A classified catalogue based on a well compiled classification
scheme, with analytical subject entries for many books and a
full alphabetical index, can be a very valuable tool for reader
and librarian alike. But a library that is not fully classified, or
one that is obliged to continue using a scheme not well suited to
a law library, would be better served by an alphabetical subject
catalogue.

Alphabetical subject catalogues

As readers almost invariably think of their information needs and problems in subject words rather than class numbers, some libraries provide a catalogue with entries under the names of subjects arranged alphabetically. Provided the reader and the librarian are using the same terms, information may be found more quickly from the single alphabetical file than through the apparently more cumbersome mechanism of the classified catalogue.

However, the great disadvantage of the alphabetical subject catalogue is the arbitrariness of the alphabetical order of words, compared with the systematic classified order. Closely related concepts, such as sale of goods, price control, consumer protection and advertising will be widely separated. Also, great care is needed in dealing with synonymous or nearly synonymous subject words so that, for example, entries are not distributed at random between conflict of laws and private international law.

These two problems are handled by the use of respectively *see also* references and *see* references (see page 532). In this way, related headings such as sale of goods and price control are linked by *see also* references and alternative headings that are not selected for use are recorded by *see* references to the chosen heading. For the use of subject headings lists to help in selecting terms see page 539.

Locating all material on a series of related topics by moving from one heading to all the other headings listed on the *see also* card (see Fig. 7 on page 532) may take as long, or longer, in the alphabetical catalogue as would a comparable search in the classified catalogue. But many librarians, particularly those obliged to use a broad or unsuitable classification scheme, or none at all, have found that a good alphabetical subject catalogue brings out aspects of the library's stock that would otherwise be hidden.

Indexes

A law librarian may need to construct a subject index to a classified file, or he may be asked to make regular contributions to a co-operative indexing project, such as the *Index to Foreign Legal Periodicals*. In the second case, he will receive specific indexing instructions. The production of indexes for publication is outside the scope of this volume.

Subject indexing differs from subject cataloguing in that an index refers the reader to a class or accession number while a subject catalogue consists of direct entries for the books. The index should contain all the specific detailed terms that are necessary. For a small library, a simple index, consisting of specific terms only, may be sufficient. But for a larger collection, especially if it is used for research, either professional or academic, an index that will relate terms to each other and demonstrate the hierarchy of subjects (see page 550) is required.

Chain procedure

The simplest method of producing a relative index is chain-indexing. It involves stating the elements that make up the class number, from the most specific to the more general, in a sequence, *eg*:

Boundaries : Treaties : International law	KC336.3
Coroners : Legal officers : Administration of justice	KL254
Revocation : Wills : Inheritance : Property	KNI25.4

Each of these would produce a 'chain' of entries such as:

Wills : Inheritance : Property	KNI25
Inheritance : Property	KNI20–43
Property	KN50–143

Vocabulary control is as necessary in indexing as in cataloguing. Subject headings lists and thesauri can be used to supplement the words used in the actual classification schedules.

Co-ordinate indexing

This method, sometimes known as uniterm indexing, may be used for detailed analysis of a limited range of documents, such as counsel's opinions, briefs, etc., for which printed indexes are inadequate or not available. Each document is assigned a unique accession number and as many subject terms as necessary. A separate record card is kept for each term in the list of terms used, usually based on a thesaurus. The document's accession number is recorded on each of the appropriate term cards.

To locate material dealing with a complex subject such as 'sentencing minors in theft cases in Scotland', the term cards for sentencing, minors, theft and Scotland would be compared. Any document whose accession number appeared on all four cards would be likely to provide relevant information. A practical version of this system is described by Miss Bull in *Law Librarian*, vol. 1, no. 3, 1970, pp. 40–41.

A number of more sophisticated indexing methods, usually known by acronyms such as KWIC, KWOC, PRECIS and SLIC have been designed, primarily for mechanized indexing. Further information is given on page 651.

Control of subject vocabulary

The English language is well known for the richness of the synonyms and near synonyms it contains. The language of law is no exception. There are, for example, many cases of modern terms like family law co-existing with older terms such as domestic relations.

There are also a large number of legal topics that require two or more words to define them, for example: administration of justice, ancient lights, appellate procedure, artificial insemination, atomic energy. Many of these subject phrases can be expressed either in plain language, as above, or in an inverted order, producing a semi-classified sequence, such as:

> Procedure, Administrative
> Procedure, Appellate
> Procedure, Civil
> Procedure, Criminal

In addition, these and many other headings can be sub-divided, for example: civil procedure – comparative law (or procedure, civil – comparative law). There are also a few terms which can have two different meanings, and which must therefore have an explanation attached, such as prohibition (liquor) and prohibition (writ).

These are some examples of the type of complication that can arise as soon as any kind of subject cataloguing is attempted. As consistency is as vitally important here as in every other part of bibliographic organization, a fully organized authority list is necessary.

Subject headings lists

The two best-known published lists of subject headings are American: the Library of Congress *Subject headings used in the dictionary catalogs* (7th edition. Washington, D.C., 1966) and *Sears' List of Subject Headings* (10th edition. New York, H. W. Wilson, 1972). The Sears list has insufficient legal detail to be any use in a specialist law library. The LC list contains a great deal of detail but, as it is a general list, the legal headings are only a small part of it. A special list, based on the LC list, was compiled by Werner B. Ellinger: *Subject headings for the literature of law and international law* (2nd edition. South Hackensack, New Jersey, Rothman for American Association of Law Libraries, 1969. AALL publications series, no. 9). The list is, naturally, biased towards North American terminology and usage and therefore requires adaptation for use in British or Irish law libraries.

Thesauri

Indexers, particularly in scientific and technical subjects, came to find that the conventional subject headings lists had insufficient detail for their needs. Also, the cross-references were too unsystematic, especially for mechanized information retrieval. For example, *see also* references are made both to related terms at the same level of division as the main heading and to terms at other levels. New specialized lists, with the name of 'thesaurus', are being compiled. There is as yet no fully accepted pattern. Some thesauri differ only a little from conventional subject headings lists, while others consist of at least two sequences for the same collection of terms, one classified and one alphabetical.

A multi-lingual list of legal headings was published in the *Index to Foreign Legal Periodicals* (volume 4, special number, February 1963). It is not a full-scale thesaurus, but has a broadly classified sequence in English, French, German and

Spanish, followed by separate alphabetical lists in each of the four languages, with English translations of the foreign terms. The English list has a considerable number of *see* and *see also* references. Mr W. A. Steiner presented a report at the 39th General Council of IFLA, Geneva, 1973, on 'Thesaurus problems as exemplified by the *Index to Foreign Legal Periodicals*' (*International Journal of Law Libraries*, volume 2, no. 1, March 1974, pp. 5–13). Another of Mr Steiner's products, the classification scheme of the Squire Law Library (see page 571), is closely associated with a list of legal subject headings. This is also in two parts, classified and alphabetical.

DEPARTMENTAL ORGANIZATION

The Cataloguing Department is responsible, in most libraries, for both cataloguing and classification, the production of catalogue cards, slips, etc., filing them in the catalogues and providing guidance for the public in the use of the catalogues. The Chief Cataloguer is responsible for allocating duties to his staff; ensuring that all books are handled expeditiously and that any priority items are dealt with immediately; recording statistics of categories of work done, *eg*, books catalogued or re-catalogued, author and subject cards filed; maintaining consistency by means of cross-checking work done and keeping up to date the authority files and departmental manual. It is desirable for all members of the department to have some typing ability, but entries for the public catalogues should be produced by trained typists, if possible. Other duties, such as duplicating cards or slips, sorting entries and preliminary filing 'on the rod' (without removing the rods from the card drawers or sheaf binders) can be performed by unqualified assistants. Filing should always be checked by a professional cataloguer.

Physical forms of catalogues

A library's catalogues should be easy for both staff and readers to use. The furniture should be reasonably compact, but not requiring users either to bend double or to stand on tiptoe to reach any part of the contents (see also page 617). From the librarian's point of view, the most important criterion is flexibility. It is an added advantage if entries can be easily copied for reporting to union catalogues.

The commonest and most flexible form of catalogue is made up of cards, one for each entry or reference, filed in drawers. The usual size of card is about 5″ × 3″ (125 mm. × 75 mm.) and the average drawer holds up to 1,000 cards. Another flexible form is the sheaf catalogue, consisting of paper slips filed in loose-leaf binders. Slips are usually about 8″ × 4″ and most binders hold 500 to 600 slips. They are housed in cabinets with shelves or pigeon-holes tailored to fit them. A strip-index: metal panels holding strips of thick card, about ½″ deep and 6″ to 8″ long, though unsuitable for a full catalogue, may be useful for a location list for serials or for titles of books on temporary reserve.

While printed catalogues have permanent value as sources of bibliographical information, their total inflexibility makes them unsuitable for use in a growing library, but the use of book-style catalogues has been revived in libraries which have completely computerized their stock records (see page 635).

Reproduction of entries

Typing is the simplest method that is consistently legible. If only three or four copies of the entry are needed, it is also the cheapest. Even an experienced typist needs careful instruction for the work, as the layout and some of the details, such as capitalization and punctuation, are likely to be different from those she is used to.

A number of duplicating methods are available, sometimes with minor modifications, for producing multiple copies of unit entries, such as: spirit duplicators, wax-stencil duplicators, xerographic copiers, offset lithography or addressing machines. Tape typewriters may be used either to produce cards or input data for computerized catalogues (see page 630). For some titles, printed cards can be purchased from the British National Bibliography or the Library of Congress.

Filing

The filing order for a classified catalogue is governed by the citation order of the classification scheme (see Chapter 15) and does not usually present many problems.

The question of arranging an alphabetical catalogue, either author/title or subject catalogue, is not quite 'as easy as ABC'. Entries in the former will be a mixture of proper names for persons, organizations and places, while in the subject catalogue will appear one-word headings, phrases and sub-divided headings. For the sake of consistency, it is essential to use a code of filing rules, such as the *ALA Rules for Filing Catalog Cards* (2nd edition. Chicago, American Library Association, 1968) or the Library of Congress *Filing Rules for the Dictionary Catalogs* (reprinted in Ann Arbor, Michigan, Finch Press, 1956). A very simple code for author/title catalogues is the British Standards Institution's *Alphabetical Arrangement and the Filing of Numerals and Symbols* (BSI, 1969. BS 1749: 1969. ISBN 0 580 05620 1).

There are two alternative basic rules of alphabetization, either word by word or letter by letter, *eg*,

Word by word	*Letter by letter*
New Brunswick	Newark, Peter
New law of theft	New Brunswick
New South Wales	Newby, Andrew
New Zealand	Newfoundland
Newark, Peter	Newlands, George
Newby, Andrew	New law of theft
Newfoundland	Newman, Barbara
Newlands, George	New South Wales
Newman, Barbara	Newspapers and the law
Newspapers and the law	Newton, Ralph
Newton, Ralph	New Zealand

Each method is favoured by some libraries, but most printed filing rules recommend the word by word method. Filing codes also deal with many other matters, such as: abbreviations, acronyms, alternative spellings (including versions of the same title in different languages), compound names, firms, foreign names, numerals, prefixes, punctuation marks and umlauts.

Several entries under an identical heading are arranged alphabetically by title. In all titles, an initial article (a, the, le,

la, der, die, das, etc.) is ignored for filing purposes, but articles
occurring in the middle of the title are taken into account.

Authority files

Every library should keep a full record of all decisions taken in
the Cataloguing Department. This is most easily done by
annotating printed codes and schedules, where used, for
decisions of principle, and maintaining authority files on cards
of all decisions on individual cases. As the library grows, the
time saved in going to and from the catalogue for constant
checking of forms of names, the existence of subject or name
references and whether series added entries are made or not,
will soon become apparent.

The authority file for the author/title catalogue should
contain a card for each name selected for use, when any element of doubt occurs. This will be only a small proportion of
the names actually appearing in the catalogue, even if, as suggested, a card is made for each corporate author heading,
whether doubtful or not. On this master card should be indicated all the *see* references made, and a copy of each reference
should also be made for the authority file (Fig. 10).

```
SILSOE, Malcolm Trustram Eve, Baron

    x Eve, Malçolm Trustram

    x Trustram Eve, Malcolm




E.M.M.
24.1.74
```

Figure 10

For future reference, it is useful to have the date and author-ship of the decision recorded on the master card.

If the library makes added entries for the titles of certain series, authority cards will be needed for the names of *all* series held, to indicate whether entries are made or not. If volumes in certain special series are classified as a series, rather than under their individual subjects, this must also be noted. Any *see* references necessary, for example for a series which has changed its title, should be made as for other names. Three possible types of series authority instructions are:

    (1) Classified as a series at KL401
        Analytics made
    (2) Classified separately
        Added entry for series
    (3) Classified separately
        No added entry for series

A library that has a subject catalogue should keep a subject authority file in classified or alphabetical order, as appropriate, for all subject decisions. The shelf-list could be regarded as a special form of subject authority file, although that is not its main function.

Authority files should be kept for any other type of decision regularly taken, such as Cutter numbers for subjects or for authors' names (see page 576).

Co-operative cataloguing

When libraries form a co-operative cataloguing arrangement, the usual intention is to produce a union catalogue recording their joint resources in a single combined record. The purposes and uses of union catalogues are described on page 394.

In compiling a union catalogue, the number of contributing libraries and the amount of detail required in recording individual holdings, especially serials, are factors in determining the physical form the catalogue should take. A normal $5'' \times 3''$ card is unlikely to be suitable. Cards and drawers are available in larger standard sizes, such as $6'' \times 4''$ and $8'' \times 5''$. Some large union catalogues are maintained in sheaf form.

Computers are being used for some union catalogues, and their use will no doubt be extended.

There are various methods of compiling union catalogues. The largest library may duplicate and circulate a list of titles it holds, which others annotate and return, for the compilers to transfer the information to the central record cards or slips. Alternatively, each contributing library may submit a list of its own holdings, possibly by photocopying the relevant entries from their own catalogues. The latter method can result in many queries having to be referred back to contributors, especially if cataloguing systems vary widely.

Great care is needed in entering reports in the central record. Mistakes can cause endless trouble, both to enquirers and to libraries. It can be useful to have cards or slips printed on the lower half with a grid of lines forming squares or oblongs. The squares are marked with the abbreviations symbolizing the various libraries and their holdings recorded in them.

Some method of keeping the union catalogue up-to-date should be agreed. For monographs, the simplest is the regular production and submission by each library of an extra copy of each new main catalogue entry produced, but accessions or *ad hoc* lists can be used instead.

Once the use of Standard Book Numbers becomes the accepted standard, they would form the briefest and simplest method of reporting and recording union catalogue information, especially in computerized systems.

Re-cataloguing

Sometimes it is necessary to consider re-cataloguing all or part of a library, for example because of faulty work in the past or because of a decision to adopt a new cataloguing code or the need to make various minor adjustments. This problem particularly affects large libraries that wish to make use of MARC tapes, or any libraries that use printed cards produced by BNB under the 1967 AACR.

The practical aspects of re-cataloguing are basically similar to those of re-classification, which are discussed on page 577.

FURTHER READING

CATALOGUING PRINCIPLES AND PRACTICE

Akers, Susan Grey. *Simple Library Cataloging.* 5th edition. Metuchen, N.J., Scarecrow Press, 1969 (ISBN 0 8108 0255 4).

Horner, John. *Cataloguing.* Association of Assistant Librarians, 1970 (ISBN 0 900092 04 1).

Needham, Christopher Donald. *Organizing Knowledge in Libraries: an introduction to information retrieval.* 2nd edition. Deutsch, 1971 (ISBN 0 233 95836 3).

CATALOGUING THEORIES AND CODES

Escreet, Phillip K. *Introduction to the Anglo-American Cataloguing Rules.* Deutsch, 1971 (ISBN 0 233 96033 3).

Lubetzky, Seymour. *Cataloging Rules and Principles.* Washington, D.C., Government Printing Office, 1953; reprinted by University Microfilms, 1970 (College of Librarianship Wales reprints, no. 6) (ISBN 0 902741 05 5).

Tait, James A. *Authors and Titles: an analytical study of the author concept in codes of cataloguing rules in the English language* . . . Bingley, 1969 (ISBN 0 85157 082 8).

also: Horner, Chapters 3–7; Needham, Chapters 2–5.

AUTHOR AND TITLE ENTRIES FOR LEGAL MATERIALS

Ellinger, Werner B. Catalog entries for primary legal sources. *Library resources and technical services,* vol. 12, no. 3, summer 1968, pp. 352–8.

Ellinger, Werner B. Non-author headings. *Journal of cataloging and classification,* vol. 10, April 1954, pp. 61–73.

Lubetzky, Seymour. Non-author headings: a negative theory. *Journal of cataloging and classification,* vol. 10, July 1954, pp. 147–154.

Moys, Elizabeth M. Cataloguing legislative materials: some problems. *Law Librarian,* vol. 3, no. 1, April 1972, pp. 6–9, 15.

Willard, D. Dean. The use of form headings in the cataloging of legal materials. *Law Library Journal,* vol. 61, no. 3, August 1968, pp. 289–93.

DESCRIPTIVE CATALOGUING

Croghan, A. *A Manual and Code of Rules for Simple Cataloguing.* Coburgh Publications, 1974 (ISBN 0 9501212 6 6).

Piggott, Mary. Uniformity in descriptive cataloguing. *Libri*, vol. 13, no. 1, 1963, pp. 45–54.

Tait, James A. *Descriptive Cataloguing : a students' introduction to the Anglo-American Cataloguing Rules, 1967*. Bingley, 1968 (ISBN 0 85157 056 9). also : Akers, Chapters 6–8 ; Needham, Chapter 13.

SUBJECT CATALOGUES AND INDEXES

Coates, Eric J. *Subject Catalogues : headings and structure*, new edition, Library Association, 1969 (ISBN 0 85365 462 x).

Haykin, D. J. *Subject Headings : a practical guide*. Washington, D.C., Government Printing Office, 1951 ; reprinted Boston, Mass., Gregg, 1972 (ISBN 0 8398 0810 0).

Shera, Jesse H. *The Classified Catalog : basic principles and practice*, by J. H. Shera and Margaret Egan. Chicago, American Library Association, 1956 (ISBN 0 8389 0026 7). also : Horner, Chapters 8–18 ; Needham, Chapters 9–10.

Indexing

Bull, Gillian. An index for opinions and other documents. *Law Librarian*, vol. 1, no. 3, December 1970, pp. 40–41.

Mills, Jack. Chain-indexing and the classified catalogue. *Library Association record*, vol. 57, no. 4, April 1955, pp. 141–8.

Sharp, John R. Indexing for Retrieval. *In Handbook of special librarianship*. 4th edition. Aslib, 1975, pp. 198–268 also : Horner, Chapters 16 and 18 ; Needham, Chapter 21.

DEPARTMENTAL ORGANIZATION

Bennett, Frederick. *Cataloguing in Practice*. Bingley, 1972 (ISBN 0 85157 141 7).

Pargeter, P. S. *The Reproduction of Catalogue Cards*. Library Association, 1960 (Pamphlet no. 20). o.p.

Trotier, A. H. Organization and administration of cataloging processes. *Library trends*, vol. 2, no. 2, October 1953, pp. 264–78. also : Horner, Chapters 25 and 33–5 ; Needham, Chapters 17 and 20.

Co-operative cataloguing

Brummel, L. *Union Catalogues*. Paris, Unesco, 1956.

Willemin, Silvère. Technique of union catalogues : a practical guide. *Unesco bulletin for libraries*, vol. 20, no. 1, January–February 1966, pp. 2–23. also : Horner, pp. 363–7 ; Needham, Chapter 19.

15. Classification

ELIZABETH M. MOYS, BA, FLA
Librarian, University of London Goldsmiths' College

PRINCIPLES OF LIBRARY CLASSIFICATION

Classification is one of the basic tools of human mental activity. Every time we refer to 'men, women and children' or to 'houses and flats' or to 'a tall fruit tree' we are classifying people or things. Library classification is a special form of this activity, as it involves books and documents which, rather than being dealt with according to their own characteristics as physical objects, are usually classified with reference to the facts or concepts contained in the printed text.

Nevertheless, books are sometimes classified by their inherent qualities, most notably those of age or size. Some books, which are specially valuable because of their antiquity or their rarity, should be kept in secure conditions, apart from the everyday practitioners' manuals or students' textbooks. Other individual volumes (as distinct from multi-volume sets occupying several feet of shelving) are so large that, if they were shelved in their normal places, a good deal of space would be wasted, and therefore they are usually kept in a separate sequence with other oversized books.

The problem of the main bulk of the books in any library is to arrange and display them so as to demonstrate the collection's resources in the way most useful to readers. It is agreed, in most general and special libraries, though not in all law libraries, that the thought content, that is the subject of the books, is the most useful criterion of arrangement. But subject classification of books and documents is also the most difficult form of classification to achieve satisfactorily. Most objects and abstractions can be classified fairly easily according to their physical or theoretical qualities. However, a single document can deal with a variety of subjects and aspects of subjects, which may be more or less inter-related. A library is also bound to take account, at least at the practical level, of bibliographical characteristics of the books, such as whether a volume is a monograph, a bibliography, a periodical, an encyclopedia or perhaps a supplement to another volume.

Classification theories

For many years, library classification was regarded as a specialist offshoot of logic and the traditional theory is concerned primarily with the logical division of subjects, establishing a fixed hierarchy, rather like a family tree. But, as authors write far more about some subjects than others, an entirely theoretical classification of knowledge tends to appear lopsided when applied to the actual literature. To meet this problem, classificationists developed the idea of 'literary warrant', making the number of divisions at each level of a scheme approximately match the existing literature. The traditional schemes attempt to enumerate all subjects and combinations of subjects, but could not anticipate all the new subjects or complex new inter-relationships that might arise.

Classificationists began to look for a new method that would be more flexible and more hospitable to new subjects and to new ways of looking at old subjects. Most of the older schemes have tables for a limited number of aspects that recur in many subjects, such as historical or geographical treatment. In effect, the new theory developed as an extension of this idea from the fringe to the core of each subject, which is analysed into its constituent categories or 'facets', such as raw materials, production methods, purposes, persons, places, periods, languages, literary forms and so on. The list of facets varies from subject to subject, according to their relevance. In a faceted classification scheme, there is a schedule or table for the contents of each facet, for example countries and towns in a place facet. The scheme will also provide a method for combining the elements from the facet tables in a suitable citation order and for indicating the inter-relationships or 'phases' such as one subject influencing another, or one subject being expounded for the benefit of specialists in another. The intention is to enable the individual classifier to build up a class number by a process of synthesis for any subject combination.

There are a number of general principles that any good classification scheme, whether it is enumerative or faceted, should follow. A scheme should not reflect a critical view of any subject in its structure. An extreme example might be putting communism among conspiracies rather than among political theories. The schedule for a subject should, as far as possible, reflect the consensus of informed opinion. The citation order, that is the order in which characteristics of division are applied in an enumerative scheme or facets are cited in a faceted scheme, should be the most suitable for the subject. The principle usually applied is that of decreasing concreteness, but flexibility in citation order can be a useful feature of a faceted scheme.

Layout of schedules

For everyday use, the schedule, however complex, must be set out in linear form. The convention is that the line goes through the 'family tree' as if it was an actual line of family succession.

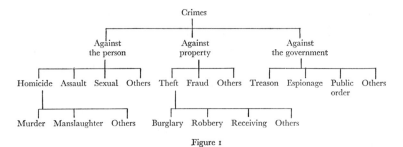

Figure 1

It is normal for the various degrees of subordination of 'son' and 'grandson', etc. to be shown by the degree of indentation. So that the subject classification shown in Fig. 1 would appear in a printed schedule as:

> Crimes
>> Against the person
>>> Homicide
>>>> Murder
>>>> Manslaughter
>>>> [etc.]

Assault
[sub-divisions]
Sexual offences
[sub-divisions]
[etc.]
Against property
Theft
Burglary
Robbery
Receiving
[etc.]
Fraud
[sub-divisions]
[etc.]
Against the government
Treason
Espionage
Public order
[etc.]

LAW LIBRARIES AND CLASSIFICATION

A considerable number of law libraries, particularly those serving professional societies, declare that they are not classified. In the strict sense, this is rarely true, as law reports, statutes and so on are almost invariably separated from the treatises, and materials on foreign or international law are kept apart from those on the local jurisdiction. It is therefore usually correct to say that these libraries are classified very broadly by jurisdiction and form, but that the treatises within a jurisdiction are not classified by subject.

Advantages and disadvantages of subject classification

One of the lawyer's first objections to subject classification is that he knows his books particularly well by author and that alphabetical arrangement is therefore the most efficient. This is true of the classic texts, such as *Chitty on Contracts* or *Ryde on Rating*. But the law is changing rapidly and new subjects are arising, such as consumer protection, environmental preservation and welfare law, for which the old standard treatises are inadequate. In an unclassified collection, the lawyer will have to make enquiries, list the authors of books that might help him, and collect the volumes together from their dispersed shelves in order to assess them. A subject arrangement would probably have all available volumes on adjacent shelves, enabling the lawyer to browse through them easily and quickly to make his selection. It would also enable him to trace a chapter on a very new topic in a more general book, before specialist volumes have been written. These arguments apply more strongly if the user is a student or a research worker.

Some arguments against classification seem to assume that because perfection is impossible (as it clearly is) the good should not be attempted. Shelf classification is a valuable tool, but is only one part of the library's information retrieval system. Allied to a good catalogue, it can help the library to function more efficiently than can an alphabetical arrangement alone. Other objections are based on the inadequacies of particular classification schemes. It is quite true that some schemes are very unsuitable for law libraries, but better schemes exist (see below).

Two disadvantages of using subject classification are that it requires more shelf space and that classifiers, especially if unqualified, can make mistakes. The only remedy for these is the expenditure of more money on space and qualified staff.

Choice of classification scheme

The decision whether to classify or re-classify, and if so by what scheme, is not always within the power of the law librarian, especially in a large general library, but he should be familiar with the problems involved so that he can offer informed advice.

A collection may be classified either broadly into a relatively small number of large categories, such as contracts, torts, property, commercial law or closely, with each class divided and sub-divided into detailed subject units, such as the law of motor vehicle insurance or the law of expert medical evidence.

For a large research library, there can be little doubt that a detailed classification, closely linked with good catalogues, is the best solution. It will enable both the practitioner with a complex case and the advanced student preparing a thesis to locate the materials needed in the most efficient manner.

A smaller library, especially if it is used primarily by practitioners, may find a broad classification more suitable. It is possible, in a small collection, for the use of detailed subdivisions for a handful of books to be unnecessarily confusing and to produce long class marks to no very useful purpose. However, all libraries tend to grow, and in time more detail may be needed. Therefore, the classification scheme chosen should be one that can be easily abbreviated or expanded, as required.

In order to assess the various classification schemes that are available, it is necessary first to identify the basic criteria for the most useful arrangement of law books and serial publications, as distinct from the classification of law itself.

CRITERIA FOR LAW LIBRARY CLASSIFICATION

It is fairly generally agreed that the two basic principles are the importance of the legal system and the distinction between primary and secondary sources. Both these principles should be incorporated in the structure of the classification scheme used in any law library. It is also advisable to consider various more practical aspects of the scheme, such as its notation, provision for up-dating and the index. Another factor that an increasing number of librarians will need to consider is the scheme's suitability for use in mechanized or computerized systems of operation (see page 652).

Any librarian seriously considering the adoption of a classification scheme will, of course, examine at first hand the schemes he thinks may suit his purposes. In this chapter, a number of published schemes are examined against the basic principles of the bibliographic classification of law, to provide a broad assessment to help in this choice. Further information about the structure and practical use of particular schemes can be found in their own introductory notes and in the material listed at the end of the chapter.

It must be emphasized that the problems involved in devising even a simple classification scheme are very considerable. It is a task that should be undertaken only by a very experienced classifier, who should be aware of the pitfalls. Anyone else, including subject experts with limited knowledge of the technicalities of constructing library classifications, is most strongly advised to make use of one or other of the schemes discussed below.

Importance of the legal system

Almost anyone using a legal collection is concerned at any particular moment with one system of law, such as English law, Scots law, Australian law, French law or public international law. A reader who says that he is looking for books on conveyancing can be assumed (with the possible exception of the known student of comparative law) to be concerned with the law of conveyancing applicable to the jurisdiction within which the library is situated. Similarly, a book entitled *The Law of Conveyancing* will almost certainly relate to the jurisdiction in which the author lives and works. If this is not the case, in either example, the reader or the author will almost invariably specify the jurisdiction with which he is concerned.

The vast majority of law books, including serial publications, deal with the whole or part of the law of a single jurisdiction. Comparative studies do exist, but are relatively rare. Therefore, to find information about wills in Scotland, it is little use consulting English or American books on wills, but any survey of Scots law will contain at least an outline of the subject.

Most classifiers are accustomed to a citation order that puts first the detailed topic, such as transistors, wages, football or computers, with the facets of purpose, process, place, time and so on following in a suitable order. This procedure is not valid for a collection of legal materials. For the reasons explained above, the first step in the arrangement of a law library is to group the volumes according to the facet of 'legal system' or 'jurisdiction'. The classification scheme used should provide for this simply and unambiguously. Most modern legal jurisdictions are much the same as the political jurisdictions listed in up-to-date place tables, such as California, Canada and Cuba. But additional provision is needed to cover books dealing with those legal systems, such as classical Roman law,

Islamic law and public international law, which do not correspond to any modern political jurisdiction.

Primary and secondary sources

In dealing with a problem in any of the common law jurisdictions (see page 59), the distinction between books containing the law itself (primary sources) and those commenting on the law (secondary sources) is also of vital importance. In legal systems based on the civil law, the distinction may be somewhat less important, but it can usually be clearly seen in the literature, and can still be useful to readers.

Some general libraries prefer to place the text of an individual statute with the treatises on the subject, for example putting an Education Act with the books on education in general, at some distance from the law section of the library. Any law library, on the other hand, and any general library maintaining a complete set of the jurisdiction's legislation, will find it essential to keep its complete sets of statutes and other primary materials all together, especially those that are serially published, and to treat the secondary materials separately.

The classification scheme should provide for separate treatment of primary and secondary materials under each jurisdiction. Primary sources are usually most suitably arranged by legal form: legislation, law reports, etc., with the digests, indexes and citators close to the volumes to which they refer. Secondary materials are usually classified (if at all) by subject content.

Practical considerations

Notation

One of the most immediately obvious characteristics of a classification scheme is its notation. A few of the older specialist schemes use words to denote main classes, but most schemes use notation made up of either letters or numerals, or a combination of the two, as code symbols to represent the subjects and concepts in their schedules. For example, the English law of evidence in civil proceedings is represented by SFH in Bliss; by

347.4206 in Dewey 18; by KD 7491–7500 in Library of Congress; by KN 390 and 347.94 in the two versions of Moys; and by KD 192 in Los Angeles.

The chief function of the notation is to reflect the order of the classes and concepts in the scheme. If possible, it should also help to show the structure of the scheme, the subordination of classes and the changes of facet and phase (see page 549). Both numerals and letters carry an obvious sequential meaning. If any other symbols, such as punctuation marks, are used, not only their meaning but their order in the sequence must be made absolutely clear.

As the notation is likely to be used on the spines of books and pamphlets, as well as in catalogue entries, brevity is an obvious advantage. It is also helpful, both to librarians and to readers, if class marks can be easily spoken and remembered. An alphabetic notation, with a potential base of twenty-six characters, will usually produce the shortest class symbols. On the other hand, a group of numbers or a mixture of numbers and letters is often thought to be easier to remember than a non-syllabic group of letters; it is especially difficult if upper and lower case letters are used with different meanings.

Up-dating

Even in a relatively conservative subject area such as law, new jurisdictions and new topics arise fairly constantly. An example of the former is the re-division of Nigeria into twelve states, instead of the previous four, and an example of the latter is the hovercraft, which is neither a ship nor an aircraft, but has some of the physical and legal characteristics of each. The classification scheme should make provision for new subjects, both by providing hospitality for them in its notation and by publishing either supplements or periodic revised editions.

Index

The need for a good subject index to the schedules should be self-evident. Almost all published schemes provide indexes of some sort, but many privately produced specialist schemes do not. The index should be as full and as specific as possible, including all synonyms or near-synonyms that the user is likely to encounter. There should be only one number in the schedules for a topic, but as many index entries to that number as may be needed. The broader the classification system, the more important it is for specific terms to be indexed. For example, if a single number is allocated to landlord and tenant, the index should include for that number a list of several terms, such as : dilapidations, dispossession, distress (rent), eviction, fixtures and fittings, furnished premises, ground rent, improvements, *landlords, leases, rent,* repairs, security of tenure, *tenancy,* tenants, unfurnished premises. Some of these terms are too specialized to be needed in a general scheme, where at least those printed in italics should appear.

GENERAL CLASSIFICATION SCHEMES

Nearly all public libraries and a number of university and college libraries are arranged by one or other of the large classification schemes that cover the whole field of knowledge. Each of these schemes includes a law class, which usually deals at least with the materials on 'lawyers' law'. But some schemes used to treat law as an aspect of various other subjects, such as trade unions, banking, public health, and did not provide specific numbers in the law class for the law of these subjects. Dispersal of legal materials in this way used to be a feature of both the Dewey Decimal and Library of Congress classifications, but this tendency has now been reversed. The new law schedules published for both these schemes have brought into the law class the greater part of the previously dispersed subjects.

However, in a general classification, there will always be a number of subjects ancillary to legal studies which must remain in other classes, such as political and social history, general sociology, ethics, philosophy, etc. Thus, law students using the legal section of a general library may have to be directed to other parts of the building for books on ancillary subjects. But a separately housed law faculty library should contain a suitable selection of books on related subjects and will normally give them the same class marks as they would have in the main library. An independent law library that uses one of the general schemes should follow the same procedure.

The four best known general schemes that are used in British and Irish libraries are briefly examined below, using the criteria already outlined.

Dewey Decimal Classification[1]

The eighteenth edition of this very well-known scheme was published in three large volumes in 1971. It includes a completely new schedule for Class 340, Law, which is a considerable improvement on the original schedule. As before, it forms a main division of Class 300, Social sciences.

As originally printed in 1971, the new schedule has serious flaws in the prescribed method of dealing with systems of law. The Dewey classification has always been above all a subject classification. The compilers were unable to accept that the legal system of each jurisdiction is a main subject in its own right, and devised a schedule involving the citation order subject – jurisdiction – subject, which was described by Mr Steiner in his review (*Law Librarian*, volume 4, no. 1, April 1973, pp. 14–15).

However, an important optional alternative has been introduced (*Dewey decimal classification: Additions, notes and decisions*, volume 3, no. 3, April 1973) 'in response to numerous requests'. Under this option, which is the only version of the DDC that can be recommended for use in law libraries, the main sub-classes are:

340	Law [general]
341	International law [public only]
	By jurisdiction
343	Ancient world
	Modern world
344	Europe
345	Asia
346	Africa
347	North America
348	South America
349	Australasia, Pacific

[1] Dewey, Melvil, *Dewey Decimal Classification*. Ed. 18. Lake Placid Club, N.Y., Forest Press, 1971. 3 vols. (ISBN 0 91068 10 5, etc.)

The number for each jurisdiction in class 343 to 349 is found by adding the area number from Table 2 to the base number 34, *eg*, the area number for England is 42, so that English law is 344.2; and the area number for New South Wales is 944, so that the law of New South Wales is 349.44.

Sub-division within a jurisdiction is achieved by adapting the schedule for classes 342 to 348 in the 1971 version of the schedule:

342	Constitutional and administrative law
343	Miscellaneous public law
344	Social law
345	Criminal law
346	Private law
347	Civil procedure
348	Law (Statutes), regulations, cases

In the original schedule, topic sub-divisions within each of these classes are preceded by a zero so that, for example, electoral law is 342.07 and the law of defamation is 346.034. The table for arranging material for each jurisdiction is made up by removing the initial 34 from these numbers and transferring the zero from the secondary position to the new initial position, *eg*:

electoral law	342.07
remove 34	207
transfer zero	027

similarly, negligence 346.034 becomes 0634.

The number so found is added to the number for the jurisdiction, so that the English law of negligence is 344.20634 and New South Wales electoral law is 349.44027. This method of classification satisfies the basic requirement for dealing with systems of law.

Primary materials, at 08, are clearly separated from secondary materials. The amount of detail in the schedule is scarcely adequate for a law library. A special extended schedule for United States primary materials has been printed and a parallel extension for United Kingdom and Irish material is needed. If required, it is possible to class individual statutes, etc., with a subject, by means of a standard table, *eg*, a statute (0263) on elections in New South Wales would be 349.440270263.

There are also tables of standard sub-divisions for bibliographical forms, etc., which can be used in the law class. For example, a periodical (05) on negligence in English law would be 344.2063405.

The notation, as the name suggests, is entirely numerical. Every class number contains at least three digits followed, if there are further digits, by a decimal point, as shown in the examples above. The structure of the scheme is clearly reflected in the notation and changes in the criterion of division are usually indicated by an intervening zero, especially in the tables of standard sub-divisions for facets such as period, persons and bibliographic forms. Class numbers tend to be long, because of the inevitable limitations of a base of ten. The same difficulty affects every decimal scheme, for example in Moys's decimal version the number for the German law of criminal procedure is 349.43059, whereas in the 1973 version of the DDC it is 344.3055, and in the 1971 version it would be 345.4305.

New subjects are catered for by the publication, about every five or six years, of a complete new edition. The fact that thousands of libraries use the scheme, and must buy each successive edition, alone makes this publication programme economically possible. Except when a 'phoenix' schedule is produced, such as Class 340, Law, in the eighteenth edition, new numbers usually have to be fitted in by sub-dividing existing numbers. Relatively minor amendments are published, in the meantime, in the bulletin of *Additions, notes and decisions*.

The published index to the whole scheme is very large and generally satisfactory. Even so, a law library is likely to find the detail insufficient, but this would probably apply equally to the index of any all-embracing classification scheme.

Universal Decimal Classification[1]

This scheme was developed, primarily on the continent of Europe, from the earlier editions of Dewey. It has grown steadily further and further from Dewey until the resemblance is now only superficial. The UDC was one of the earliest attempts to produce a faceted classification, and uses a variety of

[1] British Standards Institution. *Universal Decimal Classification*. 3rd abridged English ed. BSI, 1961. (British Standard 1000A: 1961.)

punctuation or mathematical symbols to indicate various facets and phases, such as:

=	language
(1) to (9)	place
,, ,,	time
:	relationship

In the latest available edition in English, the 3rd abridged edition, 1961, the arrangement is:

34	Jurisprudence. Law. Legislation
340	Law in general. Comparative law
341	International law. Law of nations
342	Public law. Constitutional law
343	Criminal law. Penal offences. Penology. Criminology.
344	Special penal, criminal law
347	Private law. Civil law
348	Ecclesiastical and canonical law

The degree of detail in the abridged edition is, naturally, considerably less than in Dewey 18. The fourth full edition, which is available in the definitive German and also in French translation, gives a very high degree of detail, as befits a classification designed for documents rather than treatises and other large volumes. All the class numbers in the examples below are based on the abridged edition.

Although UDC appears, like 1971 Dewey, to be based on branches of law, it is possible by somewhat stretching its facet citation order to achieve a reasonable arrangement. For example, the English law of divorce would be:

Divorce	347.627
England	(420)
complete number	34(420)7627

Among the 'Common auxiliaries of form', is a table of 'Legal sources, laws, byelaws'. This can be applied either to a particular topic or to a particular jurisdiction. For example, a French commercial code would be:

Commercial law	347.7
France	(44)
Code of laws	(094.4)
complete number	34(44)77(094.4)

while a series of the secondary legislation of Ontario would be:

Law	34
Ontario	(713)
Regulations etc.	(094.7)
complete number	34(713) (094.7)

Thus it can be seen that UDC can fulfil the two basic requirements respecting legal systems and primary materials. It should, however, be noted that the UDC Class 34, though originally based on the now discarded Dewey schedule, was developed mainly by continental documentalists and it is sometimes difficult to fit British legal publications comfortably into it. The most glaring example is the law of trusts and trustees, which has no straightforward equivalent in continental systems of law.

A major revision of the whole of Class 3, social sciences, is in progress under the auspices of the Fédération International de Documentation. A substantial quantity of numbers is being added or altered throughout class 34, law, to bring it up to date, but the procedure for agreeing to and publicising changes to UDC is lengthy. Details of the latest position can be obtained from the FID secretariat at The Hague.

This scheme, with its decimal base and its structure of auxiliary tables, almost invariably produces long class marks. But it does provide, in the full edition, more detail than any of the other schemes, with the possible exception of the Library of Congress.

Supplementation, or rather notification of occasional revisions, comes in bulletins from FID. The arrangements for English translation and publication are far from satisfactory. The English version of the fourth full edition (which has itself been substantially amended) was not complete at the end of 1975. The only index available in English is totally inadequate. There is a plan to produce eventually a computerized index, which accounts for the large number of synonyms and near-synonyms in the schedules.

Library of Congress Classification

Although Class K was assigned to law when the Library of Congress's mammoth classification was being compiled at about the turn of the century, no part of it was published until 1969, when *Sub-class KF, Law of the United States*, appeared in a preliminary edition. In 1973, *Sub-class KD, Law of the United Kingdom and Ireland*, was published. The main divisions of class K are expected to be:

K   Generalia; periodicals; philosophy of law, jurisprudence, comparative law; international legislation

KB   Ancient law; Roman law; theocratic legal systems

KD   United Kingdom; Republic of Ireland

KE   Canada; St Pierre and Miquelon; Greenland

KF   United States

KG   Latin America in general; Mexico; Central America; West Indies

KH   South America; South Pacific Islands; South Atlantic Islands

KJ   Europe in general; regional federations; Western Europe

KK   Central Europe

KL   South-eastern Europe; Northern Europe

KM   Soviet Union

KP   Asia in general; Near East; South-western Asia; Southern Asia (India, etc.)

KQ   South-eastern Asia; Far East

KR   Africa

KT   Australia; New Zealand; Oceania; Antarctic

(KX) Optional alternative to JX for International law

It can be seen that the compilers are determined to give primacy to the legal system. In the two classes that have so far appeared, very full schedules have been provided for all major jurisdictions, together with detailed tables for arranging material for individual States of the Union, cities, etc. There is a clear distinction made between primary and secondary materials and the schedules for each jurisdiction are given in meticulous detail. Inevitably the terminology has an American bias, but care has been taken to substitute or add British terms in Class KD. Some of the 'Americanisms' in the placing of specific topics, notably public property, mentioned by Moys in her review of Class KF (*Law Librarian,* volume 1, no. 2, August 1970, pp. 24–7) have been anglicized in Class KD.

The notation is the usual Library of Congress mixture of letters and consecutive numbers. A slight modification from other classes in LC is that three letters are used to denote some relatively smaller jurisdictions, such as Scotland, the Channel Islands and the individual states and territories of the United States. The notation system produces fairly short class marks, for example, the English law of fire insurance is KD 1885; the law of education in New York City is KFX 2065. As the numbers run consecutively, they do not demonstrate the structure of the scheme as clearly as do decimal numbers, but hospitality to new topics is easier to achieve by the simple expedient of leaving groups of numbers unused at likely points in the schedules.

Supplementation will doubtless be by means of LC's quarterly bulletin of *Additions and changes* and, ultimately, by the publication of up-dated editions of the schedules. New editions of the early classes may well be needed before the whole of Class K has been published. The Library of Congress cannot yet suggest when that will be achieved.

Each published sub-class has its own index, which is full and thorough. For example, the KF schedules take 277 pages in well-spaced single column format, while the index occupies 55 pages in closely printed double columns.

When the Library of Congress Class K Classification is completed, it will undoubtedly be the largest, most scholarly and best organized law classification ever seen. It is possible, though, that its very size and near-perfection may militate against its use by many libraries in the United Kingdom or in Ireland.

Bliss's Bibliographic Classification[1]

The first edition of this American scheme was completed in 1940. A second edition is being prepared under the super-

---

[1] Bliss, Henry Evelyn. *A Bibliographic Classification.* New York, H. W. Wilson, 1940–53. 4 vols. in 3. o.p.

vision of Mr Jack Mills, of the Polytechnic of North London. It is Mr Mills's wish that more attention should be paid to the second edition than the first. However, for the purposes of comparison, outlines of both editions of Class S, Law are given below.

Class S Law [1st edition]

1/9	Common sub-divisions
SA	Jurisprudence
SB	International law
	(Alternative, preferred in **Political Science**)
SC	Constitutional law
	(Alternative, preferred in **Political Science**)
SD	Administrative law
	(Alternative, preferred in **Political Science**)
	Anglo-American law
SE	General
SF	US federal law
SG	US states; Commonwealth
SH	Miscellaneous topics
SI	Equity
SJ	Civil law
SK	Local government
SL	Commercial law
SM	Property
SN	Persons, family law
SO	Criminal law and procedure
SP	Civil procedure
SQ	Administration of justice
SR	Military law (Alternative)
SS	Forensic medicine (Alternative)
	[Other modern systems]
ST/SW	France, Spain, Italy, Germany, **Austria**
SY	Other countries

Class S Law: revised schedule

1	Common form sub-divisions
2/9	Common subject sub-divisions
SA	Jurisprudence
SB	Comparative law

SC	Constitutional and administrative
	(Alternative, preferred in Political Science)
SD	International law
	(Alternative, preferred in Political Science)
	Ancient and medieval law; primitive systems
	Common law systems
	England and Wales
SE	General; primary materials
SF	Legal profession; practice and procedure
	(civil and criminal)
SG	Administration of justice
SH	Subjects of Common law
SI	Equity
SJ	Contract; agency; tort
SK	Particular torts
SL	Commercial law
SM	Property
SN	Family and social law
SO	Criminal law
SP	Constitutional law
	(Alternative, preferred in Political Science)
SQ	Conflict of laws
SR	Rest of British Isles; Australia; New Zealand
SS	USA; Canada; Caribbean
	Civil law and other systems
ST/SW	France; Spain; Italy; Germany
SX	Home country (if desired)
SY	Other countries
SZ	Religious jurisdictions

Bliss has always maintained a clear separation of legal systems and both versions show a strong Anglo-American bias in the allocation of notation. The Mills edition allows for the use of Class SX for the home jurisdiction, if desired. The original schedules did not seem to make adequate provision for primary materials, but the second edition makes full amends. For each jurisdiction, primary materials precede secondary materials and the full schedule given under England and Wales can be applied with appropriate local modifications, to any other jurisdiction.

The second edition is based on a careful study of the facet

structure of the subject and the forms of the literature, and is an improvement in innumerable ways on the original schedules. The notation, with a potential base of 26 letters plus numerals 1 to 9, is remarkably brief.

Mr Mills hopes that his version will be published in 1976. The index will include every key word and will be compiled by chain procedure (see page 537).

SPECIAL CLASSIFICATION SCHEMES

In addition to the general schemes, a number of special law classification schemes have been devised. For the most part, these schemes are tailored to the needs of particular libraries and require adaptation if transferred to other circumstances. It is usual for a special classification to provide numbers for the ancillary subjects already mentioned and also for general materials, such as bibliographies and dictionaries which would probably be found in other sections of a general classification.

Three special classifications, two at least of which are known to be used by several libraries in various countries, are examined below. From what has been said on page 563 it is clearly no accident that both of these schemes started life as substitutes for the then missing Library of Congress Class K.

Los Angeles County Law Library Classification[1]

This is probably the best known of the American Class K substitutes. It supersedes the scheme produced in 1948 by Miss Elizabeth Benyon, of the University of Chicago Law School Library, on which it is based. The main classes are:

K   General, comparative
KA   US documents, statutes, court reports, etc.
KB   US treatises, etc.
KC   Rest of America
KD   England and Wales
KE   Rest of Europe [including Scotland and Ireland] and Europe-Asia

[1] Los Angeles County Law Library. *Class K – Law.* 4th edition [The Library], 1965.

KF   Asia
KG   Africa
KH   Australia, Australasia, Oceania, Antarctica
KJ   International law, diplomacy, international relations

The treatment of modern legal systems is entirely on a geographical basis. English and United States law are completely separate (they were not in the Benyon scheme). With the exception of those two jurisdictions, countries are arranged regionally and then alphabetically. Full schedules, with separation of primary and secondary materials, are provided for the United States and England. Other jurisdictions are allocated either fifty or twenty numbers, which are to be arranged according to tables based on the main schedules.

Primary materials are arranged by form. Topics of law are classified rather broadly, with additional detail given in alphabetical lists of relatively minor topics.

The notation is of the Library of Congress type and, as the degree of detail is less than in some of the other schemes, produces fairly short class marks. For example, the Queensland law of wills would probably be KH 115. W5, whereas in 1971 Dewey it would be 346.943054.

The first edition was published in 1951 and revised editions appeared in 1956, 1958 and 1965. A small first supplement was produced in 1968 and a second in 1970.

There is a simple alphabetical index, which lists terms in the schedules, but contains few synonyms.

Moys's Classification Scheme for Law Books[1]

Unlike the schemes so far discussed, this one originated in academic libraries. It was not, however, tailored to a particular library or group of libraries. It is intended to be suitable for use in various types of libraries, academic, professional or public, anywhere in the English-speaking world. To this end, the same basic schedule has been provided with two different notations. The original was a Library of Congress type Class K, and the alternative is a Dewey-style 340. The outline is:

[1] Moys, Elizabeth Mary. *A Classification Scheme for Law Books*. Butterworth, 1968. (ISBN 0 406 30700 8.)

	K version	340 version
General material and non-national systems		
Journals and reference books	K ⎫	
Jurisprudence	KA ⎬	340
Comparative law	KB ⎭	
International law	KC	341
Religious legal systems	KD	342
Ancient and medieval law	KE	343
Modern national legal systems		
Common law		
Primary materials	KF–KH	344
Secondary materials		
General	KL	345
Public law	KM	346
Private law	KN	347
Special jurisdiction(s) (optional)	KP	348
Other countries		
Africa	KR ⎫	
Latin America	KS ⎪	
Asia and Pacific	KT ⎬	349
Europe	KV ⎭	
Non-legal subjects (optional)	KZ	DDC

There is careful separation of legal systems, but not on a strictly jurisdictional basis. A consensus of law teachers consulted at the time of compilation was in favour of keeping together all material from the main common law jurisdictions, which were defined rather narrowly as: England and Wales, Canada, Australia, New Zealand and the United States. From this decision arose a number of anomalies, particularly affecting Scotland and other Commonwealth jurisdictions such as India, which are fully discussed in the introduction to the volume. Some of the anomalies can be overcome by the use of Class KP (or 348) for any jurisdiction or jurisdictions that may be desired. It can, for example, be used for a single jurisdiction, such as Scotland, or for a federal system, such as Canada and its provinces, or for non-common law countries such as the continental members of the European Communities.

Primary and secondary materials are clearly separated, and

there are fairly full schedules for the English and United States primary materials. Schedules are given for all the general topics and systems in Classes K and KA to KE (or 340 to 343) and for legal topics in the common law secondary materials classes KL to KN (345–347). The primary materials for the other common law jurisdictions in KF to KH (344) and all materials for non-common law countries, KR to KV (349) are catered for by the allocation of groups of numbers for each jurisdiction which are sub-divided by tables. The degree of detail provided for jurisdictions varies rather arbitrarily. The tables follow the same general pattern as the schedules in Classes KF to KN (344 to 347).

The two notations closely follow the methods of the Library of Congress and Dewey classifications, with the same advantages and disadvantages. The allocation of three whole classes to legal topics in the common law system has enabled numbers there (in both notations) to be kept fairly short, although it must be remembered that for treatises the notation does not indicate the specific common law jurisdiction concerned. The law of television in England, for example, is KN 344 or 347.876 in Moys; 344.203994 in Dewey; KD 2915 in LC; SLYO in Bliss; KD 47 in Los Angeles.

So far, one general supplement has been published, as an article in *The Law Librarian* (volume 2, no. 1, April 1971, pp. 10–14). At the end of 1973 an expanded version of the common law secondary material classes: 345, 346 and 347, was privately produced in duplicated format.[1] These illustrate a difficulty inherent in special classification schemes: that they do not usually have the advantage of the backing of a large library, research foundation or commercial organization that can finance the publication of regular supplements. As some thirty libraries, spread over several countries, are known to be using the scheme, a second edition may prove possible within ten years of the original publication in 1968.

The index is substantial, occupying 127 pages, compared with 162 pages of schedules and the explanatory introduction of 41 pages. There are many entries for synonyms and near

[1] Moys, E. M. A classification scheme for law books. Supplement to Class 340: Law: expansion of Common Law classes 345, 346, 347. Goldsmiths' College Library, 1973. Mimeographed.

synonyms. Indexing of the decimal version in the 1968 edition was limited, but the expanded decimal version put this right for the common law classes.

Squire Law Library Classification Scheme, by W. A. F. P. Steiner

This scheme was originally compiled in the 1960s and circulated privately in typescript. It was first published in 1972, combined with a list of subject headings, as the second half of volume IV of the Squire Law Library's *Catalogue of International Law* (New York, Oceana Publications, 1972. ISBN 0 379 20030 9). The outline of classes is:

C   Reference works
D   Jurisprudence, philosophy, social sciences
E   Ancient and other legal systems not corresponding to that of any modern jurisdiction
F   Public international law; international transactions involving public international law *and* conflict of laws
G   Conflict of laws
H   Municipal law of modern jurisdictions, not restricted as to jurisdiction; comparative law
    Common law jurisdictions
J   United Kingdom
K   Canada
L   Australia and New Zealand
M   South Africa
N   Other British and former British territories in Africa; Cyprus; Ceylon; Hong Kong
P   Malaysia; Singapore; Pacific Islands
Q   British West Indies and Caribbean territories
R   India; Pakistan; Bangladesh; Burma
S   United States
    Non-Common law jurisdictions
T   Europe
U   Latin America
V   Rest of Asia and Africa

As Mr Steiner explains in the Introduction, the scheme is based on three facets: jurisdiction, subject and form, and a series of separate tables are provided for each. It can be seen that 'common law jurisdictions' are defined more liberally than in Moys, containing virtually all territories that have ever been under British jurisdiction.

Within each jurisdiction, the Squire divides first by subject and then by form, but it would be equally possible to reverse the order, so that the citation order would be jurisdiction – form – subject. There should be no confusion, as the tables for the three facets have entirely separate notation (see below). For example a treatise on French administrative law would be:

French law	TM
Administrative law	h
Textbook	9
complete number: *either*	TM.h.9
or	TM.9.h

It would be possible to divide first by form and then sub-divide by subject only certain forms, such as textbooks. Alternatively, as in the Squire, it is possible to place material not to be divided by subject, such as complete series of legislation, in the general class 'not restricted as to subject' at the beginning of each jurisdiction. With this flexible system, law reports can be classified either all together as a form group or, where appropriate, as subject literature.

The degree of detail in the tables varies considerably. The subject table tends to be fairly broad, for example, contract is qs and real property is qk, neither of which is sub-divided, whereas ports are jtpj. The form table, on the other hand, gives considerably more detail than most other schemes.

The scheme is presented in several sections in this order:

General synopsis
Schedule of non-jurisdictional classes
Synopsis and schedule of jurisdictions
Alphabetical index of jurisdictions
Synopsis and table of general subject divisions
Tables of subject divisions for special sections (*ie*, librarianship, ecclesiastical law, international law)
Table of general form divisions
Table of form divisions for international law
Special directions for particular main classes
Alphabetical index of form divisions

The lists of subject headings, in two sequences, classified and alphabetical, are linked to the scheme's notation and can act as a further index.

The notation is mixed, with capital letters for the main classes and for all jurisdictional divisions, *eg*, JE Scotland, NCD Botswana, TL Netherlands. Lower case letters are used for all subject divisions, *eg*, gd constitutional history, jlg compulsory purchase, ump air warfare (international law only). Form divisions are indicated by numerals, *eg*, 23 encyclopedias, 44 subsidiary legislation (non-periodical), 58 casebooks. The letters A, B, Y, Z and a, b, y, z have deliberately been left vacant to allow for their use in computerized listing (see also page 652).

Arrangements for supplementation and revision have not yet been considered by the compiler.

Most of the necessary index entries are present, but the multiplicity of alphabetical lists, separated from each other by various other tables, does not seem to make for great practical convenience. Mr Steiner is anxious to ensure that the distinction between form and subject should be applied correctly by all users, whether trained librarians or others.

Other schemes

A number of other specialist schemes have been compiled in the English-speaking world. Most of them originate in particular libraries, usually those of academic institutions, and are not intended for wider application. A few of them have been printed, but most remain in typescript and are not generally available. Many of these schemes were devised to fill the gap in the Library of Congress classification caused by the delay in the preparation of Class K, Law, and consequently use a K notation. American libraries are now, presumably, re-classifying by the new lc schedules as they appear.

Several British libraries have compiled schemes of this type, in most of which the subject classification is fairly broad – it is certainly much less detailed than in lc's new Class KD (see page 564). As the schemes were compiled several years ago, long before the entry of the United Kingdom and the Republic of Ireland into the European Communities, they tend to be very heavily biased towards English, Scots and Irish law. Some libraries are finding that their schemes are difficult to adapt satisfactorily to changed circumstances. At least two have expressed a desire, in principle, to reclassify by the Moys scheme (*Law Librarian*, volume 4, no. 2, 1973, pp. 21–22).

Another type of American scheme to be found mainly in the older universities near the east coast (*eg*, Harvard and Columbia) uses country names, or abbreviations of them, for the main classes and a table of 100 or 1000 numbers to arrange the material for each country. There is also a *Classification for International Law and Relations* by Kurt Schwerin (3rd edition, New York, Oceana, 1969. ISBN 0 379 00102 0).

PRACTICAL CLASSIFICATION

In a large or medium-sized library, classification is usually performed in the Cataloguing Department (see page 540). In a few large libraries, descriptive cataloguing may be done centrally, while classification and subject cataloguing are handled by subject librarians. In most law libraries all these tasks are likely to be undertaken by one person.

Determining the subject of the document

There is one golden rule that should be observed by all classifiers: NEVER CLASSIFY BY TITLE ALONE. Many authors and publishers take considerable care to ensure that the title of a book closely reflects the actual subject content, but others are less careful, and a few employ misleading or whimsical titles. But even meticulous authors tend to omit from their titles the name of the legal system about which they are writing, especially if it coincides with the political jurisdiction in which they live and work.

The classifier should analyse the total subject of the document by legal system (jurisdiction), legal topic(s), form of publication and any other relevant facets, such as period, special group of persons aimed at, etc., bearing in mind the construction of the classification scheme in use.

In addition to the information given on the title page, help in determining the subject can be obtained from other parts of the book, notably the list of chapters, the preface, foreword or introduction, the concluding section, the major topics featured in the index, or even the publisher's blurb (though less reliance can be placed here than on the author's own statements). Further guidance, if needed, can be found in the author's qualifications and experience or in the identity of the person who originally requested the purchase of the book, either of which may provide clues to the main branch of law concerned. If, on the other hand, the detailed legal topic of the book is clear, but its place in the field of legal literature is not known to the classifier, help can be found in legal dictionaries or the indexes to classification schemes. Valuable guidance can also be obtained from subject bibliographies. For current material, the *British National Bibliography* gives DDC numbers and the United States *National Union Catalogue* gives both DDC and LC numbers. The printed cards supplied by these two organizations give the same class numbers.

Assigning the class mark

Location symbols

Symbols are needed to lead readers to any collections of books that are detached from the main sequence for any reason, such as short-loan collections, oversize sequences, rare book collections, working collections in the acquisitions, cataloguing or other offices, and stacks containing superseded editions. These symbols are usually based on appropriate words, for example F or FOL for folio (*ie*, oversize), RB for rare books, CAT for Cataloguing Department.

Subject symbols

The class mark, in the narrow sense of the total subject symbol, is found from the classification scheme in the manner described above. The classifier will need to make frequent reference to the index of the scheme his library uses, but it must be emphasized that books must never be classified solely on the basis of an index entry. It is vital that the classifier should turn to the schedules at the number or numbers suggested in the index and examine their total subject context before deciding on the final class mark.

Alphabetical arrangement

If symbols are required for alphabetical arrangement of authors, titles, series, etc., they can be simple abbreviations of the actual words, or they can be taken from a table combining letters and numbers. One of the earliest of these tables was devised in the United States by C. A. Cutter, and symbols of this type are sometimes called 'cutter numbers'. A section of such a table might be:

Ca	11
Cai	12
Call	13
Cam	14
Camp	15
Can	16

To apply this the initial letter, in this case C is followed by the number nearest to the actual name being 'cuttered', *eg*, Caetano would be C11, Cameron C14, Campbell C15. If required, simple tables can be compiled in the library. A fuller discussion of this topic is in Phillips, W. H. *Primer of Book Classification*, 5th edition, 1961, pp. 50–54.

Copy numbers

Most libraries that wish to distinguish the various copies of a title held write '2nd copy' or 'Copy 2' on the volume. But in a few libraries each individual volume carries a unique call number. This can probably be achieved with the least difficulty by adapting cutter numbers (see above) so that, for example, the first copy of a book on a particular subject by Cameron would be C141, the second C142, and so on.

Ensuring consistency

As in cataloguing, consistency is very important. Putting books on the same subject in the same place every time is, after all, the object of classification. Most classifiers annotate the schedules and tables and, if necessary, the index each time a decision is taken to amend, amplify or interpret the scheme. Before the annotations threaten to submerge the printed text, recourse should be taken to an authority file on cards, arranged probably in classified order (see also page 544).

Guidance for the reader

Besides indicating the subject content of a book, the class mark acts as a link between the catalogue and the book on the shelf. The use of class marks in the catalogues has been dealt with on page 526. Methods of labelling the books themselves with class marks are outlined on page 496. The apparatus needed to lead the reader to the shelf he wants usually takes the form of printed or duplicated booklets, floor plans, notices, and guide labels on the stacks and individual shelves (see also page 460).

Re-classification

Occasionally, dissatisfaction either with the absence of classification by topic or with the inadequacies of the classification scheme in use reaches such a pitch that re-classification is seriously considered. With a large collection, this is a major operation, expensive and likely to cause some inconvenience to readers. However, in law libraries, especially the medium and smaller collections, the problems are greatly reduced because such a high proportion of the active book stock is in the form of statutes, law reports, journals and other largely serial-type publications. These primary materials and other serials more or less classify themselves, and can be shelved in the required order with little or no individual labelling, provided that the room and shelf guiding is adequate. If all these volumes are subtracted from the total stock of, say, 15,000 volumes in a law faculty library, the number of individual treatises, casebooks, etc. to be re-classified will be only a few thousand (the SPTL *Minimum Standards for Law Libraries* . . . recommended a text-book collection of not less than 1,250 volumes).

If the books are to be completely re-catalogued as well as re-classified, and the two often need to be done together, the average time needed per volume will closely resemble that of the normal acquisitions. For re-classification only, the time

19

will be reduced to about a third. It is almost certain that temporary extra staff will have to be recruited, so that the normal work of the library can be carried on and the re-organization can be completed in a reasonable time.

There are two main methods of effecting the physical rearrangement of the books and the catalogues. It is possible to assign new class marks to all books and cards gradually, while leaving them in their original order until the re-classification is virtually completed. It is then probably advisable to close the library to readers so that all the books can be rearranged on the shelves in their new order. If the library is being simultaneously re-catalogued, the new catalogue will, of course, be built up behind the scenes, ready to be substituted bodily for the super-seded catalogue at the appropriate moment. This method probably requires two class labels for each volume, which could be confusing to readers (though double labelling seems to have worked well enough with the decimalization of price tags in the shops).

Alternatively, it is possible to operate two parallel sequences, old and new. All new acquisitions and the gradually increasing body of re-classified books will be shelved immediately in the new sequence, while the diminishing stock of unchanged material remains as it was, except for being closed up at intervals to free more shelves for the new sequence. This method may be more difficult for readers to grasp at first, but has the advantage of demonstrating at all times the amount of progress that has been made and, if applicable, the need for extra staff to help complete the work.

FURTHER READING

GENERAL BOOKS ON CLASSIFICATION THEORY AND PRACTICE

Mills, Jack. *A Modern Outline of Library Classification.* Chapman and Hall, 1960, reprinted several times (ISBN 0 412 06530 4).

Phillips, William Howard. *A Primer of Book Classification.* 5th edition. Association of Assistant Librarians, 1961 (ISBN 0 900092 17 3).

Sayers, William Charles Berwick. *A Manual of Classification for Librarians.* 5th edition, revised by Arthur Maltby. Deutsch, 1975 (ISBN 0 233 96603 x).

CLASSIFICATION THEORY

Foskett, Anthony Charles. *The Subject Approach to Information*. 2nd edition. Bingley, 1971 (ISBN 0 85157 118 2).

Langridge, D. *Approach to Classification for Students of Librarianship*. Bingley, 1973 (ISBN 0 85157 148 4).

Palmer, Bernard Ira and Wells, Arthur James. *The Fundamentals of Library Classification*. Allen and Unwin, 1951, repr. 1961.

Ranganathan, Shiyali Ramanrita. *Elements of Library Classification*. 3rd edition. Bombay, Asia Publishing House, 1962.

LAW LIBRARIES AND CLASSIFICATION

Jacobstein, J. Myron. Alternatives to classification for law libraries. *Law Library Journal*, vol. 49, 1956, pp. 458–63.

Jennett, Charlotte. Subject classification in law libraries: a survey – 1955. *Law Library Journal*, vol. 49, 1956, pp. 17–20.

Bibliographies

Suput, R. R. Law classification bibliography. *Law Library Journal*, vol. 50, 1957, pp. 563–7.

Carlson, Elizabeth Anne. Bibliography on cataloguing and classification of legal materials. *Law Library Journal*, vol. 61, 1968, pp. 259–76.

GENERAL CLASSIFICATION SCHEMES

Dewey Decimal Classification

Mills, Chapter 7; Phillips, pp. 60–77; Sayers, Chapter 9.

Universal Decimal Classification

British Standards Institution. *Guide to the Universal Decimal Classification* (UDC). BSI, 1963 (British Standard 1000C: 1963).

Foskett, Anthony Charles. *The Universal Decimal Classification*. Bingley, 1973 (ISBN 0 85157 159 x).

also: Mills, Chapter 8; Phillips, pp. 125–40; Sayers, Chapter 10.

Library of Congress Classification

Ellinger, Werner B. Classification of Law at the Library of Congress 1949–1968. *Law Library Journal*, vol. 61, no. 3, August 1968, pp. 224–36.

Immroth, John Phillip. *A Guide to Library of Congress Classification*.

Rochester, New York, Libraries Unlimited, 1968 (ISBN 0 87287 001 4).

Matthis, Raimund E. *Adopting the Library of Congress Classification: a manual of methods and techniques for application or conversion.* New York, Bowker, 1971 (ISBN 0 8352 0493 6).

Piper, P. L. and Kwan, C. H. L. *A Manual on KF, the Library of Congress classification schedule for law in the United States.* South Hackensack, N.J., Rothman for AALL, 1972 (AALL publications series, no. 11) (ISBN 0 8377 0109 0).

also: Mills, Chapter 9; Phillips, pp. 95–109; Sayers, Chapter 11.

Bliss's Bibliographic Classification

Bliss, Henry Evelyn. *The Organization of Knowledge in Libraries.* 2nd edition. H. W. Wilson, New York, 1939.

Bliss Classification Bulletin, vol. 1– , 1954– . British Committee for the Bliss classification. (Vol. 1–3, 1945–66, published New York, H. W. Wilson.)

also: Mills, Chapter 12; Phillips, pp. 151–66; Sayers, Chapter 13.

SPECIAL CLASSIFICATION SCHEMES

Stern, William B. Law classification as practised in the Los Angeles County Law Library. *Law Library Journal,* vol. 49, 1956, pp. 449–453.

Mills, Jack. Review of Moys classification in *Journal of Documentation,* vol. 24, no. 4, December 1968, pp. 317–19.

PRACTICAL CLASSIFICATION

Merrill, William Stetson. *Code for Classifiers: principles governing the consistent placing of books in a system of classification.* 2nd edition. Chicago, American Library Association, 1939 (ISBN 0 8389 0027 5).

University of Maryland. School of Library and Information Services. Conference on reclassification, 1968. *Reclassification: rationale and problems.* College Park, University of Maryland, 1968 (ISBN 0 911808 02 7).

also: Mills, Chapter 14; Phillips, pp. 167–85; Sayers, Chapters 15–18.

16. Staff

MARGARET G. CHUBB, BA (London), MA (Dublin)
Sub-librarian i/c of Readers' Services, The Library, Trinity
College, Dublin

'Among the qualities desirable in a trainee librarian are an
ability to communicate with people generally with accuracy,
clarity, tact and understanding, intellectual curiosity, a good
memory, physical and mental stamina. There is little demand
for the shy, retiring individual hoping for a back-room job
surrounded only by books.' These are the words of advice given
by the Standing Conference of National and University Libraries to those recommending candidates for the SCONUL scheme of
library training. The main difficulty for those running a library
is how to recruit such paragons, how to train them once found
and how to keep them once trained.

RECRUITMENT

The recruitment of staff falls into two categories – the professional staff and the supporting non-professional. To recruit
it is necessary to advertise and the most useful avenues for
professional staff are the *Times Literary Supplement*, the *Library
Association Record*, and, possibly, the national newspapers. The
non-professional staff can best be recruited by advertisements in
local newspapers, contacts with careers officers in school and
technical colleges, and through local employment exchanges.
Some specialist libraries do advertise for this staff grade also in
the *Times Literary Supplement*, but this could be considered a
somewhat tedious method of finding junior staff. It is possible
for larger libraries to build up a file of stand-by applicants, both
as a result of such advertisements, and also by providing detailed
application forms to be filled in by the casual enquirer who
often calls in to a library or writes when there is no vacancy
available. Rather than merely reply that there are no posts at
present and all posts are advertised, it can be useful to build up
a holding file for the unexpected emergency.

Once the answers to the advertisement have been sifted and a short list prepared for interview, the conduct of an interview for any post is similar, the difference being in depth rather than technique, with a longer and more probing interview the more senior the post which is to be filled. In general, the chairman of the board, if it is a formal interview by more than one person, will take the candidate through his curriculum vitae and the other members will decide beforehand on the pattern of follow-up questioning. It is necessary to question any obvious gaps in the candidate's career, but the essential point to remember is to allow the candidate plenty of opportunity to talk and express his potentiality. Too many interview boards end up with the interviewers talking too much and the candidate reduced to nervous affirmatives or negatives. Elizabeth Sidney and Margaret Brown in *The Skills of Interviewing*, 1961, recognized as a standard text on the subject, emphasize the need to look at three aspects: manner and appearance, evidence relating to intelligence, and social ability. This is valid whatever post the interviewer may be trying to fill.

Staff ratios

Some special libraries continue to be staffed by one librarian alone. It can be hoped that this practice will decrease in law libraries as in other special libraries and that basic staffing will be in all instances one senior librarian with a back-up of at least one other professionally qualified or experienced librarian, plus non-professional assistance. A recommended, if optimistic ratio, has been given as three non-professional staff for every two professionals in a special library. The Parry report recommends a ratio of 51 per cent professional to non-professional staff. Generally, it is agreed it should be at least half-and-half. Whether the library's senior staff are trained as law librarians or general librarians, it is equally wasteful to have professional skills dispersed on time-consuming routine tasks more suitably done by high-grade non-professional staff. High-grade, because, in a library, there are in effect no low-grade positions. To type a catalogue card, label a book, put a book in its place on the shelf, are all routine tasks, but if, in a large library, the catalogue card is wrongly typed, the book gets the wrong label or is shelved in the wrong section, all the professional work of select-ing the book, classifying it, entering it in bibliographical guides, is wasted, as the book may never be found. This is even more true of the special library. Most special libraries are small and so are their staffs. The user on many occasions will see only the junior staff and may base his opinions of the library's efficiency and merit on its weakest members. It takes intelligence, not necessarily professional training, to know how to answer a question, indeed, how to help the questioner ask specifically for what he wants, and it needs intelligence to know when the question must be passed on to someone else. There are no backroom jobs in the special library, so all the staff will need as many of the qualities recommended in the SCONUL circular as can be got and the need is to press for staff to be paid as highly as is necessary to get these qualities.

TRAINING

Professional staff

Having decided to interview, it is essential to be clear before-hand what type of person is required and one of the immediate problems facing any special library is the type of senior librarian they wish to recruit. Mary South talks of the 'tiresome argu-ment as to the relative merits of "subject" and "library" qualifications . . . It seems obvious that a librarian must possess (in order of priority, though not of importance), lin-guistic skills, subject knowledge and "library" skills!' (Staffing the special library, in, Burkett, J. *Trends in Special Librarianship*, 1968). Her second priority is subject knowledge, but a distin-guished lawyer was heard to say that if a law student was any good, he would continue to practise law, not become a librarian. His opinion seemed to be that if the law student did become a librarian, he would, of necessity, be second-rate in both fields.

This is one view. That it is not necessarily a valid one is proved by the growth of library school courses elsewhere in law librarianship, mostly confined to those already with legal qualifications, and the anxiety of libraries to employ such graduates if they can get them. According to the Parry report (Great Britain. University Grants Committee. *Report of the committee on libraries,* 1967) 'Lawyers and medically-qualified staff although they are unlikely to be attracted into the profession, would also be most valuable additions to it'. But whether it is possible to get the expert in the subject with professional library training or considerable experience in librarianship or not, every library must have the basic strength of professional staff. It does not matter if what is needed is a special librarian to run a small specialist library, or to look after a specialist section in a large general library, the main problem of recruitment is at once obvious: the difficulty of finding suitable staff because of the interacting causes of lack of specialist training facilities and the poor career prospects for a specialized librarian compared with a general librarian.

General library training facilities tend now to proliferate in rather alarming profusion. Part-time training while working in a library has been phased out almost completely and the professional librarian will now have attended a two-year non-graduate course leading to the Library Association's diploma (A-level entry qualifications are necessary); a one-year postgraduate course leading to a Master's degree in Library Studies, in Information Studies, etc., or a library diploma; more recently a three- or four-years' undergraduate course leading to a degree in librarianship. Details of courses and where they are given can be found in Unesco's *World Guide to Library Schools and Training Courses in Documentation,* 1972. Until 1973, none of these courses, however, gave any great help in recruiting a trained law librarian. Students who were taking the Library Association part II examination, list C, could opt to do paper 304. This paper 'Bibliographical organization of the social sciences', to some extent included law bibliography. Recognizing that this could hardly be considered sufficient training, the British and Irish Association of Law Librarians has, since its inception, organized short seminars on various aspects of law librarianship for those already working in law libraries. This, to some extent, follows the developments in American practice of refresher or further training sessions. The American Association of Law Libraries, for example, holds annual rotating institutes on different aspects of legal librarianship in various centres, usually lasting for a week and preceding the annual meeting of the Association. The University of North Carolina offers a summer session every other year, lasting about ten weeks. These are ideas which might with profit be taken up by training bodies here.

Full-time courses in law librarianship were offered here for the first time in the 1973–4 academic year, when the Postgraduate School of Librarianship and Information Science of the University of Sheffield instituted an MA in Information Studies (social sciences) for graduates in law and social science disciplines, the content of the one-year course to include 'problems and skills peculiar to law libraries and legal bibliography'. A start has been made and it can be hoped this is just the beginning of such courses. In the *Recruitment check-list*, 1969, the American Association of Law Libraries tells us that 'twenty-five years ago, there was not a single course in law librarianship offered anywhere'. By 1968, twelve accredited library schools in the United States were offering special courses in law librarianship. Professor Balfour Halévy taught the first courses in Canada in the University of Western Ontario in 1970, and courses are now offered also in the University of Toronto. Growth may be small, but it is encouraging that it continues and it may be easier in the future to recruit the professionally trained *law* librarian.

Non-professional staff

The junior back-up staff may be high-level clerks or library assistants, usually school leavers with A-levels and, preferably, typing qualifications. It is essential to have one professionally trained typist in every library unit. Some libraries employ graduates with no post-graduate qualifications or library experience in assistant posts and very satisfactory recruitment is often possible from married women returning to the profession but not wishing to take on the responsibilities of more senior posts because of their own family liabilities, or having worked previously in offices. A good basic training in office routines such as filing, maintaining records, keeping accounts can be of great value to the small unit in the special library. It is encouraging when considering the recruitment of staff that D. D. Haslam talking about Manpower (*in* Whatley, H. A. *British Librarianship and Information Science, 1966–70*, 1972) says that 'For the first time since the economic depression of the 1930s there was not a serious shortage of library staff, both professional and non-professional, in all sections of the profession by the end of 1970 . . . All types of libraries have reported that there is an adequate supply of school leavers to fill vacant posts . . . although the turnover in this category of staff was higher . . . ' With the increased output of library schools and advances in school leaving age, the position for recruitment of both senior and junior staff should continue to improve rather than to deteriorate and it may be possible indeed to select staff at interview rather than be forced to take the best available, to be able to get staff at all levels with the basic essential qualities of pleasant manner and appearance, an active willingness to help a reader and the ability to transmit information to him accurately and clearly, and, above all, with an enquiring and retentive mind. In many ways, no one without this last quality will ever make a good librarian, especially a special librarian.

In-service training

Once staff are recruited they must be trained in the skills and duties necessary for the library in which they now find themselves. This applies to all levels of experience and professional knowledge. A description of the library should be available, its structure, organization and its place in the larger general library, firm or parent body. Its relationship with its readers, its function, how much, or how little it is prepared to do, or can do, for the user, need to be defined (see page 445). Guides for the reader are very necessary, guides for the staff are essential. Knowledge of library routines, methods, work-flow, budgeting, staff responsibilities and chain of command all need to be available for the new member of staff in the form of a staff manual, written instructions, information sheets, organization charts, anything rather than word-of-mouth alone (see page 434).

Law library staff, like all library staff, must have a basic knowledge of library routines, varying in depth according to professional status and responsibility. Book selection, acquisition, cataloguing, classification, circulation and control of library material, general reference tools and bibliographies, photocopying services, inter-library loans, budgeting, preparing reports on library needs and services, all are covered in standard library training and the professionally trained librarian needs to adapt this general knowledge to the library in which he or she now finds employment and the non-professional will have to be taught in sufficient depth by the trained staff to be able to fill a meaningful role in the library structure. But a law librarian, like all special librarians, must also have, or acquire, a detailed knowledge of the subject area of his library. He needs to have specialized knowledge of legal bibliography, not only in the field of British and Irish law, but also American, Commonwealth, and increasingly now, European. The standard library school requirement of at least one foreign language appears even more sensible than before with our involvement in the EEC. He needs to know the primary sources of legislative materials and judicial decisions, as well as the secondary material of law textbooks, periodicals, monographs, all this often involving the complicated handling of supplementation and up-dating of legal material and dealing with loose-leaf services. A knowledge of legal history, the constitution and organization of the law courts, the work of the legal profession and its place in the legal processes, plus an understanding of the intricacies of law publishing – all need to be covered.

A useful guide for planning necessary in-training could be the established courses in law librarianship. Where the staff are found to be deficient in knowledge can pin-point the areas needed to be covered in further training. A course given in the University of Toronto in law librarianship, for example, includes the following: an introductory course in the legal system and sources of law; courses on law libraries and law librarianship, including the types of libraries, the nature of professional associations, standards for law libraries, professional education and professional literature; general training in readers' services, covering reference tools and bibliographies, providing services such as bibliographic guides, indexes etc., instruction in circulation and control of collections, the use of special materials such as microfilms, tapes etc.; book selection and acquisition with instruction on law-book publishers and dealers, selection procedures and policies, order procedures for acquisitions, gifts, exchanges, how to maintain financial records; the basics of cataloguing and classification, with emphasis on the special needs of law libraries and instruction in card preparation and filing; the two final topics are the maintenance of collections, binding and preservation of library materials, weeding out and disposing of superseded stock, and administration, emphasizing the need to prepare annual reports, budgets, organize staff and relate the library 'to others, to the administration, to the patron, to other libraries . . . '

However well qualified or knowledgeable the library staff may be, a valuable library service will not result unless they are prepared to accept that continuous training is an essential concomitant. Time must be found to keep up with the specialist literature, both in law and in librarianship, because developments in library techniques, knowledge of how to benefit from the increasing application of computerization, and the growth of mechanical aids can all help to run the library more efficiently and deploy staff to better advantage. However small the budget, the librarian must fight to obtain his basic tools and reference works as well as those needed by the readers. Useful reference tools for the library staff are described in Chapter 10 and listed in the bibliographies to each chapter.

Staff should also be encouraged to join professional associations and attend short courses, seminars, conferences or lectures pertinent to the subject coverage of the library as, for example, the one- or two-day seminars of the British and Irish Association of Law Librarians, already mentioned, and the four weeks' summer school given in the City of London Polytechnic on English public and private law, English business law, international law, comparative law and the law of the European Economic Community. Various refresher courses are occasionally organized by the Library Association and details of these courses and others can be found in the *Directory of short courses in librarianship and information work*, published quarterly in March, June, September and December by the British Library Research and Development Department. It is not always easy to release staff to attend such courses when they are available and with the one-man library the difficulties are often insuperable. But their contribution to the efficiency of a library unit can be invaluable and it is one of the senior librarian's duties to persuade the authorities of their necessity. Once the library user has seen how a well-informed, up-to-date library staff can improve the service to him, it should be possible for him to be convinced that the cost is far outweighed by the value of the return.

STAFF MANAGEMENT AND ALLOCATION OF DUTIES

The organization and management of staff are the key to an efficient, well-run library and because a law library staff will tend to be a small staff, personal relationships can be of cardinal importance. The knowledgeable, efficient, well-trained librarian who, because of personality may irritate, offend or even antagonize in the confined quarters of a small library, not only colleagues but also the users, is a bad risk. The senior librarian must be able to impose a sense of discipline and time-keeping on his staff and still maintain their loyalty, both to him and to the library itself. Here there is often an advantage in being a small library. In the larger unit, personal relationships become more diffused and fewer people feel personally involved in the library's functions. It is often much more satisfying to be the big fish in a little pond, than the small cog in a big machine. So it is often easier to get staff to accept that, in the smaller unit, time-keeping is important, that choice of leave and time off may be restricted and there is less freedom in securing it than in a bigger library. They have to accept working to strict duty rotas, to planning leave well in advance, even, on occasions, cancelling plans already made. In return, they should have the satisfaction of a greater part in the running of their library and a recognition of greater responsibility and involvement.

A clear definition of functions, duties and responsibilities is a necessary adjunct to good management. The senior staff will normally be responsible for book-selection (the smaller the budget, the more difficult the decisions), for weeding out surplus stock, deciding on classification, producing bibliographical aids, organizing, where necessary, reader instruction or library guides, and for budgeting and preparing annual reports and statistics. Junior staff can be trained to help with indexing, routine cataloguing, recording intake, maintaining records, inter-library loan and photocopying services, ordering, checking routine enquiries on availability of material and carrying out the initial stages of more advanced information searches. The more their work can be integrated with the senior staff and the more opportunity given to them to acquire some specialist knowledge, the more likelihood there is of having an efficient, integrated staff working together as an entity.

SALARIES

Professional staff

In return, the job must be able to offer the satisfactions of a reasonable salary, and good career prospects and working conditions. It is often true that the special librarian can expect to begin his career with responsibility for a wider range of duties than his colleague in a large academic library. Early on, he may be thrust into organizing all aspects of library work, deciding what is to be bought, how it is to be catalogued, how it will be circulated, who will be allowed to borrow it and for how long, what type of services he can afford to offer the reader, how he can influence the budget-makers by producing the right sort of reports and the right sort of statistics. He may, even, do better to begin with in salary and quick promotion prospects. The problem surfaces later in his career when the career prospects and job expectations of a law librarian, like every other special librarian, tend to deteriorate. From the point of view of salary alone, the professional librarian finding employment in an academic library is more certain of becoming part of a recognized salary and career structure. A joint statement some years ago by the Association of University Teachers and the Library Association recommended that there should be straight equivalence in grades and salaries between graduate library staff and academic staff. The graduate with a good honours degree and a qualification in librarianship and/or a research degree could expect an appointment as Assistant Librarian, starting at the beginning of the lecturer's scale. The senior part of the scale is sometimes reserved for posts of sub-librarians or deputy librarians and chief librarians should be on the professorial grade. The statement also recommended that there should be no difference in the scales offered to staff in the libraries of large universities or small universities.

A national pattern is slowly emerging, but it is obvious from a study of advertised posts that it is by no means universally accepted. An assistant librarian could not guarantee that the long scale he is on in one university, which, without promotion to any higher grade, will take him to the top of the lecturers' scale, will also apply if he moves to another post. He may find himself stopped at some interim point in the scale, possibly at an efficiency bar, possibly only promotion to a higher grade and a different post will bring him above it. There are even extraordinary variants in the actual size of advertisement. An insignificant paragraph may advertise a post of chief librarian, half a page may demand the services of a library assistant with secretarial-type salary.

The position for the non-academic library is even less standard. Government librarians are likely to be on civil service grades and, therefore, on a recognized ladder of increments, pensions and retirement policies, in the same way as the academic librarian. The public librarian who is part of the local government structure also has standard scales of salary, leave, pension rights and so on. But the librarian in the independent special library is in a very different position. There are no recognized scales for independent libraries and no staff associations as yet able to put pressure on the wide-ranging type of employer to enforce any. The Library Associations in both Britain and Ireland, through their special libraries sections, are concerned about this and surveys have been made, and continue to be made, to try to establish whether any recognized pattern of salary scales exists, and if not, whether one can be established, let alone enforced.

It is not necessarily true that the law librarian working for an independent firm or organization is worse paid than his equivalent in the academic library or the public library. He may often be better paid, but he also lacks any career structure in his post, a recognized and long-range incremental salary, and sometimes there is a lack of sufficient retirement schemes and job security. The need has been recognized by the professional associations for uniformity in scales, prospects, and security for all their members in libraries of all kinds. There is, also, a corresponding need (some may consider it a liability) to establish with uniform scales, uniform requirements for entrance into the profession at each level, another standard which does not necessarily apply to recruitment for special libraries. It is likely that it will become accepted that recruitment of law librarians will be from the good honours graduate, preferably with a law degree or some legal knowledge, plus a professional library qualification. In this connection, it is interesting to note that the first recommendation of a Library Association working party set up to consider the future of the Association's qualifications is that 'after 31 December 1980, the minimum pre-entry qualification for admission to the Association's examinations and consequently to its professional Register will normally be a degree of a university in the UK or . . . an equivalent thereof' (*Library Association Record*, volume 76, no. 3, March 1974, pp. 44–6).

That there is a long way to go before any standardization can be said to exist is evident. Advertisements for assistant librarians see-saw wildly and starting salaries can vary by as much as £500 per annum, while the top incremental figures advertised differ by £1000 or more. Posts specifically asking for special librarians/information officers follow the same pattern. Some will offer no more than a reasonable salary for a clerical assistant, others will be in the upper regions of the assistant librarian scale. If librarianship is to have secure recognition as a profession, this should not be so. There should be standard professional rates of pay, based clearly on responsibility, status in the organization, number of staff employed and other variables. Salaries should be comparable in institutions employing similarly qualified staff and this will bring the additional benefit of making it easier for staff to move on a progressive scale from one library to another as their experience and ability to manage larger units develop.

Non-professional staff

The position as regards non-professional staff is even less happy. It appears to be generally accepted that even if recruitment is easy, the wastage at this level is heavy. From the viewpoint of a special library, this is serious. It may take months to train the new assistant, to inculcate some essential, if rudimentary background to the special emphasis of the library. Then the assistant is lost and the wearisome business begins all over again. The reasons that wastage is so high at this level are various. In some ways wastage is inevitable. The school leaver, if alert and ambitious, may try various fields, explore job possibilities in different areas, even in different countries before committing himself, or herself, to one position. The better the recruits, the more possibility there is of losing them for this reason if recruited straight from school, and this is inevitable if recruitment of new staff has to be at the bottom of the scale.

Again, the special library, in this case the law library, may be better able to hold the non-professional than the general library. The closer staff relationship in a small set-up, the chances of more responsibility, of more active engagement in the actual running of the library, the build-up of a personal relationship with the user as well as the colleague can help to retain staff. This integration into the staff structure can be further developed if the non-professional as well as the professional, can be encouraged to undertake some training and to develop a knowledge in some depth of the library's holdings and purpose. Most of all, if some long-term salary prospects are available. In many organizations, there is no attempt to offer any career prospect to non-qualified staff. Starting salaries are often lower than those paid to a qualified typist and long incremental scales are rare. Some libraries equate the salary structure with the scales of pay laid down by NALGO. This also has disadvantages, as the higher scales relate very closely to seniority and age and before the good junior has reached this level of experience he or she will probably have left. The University of Dublin, faced with this problem, has introduced a very long incremental scale for non-professional staff. It starts at a level comparable with the recruitment of a school leaver at 18 or 19 with honours grades in final school examinations and continues up a scale overlapping well into the professional, to provide a reasonable standard of living in maturity. With recruitment possible at different points in the scale this may provide a solution.

Difficulties of retaining staff can be eased in the large organizations where junior, as well as senior staff, share in well-established pension schemes, retirement benefits, good sick leave provision, house-loan facilities and job security, which should make it possible to recruit and retain both male and female staff at non-professional levels.

CONDITIONS

Even with a good salary structure, one of the difficulties of recruiting staff – even more in keeping them – is the irregular pattern which libraries are usually forced to follow in opening hours. In trade union parlance, librarians often work non-social hours and as this is now a bargaining point in many wage negotiations, it may be that future salary structures for both professional and non-professional staff will have to take cognizance of this. In the era of the 9 to 5, five-day week, Saturday opening, evening duty, even sometimes full weekend duty, have to be recompensed. Salaries will need to be attractive at all levels, holidays must compensate for the lack of personal freedom relative to shift-work, and reasonable working facilities, including the availability of meals at odd hours, need to be provided. The standard leave pattern in most academic libraries does appear satisfactory in this respect, with the equivalent of six weeks holiday to professional staff, sometimes in the form of a month's annual leave, with a fixed week at Christmas and Easter, plus the usual bank holidays. The leave of junior staff varies, but is normally three weeks for the first year or two, then rising to four weeks, plus, of course, the bank holidays. The hours worked per week are usually not excessive, but compensation for evening duty and weekend duty does not appear to be standard. The Standing Conference of National and University Libraries recommended to its members that time off rather than overtime rates of pay should be the normal pattern and this tends to be the case, except that increasingly in larger libraries the burden of longer opening hours is being alleviated by recruiting special staff – retired people, married women, postgraduate students – to man reading rooms outside normal working hours.

CAREER PROSPECTS

Recruits do continue to enter the profession of law librarianship and posts continue to increase, as is shown by the growth in membership of the British and Irish Association of Law Librarians since its inception in 1970, the success of its journal *The Law Librarian*, and the starting in 1973 of the first special course in these islands in law librarianship. But if the newly recruited law librarian wishes to stay in that profession, statistics are against his chances of rising to very senior status unless he leaves the field of special librarianship, and enters, or re-enters, that of academic librarianship. This is a general danger recognized by anyone working in a restricted subject field of librarianship. W. L. Guttsman says that the 'committed subject specialists will . . . feel as they get older they will thus be typecast and shunted into a siding as far as career prospects are concerned'. (W. L. Guttsman, Subject Specialization in Academic Libraries. *Journal of Librarianship*, volume 5, no. 1, 1973, pp. 1–8.) Here the oft-repeated and rather wearisome statistic that, on the whole, law libraries and staffs are small, becomes of major importance, as does the small number of entirely separate law libraries. If the law library is part of a general unit, its chief post may well not be above the rank of assistant librarian. If fortunate enough to have separate staff and a separate building, the chief librarian is most probably a sub-librarian and may even be a senior sub-librarian, the equivalent of a deputy librarian in salary scale. But unless it is a major law library in its own right, the professorial scale will not be obtainable. The IALL *European Law Libraries Guide*, 1971, lists 78 law libraries in the United Kingdom and 6 in Ireland; of these only 40 are specific law libraries and not sections of general libraries. The American Association of Law Libraries *Recruitment Checklist*, 1969, gives the information that in the United States there were then about 995 law libraries employing 1,414 law librarians. The *Bowker Annual of Library and Book Trade Information* in statistics for 1971 refers to 809 law libraries in the United States with holdings of 10,000 volumes or more, and 380 with less than 10,000 volumes. The figure given for libraries as a whole is 23,998, so it is obvious that even there law libraries are a very small proportion of the whole.

Career prospects must, however, be available or else, in the end, the best trained, the most efficient and the most valuable librarians will be forced, and, because they are of high calibre, will be able to leave the profession for the field of general librarianship, a potential wastage which it should be possible to avoid. Surveys reveal disquiet at the present prospects. In 1971, The Library Association published its *Members in special libraries staffing survey 1970*. It included in the survey only libraries, 'supported by nationalized and private industry, by commercial firms, by professional associations, by learned societies and by other independent organizations'. Presumably this is due to the belief that staff employed in universities and local government or local authority services are protected by negotiating machinery such as the Association of University Teachers, NALGO etc., whereas the private sector is not. The results are disquieting, but not unexpected. There are two obvious features: no standard qualifications for staff, who seem to range from the graduate with an FLA, to the non-graduate with no recognized qualifications, and that women do not figure at all in the higher income bracket.

The survey processed 460 replies to questionnaires, 272 from women, 188 from men. Despite the preponderance of women, only seven were earning more than £2500 compared with forty men. Even more significant, only ten (all men) were earning more than £3301. With men, the highest proportion were earning between £1901 to £2100, for women, the comparable figure was £1301 to £1500. At that period (1970), the minimum salary guaranteed by the National Joint Council to Chartered Librarians in public libraries was £1413 per annum. This alarming comparative position of women librarians is not confined to the British Isles. A salary survey on law librarians' salaries by Carlyle J. Frarey, senior lecturer in the School of Library Science at Columbia University (*Bowker Annual of Library and Book Trade Information*, 1971) indicated also that women law librarians were generally paid less than their male counterparts and were more limited in their opportunities to advance in the profession. Law librarians were 60 per cent female, but only 12 per cent of them worked in the larger law libraries holding more than 200,000 volumes. Another survey in 1970 by Miss Mariya Hughes, of the University of California Hastings College of the Law, reveals the same depressing pattern, 22 per cent of men in law librarianship then earned salaries in excess of $20,000, compared with 1 per cent of the women in the profession.

To establish the profession securely and encourage the recruitment of high-calibre staff who will not leave law librarianship when at the peak of their abilities, a development programme is necessary. The private law library, along with the publicly supported library, needs to have adequate staffing, good promotion and seniority prospects, the opportunities at the higher levels must be improved, and at all levels, salaries and prospects must not be discriminatory. It has already been said that the era of the one-man library must end, but the staffing of small, specialist libraries will always be a problem. When discussing the small library, the University of Oxford, *Report of the Committee on University Libraries*, 1966, had this to say 'there appears often to be . . . unduly heavy expenditure on staff. The normal ratio of staff to book acquisitions, circulation, and information service, does not work out evenly at the lower end . . . There is a tendency either to extravagance, or to insufficiency of staff, and the overriding factor of finance may become peculiarly acute here' (page 169). But if the usefulness of a library depends not only upon the skill of its librarians, but also the number of libraries and the supporting staff, this has to be faced in planning the overall budget. The annual reports of the University Grants Committee indicate that figures of 50 per cent or even slightly more of the total library budget is spent on salaries. The oft-quoted Parry report accepts the figures recommended by sconul of 50:50 for book grant and salaries, instead of an originally recommended ratio of 100:60 (Appendix 9, page 277). Any librarian preparing a budget and plan of staff needs for his library could find the tables given in Appendix 8, Annex C. of the Parry Report (Costs of staffing notional university library) an invaluable aid. A further and even more enviable figure, quoted for American public libraries, is $3.00 on staff for every $1.00 on books. Professor Cohen, of the Harvard University Law Library, gives his library's budget as 65 per cent for staff, 25 per cent for books and materials, 10 per cent for binding and other operating expenses. It is interesting to note that the staff structure comprises 18 professionals, 46 supporting clerical workers and 46 part-time clerical workers. (Perpetuation of excellence, *Harvard Law School Bulletin*, volume 23, 5, 1972.) All this emphasizes the necessity for adequate provision for staff to enable promotion and seniority prospects to exist.

JOB SATISFACTION

With all this gained, staff may still not remain unless job satisfaction factors are also present. Surveys are in fashion and another carried out by Norman Roberts: Graduates in academic libraries: a survey of past students of the Postgraduate School of Librarianship and Information Studies, Sheffield University, 1964/65–1970/71 (*Journal of Librarianship*, volume 5, no. 2, April 1973) enquired into job satisfaction and dissatisfaction factors. In first posts, the chief factor in making the post desirable was agreeable colleagues. This rated highly with all returns to the questionnaires. Most people left their first posts, agreeable colleagues or not, to improve their positions, and the growth of professional experience and the opportunities to use professional skills more fully were then the most important factors.

Those expressing dissatisfaction with the posts they had filled often complained that graduate professional staff were almost entirely employed on traditional book processing tasks or in administration. Readers' services tended to be operated by junior staff and this was felt by those answering the questionnaire both to give a raw deal to the reader and deprive the professional staff of any tangible end result to their processing routines, as they had no feedback from the user. Women graduates, the survey showed, were less likely than men to obtain adequate job satisfaction (this may be explained by some of the findings of the earlier surveys mentioned) and tended to leave the profession altogether more than their male colleagues (apart from leaving on marriage). As might be expected, the more experienced the librarian became, the more the future promotion possibilities, chances of a satisfying and satisfactory career structure and the use of acquired skills at a higher level determined the choice of desired post. For those engaged in staff selection and staff management, this survey is especially interesting. The early emphasis on personal relationships and the importance later of finding adequate expression for the acquired professional skills point the way a library staff should be recruited and organized. Again it can be reiterated that job satisfaction in these terms could be more easily obtained in many ways by the recruit to special librarianship, such as law, than in the necessarily more impersonal relationships of the larger unit. The difficulty is found more often in satisfying the career needs of the experienced librarian.

FUTURE PROSPECTS

Like everything else, law librarianship, even if in its early stages of development here, will not stand still. Already the social scientist and the lawyer are growing closer and it becomes harder to differentiate in the teaching and application of the one from the other. Miss Diana Priestly in an article on the libraries of the Law Society of British Columbia writes: 'Libraries containing mainly reports and statutes are no longer adequate . . . Very small staffs, or, indeed, one person managed the technical and public services of the old libraries. That is not so with a collection beginning to acquire material beyond the old narrow conception of law library books!' It is not enough to provide staff who will be sufficient to maintain and continue collections as they are. The need is to find and train those who will develop collections, ideally before the user even knows they need to be developed, who will continue to improve the facilities offered and make full use of new procedures and technical innovations, who will make the library an integral and essential part of the educational programme of its organization and the reliable and necessary tool of the profession. In return, budgets must include provision to staff and train at an appropriate level. In the end, an organization will get the library it pays for. It cannot hope to continue to get, as so often in the past it did, a far better one than it deserves.

FURTHER READING

GENERAL

Burkett, J. ed. *Trends in Special Librarianship*. Bingley, 1968 (ISBN 0 85157 058 5).
Library Association. *Management for librarians, based on a course of lectures*, ed. J. Cloke. Association of Assistant Librarians, 1968.
Neal, K. W. *British University Libraries*. 2nd edition. Altrincham, St Ann's Press, 1971 (ISBN 0 901570 03 6).

Thompson, J. *An Introduction to University Library Administration.* 2nd edition. Bingley, 1974 (ISBN 0 85157 093 3).

Great Britain. University Grants Committee. *Report of the Committee on Libraries.* HMSO, 1967. (Parry Report.)

Law libraries

Banks, M. A. *Using a Law Library.* London, Ontario, University of Western Ontario, 1971.

Finley, Elizabeth. *Manual of Procedures for Private Law Libraries.* 2nd edition. South Hackensack, N.J., Rothman, 1966 (*AALL publication series*, no. 8) (ISBN 0 8377 0106 6).

Way, D. J. *The Student's Guide to Law Libraries.* Oyez, 1967 (ISBN 0 85120 060 5).

RECRUITMENT

American Association of Law Libraries. Recruitment Committee. *Recruitment check-list 1969.* Chicago, AALL, 1969.

Gould, D. R. *Scientific Methods of Staff Selection: a recommendation for local government.* Charles Knight, 1970 (ISBN 0 85314 055 3).

Lopez, F. M. *Personnel Interviewing: theory and practice.* New York, McGraw Hill, 1965 (ISBN 0 07 038725 7).

National Institute of Industrial Psychology. *Interviewing for selection.* The Institute, 1953 (*Paper* no. 3).

Sidney, Elizabeth and Brown, Margaret. *The Skills of Interviewing.* Tavistock Press, 1961 (ISBN 0 422 70850 x).

Training

Unesco. *World Guide to Library Schools and Training Courses in Documentation.* Bingley, 1972 (ISBN 0 85157 140 9).

Rutgers University. Graduate School of Library Service. *Administration and change, continuing education in library administration.* New Brunswick, N.J., Rutgers University Press, 1969 (ISBN 0 8135 0601 8).

Wallace, E. M. *Research and development of on-the-job training courses for library personnel.* Santa Monica, Calif., System Development, 1968.

Weeraperuma, S. *In-service training in librarianship: a scrutiny of current practices with proposals for reform.* Poets Painters Press, 1971 (ISBN 0 902571 16 8).

Dalzell, Patricia M. Graduate training in Manchester public libraries. *Library Association Record,* vol. 74, 1972, pp. 2–3.

Mack, Elizabeth. In-service training in the Aslib Library and Information Department. *Aslib Proceedings,* vol. 22, 1970, pp. 260–6.

Martin, A. Practical problems and principles of in-service training. *Aslib Proceedings*, vol. 22, 1970, pp. 256–9.

SURVEYS

Hamilton, M. J. de C. and Jekyll, P. A. *Members in special libraries: staffing survey 1970.* Library Association, 1971 (ISBN 0 85365 264 3).

Roberts, N. Graduates in academic libraries: a survey of past students of the Post-graduate School of Librarianship and Information Studies, Sheffield University, 1964/65–1970/71. *Journal of Librarianship*, vol. 5, 1973, pp. 97–115.

Smith, G. C. K. and Schofield, J. L. A general survey of senior and intermediate staff deployment in university libraries. *Journal of Librarianship*, vol. 5, 1973, pp. 79–96.

17. Accommodation

MURIEL ANDERSON, BA, ALA
Deputy Librarian, Institute of Advanced Legal Studies,
University of London

A problem which most law librarians will have to face
sooner or later is that of finding space, whether to house the
ever-expanding collection or to seat the increasing number of
readers for whom the library caters. Indeed, many libraries are
already facing these problems in acute form. The accession of
the United Kingdom and Ireland to the European Communities has given a further impetus to the explosion of specialist
legal literature which has taken place over the past few decades
and which has affected both professional and academic law
libraries alike, while the expansion of student numbers, as a
result of recommendations by the Ormrod Committee on Legal
Education,[1] brings simultaneous pressure on the reader spaces
available in university law libraries.

The space problems of law libraries are accentuated by two
factors. In contrast with the largely monographic character of
collections in some disciplines and the relative obsolescence of
older serials in others, law collections are characterized both by
a high ratio of serials to monographs and by the continuing
relevance of much of the older material (particularly, but not
only, where law reports are concerned). Thus weeding the
collection in order to find the extra space needed will not
provide much relief. The speed of growth can sometimes be
moderated by sensible co-operative acquisitions arrangements
with other law libraries in the same area, and by taking account
of the law holdings of the British Library Lending Division at
Boston Spa, but there are limits to the extent to which such
interdependence can alleviate the situation. Equally, the
acceptability of off-site storage depends very much both on the
type of material being stored and the urgency with which it is

[1] Great Britain. Lord Chancellor's Department. Committee on Legal
Education. *Report.* HMSO, 1971. (Cmnd. 4595.)

likely to be required by readers. It can, at best, be a palliative. No doubt the long-term future will see the development of computerized legal information networks with ancillary full text storage on microfilm and adequate access and print-out facilities (see page 653), but work on such systems is still very much in its infancy and many expert man hours and a great deal of money must be spent before they can relieve libraries of the need to acquire an ever-increasing number of conventionally printed volumes. The more modest microfilm or microfiche editions of an increasing number of legal texts are somewhat limited in their potential for lawyers who need to turn rapidly from one volume to another. In their present form they are unlikely to make a very immediate impact on the problem.

The law librarian must still, therefore, assume that the collection will continue for some time to grow in the conventional manner and plan for adequate shelf space accordingly. This, together with reader and staff space requirements, may or may not entail either adaptation of, or extension to, existing premises or the planning and building of a completely new library. Regardless of the particular need, the factor common to all situations is the responsibility resting with the librarian to assess and draw attention to future space requirements sufficiently far ahead to allow the often slow and cumbrous machinery for bringing about improvements to have ample time to operate before the situation becomes acute. This may be a matter of several years where the acquisition or building of new premises is involved.

This chapter seeks to draw attention to a few of the factors to be considered when assessing space needs. It is this assessment which will guide the librarian and his administration in their judgment as to when and how to meet these needs, and it will form the basis of a brief to the architect when it is necessary to embark on a new building or extension. No attempt will be made here to cover the various stages and procedures of planning a new building, but reference will be made to one or two major sources of more detailed and expert information for librarians faced with that prospect. The chapter has been written during the period of conversion from the imperial to the metric systems of measurement. Imperial or metric conversions are given in parentheses for all measurements used.

In the case of metric measurements, millimetres are used for linear measurements, the traditional centimetres for the height and depth of books (in both cases to the nearest five millimetres) and square metres for areas (to two decimal places). Imperial conversions are to the nearest foot or square foot.

SHELF SPACE

When many of the law libraries in these islands were built, there were no common standards for shelving and many libraries have a legacy of variable shelf lengths, uncomfortably high bookstacks which require the use of step-ladders, and inflexible methods of shelf support which make adjustment both difficult and time-consuming. Modern methods of manufacture combined with research into the practical and ergonomic aspects of shelving have brought about a considerable degree of standardization, leading to general acceptance of a standard stack height of 7 ft 6 in. (or 2290 mm.) and bay width of 3 ft (915 mm.) (or now more usually 900 millimetres or one metre) for academic and similar libraries. The use of the term 'standard stack section' in this chapter will imply these measurements. Where adoption of this standard is possible it will bring not only financial economies but greater ease of access, combined with the complete interchangeability which results from the use of a single shelf length throughout. However, its automatic adoption depends on the existence of a suitable module or grid within which the bookstack ranges are to be fitted and will often be possible only in the case of new buildings or extensions where the optimum shelf length can dictate the module or grid size rather than vice versa. The problem of module size and its effect on shelving is discussed very fully by Keyes D. Metcalf in *Planning Academic and Research Library Buildings*, 1965, at Chapter four and more briefly by Godfrey Thompson in *Planning and Design of Library Buildings*, 1973, at page 56. A useful summary of the relationships between bookstack units and the structural grid is provided in *Library planning : structural modules* by Sally Odd (supplement to *Architects' Journal*, volume 147, 1968).

In practice, many librarians faced with the problem of adding additional shelving within an old building will find that, to some extent, circumstances will dictate their choice of shelf length. They should, however, bear in mind that the shorter the shelf length, the greater the number of uprights required and, as these are the most expensive element in a bookstack section, the greater will be the cost of the installation. If a single shelf length will not meet all requirements, every effort should be made to use not more than two throughout. If shelves significantly longer than the standard 3 ft (915 mm.) length are to be used, it will be necessary to use a thicker shelf than the normal ¾ in. (20 mm.) used in a standard steel installation, with consequent limitations on the number of shelves possible within a given height – thus again adding to cost and detracting from capacity per square foot or square metre of floor area.

As indicated earlier, the standard stack section used as a basis of calculation in this chapter is 7 ft 6 in. (2290 mm.) high and 3 ft (915 mm.) wide, the upright being slotted at one inch or 25 millimetre intervals. If non-standard sections are to be used, any figures arrived at by calculating the number of standard stack sections required will have to be further translated into terms of the particular non-standard sections to be used.

The length of shelf space and the number of bookstack sections required for the collection depends on the number of volumes already in stock, the expected rate of future growth, the period for which it is wished to make provision, and the shape and size of the books themselves. As the dimensions of the books are a critical factor, the assessment of space required will be dealt with under the headings of the height, thickness and depth (from spine to fore edge) of books. The same factors apply whether calculating the capacity of existing shelving or assessing future needs.

Height of books

The height affects the number of shelves which can be fitted into the standard 7 ft 6 in. (2290 mm.) high stack section and therefore is a factor in the total number of stack sections (and uprights) which will be required. The taller the books, the fewer the number of shelves, and therefore of volumes per section.

Metcalf (pp. 153 and 393) gives tables of book heights which show *inter alia*, that 90 per cent of books in academic libraries are 11 in. (28 cm.) or less in height, 97 per cent are 13 in.

(33 cm.) or less and only 3 per cent are more than 13 in. (33 cm.) high – percentages which suggest the most economical division of the bookstack by size, if a confusing number of different sequences is to be avoided. If the shelves on a standard height stack section are spaced at 12 in. (305 mm.) intervals (*ie*, with a clear space of 11¼ in. (285 mm.) between one shelf and the next), seven shelves per section are possible. This spacing provides economical accommodation for the 90 per cent of books which measure 11 in. (28 cm.) or less in height. There is little to be gained by spacing the shelves at less than 12 in. (305 mm.) centres, as a further useable shelf will not be gained, and to space them more widely for the sake of a small percentage of books would be wasteful. At six instead of seven shelves per stack section, however, the 7 per cent of books measuring more than 11 in. (28 cm.) but not more than 13 in. (33 cm.) high can be accommodated with the least loss of space, thus suggesting a second sequence for books with these dimensions. The spacing for the remaining 3 per cent will depend to some extent on the type of material, which will tend to vary from library to library. The heavier items should, in any case, be stored flat to avoid damage, but it is useful to know that five shelves per standard stack section are possible if the volumes measure up to 16 in. (40·5 cm.) high and only four per section for volumes measuring up to 20 in. (51 cm.) high. As will be seen later, there is usually a correlation between book height and depths which reinforces the argument for division of the bookstock into the three sizing sequences suggested above.

Thickness of books

The thickness dictates the total length of shelving which will be required for a given number of volumes and therefore the number of shelves required. This in turn affects the number of stack sections required.

Unfortunately there is considerable lack of agreement on the average thickness of a volume or, indeed, on the definition of what constitutes a volume. Is each physically separate bibliographical unit a volume, or must it be at least fifty or even 100 pages long, or be in hard covers, before it can be so defined? The definition will vary from library to library and from subject to subject. It will be affected by binding policies and will vary with the thickness of the paper on which the book is printed. Attempts have been made to arrive at an acceptable formula and Metcalf (pp. 153 and 393) prints a table, adapted from one in common use by shelving manufacturers, giving the average number of volumes which can be shelved per linear foot of shelf space for a variety of different subjects and the number which can be accommodated on a standard single-facing stack section. The figures given make allowance both for the average percentage of larger volumes in a collection and for the efficient work. ing capacity of shelves at 85 per cent full (see page 608) and are therefore useful for calculation of the number of 3 ft (915 mm.) shelves and of standard stack sections required. The figures given for law books (the largest quoted in the table) are four volumes per linear foot (305 mm.) and 84 volumes per standard single facing stack section. Those for bound periodicals (which form a higher than average proportion of the collection in a law library) are five volumes per linear foot (305 mm.) and 105 volumes per standard single facing section.

Because of the controversy over the number of volumes which can be shelved per linear foot (305 mm.), Metcalf (p. 393) suggests an alternative method of calculating the shelf space required for the existing collection, which has the additional merit of ensuring that any unbound or boxed material not qualifying for definition as a volume, but still requiring shelf space, will be provided for. This consists of measuring the actual length of shelving occupied by the total collection, excluding any gaps which have been left for expansion, in order to arrive at the number of fully packed standard single-facing stack sections which would be required to house it. To this number should be added 50 per cent to arrive at the number of standard stack sections which would be needed to house it comfortably with the shelves two-thirds full on average and leaving one foot (305 mm.) of space unused on each shelf – the point beyond which planning for new shelf space should not be delayed if it is not already available.

Two further factors need to be considered in connection with the length of shelving required. The first is the concept of efficient, as opposed to absolute, shelf capacity which has already been mentioned above. It is now generally recognized that once the shelves are more than six-sevenths (85 per cent) full they have reached the limit of efficient working capacity. Any large addition to a particular section of the library will then entail a great deal of shifting of the bookstock to make the necessary space available in the right place. This is uneconomical in staff time (both in shifting the books and amending records) and in the extra wear and tear on the books. This factor has been recognized by the University Grants Committee, which has accepted the contention of the Standing Conference of National and University Libraries that shelves 85 per cent full have reached maximum efficient working capacity. It cannot be over-emphasized that the spare 15 per cent of shelf space is *not* for further growth but is intended to maintain the collection in a workable condition.

The second factor is the estimated future rate of growth of the collection. On this will depend the period for which the existing shelving will be adequate and it is also of course a major factor in determining future shelving requirements (except in the case of new university libraries where future provision is restricted to ten years' growth from the start of building at the *current* accession rate). An estimate of the future rate of growth can only be based on the rate of accession in recent years, the policy objectives of the organization served by the library, and any known plans for expansion of coverage or more rapid growth than hitherto. Few law libraries are likely to exceed a normal annual growth rate of 5 per cent, but special circumstances may lead to a sharp short-term increase in this rate. Metcalf (p. 394) gives useful tables to show the number of years required for a collection to grow (*a*) from two-thirds to six-sevenths (85 per cent) of full capacity and (*b*) from 50 per cent to 85 per cent of full capacity at varying rates of growth. Where the provision of new shelving involves planning and building, or acquiring and adapting, new premises the librarian should remember that the process can take up to five years or even longer, and prepare accordingly.

Depth of books

This is the factor which dictates the depth of shelf required. As this, in turn, affects the square footage of floor space required to accommodate the ranges of shelves and their associated aisles, and as floor space is the most expensive part of bookstack provision, it is important to use shelves which are no deeper than necessary.

It has already been stated that there is usually a correlation between book height and depth from back of spine to fore-edge. Metcalf (p. 394) gives a table showing that 90 per cent of the books in an academic library measure 8 in. (20 cm.) or less in depth, 94 per cent measure 9 in. (23 cm.) or less, 97 per cent measure 10 in. (25·5 cm.) or less, and only 3 per cent measure more than 10 in. (25·5 cm.). He also gives a table (p. 153) which shows that these percentages correspond with the 90 per cent of books which are 11 in. (28 cm.) or less high, the 97 per cent which are 13 in. (33 cm.) or less high and the 3 per cent which are more than 13 in. (33 cm.) high respectively. Thus the 90 per cent of books which are 11 in. (28 cm.) or less in height will fit on to shelves measuring 8 in. (200 mm.) from front to back.

The 7 per cent of books measuring over 8 in. (20 cm.) but not more than 10 in. (25·5 cm.) deep, and over 11 in. (28 cm.) but not more than 13 in. (33 cm.) high, would appear at first sight to need 10 in. (250 mm.) deep shelves. However, if a bracket stack type of shelving with standard steel uprights measuring 2 in. (50 mm.) deep are used, and if the use of sway bracing (*ie*, diagonal wire stabilizers at the centre of the bookstack) is avoided, the resulting 2 in. (50 mm.) gap between the shelves on opposite sides of a double facing stack section will enable an 8 in. (200 mm.) deep shelf to accommodate 9 in. (23 cm.) deep books on opposite shelves or, if there is not a deep book immediately opposite, 10 in. (25·5 cm.) deep books. The latter problem will occur too rarely to justify the cost of deeper shelves to accommodate the few volumes concerned. It is therefore reasonable to assume that only the 3 per cent or so of books which measure more than 13 in. (33 cm.) in height and 10 in. (25·5 cm.) in depth will require shelves deeper than 8 in. (200 mm.) when the usual bracket stack type of shelving is used. In assessing the necessary depth for the larger volumes the two-inch (50 mm.) gap at the centre should always be taken into account.

In this connection, two comments are in order. Firstly, removable backstops are now supplied as a relatively standard item by most shelf manufacturers. These help to prevent smaller items slipping down through the centre gap but can be removed when larger volumes are to be housed. Secondly, it should be borne in mind that when wall strips are used, instead of the normal free-standing upright to support single facing stack sections, there is no gap available at the back of the shelf. As wall strips are considerably cheaper than free-standing uprights, it is cheaper to use deeper shelves in this situation than to substitute free-standing single facing uprights to provide the extra depth.

Aisle width

It will be seen that the dimensions and numbers of books dictate the actual shelving requirements of libraries, but the area of floor space required to accommodate the bookstacks depends also on the width of aisles between bookstacks. These are influenced by many factors, such as column spacing, length of ranges, whether bookstacks are in open or closed access areas, whether in heavily or lightly used areas, whether adjacent to reading areas, etc. There is not space to detail them here, but they are fully discussed by Metcalf (pp. 144–5, 161–2 and 330–6) and should be considered carefully before any decision on range spacing is taken. Thompson (pp. 82–3) provides useful illustrations relating the width of aisle to the various stancse and physical attitudes of the user (see Fig. 1).

The area allowed by the University Grants Committee, in the case of university libraries (*Notes on procedure 1974*[1] and *Planning norms for university buildings*[2]) for bookstacks and their associated gangways varies both with the type of volume to be housed and with the type of storage. The figures are:

	Books m² per 1000 vols.	Bound journals m² per 1000 vols.
Open access	4·65 (50 ft²)	9·35 (101 ft²)
Closed access (fixed stacks)	4·03 (43 ft²)	8·06 (87 ft²)
Closed access (rolling stacks)	2·07 (22 ft²)	4·13 (45 ft²)

[1] *Notes on procedure 1974. Capital grants.* (Mimeographed, limited distribution).

[2] *Planning norms for university buildings.* Rev. February 1974. (Mimeographed, limited distribution).

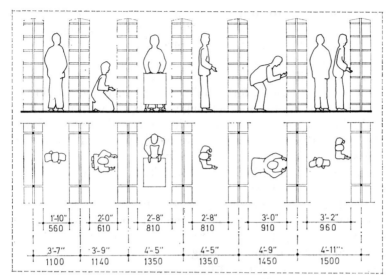

Figure 1

In addition, there is an allowance of 25·13 m² (270 ft²) per 1000 current periodical titles, assuming one-quarter of these to be on display and three-quarters to be in storage. These figures allow for the 85 per cent maximum working capacity referred to above.

In contrast with this clear specification, the Department of Education and Science *Notes on procedure for the approval of poly-technic projects*[1] make no specific provision for bookstack areas in polytechnic libraries. Total library space requirements are based on the number of full-time equivalent students, but if the bookstock increases without any corresponding increase in student numbers, there would appear to be no official standard to indicate the appropriate scale of provision for the additional shelving required. The Library Association's standard[2] of 8·36 m² (90 ft²) per 1000 volumes for open access bookstacks in polytechnic libraries does not differentiate between different kinds of volume. Metcalf quotes ten, fifteen and twenty volumes

[1] *Notes on procedure for the approval of polytechnic projects.* November 1971. (Mimeographed, limited distribution.)
[2] Libraries in the new polytechnics. *Library Association Record*, vol. 90, 1968, pp. 240–3.

per square foot (10·76 m²) as being acceptable in varying circumstances. None of these figures should be accepted uncritically and the many factors involved in each situation should be carefully considered.

The possibility of eliminating many of the aisles by using some of the various forms of compact shelving should be considered where the floor loading will take the weight involved and where the restricted access will not unduly inconvenience the reader. Only less used material should be stored in this way but shelf space per square foot or metre can be dramatically increased by this method. Both Metcalf and Thompson discuss some of the possibilities.

Finally, a word of warning is perhaps in order where new shelving is being planned. The weight of bookstacks when full is very considerable and, wherever they are to be placed, it is essential that the floor loading factor should be taken into account, whether normal or compact shelving is contemplated. This can be a very limiting factor where libraries are housed in old or adapted premises.

Types of shelving

The question of the types of shelving, either available or to be preferred, lies outside the scope of this chapter, but reference may be made to a very useful summary in Tim Poulson, *Library equipment: shelving* (supplement to *Architects' Journal*, vol. 147, 1968).

READING SPACE

Almost as controversial as the length of shelving required for a given number of volumes are the ratio of reader places to total user population which should be provided, the dimensions of the working surface, and the closely related question of the area required per work place. In planning reader space the total number of potential library users, both now and within the time-scale for which plans are being made, is a basic factor and will depend on the purposes for which the library exists and whom it is intended to serve. The figure is not a matter for decision by the librarian, but it must be known to him.

Number of reader places

Metcalf (Chapter 7) discusses at length the factors which affect the number of reader places required in academic libraries and assesses these under the headings of undergraduate students, graduate students and faculty. At pp. 389–90 he summarizes the factors on which the formula should depend and at p. 100 he indicates that, as a group, graduate students require the highest ratio of seating to their numbers, and states further that 'In general, the percentage of seats required would tend to be larger for graduates than for undergraduates, *particularly in law schools* [my italics] where up to 50 per cent or more may want to use the library at one time (or in a few schools even more)'. For university libraries in this country, the University Grants Committee *Planning norms for university buildings,* 1974, allows a ratio of one reader place to every five arts students, which, for this purpose, includes law students and also both academic staff and postgraduates. Some improvement on these figures may be permitted when a major library project is planned, to take account of reasonable requirements for future growth. In such cases an allowance of one reader place to every three arts students, based on the quinquennial planning figures, may be permitted, but this is, of course, in the expectation that the final provision would revert to 1 :5 when the expected growth in student numbers had taken place. The ratio for science students is 1 :7, but there is no further differentiation between subjects and no allowance is made for the particularly heavy use made of the library by law students. The Department of Education and Science is responsible for seating ratios in polytechnic libraries. In view of the rapid development of polytechnics, no precise standard has been laid down but, for the purpose of establishing reasonable expenditure limits, the maximum provision of readers' seats permitted would be on a scale of one to every four full-time equivalent students, depending on a number of variables.

The Society of Public Teachers of Law *Minimum standards for law libraries in England and Wales*[1] recommends for university law libraries an absolute minimum of one seat for every three law

[1] *Journal of the Society of Public Teachers of Law,* n.s., vol. 11, 1970–1, pp. 90–103.

students and staff, with a strong preference for a ratio of one seat to every two readers. This recommendation is based on the collective subjective judgment of those concerned with formulating standards. The need is recognized for a survey of the use made of libraries by law students and teachers in order to provide a firm statistical basis for any future recommendations. That the present recommendation is not unrealistic, however, is borne out by American experience. The standard laid down by the Association of American Law Schools *Executive Committee regulations : regulation 8*[1] states that libraries 'adequate for the curriculum and for research' should have 'seating accommodation, with generous table or desk space . . . for 65 per cent of the student body [*ie*, a ratio of 1 : 1·54] . . . Carrels should be provided for students doing extended legal research'. The *1970 statistical survey of Canadian law school libraries and librarians* by Marianne Scott[2] shows seating ratios which average 1 seat to every 1·86 readers. What is not in dispute and is rightly emphasized in the SPTL *Minimum Standards* is the fact that to a much greater extent than in other disciplines, books are the tools of the lawyers' trade and 'law students and law teachers spend a very high proportion of their working time in the law library'.

Dimensions of working surfaces

Another observable fact about the habits of lawyers in libraries is their need to gather round them much larger numbers of volumes at any one time than most other library users and to use these simultaneously in conjunction with each other. The question of table size and area allowed per reader is, therefore, a crucial one. Thompson (p. 102) states 'At present an acceptable figure seems to be 600 mm. × 900 mm. (2 ft × 3 ft); commonsense and personal testing agree with this . . . These figures are based on the requirements of the "average reader" or the undergraduate.' Metcalf (p. 392) gives a table of suggested minimum and adequate size working surface areas for different types of seating accommodation in which the *smallest* area per person regarded as adequate is 36 in. × 22 in. (915 mm. × 560 mm.), with areas up to 4 ft × 2 ft 6 in. (1220 mm. ×

[1] *Law Library Journal*, vol. 62, 1969, pp. 222–4.
[2] *Law Library Journal*, vol. 64, 1971, pp. 326–8.

760 mm.) plus a bookshelf for graduate students writing a dissertation. No precise standard for dimensions of working surfaces is laid down by the University Grants Committee, the Department of Education and Science or any of the associations referred to above concerned with law library standards, but a desk surface of less than 3 ft × 2 ft (915 mm. × 610 mm.) per reader should be regarded as inadequate for law students – even for undergraduates – and larger surfaces should be provided where possible, especially for postgraduate students and law teachers (helped out, if necessary, by a shelf, provided this does not impair the lighting). However, any decision on the dimensions of working surfaces must be taken within the context of the area for reader accommodation permitted by the financing authorities.

Area allowance per reader

The total area required per reader includes not only the desk space but also the space for his chair and a share of the adjacent aisle space. Metcalf (pp. 100 *et seq.*) discusses suitable allowances for different types of reader in academic libraries and summarizes these as 25 ft² (2·32 m²) per undergraduate student, 30 ft² (2·79 m²) per first-year graduate student, 35 ft² (3·52 m²) per graduate student writing his dissertation and, if closed carrels are used, a minimum of 40 ft² (3·72 m²).

For university library buildings in this country, the University Grants Committee allows 2·39 m² (26 ft²) per reader, which may be further supplemented in respect of any postgraduate research student for whom study space is not otherwise claimed in departmental buildings (*Planning norms for university buildings*, 1974).

In the case of polytechnic libraries the standards issued by the Library Association in 1968 suggest an allowance of 25 ft² (2·32 m²) per undergraduate and 35 ft² (3·25 m²) per postgraduate student. However, the Department of Education and Science, which is responsible for financing these libraries, does not quote a specific area per work place. Instead, the total library space allowance is expressed in terms of 0·8 m² (9 ft²) per full-time equivalent student (FTE), supplemented by up to 0·5 m² (5 ft²) per FTE from non-specialized teaching areas (in certain circumstances), giving a maximum of 1·29 m² (14 ft²) per FTE.

Types of reader accommodation

Some types of reading accommodation take up more space than others and this will obviously be a major factor in the choice of types to be used and the number of each. However, the saving of space obtained by the use of large tables is, to some extent, more apparent than real, as the space saved through the reduction in the number of aisles will be largely offset by the need for greater space between tables to allow access without disturbing other readers. Moreover, as few readers like to sit with someone on either side, the central seats at tables for more than four people will be avoided as far as possible and under-used. Metcalf (pp. 119–29 and 323–30) discusses the various types of seating and their arrangement in relation both to space and psychological factors and at pp. 390–2 he appends a useful summary with a table showing the approximate square-footage requirements for various types of accommodation, which is helpful for preliminary space calculations. Some lay-outs and critical dimensions are diagrammatically illustrated in L. Fairweather and J. A. Sliwa *AJ Metric Handbook*, 1970, in Section 24: Libraries at pages 129–32. For a sample, see Fig. 2.

In conclusion, each organization must come to its own decision on the appropriate scale of provision for readers, in the light of the overall space and the finance available, but, where this is subject to limitations imposed by a funding authority, the case for adequate provision for lawyers should be strongly argued.

CATALOGUE SPACE

As a library grows, so do both its public catalogue and its shelf-list, which take up an increasing amount of floor space both for the cabinets containing the drawers of cards and for the users of the catalogues. Some estimate of future requirements must be made by the librarian of the probable size to which the catalogue and shelf-list will have grown by the end of the period being planned for and of the probable number of people (both

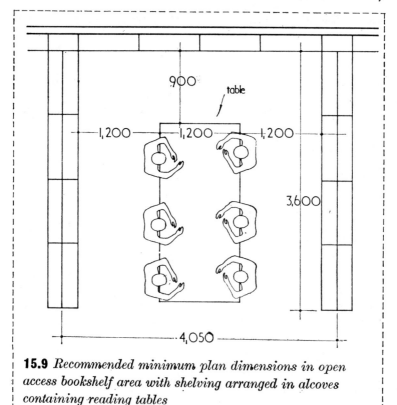

15.9 *Recommended minimum plan dimensions in open access bookshelf area with shelving arranged in alcoves containing reading tables*

Figure 2

staff and readers) who are likely to want to consult them at any one time.

Catalogue cabinets

The number of cards to be accommodated will depend both on the size of the collection and on the cataloguing policy of the library, which dictates the average number of cards required per title. An estimate of the current average of cards per *volume* can be made very easily by measuring the length of drawer space actually occupied by cards (tightly packed), assuming an average of 100 cards per inch (25 mm.) of space, and dividing the number of cards so obtained by the total number of volumes in the library. Because of the high ratio of serials to monographs in a law library, the average is likely to be somewhat lower than is usual in other libraries. If the average number of cards per volume is very low it may be advisable to use a slightly higher figure to calculate future needs, in case there should be a change in cataloguing policy. The number of cards to be accommodated ultimately will, of course, be the number of volumes expected to be held at the end of the period in question, multiplied by the average number of cards per volume. It may be necessary to add to this figure if any additional sequences of cards are maintained in the catalogue, *eg*, by form such as periodicals, law reports, etc. If so, these must be calculated in the same way, using an educated guess about the future rate of growth. Some allowance must also be made for guide cards and cross-references.

Just as the choice of bookshelves affects the space required to house a specified number of volumes, so does the choice of catalogue cabinet affect the space required for housing and consulting a specified number of catalogue cards. A further similarity is the fact that the net working capacity of a catalogue drawer is smaller than the actual net filing space of the drawer – varying from 70 per cent to 75 per cent, depending on the length of the drawer. The net filing space of a drawer (*ie*, between the front and back blocks within the drawer) is some 3 in. (75 mm.) less than the overall depth of the cabinet, for which common depths are 15 in. (380 mm.), 17 in. (430 mm.) and 19 in. (480 mm.). Thus, a drawer in a 15 in. (380 mm.) deep cabinet will have 12 in. (305 mm.) of net filing space and, at 71 per cent comfortable working capacity, will house approximately 850 cards; a drawer in a 17 in. (430 mm.) deep cabinet will have 14 in. (355 mm.) of net filing space and, at 72 per cent comfortable working capacity, will house approximately 1,000 cards; and a drawer in a 19 in. (480 mm.) deep cabinet will have 16 in. (405 mm.) of net filing space and, at 73 per cent comfortable working capacity, will house approximately 1,150 cards (Metcalf, p. 397).

The number of catalogue drawers required will, therefore, depend on the depth of cabinet chosen and this, in turn, will depend on the size of the whole installation and on the kind of use which will be made of the catalogue. Anthony Thompson in *Library Buildings of Britain and Europe*, 1963 (pp. 42–4) is probably a better guide to normal practice in this country, and in Europe generally, than Metcalf, who regards a cabinet six trays wide and ten to twelve trays high as standard. The latter are common in many American libraries, where it is normal practice to remove the required drawer completely from the catalogue and take it to a nearby consultation table. This type of catalogue cabinet is particularly suitable for very large catalogues which would otherwise require an enormous amount of floor space. They tend to be somewhat shallower in depth than some of the cabinets used in this country, as the weight of a full drawer is a significant factor when they have to be carried to a consultation point. This is obviously not a factor with the type of catalogue cabinet in general use in this country, where consultation normally takes place with the drawer in the cabinet and where the user can consult all the drawers from a standing position. To make this both possible and reasonably comfortable, cabinets do not usually exceed six drawers in height placed between 30 in. (760 mm.) and 54 in. (1370 mm.) from floor level. This type of cabinet is probably best suited to the average-sized collection in British law libraries but, although the catalogue is normally intended to be consulted without removing the drawer from the cabinet, some consultation tables or other convenient surfaces should be provided nearby for more prolonged searches.

Metcalf (pp. 335–9) discusses the *pros* and *cons* of various sizes of catalogue cabinet and (pp. 340–4) shows a variety of possible lay-outs giving useful maximum and minimum space requirements for consultation purposes. The latter will depend on the number of people expected to use the catalogue at any one time and this, in turn, will depend on the total user population, the size of the collection, whether it is largely open or closed access, and the amount of information and guidance given in the entries.

Only when the number of drawers required is known and decisions have been taken on the depth and height of cabinets, and on the space required between them and also for consultation tables, will it be possible to work out the total area requirements for this purpose.

Alternatives to the card catalogue

As explained on page 540, a number of libraries will have catalogues in either book or sheaf form and may wish to continue to use the same form. In either case, similar estimates as for card catalogues must be made of the ultimate number of entries to be accommodated. These catalogues will normally be accommodated on ordinary shelves rather than in special cabinets, but adequate and convenient consultation space should be made available.

The future may bring other developments which may make both card and sheaf catalogues obsolete. Some libraries already have catalogues on microfilm or printed by computer and these methods are likely to become more widespread in the future. They reduce drastically the amount of space required for the catalogue and, because copies can easily be duplicated and dispersed to convenient points throughout the library, they may well eliminate the normal concept of a central catalogue. Possible developments such as these must be kept in mind when assessing future space requirements for the catalogue.

Shelf-list cabinets

Unlike the public catalogue, each title or edition of a title has usually only one card regardless of the number of volumes concerned, and as libraries rarely know the number of titles held, as distinct from the number of volumes, it is more difficult to find a practical basis for calculating future needs. Indeed, it can only be done by relating the number of cards currently in the shelf-list to the number of volumes held, projecting it *pro rata* to relate to the ultimate number of volumes planned for, in the hope that the ratio of titles to volumes will remain reasonably constant, and adding a little to provide a margin of safety.

Much less circulation and consultation space will be required at the shelf-list than at the public catalogue, as it will normally be used by the staff only. If, however, readers have access to it, due allowance must be made for the greater numbers.

STAFF WORKING SPACE

This is, perhaps, the most difficult area on which to give guidelines for the assessment of space needs. So much depends on the individual circumstances of the library concerned – whether it is administered as an autonomous unit or as part of a centralized system of libraries and whether, in the latter case, either ordering and/or cataloguing functions are carried out centrally or in the law library itself.

Space must always be available at a public service point and, if recommended reading or other material for which there is exceptionally heavy demand is issued only against signature, space for an adequate number of bays of shelves must be provided in this area. If users are permitted to borrow books from the library there is likely to be greater pressure on the public service point and adequate circulation space on the readers' side of the desk is as necessary as space for the staff servicing this point. Unless there is a separate reference desk, it is here too that enquiries of all kinds will be received, with the possibility of inter-library loan work as well. Metcalf (p. 130) suggests an allowance of 100 ft^2 (9·29 m^2) per person on duty at one time and 125 ft^2 (11·61 m^2) for office accommodation if required for public service functions.

Whether or not the ordering and cataloguing of books is done in the law library itself, a private office adjacent to the public service point will be required and its size will depend both on the number of staff employed or likely to be employed within the period planned for and the number of functions carried out by the staff. In the case of some small law libraries run as autonomous units, one person may do all the work of ordering, keeping accounts, cataloguing, preparing binding and serving the readers with, perhaps, some assistance with typing and the reproduction of catalogue cards, labelling and lettering of books and other clerical tasks. Although it might appear that desk space for only one or two people is required in such cases, it must be remembered that the same books must go through several processes and will usually be stored on different shelves between processes. It is better to think in terms of the number of work stations required for various processes, keeping the work flow in mind and taking into account not only an adequate work surface for the process and for any machinery, equipment or records connected with it, but also for the associated storage of the volumes at each stage. It may be that one work station may serve more than one purpose, in which case some saving of space may be possible, but this depends on both the present number of staff carrying out the processes and any likely additional members of staff in the future, whether full time or part time.

There must also be adequate space for circulation in the staff working area for book trolleys both in and out of use and for access to the essential records such as visible indexes for periodicals, binding records, or the shelf-list, to which more than one member of the staff may require access at the same time.

In larger libraries at least the librarian in charge will have a separate office. Whether or not other senior members of the staff should also have their own offices is a question which should be carefully considered. There are many advantages in open-plan areas for all members of the staff engaged in processing the books. This allows the maximum of flexibility in lay-out in the short term and allows for easier adaptation to changes in either staff numbers or in processing methods in the longer term. This may prove to be of particular importance in the future as computers make a gradual impact on library housekeeping routines, with consequent changes in flow patterns of both books and personnel. Noisier processes may, however, have to be segregated to avoid too much disturbance to other members of the staff.

Metcalf (p. 131) suggests that for all 'processing' staff 100 ft^2 (9·29 m^2) per person expected to be employed on duty at one time should be regarded as the absolute minimum for accommodating the person and equipment, plus another 25 ft^2 (2·32 m^2) for the section head of each section with as many as five persons. He regards 125 ft^2 (11·61 m^2) or even 150 ft^2 (13·94 m^2) instead of 100 ft^2 (9·29 m^2) as much more satisfactory – particularly if there is any prospect of additional staff not otherwise allowed for. An additional 50 ft^2 (4·65 m^2) per person is suggested where there is any likelihood of employing student or similar assistance. Thompson (p. 120) gives figures of 7 m^2 to 9·3 m^2 (75 ft^2 to 100 ft^2) per member of staff in general work areas, with 7 m^2 to 8 m^2 (75 ft^2 to 86 ft^2) being adequate for staff requiring simply a single desk for their work (*eg*, typists). For more specialist staff (*eg*, cataloguers) and for

senior staff who will be consulted by colleagues, he specifies
9·3 m² to 11·6 m² (100 ft² to 125 ft²) and, for individual
offices, 9·3 m² to 28 m² (100 ft² to 301 ft²), according to
function.

It is interesting to compare these two sets of figures with those
in the Library Association standards for polytechnic libraries.
These specify 9·3 m² (100 ft²) per cataloguer, 7·43 m² (80 ft²)
per person concerned with book selection, 3·72 m² (40 ft²) per
person for clerical staff and 37 m² (398 ft²) minimum for repairs
and preparation of binding (a need which is not specifically
quantified by either Metcalf or Thompson). The figure of
13·94 m² (150 ft²) is the minimum proposed for offices for the
librarian and deputy librarian.

The University Grants Committee specifies an allowance for
administration and all other support facilities of 18 per cent of
the sum of the areas permitted for reading and bookstack
accommodation. The Department of Education and Science
gives no guidance on the subject.

The reference by the University Grants Committee to 'all
other support facilities' is a reminder that unless provision is
already made by the parent organization, space will also be
required for cleaning and maintenance staff, photocopying,
mail arrival and despatch area, staff lockers, and any other
facilities required.

BALANCE AREA

When a new building or extension is in view, the question of
balance area will arise. The balance area or non-assignable
space (sometimes called architectural space) in a building is
very much a matter for the architect once he has met the
requirements specified in his brief and, of course, within the
constraints of the cost limits set for the building. To quote
Metcalf (p. 316), 'An oversimplified definition of non-assignable
space for libraries might state that it is the difference between
gross, which is the total area of a structure, and net, which is
that part of the total which can be assigned for strictly library
purposes' – *ie*, for housing the collection, providing accommodation for readers and staff and for direct service to readers. It
must accommodate plant rooms, mechanical and electrical

services, main corridors, stairs, entrance lobbies, toilets, rest rooms – indeed everything not required for strictly library or other specified purposes. Its use by the architect will be affected by many factors, including the basic shape and size of the building site and of the building itself – and the internal arrangement of the building. It is, therefore, essential that the librarian should specify clearly any essential and desired spatial relationships between the different parts of the library and any requirements regarding the flow of either books or readers. The architect cannot be expected to appreciate, for instance, how essential it is that the library staff working area should be within easy reach of the public catalogue if much frustration, waste of staff and readers' time and generally poor service are to be avoided.

The balance areas allowed in university and polytechnic libraries are laid down by the funding authorities concerned and are normally specified as a percentage of the 'usable areas'. For polytechnic libraries, the Department of Education and Science specifies a balance area allowance of 25 per cent of the usable library accommodation. In the case of privately financed buildings, the balance area will be a matter for agreement between the architect and the client, based on many factors in which cost will figure largely. Apart from specifying spatial relationships and any other factors which may affect the balance area, the librarian will not usually be concerned with this decision.

FURTHER READING

This chapter has only touched upon some of the factors involved in assessing space needs. Frequent reference has been made to two books:

(1) Metcalf, K. D. *Planning Academic and Research Library Buildings.* New York, McGraw-Hill, 1965 (ISBN 0 07 041657 5).
The author is the acknowledged expert on the planning of academic library buildings and his book is the standard work on the subject. It deals very comprehensively with all the stages of planning a building and discusses fully the theoretical considerations lying behind the many practical issues involved. It is

essential reading for any librarian involved in accommodation planning. Although the book relates specifically to the planning of academic libraries, much of what is written has relevance to any kind of library.

(2) Thompson, G. *Planning and Design of Library Buildings*. Architectural Press, 1973 (ISBN 0 85139 526 0).

This serves as a summary and also as a useful guide to building norms on this side of the Atlantic, which are often less generous than in North America. Another useful feature of this book is the appendix of published standards for different kinds of library in this country.

Both these books have extensive bibliographies, leading the librarian to the literature on specific aspects of library planning.

Further brief but useful summaries of some aspects of library planning will be found in:

Anthony, L. J. Library Planning. *In* Ashworth, W. *Handbook of Special Librarianship and Information Work*. 3rd edition. Aslib, 1967, pp. 309–64.

Smith, D. L. and Baxter, E. G. *College Library Administration*. Oxford University Press, 1965.

An architect's view of library planning and buildings may be found in two series of studies:

Library spaces, fixtures and equipment. *Architects' Journal Information Library*, 17 February to 24 March, 1965. (Supplement to *Architects' Journal*, vol. 141, 1965.)

Library buildings. *Architects' Journal Information Library*, 21 February to 6 March, 1968. (Supplement to *Architects' Journal*, vol. 147, 1968.)

These help the librarian to understand the architect's outlook on planning procedure and the kind of information he will seek, as well as summarizing much information on spatial requirements.

The Library Association publishes useful assessments of new library buildings in this country, compiled by the Architect/ Librarian Working Party formed after the 1967 conference of the London and Home Counties Branch on planning and design of new libraries, and containing detailed assessments of all types of library buildings opened in the previous two years, with plans and statistical summaries:

Library buildings. Library Association, 1965– (ISBN 0075–9074).
Issues to date: 1965, 1966, 1967/68, 1972, 1974.

There is a section on library buildings in Whatley, H. A. *British Librarianship and Information Science, 1966–1970*. Library Association, 1972, pp. 181–212 (ISBN 0 85365 175 2). Trends and new developments over the period covered are discussed and new buildings are described in much briefer and more general terms.

Most of the available literature on specifically law libraries is to be found in periodical articles which can be traced through the *Index to Legal Periodicals*, vol. 1– , 1909– . New York, H. W. Wilson (ISSN 0019–4077). A useful bibliography on 'Library Planning' by Kate Wood is in *Library Association Library and Information Bulletin*, no. 24, 1974, pp. 4–18.

Finally, in addition to studying the literature, the value of visiting new libraries, observing their solutions to various problems and discussing their success or shortcomings with the librarians concerned cannot be overestimated. Knowledge of other people's mistakes can be as valuable as that of their successes.

18. Mechanization

P. NORMAN, BA, MA, ALA
Assistant Librarian, Institute of Advanced Legal Studies,
University of London

As many of the processes involved in library mechanization are
not peculiar to law libraries, and as such processes are treated
elsewhere in an extensive literature, it is proposed in this
chapter to treat the basic principles and terminology only in outline. The section on subject analysis is more related to the legal
field, as some work has been done in automated legal research.

It is necessary at the outset to repeat the warning that an
automated library system is not *ipso facto* an improvement on
the manual one which it replaces; preliminary studies may
reveal possible ways of improving existing systems sufficiently
without recourse to the computer. In addition, although procedures may be greatly speeded up by automation, this may be
at great financial cost, not only in purchase of equipment, but
in running and staffing the systems.

Finance is of course of major importance, as computer systems are undeniably expensive. This is in spite of the fact that,
as with television sets or pocket calculators, prices tend to
decrease as technology improves and mass production gets
under way. For this reason, few law libraries in this country are
likely to go through the whole process of automation, including
the purchase of a computer. Individual libraries may, however,
be part of a larger but integral automated system, as in a
university, or co-operate for instance in the production of
machine-readable union catalogues, which may be processed
on a computer not directly linked to any of them. In the latter
case, the problem of compatibility of records is raised.

MACHINES AND TECHNIQUES

Development

The computers in use today have a comparatively short history, beginning during the Second World War, though machines designed to perform mathematical calculations had been designed as early as 1642. The first step towards modern techniques was a system of weaving invented by J. M. Jacquard about 1810. This used cards with a series of holes punched in them to determine the pattern woven. The idea was taken up by Charles Babbage to supply information to his mechanical calculator soon afterwards. Babbage was a pioneer in the field, but suffered from an all too common lack of financial support. In 1890, however, Herman Hollerith, of the United States Bureau of the Census, invented an electro-magnetic calculator using punched cards. The instructions for a very limited manipulation of data were specified by a 'plugboard' or switchboard arrangement. Eventually the instructions themselves were put on cards in a machine designed and completed by Howard Aiken and presented to Harvard University in 1944. The first fully electronic computer, 'Electronic Numerical Integrator and Calculator' (ENIAC) was produced by the Moore School of Engineering of the University of Pennsylvania. In Britain, the first of such computers appeared in 1949 at Cambridge University. Developments since the early days have included the replacement of thermionic valves, which made the machinery bulky and unreliable, by transistors.

Computers were first designed to perform mathematical calculations, and had done so for about ten years before their use in libraries was considered, although punched cards were used to produce book catalogues at the Los Angeles County Public Library in 1953.

Telex

Before describing the working of a computer and its functions in a library, mention should be made of other machines which have been applied to library work.

The teleprinter, or Telex, is rather like an electric typewriter which is linked to identical machines in other locations by means of telephone lines. Each user has a number similar to a telephone number and calls other users by means of a dial. The message, which may be of any length, is typed by the caller, and is reproduced instantaneously and exactly on the distant machine. As it is not necessary for anyone to be present to receive the message at the time of its transmission, the problem of waiting at a telephone while a search is made can be avoided.

Before the formation of the British Library in 1973, the National Lending Library at Boston Spa made extensive use of Telex in supplying loans, being able to boast a 24-hour turn-over. With the introduction of the BLL loan/photocopy forms, the scope for Telex is likely to increase. Naturally, the greater the number of libraries with Telex, the better the service can be: it could be argued that the main sources of legal materials are well known and searches by Telex unnecessary. However, enquiries need not be confined to loan requests, but may be extended to reference or bibliographical work. In comparison with some more sophisticated equipment described below, even Telex is slow, since communications are transmitted at the speed of the sending typist and calls are charged as for tele-phones by time and distance. It is probable that in future machines will transmit messages, pre-recorded on paper tape, at speeds of up to 66 words per minute. At higher levels of mechanization, telephone lines can themselves be used to trans-mit electronically recorded data at very high speeds, though this involves the use of computers.

Punched cards

Punched card equipment has, as we have seen, had a much longer history than the computer, being in commercial use for about eighty years. Data are recorded on a card or batch of cards made of stiff good-quality paper, and normally (following Hollerith) $7\frac{3}{8} \times 3\frac{1}{4}$ inches in size. Each is divided into eighty numbered columns and twelve horizontal rows. One column represents one character, whether letter, number or other sign, which is recorded by punching holes in certain combinations of column or row. Usually there is a maximum of two holes per column to prevent card weakness.

The cards are encoded by means of a card-punch operated by a keyboard as on a typewriter. Sequences which have to be repeated are stored in a program card mounted on a revolving drum. Punches in the columns of the program card control the automatic operation for the corresponding columns of the cards being punched.

As with other automatic devices, card-punches and readers work by means of electrical impulses. In this case they are generated by brushes which make contact with a steel drum when a hole in the card passes over them. Modern equipment usually interprets the data being encoded by printing it along the top of the card, which avoids the process of passing cards through a machine in order to read their content, and renders errors immediately detectable.

Because of its long history, the punched card system has a large range of machinery, including readers and sorting devices, but these form part of an electro-mechanical system whereby the processing of data is usually performed by altering or sorting the cards themselves. The main use for punched cards is now as a means of input to a computer, but for other possible applications see for example Davies, J. Punched cards in the library and information fields. *Aslib Proceedings*, volume 12, no. 3, March 1960, pp. 101–8.

Tape typewriters

These may be thought of as a modification of the electric typewriter. As the operator types, there is generated in addition to the conventional copy, a record on paper tape. Letters or figures are represented by a system of coded holes punched across the width of the tape, usually in five or eight 'channels', with a series of sprocket holes down the centre of the tape. A record so produced can then be played back so that the data is retyped automatically at high speed. This may be repeated as often as required and by means of special keys the operator can alter the layout, though not the order, of the work as it is reproduced. A 'skip' key is provided so that sections of data may be omitted without being erased from the tape.

Thus one possible application might be the reproduction of catalogue cards in multiple copies, for instance as added or subject entries, or duplicate cards for a union catalogue. Similarly, edited versions might be used to produce a list of recent accessions. More significant perhaps is the possibility of using the tapes generated as input to a computer. An article describing the use of such machines is by Wilson, C. W. J. Use of the Friden Flexowriter in the library of the Atomic Energy Research Establishment, Harwell. *Journal of Documentation*, volume 20, no. 1, March 1964, pp. 16–24.

Computers

There are basically two types of computer, analogue and digital. The former relies on changes in electrical charge which are analogous to (that is, reflect) corresponding changes in the mathematical quantities or measurements being processed. Such machines are often built for a specific purpose, and are not the concern of the librarian. The digital computer is a machine which processes data in unit form, whether it be the transactions of a bank or the record of a library. Its smallest components, minute ferrite rings, are simply charged or uncharged with electricity, though when operating in conjunction they are capable of processing masses of data far beyond the capacity of one man or even several people within a comparable time; a computer can do in seconds what would take human beings months to accomplish.

The computer's function is to perform small and repetitive tasks on large amounts of data at a speed so great that it is calculated in thousandths of a second.

Hardware

The 'brain' of the computer, known as the central processing unit, (CPU), is unable to function without means of receiving both the material it must process and the instructions for processing it. The system therefore includes input equipment. This comprises card-readers, paper-tape readers or magnetic-tape readers and, in more advanced systems, consoles which allow direct or 'on line' access to the computer through a typewriter keyboard. Such consoles are not normally used to input large files of data. The most common method of preparing library data for computer processing is with punched cards as described above, or paper tape, though once large files of data have been collected they are read on to magnetic tape or discs. The latter are in the form of long-playing records stacked on an automatic turntable, except that the grooves are concentric, and capable of carrying between half a million and several hundred million characters. To save tracking time, reading heads are placed opposite each side of each disc. A similar device is the magnetic drum, on which data are recorded as on a phonograph cylinder. Such means of storing information not inside the computer itself are described as backing store.

Machinery is also required to reproduce the results of the computer's calculations in legible form. In most systems this consists of a line printer, which can often print 1,000 lines of 160 characters each per minute, though speeds vary with type of printer. In the most advanced systems, results can be displayed on cathode ray screens known as visual display units.

For a detailed description of the many types of computer hardware see Hayes and Becker, *Handbook of Data Processing for Libraries*, 1970, Chapters 10 to 13.

Software

This term is used to describe the range of instructions used to operate the computer and its peripheral equipment. A set of instructions to perform a specific task is a program (conventionally so spelt). Programing of computers is a specialized task normally outside the scope of the librarian, but a brief statement of the processes and their terminology may be useful.

As has been said, the computer works at a very minute level, using binary arithmetic because of the on/off basis of its construction. To write programs in the language of the machine – machine code – requires an intimate knowledge of the hardware, is detailed, laborious and slow. Manufacturers therefore provide a higher-level assembly language which interprets the functional instructions into machine code.

Even this is the work of the specialist, and so even higher level languages have been devised for the user to work in. Higher level in this context means that one instruction in such a language corresponds to many more detailed instructions in a lower level language. Computer languages in common use, though none specially designed for libraries, are FORTRAN (Formula Translator) and ALGOL (Algorithmic Language) for scientific use, and COBOL (Common Business-Orientated Language) for commercial work. Others designed for linguistic data manipulation include COMIT, developed at the Massachusetts Institute of Technology for use on IBM machines, and SNOBOL, devised at the Bell Telephone Laboratories. Programs which interpret such high-level languages into machine code are called compilers, and vary with the type of machine, whereas COBOL and the others are applicable to several makes.

The preliminary to writing a program is usually a flow-chart, which is a diagrammatic representation of the logical steps in

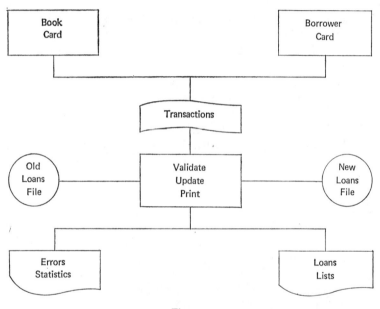

Figure 1

the task to be performed. Flow-charts are not confined to computing, but can be useful in analysing any system of operations into its logical components. Conventional signs have been developed for each type of step in the sequence, and each type of data storage device. They are the subject of a British Standard (BS 4058. 1973). See diagram, Fig. 1. The program itself is an 'ironed out' version of the flow-chart, with each step in the sequence expressed in linear form. The number of steps in a large program may run into thousands.

The main functions which a computer can be programed to perform on a file of data are the sort – arranging the file in a desired order, the search – finding a particular record within a file, and edit – the addition of a record to or its removal from a file. Of particular importance as regards the search function is the physical form in which the data are held. The records on a magnetic tape are filed sequentially from one end to the other, with gaps to allow for acceleration and deceleration of the reader. Thus the machine has to read each record in turn until it reaches the one required. On the other hand, a disc or drum file has random access – any part of the file may be read almost instantaneously. These factors also mean that it is usual to file records on magnetic tape in a specific order, *eg*, author or accession number, whereas on disc or drum the newest record may be put on the next vacant space. There are consequently both sequential or random access files and sequential or random access to those files.

Turning again to the hardware of the computer, the form in which information is handled by the machine is dependent upon the configuration of the components within the core of the machine. This is analogous to an array of pigeon-holes, each of which is of equal and finite depth. These 'pigeon-holes' are known as computer 'words', and each is numbered sequentially from zero to a number of thousands (K), so that the capacity of a computer to store data and programs is given as, for example, 256K. The number assigned to a word is its address.

Words are made up of smaller components called bits. Characters such as letters of the alphabet are represented by a group of bits, so that for the capitals alone a minimum word-length of four bits is needed, though it is usual to have words of at least eight bits to allow for upper- and lower-case, the numerals and various punctuation marks.

LIBRARY OPERATIONS

The library applications of computers fall into two main categories. First, there are the routines of library management, ranging from orders to booksellers to the production of library catalogue records or loans files. These have come to be known as housekeeping routines. Secondly, there is the ever-expanding field of information retrieval, mostly the product of automation itself, whereby hitherto impossible means of sorting, classifying and more especially selecting information have been developed. Considering first the housekeeping functions, it is perhaps best to begin with the means of acquiring new material for the library by mechanized techniques.

Ordering systems

When the library receives a recommendation for a book from a reader, the details must first be verified in such catalogues or bibliographies as may be necessary. Except in limited circumstances, the automation of this process is impracticable. This is due to the ability of the skilled librarian to make intelligent guesses where the information given is either scanty or inaccurate, and also to the need for very involved programing to enable the computer to interpret such information correctly.

However, when details have been verified, the comparison with the library catalogue to see whether the book is already held is capable of automation, if that catalogue is in machine-readable form. The user programs must of course account for minor variations between one record and the other, which may have resulted from the use of different cataloguing rules. For instance, the British National Bibliography repeats the author's name after the title statement, though the library may not do so. The machine must be told that 'Archbold's principles of pleading . . . ' and 'Principles of pleading . . . by Archbold' refer to the same book.

When it is established that a book is not already in stock, the ordering process may begin. The information requirements not only of the library and the source of supply, but also of an accounting system (possibly outside the library), or of the reader or department with special funds must be taken into consideration.

A number of elements commonly needed to identify a particular order may be considered:

Order number
Author, title, edition
Publisher

    Place (and country) of publication
    Date of publication
    Projected price
    Customer's account number
    Language – *eg*, when a translation is specifically required
    Standard Book Number
    Source of supply
    Book fund to be debited
    Number of copies

As books donated to the library may be similarly recorded, a statement as to whether the book is a gift or purchase may be included.

Although Standard Book Numbers have not perhaps yet received their due attention from booksellers or indeed publishers, they are eminently suitable for the unique identification of an item.

In addition to the above data, a current order file must be capable of storing information such as reports that a certain book is out of print, not yet published, or out of stock. It must also be possible to call up books which are overdue – the time allowed being variable as between domestic, European and other foreign publications.

For purposes of computer handling of all the above data, each element is labelled or 'tagged' so that the computer may distinguish between one category of information and another. For instance, a series of numbers might be used, two digits being sufficient to identify a large number of elements. The author statement may be given the code 01, the title 02, and so on. If the computer is instructed to list all items on order by author, it is directed to the corresponding tag for each item, and reads the information following it.

Many of these identifiers are of no interest to the bookseller, so that it may be preferable to produce the actual orders on a line printer or tape typewriter in such a way as to give only such data as are required to identify the book.

In this connection a great step forward has been made by the introduction of the International Standard Book Number (ISBN). This is an all-figure number of up to nine digits which uniquely identifies one edition of one book, distinguishing even between hardback and paperback. Its component parts are first a language digit (not always shown on English books), zero being used for English, 3 for German, and so on. Secondly comes the publisher identifier, next the number for the particular book, and finally a single check-digit, which helps to prevent errors in the reproduction of the main number. The last digit sometimes appears as x, meaning ten. The publisher number can be useful in statistical surveys, as the major publishers have the two- or three-digit codes, and the smallest ones six-digit codes.

Unfortunately, although all British books now display ISBNs, and they appear on British National Bibliography entries, since few publishers or booksellers have automated systems there is so far little scope for their use in the ordering field. However, if libraries form the habit of using these numbers in the way that we are learning to use the post codes, a great deal of effort in identification might be saved.

Returning to the elements of data in an order record, if there are many regularly used sources of supply, it may be worth while to provide a machine file of their names and addresses, with a code for each, so that it would be enough to key in the code, the line printer printing out the corresponding details on the order sheet.

At this stage, then, we have a computer file of books on order. This must be up-dated with information of the following kinds: book now received, and price amended where necessary; book out of print, not yet published, or otherwise unavailable. Information of the latter kind entails provision for projected date of arrival and its amendment in the light of suppliers' reports. Under normal circumstances one might expect British publications to arrive within a few weeks, European ones within two or three months, and American and others a good deal later. If such periods are specified, when they expire a list of overdue books can be printed out, or call-up notices produced direct. Statistical data on the actual length of time taken for books to arrive can be used to amend these projected dates.

As books are received, their records are removed from the order file and may be printed out to form process slips, with accession numbers added when necessary, and with as much available bibliographical detail as possible. The usefulness of such data depends on its source and the willingness of the cataloguing department to accept the details and format used by that source. If, for example, the library follows the Anglo-American Cataloguing Rules, as does the British National Bibliography, and can rely on the acquisitions department to follow BNB where possible, no difficulty should occur.

A representative system, operational since 1971, is that of Manchester University Library. Input to the system is by means of a Honeywell K-700 Keytape, a magnetic tape encoder, and each record consists of the equivalent of eight 80-column punched cards. The input is in two stages, the creation of a file of orders and of books received other than by order being produced first with the aid of a machine file of booksellers' names and addresses. At the second stage amendments and additions to the existing files are produced. There are weekly outputs of a list in alphabetical order of author of books on order and recently received, a list in order number order, and a set of requisition forms to send to booksellers on pre-printed stationery. At wider intervals there appear an accessions register in numerical order including statistical data, accessions lists arranged by subject fund, and lastly reminders to booksellers, again on pre-printed stationery.

Serials

In this area of library operations, the scope for automation has hitherto been somewhat limited. It is quite a trivial computer operation to list serial titles held in a library or to create a union list of the holdings of several libraries. This is little different from listing non-serial material provided that no detailed indication of holdings in one serial is required. On the other hand, the full control and listing of each issue of a serial as it is ordered, received and processed in the library involves a much more complicated set of routines.

Union catalogues

Considering first the holdings list or union catalogue, many such lists have already been produced by computer. As long ago as 1966 two such schemes were put into operation. One was a

Finding List of scientific medical and technical periodicals produced by the University of Liverpool, and the other a union list of periodicals held in Institute of Education libraries in Britain, developed with the aid of the University of Newcastle upon Tyne, a pioneer in library automation in this country. The most widely used union list is the *British Union Catalogue of Periodicals,* the data for which have been on punched cards since 1960.

Among individual libraries, the National Lending Library for Science and Technology, later the British Library Lending Division, produces a list of currently held serials, though unfortunately no indication of the completeness of particular serials is given. The task of compiling union catalogues is made easier if entries can be reduced to some form of code or acronym for search purposes. Again, this is useful if computer files are to be directly interrogated: a printed list would obviously require recognizable titles.

The coding of serial publications was started by the American Society for Testing and Materials in 1963, under the acronym CODEN. This is a six-character alphabetic code, of which the first four characters are based on the initial or early letters of significant words in the serial title. This is comparable to the standard form of abbreviation which has been developed for series of law reports, though not, it appears, for law reviews. After the four mnemonic characters comes a hyphen, followed by a letter to allow distinction between titles which may have identical four-letter codes. Finally, there is a check digit to prevent errors in transcription. These CODEN are assigned by the Franklin Institute in the United States, and appear on the cover of every issue. Although originally applied to scientific and technical journals, CODEN are now assigned to all entries in the British Union Catalogue of Periodicals.

More recently, a system of serial identification similar to the ISBN has been developed. In October 1971 the inter-governmental conference for the establishment of a World Science Information System was held at UNESCO headquarters in Paris. The proposed system has been given the name UNISIST. As part of the preparatory work, an International Serials Data System (ISDS) has already been established. It is basically a network of national centres with joint responsibility for the creation of mechanized data banks. The central administration is based at the Bibliothèque Nationale, Paris, by agreement between UNESCO and the French government.

This centre has as one of its tasks to establish an international file of serials. The file will initially be limited to scientific and technical publications, but is to be extended later to the social sciences and humanities.

At the local level, the national and regional centres will receive blocks of International Standard Serial Numbers (ISSNs) from Paris, and assign them to new serials appearing in their own area. The system of numbering itself was developed by the International Organization for Standardization, and is similar in appearance to the ISBN. The figures are arranged in two groups of four, the last one being a check digit, *eg*, ISSN: 0023–9275 (*The Law Librarian*). These numbers carry no information content comparable to the publisher code of the ISBN, nor of course can they be used to sort lists of serials in a way that would be made possible by a development of the CODEN system. ISSNs are related to the *title* of a serial, so that a change of title entails the assignment of a new number to the same journal.

Control

Some aspects of the ordering, receipt and recording of serial publications are comparable to those of monographs, considered in an earlier section. There are, however, significant differences. From the bibliographical point of view, the title of a serial fits the same part of the record as the author statement for a monograph. Similarly, the imprint can be in the same form for both types of material. The difficulties with serials are that they change title, vary in frequency, are merged and divided, and in general require continuous monitoring of their progress, both bibliographically and administratively. Binding records are another major factor peculiar to serials record systems. The bibliographic description of serials for computer systems has been dealt with by the Library of Congress in its MARC Serials Format – an extension and adaptation of the monographic format which preceded it (see the section on MARC, page 648).

No satisfactory automated system of serials control seems to have replaced adequately the manual 'Kardex' type of record (see page 490), though various projects have been under way for some time. The development of automated serials check-in systems began in 1961 at the University of California at San Diego. This involved a monthly output of punched cards representing the periodicals which were expected to arrive during that period, and from which cards were pulled manually on receipt of the relevant issue. By 1964, the Kardex records had been dropped, and the system based on a master file kept on magnetic tape.

In this country, a continuing experimental project, Periodicals Data System, is part of the work of a group at Loughborough University of Technology mentioned in connection with MARC (page 648). This was designed as a total system covering the various cataloguing, handling and administrative record requirements of serials. It was planned in three stages, the first of which was the production of a holdings list containing only selected data: title, sponsoring body, etc., for use by readers, and at the same time the input of all data elements except processing such as orders and binding.

Stage two was the addition of binding data with a provision of binding check-lists (accomplished by April 1972) and the input of subscription and order data. Finally, the addition of a 'wants' list and automated accessioning with other refinements is envisaged.

Cataloguing

For purposes of mechanization, the production of catalogues and bibliographies may be divided into two processes – the production of a bibliographical record in machine-readable form, in as many copies as necessary, dependent upon the form of the finished catalogue, and secondly the arrangement of the file of records in ways which will enable the user to find the item he requires, from whatever point of view his enquiry starts. Associated with the latter process is the insertion of new records in an existing file in the appropriate place.

These two functions are reflected in the various levels of sophistication which are possible in a mechanized cataloguing system. At the lowest level, this may be the production of

21

multiple copies of catalogue cards with the aid of a tape type-writer. This usually involves on the one hand the automatic reproduction of the main record, with manual insertion of added headings for joint authors, subjects and so on.

At the next stage, the machine-readable record, whether paper-tape or punched cards, may be read into the computer and the whole file printed out on a line printer, in various pre-determined sequences. Alternatively, if a visual display unit can be used, each record can be made to appear on a screen before being read into computer store.

In each of these processes, a visible version of the record is needed for purposes of verification and proof-correction. This ensures accuracy in a printed catalogue, and also in the machine file which it may be intended to search automatically.

The final product of the system may be, as has been said, the conventional catalogue card, but the ease and speed with which line printers operate has meant a revival of the book catalogue. Card catalogues were introduced mainly as a means of improving the currency of records in comparison with printed book catalogues (see also page 541). However, it is now possible to print out a complete catalogue as often as necessary from a machine file which may be up-dated from day to day. To reduce costs, it has been usual to print out the complete catalogue only at fairly long intervals, say annually, providing cumulative supplements between these editions.

Such systems can produce problems of a multiplicity of places to search for a particular item, especially if the machine file is supplementary to an existing traditional catalogue. This is particularly true of large libraries such as the British Museum library (see *Scope for automatic data processing* . . . para. 192–203, 261–4, and appendix B, para. 529–52).

If it is intended to publish such a book catalogue, it may be preferable, in view of the poor quality of line-printer print-out, to produce a magnetic tape which can be used to operate a computer typesetting device.

The source of the bibliographical data used to produce a computer file may be either the library's own cataloguing department or an outside agency such as the British National Bibliography. In the former case, it is usual for data to be written on specially designed stationery arranged to correspond to the computer input system. This may even be true if the data is received from outside the library, if it is simply in the form of weekly lists or centrally produced catalogue cards. Similarly, even if the record arrives in machine-readable form, this may not be compatible with the library's own cataloguing rules. In either case, it will be necessary to insert any local information such as variant subject headings, local class numbers and accession numbers.

To enable the computer to identify the various parts of a catalogue record, a means of distinguishing these must be devised. There are two possible systems for this. The simpler is to make the position of each element significant, so that the format of the record is the key to its content. The first line of a typical catalogue entry is the heading. This is followed by the title, which is on a new line, and indented say five spaces. A full stop and space at the end of the title statement may be followed by the imprint, and so on. The computer is pro-gramed to recognize the function of a part of the record by its position in relation to the rest of the record.

A disadvantage of this system, especially in view of the need for exchange of information and the compatibility of systems, is that it is dependent upon the style of cataloguing used by the library concerned, which may differ in important respects from that of other libraries.

The other, more usual, means of identifying the parts of a record is the assignment of labels or tags to each one. The tag is entered at the beginning of the part of the record to which it refers, and the end of that part is recognizable by the appearance of the tag which introduces the next part, and so on to the end of the record. The tagging device is used by the MARC service (described in the next section) which forms the most advanced type of source for cataloguing data, a file in machine-readable form supplied by a centralized agency – in this country the British National Bibliography, now part of the British Library.

Several systems of computerized cataloguing are already operational in this country, and more are planned. At the highest level, the British Library ADP Study recommends that the British Library convert its catalogue to machine-readable form, at least for current acquisitions and possibly also retro-spectively, the possible cost being under a million pounds. A project is already under way in the United States, in respect of the Library of Congress (Project RECON) see Avram, H. D. The RECON Pilot project: a progress report. *Journal of Library Automation*, volume 3, no. 3, 1970, pp. 230–51, *and* volume 4, no. 1, 1971, pp. 38–51. The conversion of the British Museum General Catalogue would entail the adaptation of headings to the new Anglo-American Cataloguing Rules 1967, in order to maintain an integrated system. At present, copyright items received by the BM Library are catalogued separately and differently by BNB and the Library itself, an unfortunate and time-wasting duplication of effort. The suitability of the AACR for a national library has been questioned, but the possibility of some adaptation has been suggested in the study.

The earliest individual library in Britain to produce its catalogue in computerized form appears to be Camden Public Libraries. This was done in 1965, when the London boroughs of St Pancras, Holborn and Hampstead were united. For a description see Maidment, W. R. The Computer Catalogue in Camden. *Library World*, volume 67, 1965, p. 40. Another public library, the West Sussex County Library, has also been a pioneer in the field. See Bearman, H. K. G. Library Computerization in West Sussex. *Program*, volume 2, no. 2, 1968, pp. 53–8.

At an intermediate level, there are schemes involving co-operation between libraries. For example, the London and South-Eastern Library Region (LASER) is likely to begin con-version of its union catalogue in the near future (1974–75). Already its member libraries are using ISBNs to identify their holdings and to notify them to central records. This notification can now form part of the ordering of cards from BNB. For a brief report on the system and future plans, see Bourne, R. Computers in the Regional Library Bureaux. *Library Association Record*, volume 75, no. 12, 1973, pp. 238–41.

MARC

As a national copyright library, the Library of Congress had for many years distributed copies of its catalogue cards for use in other libraries, thus obviating the need for local cataloguing and classification. The British National Bibliography has, since its origin in 1950, produced a similar service, though mainly used by public rather than academic or professional libraries. MARC was originally intended to provide only the data appearing on a normal Library of Congress card. The project began as a system to produce machine-readable bibliographic information for items received by the Library of Congress itself. It was first proposed in a report published in 1963 and entitled *Automation and the Library of Congress.* This report outlined the possible future for library automation, envisaging rapid growth over the following decade. It also recommended that the Library of Congress set up a pilot project to test the feasibility of producing a 'standardized machine-readable catalog record that can be manipulated and re-formatted in local institutions to serve local practices and needs'. In 1964 the Council on Library Resources authorized a study of possible methods of converting the information on Library of Congress card to machine-readable form: three of the Library's staff then produced a proposed format suggesting the content of such a record, the manner of representing data, and the concept of fixed and variable fields applied to cataloguing data.

By the end of 1965, a selection of sixteen libraries was made from forty throughout the United States which had expressed interest, and in November 1966 the first tapes were distributed to these libraries on a weekly basis. After some months' experience a formal assessment of this pilot project resulted in a change of emphasis and consequently of system design. This was prompted by the realization that the full potential of the system was not being exploited if the records were confined to traditional catalogue card data, and that it would be better to see the records produced as a means of communicating bibliographical information in much greater detail between libraries or information centres, and to allow those libraries to select the data required for their own system, arrange it as desired, and above all have access to information which, although it could not practicably be printed out on the conventional catalogue card, could be available in a machine file.

In consequence of the change of emphasis a new project, described as 'MARC II', was begun in 1967, this time in co-operation with the British National Bibliography, with the support of the newly-formed Office for Scientific and Technical Information (OSTI), now the Research and Development Department of the British Library.

Since that time, what began as a project has become a permanent system of exchange of tapes between this country and the United States, and the issue of a microfiche print-out of all English Language publications catalogued by the Library of Congress and BNB, under the title *Books in English*. The BNB weekly issues have been computer typeset since 1971, and additional subject classification added to the tapes for exchange purposes, although it does not appear in the printed version.

The preparation of a MARC record is done with the aid of manuals produced by the national organizations concerned. For details of these see the list of further reading.

The structure of a MARC record is composed of two sections – information describing the bibliographic data and the data itself. The first section is sub-divided into various parts, including one to tell the computer the length of the record, the status of the record, whether old or new, up-dated or deleted, and a 'legend' to describe the material in general bibliographic terms – form, level, part or complete work, monograph or serial, etc. The bibliographic data itself is marked by tags for each element or 'field'. More specific information about a field is given by an indicator, and at the lowest level sub-field codes identify such elements as sub-title or author statement. Some idea of the detail is given by the fact that there are over eighty tags for the several variable fields, to account for such information as corporate name, uniform title, bound with, political jurisdiction, and many others. For a brief summary see Kimber, R. T. The MARC II format. *Program*, volume 2, no. 1, April 1968, pp. 34–40. A more detailed analysis is provided in the report of the seminar on the United Kingdom MARC Project.

One interesting development in the use of MARC tapes is the production of a new series of legal bibliography entitled *Law Book Guide*, published by G. K. Hall since 1969 and based on the legal sections of the Library of Congress tapes. It includes the new 'cataloguing in publication' service, whereby books not yet received from the publisher, but about which sufficient detail is available, are given provisional catalogue entries.

Using the tagging system, a breakdown by both subject and geographical or 'area studies' is possible. The *Guide* appears monthly, and is now cumulated annually.

Apart from the production of national data banks, the MARC tapes are being used experimentally by various libraries or groups of libraries. The Birmingham Libraries Co-operative Mechanization Project was formed by the University of Aston in Birmingham, Birmingham University and Birmingham Public Libraries, to investigate ways of local co-operation in the use of the BNB MARC service, and to provide a combined bibliographical data bank.

The first participants in the Library of Congress MARC scheme were individual large libraries with a wide subject range. In this country it was felt, and the view supported by OSTI, that co-operation between a number of smaller libraries would be a feasible method of utilizing a service such as MARC.

Most of the projects have been undertaken by University libraries, *eg*, Loughborough and Southampton (reported in *OSTI Newsletter*, March 1968, p. 8). Bath University of Technology, Bristol, Exeter, the University College of South Wales and Monmouthshire, and the University of Wales Institute of Science and Technology have a joint on-line access scheme centred on Bristol.

Problems encountered at Birmingham included the compatibility of records as already used in each library, and in relation to the MARC tapes.

Work has been done on a survey of the proportion of material on MARC tapes actually received in the three co-operating libraries – an important factor in the assessment of the usefulness of MARC. It appeared that a three-year file of combined US-UK MARC records would cover over 60 per cent of the combined non-serial intake of the libraries, though this figure conceals a disparity between Birmingham University at 35 per cent and Birmingham Public Reference Library at 85 per cent.

At the same time, a survey designed to show how soon after publication the record for an item appears on MARC tapes proved that the time-lag was really too great for book selection purposes, as distinct from cataloguing, where timing is less crucial.

The Project also has a serials group, which has been studying the design of a MARC-based serials system to produce such items as a union title/sponsoring body catalogue, a subject-ordered union list and various subscription and binding lists. The Library of Congress *Serials: a MARC format* (1969) has been taken into consideration.

Especially in the serials field, close co-operation with Loughborough University of Technology has taken place, resulting in the joint publication of a MASS (MARC-based Serials System) Format, as MASS working paper no. 1. This in turn has been favourably received at a meeting of BNB and INSPEC on the setting up of the International Serials Data System (ISDS) at the Bibliothèque Nationale, Paris. For a brief history of this see the section on serials.

The only library which appears to have relied entirely on MARC tapes is that of Trinity College, Dublin which, as a British copyright library, has used the tapes since October 1969. Nevertheless, only 80 per cent of its intake appears on the tapes, so that all items received since 1972 have been put on the library's own MARC record, and the previous card catalogue is closed at that date. (See Dieneman, W. MARC tapes in Trinity College Library. *Program*, volume 4, no. 2, April 1970, pp. 70–5.)

Circulation

The requirements of a loans or circulation system vary with the type of library, and are discussed on pages 463–6. However, the suitability of one or other automated circulation system is dependent upon these differing requirements.

Mechanized circulation systems available range from simple punched cards through modest batch-processing systems to on-line loans files which can be interrogated at any time. One of the most common systems is supplied by Automated Library Systems Ltd. This uses non-magnetic metal labels which are fixed permanently inside the cover of the books, and can be read by a sensor at some distance – for example, under a counter surface across which a book is passed. The main system provided by ALS, however, is one which is intended eventually to cover all library operations. It employs a record card for book and borrower, each measuring 2″ × 3″ and edge-notched to provide a maximum of 128 characters in fifteen possible positions. At the issue point are two card-readers, one to read the book card and one the borrower card. The former will not operate without a valid card being placed in the latter. The borrower's card is held until all the cards for books he wishes to borrow have passed through the card-reader, after which the borrower's record is read and his card released. Thus each loan record consists of a string of book numbers followed by borrower number. The loans are discharged simply by passing the book card through the single discharge reader. This need not be done until after the reader has left the counter, as any fines are shown up by the normal date-for-return stamp inside the book.

The transactions in each case are recorded on paper-tape, and later processed in the computer and read on to magnetic tape to produce a daily or weekly update.

More recently, the Plessey Company has introduced its 'Data Capture System'. This employs a light-sensitive pen which reads bar-coded labels on books and borrowers' cards. On each label is a unique number assigned to book or borrower, consisting of up to fourteen digits. These numbers are also printed above the label for identification. When a transaction – issue or discharge – is performed, the information is transferred to magnetic tape cassettes, which in turn are converted by a separate machine in order to be handled by the computer. Such a system has been installed at Loughborough.

A description of several circulation systems is to be found in a symposium on computer-aided circulation systems organized by the Aslib Computer Applications Group and published in *Program*, volume 5, no. 1, 1971, pp. 1–15.

SUBJECT ANALYSIS

The attractiveness of the subject of law and computers may be attributable to the nature of legal texts. The language of law, especially statute law, is to some extent formalized. Secondly, it is argued, much of the lawyer's time may be saved by automation, not only in searching for precedents relevant to the case in hand, but also in the drafting of documents such as wills. Much of the research work could be done by a centralized agency or an information network, reducing the costs by large-scale operation, but preserving the autonomy of the individual practice.

Apart from being highly structured, the body of statute law and case-law is, especially in the common law world, very large indeed. For example, one has only to consider the great and increasing bulk of the volumes of *Public General Acts*, which seem never to be less than three large volumes per year. Statutory Instruments take up five or six volumes. In the United States there is both federal and state legislation. The 90th Congress is estimated to have enacted 2,300 pages of legislation, and in 1967–68, 44,441 measures became law in the fifty states and United States possessions. This leaves out of account the mass of bills which never reach the statute book, but which nevertheless may need to be consulted by Congressmen and others.

Similarly, case-law is produced at an alarming rate. The *English and Empire Digest* contains about 250,000 references to individual cases, to which 1,200 or so are added annually. In the United States and other federations such as Canada and Australia, there are regional and state reports. In each of a dozen or so series in the *National Reporter System* (usa), between five and ten 500-page volumes appear each year (see page 317).

All of this material is of potential relevance for an indefinitely long period – thirteenth-century British statutes are still in force and reference is still made to cases fifty or more years old. This is in contrast to some scientific fields, where published materials can be outdated very quickly.

The present means at the lawyer's disposal of tracing relevant documents have been built up over a number of years, and are described in other parts of this *Manual*. Each of these research tools – indexes, digests, encyclopedias, citators – creates problems by its bulk and the need to keep it up to date. While the main body of law remains unchanged for many years, several and crucial amendments or repeals of statutes and interpretations of precedents occur every year.

Indexing

A first step to improve those indexes might be to read them on to computer files, tagging the various elements such as index terms and citations so that they may be printed out in any desired format. This would be analogous to the MARC service already described, retaining the manual process of indexing within a pre-arranged list of subject headings, and giving the computer only the clerical tasks of listing and sorting. An example of such a scheme is the *Index to Foreign Legal Periodicals*, which has recently transferred to computer production, partly to help with the issue of its latest large cumulative volume.

Research into indexing theory and techniques has come only recently to the legal field, despite the fact that it has possessed indexes for longer than many other disciplines.

Early experiments involved a statistical analysis of the number of 'significant', *ie*, non-common words. It was assumed that words occurring most frequently would indicate the subject content of the document. Later refinements included weighting – accounting for the probable importance of paired keywords, position in the structure of the text and so on. Such systems have the advantage of uniformity and consistency which are difficult to achieve in manual operations, but suffer from the disadvantages of quantitative rather than qualitative analysis which are inevitable in automated systems.

The simplest forms of computer-produced indexes are Keyword-in-context (KWIC) and Keyword-out-of-context (KWOC). In the former, the entry word is placed in the centre of the line and the rest of the title in natural order around it:

	Use of computers to search legal literature would appear:
Use of	computers to search legal literature
to search	legal literature / Use of computers
search legal	literature / Use of computers to
computers to	search legal literature / Use of
literature /	Use of computers to search legal

The KWOC index is produced by simply placing the entry word at the beginning of the line and printing the whole of the title, or as much as will fit on the line, after it:

Computer	The Computer scene in the USA
Computer	Law and the computer
Computerization	The scope for computerization in libraries
Computers	Understanding computers

Each of these methods involves little or no intellectual effort, and can easily be performed by computer. They are usually applied to the titles of articles, though the KWIC index can serve as a means of retrieving information from a complete text. In this case, a searcher may specify a particular term, and each occurrence of the term can be printed out with a portion of the surrounding text to clarify its context.

Citation indexing is another area in which the computer has a useful role. *Science citation index* has, since the mid-sixties, been produced by scanning 2,000 scientific periodicals, and links between an article and those it cites fed into a computer. This generates a citation index, corporate index and source index. A subject 'permuterm' index is also produced which enters each item under pairs of significant words in the title.

In the area of legal documentation, a system based on keyword indexing is CREDOC, an information retrieval system for Belgian lawyers. It is based in the Maison des Notaires in Brussels, and is a non-profit-making venture paid for by subscription from its users, for whom there is no other charge.

The aim of the service is to express all terms in the legal system by means of 'concepts' which are constructed from a dictionary of about 6,500 keywords. These keywords are assigned a four-digit code and linked to the titles and abstracts of the documents in the system. The coding allows for a search in either French or Flemish. The assignment of keyword descriptors to documents is done by qualified lawyers. Users of the system frame their searches in natural language and the machine search is done through an editor. The output is in the form of citations to case law and conventional photocopies if required, or the full text of statutes.

Classification

The assignment of class numbers to documents has not so far been within the scope of the computer, as the emphasis has been on natural language indexing. However, the use of classification schemes as a means of retrieving information automatically has been accomplished. The general scheme which appears most suitable for this purpose is the Universal Decimal Classification (UDC), which is widely used to classify scientific documents. These are often published with a class mark already assigned. A great advantage of the scheme is that it is published in many languages, so that the problem of information exchange between countries is minimized. It is an information language with a simple code expressing hierarchical relationships. The Committee on Classification Research of the International Federation for Documentation has organized two seminars on the use of UDC in mechanized systems, as well as the mechanized production of the scheme itself.

In the legal field, the recently published *Catalogue of International Law* of the Squire Law Library, Cambridge, includes a newly-developed classification scheme (see page 571), the compilation of which took into account the needs of the computer and its handling of symbols. The prime consideration was the desirability of particular symbols having constant meanings, so that whenever an automatic sort is made no special instructions in the program are necessary to enable the machine to distinguish between various uses of the same symbols.

Textual analysis

The ultimate step in automation is to by-pass existing indexing methods and work with the complete texts of legal documents, whether statutes or cases. The history of this, the 'full text' approach, begins in 1959 with the Health Law Center of the University of Pittsburgh, which was given the task of finding all references in *Purdon's Pennsylvania Statutes* to 'retarded child' and changing them to 'exceptional child'. After an unsuccessful attempt, using students to read the statutes, the data was put on punched cards and read into a computer. The amendments were eventually made automatically.

The Health Law Center later became Aspen Systems Corporation, selling retrieval systems based on the full text of statutes (Aspen now has a full-text file of the laws of all the States in the Union and the United States Code). More recently a case-law service has been introduced.

In this country, a project known as STATUS (Statute Search Project) was set up at the United Kingdom Atomic Energy research laboratory at Culham in 1966. Here the full text of all atomic energy legislation was punched on cards and input to a computer. From this file a 'chained dictionary', with terms linked by logical rules, as well as a frequency analysis of the words in the text, was produced. A second stage produced an index showing, for every word in the text, a document, sentence and word number, and at the third and final stage a KWIC index was generated. (See Niblett, G. B. H. and Price, N. H. The STATUS Project: searching atomic energy by computer. UK Atomic Energy Authority Research Group Report. HMSO, 1969. CLM R101.)

The most ambitious project which, unlike STATUS, is a commercial, fully operational system, is the Ohio State Bar Automated Research System (OBAR). In 1964, the Ohio State Bar Association began to consider the feasibility of a system of computerized law searching, and such a system was eventually set up in 1968, employing a commercial company, Data Corporation, which later became a subsidiary of the Mead Corporation, as Mead Data Central.

The sophistication of the system may be judged from the fact that it involves the use of visual display units in the lawyer's office, with the possibility of modifying the enquiry in the light of information displayed on the screen. The data base, originally Ohio State law – statutes and cases – has now been extended to cover New York laws. When a satisfactory answer has been produced, the relevant document may be printed out in a variety of formats, either full text or citation, or citation plus abstract. These may be printed on a terminal in the lawyer's office, or at a computer centre and posted to the enquirer afterwards. (See Harrington, W. G. and others. The Mead Data Central system of computerized legal retrieval. *Law Library Journal*, volume 64, 1971, pp. 184–9.) In this country progress in automated legal research has been confined to a small number of dedicated pioneers such as Colin Tapper at Oxford and Brian Niblett of the Atomic Energy Authority. The only project which seems to have gone beyond showing that various systems would work if implemented appears to be that of A. Paliwala at Queen's University Belfast, where a Northern Ireland case and statute citator has been produced using an ICL 1906 computer. The project could take advantage of the relatively small data base of the *Northern Ireland Law Reports*.

A source of encouragement in Britain is the setting up of groups interested in the legal applications of computers. Again, these are of recent origin in comparison to North America; the American Bar Association having had a committee on Law and Technology for a number of years. Only in 1970 was the Scottish Legal Computer Research Trust set up, representing all branches of the legal profession in Scotland. The members are lawyers rather than computer specialists, and so much of the initial work was of 'self-education' in computer techniques. The Trust's Report, which appeared in 1972, surveys the current scene both in this country and abroad, and recommends the establishment of a full-time organization to stand between the lawyer and the commercial firm and intervene constructively in developments in the field of automated information retrieval. The Report also envisages the establishment of links first with the rest of Britain and then with Europe, stressing the importance of co-operation with other national and international centres.

In England, Paul Leach, of the Law Society, was instrumental in the formation of a Computer Study Group, also in 1972. A discussion of the Council Co-ordinating Committee led to the Secretary-General's request that Mr Leach should watch developments in the application of computers to the law and legal work. The Study Group was drawn from interested people in many fields, including publishing and local government. At its second meeting observers from the Lord Chancellor's Office, the Foreign and Commonwealth Office and Council Members from both sides of the legal profession were present. A Standards Committee and Planning Committee were eventually set up, the terms of reference of the latter being 'to prepare a programme of future action and to consider how such plans could be implemented'.

The view of government representatives appeared to be that government involvement would wait until more concrete plans had been developed by the Group through its committees.

The Law Society has also been far-sighted enough to become a member of INTERDOC, the International Association for Legal Documentation, the objects of which are 'the study and promotion of legal documentation, more generally of legal information technology; the planning on an international level of initiative on this subject matter, the co-relation in a purely scientific (as opposed to commercial) manner of existing systems'.

FUTURE PROSPECTS

As was indicated at the beginning of this chapter, the most likely contact which law libraries will have with the computer is either as part of larger library systems or as users of and contributors to a co-operative scheme of legal information transfer. Considering housekeeping routines, most of the problems are common to all types of library, and a law library new to the field has a choice of well-established systems to emulate and adapt to its own situation. Computerized cataloguing presents more problems for the special library, mainly because of the need for standardization. This is necessary both for ease of computer manipulation and for increased reliance on, for instance, centralized cataloguing services such as BNB/MARC.

But, as will be shown by a study of this *Manual*, legal materials have a special character which sometimes makes standard systems such as the Anglo-American Cataloguing Rules or a general classification scheme difficult to apply, unless special provisions are made. It is perhaps the duty of law librarians to present a united front to compilers of general schemes, so that legal materials can best be accounted for in those schemes. This is, in fact, happening, for example in the form of memoranda of the British and Irish Association of Law Librarians to the Cataloguing Rules Committee of the Library Association on possible modifications to the Anglo-American Cataloguing Rules (see page 518–9). Whether such recommendations will be acted upon is of course another question. Another aspect of standardization is legal terminology itself. The thesaurus figures largely in information retrieval systems, but most research projects in the legal field have had to produce their own word lists, and a generally accepted thesaurus of legal terms has not yet appeared; there are of course lists of subject headings used in libraries. These have usually been based on more general lists, such as Library of Congress subject headings.

If law libraries are to participate in the growing system of bibliographic information transfer, a certain amount of uniformity in the treatment of their own records appears to be desirable, or at least an agreed format with which individual library records would be compatible. This might be an advantage even for small scale projects, *eg*, regional union catalogues or specialized periodicals union lists such as have been produced by the Institute of Advanced Legal Studies.

With the advent of automated information retrieval systems, the role of the traditional library is becoming a little uncertain. Luckily, the concept of a library simply as a store-house of knowledge seems to be declining, and universities and other educational institutions are conducting library-use surveys and giving user-instruction.

Perhaps we should come to see the library as an information centre, though for legal materials the required service would depend on the type of user. The busy practitioner who needs to find documents quickly may welcome high-speed mechanized retrieval devices in a way that the academic researcher may not. Nevertheless, surveys among the profession show a great reluctance to pay for automated systems which appear to provide a not much better service than existing ones, and at much greater cost. Perhaps information scientists are too eager to try out their equipment before experiments are completed. On the other hand, they need to know the requirements of the lawyer before they can design systems.

Perhaps the future role of the law librarian will be to mediate between the automated retrieval service and its users, spending more time in helping to frame questions than in providing the answers.

FURTHER READING

BIBLIOGRAPHIES

Cayless, C. F. *Bibliography of Library Automation 1964–1967.* British National Bibliography, 1969 (ISBN 0 900220 00 7).

Tinker, L. *An Annotated Bibliography of Library Automation 1968–1972.* Aslib, 1973 (ISBN 0 85142 050 8).

GENERAL WORKS AND JOURNALS

Eyre, J. and Tonks, P. *Computers and Systems: an introduction for librarians.* Bingley, 1971 (ISBN 0 85157 120 4).

Hayes, R. M. and Becker, J. *Handbook of Data Processing for Libraries.* New York, Becker and Hayes, 1970 (ISBN 0 471 36484 3).

Kilgour, F. G. History of Library Computerization. *Journal of Library Automation*, vol. 3, no. 3, 1970, pp. 218–29.

Kimber, R. T., comp. *Automation in Libraries*. 2nd rev. ed. Oxford, Pergamon Press, 1974 (ISBN 0 08 017969 x).

The scope for automatic data processing in the British Library; report of a study into the feasibility of applying ADP to the operations and services of the British Library [directed by Maurice B. Line] HMSO, 1972. 2 vols (ISBN 0 11 270276 7).

Wilson, C. W. J., ed. *Directory of operational computer applications in United Kingdom libraries and information units*. Aslib, 1973 (ISBN 0 85142 054 0).

Journal of Documentation, vol. 1– , 1945– Aslib (ISSN UK 0022–0418).

Journal of Library Automation, vol. 1– , 1968– Chicago, Information Science and Automation Division, American Library Association (ISSN US 0022–2240).

Program: news of computers in libraries, vol. 1– , 1966– Aslib (ISSN 0033–0337) (Vols 1 and 2 published by the School of Library Studies, Queen's University of Belfast).

A series of articles on automation in law libraries also appears in the *Law Library Journal*, vol. 64, no. 2, May 1971, pp. 113–212.

INDIVIDUAL SYSTEMS

Cayless, C. F. and Kimber, R. T. The Birmingham Libraries Co-operative Mechanization Project. *Program*, vol. 3, 1969, pp. 75–79, 106–110; vol. 4, 1970, pp. 150–5.

Scott, J. W. An integrated computer based technical processing system in a small library. *Journal of Library Automation*, vol. 1, no. 3, 1968, pp. 149–58.

South-West University Libraries System Project. *A report for the period July 1969–December 1972*, prepared by R. F. B. Hudson and M. G. Ford. Bristol, SWULSP, c/o University, 1973 (ISBN 0 903910 01 2).

Wall, R. A. Automation at Loughborough – a status report. *Program*, vol. 6, no. 2, 1972, pp. 127–43.

Woods, R. G. Use of an ICL computer in Southampton University Library. *Program*, vol. 3, no. 3/4, 1969, pp. 111–14 and vol. 5, no. 2, 1971, pp. 119–21.

ACQUISITIONS

Kimber, R. T. *Automation in Libraries*. Chapter 3, Ordering and Acquisitions.

Hunt, C. J. A computerised acquisitions system in Manchester University Library. *Program*, vol. 5, no. 3, 1971, pp. 157–60.

Dowsell, J. A. M. and Earl, C. A computer book ordering system for Kent County Library using SBNs. *Program*, vol. 5, no. 3, 1971, pp. 152–6.

SERIALS

Bosseau, D. L. The University of California at San Diego serials system – revisited. *Program*, vol. 4, no. 1, 1970, pp. 1–24.

Design of information systems in the social sciences. CLOSSS – a machine readable date base of social science serials, progress report 1971–72. Bath, University Library, 1973 (*Working papers*, no. 8) (ISBN 0 900843 38 1).

Evans, A. J. *Periodicals data automation project.* Loughborough, University, 1969 (LUT/LIB/R4).

Koster, C. J. ISDS and the functions and activities of national centres. *Unesco Bulletin for Libraries*, vol. 27, no. 4, 1973, pp. 199–204.

Massil, S. W. Mechanisation of serial records: a literature review. *Program*, vol. 4, no. 4, 1970, pp. 156–68.

Vdovin, G. Computer processing of serial records. *Library Resources and Technical Services*, vol. 7, no. 1, 1963, pp. 71–80.

CATALOGUING

Avram, H. D. The RECON pilot project: a progress report. *Journal of Library Automation*, vol. 3, 1970, pp. 102–14; 230–51, and vol. 4, 1971, pp. 38–57, 159–69.

Brown, P. The Bodleian catalogue as machine readable records. *Program*, vol. 3, no. 2, 1969, pp. 66–9.

Davies, G. Computer cataloguing in Flintshire. *Library Association Record*, vol. 72, no. 5, 1970, pp. 202–3.

Dolby, J. L. *Computerized library catalogs: their growth, cost and utility.* Cambridge, Mass., Massachusetts Institute of Technology, 1969.

Jeffreys, A. E., ed. *The conversion of the catalogue into machine readable form.* Newcastle-upon-Tyne, Oriel Press, for the University of Newcastle-upon-Tyne Computing Laboratory and University Library, 1972 (ISBN 0 85362 145 4).

Jolliffe, J. W. Some problems of maintaining a computer edition of the General Catalogue of Printed Books. *Libri*, vol. 21, no. 1/3, 1971, pp. 109–17.

Plaister, J. *Conversion of a regional union catalogue into machine-readable*

form and its use as a basis for local catalogue conversion; report of a
feasibility study supported by the Office for Scientific and
Technical Information of the Department of Education and
Science. London, LASER, 1973 (*OSTI Report* 5164) (ISBN 0 903764
00 8).

Steiner, W. A. F. P. Computer catalogue for the Squire Law Library,
University of Cambridge. *Law and Computer Technology*, vol. 1,
no. 10, 1968, p. 2.

MARC

Birmingham Libraries Co-operative Mechanisation Project. *BLCMP
MARC manual: input procedures for monographs cataloguing* . . .
Birmingham, Main Library, University of Birmingham, 1972
(ISBN 0 903154 03 x).

Bryant, P. *The Bath mini-catalogue: a progress report.* Bath, University
Library, 1972 (ISBN 0 900843 21 7).

Gorman, M. and Lindford, J. E. *Description of the BNB MARC
record: a manual of practice.* British National Bibliography, 1971
(*MARC Documentation Service publications*, no. 5) (ISBN 0 900220
28 7).

Henderson, K. L. ed. *Proceedings of the 1970 Clinic on library applications of data processing: MARC uses and users.* Urbana, Ill., University of Illinois Graduate School of Library Science, 1971.

Seminar on the United Kingdom MARC project, University of
Southampton, 1969. *U.K. MARC project: proceedings* . . . ed.
A. E. Jeffreys, T. D. Wilson. Newcastle-upon-Tyne, Oriel Press,
for the Catalogue and Index Group of the Library Association,
1970 (ISBN 0 85362 086 5).

MARC II and its importance for law libraries. *Law Library Journal*,
vol. 63, no. 4, 1973, pp. 505–25 (Proceedings of a panel at the 63rd
meeting of the American Association of Law Libraries).

United States. Library of Congress. Information Systems Office.
MARC manuals used by the Library of Congress. 2nd edition. Chicago,
Information Science and Automation Division of the American
Library Association, 1970.

—— *The MARC pilot project: final report on a project sponsored by the
Council on Library Resources, inc.* Washington, D.C., US Government Printing Office, 1968.

—— MARC Development Office. *Books: a MARC format; specifica-
tions for magnetic tapes containing catalog records for books.* 5th edition.
Washington, USGPO, 1972. (The first four editions were prepared
by the Information Systems Office; the first three entitled
Subscribers' Guide to the MARC distribution service.)

—— Information on the MARC system. Washington, USGPO, 1974 (ISBN 0 8444 0130 7).

SUBJECT ANALYSIS: GENERAL

Austin, D. and Butcher, P. *Precis: a rotated subject index system.* British National Bibliography, 1969. *MARC Documentation Service publication*, no. 3 (ISBN 0 900220 12 0).

Campey, L. H. *Generating and printing indexes by computer.* Aslib, 1972 (*Aslib Occasional Publications*, no. 11) (ISBN 0 85142 047 8).

Hines, T. C. Computer manipulation of classification notations. *Journal of Documentation*, vol. 23, 1967, pp. 216–23.

Steiner, W. A. F. P. Thesaurus problems as exemplified by the Index to Foreign Legal Periodicals. *International Journal of Law Libraries*, vol. 2, no. 1, March 1974, pp. 5–13.

SUBJECT ANALYSIS: COMPUTERS AND THE LAW

Aitken, W. *Computers for lawyers: a report presented to the Scottish Legal Computer Research Trust reviewing computer applications to the law and the prospect for developments in Scotland.* Edinburgh [the Trust], 1972.

Automated law research: a collection of presentations delivered at the first National Conference on Automated Law Research, Atlanta, March 16–18, 1972 [Chicago, American Bar Association, 1973]. Conference organized by the ABA Standing Committee on Law and Technology. Gives descriptions of several operational systems such as OBAR, LITE etc.

Bigelow, R. P., ed. *Computers and the Law: an introductory handbook.* 2nd edition. Chicago, Commerce Clearing House, for the American Bar Association Standing Committee on Law and Technology, 1969.

Duggan, M. A. *Law and the Computer; a KWIC bibliography.* Collier-Macmillan, 1974 (ISBN 02 950090 7).

Myers, J. M. Computers and the searching of law texts in England and North America. *Journal of Documentation*, vol. 29, no. 2, 1973, pp. 212–28 (68 references).

Tapper, C. *Computers and the Law.* Weidenfeld and Nicolson, 1973 (ISBN 0 297 76571 x) (see especially chapters 4–11).

Jurimetrics Journal: quarterly journal of the American Bar Association Standing Committee on Law and Technology, vol. 1– , 1959– Chicago, American Bar Association.

Law and Computer Technology, vol. 1– , 1968– Washington, Section on Law and Computer Technology of the World Peace Through Law Center. (Bimonthly), set up following the Geneva

Conference of WPTLC 1967, which recommended the creation of a world-wide clearing house on automation of law by computers and other technical means.

Rutgers Journal of Computers and the Law, 1970–   (Numbered from vol. 2, 1971) Newark, N.J., Rutgers Law School. Partly concerned with legal research by computer. Bibliography in each issue.

Index of Works Cited

INTRODUCTION

All works discussed in the text or listed in the chapter bibliographies have been included in this index. Bibliographical
details for most items were supplied by the contributors, but
some have been amplified as a result of further research. In a
few instances, the details given in the index are thought to be
more up-to-date than those given in the body of the text.

The choice of entry words does not necessarily follow any
cataloguing code, such as AACR. It has been made with
reference to the manner in which items are named in the text.
For example, modern law reports are entered by title, as are
most serially published legislative and treaty collections, e.g.
Sessions Cases; *Public General Acts*; *Treaty Series* [Ireland]. On
the other hand, nominate reports (see page 144) and collections,
digests, etc., which are normally known and cited by the legal
profession according to the names of their compilers, editors,
etc., are entered under those persons, e.g. Durnford, C. and
East, E. H. *Term reports . . . King's Bench*; Martens, G. F. de
Nouveau recueil général de traités; Viner, C. *General abridgment.*

Officially published monographs, pamphlets, etc., are entered
under the name of the country with the name of the responsible
body as a sub-heading, e.g. Gt. Brit. Law Commission for
England and Wales; United States. Library of Congress.
Most official serials are entered by title, e.g. *Journal of the House
of Commons*; *Report of Her Majesty's Chief Inspector of Constabulary.*
A few exceptions were made where it appeared to be more
useful to list a number of related titles under the name of the
body responsible, e.g. Gt. Brit. H.M. Stationery Office.
Catalogue of government publications [and four other titles].

Where there was serious doubt about the method of entry
to be employed, a reference from the form not finally selected
has been made. Any reader who searches unsuccessfully for a

particular item is recommended to consult suitable terms, e.g. Collections, Legislation, Multipartite treaties, or the names of jurisdictions, etc., in the Subject Index.

International Standard Book/Serial Numbers have been included, when possible. They have not been prefaced with identifying abbreviations, ISBN or ISSN. For further details see pages 636–7 and 640.

All England Law Reports Reprint [1558–1935]. Butterworth, 1957– 1968. 36 vols.
—Extension volumes [1861–1935]. 1968–71. 16 vols. 143, 148

Allardyce, A. What can law libraries borrow direct from NCL? *Law Librarian*, vol. 3, 1972, pp. 23–5. 56

Alness, Lord. Brocards. *In* Stair Society. *An introductory survey of the sources and literature of Scots law.* Edinburgh, Stair Society, 1936, pp. 282–8. 415

American and English Annotated Cases, 1901–18 [title varies]. Northport, N.Y., Edward Thompson; San Francisco, Calif., Bancroft-Whitney, 1906–18. 53 vols. 318

American Association of Law Libraries [Annual meeting, 1972]. General session on copyright. *Law Library Journal*, vol. 65, 1972, pp. 443–53. 480

American Association of Law Libraries. *Recruitment check-list.* Chicago, The Association, 1969. 585, 595, 600

American Association of Law Libraries. Revision of the A.L.A. cataloging rules of entry for legal materials and related rules. *Law Library Journal*, vol. 48, 1955, pp. 3–39. 518

American Association of Law Schools. Executive Committee regulations: regulation 8. *Law Library Journal*, vol. 62, 1969, pp. 222–4. 614

American Decisions, 1765–1869. San Francisco, Calif., Bancroft-Whitney, 1886–8. 100 vols. 317

American Digest System, 1658– St. Paul, Minn., West Publishing Co. [several series, about 300 vols. to date] 318

American International Law Cases, ed. F. Deak, 1793– Dobbs Ferry, N.Y., Oceana, 1971– c. 10 vols. (o 379 20075 9, etc.) 346, 352

American Journal of Comparative Law, 1952– Berkeley, University of California. (us 0002–919x) 299, 302, 362

American Journal of International Law, 1907– American Society of International Law. (us 0002–9300) 350

American jurisprudence. San Francisco, Bancroft-Whitney, 1936–48. 58 vols.
—2nd ed. 1962– 320

American Law Institute. *Restatement of the law . . .* [many volumes, various editions]. St. Paul, Minn., American Law Institute Publishers. 321

American Law Reports Annotated, 1919– Rochester, N.Y., Lawyers Co-operative Publishing Co. 318

American Law Reports, Federal: cases and annotations, 1969– Rochester, N.Y., Lawyers Co-operative Publishing Co. 316, 318

American Library Association. *A.L.A. cataloging rules for author and title entries.* 2nd ed. Chicago, ALA, 1949. (o 8389 3003 4) 514

American Library Association. *A.L.A. rules for filing catalog cards.* 2nd ed. Chicago, ALA, 1968. 542

American Library Association. *Study of circulation control systems.* Chicago, ALA, 1961. 480

American Maritime Cases, 1923– Baltimore, Md., Maritime Law Association. 317

American Reports . . . 1868–87. San Francisco, Calif., Bancroft-Whitney, 1871–88. 60 vols. 317

American State Reports . . . 1878–1911. San Francisco, Calif., Bancroft-Whitney, 1888–1911. 140 vols. 317

Ames Foundation. [*Publications*]. Cambridge, Mass., Harvard U.P., 1914–43. 6 vols. 227

Amos, M. S. and Walton, F. P. *Introduction to French law.* 3rd ed. Oxford University Press, 1967. (o 19 825178 5) 298

Ancel, M. and Marx, Y. *Les codes pénaux européens.* Paris, Centre Français de Droit Comparé, 1958. 301

Ancient laws and customs of the burghs of Scotland, 1124–1707. Edinburgh,

and university libraries in the United Kingdom. Mansell, 1972. (0 7201 0299 5) 506

Blount, T. *Nomo-lexikon: a law dictionary*. Thomas Newcomb for John Martin and Henry Hemingman, 1670. 399

Bluett, J. C. *Advocate's notebook, being notes and minutes of cases heard before the judicial tribunals of the Isle of Man*. Douglas, Johnson, 1847. 184

Boase, F. *Modern English biography, 1851–1900*. Truro, Netherton & Worth, 1892–1921; rep. Cass, 1965. 6 vols. (0 7146 2118 8, etc.) 405

Bohmer, A. *Legal sources and bibliography of Czechoslovakia*. New York, Praeger, 1959. 334

Boletín de legislación extranjera, no. 1– 1910– Madrid, Cortes Españolas. 301

Boletín mexicano de derecho comparado, 1948– Mexico City, Universidad Nacional Autonoma de Mexico, Instituto de Investigaciones Juridicas. (MX 0041–8633) 299

Bolland, W. C. *Manual of year book studies*. Cambridge U.P., 1925. 254

—*The year books*. Cambridge U.P., 1921. 254

Bond, M. F. *Acts of Parliament . . . their use and interpretation*. British Record Association, 1958. 254

—The formation of the archives of Parliament, 1497–1691. *Journal of the Society of Archivists*, vol. 1, 1957, pp. 151–8. 253

—*Guide to the records of Parliament*. HMSO, 1971. (0 11 700351 4) 149, 189, 226, 294

Books in Print, 1947– New York, Bowker. (US 0068–0214) 384, 485

Bookseller: the organ of the book trade, 1858– J. Whitaker & Sons. (UK 0006–7539) 427, 484

Bosly, H. *Répertoire bibliographique de droit belge, 1919–1945*. Liège, Presses Universitaires de Liège, 1947

—*1946–1955*. Liège, 1957. Continued by supplements. 335

Bosseau, D. L. The University of California at San Diego serials system revisited. *Program*, vol. 4, 1970, pp. 1–24. 659

Bourne, R. Computers in the regional library bureaux. *Library Association Record*, vol. 75, 1973, pp. 238–41. 644

Bouscaren, T. L. and Ellis, A. C. *Canon law: a text and commentary*. Rev. ed. Milwaukee, Wis., Bruce, 1963. 364

Bouscaren, T. L. and O'Connor, J. I. *Canon law digest*. Milwaukee, Wis., Bruce, 1934–63. 5 vols. 364

Bouvier, J. *Law dictionary and concise encyclopaedia*. 8th ed. Sweet & Maxwell, 1914. 2 vols. 161

Bowker Annual of Library and Book Trade Information (Council of National Library Associations) 1955– New York, Bowker. (US 0068–0540) 595–6

Bracton, H. de. *De legibus et consuetudinibus Angliae*. Tottell, 1569. 244, 248

Bracton's notebook . . . ed. F. W. Maitland. 1887. 3 vols. 244

Bramwell, G. *Analytical table of the private statutes*, 1727–1834. 1813–1835, 2 vols. 236

Breem, W. W. S. The British and Irish Association of Law Librarians. *International Journal of Law Libraries*, vol. 1, 1973, pp. 76–8. 57

—The obligations of a law librarian. *Law Librarian*, vol. 3, December 1972, pp. 40–2. 12

—Professional law libraries of Great Britain. *Law Library Journal*, vol. 64, 1971, pp. 278–90. 38, 56

—A sketch of the Inner Temple Library. *Law Library Journal*, vol. 64, 1971, pp. 5–12. 56

Brewing Trade Review Licensing Law Reports, 1913– Brewing Trade Review. 143

Brian, R. F. Australian law libraries, 1971. *Law Librarian*, vol. 2, 1971, pp. 35–6. 57

Bridgman, R. W. *Short view of legal bibliography*. W. Reed, 1807. 388

22

Edinburgh gazette, 1793– 128, 259, 269

Edwards, Sir G. The historical study of the Welsh law book. *Transaction of the Royal Historical Society*, 5th series, vol. 12, 1962, pp. 141–55. 254

Ellinger, W. B. Catalog entries for primary legal sources. *Library Resources and Technical Services*, vol. 12, summer 1968, pp. 352–8. 546

—Classification of law at the Library of Congress, 1949–1968. *Law Library Journal*, vol. 61, 1968, pp. 224–36. 579

—Non-author headings. *Journal of Cataloging and Classification*, vol. 10, April 1954, pp. 61–73. 546

—*Subject headings for the literature of law and international law*. 2nd ed. South Hackensack, N.J., Rothman for the American Association of Law Libraries, 1969. (0 8377 0107 4) 539

Elman, P. *An introduction to Jewish law*. New York, Lincolns-Praeger, 1958. 369, 377

Elon, M. The sources and nature of Jewish law. *Israel Law Review*, vol. 2, 1967, pp. 516–65; vol. 3, 1969, pp. 88–126, 416–57; vol. 4, 1969, pp. 80–140. 369, 377

Emden, A. B. *Biographical register of the University of Cambridge to 1500*. Cambridge U.P., 1963. (0 521 04896 6) 405

—*A biographical register of the University of Oxford to 1500*. Oxford U.P., 1957–9. 3 vols. (0 19 951105 5, etc.) 405

—*A biographical register of the University of Oxford*, A.D. *1501–1540*. Oxford, Clarendon Press, 1974. (0 19 951008 3) 405

Encyclopaedia Judaica. Jerusalem, Keter, 1972. 16 vols. 369, 377

Encyclopaedia of European Economic Community Law. Sweet & Maxwell, 1973– Three series. Loose-leaf. 328–30

Encyclopaedia of forms and precedents other than court forms. 4th ed. Butterworths, 1964–73, 24 vols. (0 406 02100 7, etc.) 196

Encyclopaedia of Islam. 2nd ed. Luzac, 1954– 374, 378

Encyclopaedia of Scottish legal styles. Edinburgh, Green, 1935–40. 10 vols. 212

Encyclopaedia of the laws of Scotland. 3rd ed. Edinburgh, Green, 1926–1935. 16 vols.

—Supplement, 1931–52. 5 vols. 196, 211

Encyclopedia of the Law of Town and Country Planning. Sweet & Maxwell, 1970– 3 vols., looseleaf. 199

English and Empire Digest. 2nd ed. Butterworth, 1950–70. 56 vols.

—3rd ed. in progress. 143, 161, 164, 167–9, 177, 182, 183, 214, 308

English Reports, 1220–1865. Stevens, 1900–32. 178 vols. 148, 169, 175, 366

Ephemerides theologicae lovanienses, 1924– Louvain, Catholic University. (BE 0013–9513) 364

Episcopal Church in Scotland. *Code of Canons*. Edinburgh, Cambridge U.P., 1973. (0 521 159174 1) 369

Erskine, J. *Institute of the law of Scotland*. Edinburgh, 1773. 2 vols. 250

—*Principles of the law of Scotland*. Edinburgh, 1754. 250

Escreet, P. K. *Introduction to the Anglo-American cataloguing rules*. Deutsch, 1971. (0 233 96033 3) 516, 523, 546

Estates gazette, 1958– Estates Gazette Ltd. (UK 0014–1240) 138

European Atomic Energy Community Regulations, 1962–5. HMSO. 330

European Commission on Human Rights. *Collection of decisions* [Irregular] The Commission. Mimeographed. 345

European Communities. *Journal officiel*, 1952– Luxembourg. (LU 0022–5479) 329, 332

—Special edition (English), 1952–1972, HMSO, 1972–3. 17 vols. 330

European Communities secondary legislation, 1952–72. HMSO, 1973–4. 42 vols.

—Subject index and numerical list, 1973. 330

European Communities, treaties and

bibliographies. Washington D.C., Library of Congress, 1944. 390, 415
—Survey of Anglo-American legal bibliography. *Law Library Journal*, vol. 33, 1940, pp. 1–18. 415
The Furrow, 1950– Maynooth, Co. Kildare. (IE 0016–3120) 367
Fyzee, A. A. A. *Outlines of Muhammadan law.* 3rd ed. Oxford U.P., 1964. (0 19 635203 7) 374, 378

Gabioné, B. L. *A finding list of British Royal Commission reports: 1860 to 1935.* Cambridge, Mass., Harvard U.P., 1935. 295
Gains. *The Institutes*, translated by F. de Zulueta. Oxford U.P., 1946–1953. 2 vols. 357
Galbraith, V. H. *An introduction to the use of the public records.* Oxford U.P., 1934. (0 19 821221 6) 253
—*Studies in the public records.* Nelson, 1948. 253
Gazette of the Incorporated Law Society of Ireland [c. 1907– Dublin]. 215
Gazette of the Incorporated Law Society of Northern Ireland. New series, 1964– Belfast, The Society. (UK 0019–3526) 215
Geer, H. T. *Charging systems.* Chicago, American Library Association, 1955. 480
General abridgment of cases in equity by a Gentleman of the Middle Temple. 4th ed. Henry Lintot, 1756. 163
General Agreement on Tariffs and Trade. *Basic instruments and selected documents.* 1953– (UN 0072–0623) 283
General collection of treaties, declarations of war, manifestos and other public papers relating to peace and war among the potentates of Europe from 1648–1731 [comp. by Darby?]. 1710–32. 4 vols. 341
General report on the activities of the European Communities, 1968– Brussels. (0069–6749) 332
General Synod Measures, 1920– HMSO. 113, 365–6

Gentleman's magazine, 1731–1868. [Over 200 volumes, in 5 series, 1732–1868].
—Index to 1731–1818. 4 vols. 225
German Association of Comparative Law. *See* Gesellschaft für Rechtsvergleichung
Gesellschaft für Rechtsvergleichung. *Bibliographie des deutschen Rechts in englisher und deutscher Sprache.* Karlsruhe, Müller, 1964. 386
Gibson, Sir A., Lord Durie. *Decisions of the Lords of Council and Session . . .* 1621–42. Edinburgh, Anderson, 1690. 173
Gibson, D. B. The Home Office Library. *Law Librarian*, vol. 3, 1972, pp. 36–9. 56
Gillissen, J. *Introduction bibliographique à l'histoire du droit et à l'ethnologie juridique.* Bruxelles, Institut de Sociologie, Université Libre de Bruxelles, 1963– 302, 386
Girard, P. F. *Textes de droit romain . . .* 6th ed. par F. Senn. Paris, A. Rousseau, 1937. 354
Gjupanovich, F. and Adamovitch, A. *Legal sources and bibliography of Yugoslavia.* New York, Praeger, 1964. 335
Glanville, R. de. *Tractatus de legibus et consuetudinibus regni Angliae tempore regis Henrici Secundi compositus.* Tottell, [c. 1554]. 248
Gloag, W. M. and Henderson, R. C. *Introduction to the law of Scotland.* 7th ed. Edinburgh, Green, 1968. (0 414 00500 7) 211
Godefry, J. *Commentaires sur la coustume réformée du pays et duché de Normandie.* Rouen, Du Petit-Val, 1626. 243
Gokkel, H. R. W. Publications à feuilles mobiles. *International Association of Law Libraries Bulletin* no. 26, May 1971, pp. 3–6. 202
Goodhart, A. L. Reporting the law. *Law Quarterly Review*, vol. 55, 1939, pp. 29–34. 187
Gorman, M. *Description of the BNB/MARC record.* British National Bibliography, 1971. (0 900220 28 7) 660

Koster, C. J. ISDS and the functions and activities of national centres. *Unesco Bulletin for Libraries*, vol. 27, 1973, pp. 199–204. 659

Kreuzer, K. F. Law libraries and law collections in the Federal Republic of Germany. *Law Librarian*, vol. 2, 1971, pp. 39–42. 58

Kunkel, W. *An introduction to Roman legal and constitutional history*. 2nd ed. Oxford U.P., 1973. (0 19 825317 6) 376

La Pradelle, A. de and Politis, N. *Recueil des arbitrages internationaux, 1798–1875.* 2nd ed. Paris, Editions Internationales, 1957. 3 vols. 347, 352

Lafontaine, H. *Pasicrisie internationale: histoire documentaire des arbitrages internationaux, 1794–1900.* Berne, Union Inter-parlementaire, 1902. 347, 352

Lambert, S. *List of House of Commons sessional papers, 1701–1750.* Swift (P & D), 1968. 267, 295

Lands Tribunal Cases, 1974– Chichester, Barry Rose. 156

Lands Tribunal for Scotland reports, 1971–. *See* Scots Law Times

Langan, P. St. J. Irish material in the State Trials. *Northern Ireland Legal Quarterly*, vol. 18, 1967, pp. 428–36; vol. 19, 1968, pp. 48–53, 189–97, 299–309. 189

Langridge, D. *Approach to classification for students of librarianship.* Bingley, 1973. (0 85157 148 4) 579

Langwell, W. H. *The conservation of books and documents.* Pitman, 1957. 507

Lansky, R. *Grundliteratur zur Rechtswissenschaft* . . . Hamburg, Arbeitsgemeinschaft für juristisches Bibliotheks-und Dokumentationswesen, 1974. 336

Lasalle, C. *Répertoire du droit des Communautés Européennes*, 1952–1966. Paris, Librairies Techniques, 1967. 332

Latham, R. E. Coping with medieval

Latin. *Amateur Historian*, vol. 1, 1952–4, pp. 331–3. 252

Latin for lawyers. 3rd ed. Sweet & Maxwell, 1960. (0 421 01690 6) 402

Lavves and Actes of Parliament . . . Scotland [1424–1597] collected by J. Skene. Edinburgh, Waldegrawe, 1597. 240

—[1424–1681] collected by Sir T. Murray of Glendook. Edinburgh, 1681. 240, 241

Law and Computer Technology, 1968– Washington D.C., Section on Law and Computer Technology of the World Peace Through Law Center. (US 0023–9178) 661

Law Book Guide, 1969– New York, G. K. Hall. 308, 322, 381, 646

Law Books in Print, 1957– Dobbs Ferry, N.Y., Glanville. (US 0075–8221) 308, 322, 381, 485

Law Books in Review, 1974– Dobbs Ferry, N.Y., Glanville. 381

Law Books Published, 1969– Dobbs Ferry, N.Y., Glanville. (US 0023–9240) 308, 381, 485

Law books recommended for libraries, 1967– [US] American Association of Law Schools. 302

Law chronicle, or journal of jurisprudence and legislation, 1829–1832. Edinburgh. 4 vols. 171

Law Directory and Diary, [annual]. Dublin, Incorporated Law Society of Ireland. 409

Law Journal, 1893–1966. Law Journal. 116 vols. 151

Law Journal [*Newspaper*] *County Court Reports*, 1912–47. Law Journal, 1934–47. 14 vols. 144

Law Journal Reports, 1822–31. Law Journal. 9 vols.

—New series, 1832–1949. 118 vols. 139, 141

Law Librarian: bulletin of the British and Irish Association of Law Librarians, 1970– Sweet & Maxwell. (UK 0023–9275) 53, 54, 208, 215, 594

Law Library Journal (American Association of Law Libraries),

Mathijsen, P. S. R. F. *A guide to European Community law.* Sweet & Maxwell, 1972. (0 421 17690 3) 336

Matthis, R. E. and Desmond, T. *Adopting the Library of Congress classification*: a manual of methods and techniques for application or conversion. New York, Bowker, 1971. (0 8352 0493 6) 580

Maxwell, W. H. and Brown, C. R. *Complete list of British and colonial law reports and legal periodicals.* 3rd ed. Sweet & Maxwell, 1937.

—Supplement, 1947. 150, 169, 308

Mayers, L. *The American legal system.* Rev. ed. New York, Harper & Row, 1964. 334

Mears, T. L. *The Institutes of Gaius and Justinian*, the Twelve Tables and the CXVIIIth and CXVIIth Novels. Stevens, 1882. 357

Megarry, R. E. and Wade, H. W. R. *Law of real property.* 3rd ed. Stevens, 1966. 190

Megarry, R. E. *The lawyer and litigant in England.* Stevens, 1962. (0 420 37030 7) 91

Melcher, D. *Melcher on acquisition.* Chicago, American Library Association, 1971. (0 8389 0108 5) 506

Menger, L. E. *The Anglo-Norman dialect.* New York, Columbia University, 1904. 253

Menhennet, D. *The journals of the House of Commons.* HMSO, 1971. (0 10 831070 1) 253, 295

—The Library of the House of Commons. *Law Librarian*, vol. 1, 1970, pp. 31–4. 57

Mercati, A. *Raccolta di concordati.* Rome, Vatican Press, 1954. 2 vols. 364

Merrill, W. S. *Code for classifiers.* 2nd ed. Chicago, American Library Asssociation, 1939. (0 8389 0027 5) 580

Metcalf, K. D. *Planning academic and research library buildings.* New York, McGraw-Hill, 1965. 604–24

Methodist Church in Ireland. *Manual of the laws and discipline.* 1934. Supplement, 1954. 368

Metz, R. *What is canon law?* Burns & Oates, 1960. (0 223 29330 x) 365, 376

Mews, J. *Mews digest of English case law.* 2nd ed. Sweet & Maxwell, 1925. Supplements to 1970. 38 vols. 148, 163, 167, 169, 177

—The present system of law reporting. *Law Quarterly Review*, vol. 9, 1893, pp. 179–87.

Microdoc, 1962– Belfast, Microfilm Association of Great Britain. (UK 0026–2684) 508

Middle Temple. Library. *A catalogue of the printed books in the library . . .* by C. E. A. Bedwell. Glasgow U.P., 1914, 3 vols.

—Supplement, by H. A. C. Sturgess, 1925. 389

Middle Temple Bench book. 2nd ed. by J. Bruce Williamson. Middle Temple, 1937. 406

Middleton, B. C. *The restoration of leather bindings.* Chicago, American Library Association, 1972. (0 8389 3133 2) 507

Miller, D. H. *Treaties . . . of the United States of America* [1776–1863]. Washington D.C., Government Printing Office, 1931–48, repr. New York, Da Capo, 1969. 9 vols. (0 306 71178 8, etc.) 343

Millin, S. S. *Digest of the reported decisions of the superior courts relating to petty sessions in Ireland*, 1875–98. Dublin, 1898. 182

Mills, J. Chain indexing and the classified catalogue. *Library Association Record*, vol. 57, 1955, pp. 141–8. 547

—*A modern outline of library classification.* Chapman & Hall, 1960. (0 412 06530 4) 578

—[Review of Moys classification]. *Journal of Documentation*, vol. 24, 1968, pp. 317–19. 580

Milne, Sir D. *The Scottish Office and other Scottish government departments.* Allen & Unwin, 1957. 269

Milsom, S. F. C. *Historical foundations of the Common Law.* Butterworth, 1969. (0 406 62500 x) 90

*Registrum omnium brevium tam original-
ium qs indicalium.* W. Rastell,
1531. 248
Regulations and orders [Jersey], 1939/
1955– Jersey, Bigwood, 1966– 132
Répertoire de droit international. Paris,
Dalloz, 1968– 351
*Report of Her Majesty's Chief Inspector
of Constabulary,* 1879– HMSO. 260
Reports of tax cases. *See* Tax Cases
Report of the Scottish Law Commission,
1957– Edinburgh, HMSO. 269
Report on the affairs of British
North America from the Earl of
Durham, Her Majesty's High
Commissioner. In *Reports from
Commissioners,* 1839, XVII, HC3.
304
Report on the legal aid scheme [Scot-
land], [1951?–]. HMSO. 270
Reports of International Arbitral Awards
[1902–41]. New York, UN, 1948;
repr. New York, Kraus, 1973. 11
vols. (IX 0082–8270) 288, 347, 352
*Reports of judgments, advising opinions
and orders* (International Court of
Justice) 1946– Leyden, Sijthoff.
(IX 0074–4441) 344, 352
*Reports of Patent, Design and Trade
Mark Cases,* 1884– Patent Office.
139, 144, 152
*Reports of the Royal Commission on
Historical Manuscripts,* 1870– HMSO.
(UK 0072–7083) 222
*Rerum Britannicarum medii aevi scrip-
tores* . . . Master of the Rolls,
1858–1911. 99 vols. in 251. 220
*Review of the International Com-
mission of Jurists,* 1969– Geneva,
The Commission. (IX 0020–6393)
285
Revised Reports, 1786–1866. Stevens,
1891–1920. 152 vols. 147, 181
*Revue générale de droit international
public,* 1894– Paris, Pedone. (FR
0035–3094) 351
Revue internationale de droit comparé,
1872– Paris, Société de Législation Comparée. (FR 0035–3337)
299
Richardson, F. P. The Law Society
Library. *Law Librarian,* vol. 1,
1970, pp. 15–19. 56

Roalfe, W. R. Centralized university
library service and the law school.
Law Library Journal, vol. 50, 1957,
pp. 2–5. 441
—*How to find the law and legal writing.*
6th ed. St. Paul, Minn., West,
1965. 311
Roberts, A. A. *A guide to Voet* . . .
Pretoria, The author, 1933. 360
—*A South African legal bibliography* . . .
Pretoria, The author, 1942. 334,
362
Roberts, L. M. *A bibliography of legal
Festschriften.* The Hague, Nijhoff,
1972. 298
Roberts, N. Graduates in academic
libraries . . . 1964/65–1970/71.
Journal of Librarianship, vol. 5,
1973, pp. 97–115. 598, 601
Robertson, D. *Reports of cases on
appeal from Scotland decided in the
House of Peers,* 1707–27. Strahan,
1807. 175
Roberts-Wray, Sir K. *Commonwealth
and colonial law.* Stevens, 1966. 304
Robinson, J. *International law and
organization: general sources of information.* New York, Humanities
Press, 1967. 375, 386
Rodgers, F. *Serial publications in the
British parliamentary papers, 1900–
1968.* Library Association, 1971.
(0 85365 494 8) 295
Rolle, H. *Un abridment des plusieurs
cases et resolutions del common ley.*
1668. 2 vols. 163
Roma, E. di and Rosenthal, J. D.
*Numerical list of British command
papers, 1833–1961/62.* New York,
Arno Press, 1967. (0 87104 505 2)
266, 295
Roscoe, E. S. *Reports of prize cases,*
1745–1859. Stevens, 1905. 2 vols.
348
Ross, A. *Mona, or the history, laws and
constitution of the Isle of Man.* c.
1744. 251
Ruffhead, O. *See* Statutes at Large...
Rules of the Court of Session. Edin-
burgh, HMSO, 1965. 128
*Rutgers Journal of Computers and the
Law,* 1970– Newark, N.J., Rutgers
Law School. (US 0048–8844) 662

Twelve Tables [etc.]. Cincinatti, Central Trust, 1932; repr. New York, AMS Press, 1972. 17 vols. in 7. (0 404 11026 6) 358
Scottish Current Law, 1948– Edinburgh, Green.
—*Citator*, 1949–
—*Yearbook*, 1948– 177–8
Scottish current law statutes annotated, 1947– Edinburgh, Green. 127
Scottish jurist, 1829–73. Edinburgh, Constable. 46 vols. 171, 172, 175, 176
Scottish Land Court Reports, 1913–63. Supplement to Scottish Law Review. 171
—*1964– see* Scots Law Times
Scottish law directory, 1892– Edinburgh, Hodge, 1892– (UK 0080–8083) 409, 412
Scottish Law Gazette, 1949– Dunblane, Scottish Law Agents Society. (UK 0036–9314) 212
Scottish law reporter, 1865–1924. Edinburgh, Baxter. 61 vols.
—*Digest to volumes 1–32*, 1865–92, 1898. 171, 176, 177
Scottish law review and reports of cases in the sheriff courts of Scotland, 1885–1963. Glasgow, Hodge. 79 vols. 171, 172, 212
Sears, M. C. E. *Sears' list of subject headings*. 10th ed. by Barbara Marietta Westby. New York, H. W. Wilson, 1972. (0 8242 0445 x) 539
Selden Society. *General guide to the Society's publications . . . vols. 1–79*, compiled by A. K. R. Kiralfy and G. H. Jones. Quaritch, 1960. (0 85423 027 0) 228, 387
Select essays in Anglo-American legal history . . . comp. and ed. by a committee of the Association of American Law Schools. Boston, Mass., Little, Brown, 1907–9. 3 vols. 234
Seminar on the U.K. MARC project, University of Southampton, 1969. *U.K. MARC project:* proceedings . . . ed. by A. E. Jeffreys, T. D. Wilson. Newcastle upon Tyne, Oriel Press for the

Catalogue and Index Group of the Library Association, 1970. (0 85362 086 5) 660
Session Cases, 1906/7– Edinburgh, Oliver & Boyd, for Scottish Council of Law Reporting. 82, 170, 171, 174, 176, 177
Session notes, 1925–48. Edinburgh, Clark, for the Faculty of Advocates, 1925–45. 171, 177
Sharp, J. R. Indexing for retrieval. In *Handbook of special librarianship and information work*. 4th ed. Aslib, 1975, pp. 198–268. 547
Shaw, P. *Digest of cases decided . . . Scotland, 1800–68 and, on appeal, by the House of Lords, 1726–1868*. Edinburgh, Clark, 1869. 3 vols. 176
Shaw's directory of courts in England and Wales, 1973– Shaw, 1973– (UK 0085–6061) 412
Shepard's Citations. [Numerous series, various dates] Colorado Springs, Col., Shepard's Citations Inc. 319–20
Sheppard, W. *Epitome of all the common and statute laws . . .* 1656.
—*Grand abridgment of the common and statute law of England.* 1675. 3 vols. 235
Shera, J. H. *The classified catalog: basic principles and practice.* Chicago, American Library Association, 1956. (0 8389 0026 7) 547
Sheridan, L. A. Channel Islands. *In* Keeton, G. W. and Lloyd, D. *The British Commonwealth: the United Kingdom*, vol. 1, part 2. Stevens, 1955. 91
Sheriff Court Reports, 1922– Edinburgh, Green. 172, 212
Shorter Oxford English dictionary, ed. W. Little. Oxford U.P., 1959. 2 vols. (0 19 861105 6) 398
Shunami, S. *Bibliography of Jewish bibliographies.* Jerusalem, Magnes Press, 1965. 369
Siddiqui, M. Z. *Hadith literature.* Calcutta U.P., 1961. 373
Sidney, E. and Brown, M. *The skills of interviewing.* Tavistock Press, 1961. (0 422 70850 x) 582, 600

23

Subject Index